What to Believe When You Don't

A secular guide to life, the universe, and happiness

Paul Rogers

The Conrad Press

What to Believe When You Don't
Published by The Conrad Press in the United Kingdom
2025
Tel: +44(0)1227 472 874
www.theconradpress.com
info@theconradpress.com
ISBN 978-1-917673-56-3
Copyright ©Paul Rogers 2025
All rights reserved.
Typesetting and Cover Design by: Levellers
The Conrad Press logo was designed by Maria Priestley.
Printed and bound in Great Britain by Clays Ltd,
Elcograf S.p.A.

For Gilly, Jamie and Douglas

"This above all – to thine own self be true"

William Shakespeare, 1603

Contents

Introduction
- What is belief?
- Chapter structure
- Core "beliefs"
- Stance
- Parable

Chapter 1: Nature
- External reality and what we can "know"

PART A: Physics
- The atomic structure of matter and the sub-atomic realm
- The four fundamental forces and quantum fields
- Quantum effects
- Quantum effects in our everyday world
- Relativity
- Unifying Quantum Mechanics with Relativity
- Antimatter, dark matter, and dark energy
- The Universe in our hand

PART B: Biology
- Evolution
- Genetics
- How genes work
- Genetic similarities and differences
- Genetics and race
- Biological sex and gender identity
- Inbreeding
- What makes us who we are
- Predictability, mutability, and "flux"

PART C: Our story so far

Chapter summary

Chapter 2: Consciousness
- Consciousness main themes
- Chapter structure

PART A: What consciousness is
- The evolution of human cognition
- The brain as the centre of consciousness

PART B: The opportunity, and obligation, to exercise personal existential choice
- Personal agency and "freewill"
- The essential self
- Personality and character

PART C: How consciousness works
- Executive function and the rational brain
- Learning and development
- Joining up the dots – how our brain processes data
- Instinct, emotion, and reason as triggers for behaviour
- Cognitive bias
- "Noise"
- Categorisation

PART D: Critical faculties which form part of consciousness
- Reason
- Emotion
- Language
- Empathy and Theory of Mind
- Memory
- Imagination
- Motivation and drive

PART E: Enablers and inhibitors of consciousness
- Sleep
- Stress

PART F: Implications of consciousness for existence
- The fact that we have the freedom to exercise personal existential choice in our life means that we should actively

embrace it, and then take responsibility for the choices we make
- The fact that our consciousness is fallible means that when making choices we should consider the possibility of bias and error
- "Luck" is a fact of life, whereas "destiny" isn't
- Mindset matters: how we think about our life obviously affects how we feel about it, and can also influence outcomes
- Expectations matter: how we think about ourself and others can materially change what we and they feel and do

Chapter summary

Chapter 3: Sociability

PART A: Pro-social behaviours
- Why sociability matters
- Culture as the defining human attribute
- Sociability as the defining human behaviour
- The evolution of human sociability, and society

PART B: Anti-social behaviours

- Hierarchy and status
- Violence, bullying and intimidation
- The capacity to influence, manipulate and deceive

PART C: "Me" versus "Us"
- Cooperate or compete - the critical existential choice
- Applying Axelrod to our social reality

PART D: "Only connect" – love and affection
- Sociability feels good and is good
- Romantic love
- Sex and the capacity to entertain
- Extramarital sex
- Altruism
- Loneliness and solitude
- Relationships and subjective interpretation
- Experiencing love

Chapter summary

Chapter 4: Morality

PART A: What is moral instinct?
- Definition of morality
- Morality as sociability
- Universal moral triggers
- Empathy and "do no harm"
- Fairness

PART B: Complications
1. Morality is ultimately relative, not an absolute law of nature.
2. Moral instinct is instinctive – we feel first, and reason later.
3. Our instincts do not always prompt us to behave "morally".
4. Morality is often nuanced and contextual.
5. Morality inherently prompts us to privilege other members of our own social group at the expense of members of other groups.
6. Moral norms are not stable, but rather change over time

PART C: Practical implications
- Embrace a moral principle
- Live and let live
- Let reason, not emotion, determine the answer to complex moral issues
- "Mind the gap" between moral instinct and behavioural response

Chapter summary

Chapter 5: Happiness

PART A: Happiness as the goal of human existence

PART B: Defining Happiness
- Pain and pleasure
- Fundamental needs
- Maslow's hierarchy of needs

- Self-actualisation
- Critical assessment of Maslow's ideas
- Self-actualisation for all
- Happiness as wellbeing

PART C: Happiness in the world
- Measuring happiness
- Are people happy?

PART D: What makes people happy?
- What helps individuals to be happy?
1. Genes
2. Sense of personal agency ("locus of control")
3. Life stage
4. Relationships
5. Health
6. Money
7. Work
8. Religion
- What helps societies to be happy?

PART E: Personal meaning
1. The Meaning of Life
2. Meaning in life
3. Will to meaning
4. Experiencing meaning

- Sources of meaning

Sources of meaning - Frankl
1. Creating a work or doing a deed
2. Experiencing something or encountering someone
3. The attitude we take to unavoidable suffering
4. "Actualising" personal potential

Sources of meaning – post Frankl
5. Positive affect
6. Belonging
7. Religious and other worldviews
8. The Self
9. Mental time travel
10. Mortality awareness

- Meaning as everyday experience

Chapter summary

Summary of beliefs discussed
Acknowledgements
Index of Topics
Index of authors quoted
Selected bibliography

Introduction

This book is the product of my own lifelong curiosity about the way our world, and we ourselves, work, underpinned by the conviction that whilst both the Universe and we humans often operate in mysterious ways there are secular explanations to be found for everything, and that these answers are moreover both stimulating and entirely satisfying.

I am myself an atheist, for what that's worth. I was brought up as a Christian, sent to Sunday School, educated at a Church of England primary school and enrolled in the local church choir at an early age.

As a child I dutifully believed in the Christian God, and for example said my prayers every night before bed. Gradually, though, I lost my faith, for no single reason that I can remember but rather because I became more and more aware that what I had been taught just didn't make sense. I was clear that I no longer "believed" by the age of about 13, when it was time for me to receive confirmation into the Church. I went ahead anyway, mainly because I didn't want to upset my parents, and also because I fancied one of the girls I knew would be in the class, although I was far too shy ever to tell her so. By the age of about 17 I had thought about things more and lack of faith had morphed into committed atheism, a stance I happily maintain to this day, 50 years later.

At the same time, I have always felt an intense curiosity for the world around us – questions such as how the Universe works; where we humans have come from and what makes us "human" in the first place; what motivates people to behave the way they do; and what makes me personally who I am. These are complex topics, with the possible exception of the last. The good news is that there is an abundance of research into all of them, with the definite exception of the last.

Having spent many hundreds, maybe thousands, of enjoyable hours trying to satisfy my own curiosity I decided to take the plunge and synthesise what I have learned into a single, hopefully-coherent, narrative. The exercise has certainly helped me to formalise my own thinking. I hope it will be of some interest and, better, practical use, to others embarked on a similar journey.

I should say upfront that this is not primarily intended to be an attempt to convince individuals who may hold religious belief to give it up. In fact, much of what follows is likely to be acceptable to and compatible with many forms of religion, with the important exception that the book rejects any supernatural element to our world, along with any kind of intentional Creator.

The beliefs we will discuss are all consistent with an overarching view of the Universe as entirely "natural", that is governed by its own empirically-observable laws which have no need of or room for divine intervention.

It is of course possible to accept these natural laws whilst also believing that they were originally set in motion by a Prime Mover of some kind, albeit not that such an entity still intervenes in the world today since the natural laws themselves are inviolable. In fact, the Prime Mover hypothesis turns out to be a logical dead end, as we will in due course discuss. The point for now is simply that much, although not all, of what this book discusses will be compatible with many forms of religious belief.

In general, the book takes the attitude towards religion attributed to the celebrated French scientist Pierre-

Simon Laplace, who in 1796 published his magnum opus, the 5-volume *Celestial Mechanics*.

He presented a copy to no less a person than the Emperor Napoleon, who apparently remarked: "M. Laplace, they tell me you have written this large book on the system of the Universe, and have never even mentioned its Creator". Laplace is reported, perhaps apocryphally, to have replied: "Sire, I had no need of that hypothesis".

Following this logic, the discussion that follows will largely take as read that there is indeed a natural not supernatural explanation for everything and focus rather on what these natural explanations are. Along the way, we will see that it is not necessary to believe in a Creator to conclude that the Universe, and we ourselves as humans, move in mysterious ways which often run counter to our common-sense intuitions.

What is "belief"?

The book's title is *What to Believe When You Don't*. It therefore seems appropriate briefly to consider what we mean by the term "belief".

The Cambridge English Dictionary offers the following definition: "the feeling of being certain that something exists or is true".

We might consider "certainty" to be a high bar for most of the topics we will discuss, especially since as we shall see many aspects of the Universe and of life are ultimately governed by probability, and not by mechanistic certainty. Still, this is perhaps a semantic objection, and we could easily get round it by replacing "certain" in the definition with "confident", or some similar word.

There is a philosophical question; what if anything we can truly "know", which we'll explore further during the course of Chapter 1. In the purest sense, however, the answer is that we cannot be certain that we "know" anything at all, because our impressions of external reality are ultimately subjective, having passed through the filter of our consciousness. In this sense, literally every opinion we hold about anything should strictly be defined as a "belief".

In any case, perhaps the most important word to focus on in the Cambridge Dictionary definition is "feeling". As we'll see throughout the book, and particularly in Chapters 2 and 4 when we discuss consciousness and then morality, our beliefs are often largely a product of our unconscious mind, and are almost always heavily influenced by our emotions and instincts; albeit we can only make sense of them through the powerful if imperfect medium of language, which by definition involves using our conscious, rational, mind.

Our beliefs often have strong emotional roots because many of those that are most important to us form early in our life, when we are at the critical development stage of infancy, soaking up information and impressions like a sponge. Some beliefs form as a direct result of our primary sensory experiences, for example "it usually hurts if I put my hand into a naked flame". Many others, especially of the abstract variety, are ingested from trusted sources such as family, friends, formal institutions, and informal aspects of the culture, or cultures, to which we are exposed. Examples here might include religious, and non-religious, beliefs; and definitions of what is "moral".

The book aims to take an evidence-based approach as far as possible, acknowledging that as a practical matter we seldom have sufficient data to be rationally certain that a specific belief is in fact true, even if we leave aside for a moment the philosophical concerns about what we can truly "know". Rather, we tend to adopt a probabilistic approach, instinctively using a version of the "80:20

principle" which holds that 20% of the data which might in theory be available can often be enough for an answer in which we can be 80% confident; and that 80% confidence is in turn usually sufficient to justify moving directly to a conclusion and, where appropriate, action.

Obviously, there are exceptions to this rule. Nonetheless, the 80:20 approach is consistent with the way in which our brains itself functions, and hence with the way in which most of us embrace whatever beliefs we may hold. And the book is long even so. The hope is that the evidence quoted supports at least an 80% confidence level in the specific beliefs proposed, although each individual reader will of course be the judge.

Finally, there is an important question how open we are to changing, or modifying, whatever existing beliefs we may hold. This is relevant not simply in an abstract sense, but because I hope that readers may find that at least some of the ideas contained in this book stimulate them to challenge some of their existing ways of thinking. You are encouraged to keep as open a mind as possible.

This may be easier said than done. As we already saw, many of our most important beliefs connect powerfully with our emotions, with the result that we are each prone to a series of unconscious cognitive biases, discussed more fully in Chapter 2. A noteworthy example is "confirmation bias", which leads us, unconsciously of course, to be highly selective in emphasising data, or opinions, which support an existing entrenched belief; and de-emphasising, or ignoring, data which might undermine or contradict it. The stronger our emotional attachment to a particular belief, the more likely that confirmation bias will apply. The result is that when we encounter a viewpoint which challenges one that we ourself hold emotionally dear, the research shows that the effect is often to polarise our thinking and make our original view more deeply entrenched, even if the rational evidence is against it. You have been warned!

Core beliefs and chapter structure

The core belief of the book is that we each have a precious opportunity, amounting to an obligation, to take responsibility for our own life by embracing the ability which human consciousness gives us to choose our own actions and behaviours.

We do this in the knowledge, or more accurately belief, that we are fundamentally alone in an uncaring and entirely material Universe and so must ultimately look inside ourself for answers on how to live our life. Embracing our existential freedom to choose is the key to living a fulfilling life.

The book is divided into five chapters, loosely based on the metaphor of an "onion" which we peel layer by layer, starting, of course, with the outside, and becoming progressively more personal as we move to the centre.

Chapter 1 deals with Nature, in other words the "Big Outside World" of external reality. The core belief is that we are living in a material world, with no need of or room for any element of supernatural explanation.

This is underpinned by two subsidiary beliefs:

- the Universe is governed by a set of inviolable natural laws, notably including quantum theory, which is inherently probabilistic not deterministic; and relativity, which reveals that even a concept as fundamental as time which may seem to us to be absolute is in fact relative.

- all life, including human life, is a product of the natural process of biological evolution, mediated through our genes and gene-combinations. Experience acts on our genes to make us who we are, and since our specific genetic profile and personal experiences are unique to each of us as individuals it follows that we are ourself ultimately unique.

Chapter 2 addresses the distinctive faculty of human consciousness: our "Inner World". The core belief is that "I am the captain of my soul", meaning that we each have some level of personal agency and are ultimately free to choose our own actions. However, our freedom is constrained in important ways, and our judgement can be fallible. Underpinning beliefs are:

– human consciousness creates "freewill": the possibility, in effect the obligation, to exercise conscious choice over our own life and behaviour; acknowledging that our genes and experiences strongly predispose us to respond in certain ways to particular triggers and therefore heavily influence but do not entirely predetermine our behaviour.

– consciousness is fallible. In exercising personal choice, we need to be aware of the possibility of cognitive error, psychological bias and random "noise", often operating below our conscious mind. We do well to cultivate self-knowledge about our own personal predilections.

Chapter 3 deals with Sociability, defined as the capacity to relate to and cooperate with others, including with strangers. This is the behaviour which most distinguishes humans from other species. The core belief is "only connect...", meaning that we should focus our discretionary energy on building and sustaining meaningful personal relationships above all else. Subsidiary beliefs are:

– we are social animals first and foremost. We are hardwired to behave in "groupish", which is to say cooperative, ways, anchored by powerful emotions such as love, friendship and fellowship. We are also each capable of anti-social, "selfish", behaviour.

– some of the most important existential choices we make are therefore when to cooperate, privileging the interests of other people; and when to "compete", privileging our own. We do well to bias towards cooperation, but also to recognise that the appropriate answer in any particular situation is circumstantial.

Chapter 4 discusses Morality, acknowledging that we each experience strong moral instincts, and these exert a powerful, often subconscious, influence on our behaviour. The core belief is "there is nothing either good or bad, but thinking makes it so": morality is essentially a human invention and therefore ultimately subjective and relative. Subsidiary beliefs are:

– we each have an innate moral sense, which drives our feelings and behaviour in significant, often unconscious, ways, generally serving to reinforce pro-social, which is to say cooperative, behaviours especially towards people we perceive to be members of our own social group.

– however, moral judgements that we may experience as being binary may often turn out to be nuanced and circumstantial when subjected to closer scrutiny. Our moral instincts can be particularly problematic when it comes to people we perceive as "other", often serving to alienate rather than bind us.

Chapter 5 focuses on Happiness, the centre of our metaphorical onion. The core belief is "live, love, laugh and be happy", in other words that we should take responsibility for our own happiness by embracing the opportunities that life affords. Subsidiary beliefs are:

– personal happiness is the legitimate goal of our existence, broadly defined as achieving a sense of well-being, which includes both sensory and aesthetic pleasure as well as deeper psychological fulfilment. Happiness is eminently achievable, although certainly not guaranteed.

– it is for us each to take responsibility for our own happiness. The specific answer will be unique to each of us as indiviudals. For most people it will be found mainly through embracing the business of everyday living; and, social creatures that we are, relationships will be at the core.

Stance

The book is written from the perspective of a layman. It could not be written any other way since my qualification as author is that I have striven to satisfy my own curiosity by researching extensively amongst subject-matter experts on each of the topics covered, not by conducting independent research of my own.

This is not, however, to imply that the content is somehow whimsical or superficial. On the contrary, the intention throughout is to review not just abstract concepts and ideas but also the evidence which supports them. The hope is that the book will appeal to the same kind of "serious layman" that I consider myself to be.

The book draws heavily on the thoughts of a whole panoply of experts in specific fields, often quoting from them directly and sometimes at length. Paying respectful homage to Isaac Newton, I can assert that any merit it may have is unequivocally because I have been able to scramble onto the shoulders of a large number of giants in their own fields. I have been as diligent as I can in attributing my debts to this rich variety of sources. I hasten to add that the undoubted errors, omissions, and misunderstandings are entirely my own. In any case, unlike Newton I cannot and do not claim to have seen further in any particular area. My hope is rather that I have managed to make accessible topics that can sometimes be remote and hard to fathom; and also to have created a single coherent narrative, linking a broad range of topics into an integrated "worldview".

I acknowledge that since the book is grounded in my own reading and experiences, it tends to a decidedly "Western" slant, with a predominance of "Western" sources. There is not a great deal I can do about this, other than to recognise that there are surely other sources which would potentially enrich the beliefs discussed but with which I am sadly not sufficiently familiar.

In terms of authorial voice, I have opted after some deliberation for a "we/ourself" formulation throughout, which I realise some readers may find unsettling. I made this choice because my hope is that it will encourage readers to think about how the various topics might apply to them personally. It is worth reinforcing, however, that throughout the book "we" is intended as the plural English form, which is to say "all of us together". I specifically do not intend to convey the kind of grandiose, and archaic, "Royal We" that we might find for example in the mouths of Shakespearean monarchs. If it comes across that way in places, I can only assure you that this is never the intention.

In the same way, "ourself", rather than "ourselves", is intended to encourage the reader to identify personally with whatever topic is being discussed, reinforcing the book's core message that ultimately all these ideas are helpful not as points of academic interest but rather because they can help each of as individuals to make sense of our own personal existence.

I should also draw attention to a couple of stylistic decisions which I judged necessary for reasons of consistency. I have Anglicised all spellings throughout, even when quoting from, for example, US sources. Also, in acknowledging my many expert sources I have generally opted to give the birth name and surname plus a broad description of their field of expertise, but have avoided further details, such as titles, including job titles; middle initials; and so on. In most cases I mention nationality, on the grounds that this will give readers some feel for the likely cultural frame of reference.

Finally, at different points in the book we'll use numbers for support, although certainly not any complex maths. Some of the numbers are large, and this invites a potential problem, which is that most of us do not have an intuitive appreciation for large numbers since we rarely encounter them in our everyday life.

To mitigate this, I'll share an insight recently vouchsafed by my builder, which certainly helped me at least to gain a new appreciation for the matter. In turns out that 1 million seconds is equal to about 12 days. However a billion (that is, a thousand million) seconds is about 31 years. And a trillion (thousand billion) seconds translates to no less than 31,688 years. The point being that whilst the words we use to describe large numbers can make them sound similar, in fact the difference between "large", say a million, and "huge", say a trillion, can be unimaginably vast.

Message

I have consciously resisted trying to distil the book's content into a handful of prescriptive "lessons", on the grounds that whilst as humans we obviously have much in common we are nonetheless each unique as individuals, and our path to personal happiness is ultimately subjective and specific to our own self.

Having said this, each chapter explores between six and eighteen specific beliefs which support the over-arching core belief on which it is built. These are summarised at the end of the chapter and then collected together at the end of the book. Readers wishing to cut to the chase may choose to go straight there.

Other readers may crave more explicit guidance on the implications of all these beliefs for how we should each live our individual life. For them, and with some trepidation, I offer the following:

Believe in *yourself*:

- embrace your freedom to choose what to do and how to behave, and own the consequences.

- cultivate self-knowledge of your own predispositions, strengths and weaknesses, so that you can take due account of them in the choices you make.

- take responsibility for your own happiness. Focus energy on:
– maintaining your health, and achieving a level of material wealth and security for you and your loved ones.
– building and sustaining high-quality personal connections, characterised by mutual feelings of love, friendship, or fellowship, and which help you to feel that you truly belong.

- achievements that you personally consider to be meaningful.
- behaviours which you feel reflect your best Self.

I am conscious that this advice may seem obvious, even trite. If so, I'll counter with two observations.

First, it is true that for most of us the main satisfaction in life is to be found through the business of everyday living, rather than in grand gestures or high drama.

Second, my aspiration is indeed to be simple, without however being simplistic. I hope to meet the hurdle set by the 20th century American jurist and Supreme Court member Oliver Wendell Holmes, who is reported to have said: "for the simplicity on this side of complexity, I wouldn't give you a fig. But for the simplicity on the far side of complexity, for that I would give you anything I have". Many of the topics we will cover are complex, the devil is generally in the detail, and readers who stay the course will appreciate that their ability to live according to these simple principles will be greatly enhanced by understanding at least some of the intricacy which underpins them.

Still, there is inevitably a good deal of subjective judgment on my part in choosing which topics to include and how much supporting detail to provide. For readers who may feel I have erred on the side of "too much", I can only offer a diffident apology. Readers who may feel the reverse is true and who may want to explore particular issues in more depth are referred to the Bibliography for authoritative texts on every major topic. These will handsomely repay the investment needed to engage.

Finally, I'll share two concepts which will likely seem out of context now, but will hopefully be of value as the book unfolds. First is how to define success in our life. A wise colleague was fond of quoting the formula: *"Success =*

Outcomes plus or minus Expectations" ("Expectations" can also be replaced with "Aspirations"). This turns out to be quite profound. Our expectations colour not only how we feel about a particular outcome but can even influence the outcome itself, as we will later discuss.

The second I'll call The Goldilocks Principle, after the fable of Goldilocks and the Three Bears. This is potentially relevant as we contemplate the various existential choices with which we are faced. In short, Goldilocks is a (human) girl, who walks into the Bears' cottage in the woods whilst they are out. She is hungry, so she samples the porridge which has been left on the table. Daddy Bear's is too hot, Mummy Bear's is too cold, and little Baby Bear's is just right, so she eats it. Goldilocks feels tired, so she decides to take a nap on one of the Bears' beds. Daddy Bear's is too hard, Mummy Bear's is too soft and (of course) Little Baby Bear's is just right, so she sleeps on it. And so on.

The point of this story is absolutely not to imply that some kind of compromise is automatically right in every circumstance. There are many situations in which a choice really is binary, or where the best choice lies at one end of whatever spectrum. The point is rather to emphasise that we should beware prescriptive solutions. We are each ultimately unique as individuals and, like Goldilocks, should look to make choices that are "just right" for us personally.

Parable

I'll close by sharing a modern parable which had a profound impact on me, as well as on many of my then-colleagues, when we first heard it long ago.

The context was that the company we worked for at the time was in danger of going out of business. The wounds were mainly self-inflicted, but they were deep. Our very survival was in question, as an enterprise and as a group of companions. As we considered this rather forbidding landscape and what it might require from each of us, our Chairman (in fact a woman) offered the following story, inspired I believe by her husband who was and for that matter still is a solo long-distance yachtsman.

Picture yourself alone, on a small boat in the middle of the ocean. Unexpectedly, a violent electrical storm blows up, disabling all your communication systems and leaving only your compass working.

If you have a magnetic compass you will surely die, because the impact of the electrical storm will be to make it whirl around in circles and effectively render it useless.

But if you have something called a gyroscopic compass you will be fine because, crucially, this instrument consults its own inner workings to keep pointing resolutely in the right direction, no matter how hostile or unpredictable the external environment may be. However terrible the storm outside, at least it will be clear in which direction you should head.

The moral is (hopefully) obvious, and, to me at least, uplifting. The key to navigating through life's many challenges is to stay focused on our own internal compass, and ultimately to look inside ourselves for the answers. Life is not only about surviving metaphorical electrical storms of course – beside whatever challenges we may face there are hopefully also many opportunities. But the metaphor applies just the same.

My hope is that the contents of this book will be helpful to the reader in helping you to set your own internal compass as you make the choices that will set and keep you on course for a fulfilling life.

Chapter 1:

Nature

"We are living in a material world"
Madonna, 1984

The foundational belief about Nature is that we live in an entirely natural Universe, with no need of or room for any element of supernatural. And the foundational belief about humans is that we are the entirely material product of this Universe, built from the same fundamental matter particles as everything around us and having developed alongside all other life forms through the entirely natural process of biological evolution.

These beliefs have important implications for how we think about our life. We are essentially alone, in a Universe which whilst not actively hostile is indifferent to our existence. In deciding how to live we must therefore look internally, to our own self; not externally, for example to some supernatural "saviour". We are also mortal. The fundamental matter from which we are made may be imperishable, but we ourselves are not. We exist once as a living organism, and then we are gone.

In this chapter we will see that the Universe and everything in it is governed by a set of natural Laws, which are "universal" in a literal sense. They are immutable and absolute, so that everything that happens happens in accordance with them, with no exceptions, in any place or at any time. We will focus in particular on the laws of physics, which explain how the Universe itself works; and the laws of biology, which govern life on Earth, specifically including human life.

These are complex topics, and it is important to acknowledge that we do not yet have a complete understanding of either. It is conceivable that we never will. Still, we know a great deal, sufficient to be able to assert with confidence that a material explanation for reality in its entirety is there to be found, if we are ever capable of finding it.

We'll first ground our discussion by briefly reviewing a topic which has vexed philosophers down the ages: how and to what extent we can truly know that an external reality exists in the first place. Fortunately for the rest of the book, we'll conclude that it is reasonable to believe this, although not necessarily easy to prove.

We'll then discuss the Universe around us. We'll explore the most fundamental level of physical reality: the atomic and sub-atomic particles, or, more accurately, wave-particles, which make up all matter throughout the Universe, including organic life forms such as humans.

We'll discuss the strange world of quantum mechanics, which operates according to laws which are quite different from what we might expect based on our commonsense intuitions, arising as these do from our experiences of the everyday, macroscopic, world. We'll also look at the "macro" level of the entire Cosmos, in particular Relativity Theory. Here, we'll see that ideas as basic to our everyday life as Space and Time, which we subjectively experience as absolute, are in fact robustly relative, which is to say that they are in reality different for objects (and, at least in theory, people) moving at (hugely) different speeds.

We'll then turn to evolutionary biology and see how as humans we are just one among countless species of life on Earth, and not in any meaningful sense some kind of "chosen people"; how the nature of the evolutionary process is such that over enough generations it can, and does, produce organisms of great complexity without any need or indeed room for an external "Creator"; and how our own unique combination of genes shapes who we are in important ways, combining with our experiences to influence not only our physical self but also how we think, feel and behave. Along the way we'll observe that Nature is inherently amoral, so that any concept of "natural justice" is essentially meaningless.

Finally, we'll look at how the combination of fundamental physics and evolutionary biology allows us to tell the fascinating, and entirely material, story of how the Universe, life, and we ourselves have developed – where we have come from, and the forces that shaped us.

External reality and what we can "know"

How do we know that an objective external reality actually exists, and that for example we are not all just projections of some other entity's imagination, like characters in *The Matrix*?

This may seem like an abstract question. And as it happens it turns out to be surprisingly difficult to provide rigorous proof that an objective external reality exists, of a standard sufficient to satisfy philosophers, because ultimately every aspect of the "reality" we experience is filtered through the medium of our human senses, and, powerful as these undoubtedly are, they are also fallible and ultimately subjective, a topic we will explore in some detail in Chapter 2.

The 17th century Irish philosopher Bishop Berkeley took a strong stance on the issue with his famous dictum that "to be is to be perceived", in other words asserting that external reality exists only if a third party is present to perceive it. The example most often cited to make the proposition concrete is also typically credited to Bishop Berkeley although may in fact be apocryphal: we are invited to consider whether if a tree falls in the middle of a forest and there is no-one around to hear it, it can be said to make a sound; and, how we can know.

Whatever the origin of the "falling tree" question, the generally accepted answer focuses on the underlying physics and asserts that in falling the tree disturbs the surrounding air and creates soundwaves. However, these are not experienced as "sound" if there is no-one present to hear them, because experiencing something as sound requires that the soundwaves be processed by the auditory system of a brain. So in a strictly technical, if pedantic, sense there are soundwaves but no "sound".

Further, we cannot know for certain that soundwaves were produced, given that by the terms of the thought-experiment no-one was within earshot to record them. However, we can hypothesise that soundwaves were produced, and can place high confidence in this hypothesis, because we can infer it from the many similar events where a human *was* present to witness the falling of a tree, and heard a crashing sound on every occasion.

Separately, our knowledge of the laws of physics tells us that when a tree falls in Earth's atmosphere it inevitably disturbs the surrounding air, and the effect is to produce soundwaves regardless of whether a brain happens to be within earshot to hear them. In sum, we cannot technically "know" that the falling tree made a sound, but we can confidently infer it. As a practical matter, we are justified in believing that the falling tree made a sound which would have been heard had there been someone there to hear it.

And in this book overall, we will take as our starting point the belief that there indeed exists an external material world which can meaningfully be said to be "real" independent of us as the perceivers.

It is of course a separate question how far we are capable of accurately perceiving this external reality. As already noted, our impressions are filtered by our senses, which are subjective and fallible. What is more, we might logically expect our senses to be adapted to presenting us with the view of external reality best adapted to our own survival, rather than necessarily giving us the most accurate representation of reality itself. "(Evolutionary) fitness beats truth", as the American cognitive scientist Donald Hoffman puts it in his 2019 book *The Case Against Reality – How evolution hid the truth from our eyes*. Among many examples, Hoffman gives that of oxygen, pointing out that our senses and physiological response mechanisms are attuned not to making an accurate assessment of the actual level of oxygen in our environment, but rather to whether or not there is the right level for us to be able to breathe. Hoffman's central point is not that an underlying reality does not exist, but rather that we should not expect our human senses to be adapted to perceiving it directly. The implication is that it should not surprise us if the way reality works turns out to be different from what we might predict based on the evidence of our own intuitions and senses; an insight which the pages that follow will certainly confirm.

Finally, it is important to acknowledge that a healthy level of humility is appropriate as we review the workings of our natural world. We know a lot, but we certainly do not know everything. This is why the specific beliefs we'll discuss in the pages which follow are generally framed as "hypotheses", or alternatively "theories", rather than asserting absolute certainty, or "knowledge".

This is partly stylistic, in deference to the epistemological concerns raised by Bishop Berkeley and others about our ability to be 100% certain of anything. Mainly, though, it reflects the application of the scientific method, which works through a process of developing hypotheses, subjecting them to experimental testing, and then refining or in some cases replacing them as we learn more. To be clear, though, the terms "hypothesis" and "theory" do not imply "tentative" or "superficial".

On the contrary, the beliefs we will explore are almost without exception the product of rigorous scientific research. And whilst specific ideas will continue to evolve as our knowledge grows, there is no reason to suppose that this will change the foundational belief for this chapter: that a material explanation exists for everything in the natural world, which is to say the Universe and everything in it, including humans. Whatever new insights appear in the future are simply likely to give us better material explanations.

Thus armed, let us turn to a discussion of external reality in its purest form: the natural laws which govern the Universe.

PART A: Physics

The Introduction noted that this book will explicitly and unashamedly seek to stand on the shoulders of "giants", in other words subject-matter experts in each of the topics covered. Our first giant is the French physicist Christophe Galfard, who in addition to his own impressive list of accomplishments worked closely for many years with the celebrated British physicist Stephen Hawking. In 2015 Galfard published a book called *The Universe in Your Hand*, and we will use this as our main point of reference throughout this section.

In his Foreword, Galfard states a bold ambition: "my ambition...is that in this book I will not leave any readers behind. You are about to start a journey through the universe as it is understood by science today. It is my deepest belief that we can all understand this stuff".

Hopefully, Galfard's ambition to make complicated ideas simple enough to be generally accessible will be realised in the sections that follow, indeed throughout this book more generally. Having said this, we will explore the world of physics in some detail, because this is necessary to give substance to the overarching belief that there is a material explanation for everything, and also because the topics are interesting and in some cases provocative. Still, this may not be to every reader's taste, in which case it is possible to browse the main ideas then go straight to Part B, in which the discussion turns to biology.

The atomic structure of matter and the sub-atomic realm

All matter throughout the Universe is composed of atoms, including the biological cells from which the human body and brain are made. Atoms are made from a variety of sub-atomic particles which are themselves "fundamental", or alternatively "elementary", meaning they cannot be further sub-divided. Fundamental particles are therefore the most fundamental level of external reality, as their name implies.

Each type of fundamental particle is identical to all others of that type, wherever they may be in the Universe at whatever time. Differences in the physical and chemical properties of different forms of matter are therefore due to the way in which the fundamental particles which comprise it are arranged, not to differences between the fundamental particles themselves.

The full list of fundamental particles is long enough to be confusing, and fortunately it is not necessary to explore it in detail. In brief, there are two categories: Fermions and Bosons. All fundamental particles throughout the Universe belong to one or other of these two categories: "there is no third kind of subatomic particle", as American philosopher and scientist Alex Rosenberg tells us on p21 of his 2011 book *The Atheist's Guide to Reality*. Fermions are generally associated with matter, whereas Bosons typically do not have mass but rather are carriers of the four fundamental forces which permeate the Universe, and which we will explore in due course.

For those interested in the details, CERN, the European Organisation for Nuclear Research, provides a full description of Fermions in a website module called *The Standard Model*, in a section titled *Matter Particles*: "all matter around us is made of elementary particles, the building blocks of matter. These particles occur in two basic types called quarks and leptons. Each group consists of six particles, which are related in pairs, or "generations". The lightest and most stable particles make up the first generation, whereas the heavier and less-stable particles belong to the second and third generations. All stable matter in the universe is made from particles that belong to the first generation; any heavier particles quickly decay to more stable ones. The six quarks are paired in three generations – the 'up quark' and the 'down quark' form the first generation, followed by the 'charm quark' and 'strange quark', then the 'top quark' and 'bottom (or beauty) quark'.

Quarks also come in three different 'colours' and only mix in such ways as to form colourless objects. The six leptons are similarly arranged in three generations – the 'electron' and the 'electron neutrino', the 'muon' and the 'muon neutrino', and the 'tau' and the 'tau neutrino'. The electron, the muon, and the tau all have an electric charge and a sizable mass, whereas the neutrinos are electrically neutral and have very little mass".

Moving back to the level of the atom itself, every atom possesses a nucleus surrounded by one or more electrons. The electrons are fundamental, and carry a negative electrical charge. The nucleus comprises one or more protons, which carry a positive electrical charge; and one or more neutrons, which are electrically neutral. Each proton is made from two up quarks and one down quark, all of which are fundamental; and each neutron from two down quarks and one up quark. When the number of protons in an atom matches the number of electrons it is electrically neutral; if an atom gains or loses an electron then it becomes electrically charged, or "ionised".

Atoms all exhibit this same basic structure. But they are not all the same. Rather, they vary in size according to the Periodic Table, first published in something resembling its modern form by Russian chemist Dmitri Mendeleev in 1869. Atomic size, or "number", denotes the number of protons within the nucleus, and therefore the number of circulating electrons required to balance the resulting electrical charge if the atom itself is to remain neutral. The smallest atom is hydrogen, which has just one proton and one electron. Next is helium, with two of each; and so on up.

Gold, for example, has an atomic weight of 79, meaning it has 79 protons and typically 79 circulating electrons. There is some dispute about the largest naturally-occurring atom found on Earth, although this is generally recognised to be uranium, with an atomic weight of 92. Atoms with a higher atomic number are in theory possible and indeed some have been produced synthetically in laboratories, the highest atomic weight achieved so far being 118 for an element named Oganesson. However, atoms at this end of the atomic number scale tend to be highly radioactive and unstable, quickly decaying into smaller constituents.

In the distant past, when the Universe was young, hydrogen and helium accounted for virtually all the atoms there were – 100%, or close, of the Universe's matter. Heavier atoms, which is to say all those with an atomic number higher than 2, have been produced over time either in the high-energy hearts of stars or, in the case of the heaviest atoms, as a result of a supernova, when a massive star explodes or collapses in on itself at the end of its life, releasing even higher energy.

On p18 of *The Universe in Your Hand* Galfard describes the process by which heavier atoms are made inside a star. He imagines that we embark on a journey to the centre of our own Sun to witness the process at first hand: "you dive deeper and deeper inside the Sun; the temperature rises, and becomes mind-bogglingly hot. As you reach its core, we are talking 16 million degrees Celsius. Maybe even more. And there are plenty of hydrogen atoms everywhere, although they have been stripped naked by the surrounding energy: the electrons are loose, leaving bare nuclei. The pressure is so high, these nuclei are so tightly packed by the (gravitational) weight the whole star exerts on its own heart, that they barely have any freedom to move at all. Instead, they are forced to fuse into one another to become a bigger nucleus. You see it happening right in front of you: a *thermonuclear fusion reaction* (author's emphasis), the creation of big atomic cores out of smaller ones...once built, as they move out of the furnace that gave them birth, these heavy cores will team up with the lone, free-moving electrons that were stripped away from the hydrogen nuclei, and become new, heavier, atoms: nitrogen, carbon, oxygen, silver...all the heavy atoms the Earth is made of, all the atoms that are necessary for life, atoms that your body contains, were once forged in the heart of a star".

Once formed, these heavier atoms are distributed throughout Space as the stars which forged them reach the end of their life and explode or collapse, producing clouds of spacedust which eventually coalesce to form next-generation stars, and planets such as Earth. It is precisely because the Earth contains the mix of heavier atoms it does that we can deduce that our Sun, formed from the same spacedust which created Earth, must itself be at least second-generation. Galfard explains, on pp19-20: "since we are not made out of hydrogen and helium alone, since our bodies and the Earth, and everything that surrounds us also contain carbon and oxygen and other atoms, we know that our Sun is a second – or maybe even third-generation star. One or two generations of stars had to explode before their dust became the Sun, and the Earth, and us".

The fundamental particles are called "particles" as a kind of shorthand, and because in classical (for example, Newtonian) physics they were conceived of as being tiny spheres of solid matter. Nowadays, however, we know that in most circumstances they are more accurately thought of as wave-particles, because much, although not all, of their behaviour reflects that of a wave rather than of a solid object. Galfard offers what is therefore a more accurate description, on p184: "all atoms in the universe have this structure: a core (my note: in other words, nucleus) of varying size, surrounded by one or more electrically charged waves". We will return to the topic of wave-particle "duality" in our discussion of quantum mechanics, later in this chapter.

For now, though, we will continue with the discussion of atomic structure. Electrons cannot arrange themselves just anyhow around the nucleus of the particular atom to which they belong, but must rather conform to a rigid pattern. Galfard explains, on p197: "however identical they may all be to each other... electrons do not share their territory at all. Ever. They simply and plainly avoid being at the same place at the same time, because it so happens that nature forbids them from doing so: whatever the atom they belong to, their wavy selves overlap nowhere, thus imposing very strict conditions on their potential cohabitation within any atom. They have no choice but to arrange themselves in layers, like an onion, around the nucleus, and that is exactly what they do. Only two electrons can fill the first, innermost layer. Only eight can settle in the second, eighteen in the third, thirty-two in the fourth, and so on...Hydrogen, the smallest of atoms, has one electron whose orbital lies within the first electronic shell. Helium has two electrons. Their orbitals fill up the first shell. Neon, to take a third atom at random, has ten electrons. Its first two electronic shells are saturated. The chemical and mechanical properties of all the atoms are related to how full their external atomic shell is".

Atoms can themselves combine to form molecules. Again, the basic principles which govern molecular structure are always the same: molecules are formed by atoms sharing their electrons. Galfard explains, on pp199-200: "although electrons like their privacy, they do not mind being shared. And this allows them, rather fortunately for us, to build the matter we are made of...(for example) oxygen, with...eight electrons. Its first atomic shell is filled, but there is room for two more in its outermost shell, the second one, which has six electrons and could contain eight. The hydrogen atom's lone electrons are not about to let such an opportunity pass. (Imagining) there are two hydrogen atoms nearby...as soon as oxygen passes by, *hop* (author's emphasis), the first hydrogen's lone electron jumps over and settles down within the oxygen family, never to be alone again. And *hop* (author's emphasis, again)...the other hydrogen's electron fills in the last spot. And since all the electrons in the universe are exactly identical, no one can tell who was there in the first place and who arrived later. The perfect assimilation...the (hydrogen) nuclei here have no choice but to follow them, and so the three atoms are now stuck to one another.

Two hydrogens and one oxygen are forced to cohabit. This done, there is no more space available for any extra electron. The whole construction is stable. By sharing the electrons as above, atoms become part of larger structures, which are called *molecules* (author's emphasis). The molecule you've just seen being built is made of two atoms of hydrogen and one of oxygen. Two Hs and one O. H2O. It is water: the most precious molecule for life as we know it".

We saw that heavier atoms are formed in the heart of stars, and molecules also are often formed in Space. Indeed, the leading hypothesis for how the water molecules we drink and shower in as part of our everyday life were formed is that this probably did not happen on Earth, but rather in some distant part of outer space with the molecules then being brought to Earth, perhaps by comets or asteroids.

Galfard explains, on p200: "on a universal scale, water is...usually assembled in...outer space, inside the huge clouds of stardust that are scattered within galaxies, and which astronomers called *nebulae* (author's emphasis). Within these nebulae, the oxygen forged in exploded stars mixes with hydrogen, which can be found everywhere. When stars die, they send their seeds away, paving the way for water molecules to be built. And many other molecules as well".

And just as atoms vary in size and complexity, so do molecules. Galfard summarises, on p200-1: "by sharing one or more of their electrons, many atoms can be bound together, in many different ways, to form chains of various complexity. Nature has built molecules of different sizes and properties this way, from rather tiny ones (water molecules are made of three atoms only) to extraordinarily long ones, such as your own DNA, which, with its billions of joined atoms, carries all the information needed to build someone like you".

The degree to which atoms share their electrons determines the physical characteristics of the resulting matter, including whether it is solid, liquid or gas. Galfard explains, again, on pp201-2: "since both you and the air are made out of...atoms sharing their electrons, how is it, then, that you (very fortunately) can walk through air, but can't walk through a wall?...the answer is that the atoms in the air are not all sharing their electrons and hence don't hold onto each other that much whereas, forming a solid, yours are. Instead of stopping you from moving at all, the electrons that surround the atoms that make up air move away as yours force their way through, incidentally bumping into each other, creating some wind. That, incidentally, again, is the difference between a gas and a solid. In liquids, nearby atoms are a little more tightly bound to each other, but not enough to stop you, unless you try and enter too fast, like when diving off a cliff into the iron-grey sea. In solids, atoms don't move aside unless you force them hard to do so – think of sharp scissors cutting through paper".

With at least 92 different naturally-occurring atoms on Earth, there is of course potential for an enormous variety of different molecules. It is sobering to realise that the basic requirements for organic life as we know it on Earth were relatively modest. On p201 Galfard tells us: "only six atoms were necessary to build all the molecules required for life to thrive on Earth: carbon, hydrogen, nitrogen, oxygen, phosphorus, and sulphur".

The four fundamental forces and quantum fields

We saw earlier that the second category of fundamental particle is the Boson, and the different kinds of Boson are in turn associated with the four fundamental forces which govern all physical interactions throughout the Universe. Specifically:

• *The strong nuclear force*, which binds quarks together to form protons and neutrons, the components of an atomic nucleus. This is the strongest of the four forces, but is effective only at very short, sub-atomic, range.

• *The weak nuclear force*, which causes individual quarks within a proton or neutron to change "flavour", resulting in the radioactive decay of an unstable atom into smaller constituents, and also playing an important role in nuclear fusion. This force is also effective only at short, sub-atomic, range.

• *Electromagnetism*, which governs the way electrons interact with an atomic nucleus, and operates both at sub-atomic levels and also much longer, effectively infinite, ranges.

• *Gravity*, which governs how larger objects interact, including macroscopic objects such as humans and also stars, planets and indeed entire galaxies. Gravity is the weakest of the four forces but is effective over an infinite range. It exerts enormous influence on a cosmic scale but typically has little effect at the sub-atomic level.

Each of the first three of these fundamental forces has been shown to have its own force-carrying particle or particles, the Bosons. These interact with, which is to say exchange energy with, their corresponding fundamental matter particles, the Fermions. The CERN website again provides a helpful summary, in the same website module referenced above but in a different section called *Forces and carrier particles*: "three of the fundamental forces result from the exchange of force-carrier particles, which belong to a broader group called 'bosons'.

Particles of matter transfer discrete amounts of energy by exchanging bosons with each other. Each fundamental force has its own corresponding boson – the strong force is carried by the 'gluon', the electromagnetic force is carried by the 'photon', and the 'W and Z bosons' are responsible for the weak force". As an aside, photons are otherwise known as "particles" of light (the quotation marks are because they also behave as waves, as already noted), being the smallest possible packets of electromagnetic energy. Finally, a force-carrying particle for gravity has not yet been experimentally observed, but scientists hypothesise that one exists and have named it the "graviton" in anticipation.

The first three "forces" are in reality best conceived as "fields", specifically "quantum fields". Again, physicists hypothesise that gravity may eventually be explained in the same way, but so far this remains unproven. Each field permeates the entire Universe and effectively gives rise to what we observe as elementary matter particles.

Galfard explains, on p305 of *The Universe in Your Hand*: "quantum field theory asserts that as soon as there are fields around, these fields can create small packets of energy, or small packets of matter, which are called *quanta* (author's emphasis). The basic quanta of the electromagnetic field are the least energetic states of its elementary particles, the photons and the electrons. Similarly, the basic quanta of the strong nuclear force field give the quarks and gluons". The fundamental fields are essentially separate, although Galfard comments on pp210-1 that: "nothing prevents particles from (belonging to more than one field)...being electrically charged, the quarks belong to the electromagnetic field, as well as to the strong interaction one. They can interact with the force carriers of either: through light *and* (author's emphasis) gluons".

The fundamental fields do not exist independently from the fundamental matter particles with which they associate. Rather, the matter particles are an integral part of the relevant field, in effect an expression of it. Galfard gives the example of how an electron relates to the electromagnetic field, on pp188-9 of *The Universe in Your Hand*: "the electromagnetic field is everywhere, and every single electron that exists in the universe not only belongs to it, but also is exactly identical to any other electron, anywhere, and anywhen. Interchange two of them, and the universe won't notice. Because of that, because of the quantum field they are an expression of, electrons cannot be described as one would describe a macroscopic object. They belong to the field. They are part of it, like a drop of water in the vast ocean, or a gust of wind in the night air, a drop or a gust you cannot localise. As long as one does not look, drops and gusts are just like the ocean itself, like the wind. Mingled into an entity much vaster than themselves, they have no identity of their own".

In conclusion, the fundamental matter particles and the four fundamental forces of which they are an expression combine to create the Universe, including the world we experience. Galfard summarises, on p233: "Earth (is)...a lump of matter, made out of the three quantum fields known to mankind, held together by gravity, the so-called fourth force...floating within and through spacetime".

Quantum effects

The quantum world is perhaps the realm in which external reality diverges most from what our human senses might intuitively expect, developed as they are to help us survive and thrive in our everyday macroscopic life. Galfard is explicit, on p240: "the rules obeyed by quantum particles are not the same as the ones that rule your everyday life. Your senses and intuition are of no use with particles. Forget about them".

Of course, this does not make the quantum realm less real, nor less relevant or interesting. We'll therefore briefly review some of its most salient characteristics.

The quantum world is inherently probabilistic. This contrasts with the deterministic approach to reality taken by classical physics. Classical physics asserts that all matter is linked in an unbroken chain of cause and effect such that if we were ever once to have perfect knowledge of the past, we could predict with certainty the future. Quantum tells us instead that at the most fundamental level reality is governed by probabilities, and therefore that chance plays an important role.

Quantum uncertainty is encapsulated in the famous Heisenberg Uncertainty Principle, postulated by the German physicist Werner Heisenberg in 1927. This asserts that there is a fundamental limit to the accuracy with which the physical properties of a particle can be predicted, for example its speed and position. If we succeed in obtaining a precise measurement of an object's speed, it is a condition of the natural world that we cannot be certain about its position, and vice versa. This uncertainty is ontological not epistemological, which is to say that it is a feature of underlying reality, not of a shortcoming in our ability to have knowledge of that reality. It is therefore sometimes called the "indeterminacy principle", a label which is probably more accurate but has not caught the popular imagination in quite the same way.

Separately, it is worth noting that Heisenberg's Uncertainty Principle not the same as the "observer" effect, which Heisenberg also used. The observer effect states that one cannot observe something without in some way changing it. This is also called the Hawthorne effect when applied to human behaviour, named after studies conducted at the Hawthorne works in Chicago between 1924 and 1932 which concluded that the very act of observing workers resulted in changes in their productivity, independent of whatever process changes were supposedly being tested.

Galfard reinforces the uncertainty point, on p189 of *The Universe in Your Hand*: "in the quantum world, as soon as you look, the electrons do become particles with given properties, like drops taken out of the ocean, but their properties are like nothing you've ever seen. They do not behave as expected – or at least as our senses might expect from our experience of everyday life. If you know where an electron is, you *cannot* (author's emphasis) know how fast it is moving: its speed becomes unpredictable... in a similar way, if you know how much energy an electron has, you *cannot* (again, author's emphasis) know how long it will keep it".

He adds, on pp244-5: "the quantum world turns what we thought were certainties into possibilities, or probabilities, for us to probe with experiments, the outcome of which no one can guess with total confidence. Just like flipping a coin or rolling a dice. Scientists have thought that this uncertainty was linked to something missing in their knowledge, but it was proven that it is not thanks to a celebrated theorem published in 1964 by Northern Irish physicist, John Stewart Bell. Bell's theorem allowed French physicist Alain Aspect to experimentally show that the existence of possibilities rather than certainties is a property of the very small we'll just have to accept". As an aside, the full implications of Bell's theorem remain a matter of debate among scientists and mathematicians. For example, one interpretation appears to suggest the existence of communication faster than the speed of light, which would contradict a central tenet of modern physics. Fortunately, a fuller discussion of the theorem is beyond the scope of this book, and indeed this author.

Returning to our main discussion, quantum uncertainty extends to our ability to predict *where* a particular particle will be when we measure it. One of the strangest features of the quantum world is that a particle is best thought of as taking all possible paths between two points, such that the specific path it takes, and where on this path it is found, are crystallised only by the act of observation itself and cannot be predicted with certainty.

Galfard explains, on pp237-8: "a particle really does take *all* (author's emphasis) paths one can possibly imagine, whether they sound reasonable or not, as long as one does not look. Particles move and behave like nothing you've ever seen or experienced in your daily life…belonging to a quantum field means that particles really do split into many images of themselves, all the time. And the paths taken by all these images fill in every spot there is in space and time, with you having only a chance, a probability really, of finding a particle at *one* (author's emphasis) particular time and place".

Moving along, sub-atomic particles also exhibit "wave-particle duality", as already noted. This literally means that they are capable of behaving as *both* a wave, pictured, for example, as the ripples on the water when a stone is thrown into a pond; and *also* as a particle, often pictured as a tiny spherical ball.

Light is a celebrated example. For centuries physicists argued about whether light was most appropriately thought of as a particle or a wave. Around 1700 CE Isaac Newton concluded that it is made of particles (now called "photons", as we saw), and this view prevailed for about

100 years, at which point the scientific consensus swung the other way behind wave theory.

Then in 1905 a certain Albert Einstein published the paper which won him a Nobel Prize, demonstrating that light exists as tiny packets ("quanta") and that these exhibit the properties of *both* waves *and* particles. This remarkable insight has subsequently been extended to include all sub-atomic particles, meaning that *all* fundamental particles are more appropriately described as wave-particles.

The next point about the quantum world is that physical characteristics such as energy and momentum are restricted to discrete values, and these are finite i.e. not infinitely divisible. What this means is that a particular quantum particle can notionally have a physical property with a value of say 1 or 2, but not 1.5 or any other intermediate value in between 1 and 2. There is also always a minimum "quantum" value, which cannot be further reduced or divided. By contrast, classical physics assumes an unbroken continuum, in which any and all intermediate values are possible; and has no minimum values, but rather allows for values to be reduced to infinity. These may seem like abstract distinctions, but they turn out to have important consequences for our understanding of how the natural world works.

The next noteworthy feature of quantum particles is that are capable of performing the famous "quantum leaps", also known as quantum jumps. A particular particle might literally disappear from one position and appear in another, without passing through any intermediate points. This is of course consistent with the observation above that the quantum world only allows for discrete, not intermediate, values. It also conforms to the principle of "allowed states", whereby a quantum object will only ever be observed in certain very specific states, never in any intermediate ones.

American physicist Chad Orzel explains, on p73 of his 2010 book *How to Teach Quantum Physics to Your Dog*: "an electron orbiting the nucleus of an atom can only be found in certain very specific states. Each of these states has a particular energy, and the electron will always be found with one of those energies, never in an in-between state. Electrons can move between those states by absorbing or emitting light of a particular frequency – the red light of a neon lamp, for example, is due to a transition between two states in neon atoms – but they make those jumps instantaneously, without passing through the intermediate energies. This is the origin of the term 'quantum leap' for a dramatic change between two conditions – the actual energy jump is very small, but the change in the state happens in no time at all".

Quantum particles also spontaneously appear and disappear, everywhere throughout space and time. Far from being an empty vacuum, space is therefore filled with a maelstrom of fundamental matter particles appearing and disappearing apparently at random as they interact with their force fields. On pp245-6 of *The Universe in Your Hand* Galfard imagines a thought-experiment in which a (highly) miniaturised version of you is able to observe this happening at first hand: "you are back in the middle of what seems to be the cosmic night, alone, surrounded by nothingness...it is as if...a particle (or maybe there were two, you aren't sure) just appeared right in front of you, before vanishing in a puff of light. There was nothing around, and then there was something, and now there isn't anything any more. Strange. And now it happens again. And again. And countless other times, everywhere. What you are witnessing is the apparently spontaneous creation of particles out of nothing...but how can they just pop out of nothing? Well, it is not nothing that surrounds them. There are quantum fields around. To appear, particles have to borrow some energy from the quantum field. And since those fields fill in every place in space and time, particles can literally appear anywhere, at any time. That is the reason why there is no such thing as true emptiness, anywhere in the universe".

Particles within a particular quantum field can also interchange. For example, within the electromagnetic field electrons can literally turn into the force-carrying photons (otherwise known as light particles) and vice versa; and within the strong nuclear field quarks can turn into gluons, and gluons into quarks. Galfard comments, on p194: "the most well-known fundamental particles of the electromagnetic field, namely the electrons and the photons, can and do interact with each other...electrons and photons can turn into one another...it is such an incredible discovery that I here say it again: matter and light can, and do, turn into one another".

And on p213: "just as light can be transformed into an electron, (so)...gluons (can) transform themselves into...quarks". This ability to morph from one state to another is incredible in its own right, of course, and also because it is the concrete manifestation of one of Einstein's central theories which we will shortly review in our discussion of Relativity, namely that energy and mass are themselves interchangeable, different expressions of essentially the same fundamental thing. Electrons and, especially, protons and neutrons (both made from quarks) have mass; whereas photons and gluons have energy but no mass. As it happens, an electron has only about one two-thousandth the mass of a proton or neutron, which is to say that almost the entire mass of an atom is concentrated in its nucleus. But the principle is the same regardless.

Finally, total system energy is always conserved. This is sometimes stated as the First Law of Thermodynamics, although the modern definition includes not just heat but all energy and matter throughout the Universe. Simply stated, all the energy in the Universe was present at its origin (the so-called "Big Bang") and will still be there at its demise. What this means at the sub-atomic level is that individual particles may come and go, but they never "die", in the sense that the energy they represent is always maintained even if in a different form.

Quantum effects in our everyday world

An obvious question is: why do we not observe quantum effects in our everyday life? Why, for example, do we not see a macroscopic object such as a chair, or indeed a person, spontaneously disappear, or conversely appear, in the way that fundamental particles do? Alternatively, if reality is inherently probabilistic how is it that we can predict with confidence the orbit of the Moon around the Earth, or the movements of the planets in general?

The short answer is that larger structures mostly lack "coherence", which is to say that the individual wave-particles from which they are made behave randomly rather than in unison. This means that the quantum wavefunctions of each particle tend to cancel out, even as each particle itself behaves in a quantum way.

There are nonetheless some exceptions, and the American physicist Christopher Baird provides a more detailed answer, in an article called *Why do quantum effects only happen on the atomic scale?*, published online on 22 April 2014 as part of a series called *Science Questions with Surprising Answers*. It's a long quote, reflecting the complexity of the topic:

"Quantum effects are not only confined to the atomic scale. There are several examples of macroscopic quantum behaviour. Quantum physics describes matter and energy as quantum wavefunctions, which sometimes act like waves, and sometimes acts like particles, but are actually more complicated entities than just waves or particles. In reality, every object in the universe (from atoms to stars) operates according to quantum physics. In many situations, such as when throwing a baseball, quantum physics leads to the same result as classical physics. In such situations, we use classical physics instead of quantum physics, because the mathematics is easier and the principles are more intuitive. The laws of quantum physics are still operating in a baseball thrown across the field, but their operation is not obvious, so we say the system is non-quantum.

A situation is described as quantum when its quantum behaviour becomes obvious, even though it is really always quantum. A 'quantum effect' is therefore an effect that is not properly predicted by classical physics, but *is* (author's emphasis) properly predicted by quantum theory. Classical physics describes matter as composed of little, solid particles. Therefore, any time we get the pieces of matter to act like waves, we are demonstrating a quantum effect. (Classical waves such as sound and sea waves don't count as quantum because the motion is a wave, but the pieces are still little solid balls. In order to be a quantum effect, the particle itself must be acting like a wave.)...while quantum effects are not strictly confined to the atomic scale, they certainly are more common at the atomic scale.

Why is this? Let's look at matter. To be a quantum effect, we have to get matter to act like waves. To be a macroscopic quantum effect, we have to get many bits of matter to act like waves *in an organised fashion* (author's emphasis). If all the bits of matter are acting like waves in a random, disjointed manner, then their waves interfere and average away to zero on the macroscopic scale. In physics, we refer to an organised wave-like behaviour as 'coherence'. The more the wave-like natures of the bits of matter are aligned, the more coherent is the object overall. And the more coherent an object, the more it acts like a wave overall. As a rough analogy, consider a group of kids splashing about in the swimming pool. If the kids are all doing their own thing, then the water waves they create when they splash will be random. A bunch of random water waves adds up to approximately zero. This system is non-coherent and the water waves are not obvious, unless you look closely.

Now, if the kids line up and all splash the water at the same moment every two seconds, all of their little waves add up to one giant wave of water. This system is coherent, and the water wave in the pool is obvious. The swimming pool is only an analogy. Water waves act like waves of little solid particles, and are therefore classical and not quantum. In order to act like quantum waves, bits of matter must not just have their motions aligned, the bits of matter must also have their quantum wave natures aligned...the key here is that a large-scale, coherent state is improbable as long as the individual parts are behaving randomly. There are only a handful of possible ways to have a system of pieces act in a coordinated fashion, while there are far more ways to have the system act in an uncoordinated fashion.

Therefore, coordinated behaviour is less likely than uncoordinated behaviour, although not impossible. For example, if you roll 5 traditional dice, there are six ways to get all the numbers to be the same in one roll. In contrast, there are thousands of ways to get all the numbers to *not* (author's emphasis) be the same. Getting the dice to show the same number is improbable but not impossible. In a similar way, quantum coherence on the macroscopic scale is improbable, but not impossible. If the quantum wave natures of the individual bits of matter can be aligned into a coherent state, then quantum effects will become evident on the macroscopic scale. Below are some examples of macroscopic quantum effects.

- *Superconductivity.* When a conducting material is cooled enough, its conduction electrons spread out into large-scale, coherent wave states. These coherent wave states are able to flow past impurities and atoms without being perturbed, so that a material with zero electrical resistance results. Superconductivity leads to interesting macroscopic affects such as quantum levitation (the Meissner effect).

- *Superfluidity.* When certain materials are cooled enough, their atoms can spread out into coherent wave states that resist surface tension, allowing the material to flow like a liquid with zero viscosity.

- *Bose Einstein condensate.* When certain materials are cooled enough, their atoms spread out completely into a single, giant, coherent wave state. A macroscopic chunk of matter that has condensed in this way acts like a wave and exhibits wave properties such as interference".

So there we are. Quantum activity is all around us all the time at the most fundamental level of external reality, somewhat spookily including within our own body. With rare exceptions, however, we are unlikely to observe or be aware of it at the macroscopic level in which we live.

Relativity

Albert Einstein published his theory of Special Relativity in 1905, and his theory of General Relativity in 1915. Together, they are the foundation for our modern understanding of cosmology - how very large, planet-sized objects interact in the Universe. Like quantum mechanics, Relativity also produces some startlingly counter-intuitive conclusions, which again challenge our commonsense notions of how things work in our everyday human lives.

Special Relativity explains how space and time are linked for objects that are moving at a consistent speed in a straight line. It is "special" because it deliberately makes this simplifying assumption to avoid having to deal with the effects of gravity, addressed in the General Theory.

Special Relativity takes as its starting point the speed of light. In the 1880s, the American physicist Albert Michelson had shown that the speed of light is a constant. Einstein's equations show it to be the speed limit of the Universe, which is to say that it is not possible for *anything* to move faster. Building on this, the Special Theory of Relativity goes on to provide proof that the underlying laws of nature are the same for observers in all reference frames. In this sense, these laws can legitimately be said to be absolute – they apply in exactly the same way at all times, everywhere in the Universe. What differs is an observers' subjective, relative, experience of say space and time, which varies with their particular circumstances and point of reference. Said another way, there is no such thing as a truly objective frame of reference. Rather, our experiences and observations are strictly relative, shaped by our own position and momentum relative to that of others.

An important finding of the Special Theory is that space and time are not separate, but are aspects of a single underlying reality, Spacetime. And one of the most unsettling conclusions is that neither are universal constants as we might think, but are in reality different for observers moving at different relative speeds, a phenomenon known as kinetic "dilation" of time and/or space ("length" is sometimes used as another word for "space": for our purposes they are synonymous). What this means is that time literally moves relatively more slowly for an object travelling at a relatively higher speed; and in the same way length literally contracts. Conversely, velocity, for example the speed of light, is what it is. Galfard summarises, on p152 of *The Universe in Your Hand*: "velocities are not observer-dependent. Only time and lengths are".

To illustrate, if it were possible for two identical twins to travel through spacetime at vastly different velocities, the twin travelling fastest would experience time moving significantly more slowly, relative to his or her fellow twin. Galfard explains, on pp142-3 of *The Universe in Your Hand*: "let us imagine twins...French physicist Paul Langevin calculated, using special relativity, that if one of the twins was sent in a rocket for a six-month round trip away from Earth at 99.995 per cent of the speed of light, the one who stayed on Earth would have to wait 50 years to see his sibling come back. So according to Einstein, six months lived by the one who left in the rocket ship should equate to fifty years for the one who stayed on Earth, and for the whole of humanity too: our planet would orbit the Sun fifty times during the travelling twin's voyage. Although they are twins, they would end up not having the same age at all, one being forty-nine years and six months older than the other".

And although we are unlikely to experience such extreme levels of relative difference in our everyday life, time dilation nonetheless has practical application.

For example, GPS navigation systems rely on signals which pass between orbiting satellites and earth-bound receivers, and as part of their calculations GPS engineers must account for the effects of kinetic time dilation on these signals. Since the satellites have a higher velocity relative to the earth-bound receivers, kinetic time dilation causes time to move relatively slower for the satellites, not to the same extent as for Langevin's imaginary twins of course, but still to a level that would quickly make the system unusable if not accounted for. Not to confuse things, the engineers must also factor in the time dilation caused by gravity, a finding of the later

General Theory of Relativity whereby time also flows more slowly when gravity is relatively stronger. Gravitational time dilation is a counter-effect because in this case it is the receivers for which time flows more slowly, since they are closer to the Earth's centre and therefore exposed to relatively higher gravity.

The specifics are explained in an article titled *Real-World Relativity: The GPS Navigation System*, authored by Richard Pogge and published on the Ohio State University website on 11 March 2017. Pogge calculates that time moves faster overall for a satellite relative to a receiver by about 38 microseconds per day, being the net of -7 microseconds due to kinetic time dilation, and +45 microseconds as a result of gravitational time dilation. A difference of 38 microseconds per day may not seem much, but Pogge points out: "if these effects were not properly taken into account, a navigational fix based on the GPS constellation would be false after only 2 minutes, and errors in global positions would continue to accumulate at a rate of about 10 kilometres each day! The whole system would be utterly worthless for navigation in a very short time".

Space, or length, also dilates. Simply put, this means that distance shrinks as speed increases. It is not just that a higher speed allows us to reach a given destination more quickly: the actual distance we have to travel reduces.

Galfard explains, on p150 of *The Universe in Your Hand*: "a metre is always a metre, you might think? Well, that is not correct. It depends on who is looking at it. Space and time are linked to one another: if time changes, distances also have to give".

He elaborates in the form of another thought-experiment, on pp151-2: "in outer space, light travels at around 300,000 kilometres per second. An Earth-based observer watching you fly at 87 per cent the speed of light would see you travel 260,000 kilometres in one of his seconds. Flying that fast, however, you must remember that the seconds you experience are now different from his. At 87 per cent the speed of light, one second of yours equates to *two* seconds on Earth – and in those two seconds the Earth-based observer sees you travel 520,000 kilometres. That's twice the distance he sees you cover in one second. Nothing peculiar here, right? Wrong. Because, although you'd have travelled 520,000 kilometres in two of *his* seconds, only *one* of yours has passed. That's 520,000 kilometres per second, as far as you are concerned. The speed of light being 300,000 kilometres per second, you'd have smashed the universal record...but this is forbidden. Not by the police, but by nature. Remember: *nothing* can travel faster than light...in (Einstein's) theory of moving bodies, the special theory of relativity, times and distances have to dilate and contract in such a way that, whoever is watching, no object can ever cross the light-speed limit from anyone's point of view. An Earth-based observer's time flows twice as fast as yours? Then the distances you travel are, from your point of view, half the ones the observer sees you cross. Flying at 87 per cent the speed of light you do *not* travel 520,000 kilometres every second, but 260,000. What seems to be a kilometre for an Earth-based observer is actually half a kilometre for you. Your speed is always the same, whoever measures it, be it you or anyone else (author's emphases throughout)".

Finally, on p152 Galfard tells us that the effects of space dilation apply to objects, as well as distances: "objects themselves shrink with speed too...at 87 per cent the speed of light, flying like Superman, fist stretched out ahead, you (would shrink) to half your length as measured by someone on Earth. And someone flying with you would not (notice it), for their tape measure would also (shrink). This is all a consequence of accepting a fixed, finite and unbeatable speed for light".

A third feature of special relativity is Einstein's celebrated insight that energy and mass (in other words, matter) are interchangeable - in effect different expressions of a single underlying reality. What is more, Energy and Mass have a specific rate of exchange, expressed, of course, in surely the most famous equation in physics: $e = mc2$. Specifically, a given amount of Energy ("e"; measured in joules) is equal to the resting mass ("m"; measured in kilograms) of an object, multiplied by the speed of light ("c"; measured in metres per second) squared. The speed of light is around 300,000 kilometres (around 186,000 miles) per second. Hence "mc squared" almost inevitably produces an enormous number, meaning that a huge amount of energy can be obtained from a small amount of mass. The reverse is also true - a large amount of energy is needed to create a small amount of mass. The critical insight is that energy and mass are different manifestations of the same fundamental physical thing; or alternatively, that mass can be thought of as simply a different form of energy.

Like Spacetime dilation, $e = mc2$ has robustly practical application to our everyday world. Most obvious is the nuclear industry, including bombs of course and also civil power generation. Contemporary technologies for power generation rely on nuclear fission, in which the atoms of an unstable element such as certain kinds of uranium, or alternatively plutonium, are split and decay into smaller, more stable atoms, in the process releasing a tremendous amount of energy and also producing some unfortunate by-products with the capacity to harm, such as alpha particles and gamma rays. As we saw earlier, however, there is an altogether different source of nuclear power called nuclear fusion, which is what powers our Sun and indeed all other stars in the Universe. In this, atoms of hydrogen are "fused" into helium, releasing energy in the process. There are hopes that nuclear fusion may eventually be harnessed for commercial application on

Earth, and this would surely be a good thing since hydrogen is plentiful as a fuel source, and the process of nuclear fusion does not produce harmful by-products in the way that fission does.

The main point for our purposes, though, is that in their different ways nuclear fission and fusion are both examples of Einstein's insight that mass can be turned into energy, at a highly favourable rate of exchange.

The reverse process, of energy turning into mass, also occurs. Indeed, it becomes inevitable at speeds approaching the speed of light. Galfard explains, on pp149-50 of *The Universe in Your Hand*: "nothing with any mass can reach the speed of light, let alone break that speed. That's a law. So the faster anything with mass is travelling, the more difficult it gets to accelerate it.

To see what this means in practice, picture yourself flying so fast that adding only 1 km an hour to your tachymeter would mean reaching the speed of light. You then take a tennis ball out of your pocket, and throw it ahead of you. Let's say for the sake of argument that you throw it at 20 kilometres per hour...on Earth, that'd be easy. But right now, it isn't. In fact, it is impossible *Nothing* (author's emphasis) can move faster than light.

So as you fly along at just 1 kilometre per hour short of light speed, your ball simply *couldn't* (author's emphasis again) go 20 kilometres per hour faster...nothing prevents you from throwing the ball, that's true – but if the ball can't travel faster than the speed of light, than clearly something else will have to give as you hurl it into the void ahead of you. And the answer is given by our old friend $e = mc2$: the extra energy you give the ball by throwing it forwards is turned into mass, since it cannot turn into speed. (To be more precise, at such extraordinary velocities, Einstein's equation needs some corrections (and Einstein is the one who found them), but the idea is basically the same)".

Turning to General Relativity, this explains how large objects move relative to one another through Spacetime, effectively replacing Newton's Laws of Gravity.

Newton's concept was that objects with mass exert an attractive force on one another, and whilst the resulting maths is accurate in the majority of situations relevant to our everyday lives, anomalies were also observed. For example, some specific movements of the planets were shown to be aberrations according to Newton's Law but are perfectly predicted by General Relativity.

The central idea behind General Relativity is that energy, whether from matter, momentum or radiation (for example heat), curves Spacetime in ways that are predictable and observable, at least when sufficiently large amounts of energy and therefore curvature are involved. Massive objects then "fall" in predictable trajectories, proportional to the geometric curvature of Spacetime in whichever region they happen to be.

A popular analogy is to imagine a rubber sheet held in such a way that it curves in the middle. If a marble were dropped onto this sheet on any surface at the top, it would inevitably fall to the middle, following the curvature of the sheet. This curvature of Spacetime is what we think of as gravity, and it affects everything in the Universe. For example, even light "bends" in proportion to the curvature of Spacetime in whichever part of the Universe it happens to be, causing it to change wavelength in predictable and measurable ways.

Finally, another noteworthy feature of General Relativity which has caught the popular imagination is that it also predicts the existence of "Black Holes" – regions of Spacetime in which the concentration of energy is so dense that even light cannot escape its gravitational pull. Black Holes exist at the centre of each of the billions of separate galaxies which populate Space, including our own, and in other places besides.

Unifying Quantum Mechanics with Relativity

Quantum Mechanics does an excellent job explaining events in the subatomic realm, specifically through something called the Standard Model of Physics which integrates three of the four fundamental forces: the Strong and Weak Nuclear Forces and Electromagnetism. General Relativity does an excellent job explaining how the Universe works at a cosmological scale, through the curvature effect of the fourth "force", gravity.

Unfortunately, however, the two theories are not compatible with each other.

For example, when the predictions of General Relativity are scaled down to the quantum world of subatomic particles the maths simply does not work, yielding infinite values in its description of gravity. Conversely, scaling up quantum predictions to a cosmic level also gives nonsensical answers, predicting the existence of so much energy that the Universe would inevitably collapse in on itself.

This failure to agree is not trivial to resolve. Indeed, it is a difference of underlying concept, not just maths. In an article titled *Relativity versus quantum mechanics: the battle for the universe*, published online by the UK *Guardian* newspaper on 4 November 2015, American science journalist Corey Powell quotes Sean Carroll, an expert in cosmology at Caltech: "the real issue is not general relativity versus quantum mechanics, but classical dynamics versus quantum dynamics. Relativity, despite its perceived strangeness, is classical in how it regards cause and effect; quantum mechanics most definitely is not".

Specifically, at its core Relativity assumes a deterministic view of how the Universe works, in line with classical physics from the Ancient Greeks to Newton. As we saw earlier, in such a world a given "cause" will certainly and always produce a corresponding "effect", so that if we were to have perfect information about a cause, we could predict with certainty what would be its consequence.

This implies that if we could ever achieve perfect knowledge of the present and the past, we would in principle have similarly perfect knowledge of the future, a concept known as scientific determinism.

Pierre-Simon Laplace (he of "I had no need of that hypothesis" fame) is reckoned to be the first to frame the implications of such of a view, in what has become known as "Laplace's demon", described in his *A Philosophical Essay on Probabilities*, published in 1814: "we may regard the present state of the universe as the effect of its past and the cause of its future. An intellect which at a certain moment would know all the forces that set nature in motion, and all positions of all items of which nature is composed, if this intellect were also vast enough to submit these data to analysis, it would embrace in a single formula the movements of the greatest bodies of the universe and those of the tiniest atom; for such an intellect nothing would be uncertain and the future just like the past would be present before its eyes".

Relativity also aligns with classical physics in assuming that Spacetime is smoothly continuous and infinitely divisible. Obviously there are other topics on which Relativity differs from the classical view, for example the insight that Spacetime is a single, relativistic, entity. But this is beside the point for the present discussion.

In the Quantum world, by contrast, events have probabilistic not definite outcomes – in other words, even if we have perfect information about a cause we can predict its effect only in terms of a probability, not a certainty. In the quantum world, then, achieving perfect knowledge of the past would *not* mean that we could be certain about the future.

Also, as we saw quantum phenomena can only have discrete values, or "quanta". Events produced by the interaction of subatomic particles do not happen along a smoothly continuous spectrum of outcomes but rather in jumps - the famous "quantum leaps" that we briefly reviewed earlier. There is always a minimum value (or quantum) for any entity, below which it cannot be further divided or reduced.

Relativity and Quantum are therefore incompatible in important ways, even though they each do an excellent job of describing their respective fields of focus. The search for a single "unified theory" has been ongoing for the past hundred years and remains in many ways the Holy Grail of contemporary physics.

Einstein passionately believed at an intuitive level in the classical view, notwithstanding the irony that it was his own work which had overturned it and given birth to quantum theory. Indeed, he spent most of the second part of his career fruitlessly trying to find evidence to support his classically-aligned intuition. Einstein's famous comment that "God does not play dice" is best understood in this context, as an endorsement of classical determinism, rather than as an avowal of religious sentiment (as an aside, and for what it is worth, Einstein disavowed the notion of any kind of personal god, concerned with humanity, nor did he believe in life after death. He nonetheless stopped short of calling himself an atheist, for example asserting in a letter to a correspondent called Joseph Dispentiere dated 24 March

1954: "I do not believe in a personal god...if there is something in me which can be called religious then it is the unbounded admiration for the structure of the world so far as our science can reveal it").

Still, quantum and Relativity cannot ultimately both be right; something will have to give. And these days much, although certainly not all, of the smart money believes that some form of the quantum view will ultimately prevail. Sean Carroll from Caltech, again quoted in Powell's *Guardian* online article, summarises: "most of us in the game believe that quantum mechanics is much more fundamental than general relativity is". In other words, that the entire natural world is ultimately driven by probability and therefore chance, and not by deterministic certainty.

It is possible that the problem will be solved by incorporating into Relativity the hypothesis that space and time are themselves quantised rather than operating as a smooth, infinitely-divisible continuum. This in turn would mean that there is a minimum unit value to which the mathematical equations should be applied, and there is hope that such an explanation would eliminate at least some of the mathematical problems which result from scaling-down Relativity.

In the meantime, quantum, in the form of the Standard Model, co-exists alongside General Relativity. Fortunately, this works for the majority of applications because, as the weakest of the four forces, gravity typically does not materially affect the sub-atomic world.

CERN explains, in the same website module *The Standard Model* referenced earlier: "the Standard Model includes the electromagnetic, strong and weak forces, and all the carrier particles, and explains well how these forces act on all of the matter particles. However, the most familiar force in our everyday lives, gravity, is not part of the Standard Model, as fitting gravity comfortably into this framework has proved to be a difficult challenge. The quantum theory used to describe the micro world, and the general theory of relativity used to describe the macro world, are difficult to fit into a single framework. No one has managed to make the two mathematically compatible in the context of the Standard Model. But luckily for particle physics, when it comes to the miniscule scale of particles, the effect of gravity is so weak as to be negligible. Only when matter is in bulk, at the scale of the human body or of the planets for example, does the effect of gravity dominate. So the Standard Model still works well, despite its reluctant exclusion of one of the fundamental forces".

Antimatter, dark matter, and dark energy

Our understanding of the Universe includes three other phenomena which we will mention for completeness but touch on only fleetingly, in the interests of brevity.

First, a characteristic of the quantum fields is that each fundamental particle has an anti-self. In other words, matter is balanced by anti-matter. Galfard explains, on pp260-1 of *The Universe in Your Hand*: "an electron never appears alone. It must appear alongside a particle that is identical to it, except for its charge, which is opposite. Such a particle is called an *anti-electron* (my note: also called a 'positron')...the process by which an electron and its anti-self appear out of nothing is called a particle-antiparticle *pair creation*, and the opposite process also exists: when an electron meets an anti-electron, they *annihilate*, they disappear, *puff!* gone, their mass transformed back into energy, into light, in an instant. Electrons and their anti-selves are created out of the electromagnetic field, and they melt back into it when they annihilate (author's emphases throughout)."

All fundamental particles have anti-selves, as Galfard explains on p262: "what is true for the electron is true for all particles. They all have their anti-selves. Anti-quarks, exist, and so do anti-neutrinos, and anti-photons. But some particles, ones that do not carry a charge, can play both sides and be their *own* (author's emphasis) antiparticles. Light is a good example: because photons and anti-photons carry no charge, they are identical".

He continues: "so why don't we see...antiparticles around us, everywhere we look? The answer is that they *are* (again, author's emphasis) there, around us, around you, but not in large quantities, because, whenever one appears, it only lives for a very, very short time (before it annihilates)".

The existence of antimatter prompts the question how it is that matter has come to dominate in the Universe. If matter and antimatter particles are always produced together and then rapidly annihilate, how come there is any surviving matter at all?

CERN describes this question as "one of the greatest challenges in physics", in an entry on their website titled *The matter-antimatter asymmetry problem*. They go on to hint at a possible, albeit as yet non-specific, solution: "matter and antimatter particles are always produced as a pair and, if they come in contact, annihilate one another, leaving behind pure energy. During the first fractions of a second of the Big Bang, the hot and dense universe was buzzing with particle-antiparticle pairs, popping in and out of existence. If matter and antimatter are created and destroyed together, it seems the universe should contain nothing but leftover energy. Nevertheless, a tiny portion of matter – about one particle per billion – managed to survive. This is what we see today. In the past few decades, particle-physics experiments have shown that the laws of nature do not apply equally to matter and antimatter...researchers have observed spontaneous transformations between particles and their antiparticles, occurring millions of times per second before they decay. Some unknown entity intervening in this process in the early universe could have caused these 'oscillating' particles to decay as matter more often than they decayed as antimatter".

Time, and further scientific research, will hopefully tell.

As with the dilation of time and space, the existence of anti-matter may seem abstract but in fact has robust practical application to humanity, for example underpinning the operation of positron emission tomography (PET) scanners, used for a range of advanced medical diagnoses. Positrons are emitted by radioactive samples injected into a patient, and when these positrons encounter an electron they both annihilate, emitting gamma radiation which is then detected by the machine and used to produce detailed three-dimensional images of the inside of the body.

The second phenomenon is "dark matter", a term coined by the Dutch astronomer Jan Oort who in the 1930s identified that the amount of ordinary matter in the known Universe is insufficient to account for the gravitational movements of the stars at a cosmic scale, for example the rotation of our Sun around the centre of our galaxy, a rotation which incidentally requires 250 million years for a single orbit.

Oort's studies confirmed that there should be around five times more matter in the Universe than we previously knew existed. This extra matter is "dark" precisely because it is invisible to our human senses and even to our current scientific instruments.

And the third phenomenon is "dark energy". As with dark matter, we infer the existence of dark energy rather than being able to observe it directly.

Galfard explains, on pp339-40 of *The Universe in Your Hand*: "in 1998, two independent teams...published their results. One was led by US astrophysicist Saul Perlmutter and the other by US astrophysicists Brian Schmitt and Adam Riess. Both teams found out that about 5 billion years ago, after more than 8 billion years of normal behaviour, the universe's expansion started to accelerate...at large scales, it is Einstein's general relativity that rules everything and Einstein's gravity, like Newton's, only allows for objects to attract one another. Whatever fills in the universe, be it matter or antimatter or dark matter, must hence, in the long run, slow down any expansion. Not accelerate it...the only possible way out of this contradiction was for something very new to be introduced to account for such an acceleration. And this something had to fill the entire universe. And it needed to have an extraordinary property: it had to be acting as an *anti-* (author's emphasis) gravitational force, repelling matter and energy, instead of attracting them. For some unknown reason, this new force overcame all the other large-scale forces in our universe about 5 billion years ago. Before that, its effect was zero".

Dark matter and dark energy may be invisible to us as humans, but they exert an enormous influence on the cosmos. Galfard summarises, on p340: "today, according to NASA's satellite estimates...the energetic content of our universe...consists of the following: dark energy: 72%; dark matter: 23%; the matter we know (including light): 4.6% (the total does not add up to 100%, because there are always some uncertainties in the numbers obtained)".

The Universe in our hand

Putting all this together, and accepting that for the moment we have no synthesis between quantum mechanics and gravity, our understanding of how our Universe works allows us to create a seamless picture:

from the largest possible scale, that of the Universe itself; down to the smallest possible, which is to say the fundamental particles, the fermions and bosons.

Galfard has been our main guide throughout this section and it is therefore appropriate to give him the final word.

On pp391-2 he imagines taking us on a journey which starts by seeing the Universe in its entirety and progressively narrows in scope: "our whole visible universe is a sphere 13.8 billion light years in radius. From such a gigantic perspective, one first sees filaments of giant clusters of galaxies, bathed within gases and dark matter, and, more fundamentally, all the quantum fields there are. These can't be seen from that far up, but they can be felt...you are out there, watching it all, and you start zooming in...you see galaxies...with their hundreds of billions of stars. Their supermassive central black holes spit jets of the most energetic light and matter there is. You see the dark matter's presence. You see it preventing the galaxies from being torn apart because of their own spinning. Keep zooming in. You are at the scale of stars, huge balls of burning-hot plasma, shining the light that we humans use to probe the distant universe. Then come the planets, spherical worlds too small ever to become stars. Smaller yet, there are the asteroids, the comets, the living beings that our planet harbours beneath 100 kilometres of atmosphere. And then come the microbes, the cells, the molecules, the atoms, the electrons and photons, the protons and neutrons, the quarks and the gluons. Keep zooming in. You are back into quantum-field territory".

The defining feature of this extraordinary, indeed beautiful, picture is that it is entirely material – there is no need of, or room for, any supernatural element.

PART B: Biology

Evolution

Quantum mechanics and Relativity tell us much about the physical Universe. They are less helpful when it comes to the question of life itself, and the natural laws which govern that.

For this we need to turn to the celebrated Victorian English naturalist Charles Darwin, and his theory of evolution by natural selection. Darwin published *On the Origin of Species by Means of Natural Selection* in 1859, although much of the content had been developed 20 years earlier. His caution in publishing was largely because he anticipated that his findings would prove controversial to a scientific world where the prevailing orthodoxy was that all species were the fixed and essentially unchanging product of a divine Creator, with humans specially selected by said Creator to "rule" an Earth created expressly for their own convenience and pleasure. According to this view, humans are above all "special", separate from and superior to other life forms.

Darwin was right to anticipate that his theory would prove controversial. Approaching 200 years later, however, he has also been proved right in a more important sense, in that evolution by natural selection is established as the definitive theory for how life developed, and continues to develop, on Earth. There is overwhelming evidence to support it, and not a shred of evidence so far found which clearly contradicts it, despite many efforts with that objective in mind. This is not to say that everyone agrees on the finer details of how evolution works specifically, but that is a different point.

Evolution as a concept has also been found to be relevant in a wide range of other domains, well beyond the biological realm in which it was conceived: for example in fields such as anthropology, sociology, psychology, economics, politics, computer science, and culture. Unfortunately, it must be acknowledged that there are also cases in which the idea has been misused, such as the infamous experiments conducted in the early to mid-20th century in the fields of eugenics and racial engineering.

The core idea is disarmingly simple, more intuitive than many of the insights that we have reviewed from modern physics. In a competitive world, individuals who are better equipped to survive and reproduce will by definition tend to have relatively more offspring. These offspring will inherit whatever the characteristics are which made the parents successful. And so over multiple generations these preferred characteristics will become relatively more prevalent in the population at large, as the individuals who possess them out-compete and out-reproduce those who do not. Given enough generations, and assuming a sufficient margin of superiority, the favoured characteristics will come to dominate and those less favoured will disappear.

The operation of this process on biological life explains how species develop, flourish, and eventually go extinct as either more successful competitors develop or the prevailing environment changes such that characteristics which were previously helpful lose their advantage.

The key point is that, in biology as in all other domains in which the evolutionary process operates, selection pressure ensures that variations ("mutations") which are better adapted to the prevailing environment out-compete, that is are more successful in surviving and replicating than, versions which are less well suited. Therefore, over time these "fitter" variations will tend to become relatively more prevalent in the population.

To quote from the original source, in the Introduction to *On the Origin of Species* Darwin posits a natural world in which all living things are engaged in a quotidian struggle for survival, essentially because the reproductive capacity of Earth's many species is greater than the resources necessary to support them, and whilst reproductive capacity is in principle exponential, resource supply is not. In such a world, it is inevitable that an organism which is better adapted in some way to compete for the available resources will prosper, at the expense of one which is not, and will therefore bequeath relatively more copies of itself to posterity – a process Darwin calls "natural selection".

He defines this on p14 of *On the Origin of Species*: "the Struggle for Existence amongst all organic beings throughout the world, which inevitably follows from their high geometrical powers of increase...as many more individuals of each species are born than can possibly survive; and as, consequently there is a frequently recurring struggle for existence, it follows that any being, if it vary however slightly in any manner profitable to itself, under the complex and sometimes varying conditions of life, will have a better chance of surviving, and thus be *naturally selected* (Darwin's emphasis). From the strong principle of inheritance, any selected variety will tend to propagate its new and modified form".

To simplify, we might summarise evolution as the application of a 3-step process, or algorithm, repeated over many generations. The 3 steps are: "replicate; vary; select", and the mechanics are as follows.

Something makes a copy of itself, through biological reproduction in the case of a living organism. This is step 1: "replicate". It is important that the copy is high-fidelity, which is to say that it closely resembles the original, and fortunately this is exactly what happens in biological reproduction.

However, for the process to work a small number of random copying errors, otherwise known as "mutations", must also occur, giving rise to step 2: "vary". This is again exactly what happens in biological reproduction.

Because mutations are random, only a small proportion of them will tend to improve the life chances of an organism. Such mutations are said to be "adaptive", serving to increase the organism's "fitness", in other words its ability to survive and successfully reproduce. By definition proportionally more copies of an adaptive mutation will appear in successive generations, as those organisms carrying it out-compete those which do not.

Conversely, mutations which do not enhance, or dilute, the organism's life chances will tend to disappear over time as their host organisms are out-competed by other, "fitter", individuals. This is step 3: "select."

As an aside, it is perhaps obvious but nonetheless worth reinforcing that "fitness" in this context does not necessarily mean building stronger muscles, or any of the other health-related associations the word has come to have in everyday modern usage. It simply means the ability of an organism to survive and successfully reproduce in a particular environment. Similarly, "mutation" does not automatically carry a pejorative meaning, as it might in colloquial parlance. The majority of mutations are indeed bad, or at least neutral, for their host; but a few are highly beneficial. And if mutations did not occur, the evolutionary process itself would grind to a halt because without variation there would be no possibility of natural selection.

Specific evolutionary changes tend to be small and relatively incremental ("evolutionary" rather than "revolutionary"), for the same simple reason that in a natural state mutations are random. The probability that any one mutation will be beneficial is therefore much lower than that it will be neutral or detrimental (as the celebrated British biologist Richard Dawkins puts it: "there are many more ways to be dead than alive").

And the odds of a variation having a positive impact decrease exponentially as the magnitude of the mutation increases. It is not impossible that a single large mutation might produce a "revolutionary" change, but it is highly improbable. This is not at all to say that evolution is not capable of revolutionary change. On the contrary, given enough cycles of the 3-step process, it is entirely possible that the eventual end result will be radically different from the starting point, and also that complexity will increase. It is just that whatever changes occur will be achieved through a series of smaller, individually-incremental changes along the way. "Revolution through evolution", we might call it.

A vivid example of an evolutionary process in action is provided by the American author Jonathan Weiner in his classic work *The Beak of the Finch*, published in 1994. This charts the 20-year (at that time) labour of husband-and-wife team Peter and Rosemary Grant to observe, and measure, a colony of Darwin Finches in the Galapagos Islands. There is a pleasing symmetry in that observation of this species was an important contributor in helping Darwin himself develop his original theory of evolution, during his voyage on *The Beagle* in the 1830s. Hence presumably how the species comes to bear his name, and perhaps why Peter and Rosemary Grant chose to study it.

The Grants made an annual visit to an island called Daphne Major, and on each visit they made careful physical measurements of the population of Darwin finches they found there. The most striking finding, which gave the book its title, related to the changes they observed in the average size and shape of the birds' beaks.

In a year of drought, larger individuals with longer beaks were advantaged: there were relatively fewer seeds available because of the lack of water, the supply of smaller, softer seeds was quickly exhausted, and the larger birds with longer beaks were better able to access and consume the bigger, harder seeds which were available. A higher proportion of larger birds therefore survived into the breeding season, and hence passed their genes to the next generation, so that the following year the Grants observed a pronounced shift in the average finch population towards larger birds with longer beaks.

Had droughts continued to be the norm, this trend would surely have continued, and over time the finch population would have become steadily larger and longer-beaked, up to some notional point at which the advantages of increased size started to be outweighed by disadvantages.

However, the reverse effect in fact occurred a few years later. Abundant rains produced lush vegetation, which ultimately favoured the production of smaller, softer seeds, requiring more dexterity to access. Larger birds with longer beaks were now relatively disadvantaged, smaller birds with shorter beaks flourished, and sure enough the average size and beak length of the finch population shifted back decisively in this direction, for exactly the same reason in reverse as had caused the earlier shift – relatively more of the smaller birds now survived and reproduced.

The finch example serves to illustrate three important characteristics of the evolutionary process.

First, evolutionary selection happens as a function of the ability of an organism to survive, and successfully reproduce, in a particular environment. In other words, it is contextual.

Second, the environment itself is not necessarily, indeed usually isn't, a constant, so that as an environment changes over time so does the definition of "fitness" i.e. how successful a given adaptation will be and therefore how likely it is to continue to be "selected".

Third, the direction of change for a particular environment is not necessarily one-way or irreversible over time. It might be, of course, for example if land is progressively deforested, or if average temperatures inexorably rise, or fall. But, as the finch example shows, it is also possible for environmental changes to oscillate backwards and forwards, with the consequence that the selection pressures for a particular adaptation, or even an entire species, do too.

It is worth reinforcing that although the word "selection" has come to be the definitive description of the third, vital, evolutionary step, there is no suggestion that there is any kind of conscious agency at play, certainly as far as evolution in the natural world is concerned. Mutations are random, and selection is "natural", operating through the simple mechanism that a mutation which enhances "fitness" will propagate because relatively more copies of it will pass into the next generation.

Artificial selection is also possible, of course, whereby a conscious agent, typically a human, deliberately regulates breeding in order to produce more, or less, of a particular characteristic. Indeed, many of Darwin's own examples are taken from programmes intentionally designed by human breeders to promote specific attributes in particular species, most notably pigeons.

The 3-step process is the same whether the selection taking place is natural or artificial. The important difference is that "natural" selection is undirected; whereas "artificial" selection has a high degree of intentionality from a guiding, human, influence.

It is also worth a brief digression on the potential for what Darwin called "sexual" selection. Many evolutionary changes tend to improve fitness in a strictly functional sense: they help an animal to run faster, or camouflage better to hide from its predators, or have better night vision, or whatever.

But Darwin's theory also explicitly allows for the possible influence of more subjective factors. Evolutionary theory predicts that in most species, females will be "choosier" than males when it comes to deciding with whom they will mate, because in most species the female invests proportionally more resources than the male in carrying and rearing the offspring.

Human females, for example, give birth to (usually) just one child at a time, and are then close to irreplaceable, at least historically, as a source of maternal milk during weaning, which in earlier societies might have lasted anything up to 3 years per child or even longer. The longer a particular mother weans her child, the longer the gap before she is biologically able to have another.

Human males, on the other hand, have the physical capacity to impregnate dozens or even thousands of females per year, at least in theory, and are not critical to the health of any resulting children in the same way that a mother is through her milk.

The effect of this imbalance is to create competition amongst males to mate with the most desirable females, in turn leading to males typically being physically bigger and stronger, the better to compete with one another, a phenomenon known as sexual size dimorphism. Females for their part are more likely to choose bigger, stronger males as their mating partner because this gives their offspring the best chance of themselves having the characteristics needed for reproductive success.

In at least some species, however, females have found ways to guide their choice of mate which involve criteria other than just physical size and power. And crucially, if a "subjective" female preference once becomes established, this alone can be sufficient to drive evolutionary adaptations towards whatever this preference is amongst the males seeking their favours.

An example which is often cited to illustrate the concept of sexual selection is the fabulous tail of the male peacock.

It seems obvious that this can have no functional benefit. It surely has some serious disadvantages, for example making the male more visible to potential predators and also less agile, and hence less able to escape them.

The theory of sexual selection explains this apparent paradox by proposing that at some point in the remote past a positive feedback loop developed whereby a longer, showier male tail became attractive to peahens. The reasons for this are necessarily speculative but might perhaps be because a flashier male tail signalled virility and underlying health, desirable characteristics in a potential father for your pea-children.

Whatever the cause, once this preference became established, it led to a kind of peacock-tail arms race, in which males with the longest, most impressive tails were more successful at wooing females and reproducing, in turn ensuring that relatively more offspring were born who themselves had long tails if they were male, and a preference for long tails if they were female. In this way, male peacock tails gradually became longer and more elaborate through successive generations, until reaching some notional point of equilibrium at which the benefits of an even bigger tail ceased to outweigh the costs.

Finally, evolutionary change may typically be incremental and gradual, but this is not to say that it is necessarily continuous, or that when it occurs it proceeds with a smooth unbroken trajectory of change. In the 1970s the British evolutionary biologist John Maynard Smith coined the terms "evolutionarily stable state" and the related "evolutionarily stable strategy" (or "ESS") to describe situations in which an entity becomes so well adapted to its environment that selection pressures tend to reinforce rather than change the status quo, so long as disruptions to the external environment are not too great. To take one example, this explains why crocodiles have evolved only modestly since the time of the dinosaurs: they had already become so well adapted that the scope for further improvement is small, so long as their environment itself does not change too much. It is not that crocodiles have somehow stopped evolving, merely that already by the time of the dinosaurs they had developed a body plan and life strategy so well suited to their environment that few subsequent mutations have proved to be further adaptive.

ESS is an important concept in evolutionary theory, and it's worth a brief digression to elaborate.

An oft-used example is the sex ratio, which tends towards an evolutionarily stable 50:50, or 1:1, in most sexually-reproductive species. The logic for this is known as the Fisher Principle, named after the British geneticist Ronald Fisher who first outlined it in his 1930 book *The Genetical Theory of Natural Selection*. The Fisher Principle was in turn pithily summarised by the English evolutionary biologist WD Hamilton in his 1967 paper on *Extraordinary sex ratios*:

1. Suppose male births are less common than females
2. A newborn male then has better mating prospects than a newborn female, and therefore can expect to have more offspring

3. Therefore parents genetically disposed to produce males tend to have more than average numbers of grandchildren born to them

4. Therefore the genes for male-producing tendencies spread, and male births become more common

5. As the 1:1 sex ratio is approached, the advantage associated with producing males dies away

6. The same reasoning holds if females are substituted for males throughout. Therefore 1:1 is the equilibrium ratio

As regards the evolutionary change process itself, many scientists subscribe to the theory of "punctuated equilibrium", which holds that evolution in particular species tends to develop in fits and starts between periods of relative stability. The point remains, however, that even in periods of relatively significant change, they typically manifest in a series of gradual, incremental steps. After many generations there may be big differences between the members of a species and their remote ancestors, but each generation along the way is likely to have been similar in most respects to those which came immediately before and after.

Finally, evolutionary theory gave rise to Darwin's famous "Tree of Life", in which all living things can ultimately be traced back to a single common ancestor, and all the similarities and differences between existing, and past, life forms can in principle be explained. Far from being some kind of "chosen race", humans are just one among countless species to have existed, with a heritage shared ultimately with all other life forms.

It is a remarkable, and remarkably powerful, idea. It is also humbling to realise that in order for us each individually to exist not only did our own parents have to be successful in conceiving and rearing a surviving child, us; but so did their parents, and their parents' parents, and their parents' parents' parents, and so on in an unbroken chain across the many thousands of generations which ultimately stretch back through the ancestors of our species, to the species which gave rise to them, and so on back to the very earliest life forms. If just one link had been broken anywhere in this chain, we ourself would not exist.

Darwin revolutionised our understanding of how organic life developed on Earth. He identified heredity as being critical to the process. One thing he was not able to do, however, was to identify the physical mechanism through which heredity happens. It was only with the emergence of the science of genetics that this became clear.

Genetics

Genetics is defined by the Cambridge English Dictionary as "the study of how, in all living things, the characteristics and qualities of parents are given to their children by their genes".

This particular branch of science is acknowledged to have originated in the mid 19th century with the work of Gregor Mendel, an Augustinian friar in what is now the Czech Republic. Mendel first published his ideas in 1865 but it was not until early in the 20th century, after his death, that they gained widespread currency.

In essence, he conducted a series of experiments with pea plants which for example showed how crossing a plant which produced green peas with one which produced yellow peas always produced yellow offspring in the first generation, then a predictable ratio of one green to three yellow subsequently. Mendel's major insight was to identify the process by which this happens: through discrete heritable units, now called "genes", which could be mathematically explained and therefore measured.

The term "gene" itself was coined by Danish biologist Wilhelm Johansen in the early 1900s. As an aside,

Johansen also gave us "phenotype", defined by the Cambridge English dictionary as "the physical characteristics of something living, especially those characteristics that can be seen", in other words the physical effects which the genes produce; and "genotype", defined as "the particular type and arrangement of genes that each organism has".

Experiments in the 1940s and 1950s identified DNA (deoxyribonucleic acid) as the molecule from which genes are made. A major milestone occurred in 1953, when James Watson and Francis Crick published the paper identifying the famous double-helix structure of the DNA molecule.

The basic idea is, again, relatively simple. Genes are the fundamental building blocks of life because they contain the instructions for the proteins from which a body is built and then renewed over time. This means that genes determine, or more accurately significantly influence, the characteristics of whatever organism is their "host", including physical attributes such as size, power, appearance, and health; and non-physical features such as intellectual capacity, temperament, and personality.

Our genes influence these things but do not completely determine them, because, as we'll see later, the experiences the organism has and the environment in which it lives also have an important modifying effect on how the genes are activated, or "expressed". Still, the point is that our genes matter, enormously.

Many species reproduce sexually, including humans, mammals and many other animals, and a surprising number of plants. In sexually-reproducing species every individual organism has its own unique genetic profile, which is to say its own unique set of genes, arranged in a unique combination. A given species will have a common "gene pool". But no two individuals within it will have the exact same collection of genes, arranged in the same way.

And it turns out that the gene, or at least the gene-combination, is the level at which Darwin's process of evolution by natural selection actually operates. Genes which confer some survival or reproductive advantage on their host organism prosper, by helping their host to flourish at the expense of other hosts whose genes do not confer the same adaptive advantage.

The gene is therefore the main unit of heredity, to the extent that it is possible to think of host organisms as being little more than passive vehicles for carrying successful genes and gene-combinations down from one generation to the next – "survival machines", as the British biologist Richard Dawkins famously christened them. The seminal work in which this gene-centred view is described is Dawkins' book *The Selfish Gene*, first published in 1976 and updated and republished in multiple editions since. Dawkins is also famous for his militant atheism, but entertaining as his thoughts on that topic are we will concentrate here just on his contributions to our understanding of biology, which are multiple and significant.

How genes work

All living things have DNA in their cells: clearly DNA itself evolved very early in the Tree of Life. Our cells also contain RNA (ribonucleic acid), which it is speculated may have been the primary replicator in the very earliest life forms. Still, whilst RNA today provides important support in helping our body to function, sometimes described as a "messenger" role, it is DNA where the main action occurs and on which we will therefore focus.

The chemistry of DNA is fairly well understood, although somewhat complex. Readers who might like a fuller explanation are referred to a helpful summary on the US Centers for Disease Control and Prevention website, which features a specific module called *DNA Structure*. To summarise, a DNA molecule is made from five atoms: carbon, nitrogen, oxygen, phosphorous and hydrogen. These atoms combine into two structures: a five-carbon sugar molecule called deoxyribose, which gives DNA its name; and one of four nitrogen "bases". The four base chemicals are usually known by their initial letter, A (for adenine), T (thymine), G (guanine), and C (cytosine).

DNA is not produced as a single strand, but on a template formed by a preexisting DNA strand, the strands twisting around each other to give the famous double-helix shape. The nitrogen bases protrude from each strand and combine to bind the two strands together, in a formulation where the chemicals always pair: A with T, and G with C. A strand of DNA therefore comprises a series of base pairs in the form AT and GC, combined in different sequences and lengths.

Human DNA contains a total of around 3 billion base pairs, otherwise known as the human genome. Interestingly, the size of a species' genome does not seem to correlate to the complexity of the organisms it produces. For example, the genome of frogs and sharks both contain about the same number of base pairs as humans. By comparison the newt genome contains about 15 billion base pairs, and a lily almost 100 billion. It seems that the number of base pairs an organism has is much less significant to how complex it is than how these pairs are arranged.

One of the remarkable features of DNA is that it self-replicates, that is makes copies of itself. It therefore satisfies the first, "replicate", step of the 3-step evolutionary algorithm.

In fact, DNA replicates with astonishingly high, but fortunately not completely foolproof, accuracy. The website *basicbiology.net* tells us that on average one copying error, or mutation, is made for every 100,000 base pairs copied. This may not sound like much, but all other things being equal the result would be that the DNA of an average human would contain about 30,000 mutations. All other things are not equal, however, because DNA also has its own built-in error-detection system, the effect of which is to reduce the proportion of copying errors which actually enter the genome.

The net effect is that on average we each carry 100-200 new mutations, according to research conducted by the Wellcome Trust Sanger Institute and cited in an article titled *We Are All Mutants: Measurement Of Mutation Rate In Humans By Direct Sequencing*, published on *ScienceDaily* on 1 September 2009. The article reassures readers that, as previously discussed: "fortunately, most of these are harmless and have no apparent effect on our health or appearance".

These surviving mutations are the second, "vary", step in the evolutionary algorithm, and they are what underpin genetic innovation. To reinforce, most are likely to have a neutral effect on the "fitness" of their host organism.

A few may have a negative effect, in which case Nature will by definition tend to select against them. A few others may confer adaptive advantage, enabling their host to out-compete others in the Darwinian struggle for survival and successful reproduction and therefore tending to propagate into subsequent generations. This is the third, "select", step of the algorithm.

DNA is packaged into thread-like structures called chromosomes, located inside the nucleus of biological cells. Most humans have 46 chromosomes, although some might have 45 or 47. We each receive half our chromosomes from our mother and half from our father, and they are paired, so that in effect we have two parallel sets of instructions for how our body should be made, which our body then "chooses" between based on a complicated set of chemical interactions. Still, if our parents are themselves genetically similar in some respect – say they both have brown eyes - then it is likely that we will inherit this characteristic, since both parallel sets of genetic instructions are likely to code for it.

Even here there may be exceptions, though, because our parents themselves carry two sets of genetic instructions and whilst they may pass onto us the version which they themselves "expressed", in this case for brown eyes, it is also possible that they may instead pass on the version which did not activate in them but may under some circumstances in us, and which in this example might code for say blue eyes.

Separately, whilst we inherit half of our chromosomes from each of our biological parents, we also inherit a good deal more besides from our mother, because she provides the egg whereas our father just provides the sperm. American cognitive scientist Cat Bohannon explains, on p346 of her 2023 book *Eve: How The Female Body Drove 200 Million Years Of Human Evolution*: "while half of your DNA came from your dad and half from your mom, most of your mitochondria and cytoplasm came from your mother. Sperm are basically an information delivery system that dumps the father's DNA into the egg, whereas eggs have to provide all the construction materials to build that embryo. And that's the major reason eggs are about four thousand times larger than sperm: they're not just half a set of blueprints; they are half a set of blueprints plus the entire factory".

In any case, the one chromosome for which we do not inherit a paired copy from each parent is our so-called sex chromosome. Here, females inherit two copies of an "X" chromosome and males typically one copy each of an "X" and a "Y". Interestingly enough, the X chromosome is roughly three times larger and contains about 900 genes compared with about 55 for a Y. At conception, the mother always gives an X chromosome to the child, logically enough since the mother is by definition XX. The father may give either an X or a Y, determining whether the baby will be biologically female or male.

Our chromosomes are created through a process known as "meiosis", or recombination, in which the chromosomes each parent donates to their egg or sperm are a mish-mash of their own chromosome pairs, not copies of single entire parental chromosomes. The effect is to ensure that offspring are genetically distinct from their parents – in other words, unique.

What is more, each *individual* parental egg and sperm has a different mashed-up combination of parental genes and is therefore unique, which is why dizygotic ("fraternal") twins, fertilised from two different eggs and two different sperm, are not identical; and monozygotic ("identical") twins, fertilised from a single egg and sperm, essentially are. For completeness, in turns out that even identical twins exhibit minor differences of perhaps a few hundred base pairs across their personal genome, because of embryonic mutations which occur after the point of fertilisation.

Whatever, once a specific sperm has fertilised a particular egg, the cells which are then created in the resulting organism all have exactly the same chromosomes as one another. Hence, every individual cell in a particular body contains exactly the same genes as all the other cells in that body, arranged in exactly the same order.

Species have widely varying numbers of chromosomes, from as many as 254 in a species of hermit crab, down to just 2 in a species of roundworm. As with base pairs, though, what seems to matter is not the number of chromosomes, indeed this seems to be fairly random across species, but rather the specific genes and gene-combinations the chromosomes contain.

And when it comes to individual genes, the picture is complicated by the fact that there is no standard shape, size or even definition. A "gene" is typically understood as a discrete number of base pairs arranged in a specific sequence, as part of a strand of DNA, contained in a specific location on a particular chromosome. But there is no rule, or discernible pattern, governing how many base pairs are definitive, or in what kind of sequence.

What's more, comparatively minor differences are possible in a sequence, meaning that multiple viable versions of the same gene can be possible. These are called alleles, and we might think of them as being like different flavours of the same basic thing. For example, a gene which codes for pigment in hair might have a number of alleles which code for lots of dark pigment, producing black hair; or alternatively for different shades of brown, red or blond hair.

Finally, it is rare that a single gene directly produces a specific phenotypical effect. It is much more usual that these effects are the result of interactions between a number of genes. For example, whilst it seems clear that different forms of human sexuality are due at least in part to underlying genetic differences, searching for a single specific "gay gene" is almost certainly a fruitless quest.

Each human is estimated to have somewhere in the order of 30,000 individual genes, according to the website of the National Human Genome Research Institute, and, adding to the complexity, each gene makes an average of three different proteins. Other sources put the total number of human genes at 20-25,000, which serves to underscore the challenge of determining whether a particular base pair sequence does or does not constitute a "gene". Fortunately, the difference doesn't matter for our purposes.

Within this overall number, there are huge differences between individual chromosomes, and also between individual genes. For example, human chromosomes range in size from about 50 million to about 300 million base pairs. A typical gene might contain around 27,000 base pairs, but some have as many as 2 million. Hence, each strand of DNA on each of our 46 chromosomes contains anything from hundreds to thousands of individual genes.

It also turns out that all genes are not equal in their effect, to a surprising degree. Identifiable genes in the most literal definition, that is base sequences which contain actual instructions for coding the proteins from which our bodies are made, account for only around 1.5% of the total number of base sequences contained in our DNA. So, of the 3 billion base pairs in our genome, only around 45 million are part of a sequence which can actually be shown to code for proteins, and therefore directly impact how our body works.

When this was first realised in the 1960s the remaining 98.5% was given the unfortunate name "junk DNA" because it appeared to serve no useful biological purpose. However, more recent research suggests that this is a misnomer, and that much of this material might be useful after all. Indeed, the evidence is that differences in our "junk" DNA may be largely what make us our unique self: the base sequencing of our "active" genes, that is the DNA which directly codes for proteins, varies by only about 0.025% across all humans, whereas the sequencing of our non-coding, "junk", DNA varies by anything between 1 to 4%. And an emerging theory described in an entry titled *"What Makes You Unique?"* on the *Stanford Medicine News Center* dated 18 March 2010 suggests that at least some portions of our non-coding DNA may play a crucial role in stimulating specific active genes to activate.

In summary, each species is heir to a particular "gene pool" which contains a collection of specific genes carrying the chemical blueprint for how an organism in that species is assembled and functions. Each member of a sexually-reproducing species has their own unique combination of genes, inherited from their parents but "scrambled" to ensure that it is distinct. Most individuals acquire a small number (relative to their total genome) of gene mutations, a few of which might prove to be adaptive although most will not. The evolutionary algorithm ensures that mutations which are adaptive, and which confer sufficient "fitness" advantage, permeate the broader species gene pool over time, through the process of evolution by natural selection.

Genes therefore emerge as the core unit of heredity, with the science of genetics providing the underlying biological explanation for how the effects observed by Darwin actually come to happen: how it is that, say, parent finches who are larger with longer beaks tend to pass these same characteristics on to their offspring by passing on the genes which code for them.

Genetic similarities and differences

Genetics enables us to measure with mathematical precision the similarities and differences between humans and other species; and also between individual humans, and groups of humans, now and back in time.

For example, the laws of exponential maths help us to understand how we can essentially guarantee that every human is genetically unique. UK science journalist Matt Ridley explains, on p2 of his 2003 book *Nature via Nurture*: "...just 33 genes, each coming in two varieties (such as on or off), would be enough to make every human being in the world unique. There are more than 10 billion ways of flipping a coin 33 times. So 30,000 (my note: the total number of genes that we each have) does not look like such a small number...two multiplied by itself 30,000 times produces a number larger than the total number of particles in the known universe".

On a point of detail, genetic difference is measured not simply, or even mainly, through detecting entirely different standalone genes, but rather through subtler differences in the type and location of base pairs within a particular gene. Ridley explains, on p26 of *Nature via Nurture*: "... there are about 30,000 human genes. That is, scattered throughout the genome are 30,000 distinct stretches of digital information that are directly translated into protein machinery to run and build the body; a gene being a recipe for a protein. Chimpanzees almost certainly have roughly the same number of genes. Since 1.5 per cent of 30,000 is 450 (my note: the relevance being that the human genome differs from that of chimps by about 1.5% overall), then it seems to follow that we have 450 different, uniquely human genes. Not such a big number. The other 29,550 genes are identical in us and chimps. But this is actually most unlikely. It could instead be that every single human gene is different from every single chimp gene, but only 1.5 per cent of its text is different. The truth is bound to lie somewhere between the two. Many genes will be identical in closely related species; many will be slightly different. A very few will be utterly different".

Confusingly, different measures are typically used to quantify the degree of genetic overlap between humans and other species; and between individual humans or groups of humans. This is why statements can co-exist such as "humans share 98.5% of our genes with chimpanzees" and "individual humans share 50% of their genes with each of their parents". Both these statements are quantifying an observable level of genetic overlap. However, the denominator for the first is the entire genetic sequence, which as we saw amounts to around 3 billion base pairs for humans; whereas the denominator for the second is just those genes which typically vary between individual humans, equating to 0.1% of the total or around 3 million base pairs.

Comparing across species, and depending on one's preconceptions, it is possible to find the levels of both similarity and difference surprising. For example, on p25-6 of *Nature via Nurture* Ridley elaborates on the degree of genetic difference between humans and chimpanzees: "the human genome contains about three billion 'letters' of code. Strictly speaking, these are chemical bases on a molecule of DNA, but since it is their order, not their individual properties, that determines what they produce, they can be treated as digital information. The difference between two individual human beings amounts, on average, to 0.1 per cent, so there are three million different letters between me and my neighbour. The difference between a human being and a chimpanzee (our closest biological 'cousin') is about 15 times as great, or 1.5 per cent. That equates to 45 million different letters. That is about ten times as many letters as there are in the whole Bible...the book of digital differences between our two species, unannotated, would fill eleven feet of bookshelf. (The bookshelf of similarities, by contrast, would stretch to 250 yards)".

In any case, even a modest level of genetic variation can produce major differences in outcome. The *Scientific American* summarises, in an article titled *What does the fact that we share 95 percent of our genes with the chimpanzee mean? And how was this number derived?*, published online dated 1 March 2004: "it is worth noting that individual humans generally differ by about 0.1 per cent genetically. Thus, chimps differ from humans by about 15-fold more, on the average, than humans do from one another. The 0.1 per cent human divergence certainly results in significant variation in physical appearance and traits among humans. Therefore, perhaps we shouldn't be so surprised that chimps could be 98.5 percent related to humans. Relatively small genetic changes can produce major phenotypic changes". (The article also explains how different ways of measuring genetic variation can produce answers that humans differ from chimps by either 98.5% or 95%, depending which approach is used. These are technical differences which have no impact on the conclusions relevant to this book.)

In fact, we turn out to share a surprising amount of our genes with *every* multi-cellular life form – for example, we share around 50% with a banana. This shows how much of the basic machinery needed for life is common across species, inherited by all of us from much earlier common ancestors, reinforcing the point that humans are but one small part of a single giant biological eco-system, directly sharing our genetic inheritance, and even many of our specific genes, with all other life forms on Earth.

Ultimately, genetics enables us to map with confidence the Darwinian "Tree of Life", showing amongst other things how far back in time each species shared a common ancestor. As examples: the most recent common ancestor of all humans alive today lived around 150,000 years ago; the branch of the Tree of Life which eventually became modern humans split from the branch which became modern chimpanzees and bonobos (otherwise known as pygmy chimpanzees) around 7 million years ago, the split between chimpanzees and bonobos themselves occurring more recently; and the branch which eventually became apes, including humans, chimpanzees, bonobos and other apes such as gorillas and orang-utans, split from the branch which instead went on to become the various species of monkey around 21 million years ago.

The notion of a "common ancestor" is perhaps worth emphasising. It is not that humans are descended directly from monkeys, as some of Darwin's most vituperative critics contended he said, although in fact he did not. Rather, humans, modern apes and modern monkeys are together descended from a common ancestor, which would logically not have the name of human, ape or monkey but could be called by a more general name, say "ancestral primate".

Going further back in time, this early primate common ancestor would itself have had a common ancestor with other mammalian species. For example, genetics reveals that primates split from other mammals around 65 million years ago, around the time that dinosaurs became extinct. Eventually, we can trace common ancestry for all animals, including humans, with the two other major "kingdoms" of plants and fungi, the connection being that all organisms within these categories are "eukaryotic", which is to say they are made from cells which have a nucleus bound within a membrane. Even further back is the common ancestor with other surviving life forms such as bacteria and other micro-organisms until eventually we reach the very earliest, primitive life forms which are the common ancestor of every organism which ever has and presumably ever will exist, at least here on Earth.

It's a fascinating story, and readers interested in the details are referred, again, to Richard Dawkins, who has told it brilliantly at least twice - working forwards from the earliest life forms in *River out of Eden*, published in 1995; and in reverse order, that is working back from modern humans, in *The Ancestor's Tale*, co-authored with Yan Wong and published in 2004.

Turning to the second, narrower, measure used to assess genetic differences between humans, genetics also enables us to quantify the degree to which we share our genes with various relatives. As we have seen, the closest genetic bonds are between identical twins, who share almost 100%. We share 50% with each of our parents, and also with any brothers and sisters assuming they are full siblings, that is, that they have the same two biological parents that we do. Obviously, if we have more than one sibling the 50% of genes we share with each one are not likely to be the same specific genes. We share 25% of our genes with each of our grandparents, again obviously not the same specific genes, and so on.

Genetics therefore explains why kin groups are typically so important as a social unit in so many species, including humans. Given that the best way to understand the evolutionary process is at the level of the individual gene and gene-combination, and that the evolutionary function of a host organism is to secure the transfer of its own genes into the next generation, it follows that any individual organism has a built-in incentive to act in favour of close relatives rather than random strangers. The biggest mathematical incentive is to pass on one's own genes directly, of course, resulting in a child which inherits 50% of them. Still, if a (full) sibling is successful in reproducing, this means that 25% of one's own distinctive genes survive; compared with effectively zero in the case of a random stranger.

Genetics and race

Genetics also provides a powerful analytical lens through which to explore the emotive topic of race.

The headline is that there is no basis in science to support historical race theory, in which a particular race, almost invariably "white", is deemed to be inherently superior to others because of "better" genes.

In fact, in turns out that there is quite limited genetic variation across what were historically thought of as different "races". It is true that in some cases differences in outcomes are observed between "racial" groups, but with some specific and generally relatively superficial exceptions these can generally be attributed to differences in experience and environment rather than to any underlying difference in genes.

At the heart of the issue historically are the beliefs first that distinct "races" exist, generally denoted by skin colour and perhaps facial features; and second that members of the "white" race are inherently, in other words genetically, superior to all others in general and to "blacks" in particular, including in the case of the British Raj native Indians, otherwise known as "Hindoos". This inherent superiority was supposed to manifest in a variety of ways, including higher intelligence and a more "civilised" temperament leading to a more civilised culture, often including belief in the Christian god, who in some versions had "chosen" this superior white race to bring His word to these other less favoured peoples.

It is easy to see that such a belief might be attractive to, for example, European colonialists, providing an intellectual and even moral justification for their actions, at least according to their own subjective moral perceptions (we will explore how morality is ultimately relative and subjective in Chapter 4).

And it is not an endorsement to acknowledge that back in the day it was possible to think of such a view as intellectually credible. After all Europeans and their colonial descendants outside Europe, generally with light ("white") skin, enjoyed obvious massive technological and economic advantages over the rest of the world accruing from the Industrial Revolution. It is arguably a relatively short step from early Darwinism to conclude that this superiority might itself be based on some kind of difference in innate biological "fitness".

Still, there were problems with the theory even at the time. For example, there was no rigorous way to classify different "races". Attempts were made, of course, one example being a 1757 effort by the celebrated Swedish botanist Carl Linnaeus, who is famous for also devising the taxonomy by which animal and plant species are still classified today. It is fair to say that this work has stood the test of time rather better than his work on races.

In his 2005 book *Anthropology the basics*, US anthropologist Peter Metcalf summarises Linnaeus' five proposed racial categories: "American" (nowadays we would probably use the term "Native American"); "European"; "Asiatic"; "African"; and "wild man", the last seemingly being a category to cover all peoples who did not easily fit into one of the four other definitions.

In fairness to Linnaeus, he did not have access to genetic analysis. We do, however, and what it shows is that in fact only around 0.1% genetic variation is observed between "races". This is not quantitatively different to and may even be less than the level of variation seen between individuals *within* a given "race". It is entirely possible that two individuals of say "white European" descent may each be genetically more similar to someone of "Asian" descent than they are to each other.

Such genetic differences as do exist turn out to relate mainly to the kinds of variation in physical characteristics which Linnaeus observed, such as skin colour, eye shape and hair type, which in turn relate to differences in the physical environments in which these adaptations were acquired. These are in reality superficial, however outwardly striking they may appear. No systematic variation has been found in more basic physical attributes such as average height, weight, or blood type, although of course all these things do vary considerably within particular "races".

Perhaps the most controversial topic is the historical belief that there are racial differences in innate intelligence. And it is true that numerous studies, especially in the US, have indeed shown "blacks" underperforming "whites" on IQ and various other cognitive tests, with more recent studies incidentally also showing "East Asians" outperforming both groups.

The question this obviously begs is the extent to which such differences are the product of "nature", that is, inherited genes; or "nurture", namely educational and broader cultural experience. And these days the generally-accepted view is that "nurture" is entirely responsible: where differences in outcomes are observed between groups, this is generally the product of circumstance, including in some cases culture, not of underlying genes.

To give a few examples, in the abstract of his 2007 article *Biology and intelligence – the race/IQ controversy*, psychologist Mike Anderson concludes: "there is no good reason to believe that the difference in group means that exists between black and white Americans in measured IQ is either genetically based or based on race differences in biology".

In an article titled *Racial IQ Differences among Transracial Adoptees: Fact or Artifact?*, published on the *National Library of Medicine* dated 5 March 2016, American biologist Drew Thomas summarises: "I conclude that East Asian adoptees raised by Western Whites score about on par with non-adopted Western Whites, and that there is no consistent IQ difference between Black adoptees raised by Whites and White adoptees raised by Whites".

And in an article titled *The unwelcome revival of 'race science'*, published in *The Guardian* on 2 March 2018, British psychologist Gavin Evans quotes the view of Craig Venter, the American biologist who led the pioneering effort to decode the human genome in the early 2000s: "there is no basis in scientific fact or in the human genetic code for the notion that skin colour will be predictive of (underlying) intelligence".

None of this is to say that there are no genetic differences at all between different groups of humans. On the contrary, we would expect to see some level of genetic divergence over time between populations living in isolation from one another. As biologists Jerry Coyne and Luana Maroja, American and Brazilian respectively, observe in an article titled *The Ideological Subversion of Biology*, published by *Sceptical Inquirer* dated July/August 2023: "given restricted movement in the past, human populations evolved largely in geographic isolation from one another...(and)...as every evolutionary biologist knows, geographically isolated populations become genetically distinct over time". The authors go on to show that some level of genetic variation can be seen even at the level of quite local geography: "genetic analysis of Europeans shows that, remarkably, a map of their genetic constitution coincides almost perfectly with the map of Europe itself. In fact, the DNA of most Europeans can narrow down their birthplace to within roughly 500 miles".

The point is not that genetic differences do not exist between historically-isolated groups, but rather that the levels of difference that are seen tend to be superficial.

In his *Guardian* article referenced above, Evans points to a possible explanation: there simply has not been enough time for more complex genetic divergence to occur. Evans says: "one of the remarkable dimensions of the human genome is how little genetic variation there is.

DNA research conducted in 1987 suggested a common, African ancestor for all humans alive today: 'mitochondrial Eve', who lived around 200,000 years ago. Because of this relatively recent (in evolutionary terms) common ancestry, human beings share a remarkably high proportion of their genes compared to other mammals. The single subspecies of chimpanzee that lives in central Africa, for example, has significantly more genetic variation than does the entire human race".

Other sources date mitochondrial Eve to around 150,000 years ago. But the difference does not matter for this discussion, and in any case this more recent estimate would afford even less time for major divergence.

There is also a male equivalent, "Y-chromosomal Adam", the common ancestor through the male line of all humans alive today, who is believed to have lived between 2-300,000 years ago. This is also recent in evolutionary terms, when compared for example with the 7 million years or so that have passed since our earliest hominid ancestors diverged from our closest primate cousins.

Evans goes on to point out that the comparative recency of the last common ancestor for all modern humans is particularly relevant to the question of genetic differences in intelligence: "the second plank of the race science case goes like this: human bodies continued to evolve, at least until recently – with different groups developing different skin colours, predisposition to certain diseases, and things such as lactose tolerance. So why wouldn't human brains continue evolving too? The problem here is that race scientists are not comparing like with like. Most of these physical changes involve single gene mutations, which can spread throughout the population in a relatively short span of evolutionary time. By contrast, intelligence – even the rather specific version measured by IQ – involves a network of potentially thousands of genes". Evans asserts that intelligence "probably takes at least 100 millenia to evolve appreciably", and whilst it is not obvious how he arrives at this specific number his broader point is clear.

Finally, Evans highlights how, unlike genes, environmental changes *can* have a material impact on the average IQ of a population group over relatively short timescales: "perhaps the most significant IQ researcher of the last half century is the New Zealander Jim Flynn. IQ tests are calibrated so that the average IQ of all test subjects at any particular time is 100. In the 1990s, Flynn discovered that each generation of IQ tests had to be more challenging if this average was to be maintained. Projecting back 100 years, he found that average IQ scores measured by current standards would be about 70. Yet people have not changed genetically since then. Instead, Flynn noted, they have become more exposed to abstract logic, which is the sliver of intelligence that IQ tests measure. Some populations are more exposed to abstraction than others, which is why their average IQ scores differ. Flynn found that the different averages between populations (my note: for IQ) were therefore entirely environmental".

This all serves to create the potential for a pernicious interplay between "nature", or more accurately *perceptions* of "nature", and "nurture". If a belief once becomes established that a particular group has lower innate aptitude for a specific attribute, for example intelligence; and if this in turn leads to different, lesser, developmental experiences being provided for the members of that group, then they are indeed likely to end up performing more poorly over time, in a cruel irony potentially providing evidence which apparently supports the initial misguided prejudice.

What is really happening in such a situation, though, is not that the group members start with lower innate potential, but rather that they are less able to fulfil their potential because of the environment they are in and the experiences they have. There may indeed end up being a measurable difference of outcome. But the root cause is nurture not nature; experience and environment, not underlying genes.

Such an effect may apply to perceptions of race, but it is clearly not limited to these. It could also apply to any group to which is perceived as having low innate aptitude, however erroneously.

An obvious example is the distinction that some societies historically made, and some still make, in the educational opportunities available to boys compared with girls.

And, turning the telescope around, what is true for a social group can also apply at the level of the individual. For example, a person who thinks they have lower innate intelligence than they do, and as a result does not engage fully with whatever educational and other learning opportunities may be available to them, is sadly likely to end up demonstrating lower achieved intelligence than their actual genetic potential would have supported.

Of course, none of this is to imply that all individuals *within* a particular group, racial or other, have equal genetic potential. Manifestly this is not the case, for intelligence any more than for attributes such as height, weight or physical strength. The point is simply that there is no evidence to support a meaningful difference in *average* potential across groups, particularly insofar as historical distinctions of "race" are concerned.

Finally, it is also not to suggest that such differences as do exist between genetically-distinct groups are not worthy of study. Some of these groupings may be categorised as "racial", although a more neutral term such as "population group" may be preferable. For example, in their *Sceptical Enquirer* article referenced above, Coyne and Maroja make a plea that racial sensitivities should not inhibit research into certain medical conditions which appear to be particularly prevalent in some ethnic groups: "there is medical value in genetic studies of populations. A fair number of genetic diseases...are associated (though not absolutely) with ethnicity: maladies such as Tay-Sachs disease, sickle-cell anaemia, cystic fibrosis, and hereditary haemochromatosis".

The general point is that genetics shows there is simply no scientific basis for historical racism. Some genetic differences indeed exist between different population groups, but these tend to be minor in the scheme of things, with less variation in most cases between different groups than within them. There is no basis for historical tropes such as a particular race possessing "superior" genes for intelligence, or other cognitive faculties.

We must also beware confusing biology with environment. In particular there is a risk that an initial misplaced prejudice about an illusory, or exaggerated, biological difference may became self-fulfilling if it then results in negative consequences for the *experiences* of the group about whom the prejudice is held.

Biological sex and gender identity

There is one obvious genetic segmentation which can classify more or less the entire human race into just two groups – females, with their XX chromosome; and men, with XY. What is more, the separation of at least this part of our biology has endured not just for millenia but for aeons, potentially stretching back all the way to the last eukaryotic common ancestor which existed around 2 billion years ago, according to the Wikipedia entry on *Eukaryogenesis*.

As an aside, the same entry hails the development of the eukaryotic cell as "a milestone in the evolution of life", involving as it most likely did the symbiotic union of archaea and bacteria and subsequently giving rise to the ancestors of animals, plants and fungi as well as a diverse range of single-celled organisms. For those interested in the details, a eukaryotic cell is one which possesses a clearly-defined nucleus, and the Wikipedia article cites as its source for the estimate of 2 billion years papers authored by Toni Gabaldon (*Origin and Early Evolution of the Eukaryotic Cell*, published by the *National Library of Medicine* dated 3 August 2021); and separately Carl Woese, Otto Kandler and Mark Wheelis (*towards a natural system of organisms: proposal for the domains Archaea, Bacteria, and Eucarya*, also published by the *National Library of Medicine*, dated 26 March 1990).

The point is that we might legitimately speculate that sufficient evolutionary time has passed for some level of genetic difference to develop between the sexes. We will therefore move swiftly to our next hot-potato topic: biological sex and gender identity.

There are at least three levels to the discussion, and since they point in different directions it should perhaps not be a surprise that contemporary public discourse on the issue should sometimes be confused.

The first and most basic level is our reproductive system, which defines what we will call our biological sex. The distinction here is essentially binary – almost every human is biologically either categorically "female" or categorically "male". A small minority are born "intersex", and for these individuals the categorisation is less obvious. But even in these cases the strict biological definition ultimately holds because each individual must still reproduce as either male or female, if they are to reproduce at all.

To dig a level deeper, nature has evolved two viable strategies for reproduction, asexual and sexual.

Organisms which replicate asexually, such as stick-insects, do not need a mate, but rather produce a copy of their own entire genome, so that a child is an exact genetic copy of its parent. The mutations necessary for the evolutionary algorithm to do its work can still occur but the process is relatively less dynamic, which is presumably why asexual species are in the minority in Nature despite the obvious efficiency benefits of, for example, not having to find a mate.

Organisms which replicate sexually, on the other hand, do so by randomly combining the genes from two separate individuals to form a third, distinct, genome, through the process called meiosis. Humans are an example of a sexually-reproducing species, of course, together with the majority of other animals and a surprising number of plants and fungi.

The advantage of sexual reproduction is that it improves genetic diversity and therefore the chances that at least some offspring will survive in an unpredictably variable environment, for example by staying one step ahead of whatever parasites are likely to be evolving in parallel. A less dynamic gene pool carries a greater risk that a particular parasite might gain a decisive generational advantage, with potentially catastrophic consequences.

In all sexually-reproductive species, reproduction requires a "male" and a "female" organism to exchange and mix their genes through some form of physical mating process. These roles are binary, and not interchangeable, because the sexual apparatus required for each role is so comprehensively different. Coyne and Maroja explain, in *The Ideological Subversion of Biology*, referenced in the previous section: "your biological sex is determined simply by whether your body is designed to make large, immobile gametes (eggs, characterising females; my note: a gamete is a cell capable of combining with another of the opposite sex to form a zygote, in effect a fertilised egg), or very small and mobile gametes (sperm, characterising males). Even in plants we see the same dichotomy, with pollen producing the tiny sperm and ovules carrying large eggs. Size difference can be huge: a human egg, for instance, has *ten million times* (authors' emphasis) the volume of a single sperm. And each gamete is associated with a complex reproductive apparatus that produces it. It is the bearers of these two reproductive systems that biologists recognise as 'the sexes'".

They continue: "because no other types of gametes exist in animals or vascular plants, and we see no intermediate gametes, there is no third sex. Although many species of animals and flowering plants have hermaphrodites, these simply combine male and female functions (and gametes) within single individuals and don't constitute a 'third sex'. Further, developmental issues can sometimes produce people who are intersex, including hermaphrodites. Developmental variants are very rare, constituting only about one in 5,600 people (0.018 percent), and also don't represent 'other sexes'. (We know of only two cases of true human hermaphrodites who were fertile, but one individual was fertile only as a male and the other only as a female)".

It is worth noting that although an incidence of 0.018 per cent for people who exhibit differences in sexual development (DSD for short) of course means that they are rare as a proportion of the total population, with 8 billion people alive in the world today this still equates to around 1.5 million individuals globally. Estimates of the incidence of DSDs vary, and the actual number may be significantly higher: for example, an incidence of 0.1% would equate to around 8 million individuals.

Whatever the total number, multiple DSD conditions exist within it, encompassing both XY "males" and XX "females". To give one topical example, some people born with an XY chromosome have an abnormality in the sex-determining region of their Y chromosome, known as the SYR region, in which three genes (SRD5A1, SRDA2 and SRDA3) code for the production of enzymes which then cause the development of male genitalia. An abnormality in these genes can cause an XY "male" baby to be born with ambiguous or female type external genitals, perhaps with testicles which are retracted inside the body and not obvious externally. In such a case, it is easy to see that the individual might be classified as female at birth, and brought up as such in whatever the prevailing culture happens to be. Later, at puberty, testosterone is released, as is typical for XY "males", and this potentially leads to the development of male secondary sexual characteristics such as a deep voice, muscles, hair on the body and so on.

In such cases, babies identified by doctors as female at birth can, at puberty, become rather male in appearance and body design. However, just to complicate matters, such development is not inevitable. For example, there is a second condition called androgen insensitivity syndrome, in which XY individuals produce testosterone and, presumably, the enzyme required to produce male genitalia, but the receptors in their cells do not respond to it. This can also result in a range of appearances in the newborn baby from typical male to typical female and the full range in between; and inhibit or even eliminate the bodily effects of testosterone surge at puberty.

Our growing knowledge of the various DSD conditions feeds the broader "culture war" debates concerning, for example, eligibility for participation in elite women's sport. Prominent recent examples are the gold medal-winning female boxers Imane Khelif and Lin Yu-ting at the 2024 Paris Olympics. At the time of writing the biological profiles for these individuals are not publicly available, and so it is hard to comment on their specific cases. From what is in the public domain it seems likely that both are examples of the kind of condition described above, classified as girls at birth and raised as such, then subsequently developing secondary male characteristics such as muscle mass and increased power at puberty.

It is easy to empathise with the experience of the individuals themselves, raised as they were to think of themselves as being entirely female and likely confused and emotionally threatened by the sudden clamour that in fact they might not be. It is also easy to appreciate the concerns of their opponents, and of commentators more generally, particularly with respect to physical safety in a contact sport such as boxing.

Of course, a binary decision about participation must be made for specific individuals wishing to compete in particular sports events. It is however not straightforward to develop a simple set of scientific rules to cover all eventualities, because the topic is complex and our understanding remains far from complete. UK journalist Sofia Bettiza summarises, in an article titled *What does science tell us about boxing's gender row?* dated 9 August 2024 and published on the BBC Sports website: "there are a group of about 40 conditions involving genes, hormones and reproductive organs that develop in the womb...for now, science is not yet able to offer a definitive view on how people with different chromosomal make-ups should be categorised for the purposes of elite sport. For those who spend their lives trying to make sense of the science, their hope is that this latest row will propel much-needed research".

Science may certainly provide further illumination. The likelihood is that it will never provide definitive answers, though, because at some point the question of which individuals should be eligible for particular competitions becomes a matter of social judgement. Still, the hope is that improved scientific understanding will help shape more informed judgements, benefitting all parties including the individuals at the centre of the debates.

Moving to the second level of our broader discussion, meaningful differences exist between biological males and biological females across a whole host of dimensions when we consider average values for each sex, including physical and, more controversially, cognitive and psychological characteristics. Admittedly, some of the latter in particular are potentially complicated by the kinds of "nature versus nurture" issues we touched on in the previous section, whereby a belief in a difference in say innate intelligence might prove self-fulfilling because the very expectation can result in differences of experience which then paradoxically create the predicted outcome even though in reality this may have nothing to do with the underlying genes.

In any case, in this as in other situations averages can be misleading when it comes individual cases. For both sexes the values of any given trait are typically distributed in what is called a "normal" distribution around the average value for the particular sex, meaning that the highest number of individuals cluster around the actual average, and then there are progressively fewer instances in equal proportion as the value increases or decreases from the average. Crucially, these distribution curves tend to overlap, describing what American/Canadian psychologists Yanna Weisberg, Colin DeYoung and Jacob Hirsh call a "camel's hump bi-modal" pattern, in an article titled *Gender Differences in Personality across the Ten Aspects of the Big Five*, published on 1 August 2011 in *Frontiers in Psychology*. This means that for any given trait there will always be some biological females who possess more of it than do some males; and for many traits some females who possess more than the *average* male. The reverse is true – for any particular trait, there will be some biological males who possess less of it than some biological females, and some smaller number who possess less than the *average* female.

Physically, for example, the average human male is taller and heavier than the average female, with greater muscle mass and a lower proportion of body fat. For weight specifically, research from the US CDC (Centers for Disease Control) suggests that the average American man in 2020 weighed around 200 pounds, or 91 kg; roughly 17% more than the weight of the 2020 average American woman, at around 171 pounds, or 78kg.

As an aside, average weights for both sexes are markedly higher than their counterparts back in time, for example in the 1960s. This is the obesity epidemic in action. However, the *relative* average weights were not observed to have changed significantly over time.

And the point is that within these 2020 average values there were, of course, some individual women who weighed more than 78kg, including some who weighed more than 91kg; and likewise some individual men who weighed less than 91kg, including some below 78kg.

In short, whilst it is statistically accurate to say that the average woman weighs less than the average man, and we can arguably infer that the heavier someone is the more statistically likely they are to be male, we cannot make categorical gender distinctions for individuals based solely on their weight, or indeed on pretty much any other attribute other than reproductive organs.

There are of course many physical differences between the sexes on average. A 2024 article titled *25 Fun Facts About What Makes Men and Women Different*, on the *Ask the Scientists* website, lists examples such as: males typically have around 25% thicker skin; males have significantly higher levels of testosterone; the second longest finger for males is usually the ring finger whereas for females it is the index finger; males have more pronounced Adam's apples because they tend to have larger voice boxes; females tend to have better senses of smell and taste than males; and so on. The full list of differences runs to many more than 25.

There are also observable differences in the physical structure of "typical" male and female brains, described in the same *Ask the Scientists* article referenced above: "there are differences in the way male and female brains are structured, how they process information, and interact with chemical signals. Some examples: men have more information-containing grey matter, but women have more white matter, which connects different parts of the brain. Also, women have bigger memory centres than men".

Admittedly, these differences between male and female human brains are less pronounced than they are for many other mammal species, as Cat Bohannon observes on pp245-6 of *Eve*: "after spending years digging through the literature on the subject from dozens of different angles, I can actually report that the oddest thing about our species might be that the female human brain doesn't seem to be all that functionally different from the male...that's not true of rodents: male rodents have distinctly rodent-masculine brains, and the females have pretty obviously female brains; both are clearly about the same *size* (author's emphasis), proportional to their bodies, but the way a female rodent's brain reacts to something like a particular pheromone is drastically different from what a male brain does. And these kinds of differences between male and female brains exist across the mammal kingdom".

Still, the point is that some observable differences exist in how male and female human brains are structured, and it seems reasonable to infer that this might lead to some differences in how they function. As an example, small but statistically meaningful variations are observed in the average personalities of males compared with females. In fact, differences are seen across *every* dimension of the "Big 5" personality profile, generally accepted as the best framework yet devised for measuring personality and to which we will return in the next chapter.

Weisberg, DeYoung and Hirsch tell us, in the same *Gender Differences in Personality* article referenced above: "this paper investigates gender differences in personality traits, both at the level of the Big Five and at the sublevel of two aspects within each Big Five domain. Replicating previous findings, women reported higher Big Five Extroversion, Agreeableness, and Neuroticism scores than men. However, more extensive gender differences were found at the level of the aspects, with significant gender differences appearing in both aspects of *every* (my emphasis) Big Five trait".

To decode this, the Big 5 personality model identifies five dimensions along which it has been found to be statistically meaningful to assess personality differences and similarities. These are: openness to experience; conscientiousness; extraversion; agreeableness; and neuroticism. These 5 dimensions can themselves be further divided into 10 "aspects": volatility; withdrawal; enthusiasm; assertiveness; intellect; openness; industriousness; orderliness; compassion; and politeness.

There is not space, and nor do we need, to get into the details of what the differences between the sexes are along all these parameters. Two examples will suffice to illustrate the broader point: the research confirms with statistical rigour that on average females are more nurturing, and males more prone to aggression. To repeat, though, the research deals with averages. The "overlapping camel's hump" distribution ensures that on these dimensions as on others some individual females will be less nurturing and/or more aggressive than some individual men, and vice versa.

Many studies have been conducted on the question of whether differences in intelligence exist between human males and females. Although the results are not universally consistent, the clear consensus is that *no* meaningful differences exist on average at the level of general intelligence. Differences are seen, however, in some specific cognitive faculties. For example, on average females do relatively better at tasks which require verbal ability, such as reading and writing. Conversely, males tend to have better spatial awareness. Again, we are dealing with averages...

Interestingly enough, there is also data to suggest that males tend to have a higher-than-justified impression of their own IQ whereas females tend to undervalue theirs. Australian psychologists David Reilly, David Neumann and Glenda Andrews comment, in an article titled *Gender Differences in Self-Estimated Intelligence: Exploring the Male Hubris, Female Humility Problem*, published on the *National Library of Medicine* website dated 7 February 2022: "despite evidence from cognitive psychology that men and women are equal in measured intelligence, gender differences in self-estimated intelligence (SEI) are widely reported with males providing systematically higher estimates than females".

The authors spend the bulk of their paper exploring why this should be so, concluding that whilst a number of factors are likely to be involved, a female tendency towards lower self-esteem is probably an important contributor. Whatever the cause, the authors point out that the divergence is potentially harmful to both groups: "while a mild self-enhancing bias may be protective and to some degree self-fulfilling, the psychological consequences of inaccurately calibrated estimates of intellectual ability can also be damaging. Unrealistically inflated estimates may set students up for future discouragement and failure if their reach exceeds their grasp...perhaps even more problematic though is the effect of underestimation on achievement motivation, course selection and educational aspirations: if you tell yourself that you can't, then you're right – you won't".

We are now firmly into territory which begs the familiar question, discussed during our review of race, of the extent to which whatever cognitive and psychological differences are observed between the sexes on average might be the product of "nature", hardwired into our brain by our genes; or alternatively "nurture", the result of learned experiences prompted, for example, by assigned social roles and experiences in the specific culture in which we happen to live.

Weisberg, DeYoung and Hirsh make the case that at least some element of "nature" is likely to be involved: "it's certain that, over millions of years, natural selection caused some behaviours of males and females to diverge. How do we know this? By using multiple criteria, including evaluating the general likelihood of an adaptive explanation; looking for behavioural parallels in other species (especially our closest primate relatives); determining whether a sex difference in behaviour is ubiquitous among different human cultures, including hunter-gatherers; testing whether the behaviour is influenced by reproductive hormones, such as testosterone; and seeing if the behaviour appears at the expected time of development. Risk-taking and male-male aggression, for example, are strongest during the peak reproductive years of young adulthood – just as we expect if these are behaviours that evolved to help men secure mates".

As an aside, the authors also mount a spirited defence of evolutionary psychology in general: "the fundamental premise of evolutionary psychology is simply this: *our brains, and how they work – which yield our behaviours, preferences, and thoughts – sometimes reflect natural selection that acted on our ancestors* (authors' emphasis). Nobody denies this for our bodies – palimpsests of once-adaptive traits that are no longer useful (wisdom teeth, tailbones, and transitory coats of hair in embryos) – but opponents of evolutionary psychology deny it for our behaviours. But there is no scientific reason for such duality. Why on earth should our bodies reflect millions of years of evolution, while behaviours, thoughts, and psychology, moulded by the very same forces, are somehow immune to our past? The only way this could be true is if human behaviours lacked genetic variation, a *sine qua non* for evolution. Yet research has shown that our behaviours are among the most genetically *variable* (authors' emphasis) human traits!"

To summarise, the critical point for this second level of discussion is that a wide range of physical, cognitive and psychological differences exist between the sexes on average, albeit for any specific trait there is typically a distribution around the average for each sex, which tends to overlap that of the other sex. Whereas biological, which is to say reproductive, sex is essentially binary, then, Weisberg, DeYoung and Hirsh point out that when it comes to other attributes there are: "many more intermediates than we see for biological sex".

Viewed through this lens, at the second level of discussion it becomes harder to give a succinct answer to the popular tabloid question "what is a woman?". More accurately, it is easy enough to define this at the level of the "average" woman, or indeed man, but potentially more challenging for specific individuals.

Finally, the third, and deepest, level of complexity arises when we introduce the question of personal identity - what it feels like to be "me" or, said differently, our sense of Self. We will explore the topic of Self more fully in the next chapter. Suffice for now to say that it is by definition personal, subjective, and ultimately unique to us as an individual. Whilst gender is just one of many dimensions along which we may define our Self, the "camel's hump" nature of the many average physical and psychological differences which exist between the sexes makes it easy to see how at least some individuals may resist binary categorisation of their own identity, even before the additional complexities which may confront individuals who exhibit some form of DSD.

The broader topic of transgender individuals has received particular attention in recent years, and on p215 of his 2017 book *Behave* American neurologist Robert Sapolsky has this to say: "remarkably, studies have examined brains of transgender individuals, concentrating on brain regions that, on the average, differ in size between men and women. And consistently, regardless of the desired direction of the sex change and, in fact, regardless of whether the person had undergone a sex change yet, the dimorphic brain regions in transgender individuals resembled the sex of the person they had always felt themselves to be, not their 'actual' sex. In other words, it's not the case that transgender individuals think they are a different gender than they actually are. It's more like they got stuck with the bodies of a different sex from who they actually are".

In sum, biological sex as defined by our reproductive system is essentially binary and immutable; many meaningful physical, cognitive and psychological differences exist on average between the biological sexes but for any given trait there are likely to be specific individuals who exhibit more, or less, of it than the average value for the opposite sex; and our sense of personal identity is unique to us as an individual, along many dimensions potentially including gender.

These three levels of complexity help to explain why easy answers are not always forthcoming on public policy questions such as whether a biological male identifying as a female should be allowed access to a female public toilet. As with the question of participation in elite, and indeed non-elite, sport, the science can help inform the judgement needed to answer such questions but is unlikely ever to provide a definitive resolution. And, cop-out though it may be, public policy is fortunately beyond the scope of this book.

Inbreeding

Genetics also helps us to understand the mechanics of inbreeding, defined by *ScienceDirect.com* as: "the production of offspring from the mating of individuals related by ancestry. This includes self-fertilisation, brother-sister, parent-offspring, and cousin matings, as well as matings between more distant relatives".

Inbreeding may be inevitable if a population is very small, meaning that it must have occurred at some level in human populations of the remote past. There have also been, and to an extent remain, some human cultures which promote it, for example through cousin marriage, and typically for dynastic or clan reasons. Generally, though, inbreeding has a deservedly bad rap because in many species, certainly including humans, it is associated with health problems of various kinds as well as with a phenomenon called "inbreeding depression", which is not a psychological condition but rather a technical term describing a reduction in the ability of an inbred population to survive and reproduce.

A celebrated example of the potentially pernicious effects of inbreeding is the Royal House of Hapsburg, "one of the most powerful dynasties of Medieval and Renaissance Europe...which controlled land from the Philippines to the Americas", according to an article titled *The*

Hapsburg Jaw: How Inbreeding Ended a Dynasty published as a blog on the *23andMe* website and dated 4 June 2024. The article continues: "their expansion and hold on power came about in part through inter-family marriages...the Hapsburgs are known not only for controlling vast tracts of Europe but also for maintaining control by rarely marrying outside the dynasty...by the end of the 17th century, the results of their marital practices had become apparent. Family members had distinctive protruding lips, a high rate of infant mortality and a host of other health problems".

Matters finally came to an inbred head in the unfortunate personage of Charles II, King of Spain and much else besides, who was born in 1661 and died in 1700, aged 38. The story proceeds: "from 1516 to 1700, it has been estimated that over 80% of marriages within the Spanish branch of the Hapsburg dynasty were consanguineous. In other words, they were marriages between close blood relatives...infant and child mortality rose to 50% among Spanish Hapsburgs, much higher than the average for the period... the final Hapsburg King of Spain, Charles II, was perhaps the most unfortunate result of these unions. Also known as "El Hechizado" ("The Hexed"), Charles was severely deformed...the so-called "Hapsburg Lip"...(made it) difficult for him to speak. An enlarged tongue, gastrointestinal problems, mental retardation, and possible growth problems meant that Charles was raised almost as an infant until the age of 10. Even as he grew older, he was never able to govern effectively. His rule saw the rapid decline of the empire, only exacerbated by his death". In fact his death precipitated a succession crisis because he died childless, unsurprisingly given that an autopsy revealed that by the time of his demise he had only one testicle, which had itself atrophied.

The root cause of inbreeding depression is that inbreeding reduces genetic diversity. One important implication, as we saw earlier, is that this increases the risk of disaster to an inbred population as a result of exposure to a particular virus or disease which it is not genetically equipped to defend against.

Inbreeding also increases the risk that harmful "recessive" genes will become active. To explore this requires that we briefly review the topic of "recessive" as distinct from "dominant" genes.

We saw earlier that we inherit two copies of each of our genes, one from each parent. British journalist Alfie Shaw explains, in an entry called *What are the effects of inbreeding?*, published on the *BBC Earth* website and undated: "genes determine different aspects of your appearance, like hair and eye colour, as well as biological factors such as your blood type. These genes fall into two categories, dominant and recessive. If one of the genes in the pair is dominant, then the result is you gain the trait of the dominant gene. However, for traits that originate from the recessive gene, you need both genes to be recessive. For example, the gene for brown eyes is dominant and so having just one of these in a pair will result in your eyes being brown. However, the gene for blue eyes is recessive so you'll need both of them to get blue eyes".

The technical term for these gene copies is alleles, and the natural variation that we have seen is at the heart of the evolutionary algorithm means that some specific gene "flavours", or alleles, will be neutral in terms of their impact on biological fitness (for example whether one has brown or blue eyes is unlikely to affect one's chances of survival and reproduction, at least so long as no marked female preference emerges for one or the other in males); some gene variations will be beneficial (for example, those which promote physical or cognitive excellence), and finally some will reduce fitness. This last category are classified as deleterious genes, and include those that code for all manner of hereditary conditions, such as various forms of cancer, heart disease, cystic fibrosis, colour blindness, and so on.

If a deleterious gene is dominant, and sufficiently severe in impact, it will tend to disappear from the population over time for the obvious reason that it will disadvantage its host, who will then be out-competed by others in the evolutionary struggle to survive and reproduce.

When a deleterious gene is recessive, however, it will likely be masked in most cases by the presence of the non-deleterious dominant alternative, and so may persist for generations without ever being expressed. Simply put, the problem with inbreeding is that it increases the probability that two such deleterious recessive genes will occur together in an individual and so be expressed.

Further explanation is provided by an entry called *Inbreeding depression*, part of *Understanding Evolution*, published on the Museum of Paleontology website, itself affiliated to Berkeley University: "over time, natural selection weeds deleterious alleles out of a population – when the dominant deleterious alleles are expressed, they lower the carrier's fitness, and fewer copies wind up in the next generation. But recessive deleterious alleles are 'hidden' from natural selection by the dominant non-deleterious counterpart. An individual carrying a single recessive deleterious allele will be healthy and can easily pass the deleterious allele into the next generation...when the population is large, this is generally not a problem – the population may carry many recessive deleterious alleles, but they are rarely expressed. However, when the population becomes small, close relatives end up mating with one another, and those relatives likely carry the *same* recessive deleterious alleles. When the relatives mate, the offspring may inherit *two* (author's emphasis in both cases) copies of the same recessive deleterious allele and suffer the consequences of expressing (it)".

In some circumstances, inbreeding can have positive effects, if the reduction in genetic diversity serves to promote and homogenise "desirable" genes in a population rather than to spread malign ones. "Pure bred" dog breeds, for example, have generally been created by a process of artificial selection in which successive generations descend from a limited pool of common ancestors, so that particular characteristics of physical appearance and temperament are preserved and amplified over time. There is a catch, though. Many such breeds suffer disproportionately from a variety of health complications, such as weakened immune systems, heart conditions and even cognitive impairments.

A second example of controlled inbreeding is laboratory mice. These are specifically inbred to be clones, in other words genetically identical, so that, say, alternative medical treatments for a particular condition can meaningfully be tested.

However, the process to produce such clones is not straightforward. Early attempts were often thwarted when one disease or another wiped out entire colonies, their lack of genetic diversity leaving them particularly vulnerable to this form of catastrophe. Nowadays, the typical process involves breeding a minimum of twenty generations of brothers and sisters, all descended from one original mating pair. Those individuals unfortunate to inherit two copies of a deleterious gene express it and are eliminated from the population, one way or another. Those who inherit one deleterious and one dominant, non-deleterious copy have a 50% chance of passing on either when they themselves reproduce. Statistically, a few populations will tend disproportionately to pass on the non-deleterious version, and if this imbalance continues over enough generations then the deleterious version might eventually disappear. Eventually, it is only the populations within which this happens who become viable. Clearly there would be significant ethical, not to mention practical, challenges in applying such a process to a human dynasty, or indeed to any human population.

How large a population is needed to mitigate the risks of inbreeding and ensure viability over time? There is no consensus on the answer, partly because it leaves open the question of what level of residual risk is acceptable.

In 1980 the Australian geneticist and the American biologist Michael Soule proposed a generalised rule of "50/500", specifically that for many species just 50 genetically-diverse breeding individuals would be sufficient to mitigate the health risks from inbreeding, and 500 to mitigate the risks of "genetic drift", in which small populations are exposed to random changes in the genome becoming endemic. Many scientists since have expressed the view that these numbers are too low, and also that the answer is likely to vary by species, such that species with high reproductive capacities, for example rodents, would be able to support a lower minimum viable population than those with lower reproductive capacities, for example large mammals.

Matthew Flinders, Professor of Global Ecology at Flinders University suggests that for most species "a number in the 1000s (preferably the high 1000s)" is a more appropriate benchmark, in an entry titled *We're sorry, but 50/500 is still too few*, published on *ConservationBytes.com* and dated 28 January 1 2014. With the possibility of inter-planetary space travel looming, various experts have opined on how large a human population might be needed for an extra-terrestrial colony to be biologically viable, and an entry on the *NBC News* website titled *MACH: how many humans would it take to keep our species alive?* and dated 13 August 2018 quotes an estimate as low as 98, from Frederic Marin, a French astrophysicist; and as high as 14,000 from Cameron Smith, an American anthropologist. There is no single "magic number" which answers the question, then, but rather a range from as low as around 100 to as high as around 14,000.

In any case, the broader point is that genetics helps us to understand just why inbreeding is generally a bad idea, specifically for humans. An article titled *What Scientists Found After Analysing Cases of Human Inbreeding in the UK*, published on the *Discover* website and dated 22 December 2022 comments on the risks to general health: "scientists from the University of Queensland, in Australia, sifted through some 450,000 genomes from people of European ancestry born between 1938 and 1967...the team determined that 125 people, or one in roughly every 3,600, met their criteria for inbreeding, meaning the parents were likely either first-degree relatives (siblings, for example), or second-degree relatives (aunts or uncles, among other possibilities)...inbred children commonly displayed decreased cognitive abilities and muscular function, reduced height and lung function, and are at greater risk from diseases in general, they found. The inbred children are also at higher risk of rare recessive genetic disorders, though the researchers didn't include any data on those".

For completeness, the article also caveats that the research sample is not completely representative of the UK population, tending to be slightly more educated and healthier than average; and also that the severity of the health effects observed was "somewhat limited...so inbreeding hasn't necessarily caused people in the (sample) irreparable harm".

And Alfie Shaw comments on the specific risks from the propagation of recessive genes, in the same *BBC Earth* entry referenced above: "certain congenital defects and genetic diseases, such as cystic fibrosis, are carried by recessive alleles. Inbreeding stacks the odds of being born with such conditions against you. As blood-relative mating partners have similar DNA, the chances of them carrying the same recessive gene is greatly increased. According to a 2011 study, the rate of near natal and childhood death increases if the child comes from a first cousin union, nearly doubling in certain countries".

Overall, the message is clear that in general, inbreeding is best avoided. This is presumably why incest came to be taboo in most of the world's cultures; and things ultimately ended badly for the few exceptions that we know of, such as the Egyptian Pharaohs and the Hapsburgs, even if multiple generations were needed for the full effects to be felt.

What makes us who we are

Our unique set of genes profoundly influences who we are and how we behave. It does not completely determine this, however. Rather, it is the interaction of our genes with our experiences and environment which combine to make us "us".

We briefly touched on the question of "Nature versus Nurture" in our discussions of race and biological sex, and it turns out that this issue more broadly stated has been a topic of contention for centuries.

At one pole of the debate is the idea of "genetic determinism", which flourished in the late 19th and early 20th centuries. At its most extreme, this proposed that our genes determine virtually everything we do. Francis Galton, cousin of Charles Darwin, was one early advocate, for example asserting on p241 of his 1883 publication *Inquiries into Human Faculty and Its Development* that: "there is no escape from the conclusion that nature prevails enormously over nuture...".

Galton is credited with inventing, or at least popularising, the very framing of the debate as "nature versus nurture"; and also with pioneering the altogether more sinister "science" of eugenics, aiming to improve the human gene pool through applying to human populations the kinds of selective breeding practices typically used for livestock and other animals, for example advocating the forced sterilisation of individuals considered "unfit" to reproduce; and also embracing the kind of "scientific racism" which we saw earlier has since been discredited by the advances of genetics, ironically enough.

At the other end of the spectrum lies the *tabula rasa* school of thought, literally translated as "blank slate". This essentially holds that our mind is completely unformed at birth, and that our thoughts, personality and behaviour are entirely determined by our experiences.

This approach has ancient and distinguished origins - the blank slate image itself is attributed to Aristotle, along with his famous if somewhat chilling dictum "give me a child until he is 7 and I will show you the man". Similar ideas are found in ancient Hindu tradition. The notion that we are entirely a product of our experiences gave rise to the influential school of Empiricist philosophy, and achieved renewed impetus in the 20th century through the work of the American psychologist BF Skinner and his fellow Behaviourists.

The modern synthesis is that the correct answer is a synthesis: our genes and our experiences both play important roles in making us who we are. *Nature via Nurture*, as Matt Ridley titles his 2003 book on the topic.

This conclusion may seem intuitively obvious to a contemporary audience, but if so the clarity is relatively recent. In any case, what is perhaps more interesting is how the interplay between nature and nurture plays out at a biological level. Our experiences have the effect of causing particular genes to "express" or not, which is to say to switch on or off. This process is at the heart of the emerging science of epigenetics, defined by American science journalist Rachael Rettner in an article called *Epigenetics: Definition & Examples*, published on *Live Science* on 24 June 2013: "epigenetics...refers to external modifications to DNA that turn genes 'on' or off'. These modifications do not change the DNA sequence, but instead they affect how cells 'read' genes".

In effect, our genes create the propensity for us to develop and act in certain ways, and our experiences and environment determine how these propensities are actualised. Matt Ridley summarises, on p6 of *Nature via Nurture*: "it is genes that allow the human mind to learn, to remember, to imitate, to imprint, to absorb culture and to express instincts. Genes are not puppet-masters, nor blueprints. Nor are they just the carriers of heredity. They are active during life; they switch each other on and off; they respond to the environment. They may direct the construction of the body and brain in the womb, but then they set about dismantling and rebuilding what they have made almost at once – in response to experience. They are both cause and consequence of our actions".

And this dynamic interplay is made easier because of the remarkable rate at which our body regenerates. For example, US journalists Mark Fischetti and Jen Christiansen report, in an article published on 1 April 2021 in the *Scientific American*, titled *Our Bodies Replace Billions of Cells Every Day*: "about 330 billion cells are replaced daily, equivalent to about 1 percent of all our cells. In 80 to 100 days, 30 trillion will have replenished – the equivalent of a new you".

American biologist Robert Sapolsky explains the biochemistry, on p70 of his 2023 book *Determined*: "genes are turned on and off by environment. What is meant here by *environment*? (author's emphasis). It can be the environment within a single cell – a cell is running low on energy, which generates a messenger molecule that activates the genes that code for proteins that boost energy production. Environment can encompass the entire body – a hormone is secreted and is carried in the circulation to target cells at the other end of the body, where it binds to its distinctive receptors; as a result, particular genes are turned on or off. Or environment can take the form of our everyday usage, namely events happening in the world around us. These different versions of environment are linked. For example, living in a stressful, dangerous city will produce chronically elevated levels of glucocorticoids secreted by your adrenal glands, which will activate particular genes in neurons in the amygdala, making those cells more excitable".

Sapolsky emphasises the vital role that experience plays. He points out that the frontal cortex region of the human brain does not mature fully until our early to mid-20s. This is the region which most distinguishes the human brain from those of other species, associated with faculties such as executive function, long-term planning, gratification postponement, impulse control, and emotion regulation. Sapolsky observes, on pp61 2: "by definition, if the frontal cortex is the last part of the brain to develop, it is the brain region least shaped by genes and most shaped by environment...if this is the brain region central to doing the right thing when it's the harder thing to do, no genes can specify what counts as the right thing. It has to be learnt the long, hard way, by experience...this suggests something remarkable – the genetic program of the human brain evolved to free the frontal cortex from genes as much as possible".

Still, our genes are foundational. The majority of the activity that they promote is concerned with the essential if unglamorous task of simply keeping us alive. The emphasis here is much more on similarity than difference, similarity not only with other humans but with other life forms more generally since as we saw we share much of our basic body chemistry, meaning a high proportion of our genes, with other species: for example the 50% of our DNA that we share with a banana.

Essential activities include core biological processes such as manufacturing the proteins to create cells; assembling these cells into a coherent body plan; regenerating them over time; converting the energy we take in from whatever source into usable energy for our body; operating our vital organs such as our liver, kidneys, heart, lungs and of course our brain; and a host of other similarly important if mostly invisible functions. On p88 of his book *Burn – The Misunderstood Science of Metabolism*, published in 2021, the American anthropologist Herman Pontzer tells us that the energy needed to power these basic activities accounts for the majority of the energy our bodies burn: "with all of your organs toiling away all day, it's little wonder that (they) account for most of the calories you burn each day - around 60% for most of us".

By definition, though, these essential processes do not explain what makes us uniquely "us". And, here it turns out to be quite difficult to isolate the relative effect of "nature", that is, our genes, from that of "nurture", our environment and experiences. Some of the most interesting evidence comes from studies of twins, especially identical (monozygotic) twins, who are born from a single fertilised egg and who as we saw earlier therefore share close to, although not quite, 100% of their genes. It follows that differences observed between identical twins can be assumed to be almost entirely a function of their different experiences, and the environments in which they obtained them.

As it happens, Francis Galton was something of a pioneer in the field of twin studies too. But US psychologist William Bouchard was the first person to undertake rigorous research in the field in the modern era. Bouchard started his work at the end of the 1970s, and focused in particular on identical twins who had been separated soon after birth and had therefore grown up in different families, with shared genes but diverse experiences. By now there have been many twin studies of various kinds, in many countries. These use a variety of methods to control for environmental factors, for example comparing findings for identical twins with those for fraternal (dizygotic) twins, or with parents or non-twin siblings who live in the same household and therefore might reasonably be expected to have broadly similar lifestyle and experiences.

In general, twin studies repeatedly reinforce the finding that our genes strongly influence the person we become, shaping for example our physical and intellectual characteristics, our psychological profile, and our personality. At the same time, the studies also consistently tell us that our genes do not completely determine these things. Experience and environment have an important effect too.

To demonstrate the effect our genes have on our physical body we'll look at a single concrete example among many possible: that of weight. On p83 of *Nature via Nurture* Matt Ridley tell us: "the correlation between two siblings in weight, according to one study, is 34 per cent. The similarity between parents and children is a little lower, at 26 per cent. How much of this similarity is due to the fact that they live together and eat similar food, and how much to the fact that they share many of the same genes?

Well, identical twins reared in the same family have a correlation of 80 per cent, while fraternal twins reared together have only 43 per cent similarity, which suggests that genes matter rather more than shared eating habits. What about adoptees? The correlation between adoptees and their adoptive parents is only 4 per cent, and between unrelated siblings in the same family it is just 1 per cent. By contrast, identical twins reared apart in different families are still 72 per cent similar in weight". The conclusion is clear – for weight specifically, genes have a significant impact, albeit still not entirely deterministic.

Turning to psychology, we'll again look at just one representative example: in this case depression. On p288 of his book *Why Zebras Don't Get Ulcers*, first published in 1994 with subsequent editions in 1998 and 2004, Robert Sapolsky explains that a tendency to depression clearly has an important genetic component: "the more closely related two individuals are, the more genes they share in common and, as it turns out, the more likely they are to share a depressive trait. As one of the most telling examples of this, take any two siblings (who are not identical twins). They share something like 50% of their genes. If one of them has a history of depression, the other has about a 25% likelihood, considerably higher than would be expected by chance. Now, compare two identical twins, who share all of their genes in common…if one of them is depressive, the other has a 50% chance".

Sapolsky highlights that personal experience plays a vital role in determining whether someone born with a genetic propensity for depression actually goes on to develop it, in particular how exposed they are to different kinds of stress. He summarises, on p293: "back to that business about there being a genetic component to depression. Does this mean that if you have 'the gene' (or genes) 'for' depression, that's it, you're up the creek, it's inevitable? Obviously not, and the best evidence for this is the factoid about identical twins. One has depression and the other, sharing all the same genes, has about a 50 per cent chance of having the disease as well, a much higher rate than in the general population. There, pretty solid evidence for genes being involved. But flip this the other way. Share every single gene with someone who is depressive and you still have a 50 per cent chance of *not* (Sapolsky's emphasis) having the disease".

Later on p293 Sapolsky reinforces the broader point. Genes play an important role, but: "(they) are rarely about inevitability, especially when it comes to humans, the brain, or behaviour. They're about vulnerability, propensities, tendencies. In this case, genes increase the risk of depression only in certain environments: you guessed it, only in stressful environments".

Finally, the picture is similar for the effect genes have on our personality: our genes and experiences both play a significant role. Matt Ridley, again, summarises, on p83 of *Nature via Nurture*: "...personality is about as heritable as body weight...a little over 40 per cent of the variation in personality is due to direct genetic factors, less than 10 per cent due to shared environmental influences (i.e., mostly the family), and about 25 per cent due to unique environmental influences (everything from illness and accident to the company he or she keeps at school). The remaining 25 per cent or so is simply measurement error".

So there we have it. We each have a unique genetic profile which plays a critical role in making us who we are, including shaping our physical attributes and physiology; our mental capacities and psychology; and our personality. But for the most part our genes do not completely determine any of these things. Rather, they create the potential for us to develop in certain ways – they hardwire us with certain "propensities", as Sapolsky puts it. What we ultimately become is then the result of our experiences and environment acting on our genes, in other words the impact of our personal "nurture" on our unique genetic "nature". And, whilst the specific role that nature plays relative to nurture obviously varies considerably across both traits and individual situations, a surprising number of studies conclude that in many cases the impact tends to be about 50:50.

Predictability, mutability, and "flux"

A defining characteristic of the natural world is that it is in a constant state of change, and also subject to random, or apparently-random chance.

Earlier in the chapter we saw how the quantum world, the most fundamental level of external reality, is inherently probabilistic so that even if we were somehow to possess perfect information about the state of things, we could not be certain how they would subsequently develop.

Turning to the macro world in which we live, the ability to embrace and adapt to change is at the heart of evolutionary success, a sentiment captured in the celebrated quote generally attributed to Charles Darwin and with which he would presumably have agreed even though extensive searches have failed to reveal any text in which he actually uses these specific words: "it is not the strongest of the species that survives, nor the most intelligent. It is the one that is most adaptable to change".

As humans we are programmed to look for cause and effect relationships in the world around us, but even when these exist they are not always obvious or easy to predict. Chaos Theory is a noteworthy example, the idea being that if a particular effect is highly sensitive to initial conditions, and if these in turn are sufficiently hard to understand in detail, then accurate prediction becomes impractical so that an outcome appears random even though it is in reality ultimately causal. To illustrate the point, the American meteorologist Edward Lorenz coined the term "the butterfly effect", in which the suggestion is that the effect of a butterfly flapping its wings in say Brazil might eventually be to cause a tornado in say Texas. There would be no way to predict this from observing the butterfly, even though the event is in reality causal.

The point is that whilst our understanding of the natural laws which govern our world is well developed and affords us a measure of control or at least influence over nature and our personal environment, there remains much that we do not understand and certainly much that we do not control. The implication is that as individuals we do well to remain open to change, in our environment and in ourself. At the same time we must accept that to an important degree our existence remains subject to the slings and arrows of outrageous fortune; in other words, probability and chance.

PART C: Our story so far

Putting together the insights from fundamental physics and evolutionary biology gives rise to an unbroken story of how the Universe and we ourselves have come to be, starting at the very beginning, which is to say the moments immediately after the Big Bang, and continuing all the way to us as the unique individuals that we each are. This story is not fantasy or myth, but rather entirely "natural", backed by a tsunami of scientific evidence and support. It is said that truth can be stranger than fiction and indeed it's quite a story...

About 13.6 billion years ago Big Bang unleashed an unimaginably large amount of energy. This energy was so great that in the immediate aftermath all sorts of exotic matter and antimatter particles formed, many of which were not stable except in these extremely high energy conditions. Very quickly, as measured in the time units that are meaningful to us, this alphabet soup of particles decayed into the range of subatomic particles which are still with us today, both the matter particles and their anti-matter equivalents. These include both the Fermions, the various matter particles; and the Bosons, the force-carrying particles for the four fundamental forces which permeate the Universe: the Strong and Weak Nuclear Forces, Electromagnetism, and Gravity.

Most of the matter and anti-matter particles collided and were quickly annihilated, but fortunately, for reasons we do not yet understand, there was a slight asymmetry and some matter particles remained – enough to account for the entire mass of the Universe today.

The Universe started to expand rapidly, and to cool as it did, a process that remains ongoing. The particles in this early stage formed a kind of spacedust, evenly distributed but crucially with slight fluctuations in density. Hydrogen and helium atoms abounded, a few lithium atoms existed, but almost no other atoms were yet formed. Gradually, the regions in which the spacedust happened to be distributed most densely started to coalesce and to experience the effect of gravity, and a positive feedback loop developed whereby the denser they became, the more they curved their local spacetime so that surrounding matter "fell" towards them.

This in turn led to the formation of networks of "filaments", creating the conditions for the first stars to form, maybe as early as 100 million years after Big Bang. The same process operating on a wider scale formed the first galaxies, which appeared after about a billion years. The first stars were super-massive objects, possibly as much as one million times bigger than our Sun. Because they were so huge, these early stars had a short lifespan, at least in cosmic terms, of just a few million years. They began to contract because of their own enormous gravity. This in turn caused the temperature of the gases inside the star to increase, to a surface temperature maybe 17 times hotter than that of our own Sun. As they collapsed in on themselves, the nuclear fusion processes inside them produced the range of atomic structures we observe in the Universe today – the "heavier elements" or "metals". Many of these stars ultimately exploded as supernovae, creating yet heavier atoms and distributing them as particles across the early Universe. The most massive stars collapsed to form Black Holes, and gravitational forces eventually caused these Black Holes to merge with others in the same vicinity to create even larger Black Holes, such as we observe today at the centre of galaxies, including our own.

The radiation emitted by these stars also ionised the gas remaining in the early Universe. As the conditions evolved, a second generation of stars was born, from coalescing clouds of the now-ionised gases and spacedust, including some of the particles of heavier elements released by the first generation of stars. This second generation of stars was typically smaller than the first, partly because of the presence of the heavier elements, which altered the physics governing their size. These stars emitted radiation in the visible light spectrum, lighting up the Universe in the way we see today. Over time, these stars also started to "die" (that is, explode as supernovae or collapse into Black Holes), a third generation of stars emerged, richer still in the trace metals; and so the cycle continues.

The most intense period of star and galaxy formation occurred a few billion years after Big Bang. The process remains ongoing, albeit at a declining rate. Still, one estimate suggests that just in our own galaxy, the Milky Way, a new star is born on average roughly every year, although this does not happen in a predictable pattern but rather in bursts of activity followed by periods of relative inactivity.

Around 4.6 billion years ago, some spacedust coalesced to form what would become the Solar System, including our Sun and its satellites, among them planet Earth.

Within the first 100 million years of the Earth forming, it experienced a collision with a huge object, possibly as big as the planet Mars, causing the Earth to eject material which then coalesced to form the Moon. As the Earth cooled from a molten state to below the temperature of boiling water, a crust formed, an atmosphere was created by the gravitational effect of Earth's mass on the gases spewing out of the volcanoes which dominated the early landscape, and moisture was released from the molten rocks which then fell as rain, creating the primitive oceans by about 3.8 billion years ago.

The earliest undisputed evidence of life on Earth has been dated to 3.5 billion years ago. Some estimates put the date even earlier, as little as 750 million years after Earth itself was formed. The very first, simple microorganisms emerged from the primordial soup, that is the early oceans. We do not yet have a generally-accepted hypothesis for how this life began, although there is broad scientific consensus that a natural explanation exists. Probably, chemical effects based mainly on the interaction of carbon and water led to the gradual emergence of self-replicating chemical compounds, which evolved into macromolecules, acquired cell membranes (a major innovation) and finally evolved into what we now know as organic life. It is possible, although certainly not proven, that the process was helped by chemicals brought from Space by meteors, or even that life itself developed somewhere out in Space and was transported to Earth on one, or more, of the meteors which were abundant in this period.

Once they appeared, cell structures grew gradually more complex. A critical milestone was the evolution of the "eukaryotic" cell, first appearing perhaps 2 billion years ago and thought to be the symbiotic union of bacterial and archaeal cells. Crucially, eukaryotic cells contain a nucleus in which the genetic material is separated from the surrounding cytoplasm, in contrast to the earlier "prokaryotic" cell, a simpler structure which nonetheless continues to prosper in the form of bacteria and viruses.

The evolution of the eukaryotic cell enabled the development of multi-cellular life forms, eventually producing the complex organisms we see in the world today through the process of Darwinian evolution ("replicate; vary; select"). As we have seen, the power of the evolutionary algorithm is such that whilst no specific life-form (such as humans) could be predicted, a general progression towards more complex life forms certainly could be, given enough time for the algorithm to do its work, and the absence of environmental shocks sufficient to destroy, or fundamentally impair, the whole system.

Of course, the environment did not remain completely stable but rather changed over time, partly due to changes in the physical conditions and geography of Earth, and partly driven by the different selection pressures exerted by the evolving life forms themselves. Life forms which were less successful in adapting to this changing competitive landscape declined and eventually became extinct. Neither Nature nor the evolutionary algorithm are sentimental, and it is estimated that as many as 99.9% of all the species which have existed on Earth to date have become extinct.

The atmosphere of the young Earth contained very little oxygen, comprising mainly hydrogen sulphide, methane and carbon dioxide. Between 2.4 and 3.3 billion years ago primitive organisms developed the ability to photosynthesise, and thus began a process of enriching the atmosphere with oxygen. Gradually, maybe around 1.1 billion years ago or so, eukaryotes evolved into the separate "kingdoms" that we recognise today, including plants, animals, fungi and protozoa. Still these organisms were all tiny, single-celled creatures, until about 580 million years ago when multi-celled organisms started to appear, at least within the first three "kingdoms". A period of intense species proliferation followed, beginning about 540 million years ago and lasting about 50 million years – what is known as the Cambrian Explosion. This is when most of the phyla (that is, the sub-categories within each "kingdom") that we observe today first developed, including the first, ocean-dwelling, vertebrates in the form of fish.

Bacteria had probably moved onto land as early as 2.6 billion years ago. Plants and fungi then started to colonise land close to the ocean edge, possibly a billion years ago in the case of fungi, and maybe 700 million years ago for plants. These evolved to flourish in their new habitat. The earliest clear evidence for animals moving onto land is around 450 million years ago.

There followed oscillating periods of proliferation of species, offset by several mass extinctions, mainly driven by changes in climate. Mammals first appeared about 200 million years ago, "only" 30 million years or so after the first dinosaurs. These early mammals were small, probably nocturnal, creatures. They were successful, insofar as they survived. But mammals only really began to flourish and diversify after the extinction of the dinosaurs, about 65 million years ago, which is to say around 135 million years after mammals themselves had first appeared. The leading hypothesis for the cause of the sudden extinction of the dinosaurs is a 10-kilometre asteroid which struck the Earth in what is now Mexico, throwing enormous quantities of dust and other matter into the atmosphere and blocking sunlight so that photosynthesis was catastrophically impaired, many herbivores starved to death, and hence so did many of the carnivores which relied on them for prey. Not just the dinosaurs but 75% of all life forms alive at that time became extinct, and life on Earth would surely be very different today had that giant asteroid not struck.

Whatever, mammals began to flourish. The oldest accepted fossil record shows that primates had clearly diverged from other mammals by around 55 million years ago, although some scholars suggest the split happened much earlier, maybe as long ago as 80 million years, which is to say well before the extinction of the dinosaurs.

Be that as it may, our early primate ancestors had adapted to become tree-dwellers. Apes diverged from other primates around 21 million years ago, and eventually, around 7 million years ago or so, "hominids", the ancestors of modern humans, diverged from our common ancestor with chimpanzees and bonobos, in what is now Africa.

For a long time hominids remained essentially tree-dwelling, with a mainly vegetarian diet. Fairly quickly, it seems, they transitioned from a social structure based on dominance and promiscuity to one favouring pair-bonding and fidelity, a shift we will explore further in Chapter 3. Eventually, maybe around 4 million years ago, hominids came down from the trees, likely in response to climate changes which reduced the amount of forest and created more savannah. A plausible scenario is that the loss of rainforests led to a shortage of food, and increased competition with other species for what food there was. Our ancestors' response was to range more widely over grassland in search of new food sources. Bipedalism, that is walking on two legs, developed, the advantage being that it is more economical for covering long distances, and enables those who practice it to see further across a savannah terrain. Diet changed to become omnivorous and specifically to include more meat, making the species more resilient to temporary changes in the availability of particular foods. This new diet also provided more calories, fuelling larger brains which themselves were required for and in turn enabled novel developments in social behaviour and technology, for example sharing and tool use, also topics we will discuss further in Chapter 3.

By 3 million years ago there is some evidence of a modest increase in brain size, to around one-third the size of our modern brains, as well as evidence of the use of rudimentary stone tools. Around 2.5 million years ago we see the first evidence of primitive stone tools, and also of the hunting of larger game, so that we can infer that sharing food, and possibly other resources such as shelter, had become an established behaviour. It is also around this time that what we now call the "hunter-gatherer" lifestyle began. Around 1.5 million years ago the first tear-shaped hand axes appear, and by around 700,000 years ago we see evidence of spears. The earliest evidence of systematic use of fire can confidently be dated to around 400,000 years ago, although some researchers speculate that fire may have been used opportunistically by our ancestors well before this time, perhaps as early as 1.5 million years ago.

Over time, a variety of different hominid species developed, although it is only our own, *homo sapiens*, which now survives. Distinct hominid species included for example *homo habilis*; *homo heidelbergensis*, the Denisovans, and the Neanderthals, as well as *homo floresiensis*, otherwise known as the "Hobbit" due to its small average height of not much more than 3 feet, or about 0.9 metres.

There is evidence of Neanderthals specifically from maybe 400,000 years ago; well before the earliest evidence of our own direct ancestors, *homo sapiens*, which dates back around 200,000 years albeit some tantalising recent clues suggest an earlier date of maybe 300,000 years. Whatever, these early *homo sapiens* had a body design, and brain size, essentially the same as we have today, and once they appear there is evidence of more advanced stone tools, and even some hints of local trade networks. Around 150,000 years ago we see the first evidence of what were labelled *homo sapiens sapiens*, which is to say entirely modern humans, again in Africa. This distinction was introduced in an era when it was thought that separate species of contemporary human existed, in the form of different "races" as previously discussed. As we saw, this subsequently turned out to have no basis in biological reality, and it is no longer clear that there is a biologically meaningful distinction to be made between *homo sapiens* and *homo sapiens sapiens* either. Hereafter we'll just use *homo sapiens* for simplicity.

It is generally accepted that the majority of early hominid development occurred in Africa. Over time, there were a series of "Out of Africa" migrations, and although it seems likely that many of these early populations eventually became extinct or retreated back, eventually of course modern humans colonised most of the planet. The first significant migration is thought to have happened around 1.8 million years ago, by a hominid species called *homo erectus*. Within 100,000 years this species had spread through central Eurasia to east Asia, including what is now China and Indonesia.

There is some evidence for an expansion of *homo sapiens* as much as 200,000 years ago, early in its existence, and more definite evidence for another around 125,000 years ago. However these populations eventually went extinct. The definitive migration, from which the majority of modern humans are descended, occurred some time around 60,000 years ago, reaching Europe around 50,000 years ago. These people encountered Neanderthals in the Middle East and Europe and lived alongside them for possibly 7,000 years, interbreeding for that period.

Around 40,000 years ago Neanderthals went extinct, as did the population of *homo sapiens* living in Europe at the time. It is not clear why this happened but the leading hypothesis these days is that climate fluctuations were likely responsible, replacing earlier theories such as that humans inflicted genocide on Neanderthals. In any case, by this time the interbred offspring of the *homo sapiens* population had spread out further in the world, and went on to colonise most of the planet including re-populating Europe. The consequence is that all modern humans outside Africa have 1.5-2% Neanderthal DNA, and it is possible that this was in fact crucial to our ancestors' ability to resist novel pathogens which their *homo sapiens* forebears had not encountered in Africa, but which Neanderthals had.

It is not that the hominid lineage enjoyed a smooth unbroken ascent. On the contrary, it is clear that along the way there were ebbs and flows in the population, including several "population bottlenecks" during which the species came close to extinction. For example, genetic research by a team at the Sapienza University of Rome suggests that between 800-900,000 years ago our ancestors' total population declined to as few as around 1,280 breeding individuals, remaining at roughly that level for as long as 117,000 years (reported in *The Guardian* in an article by Hannah Devlin titled *Population collapse almost wiped out our ancestors, say scientists*, dated 31 August 2023).

The relatively low level of diversity within the human gene pool strongly suggests an even more recent population collapse, although there is not yet a consensus explanation for the specifics. One theory which was popular in the late 1990s but has since been challenged is that the catastrophic explosion of the Lake Toba supervolcano around 74,000 years ago, incidentally a definite historical event and one of the largest known volcanic eruptions in the Earth's history, precipitated a decline in the global human population to as few as

10,000 individuals, all living in Africa. Other research suggests the possibility of a bottleneck over a much longer timeframe, with numbers dropping as low as 2,000 and remaining low for as long as 100,000 years, described in the *Wikipedia* entry *Population bottleneck*.

Be that as it may, clearly the species survived and, eventually, started to prosper. The earliest known cave paintings date from 35,000 years ago, and the earliest pottery from 30,000 years ago. Around 25,000 years ago modern humans arrived in the Americas, the last continent to be peopled. The numbers involved may have been small – one theory, mentioned in the same Wikipedia article quoted above, suggests that the entire pre-1492 population of the Americas may have descended from as few as 70 individuals who crossed the original land bridge between Asia and North America. The last Ice Age ended around 13,000 years ago, and the earliest agriculture came soon after, around 12,000 years ago, or around 10,000 BCE, famously originating in the so-called Fertile Crescent in Mesopotamia, and, less famously, independently in as many as ten other places around the world, more or less at the same period.

For those people who embraced it, a number which grew rapidly and eventually became a sizeable majority, agriculture ended the hunter-gatherer lifestyle which had persisted for the preceding 2.5 million years, or possibly more, and ushered in what became an entirely new way of life, for better and in some respects worse. In particular, agriculture created the possibility of economic surpluses, so that not every member of the group had to rely on their own resources to eat each day. This opened the door to the division of labour, and eventually to specialisation of various kinds. Larger social groups and settlements became possible, because there was enough food to feed the population, and because it was no longer necessary to keep moving to wherever the food was. This in turn created the opportunity, and arguably the need, for hierarchies to develop, to organise and control larger, more complex communities. There is intriguing evidence of a culturally-induced population bottleneck occurring around 5,000 years ago and which may be presumed to relate to hierarchy. The same Wikipedia entry referenced above highlights data suggesting that genetic diversity in the male Y chromosome "dropped precipitously to a level equivalent to reproduction occurring with a ratio between men and women of 1:17". The entry comments, somewhat drily, that: "the research suggests that the reason for the bottleneck was not a reduction in the number of males, but a drastic decrease in the percentage of males with reproductive success".

The pace and scale of technological change began to increase, for example with the earliest evidence of copper smelting around 5,000 BCE. The first cities emerged, around 3,500 BCE in Sumeria, in what is now Iraq. The wheel was invented around the same time, first used in the Tigris-Euphrates valley. By around 3,000 BCE there is evidence of iron and glass. This is also when writing emerges, again in Sumeria, apparently for the purpose of recording and perhaps regulating business transactions.

This also marks the point at which recorded history begins, and we will therefore leave the story there; other than to celebrate the remarkable, if admittedly solipsistic, fact that during this period as in all others since life itself began there existed some specific organisms whose success in reproducing and helping their offspring to survive led in an unbroken chain to - us.

Chapter summary

We have seen that natural laws exist which govern the development and operation of the Universe and of the Earthly life it contains, specifically including human life. The specifics of these laws are often complicated and also counter-intuitive to our common sense expectations, but they nonetheless provide rational, material explanations for some of the most fundamental questions, such as how the Universe developed and operates, and how human life on Earth emerged. They are sufficiently compelling to support an overarching belief that the world we live in is entirely material, so that natural, rather than supernatural, explanations exist for everything.

This allows us to infer what we might call the boundary conditions for our own life. In particular, we cannot assume that there is some kind of benevolent deity somehow looking out for us, nor is there any reason to assume that our existence will extend beyond our lifespan here on Earth. On the contrary, we are fundamentally alone, for better or worse; and must ultimately look inside ourself and not to some external "authority" to make the most of the opportunity that the fact of our existence affords us.

As we contemplate this, a number of specific conclusions, or "beliefs", emerge:

- The Universe, including human life, is entirely natural, which is to say that it is entirely material, governed by a set of natural laws which are themselves inviolable. The supernatural is "real" only within the subjective world of the human mind, not in any objective external sense.
- All matter throughout the Universe, including human beings, is composed of fundamental particles, more accurately "wave-particles", which are themselves an expression of, and interchangeable with, underlying force fields which permeate the Universe. The total amount of energy these particles represent does not change, even as their distribution does.
- At a microscopic scale reality is probabilistic, meaning that random chance plays an important role.

- Things we may subjectively experience as absolute are in fact relative, specifically including Time and Space.
- Nature is inherently amoral, subject to the evolutionary algorithm: "replicate; vary; select".
- Humans are just of one of many species which all ultimately developed from a common ancestor in the 3.5 billion years or so since life on Earth began. Humans are not a "chosen" species, simply one which has been successful at out-competing other species, albeit for a relatively short period in terms of evolutionary time.
- As individuals, we each have a specific genetic profile which is unique to us, inherited from our biological parents. Our genes significantly affect, but do not completely determine, who we are. Our experiences and environment are important influences too.
- The natural world is in a constant state of flux, and there is much that we cannot predict or control, implying amongst other things that we ourself should remain open to change.
- We are each part of a remarkable story which starts with Big Bang 13.6 billion years ago and continues right through until...us.

Chapter One has focused on the beliefs appropriate to what we might call the Big Outside World. In the next chapter we'll shift gears and turn our attention inwards, to our own Inner World as mediated by the remarkable faculty of human consciousness.

Timeline summary ("chronology of the human brain")

Years ago	Event
13,800 billion	Big Bang
4,600 billion	Earth forms
3,500 million	Life on Earth begins, in the oceans ("the primordial soup")
2,000 million	Eukaryotic cell develops
1,500 million	Oldest known fossil of multi-cellular organism
520 million	Oldest "complex" brain found (worm-like arthropod)
500 million	First plant life on land
430 million	Oldest known fossil of land-dwelling creature (millipede found in Scotland)
375 million	Four-legged fish-like creatures move onto land
200 million	Earliest mammals
80-55 million	Earliest primates diverge from other mammals, becoming tree-dwelling, and developing a slower metabolism with a slower reproductive cycle and longer lifespan
65 million	Dinosaurs become extinct.
21 million	Apes diverge from other primates. Live in social groups, characterised by in-group competition, dominance and promiscuity. Rudimentary cognition develops ("individual intentionality")
7 million	Hominins (the lineage from which humans descend) diverge from other apes, subsequently evolving into a variety of hominin species (e.g. *Homo erectus*, *Homo*

	Habilis, Homo Heidelbergensis etc). The early hominin diet is almost entirely vegetarian, mainly fruit. Transition to pair-bonding as the primary basis for mating and child-rearing, leading to reduced male-male competition and associated physiological, and psychological, changes.
4 million	Hominins move from tree-dwelling to roaming the savannah, likely in pursuit of new food sources in response to climate change. Bipedalism develops, with other physical changes such as hair loss and sweat glands. Diet evolves to include meat.
3-4 million	*Australopithecus*. Earliest evidence of rudimentary stone tools.
2.5 million	Dawn of the hunter-gatherer lifestyle. More developed, but still primitive, stone tools; first signs of butchery of large animals. Evidence of sharing, likely in conjunction with collaborative foraging, leading to and reinforced by "joint intentionality". Earliest evidence of an increase in brain size.
2 million	Brain size around 20% larger than Australopithecus. Endurance running develops
c1.8 million	*Homo erectus*: Out of Africa expansion. Brain size increases significantly, eventually tripling over the course of two million years
1.5 million	Tear-shaped hand axes
9-800,000	Population bottleneck: humanity reduced to as few as 1280 breeding pairs
500,000	Earliest spears
4-500,000 (maybe earlier)	Hominins are controlling fire, for warmth, cooking, and protection from predators

2-300,000	*Homo sapiens* diverges from other species of hominin. Shift to larger, more integrated social groups, likely in response to population growth and between-group competition. "Collective intentionality" develops, with cognition similar in many respects to modern humans. Signs of advanced tools and hints of local trade networks. Brain stops getting bigger (average human brain size relative to body size has actually shrunk 3-4% in the most recent 10-15,000 years)
	"Y-chromosomal Adam": the most recent male from whom all living humans are descended through the male line
c150,000	"Mitochondrial Eve": the most recent female from whom all living humans are descended through the female line
c125,000	*Homo sapiens* Out of Africa expansion, eventually going extinct
70,000	Population bottleneck: humanity reduced to maybe 10,000 people globally, for reasons which remain unclear. Earliest evidence of bows and arrows
c60,000	"Great leap forward", jewellery, standardised stone tools
c50,000	Out of Africa expansion, of the common ancestors for all humans alive today
c40,000	*Homo sapiens* arrive in Middle East and Europe, where they overlap, and interbreed, with the last remaining Neanderthals for around 7,000 years.
	Neanderthals become extinct. *Homo sapiens* is the last remaining hominin species, albeit with c2% Neanderthal genes for all

	populations outside Africa
35,000	Earliest known cave paintings
30,000	Earliest evidence of pottery
25,000	Humans arrive in the Americas, the last continent to be peopled
13,000 BCE	Last Ice Age ends
c10,000 BCE	Agriculture begins
c8,000 BCE	Sheep and goats domesticated
c6,400 BC	Cattle domesticated
c5,000 BCE	Earliest evidence of copper smelting
c3,500 BCE	Earliest cities (Sumeria in the Middle East)
	First use of the wheel, in Tigris-Euphrates valley
3,000 BCE	Earliest evidence of iron and glass. Emergence of writing. Recorded history begins.

Chapter 2:

Consciousness

"I am the captain of my soul"
William Ernest Henley, 1875

Conscious experience is the defining feature of what it means to feel human. It helps us to shape our existence, through a combination of reason, emotion and instinct (in other words, the combination of our conscious and unconscious mind), which together prompt our behaviour. Consciousness creates the possibility for a varied, textured mental life, rich with fantasy and feeling. Last but not least, consciousness gives us each the ability to achieve some perspective on ourself and on the external world, through the "little voice" inside our mind.

The consequence of all this is that it seems reasonable to believe, although virtually impossible to prove, that as humans our subjective experience of existence is, or at least has the potential to be, enormously richer and more nuanced than that of other species. It is, of course, for each of us to make the most of the precious opportunity that this affords us.

Most important, consciousness gives us agency - the freedom to choose how to live our life, and how to behave in response to a particular event, person, or stimulus. This freedom is obviously not absolute. Our choices are inevitably constrained, by our physical circumstances, and by the combination of our genes and prior experiences which predispose us to behave in particular ways in response to specific "triggers". Still, to predispose is not necessarily to predetermine, and it is specifically in embracing our existential freedom to make our own choices and then accept responsibility for the consequences that we are able to create subjective "meaning" in our life, in turn giving us the best chance of achieving personal fulfillment and happiness.

Powerful as our consciousness is, it is also subjective and fallible in various ways, most of which are not readily obvious to our rational mind. As we seek to exercise personal agency we therefore do well to remain sanguine about the extent to which we can truly be said to be the author of our own good fortune, or misfortune; and also to cultivate a degree of self-knowledge about our most salient personal predispositions, so that, whilst we certainly cannot avoid being subject to these largely-unconscious prompts, we are at least able to make some allowance for them in what we experience as our conscious decisions.

Consciousness main themes

The starting belief is that consciousness is an entirely material phenomenon, like the Universe itself. Specifically, consciousness happens inside, and as a result of, the remarkably sophisticated organ that is the human brain: "the most complex thing we have yet discovered in our universe", according to the Foreword to the online article *Discovering the Brain*, published by the *NCBI* (the US *National Centre for Biotechnology Information*), dated 1992.

It is perhaps obvious, but worth reinforcing, that there is no room in this model for any kind of separate, immaterial "soul", that somehow has an existence independent from our body. Of course it follows that if there is no separate soul, it cannot be immortal. Consciousness is a product of our material brain, and ceases when our brain itself stops functioning, which is to say when we die.

How consciousness happens in a physical sense is frustratingly not yet clear, and may not be for a long time yet. Much progress has been and continues to be made in understanding the biochemistry of the brain, but even so "most neuroscientists agree that we are decades away from knowing the intricacies of how our brain works, let alone how it creates consciousness", as the Canadian-American psychologist Lisa Feldman Barrett puts it on p82 of her 2017 book *How Emotions Are Made – the secret life of the brain*. The American philosopher Alex Rosenberg, whom we met briefly in the previous chapter, suggests that the challenge is such that it may take another 200 years before we have a complete understanding, on p149 of *The Atheist's Guide to Reality*. In short, there is much we still don't know.

And what we do know creates something of a paradox. We have an account of our neural biochemistry which cannot explain conscious experience (indeed often does not even seek to explain it, on the grounds that it is assumed to be somehow illusory and therefore irrelevant); and conversely an account of conscious experience and cognition which cannot be explained in terms of the underlying biochemistry. There is something of an echo of the situation in particle physics whereby both relativity and quantum have considerable descriptive power, and supporting evidence, but cannot currently be reconciled.

Part of the challenge lies in the fact that although no-one denies that our conscious experiences are subjectively real, we also know that our brain is essentially constructive and therefore potentially an unreliable guide to objective reality. Specifically, our brain does not perceive external reality directly but rather filters the continuous stream of data it receives from our senses and from our own body to create an internal representation of reality. It then draws on our past experiences to determine our response to a particular stimulus.

The result is that: "introspection is a process not of *perception* but of *invention* (author's emphasis in both cases): the real-time generation of interpretations and explanations to make sense of our own words and actions", as the British behaviourial scientist Nick Chater explains on p5 of his 2018 book *The Mind is Flat – The Illusion of Mental Depth and the Improvised Mind*, adding on p14: "in reality...the rich mental world we imagine that we are 'looking in on' moment-by-moment, is actually a story that we are inventing moment-by-moment".

This quickly raises a practical problem because, unreliable as they may be, introspection, and cognition more broadly, are the faculties which evolution has bequeathed us to help navigate the world. So, whilst modern research is showing that we must treat their promptings with considerable caution we also have no realistic option to abandon them entirely. Perhaps neuroscience will eventually develop further, to a point where it might enable us to adopt an alternative mental approach. But, as we just saw, this might require as much as another 200 years and in the meantime we have little alternative but to use the mental equipment we have, although we may certainly hope that understanding what the science tells us about its main features and limitations will help us to use it more effectively.

Of particular consequence for this book is our subjective experience of reason: thinking rationally about our world and ourself in ways which in turn enable, or seem to enable, us to exercise conscious choice over our decisions and actions. The choices we make about how to exercise this personal agency ultimately define us. Simply put, we each experience at least some level of opportunity to choose the person we want to be, and then to regulate our day-to-day actions and behaviours in support of this, adapting over time as we feel appropriate. Of course, we must do this whilst taking appropriate account of our circumstances and environment, as well as the relevant features of what we experience as our own "self", including for example our personal triggers, predispositions and biases. Ultimately, though, it is for us each to embrace our existential freedom to choose; take active responsibility for the precious opportunity afforded by our own existence; and make whatever allowances we feel are appropriate for the unreliability and volatility of our inner promptings.

Our existential freedom takes a number of forms and must be exercised in the face of a multitude of constraints. At a practical level, for example, we don't choose our biological parents, and therefore our genetic inheritance. But we do have some ability to acquire self-knowledge over time about what the impact of our genes and upbringing is on, say, our own relative strengths, weaknesses, predilections and preferences. We obviously do not choose the circumstances into which we are born, or to a large extent those in which we are raised. We do, however, have a certain amount of discretion over how we respond. Depending on the specific culture we live in, and the choice we make about how closely to conform to it, we have agency over big "life" decisions such as which romantic partner, or partners, and career, or careers, to pursue, and when to change course in some way. Last, and perhaps most important, we are always in principle free to choose how we behave in response to the hurly-burly of everyday life: the many situations in which must decide how to react to a particular circumstance or event, or the behaviour of another individual or group.

We must accept that the choices we make are complicated by the fact that our consciousness is inherently subjective, constrained, and fallible. Subjective, because as we briefly discussed, consciousness essentially works by taking data from our senses, feeding this into our brain, and creating a representation inside our mind of what this tells us about external reality. Constrained, because we are to a large extent the product of our own biological history and experiences, and therefore heavily predisposed to behave in certain ways in response to particular triggers. Fallible, because the picture of external reality formed by our mind may itself sometimes be mistaken, and also because our minds have evolved to dictate our behaviours based on a complex interplay between instinct, emotion and reason so that choices which we may experience as appropriate or rational in the heat of a particular moment may turn out on subsequent reflection not to be.

With all these caveats, then, we return to the main point. It is a central belief of this book that consciousness gives us the opportunity to exercise existential choice in our life, and therefore to shape and ultimately to define our own existence. It is for each of us individually to make the most of this opportunity, and to embrace personal responsibility for the choices we make. However, we must do this in the knowledge that our consciousness is also subjective, constrained and fallible.

Chapter structure

There is a lot of ground to cover, and it may therefore be helpful to review the structure of this chapter before getting into the detail:

- Part A seeks to define what consciousness is, including discussing the brain as the centre of consciousness and the evolution of human cognition.
- Part B focuses on the crucial opportunity, and in a sense obligation, which consciousness gives us to exercise our freedom to make personal existential choices:

- the time-honoured question of the extent to which we can be said to have personal agency, or "freewill", and therefore genuine freedom to exercise existential choice;
- the concept of the essential "Self", which makes these choices;
- the related topic of our personality and character.
- Part C looks at critical aspects of how consciousness works. In particular:
- executive function and the rational brain;
- learning and development;
- joining up the dots - how our brain processes data;
- instinct, emotion and reason as triggers for behaviour;
- cognitive bias;
- "noise";
- categorisation.
- Part D explores specific faculties which form part of consciousness, including:
- reason;
- language;
- emotion;
- empathy and Theory of Mind;
- memory;
- imagination;
- motivation and drive.
- Part E discusses two factors which can both have an important impact on how our consciousness functions in practice, specifically:
- sleep, and;
- stress.
- Finally, Part F explores some of the most important implications of consciousness for our own existence, including:
- the fact that we have the freedom to exercise personal existential choice in our life means that we should actively embrace it, and then take responsibility for the choices we make.

– the fact that our consciousness is fallible means that when making choices we should give appropriate consideration to the possibility of bias and error.
– "luck" is a fact of life, whereas "destiny" isn't.
– mindset matters: how we think about our life obviously affects how we feel about it, and can also influence outcomes.
– expectations matter: how we think about ourself and others can change what we and they feel and do.

PART A: What consciousness is

The American version of the Cambridge English Dictionary defines consciousness as: "the state of being awake, aware of what is around you, and able to think".

The American author Kendra Cherry elaborates, in an article titled *What is Consciousness?*, posted on *verywellmind* and dated 13 May 2020, highlighting that consciousness is inherently subjective, has both an internal and external dimension, and is intimately connected with our ability to use language: "consciousness refers to your individual awareness of your unique thoughts, memories, feelings, sensations, and environments. Essentially, your consciousness is your awareness of yourself and the world around you. This awareness is subjective and unique to you. If you can describe something you are experiencing in words, then it is part of your consciousness".

As humans, we each experience consciousness mainly as a "little voice" inside our heads, specifically inside our brain. This "voice" is crucial to our mental life and our experience of existence. One of its most peculiar, and spectacular, features is that it allows us to introspect: to think about thinking, as it were; sitting outside of our bodies, in a metaphorical sense, and conducting a dialogue with ourself about our thoughts, feelings, motivations and actions. It also allows us to imagine the thoughts and feelings of others, although obviously we cannot know those with the same intimacy or apparent precision as we do our own.

We'll include emotions in our discussion of consciousness because, as we'll see, it is often the interaction between our emotions and what we might call our rational brain which prompts us to make decisions and take actions. Indeed, our emotions often play a pivotal role, in ways which may not be obvious even for decisions which we may subjectively experience as rational. Emotions are of course also fundamental to our actual experience of existence, sometimes dominating our sensibility to the point of feeling overpowering. Indeed, including emotions in this way requires that we stretch Cherry's definition of consciousness somewhat, because strong emotions can sometimes be difficult to capture adequately in words.

There is legitimate debate about whether it is only humans who have consciousness, or whether animals and possibly other life forms do too; even in extreme versions objects that we might typically think of as inanimate, such as computers and smartphones, especially as we contemplate current and potential future developments in the field of artificial intelligence.

The answer lies largely in how we define "consciousness". As we will shortly explore, our great ape cousins have some cognitive abilities which we might feel justify the label of consciousness, such as an understanding of causality in tool use and of intentionality as it relates to others in their social group. It seems obvious that at least some animals experience feelings which we would characterise as emotions – a dog for example clearly appears to experience pleasure, affection, pain and fear. In this sense, dogs, and by extension other animals, can be said to have a basic inner life, and therefore a form of consciousness. On the other hand it also seems obvious, although hard definitively to prove, that a dog does not have many of the faculties that a human typically does, for example, the same sense of self-awareness, or the ability to put itself in the shoes of others, or to perform rational analysis, or to plan. We may like to imagine that our own family dog can do all these things, but that is another story.

The Australian philosopher of science Peter Godfrey-Smith suggests, on p258 of his 2020 book *Metazoa: animal minds and the birth of consciousness*, that whilst animals indeed possess some attributes relevant to consciousness there are also important differences when compared with humans: "...taken all together, this suggests that some other animals do have offline processing of possibilities, and offline experience, too. A lot of animals spend a considerable amount of time just sitting. When they do, I don't think it is all blank in there, and I doubt that they experience a fixed monotonous slide of the here-and-now scene, either. The self-propelled dynamic patterns in animal brains have more going on in them than that. I think many animals spend a fair amount of time elsewhere. A likely difference between human and non-human cases is not the existence of elsewhere-experience, but the extent of its deliberate control. A feature of human cognition that really does seem to differ greatly from what goes on in other animals is something psychologists call 'executive control,' the ability to direct oneself on a task, suppress momentary urges, and marshal one's various abilities in pursuit of a consciously represented goal. Through this side of human cognition, in concert with tools such as language as an organiser of thought, we can deliberately induce and control our offline journeys, rather than just having them happen. We can set out deliberately to some particular elsewhere, though we might also meander, drift off, and dream".

Overall, then, it seems reasonable to suppose that there is something qualitatively different and special about the human experience of consciousness. It may well be that consciousness lies on a kind of continuum, and that humans are simply further along it than other sentient beings. If so, the gap is surely sufficiently large to regard our case as being substantively different. And since the focus of this book is on human existence, from here on we'll focus just on consciousness as it relates to humans.

This prompts the question at what point an individual human can themselves meaningfully be said to possess consciousness. A similar spectrum-based answer potentially applies, as explained by the British pharmacologist Susan Greenfield on pp139-40 of her 1997 book *The Human Brain, a guided tour*: "since the brain develops slowly and gradually, perhaps consciousness does also. It could be the case that consciousness is not an all-or-none phenomenon, but that it grows as brains do. If we accepted that consciousness were a continuum in this way, then it would follow that the foetus is conscious, but conscious to a far lesser degree than the human adult, or even the human newborn". Greenfield goes on to make the comparison with animals explicit: "this way of looking at consciousness would also help with regard to the riddle of whether non-human animals were conscious. The less sophisticated the brain, the less the degree of consciousness. Hence, animals would be conscious, but a chimpanzee would be conscious to a lesser degree than its human counterpart, as the brains of the two species, so similar at birth, then follow different fates".

Through the ages, our subjective experience of a "little voice" which feels somehow independent of our physical body on the one hand, and our emotions on the other, has given rise to much philosophical speculation that the separation is real. This in turn has underpinned a long tradition of metaphysical belief in the existence of a separate "psyche", or "soul", underpinning a further belief that this soul is immaterial and indeed immortal. These beliefs have been pervasive. Elements of them can be found in many belief systems of the ancient world including, for example, Ancient Egypt, Assyria and Babylon. They found clear expression in the works of leading classical Greek philosophers, most notably Plato, living around 428-348 BCE. Arguably, they reached their apotheosis as they were incorporated into the belief systems of the major monotheistic religions, especially Christianity and Islam. Belief that an immaterial, and immortal, soul exists and is fundamentally separate from the physical body is also at the heart of the philosophical movement known as Dualism, popularised above all by Rene Descartes, the 16th century French philosopher. In short, the notion of a separate, immortal, soul has a long and venerable heritage.

Of course, just because a belief is pervasive does not necessarily mean that it is correct, any more than say the ancient belief that the Earth was at the centre of the Solar System, or that thunder was an expression of the anger of the gods. And, as already discussed, this book espouses the alternative belief that consciousness is an entirely material product of the human brain, leaving no room for immateriality or, sadly, immortality.

Godfrey-Smith explains, on p20 of *Metazoa*: "minds are evolutionary products, brought in to being by the organisation of other, non-mental ingredients in nature...a materialist view does not claim that the mind is an *effect* of physical processes in our brains, a consequence or product of them...the idea, instead, is that experiences and other mental goings-on are biological, and hence physical, processes of a certain kind. Our minds are arrangements and activities in matter and energy. Those arrangements are evolutionary products; they are slowly brought into being. But those arrangements, once they exist, are not *causes* of minds; they *are* minds. Brain processes are not causes of thoughts and experiences; they *are* thoughts and experiences (author's emphases throughout)". Far from being separate from our material self, consciousness is intimately, and entirely, bound up with it.

Why do we believe that consciousness is a product of our material bodies? We cannot empirically demonstrate this, and it is hard to see how we ever will given that consciousness is above all a subjective phenomenon. Rather we infer materiality by combining a number of other findings and assumptions:

- as we saw in the previous chapter, a material explanation is sufficient to explain the entire Universe and natural world, since both began. It would be strange if human consciousness were the sole exception.
- we know and continue to learn a great deal more about the human brain as the presumed centre of consciousness. We know that almost every physical stimulant to consciousness, in the form of our sensory perceptions of the outside world, passes through the brain. The brain is where almost all observable cognitive faculties reside, and nowadays we can actually see many of these in action using various kinds of brain scanner, for example observing how different brain parts activate when we process rational thoughts, feel emotions, respond to different sensory stimuli, and so on.
- we know that physical changes to the material brain, for example through brain damage or narcotics, are capable of producing significant and tangible effects on both the behaviour and lived experience of the affected individuals, in ways which clearly impact their consciousness, that is their rational and emotional functioning, and their sense of "self".

- we may not yet have a consensus view of how consciousness works at a biological level, but there is broad consensus that a material explanation is possible and overwhelmingly likely. Indeed, this is one of the few topics on which almost all researchers agree. There is also broad agreement that the brain has no separate "centre of consciousness" in the sense of a specific area of the brain where consciousness happens – no "Cartesian Theatre", as the American philosopher Daniel Dennett describes it in his book *Consciousness Explained*, published in 1991. Likewise, there is no area of the physical brain which can credibly be associated with a "soul". Rather, consciousness and cognition are the product of neural connections within our brain.
- in any case, there is no plausible alternative to a material explanation for consciousness, and certainly not an alternative supported by any evidence beyond (fallible) reported subjective experiences, usually invoking religious or other supernatural phenomena which we have already seen are incompatible with our understanding of the natural world itself.

The brain as the centre of consciousness

Our starting point is that consciousness is a product of, and takes place within, the remarkable organ that is the human brain.

Of course, humans are not the only creatures to possess a brain. On the contrary, something at least resembling one is found in all animals, that is to say all life forms whose strategy for existence involves them moving around. Susan Greenfield summarises, on pp42-3 of *The Human Brain*: "you only need a brain when you are moving. For stationary life forms, a brain is no longer necessary. The whole point is that for an animal moving around, there is an interaction with an environment that is incessantly changing. You need a device to tell you very quickly what is happening and, most importantly, to enable you to respond to what is happening, to get out of the way of predators or to chase after prey. So the brain, in whatever shape, size, and degree of sophistication, is somehow connected in a very basic way to ensuring survival as both a consequence and cause of movement". By way of illustration, also on p42, Greenfield cites the example of the sea-squirt, which swims around quite freely as a larva then in maturity attaches itself to a rock and becomes immobile for the rest of its life, at which point it eats its own brain since it no longer needs it.

At its simplest, a brain is a kind of control centre which takes in information about the outside world through a network of nerves; combines this with information about the organism itself, for example, whether it needs food and how urgently; processes this information; and then issues "instructions" to the host body about what action to take. It is in effect a machine, albeit one which works primarily through biological and chemical rather than mechanical processes. Our brain accesses huge quantities of external data from our sensory organs – sight, sound, taste, touch and smell. It then processes this to create representations of the "real", outside, world, combining this with the information it also receives about the state of our body and with its own store of past experiences to direct relevant parts of our body to respond. The information flows via electrical signals along the nervous system, in both directions, which is to say from the nerves to the brain, and from the brain back out to the rest of the body.

It is not the possession of a brain which makes humans different, then, but rather the complexity and power of the specific human brain to which we are heir.

It's not that it is all that remarkable to look at. It typically weighs about 1.5 kg in an adult male, and a bit less on average in an adult female. It's made from a greyish spongy matter, wrinkled and folded over on itself rather like a walnut. It has no mechanically-moving parts, unlike say the heart or the lungs. An interesting paradox is that although the brain is where our "feelings" are located, in the sense that signals of say pain are transmitted by the nervous system from whichever part of the body they originate in and are then decoded by the brain to produce the sensory experience we recognise as "pain", the brain itself has no nociceptors and therefore does not itself directly feel pain. We can experience headaches of course. But this is because parts of the body close to the brain do possess nociceptors, for example blood vessels, nerves and muscles in the neck, face and scalp. Headaches do not stem from the brain itself.

What starts to be remarkable is that the brain accounts for around 2% of our body mass, but consumes around 20% of the energy we burn as adults, and as much as 60% of the energy we burn as children, when we are at the stage of our life in which we are learning the most (this data is taken from pp84-8 of *Burn: the Misunderstood Science of Metabolism*, authored by Herman Pontzer and published in 2021). Our brain must obviously be doing something important for our overall life chances for evolution to favour such an asymmetric use of resources.

There are also elements of the human brain's physical structure which set it apart, at least to some extent. In particular, humans have a much more developed cerebral cortex than other mammals, especially when considered as a proportion of body size. The cerebral cortex is the outer layer of brain tissue, and is the part of our brain which developed most recently in our evolutionary history. It seems to be particularly important to fine motor skills, for example toolmaking and more recently writing; to receiving and processing information from the senses, particularly vision, hearing and touch; and to stimulating neural connections within the brain itself, which enhance our ability to create representations of the world we are experiencing, and also to engage in abstract thinking and complex language.

Greenfield explains, on p18 of *The Human Brain*: "the brain region that has undergone the most change during evolution is the outer layer of the brain, the cortex...an important clue to brain function is that in more sophisticated animals the cortex is folded – convoluted – so that its surface area has been able to increase while respecting the confines of a relatively small skull. Flattened out, the rat cortex would be the size of a postage stamp, that of the chimp would be the size of a piece of standard typing paper, while the human brain would be four times greater still! Humans have the least stereotyped, most flexible lifestyle of all animal species, and it is believed the cortex must therefore in some way be related to liberating the individual from fixed, predetermined patterns of behaviour. The more extensive the cortex, the more an individual will be able to react in a specific, unpredictable fashion in accordance with the dictates of a complex situation. The more extensive the cortex, the more an animal will be able to think for itself".

The Irish neuroscientist Kevin Mitchell expounds on the critical role played by the neocortex, on p121 of his 2023 book *Free Agents – how evolution gave us freewill*: "the elaboration of the neocortex allowed more sophisticated perception aimed at extracting meaningful information – identifying objects of interest in the world and creating a map of where they are and how they are moving, all relative to the organism itself. Perception became more and more internalised as additional cortical areas evolved and were recruited to the task of extracting higher- and higher-order features. It also became more subjective, in the sense of being tuned by prior experience and top-down expectations, allowing organisms to internally represent beliefs about what is out in the world. All of that neural machinery is expensive to build and to operate. Those costs are worthwhile only because that information could be profitably put to good use guiding behaviour".

For a long time it was thought that the brain operated like a kind of industrial machine, with different "component" areas specialising in different activities. This gave rise to perhaps the best-known model of the brain, the so-called Triune model first proposed by the American physician and neuroscientist Paul MacLean in the 1960s. MacLean suggested that the brain comprised three largely-autonomous sub-brains, and that each of these systems had been built by evolution on top of the previous one. First, and earliest, was the memorably-named "reptilian" brain, corresponding to the area known as the basal ganglia and associated mainly with our autonomic nervous system which controls our core bodily functions such as breathing, heartbeat and so on. Second was the "mammalian brain" (MacLean called it the "paleomammalian brain"), corresponding to the region known as the Limbic System, thought to control our emotions. Third, and most recently evolved, was the "rational" brain (MacLean called it the "neomammalian brain"), corresponding to the neocortex and associated mainly with the higher cognitive functions such as rational and abstract thought, language and planning, and including the cerebral cortex. Memorable as it undoubtedly is, however, the Triune model has since been discredited on the basis that the different brain regions are in fact inter-connected not separate and, moreover, far from humans being unique in having all three systems, we now know that they are present in some form in the brains of all vertebrates. Indeed, Barrett dismisses it with a single quote, on p18 of *How Emotions Are Made*: "humans don't have an animal brain gift-wrapped in cognition, as any expert in brain evolution knows. 'Mapping emotion onto just the middle part of the brain, and reason and logic onto the cortex, is just plain silly,' says neuroscientist Barbara Finlay, editor of the journal *Behaviour and Brain Sciences*: 'all brain divisions are present in all vertebrates'".

And it is specifically the networks of connections between the individual neurons throughout the brain which appear to hold the key to its operation, and therefore to what we experience as consciousness. The average human brain contains around 86 billion neurons. Each has the potential to connect with any other, through connection points known as synapses. This means there are more potential connections in a single human brain than there are atoms in the known Universe, according to Messrs Al-Chalabi, Turner, and Delamont in their book *The Brain*, published in 2006 (the reference is on p18).

In practice, a single neuron can connect with anywhere between 10,000 and 100,000 others, and it is the combined effect of all of the connections to a particular "host" neuron which determines how it "fires", which is to say what specific electrical pulse it emits. What is more, the process is mediated by a variety of chemicals, called neurotransmitters, and each neurotransmitter has its own signature impact, and is also capable of coming in different doses, with correspondingly different effects. Greenfield explains, on p102 of *The Human Brain*: "consider once more how many inputs can form synapses with a target cell (that is, neuron): as many as a hundred thousand. In each case...different amounts of transmitter will be released...the activation of the neuron is not fixed but can be *varied* (Greenfield's emphasis) in up to a hundred thousand individual cases. Moreover, by having many different chemicals, each working on its own custom-made target, different transmitters will have different effects on the final voltage". She elaborates, on p106: "the brain is built up from single neurons in increasingly complex circuits. These connections are not like a row of people just holding hands in a line or like the children's game where messages are passed from one end of a row to the other and end up completely distorted. Instead, remember that between ten thousand and one hundred thousand neurons make contact with any particular neuron. In turn, any particular neuron will become one of many thousands of inputs for the next cell in the network. If we took a piece of brain the size of a matchhead alone, there could be up to a billion connections on that surface".

The picture that emerges is of a brain in which individual areas may be associated with a particular functionality, for example vision or speech, but where the action is ultimately driven by networks of neurons whose connections are not limited to specific locations. Mitchell explains, on pp215-6 of *Free Agents*: "it is not really correct to think that the various components of an organism are parts, in the way we think of the separable parts of a machine. Instead, *they play parts* (author's emphasis). It is their functional relations to each other that comprise the pattern of organisation. We often draw simplified diagrams of systems with various elements – A, B, C, and so on – in little boxes and arrows drawn between them. The key point to realise is that the organism is not made of the boxes: it's made of the arrows. It is not an organisation of stuff; it's an organisation *of processes* (again, author's emphasis) in mutual relation to each other. The activity of each process is constrained by the collective activities of all the other processes, and these collective activities are constrained to be goal directed, with functionalities that are fitted to the environment, designed to ensure the thriving of the organism and its lineage in its environment".

And on p260 Mitchell reinforces that even the neocortex, important as it is, does not operate independently from the rest of the brain: "it is important to emphasise that although prefrontal regions sit at the top of a hierarchy in one sense, that does not mean they make all the decisions in isolation. Prefrontal regions do have a privileged position in receiving inputs from across the brain. But it is not accurate to think that all that information is just funnelled to the prefrontal cortex where decisions are made, with orders then transmitted down to the rest of the brain. Instead, the process of guiding behaviour involves reverberating conversations up and down the hierarchy, with different regions at different levels concerned with different aspects".

As an aside, an additional roughly 100 million neurons have been discovered to reside in our gut, connecting with the "main" brain in our skull via neurotransmitters in much the same way that the neurons located there connect with one another. Unsurprisingly these gut neurons are associated with the regulation of digestion and the evacuation of waste, and may also impact at least some aspects of our emotional state, bringing a new significance to the neural legitimacy of "gut feelings".

It is because of this exquisite complexity, and the potential it carries for an almost infinite variety of responses, that Greenfield asserts, on pp104-5, that whilst we may consider the brain to be a kind of machine, comparisons with a conventional computer are wide of the mark: "this molecular symphony can hardly be regarded as comparable to the scenario inside a computer. First, and most obviously, the brain is fundamentally a chemical system – even the electricity it generates comes from chemicals. More significantly, beyond the fluxes of ions into and out of the neuron, a wealth of chemical reactions are occurring incessantly in a bustling but closed world inside the cell. These events, some of which determine how the cell will respond to signals in the future, do not have a direct electrical counterpart or any easy analogy with a computer...second, the chemical composition of the neurons themselves is changing, and hence there is no separate and unchanging hardware, in contrast to a programmable range of software. Moreover, the ability for incessant change within the brain leads to a third distinction from systems in silicone: of course, computers can 'learn,' but few are changing all the time to give novel responses to the same commands".

Chater takes the computer analogy a stage further, on pp127-8 of *The Mind is Flat*: "our brain is a remarkable computer, but it is a very unconventional computer...the power of the familiar digital computers – including our PCs, laptops and tablets – comes, largely, from carrying out simple calculation steps at phenomenal speeds: many billions of operations per second. By comparison, the brain is dreadfully slow. Neurons – the basic computational unit of the brain – calculate by sending electrical pulses to each other across hugely complex electro-chemical networks. The very highest rate of neural 'firing' is about 1,000 pulses per second; neurons, even when directly recruited to the task in hand, fire mostly at far more leisurely rates, from five to fifty times per second. So our neurons are leisurely compared with the astonishing processing speed of silicon chips. But while neurons may be slow, they are numerous. A PC has one or at most a few processing chips, processing at a phenomenal rate, while the brain has roughly one hundred billion sluggish neurons, linked by roughly one hundred trillion connections...so the spectacular cleverness of the human mind must come not from the frenzied sequences of simple calculations that underpin silicon computation. Instead, brain-style computation must result from *cooperation* (author's emphasis) across the highly interconnected, but slow, neural processing units, leading to coordinated patterns of neural activity across whole networks or perhaps entire regions of the brain".

One consequence is that we are only capable of consciously conceiving of one thing at a time, as Chater describes on p128 of *The Mind is Flat*: "it is hard to see how a vast population of interconnected neurons can coordinate on more than one thing at a time, without suffering terrible confusion and interference...if the brain solves problems through the cooperation computation of vast networks of individually sluggish neurons, then any specific network of neurons can work on just one solution to one problem at a time...if interconnected neurons are working on entirely different problems, then the signals they pass between them will be hopelessly at cross-purposes – and neither task will be completed successfully: each neuron has no idea which of the signals it receives are relevant to the problem it is working on, and which are just irrelevant junk".

Nonetheless, our "biological computer" has enormous power, as Chater explains on p129 of *The Mind is Flat*: "by cooperatively drawing on a vast population of interconnected neurons – each contributing only a little to the overall solution to the problem in hand – (our brain) has the potential to answer questions of enormous difficulty: for example, decoding a facial expression, predicting what will happen next in a complex physical and social situation, integrating a fast flowing input of speech or text, planning and initiating the spectacularly complex sequence of actions to return a tennis serve thundering down at more than 100 mph. Each of these processes would, to the extent that it can ever be successfully simulated on a conventional computer at all, correspond to millions or even billions of tiny steps, implemented with almost unimaginable speed, one after the other. But the brain takes a different tack: its slow neural units split up the problem into tiny fragments and share their tentative solutions in parallel across the entire, densely interconnected network".

Somewhere in all this neural activity, consciousness occurs. As already noted, we currently have no generally-accepted biological explanation for how this happens, frustrating as this may be. As Chater puts it on p35 of *The Mind is Flat*: "one of the deepest challenges in science is to figure out...how electrical and chemical activity in our neural circuits can somehow generate our stream of thought and actions".

What we do have is our own subjective experience of an inner life. Of course this may not be an entirely reliable guide. Rosenberg goes so far as to dismiss it altogether, on pp147-8 of *The Atheist's Guide to Reality*: "science reveals that introspection – thinking about what is going on in consciousness – is completely untrustworthy as a source of information about the mind and how it works. Cognitive neuroscience has already established that many of the most obvious things introspection tells you about your mind are illusions. If the most obvious things consciousness tells us are just plain wrong, we can't trust it to tell us anything about ourselves". This is an extreme position, clearly. Still, we don't need to go as far as total rejection of conscious experience to accept that it may have limitations. And it is evident that it can indeed be fallible in many ways, the most salient of which we will explore later in this chapter.

Our brain is a constant hive of activity, described by Barrett on p58 of *How Emotions Are Made*: "your brain's 86 billion neurons, which are connected into massive networks, never lie dormant awaiting a jump-start. Your neurons are always stimulating each other, sometimes millions at a time. Given enough oxygen and nutrients, these huge cascades of stimulation, known as *intrinsic brain activity* (author's emphasis), continue from birth until death. This activity is nothing like a reaction triggered by the outside world. It's more like breathing, a process that requires no external catalyst... the intrinsic activity in your brain is not random; it is structured by collections of neurons that consistently fire together, called *intrinsic networks* (again, author's emphasis). These networks operate somewhat like sports teams. A team has a pool of players; at any given moment, some players are in the game and others are on the bench, ready to jump in when needed. Likewise, an intrinsic network has a pool of available neurons. Each time the network does its job, different groupings of its neurons play (fire) in synchrony to fill all the necessary positions on the team...intrinsic networks are considered one of neuroscience's great discoveries of the past decade... you might wonder what this hot bed of continuous, intrinsic activity is accomplishing, besides keeping your heart beating, your lungs breathing, and your other internal functions working smoothly. In fact, intrinsic brain activity is the origin of dreams, daydreams, imagination, mind wandering, and reveries...collectively called simulation. It also ultimately produces every sensation you experience, including your interoceptive sensations, which are the origins of your most basic pleasant, unpleasant, calm, and jittery feelings".

As an aside, "interoceptive" is the term Barrett uses for the picture the brain creates of the state of our own body, offering the following definition on p56: "interoception is your brain's representation of all sensations from your internal organs and tissues, the hormones in your blood, and your immune system. Think about what's happening within your body right this second. Your insides are in motion. Your heart sends blood rushing through your veins and arteries. Your lungs fill and empty. Your stomach digests food. This interoceptive activity produces the spectrum of basic feeling from pleasant to unpleasant, from calm to jittery, and even completely neutral". She also explains that the summary term for "the spectrum of basic feeling from pleasant to unpleasant, from calm to jittery, and even completely neutral" is "affect", a concept which turns out to be critical both to our decision-making and our happiness, as we will in due course discuss.

Perhaps the defining characteristic of all this neural activity is that the brain is *constructive*, which is to say that it creates its own internal representations, or simulations, of reality rather than necessarily creating an accurate picture of reality itself. This means that our perception of reality, and even of our own bodily state, is ultimately subjective: our brain interprets the data it receives to create subjective "meaning", as the basis for then determining how to direct our body to act. In doing this, it is reasonable to suppose that it will emphasise those representations which are most effective in helping it achieve its basic tasks of survival and reproduction, rather than necessarily creating the most accurate picture of reality itself: "(evolutionary) fitness beats truth", as we saw earlier that the American cognitive scientist Donald Hoffman puts it, on pxv of the Preface to his 2019 book *The Case Against Reality, How evolution hid the truth from our eyes*. Still, our subjective representations must be somewhat congruent with reality at least as far as the fundamental laws of physics are involved. To give an obvious example, if you tie yourself to the track in front of a speeding train and your brain then somehow convinces itself that you are lying in a grassy meadow with a glass of something soothing, a sticky end is surely in prospect for you and your brain together.

The point is that the brain occupies itself mainly with simulation: with creating a representation of reality rather than directly recording it. On pp84-5 of his 2006 book *Stumbling on Happiness* the American psychologist Dan Gilbert explains how this important development in our understanding traces back almost 250 years, to the German philosopher Immanuel Kant: "philosophers had thought of the senses as conduits that allowed information about the properties of objects in the world to travel from the object and into the mind. The mind was like a movie screen in which the object was re-broadcast...when the senses were working properly, they showed what was there (my note: he is referring to the philosophical school called "realism")...but in 1781...Kant's new theory of *idealism* (Gilbert's emphasis) claimed that our perceptions are not the result of a physiological process by which our eyes somehow transmit an image of the world into our brains, but rather, they are the result of a psychological process that combines what our eyes see with what we already think, feel, know, want, and believe, and then uses this combination of sensory information and pre-existing knowledge to construct our perception of reality...the historian Will Durant performed the remarkable feat of summarising Kant's point in a single sentence: 'the world as we know it is a construction, a finished product, almost – one might say – a manufactured article, to which the mind contributes as much by its moulding forms as the thing contributes by its stimuli'".

And on pp26-7 of *How Emotions Are Made* Barrett offers a vivid illustration of the power of simulation: "think of the last time someone handed you a red, juicy apple. You reached out for it, took a bite, and experienced the tart flavour. During those moments, neurons were firing in the sensory and motor regions of your brain. Motor neurons fired to produce your movements, and sensory neurons fired to produce your sensations of the apple, like its red colour with a blush of green; its smoothness against your hand; its crisp, floral scent; the audible crunch when you bit into it; and its tangy taste with a hint of sweetness. Other neurons made your mouth water to release enzymes and begin digestion, released cortisol to prepare your body to metabolise the sugars in the apple, and perhaps made your stomach churn a bit. But here's the cool thing: just now, when you read the word 'apple,' your brain responded to a certain extent as if an apple were actually present. Your brain combined bits and pieces of knowledge of previous apples you've seen and tasted, and changed the firing of neurons in your sensory and motor regions to construct a mental instance of the concept 'Apple'. Your brain simulated a non-existent apple using sensory and motor neurons. Simulation happens as quickly and automatically as a heartbeat".

Simulation allows the brain to impose meaning on what would otherwise be a random stream of data, as Barret explains on p27: "simulations are your brain's guesses of what's happening in the world. In every waking moment, you're faced with ambiguous, noisy information from your eyes, ears, nose, and other sensory organs. Your brain uses your past experiences to construct a hypothesis – the simulation – and compares it to the cacophony arriving from your senses. In this manner, simulation lets your brain impose meaning on the noise, selecting what's relevant and ignoring the rest".

Finally, on p59 and then p64 of *How Emotions Are Made* Barrett explains that what the brain constructs is in fact a *prediction* of reality. What is more, the most important data source in making these predictions tends to be the information the brain is receiving about the state of our body, so that the data it receives about external reality are often of secondary importance: "through prediction, your brain constructs the world you experience...the brain is not a simple machine reacting to stimuli in the outside world. It's structured as billions of prediction loops creating intrinsic brain activity. Visual predictions, auditory predictions, gustatory (taste) predictions, sensory (touch) predictions, olfactory (smell) predictions, and motor predictions travel throughout the brain, influencing and constraining each other. These predictions are held in check by sensory input from the outside world, which your brain may prioritise or ignore". She continues, on pp64-5 and then p80: "your brain works like a scientist. It's always making a slew of predictions, just as a scientist makes competing hypotheses. Like a scientist, your brain uses knowledge (past experience) to estimate how confident you can be that each prediction is true. Your brain then tests its predictions, comparing them to incoming sensory input from the world, much as a scientist compares hypotheses against data in an experiment...you might believe that you are a rational creature, weighing the pros and cons before deciding how to act, but the structure of your cortex makes this an impossible fiction. Your brain is wired to listen to your body budget. Affect is in the driver's seat and rationality is a passenger. It doesn't matter whether you're choosing between two snacks, two job offers, two investments, or two heart surgeons – your everyday decisions are driven by a loudmouthed, mostly deaf scientist who views the world through affect-coloured glasses".

So there we have it. Consciousness is a product of the human brain, the most complex object yet discovered in the Universe. The brain's main activities are conducted by complex networks of inter-connected neurons, which process information received via our senses; and also, importantly, from our body. Our neural networks combine this information with past experience to impose meaning, constructing simulations and predictions which ultimately lead to some form of action. Critical elements of the process include the way in which our brain represents external reality in a particular moment; the interpretation it makes of the data it receives about the state of our body, this being particularly influential; and the stored experiences which it accesses.

The evolution of human cognition

We do not yet understand how the biochemical activity of our neurons produces our experience of conscious thoughts. We do, however, have a compelling theory for how human cognition itself developed, this being the faculty which underpins arguably the most critical aspects of consciousness; namely the ability to introspect, and to discern causal and/or intentional relationships in the world, in other words that X happens as a consequence of Y, or that an individual is likely to react in a certain way to a particular stimulus.

Here we are indebted to the work of the American social psychologist Michael Tomasello and his 2014 book *A Natural History of Human Thinking*. All quotes in this section are from this book unless otherwise stated. We will also hear from the British psychologist Simon Baron-Cohen and his 2020 book *The Pattern Seekers*.

In a nutshell, Tomasello proposes that our last common ancestor with the other great apes, living around 6-7 million years ago, already possessed somewhat advanced cognitive capacity. Tomasello labels this "individual intentionality", defined as a rudimentary ability to recognise and take account of the intentions of others within one's own group, as well as some primitive understanding of causality relating to tool use. Early humans then built on this capability through two further major evolutionary developments, both driven by selective pressures resulting from fundamental lifestyle changes which were themselves brought on by changes in the environment, and which featured progressively greater levels of cooperation between individuals.

The first was a shift to collaborative, as distinct from competitive, foraging, which both required and enabled "joint intentionality". The second was a further change to foraging in larger, inter-dependent groups, associated with the development of "group intentionality" and producing essentially the full range of cognitive skills possessed by modern humans.

Baron-Cohen focuses on one specific cognitive capability which he calls "the systemising mechanism", defined on p12 of *The Pattern Seekers* as the ability to discern "*if-and-then* (author's emphasis) patterns". This developed relatively recently, at least in evolutionary terms, crucially enabling us to understand causality in a system and therefore to innovate and to exert an increasing level of control over our surroundings.

Tomasello's starting point is that it is reasonable to infer that cognitive faculties observed in all four surviving nonhuman great ape species were also shared with our last common ancestor. He says, on p15: "we begin our natural history of the evolutionary emergence of uniquely human thinking with a focus on the last common ancestor of humans and other extant primates. Our best living models for this creature are humans' closest primate relatives, the non-human great apes (hereafter, great apes), comprising chimpanzees, bonobos, gorillas, and orangutans – especially chimpanzees and bonobos, who diverged from humans most recently, around 6 million years ago. When cognitive abilities are similar among the four species of great ape but different in humans, we presume that the apes have conserved their skills from the last common ancestor (or before) whereas humans have evolved something new".

And modern great apes exhibit relatively advanced powers of cognition, which we may presume gave our hominid ancestors a head start in their own evolutionary journey. Tomasello explains, on p2: "great apes, as the closest living relatives of humans, already understand in human-like ways many aspects of their physical and social worlds, including the causal and intentional relations that structure those worlds. This means that many important aspects of human thinking derive not from humans' unique forms of sociality, culture, and language but, rather, from something like the individual problem-solving abilities of great apes in general".

Specifically, great apes show a basic understanding of causality, as Tomasello explains on p16: "what great apes are especially skilful at, compared with other primates, is tool use – which one might characterise as not just understanding causes but actually manipulating them...classically, tool use is thought to require the individual to assess the causal effect of its tool manipulations on the goal object or event (Piaget, 1952), and so the flexibility and alacrity with which great apes succeed in using novel tools suggest that they have one or more general cognitive models of causality guiding their use of these novel tools".

Great apes also demonstrate a propensity for understanding intentionality, which is to say predicting the intentions of others, albeit a crucial point is that they do this mainly in the context of competition rather than cooperation. On p20: "primate cognition of the social world evolved mainly in the context of competition within the social group for food, mates, and other valued resources...in order to outcompete groupmates, individual primates evolved the approximate goals, representations, and inferences for (1) recognising individuals in their social group and forming dominance and affiliative relationships with them and (2) recognising third parties' social relationships with one another, such as parent or dominant or friend, and taking these into account. These abilities enable individuals to better predict the behaviour of others in a complex 'social field' (Kumar, 1972). Despite important species differences of social structure and interaction, in these most basic skills of social cognition all primates would appear to be generally similar".

On p30 Tomasello puts this into a specific evolutionary context: "and so we may imagine a common ancestor to humans and other great apes. Its daily life was like that of extant non-human apes: most waking hours spent in small bands foraging individually for fruit and other vegetation, with various kinds of social interactions, mostly competitive, interspersed. Our hypothesis is that this creature – and also probably australopithecines for the ensuing 4 million years of the human lineage – was individually intentional and instrumentally rational. It cognitively represented its physical and social experience categorically and schematically, and it made all kinds of productive and hypothetical inferences and chains of inferences about this experience as well – all with a modicum of cognitive self-monitoring. And so, the crucial point is that well before the emergence of uniquely human sociality, much less culture, language, and institutions, the foundation for human thinking was securely in place in humans' last common ancestor with other apes".

On p31 Tomasello reinforces that there is nonetheless an important difference in how great apes live, and therefore think, when compared with modern humans; specifically, that apes are fundamentally wired to compete, whereas humans demonstrate a much greater tendency to cooperate: "in virtually all theoretical accounts, great apes' skills of social cognition evolved mainly for competing with others in the social group: being better or quicker than groupmates at anticipating what potential competitors might do...and indeed a number of recent studies have found that great apes utilise their most sophisticated skills of social cognition in contexts involving competition or exploitation of others as opposed to contexts involving cooperation or communication with others (e.g., Hare and Tomasello, 2004; see Hare, 2001). Great apes are all about cognition for competition...human beings, in contrast, are all about (or mostly about) cooperation. Human social life is much more cooperatively organised than that of other primates, and so, in the current hypothesis, it was these more complex forms of cooperative sociality that acted as the selective pressures that transformed great ape individual intentionality and thinking into human shared intentionality and thinking".

Cooperation itself does not inevitably produce human-style cognition. Rather, it is because our ancestors already benefited from the relatively advanced cognitive skills they shared with other apes that they were then able to develop more advanced capabilities. On p33: "cooperation by itself does not create complex cognitive skills – witness the complex cooperation of the cognitively simple eusocial insects and the cooperative childcare and food sharing of the not-so-cognitively-complex New World monkeys, marmosets and tamarins. The case of humans is unique, from a cognitive point of view, because the common ancestor to humans and other great apes had already evolved highly sophisticated skills of social cognition and social manipulation for purposes of competition (as well as highly sophisticated skills of physical cognition for purposes of manipulating causality in the context of tool use)".

On p5 Tomasello summarises the two major changes in ecology and lifestyle which underpinned the changes in human cognition: "there were two key evolutionary steps. The first...involved the creation of a novel type of small-scale collaboration in human foraging. Participants in this collaborative foraging created socially shared joint goals and joint attention (common ground), which created the possibility of individual roles and perspectives within that ad hoc shared world...to coordinate these newly created roles and perspectives, individuals evolved a new type of cooperative communication based on the natural gestures of pointing and pantomiming...to self-monitor this process the communicator had to simulate ahead of time the recipient's likely inferences...the second step...came as human populations began growing in size and competing with one another. This competition meant that group life as a whole became one big collaborative activity, creating a much larger and more permanent shared world, that is to say, a culture. The resulting group-mindedness among all members of the cultural group (including in-group strangers) was based on a new ability to construct common *cultural* (author's emphasis) ground via collectively known cultural conventions, norms, and institutions. As part of this process, cooperative communication became conventionalised linguistic communication. In the context of cooperative argumentation in group decision-making, linguistic conventions could be used to justify and make explicit one's reasons for an assertion within the framework of the group's norms of rationality. This meant that individuals could now reason 'objectively' from the group's agent-neutral point of view ('from nowhere')".

It is not clear when the shift to collaborative foraging occurred, although on p36 Tomasello suggests that it may have begun around 2 million years ago or so, "soon after the emergence of the genus *Homo*... during this period there was a great expansion of terrestrial monkeys, like baboons, that might have outcompeted humans for their normal fruits and other vegetation. Humans then needed a new foraging niche. A beginning might have been scavenging meat, which would probably have required a kind of coalition of individuals to frighten off the animals that made the initial kill. But at some point there began more active collaborative hunting of large game and gathering of plant foods, typically in a mutualistic stag hunt-type situation in which both individuals could expect to benefit from the collaboration – if they could somehow manage to coordinate their efforts. This is the collaborative creature we are imagining here, and for the most clarity we may focus on its culmination in hominins of about 400,000 years ago: the common ancestor to Neanderthals and modern humans, the ever mysterious *Homo heidelbergensis*. Paleoanthropological evidence suggests that this was the first hominin to engage systematically in the collaborative hunting of large game, using weapons that almost certainly would not enable a single individual to be successful on its own, and sometimes bringing prey back to a homebase (Stiner et al, 2009). This is also a time when brain size and population size were both expanding rapidly".

Whatever, "more important than when is how", as Tomasello tells us on p37, adding: "in the hypothesis of Tomasello et al. (2012), obligate collaborative foraging became an evolutionary stable strategy for early humans because of two interrelated processes: interdependence and social selection. The first and most basic point is that humans began a lifestyle in which individuals could not procure their daily sustenance alone but instead were interdependent with others in their foraging activities – which meant that individuals needed to develop the skills and motivations to forage collaboratively or else starve. There was thus direct and immediate selective pressure for skills and motivations for joint collaborative activity (joint intentionality).

The second point is that as a natural outcome of this interdependence, individuals began to make evaluative judgements about others as potential collaborative partners: they began to be socially selective, since choosing a poor partner meant less food. Cheaters and laggards were thus selected against, and bullies lost their power to bully. Importantly, this now meant that early human individuals had to worry, in a way that other great apes do not, both about evaluating others and about how others were evaluating them as potential collaborative partners (i.e., a concern for self-image)".

Eventually there was a second major shift, to the much broader form of collaboration which characterises modern humans to this day, described by Tomasello on pp82-3: "the small-scale, ad hoc collaborative foraging characteristic of early humans was a stable adaptive strategy – for a while. In the hypothesis of Tomasello et al. (2012), it was destabilised by two, essentially demographic, factors...the first factor was competition with other humans. This meant that a loose pool of collaborators had to turn into a proper social group in order to protect their way of life from invaders...this meant that group members were motivated to help one another, as they were all now clearly interdependent with one another at all times: 'we' must together compete with and protect ourselves from 'them'...the second factor was increasing population size. As human populations grew, they tended to split into smaller groupings, leading to so-called tribal organisation in which a number of different social groupings were still a single supergroup or 'culture'. This meant that recognising others from our own cultural group became far from trivial – and of course we needed to ensure that they could recognise us as well. Such recognition in both directions was important because only members of our cultural group can be counted on to share our skills and values and so be good and trustworthy collaborative partners".

A feature of this second step towards more integrated cooperation was a pressure to conform to distinct group cultures, in turn leading to a "ratchet effect" in which aspects of culture could endure through time, a process described by Tomasello on pp83-4: "and so early humans' skills of imitation became modern humans' active conformity, both to coordinate activities more effectively with in-group strangers and to display group identity so that others will choose me as a knowledgeable and trustworthy partner. Teaching others to do things, perhaps especially one's children, became a good way to assist their functioning in the group and to ensure even more conformity in the process. Teaching and conformity then led to cumulative cultural evolution characterised by the 'ratchet effect' (Tomasello et al, 1993; Tennie et al, 2009; Dean et al, 2012) in which modifications of a cultural practice stayed in the population rather faithfully until some individual invented some new and improved technique, which was then taught and conformed to some still newer innovation ratcheted things up again. Tomasello (2011) argues that great ape societies do not display the ratchet effect or cumulative cultural evolution because their social learning is fundamentally exploitative and not cooperatively structured in the human way via teaching and conformity, which constitute the ratchet that prevents individuals from slipping backward...the new sense of group identity characteristic of modern humans was thus extended not just in space to in-group strangers but also in time to ancestors and descendants in the group: this is the way 'we' have always done things; it is part of who 'we' are...human populations thus became more than a loosely structured pool of collaborators; they become self-identified cultures with their own 'histories'. Once again, precisely when all this happened is not crucial to our story, but the first clear signs of distinct human cultures appear with *Homo sapiens sapiens*, that is, modern humans, beginning at the earliest some 200,000 years ago".

These seminal changes in lifestyle and social environment had important implications for cognition. For example, on p59 Tomasello highlights that effective collaboration requires that one take some account of one's partner's perspectives and intentions, a process known by modern psychologists as "Theory of Mind":

"and so, the kind of thinking that goes on in human cooperative communication is evolutionarily new in that it is perspectival and socially recursive. Individuals must think (simulate, imagine, make inferences) about their communicative partner thinking (simulating, imagining, making inferences) about their thinking – at the very least. Great apes show no signs of making such inferences...human thinking in cooperative communication also involves a new kind of social self-monitoring, in which the communicator imagines what perspective the recipient is taking, or will take, on his intentions toward her intentions – and so imagines how she will comprehend it".

Related to the ability to consider different perspectives is the ability to categorise, helping organise into manageable groupings what would otherwise threaten to be an overwhelming number of individual entities and, eventually, concepts. Tomasello elaborates, on p62: "the vast majority of communicative conventions in a natural language are category terms. That is, common nouns and most verbs are conventionalised for reference to categories of entities such as *dog* and *bite*, which means that to make reference to a specific dog or instance of biting, we must do some kind of pragmatic grounding (such as with *the* or *my dog*, or *the dog who lives next door* in the case of nouns; or tense and aspect markers, as in *is biting* or *bit*, in the case of verbs)...the categorical dimension is bound up with perspective in the sense that calling someone either Bill or Mr. Smith is not perspectival because these are not category terms, but calling him a father or a man or a policeman is perspectival because it puts him 'under a description', that is, it "perspectivises' him differently on different occasions for different communicative purposes" (author's emphases throughout).

On p81 Tomasello describes how more advanced, group-wide cooperation also requires a sense of objectivity - the ability to take a generic perspective into account, not just that of another specific individual; as well as the ability to reason, so that informed dialogue is possible: "in terms of thinking, early humans imagined the world in order to manipulate it in thought via perspectival cognitive representations, socially recursive inferences, and social self-monitoring – which prepared them to coordinate with other specific individuals. But group-minded and linguistically competent modern humans had to be prepared to coordinate with anyone from the group, with some kind of generic other. This meant that modern human individuals came to imagine the world in order to manipulate it in thought via open 'objective' representations (anyone's perspective), reflective inferences connected by reasons (compelling to anyone), and normative self-governance so as to coordinate with the group's (anyone's) normative expectations".

On pp96-7 Tomasello explains how the standardisation of language required for the members of a large social group to communicate effectively results in more arbitrary conventions. For example, the word "banana" signifies a curved yellow fruit because we all agree it does, not because there is any inherent connection between the word and the object it describes, as there might be if we were using sign language.

This in turn enables a massively enhanced capacity for abstract thought: "communicating conventionally with arbitrary devices also creates, or at least facilitates, two other new processes of cognitive representation. The first is that the arbitrariness leads to a higher level of abstractness. Thus, when gestures are purely iconic, the level of abstraction is typically low and local. For example, with spontaneous iconic signs, opening a door is pantomimed in one way whereas opening a jar is pantomimed in another...however, in a community, as the iconicity fades for new learners, and arbitrary conventions arise, there comes a more stylised depiction of *open* (author's emphasis) that is highly abstract and resembles no particular manner of opening...the second new process...also involves abstractness, but of a different type. Many of the most abstract conceptualisations in contemporary languages are single items for highly complex situations involving multiple agents doing things over time; for example, to define a term like *justice* (author's emphasis), one would most naturally proceed with a kind of narrative: justice is when someone...and then someone...it is difficult to imagine how to indicate for others complex situations and events such as *justice* (again, author's emphasis) in pantomime, except by acting out a kind of full narrative...but with arbitrary signs one may simply designate these complex situations with a single sign. This means that, in essence, arbitrary signs open up the novel possibility of symbolising aspects of the relational, thematic, or narrative organisation of human cognition...which expands the range and complexity of human thinking immensely".

And on pp110-2 Tomasello describes how the communication needed to support collaborative foraging logically leads to, and is reinforced by, the ability to reason; and how this, when combined with the need to anticipate how a counterparty might potentially react, in turn allows for our "little voice", in other words our ability to introspect: "the proposal that human reasoning, including individual human reasoning, has a social-communicative origin is almost certainly correct...the key social context is joint or collective decision-making, as it occurred regularly in collaborative activities. Thus, on a hunting trip, perhaps you think we should hunt for antelopes in this direction, and I think we would be better off going in that direction. To make your case, you make your reasoning more explicit in our conventional language by, for instance, noting that there is a watering hole to the south. I counter, also in language, by making explicit my reasoning that at this time of day it is likely that lions will be at the watering hole and so no antelopes will be – and besides, here are some antelope tracks going to the north. You say these tracks look old, but I think that is because they were in the direct sunlight this morning and actually they are from around dawn or so. And on and on.

The key point is that arguing in this way assumes a cooperative context...the capstone of all of this – recognised by all modern thinkers who take a sociocultural view of human thinking – is the internalisation of these various interpersonal processes of making things explicit into individual rational thinking or reasoning. Making things explicit to facilitate the comprehension of a recipient leads the communicator to simulate, before actually producing an utterance, how his planned communicative act might be comprehended – perhaps in a kind of inner dialogue. Making things explicit to persuade someone in an argument leads the disputant to simulate ahead of time how a potential opponent might counter his argument, and so to make ready, in thought, an interconnected set of reasons and justifications – again, perhaps, in a kind of inner dialogue".

Tomasello summarises the main phases of the process through which human cognition plausibly developed, in extracts taken from pp135-42 of *A Natural History of Human Thinking*:

"1. *Competition with groupmates led to sophisticated forms of nonhuman private social cognition and thinking without human-like forms of sociality or communication* (my note: Tomasello terms this 'individual intentionality')...basic mammalian sociality is simply the motivation to live in a social group. Within-group competition engenders social relations of dominance and, along with other factors, affiliation...great apes collaborate – that is, actually work together – very little, and when they do, it is best characterised as what Tuomela (2007) calls 'group behaviour in I-mode,' as in chimpanzees' group hunting in which each individual is attempting to capture the monkey for itself...great ape communication is almost exclusively about attempting to direct the recipient's attention and behaviour in some desired ways, not to inform them of things useful to them. There are no human-like joint goals; there is no cooperative communication for coordinating actions.

2. *Early human collaborative activities and cooperative communication – employing new forms of social coordination – led to new forms of human thinking without either culture or language* (my note: 'joint intentionality'). For more than 5 million of the 6 million years that humans have been on their own evolutionary pathway, their thinking was mainly ape-like...but then there was a change in ecological conditions that forced some early humans to begin collaborating in new ways to obtain food. This made individuals interdependent with one another in an especially urgent way. In mutualistic activities such as these, communication could become fully cooperative since it was in the interest of each individual to coordinate with others toward their mutualistic goal and to inform them of things useful to them in their role. And so were born early humans who could survive and thrive only by collaborating and communicating cooperatively with social partners.

3. *Modern human processes of conventionalised culture and language led to all of the unique complexities of modern human thinking and reasoning* (my note: 'collective intentionality'). Modern humans faced some

social challenges due to increases in group sizes accompanied by competition among groups. For survival, modern human groups had to begin operating as relatively cohesive collaborative units, with various division-of-labour roles (see Wilson, 2012). This created the problem of how individuals could coordinate with in-group strangers, with whom they had no personal common ground. The solution was the conventionalisation of cultural practices: everyone conformed to whatever everyone else was doing, and expected others to conform as well (and expected them to expect them to, etc.), which created a kind of cultural common ground that could be assumed of all members of the group (but not other groups). Modern humans' ways of communicating were conventionalised in the same way as well, which meant that individuals operated in a cultural common ground comprising a kind of group perspective and with conventionalised linguistic items and constructions that could be used effectively with anyone in the group.

4. *Cumulative cultural evolution led to a plethora of culturally specific cognitive skills and types of thinking.* Most likely, the first step of joint intentionality evolved in Africa before the split between the Neanderthals and modern humans and so characterised both species. The second step of collective intentionality likely evolved in a population of modern humans in Africa before they migrated out into other parts of the world after 100,000 years ago. But once they started migrating out and settling in highly variable local ecologies, differences in cultural practices became pronounced. Different human cultures created very different sets of particular cognitive skills, for example, for navigating across large distances, for building important tools and artefacts, and even for communicating linguistically. This meant that different cultures created, on top of their species-wide cognitive skills of individual, joint, and collective intentionality,

many culturally specific cognitive skills and ways of thinking for their own local purposes....as one dramatic example in the contemporary world, we may point to what are arguably the most abstract and complex forms of human thinking, that is, those involved in Western science and mathematics. The point here is that these forms of thinking are simply not possible without special forms of socially constructed conventions, namely, those in written form, that developed over historical time in Western culture. This point is stressed especially by Peirce (1931–1958) and is summarised in the classic text of modern logic by Lewis and Langford (1932, p4): 'had it not been for the adoption of the new and more versatile ideographic symbols, many branches of mathematics could never have been developed because no human mind could grasp the essence of their operations in terms of the phonograms of ordinary language'...cultures that have not created and do not currently possess any of these kinds of graphic symbols cannot currently participate in these activities".

Baron-Cohen adds to this picture the emergence of a specific, landmark, development in human cognition which he calls the "systemising mechanism" "Systemising" is in essence the ability to apply causal logic to a system using what Baron-Cohen labels an *if-and-then* formulation, terms which he tells us he has himself borrowed from the 19th century English mathematician George Boole. The point being that if we once understand something about the causal relationships within a system then we have the potential to exercise some level of control over it, and moreover to experiment, so that we continue to improve our understanding, and control, over time. To give one example from many, on p17-8 of *The Pattern Seekers* Baron-Cohen explains: "here's one of my favourite examples of a mechanical system, invented about 5,000 years ago to address a big question: how can a massively heavy object be moved? Back then, someone must have looked at a heavy stone, for example, and then looked at their ox for its potential use in an *if-and-then* pattern. What I like about this example is that the ox already existed, but a human looked at the ox in a new way: '*if* the stone is hugely heavy, *and* I harness it to my ox, *then* the heavy stone moves'. The ox was no longer just an ox but now was seen as a causal operation in an *if-and-then* algorithm. Historians think this is how the huge stones at Stonehenge in England were transported to their eventual location 5,019 years ago. This invention most likely built on an earlier new tool, the wheel, invented about 500 years earlier. Combining these two inventions yielded the ox pulling the hugely heavy stone on rollers, or on a sledge" (author's emphases throughout).

Baron-Cohen dates the earliest evidence that humans were capable of "systemising" to only around 70-100,000 years ago, comparatively recent in evolutionary terms and at least 100,000 years after the emergence of *homo sapiens* as a species. His logic is that this the earliest time for which we have evidence of the kind of serial, complex innovation which "systemising" enables, and for which it is required. For example, on pp86-8 of *The Pattern Seekers* Baron-Cohen tells us that there is evidence of engraving 77,000 years ago in what is now South Africa, "a clear sign that humans were producing specialised tools"; what some archaeologists interpret to be the earliest known jewellery dates back 82,000 years and 75,000 years respectively; and the earliest evidence of bows and arrows is from around 71,000 years ago.

The point is that the impact of this particular cognitive skill was and continues to be profound, because, on p21 of *The Pattern Seekers*: "once we analyse the *if-and-then* rules governing a system, we understand how the system works. Of course, often there's more to learn, but systemising is iterative – we can keep exploring the system further to learn more about its inner workings, but the method is always the same: *if-and-then*" (again, author's emphasis throughout).

And the "systemising" approach can be applied not just to mechanical systems such as teams of oxen pulling heavy loads, but to literally *any* system to which the laws of causality apply. As Baron-Cohen puts it, on p20 of *The Pattern Seekers*: "when we gaze at the world, we also see a myriad of *natural* systems – the changing weather as snowflakes fall, the movement of the wings of a dragonfly, the motion of tidal waves – all amenable to an *if-and-then* pattern analysis, and which we can use to make predictions: *if* there are cumulonimbus clouds in the sky, *and* there is thunder, *then* there will be severe weather" (author's emphasis throughout).

Last but by no means least, "systemising" is what enables us to innovate, by using our understanding of causality as a basis for novel solutions which, moreover, can be tested and either rejected if ineffective, or adopted and further improved over time. Agriculture and medicine are just two examples, described later on p20 of *The Pattern Seekers*: "*if* a tomato seed is in the soil, *and* the soil is moist, *then* the seed will grow into a tomato...*if* I have a headache, *and* I eat willow bark, *then* my headache goes away" (again, author's emphasis throughout).

To be clear, Baron-Cohen does not suggest that "systemising" is the only distinctive feature of human cognition. It is at its most powerful when applied to systems which are wholly or largely inanimate, and which are therefore largely predictable and repeatable if we once understand the relevant causal relationships: the Laws, or "rules", which govern them. This obviously includes mechanical objects and indeed many of the features of the natural world. However, it can be more problematic when it comes to human society, and especially to individual humans.   Baron-Cohen acknowledges, on p34 of *The Pattern Seekers*, that: "most of our everyday behaviour is not rule-based...when we chat with friends, we don't have the very same conversations every time. And systemising other people's thoughts and feelings will inevitably fail: when we experience emotions, they don't bubble up exactly the same way, responding to the same triggers...so systemising fails us in most of our social interactions".

In situations like these we mostly need to rely on what Baron-Cohen describes as our "empathy circuit", defined on p34 in terms which echo Tomasello and hence bring us full circle: "the empathy circuit allowed us to think about the thoughts and feelings of others and to think about our own thoughts and feelings, rapidly, second by second, in real time in a dynamic social context. By enabling us to imagine other people's mental states (their thoughts, feelings, intentions and desires), not in a rule-based way but flexibly, we could anticipate what they would be likely to do next, in real time, and to react to their thoughts and feelings rapidly with an appropriate emotion of our own".

To conclude, the result of these remarkable cognitive developments was to equip humans with the faculties necessary to experience consciousness in the way we do, including, although not limited to:

- *pattern recognition* – the ability to see meaning in what might otherwise be random streams of data.
- *causality* – the ability to discern causal relationships, so that given sufficient information the effects of a potential action can confidently be understood and predicted or at least trialled.
- *intentionality* – the ability to recognise and imagine another person's intentions and, possibly, motivations.
- *perspective* – the notion that more than one viewpoint is possible in a situation, leading to the ability to

"objectivise", that is to conceive of the possibility that one perspective is objectively "right".

- *categorisation* – the ability to conceive of objects, or concepts, as belonging to particular groupings, so that for example "X is similar other Xs but not to Ys".
- *abstraction* – the ability to conceive of, and describe, intangible concepts, such as "justice", or "freedom".
- *reasoning* – the ability to assess and articulate why a particular perspective may be more valid than another.
- *introspection* – the ability to think about our own thoughts and urges/motivations, and to conduct a dialogue with oneself via the "little voice" inside our head.

PART B: The opportunity, and obligation, to exercise personal existential choice

Personal agency and "freewill"

Perhaps the most fundamental premise of this book is the belief that we can, and from a practical standpoint must, assume that consciousness gives us meaningful agency in the world – that we are in some sense "the captain of our soul", ultimately free to choose what we do and how we behave. What is more, once we accept that we have this essential existential freedom, we have what amounts to an obligation to embrace it: to exercise it actively and thoughtfully, and then to accept responsibility for the decisions we make and the actions we take.

For most of us, this capacity to choose is such a familiar feature of our everyday, subjective, life that we largely take it for granted, accepting that we may also experience frustration when we feel that our freedom is constrained in some way, by external forces or by our own personality or character. However, the extent to which we can be said to possess genuine freewill has been the topic of heated philosophical and scientific debate through the ages, and the discussion continues to this day.

The belief that we each have at least some level of meaningful freewill is one of the most critical beliefs advocated in this book, and we will therefore take time to review the arguments on both sides. We will eventually conclude that a belief in personal agency is both legitimate and pragmatic. As we saw earlier, though, it is also clear that the choices we make are constrained. Our behaviours are heavily influenced by factors which we do not ultimately control and that tend not to be easily accessible to our conscious mind; in particular our personal genetic profile and past experiences which predispose us to act in certain ways. It follows that in exercising agency we do well to proceed with an appropriate level of humility and caution.

The historical debate tended to centre on how humans could be said to have agency in a Universe designed and run by a presiding Deity. This is indeed a tricky problem if your starting point is belief in such a God. For example, it is hard to see what the point (or "justice") of divine judgement would be if everything were pre-ordained; or if an engaged, "benevolent", omniscient and omnipotent God had chosen not to intervene in a particular situation despite knowing that an individual was imminently about to commit a bad act, or think an impure thought, sufficient to condemn them to eternal damnation when the final Judgement inevitably came. Fortunately, we don't need to be concerned with this strand of theological circle-squaring.

We do need to address the modern secular equivalents, though, and these come in two, related, forms.

First, "physical predeterminists" suggest that everything that happens in the Universe is the inevitable consequence of a prior cause, simply leaving no room for human freewill. The contention is that everything ultimately happens as the result of interactions between fundamental, subatomic, particles, acting in accordance with the immutable laws of physics; and since there is an unbroken chain of interactions with one particle acting on another all the way back to Big Bang, it follows that everything that ever has happened or ever will happen is predetermined. This idea was famously framed in 1814 by Pierre-Simon LaPlace (he of the "Sire, I have no need of that hypothesis" fame) in a proposition which came to be known as "LaPlace's Demon", the "Demon" being the "vast intellect" which features in the passage: "we may regard the present state of the universe as the effect of its past and the cause of its future. An intellect which at any given moment knew all of the forces that animate nature and the mutual positions of the beings that compose it, if this intellect were vast enough to submit the data to analysis, could condense into a single formula the movement of the greatest bodies of the universe and that of the lightest atom; for such an intellect nothing could be uncertain and the future just like the past would be present before its eyes".

We heard in the previous chapter from the American neurobiologist Robert Sapolsky and his 2023 book *Determined - Life Without Freewill*. He paraphrases LaPlace, on p15: "if you had a superhuman who knew the location of every particle in the universe at this moment, they'd be able to accurately predict every moment in the future. Moreover, if this superhuman (eventually termed 'Laplace's Demon') could re-create the exact location of every particle at any point in the past, it would lead to a present identical to our current one. The past and future of the universe are already determined".

And on pp236-7 of *The Atheist's Guide to Reality* Rosenberg applies a similar logic to the physics of the human brain: "science's argument against the possibility of free will is disarmingly direct...the mind is the brain, and the brain is a physical system, fantastically complex, but still operating according to all the laws of physics –

quantum or otherwise. Every state of my brain is fixed by physical facts. In fact, it is a physical state. Previous states of my brain and the physical input from the world together brought about its current state. They were themselves the result of even earlier brain states and input from outside the brain. All these states were determined by the operation of the laws of physics and chemistry. These laws operated on previous states of my brain and on states of the world going back to before my brain was formed...they go back through a chain of prior events, not just before anyone with a mind existed, but back to a time after life began on this planet...when I make choices – trivial or momentous – it's just another event in my brain locked into this network of processes going back to the beginning of the universe, long before I had the slightest 'choice'. Nothing was up to me. Everything – including my choice and my feelings that I can choose freely – was fixed by earlier states of the universe plus the laws of physics. End of story. No free will, just the feeling, the illusion in introspection, that my actions are decided by my conscious will".

Later on p15 of *Determined*, Sapolsky acknowledges that "science since LaPlace's time shows that he wasn't completely right", Kevin Mitchell highlights quantum mechanics as a specific scientific advance which challenges the idea that the way in which the Universe developed was predetermined. On p159 of *Free Agents* Mitchell says: "the observed organisation of matter in the universe depended on the presence of quantum fluctuations in the phase of 'cosmic inflation' that preceded the 'hot' Big Bang. As the universe was rapidly expanding, it was initially a homogenous field of energy. Without the random quantum fluctuations that broke up this symmetrical field, matter and energy would have been so evenly distributed that pretty much nothing would have happened. Instead, these tiny blips introduced enough inhomogeneity into gravitational fields that galaxies and stars and planets could form".

Mitchell reminds us, on p162, that quantum uncertainty remains a feature of our contemporary world, present in even the very largest objects albeit as we saw in the previous chapter the effects are muted at larger scales: "the wavelike nature of quantum particles means that their position and momentum are both probabilistic and are mathematically related in such a way that narrowing the range of probabilities for one of them necessarily increases it for the other. In fact, this is true even for classical-sized objects: it's just that the margin of error – the fuzziness of these parameters – is negligible relative to the size of the object".

And as an intriguing aside, on pp159-61 Mitchell speculates that quantum uncertainty may be best understood as a temporal rather than spatial phenomenon: "physicists Lee Smolin and Clelia Verde have proposed that the quantum-to-classical transition does not reflect spatial scale at all, but rather the flow of time. In fact, they argue that what we experience as the present is simply the period in which the indefinite becomes definite. In this view, all systems have quantum properties in the future. That is, the properties of the individual particles are probabilistic – they are inherently undefined. It is only when the particles interact that these properties resolve into definite values. What we call 'the present' is that period of transition from a future that is indefinite, in which multiple possibilities exist, to a past that can no longer be changed...the upshot of these views is that the future is open: indeed, that is what makes it the future. Because we only inhabit the present, we don't experience this indeterminacy firsthand. We can't directly experience the future as it currently is (if it even makes sense to think in those terms); we can only predict what it will be like when we get there (or when it gets here). By definition, at that point it will be the present, and things will have become definite, in a kind of just-in-time reality. If we could really glimpse the future, we would see a world out of focus. Not separate paths already neatly laid out, waiting to be chosen – just a fuzzy, jittery picture that gets fuzzier and jitterier the further into the future you look".

Be that as it may, the significance of quantum uncertainty for a discussion of physical predeterminism is succinctly captured by American physicist Tim Andersen in an article titled *Quantum mechanics and the return of free will*, published by *IAI* (The Institute of Art and Ideas) *news* on 3 July 2023: "in a classical, deterministic world...all pasts have the same future, but...in a quantum world...all pasts do not share the same future". And, whilst certainly not sufficient to prove that freewill exists, a world in which all pasts do not share the same future opens the door to at least the possibility that it could.

This brings us to the second important argument levelled against freewill, which is that our growing, albeit still far from complete, understanding of neurobiology is incompatible with it.

For example, on pp3-4 of *Determined* Sapolsky suggests that the workings of our brain are "causally determined", meaning that our response to any given situation is essentially automatic, a product of how our brain has developed over time: "once you work with the notion that every aspect of behaviour has deterministic, prior causes, you observe a behaviour and can answer why it occurred...because of the action of neurons in this or that part of your brain in the preceding second. And in the seconds to minutes before, those neurons were activated by a thought, a memory, an emotion, or sensory stimuli. And in the hours to days before that behaviour occurred, the hormones in your circulation shaped those thoughts, memories, and emotions and altered how sensitive your brain was to particular environmental stimuli. And in the preceding months to years, experience and environment changed how those neurons function, causing some to sprout new connections and become more excitable, and causing the opposite in others. And from there, we hurtle back decades in identifying antecedent causes. Explaining why that behaviour occurred requires recognising how during your adolescence a key brain region was still being constructed, shaped by socialisation and acculturation. Further back, there's childhood experience shaping the construction of your brain, with the same then applying to your fetal environment. Moving further back, we have to factor in the genes you inherited and their effects on behaviour. But we're not done yet. That's because everything in your childhood, starting with how you were mothered within minutes of birth, was influenced by culture, which means as well by the centuries of ecological factors that influenced what kind of culture your ancestors invented, and by the evolutionary pressures that moulded the species you belong to. Why did that behaviour occur? Because of biological and environmental interactions, all the way down".

Sapolsky summarises, on p240: "evolution produces genes marked by the epigenetics of early environment, which produces proteins that, facilitated by hormones in a particular context, work in the brain to produce you. A seamless continuum, leaving no cracks between the disciplines into which to slip some free will".

This line of reasoning has echoes of that expressed by Rosenberg above. And indeed Rosenberg himself goes on to suggest that all human behaviour is the product of encoded "stimulus-response" experiences: in essence, that all human behaviour is learned behaviour, and not in any meaningful sense discretionary or intentional.

Specifically, in extracts taken from pp180-3 of *The Atheist's Guide* Rosenberg cites research into stimulus:response patterns in sea slugs which won Eric Kandel the Nobel prize in Physiology or Medicine: "Kandel started out by discovering how the sea slug learns things...like Pavlov's dogs, only more easily, the sea slug can be subjected to conditioning experiments. Recall Pavlov's famous experiment: by presenting a dish of meat (the unconditioned stimulus) to dogs and ringing a bell at the same time over and over again, he was able to get them to salivate at the sound of the bell without the meat. The sound of the bell was the 'conditioned' stimulus. Similarly, the sea slug can learn to withdraw its gills and its siphon from a conditioned stimulus. For example, combine a harmless electrical stimulus (the conditioned stimulus) on one nerve with a painful stimulus (the unconditioned stimulus) on another nearby nerve. The sea slug will soon respond to the painless electrical stimulus alone the way it originally responds to the combined painful and painless stimuli. It will withdraw its gill and siphon. *Voilà!* Learning by classical conditioning...the real beauty of sea slug training is that Kandel was then able to see how the conditioning changed the neurons...the changes are broadly of two types, depending on the conditioning experiments. Pair the unconditioned stimulus (the painful shock) and the conditioned stimulus (the harmless one) a few times. Then the sea slug will respond to the harmless stimulation alone once or twice, but will soon cease to respond to it. Pair the unconditioned and the conditioned stimulus several times, and the slug will continue to respond to the unconditioned stimulus – the harmless one – for a long time. Kandel discovered the source of the difference. A little training releases proteins that open up the channels, the synapses, between the neurons, so it is easier for molecules of calcium, potassium, sodium, and chloride to move through the gaps, carrying electrical charges between the neurons.

This produces short-term memory in the sea slug. Training over a longer period does the same thing, but also stimulates genes in the neurons' nuclei to build new synapses that last for some time. The more synapses, the longer the conditioning lasts. The result is long-term memory in the sea slug...now the slug does not actually learn any information that could be expressed in thoughts *about* (author's emphasis) stimuli. It doesn't have the thought, 'uh oh, painless electrical stimulation in neuron 1. That means painful stimuli is coming in neuron 2, so it's time to pull back the gill'. What the sea slug has learnt is not some new fact *about* (author's emphasis again) the world. It has acquired a new habit to do something, under certain conditions. It did this because its neurons were rewired into a new input/output circuit, creating the new habit. The sea slug has learned to respond to a particular stimulus and retains that response pattern for a long while. It's learned to do something; it hasn't acquired a thought *about* (author's emphasis again) something...what goes on in the human hippocampus is the same as what goes on, neuron by neuron, in...the sea slug's neurons when they store its response to a mild electrical stimulus...the big difference is one of degree, the number of neurons involved. In the human hippocampus (and the rest of the cortex, too), there are vastly more neurons to be changed...but the basic process is the same".

These neurobiological arguments against the existence of genuine freewill are complemented by philosophical reasoning tracing back at least as far as the 17th century Dutch philosopher Baruch Spinoza's assertion that: "men believe themselves free, simply because they are conscious of their actions and unconscious of the causes whereby those actions are determined", echoed by the 19th century German philosopher Arthur Schopenhauer's equally-celebrated observation that: "man can do what he wills; he cannot will what he wills".

The case for the defence, which is to say in support of freewill, rests largely on the belief that Rosenberg's sea slug example is an incomplete explanation of the workings of the human brain. It is not in dispute that as humans we are of course susceptible to the kind of behavioural "operant conditioning" that Rosenberg and Sapolsky both describe, and which we will shortly discuss further. The critical question, however, is whether this tells the full human story. A belief in freewill is logical if we allow the possibility that somewhere in the vastly greater number of neurons which the human brain contains, networks have developed which genuinely enable the kind of "feedback control" cognition we subjectively experience, for example consciously weighing alternative options and choosing one in particular from among them.

Tomasello explains, on pp7-8 of *A Natural History of Human Thinking*: "all organisms possess some reflexive reactions that are organised linearly as stimulus-response linkages. Behaviourists think that all behaviour is organised in this way...the alternative is to recognise that complex organisms *also* (my emphasis) possess some adaptive specialisations that are organised circularly, as feedback control systems, with built-in goal states and action possibilities. Starting from this foundation, cognition evolves not from a complexifying of stimulus-response linkages but, rather, from the individual organism gaining (1) powers of flexible decision-making and behavioural control in its various adaptive specialisations, and (2) capacities for cognitively representing and making inferences from the casual and intentional relations structuring relevant events...adaptive specialisations are organised as self-regulating systems, as are many physiological processes such as the homeostatic regulation of blood sugar and body temperature in mammals. These specialisations go beyond reflexes in their capacity to produce adaptive behaviour in a much wider range of circumstances, and indeed, they may be quite complex, for example, spiders spinning webs...cognition and thinking enter the picture when organisms live in less predictable worlds and natural selection crafts cognitive and decision-making processes that empower the individual to recognise novel situations and to deal flexibly, on its own, with unpredictable exigencies. What enables effective handling of a novel situation is some understanding of the cause and/or intentional relations involved, which then suggests an appropriate and potentially novel behavioural response".

Mitchell goes further, on p218 of *Free Agents*: "I claim that agency – the capacity of organisms to act with causal power in the world, for their own reasons – is the defining feature of life itself". He acknowledges that our personal brain chemistry and personal history of stimulus:response experiences have an important influence on our behaviour, but, like Tomasello, argues that this does not negate freewill because, again, these things do not tell the whole story – they are not "causally comprehensive" as he puts it, on p164.

The critical point is that causality in a system does not, or at least need not, always flow from the lowest level up: it can also derive from the higher-order features of a system and in effect flow top-down. And, as Mitchell points out on p165 of *Free Agents*: "if higher-order features...can exert causal power in a system – then causal determinism poses no threat to concepts of agency and freewill. The agent itself can be the cause of something happening".

How might these higher-order cognitive faculties operate at the level of our brain chemistry? The short answer is that we don't know. Mitchell offers a couple of possible pointers, although they are no more than directional.

First, on p165 Mitchell proposes a potentially causal role for "purpose", the idea that something, in this case an organism, might have a specific goal towards which to direct its activities. Mitchell acknowledges that he is on sensitive ground here because of the possible confusion with teleology, the notion that "things in nature are the way they are because they have been driven that way by some overarching purpose, thereby implying the hand of some intelligent designer". He rejects notions of a Cosmic Designer, asserting that nonetheless: "although the universe itself may not have a purpose, living organisms certainly do. That is, in fact, their defining characteristic". Elsewhere he summarises this purpose as "to persist", in other words to embody the Darwinian imperative to survive and reproduce.

Second, Mitchell suggests that the way a system is organised can have a causal effect on how its constituent parts behave. The implication is, again, that somewhere in the complicated morass of neural networks which comprise the human brain structures have developed which regulate and give direction to the activities of other networks. By way of illustration, Mitchell introduces the analogy of the impact a football coach has on the behaviour of the individual team members, on pp166-7: "(the brain's) subsystems work in ways that ultimately increase survival and reproduction...it's important to emphasise that the resultant functionalities – the specific architectures that carry out various operations – do not just *emerge from* (author's emphasis), the lower-level components, any more than the strategies of a football team emerge from what the individual players are doing. The relationship is precisely the converse: the functional architectures or the strategies have an independent origin and *constrain* (again, author's emphasis) the actions of the individual components. Paradoxically, as philosopher Alicia Juarrero argues, constraining the actions of components allows the whole system greater freedom to pursue higher-order goals. We pay football coaches so much because organisation matters".

Whatever the explanation, there is no challenge to the belief that consciousness itself is robustly material. Mitchell summarises, on pp168-9: "there is nothing in the laws of physics that rules out the possibility of agency or free will, a priori. The universe is not deterministic, and as a consequence, the low-level laws of physics do not exhaustively encompass all types of causation. The laws themselves are not violated, of course – there's nothing in the way living systems work that contravenes them, nor any reason to think they need to be modified when atoms or molecules find themselves in a living organism. It's just that they are not sufficient either to determine or explain the behaviour of the system".

And, on pp267-8: "*thoughts are not immaterial*: they are physically instantiated in patterns of neural activity in various parts of the brain, which can naturally have effects on how activity evolves in other regions...thoughts are not *just* patterns of neural activity: *they are patterns that mean something*...it is the meaning of the neural patterns that drives the unfolding of neural activity in the brain – the low-level physical details are often incidental. So, although thoughts must be instantiated in some pattern of neural activity, such patterns only have causal power in the system by virtue of what they mean. Some subset of those meanings are consciously apprehended. When they are, that *just is* you thinking. And when you are manipulating those cognitive representations and consciously working out what to do, that *just is* you deciding. It's not an illusion or an epiphenomenon or a post-hoc rationalisation. Mental causation is a perfectly real and naturalisable phenomenon...there is nothing spooky at work, but neither can it be reduced to mechanism (author's emphasis throughout)".

What this all adds up to is the crucial belief that as humans we indeed have a genuine capacity for self-reflection and self-control, which is to say for consciously intervening to regulate our own actions and behaviours. Introspection may be fallible, but that does not mean it is purely illusory or irrelevant, as Rosenberg suggests.

Mitchell elaborates, arguing on p219 of *Free Agents* that: "we...have the capacity for reflective cognition, which means our subconscious psychology is not always opaque or cryptic to us. We have powers of introspection and imagination and metacognition that let us identify and think about our own beliefs and drives and motivations, examine our own character, and consciously adopt new goals or set new policies that guide our future behaviour. We have, in short, the capacity of self-awareness...and we have the capacity of self-control. We have, in real time, the means to intentionally adjust our behaviour by selecting the objects of our attention and the different options for action that we consider and prioritise".

He echoes Tomasello in adding, on pp276-7: "the final stage in our evolutionary story – the admittedly egocentric story of our own lineage, that is – is the emergence of the ability to reason about our reasons. The expansion of the prefrontal cortex in primates, especially in humans, added more levels to our cognitive hierarchy. We moved beyond having a model of our bodies and a model of the world. Now we could have a model of our own minds – of our goals and desires and beliefs and the certainty we should attach to them. We could operate on those ideas in a common cognitive space. Being able to reason about our reasons meant we could intervene in them: we could exercise top-down cognitive control, in the moment. And we could consciously make decisions prospectively for future actions, adopting policies and commitments to guide future behaviour, in the process, shaping our own character and actively constructing ourselves as we interacted with the world".

On pp277-8 Mitchell makes a tentative suggestion for how conscious experience may have developed, again echoing some of the ideas that we heard earlier from Tomasello: "the conscious aspects of those processes remain mysterious...(but) at some point in evolution, our internal models became so abstract and recursive that they gave rise to mental experience...perhaps expanding the cortex...adding new levels to the recursive hierarchy, necessarily leads to the system modelling its cognitive processes. And perhaps modelling one's own thoughts necessarily entails conscious mental experience. But it's also possible we're missing some other essential element...the leading hypothesis is that the emergence of some kind of primitive language allowed humans to develop culture, and to share hard-won knowledge with our fellows and, crucially, with our offspring, accumulating the abilities to control our environments over generations. This likely provided some positive feedback for our move into the cognitive niche, with each new advance opening up new possibilities in a self-amplifying process. Thus, through both biological innovations and cumulative cultural evolution, humans developed capacities for creative, open-ended, recursive, thought and boundless imagination that truly set our minds free to combine and manipulate ideas in more and more abstract ways".

Finally, Mitchell cites the famous two-stage model pioneered by the American psychologist and philosopher William James in 1884 as a possible explanation for how freewill actually happens, on pp187-8 of *Free Agents*: "this (model)...incorporates a degree of indeterminism in our cognition while protecting the causal role of the agent in actually deciding what to do. In the first stage, in any given situation, some set of possible actions occur to the organism. In this process, James proposed that some degree of randomness is at play, but the randomness does not decide the outcome – the organism does. The options are presented for consideration, and the organism selects the one that is most congruent with its current goals and beliefs, and that has the highest predicted utility. That is, the organism selects from the range of presented options, *based on its current reasons* (author's emphasis)...in terms of our current understanding of the neuroscience of action selection...the possible actions would be represented by patterns of activity arising in cortical areas. These patterns would then be evaluated through extended interlocking circuit loops among the cortex, basal ganglia, thalamus, and midbrain. This evaluation process biases the ongoing competition among the patterns of activity in the cortex, 'up-voting' some and 'down-voting' others, which ultimately results in one possible action winning the competition and being released while all the others remain inhibited".

Of course, the two opposing viewpoints represented by Sapolsky and Rosenberg on the one hand and Mitchell and Tomasello on the other cannot both be right. We are forced to choose between them, ironically enough.

There is some common ground. No-one disputes that we each subjectively experience conscious thoughts and choices. All parties agree that these are the material product of our physical brain, that our current understanding of our brain chemistry is not adequate to explain how these sensations are produced, and that our understanding is nonetheless sufficiently advanced to conclude with confidence that our behaviour is heavily influenced by our personal genes and history in ways of which we are often not consciously aware.

It is at this point that we must choose, however: either to believe that our behaviour is always and inevitably determined by the mechanistic impact of stimulus:response experiences on our particular collection of neurons, so that what we experience as cognition and choice are simply illusory; or that our experience of personal agency has at least some level of validity deriving from higher-order cognitive capabilities which exert a level of control over the more basic neural activity, albeit we cannot explain how this happens at the level of our underlying brain chemistry.

Both positions beg important questions for which we do not have satisfactory answers. For example, Sapolsky does not explain why evolution should have gone to the trouble of developing our subjective feeling of agency, or cognition more broadly, if they are purely illusory; and Mitchell acknowledges that there is not a robust explanation for how our biochemistry produces the sensation of choice (in fact this would still need explaining even in Sapolsky's world in which freewill is an illusion, because, again, no-one doubts that we each subjectively experience it).

This book opts firmly for the Mitchell/Tomasello position, that our sense of agency is meaningful and real. It would obviously be more satisfying to have conclusive evidence on such a vital question. But it is what it is given our current state of knowledge.

Importantly, taking this position does not imply that our freewill is anywhere close to all-encompassing. Operant conditioning and stimulus:response reflexes are important influences on human behaviour, as they are for sea slugs and all other animals. Indeed, it is likely that these things dictate or at least influence much of our behaviour, at a level below that of our conscious mind. It is just that in some situations humans have some level of cognitive capacity to take a different, more intentional, approach. In sum, freewill is real but is also heavily constrained, in ways that are often not easy for our conscious mind to access.

As it happens, Sapolsky indicates that he is himself willing to settle for a less extreme position. On p6 of *Determined*, he explains that his goal is to convince the reader that: "there is much *less* (author's emphasis) free will than generally assumed"; and he returns to the same theme on p242: "I'll settle for merely significantly challenging someone's free-will faith. Sufficiently so that they will reframe their thinking about both our everyday lives and our most consequential moments".

And Mitchell for his part agrees that freewill has its limits. On p279 of *Free Agents* he says: "the question of whether we have free will does not have a yes-or-no, all-or-nothing answer". He adds, on p281: "the idea that we are not fully free because some prior causes that we did not control influenced the way our brains are configured has some merit to it. We are indeed somewhat constrained by evolution and our genetics and the way our brain happened to develop. All those elements did contribute to our psychological predispositions".

The point nonetheless is that: "those predispositions do not *determine* (Mitchell's emphasis) our behaviour, on a moment-to-moment basis...rather, they shape the ways in which we adapt to our worlds, choose and craft our environments, pursue our interests, and actively construct our character".

Finally, there is a practical question. It is not clear how we could function in our daily existence without embracing at least some notion of personal agency. Sapolsky himself hints at this on p9 of *Determined*, confiding that: "even I think it's crazy to take seriously all the implications of there being no free will".

There are least three ways in which to deny agency entirely would be to risk making life impractical.

First, evolution has wired us to experience the sensation of rational analysis and conscious choice, and it is hard to see how we could operate day-to-day whilst somehow repudiating or ignoring this. In effect, our experience of existence presents as largely an endless stream of decisions, each requiring us to exercise what our brain tells us is conscious choice. These include "big", albeit generally infrequent, decisions such as relationship and career choices; and countless "small", even trivial, decisions which frame our daily life and may often recur; for example whether to get out of bed when our alarm goes or sleep an extra ten minutes; whether to set an alarm in the first place; what to wear; whether to breakfast and what to consume if we do; how to show up in terms of our specific behaviour when we interact with our partner, family, work colleagues and strangers we meet during the course of the day; and so on and on.

As a practical matter, it is difficult to imagine how we might live if we were somehow to seek to deny our ability to exercise rational choice. The 1971 novel *The Dice Man*, by American author George Cockcroft, proposes one possible response, in which the protagonist decides he will literally follow the dictates of a dice throw for a series of life decisions. It creates chaos, of course, for him and those around him, to the extent that it is ultimately not sustainable. And even whilst attempting to live this way he cannot avoid exercising some degree of agency, or what seems to him like agency, for example in deciding which decisions will and will not be subject to the dice process, and how to frame those that are.

The upshot of all this is that from a practical perspective to embrace a belief that freewill is entirely illusory is to enter a world in which either one gives up altogether on the exercise of cognition and choice and lapses into a fatalistic, even vegetative state; or engages these faculties whilst simultaneously believing them to be illusory and therefore futile, a position likely to result in a serious case of an uncomfortable psychological condition called cognitive dissonance, which mainly occurs when an individual feels that there is a fundamental disconnect between their actions and beliefs.

The second practical problem if we deny agency is that this would create profound social challenges, because it would be unreasonable to hold ourself or others accountable for our actions and any notion of personal responsibility would therefore be defunct. Sapolsky devotes the second half of *Determined* to arguing that humanity has successfully adapted to changes of this kind before, for example in attitudes to various mental conditions and cases of what a lawyer might call diminished responsibility. Still, important as these have undoubtedly been, it would surely be a much bigger step to abandon *all* notion of personal accountability.

Third, research shows one of the factors which contributes to our happiness is a feeling that we possess some appropriate level of agency. To deny agency altogether would therefore be to risk jeopardising this.

The conclusion from all this is that a belief in personal agency is both justified and pragmatic. We are heavily influenced by our genes and history, but we are not mere prisoners of them. As Richard Dawkins urges on p201 and then p331 of *The Selfish Gene*: "we (humans), alone on earth, can rebel against the tyranny of the selfish replicators (that is, genes)...it is perfectly possible to hold that genes (my note: and our broader history) exert a statistical influence on human behaviour while at the same time believing that this influence can be modified, overridden or reversed by other influences".

The ability to exercise conscious choice is surely the most important of these "other influences".

And, once we embrace a belief in personal agency, it is a short step to the assertion that how we choose to exercise it is crucial to our very humanity. This was certainly the view of the 20th century Austrian psychiatrist (and death-camp survivor) Viktor Frankl, credited by many as the founding father of what we now call psychotherapy.

The quote most often used to summarise Frankl's view has a history of its own because it is not clear that Frankl himself ever said or wrote these actual words. The derivation seems to be that the American author Stephen Covey read about Frankl in a library book and popularised this framing without noting the original source. In any case, the quote is generally acknowledged to be an accurate summary of Frankl's belief:

"Between stimulus and response lies a space. In that space lies our freedom and power to choose a response. In our response lies our growth and our happiness".

This important idea is sometimes paraphrased as an exhortation to "Mind the Gap" between a stimulus and how we choose to respond, and we will return to it several times during the rest of this book.

So there it is. The foundational belief is that we each have an important measure of personal agency: the ability to engage in self-reflection and to exercise some degree of self-control over our own actions and behaviours. We can meaningfully be said to be the "captain of our soul", using "soul" in a strictly metaphorical sense of course.

At the same time, we must exercise this agency in the knowledge that our decisions and behaviours are heavily influenced by our unique genes and history, specifically by the impact these things have on the design and functioning of our brain, the effect of which is powerfully to predispose us to act in particular ways in response to specific triggers. In short, conscious experience and cognition are real; but so are our behavioural predispositions, which are themselves often not easily accessible to our conscious mind.

It follows that our ability to exercise our agency effectively will be enhanced by cultivating a degree of self-knowledge about our own predispositions and the associated "mind traps" into which we risk falling. It is to these topics that we will now turn our attention.

The essential self

The Greek writer Pausanias tells us that the exhortation to "know thyself" was the first of three maxims inscribed in the forecourt of the Temple of Apollo at Delphi, home of the Oracle, known and respected throughout classical Greece. (The other two maxims were "nothing to excess" and "surety brings ruin", presumably exhorting followers to embrace the fundamental unpredictability of human existence.) And one of the most celebrated quotes from the whole of Shakespeare is the advice given by Polonius to his son Laertes as the latter sets off on a potentially perilous journey, advice which indeed forms the epigraph to this book: *"this above all: to thine own self be true"* (*Hamlet*, Act 1, Scene III, line 78).

As an aside, there is a potentially unsettling debate to be had about how we should interpret this advice since Shakespeare chooses to put it in the mouth of a character who is shallow, vain, and generally unreliable. For the purposes of this book the assumption is that we can take the comment at face value, in effect a pearl of wisdom direct from Shakespeare himself. Drama scholars may of course demur, but that is a discussion for another day, not to mention a different book.

Returning to the main narrative, what is a "self", exactly? The answer is not entirely straightforward, perhaps not surprisingly for something inherently so subjective.

The Cambridge English Dictionary offers the following definition: "the set of someone's characteristics, such as personality and ability, that are not physical and make that person different from other people".

It is not obvious why the Cambridge Dictionary chooses to exclude physical characteristics, and many other definitions include them. For example, the Merriam-Webster Dictionary offers: "the union of elements (such as body, emotions, thoughts, and sensations) that constitute the individuality and identity of a person".

In an article called *Self Concept*, published in *Simply Psychology* in 2008, British psychologist Saul McLeod suggests that: "the list of answers to the question 'who am I?' probably include examples of each of the following four types of responses:

1) *Physical Description*: I'm tall, have blue eyes...etc.

2) *Social Roles*: we are all social beings whose behaviour is shaped to some extent by the roles we play. Such roles as student, housewife, or member of the football team not only help others to recognise us but also help us to know what is expected of us in various situations.

3) *Personal Traits*: these are the third dimension of our self-descriptions. 'I'm impulsive'...'I'm generous'...'I tend to worry a lot'...etc.

4) *Existential Statements* (abstract ones): These can range from 'I'm a child of the universe' to 'I'm a human being' to 'I'm a spiritual being'...etc."

And the American business academic Russell Belk quotes William James, again, pointing out that our definition of self can also include external elements such as material possessions. In an article titled *Possessions and the Extended Self*, published in the *Journal of Consumer Research* Vol 15, in September 1988, Belk says: "William

James (1890, PP. 291-292), who laid the foundations for modern conceptions of self, held that: 'a man's self is the sum total of all that he can call his, not only his body and his psychic powers, but his clothes and his house, his wife and children, his ancestors and friends, his reputation and works, his lands, and yacht and bank-account. All these things give him the same emotions. If they wax and prosper, he feels triumphant; if they dwindle and die away, he feels cast down, - not necessarily in the same degree for each thing, but in much the same way for all.'...if we define possessions as things we call ours, James was saying that we are the sum of our possessions".

Whatever dimensions we may feel best capture our own sense of "self", a somewhat different challenge is involved if we are to follow Polonius' advice, and "to (our) own self be true." Here, we are helped by the work of the 20th century American psychologist Carl Rogers (sadly no relation), specifically by his ideas on what he called "humanistic" self-concept. These are summarised by Saul McLeod, again, in a different entry for *Simply Psychology* titled *Carl Rogers*, updated in 2014: "according to Rogers (1959), we want to feel, experience and behave in ways which are consistent with our self-image and which reflect what we would like to be like, our ideal-self. The closer our self-image and ideal-self are to each other, the more consistent or congruent we are and the higher our sense of self-worth...the humanistic approach states that the self is composed of concepts unique to ourselves. The self-concept includes three components:

– *Self-worth*: self-worth (or self-esteem) comprises what we think about ourselves. Rogers believed feelings of self-worth developed in early childhood and were formed from the interaction of the child with the mother and father.

– *Self-image*: how we see ourselves, which is important to good psychological health. Self-image includes the influence of our body image on inner personality. At a simple level, we might perceive ourselves as a good or bad person, beautiful or ugly. Self-image affects how a person thinks, feels and behaves in the world.

– *Ideal-self*: this is the person who we would like to be. It consists of our goals and ambitions in life, and is dynamic - i.e., forever changing. The ideal self in childhood is not the ideal self in our teens or late twenties etc".

We may feel an important sense of continuity in our "self" through the course of our life, but in fact many elements are subject to change. For example, in an article titled *Does your body really replace itself every seven years?*", published on *How Stuff Works* and dated 14 April 2021, American journalist Chris Opfer tells us that the impact of cell regeneration is to replace almost our entire physical body every 7-10 years, apart from a few cell types which never regenerate, interestingly enough including the lens in our eye and the neurons in our cerebral cortex. However, whilst at least some neurons may not replenish, the network of connections between our neurons certainly does continue to evolve throughout our life, meaning that the wiring of our brain changes over time. Memory provides a salient example. We are constantly laying down new memories as we have new experiences, these memories are stored in the form of neural connections, and memory is obviously of crucial importance when it comes to our sense of who we are. Beyond this, in the same article referenced above Saul McLeod highlights that even the way in which we conceptualise our "self" may change over time, so that we give different weight to different factors as we age: "typically young people describe themselves more in terms of personal traits, whereas older people feel defined to a greater extent by their social roles".

Finally, our sense of "self", or at least how we choose to project it, may vary situationally. Often, this will take the form of role-playing, sometimes consciously but frequently not. For example, we are likely to behave in a different way when we play the role of watchful, or alternatively nurturing, parent; compared with say that of an eager subordinate at work; or a loving romantic partner on a date. We may find ourself behaving differently with one group of friends when compared with another, and so on. In effect, we are projecting a different aspect of our overall "self" in these different situations: what we might call a different "persona", a word derived from the Latin for a theatrical mask like those used in classical Roman, and Greek, theatre. In such a case we literally act out a role, and our choices and behaviours are shaped by our preconceptions of what might be expected from someone in that role.

Lisa Barrett explains, on pp190-1 of *How Emotions Are Made*: "my scientific definition of the self is inspired by the workings of the brain...the self is part of social reality. It's not exactly a fiction, but neither is it objectively real in nature like a neutron. It depends on other people. In scientific terms, your predictions in the moment, and your actions that derive from them, depend to some extent on the way that others treat you. You can't be a self by yourself... if the self is a concept, then you construct instances of yourself by simulation. Each instance fits your goals in the moment. Sometimes you categorise yourself by your career. Sometimes you're a parent, or a child, or a lover. Sometimes you're just a body. Social psychologists say that we have multiple selves, but you can think of this repertoire as instances of a single, goal-based concept called 'the self' in which the goal shifts based on context".

Stepping back, our sense of "self" is our most personal psychological feature. It is our very identity, our innermost core, what makes us "us" and not some other, generic, being. It is unique, of course. As already discussed, we experience our psychological "self" largely as the "little voice" inside our mind. And, despite the many changes which undoubtedly occur, we carry some sense of continuity throughout our life, from our earliest conscious awareness right until our death, with the caveat that this can be tragically undermined if we are unfortunate enough to be afflicted with dementia or some similar degenerative brain condition as we age.

The critical point is that the Delphic Oracle was surely right. The better we "know ourself" as we embrace the existential choices in our own life, the better able we will be to act in ways that are congruent with whatever we feel our essential self to be.

Personality and character

Personality and character are important expressions of "self", each worth a brief discussion.

The Cambridge English dictionary defines personality as: "the type of person you are, shown by the way you behave, feel and think". And, as with the self more generally, at the most fundamental level our personality is unique. There has never been, and never will be, anyone else who behaves, feels, and thinks, exactly like you, or me, or any other individual past, present or future.

Still, a good deal of interesting work has been done on the topic of personality profiling, which typically clusters people into discrete groups. The idea is not to imply that members of the same group have the exact same personalities, of course, but rather that at a certain level of abstraction they exhibit broad traits which can meaningfully be said to make them similar to others in the same group, and different to people in other groups. This kind of framework can be helpful in giving a basic structure within which we can assess our own individual profile and so cultivate self-knowledge.

There is not a single definitive approach. However, the so-called "Big 5" framework probably comes closest. This builds on work originally done by Tupes and Crystal in the US in the 1950s, and proposes 5 core personality traits which together form the acronym OCEAN. The model seeks to be descriptive rather than prescriptive, meaning that it explicitly does not suggest that any particular profile is somehow inherently "better" than another, although it does propose that some profiles are better suited to some environments. If you'd like to explore your own profile, there are plenty of tests available online which use the OCEAN framework, many of which are free.

The "Big 5" traits are:

- *Openness*. People who demonstrate high openness typically have a wide variety of interests, and enjoy seeking out new experiences. People who don't are more focused and conservative (with a small "c" i.e. not necessarily implying a specific political affiliation).
- *Conscientiousness*. People who demonstrate high conscientiousness are organised, reliable and thorough. People who don't are more fluid, and less stressed about deadlines, for example.
- *Extroversion*. People who are highly extroverted get their energy mainly from interacting with other people. Conversely, people who are highly introverted get their energy mainly from within themselves. As an aside, this is not to say that introverts necessarily lack social skills, or somehow do not value building relationships; nor that an extrovert will always be the life and soul of a party. The fundamental question is simply whether an

individual finds it relatively more or less energising to be with other people, especially people they don't know well, and especially in groups.
- *Agreeableness.* People who demonstrate high levels of agreeableness are typically friendly, compassionate, and collaborative. They may not be highly competitive, indeed this is more likely to be a characteristic of individuals at the other end of the agreeableness spectrum. There is some evidence that people who enjoy higher levels of career success tend to score relatively lower for agreeableness, at least if we measure "career success" in a traditional way, for example by the amount of material wealth generated.
- *Neuroticism.* People who are highly neurotic tend to experience larger and more frequent mood swings – the classic emotional "highs" and "lows". People who are not tend to be more emotionally stable over time; in other words they experience, and demonstrate, a narrower emotional range.

Turning to "character", the distinction is that this typically has a moral dimension, in contrast to personality which, as we just saw, is essentially neutral from a moral standpoint. In addition, personality tends to be somewhat fixed whereas character can change over time. Finally, we have limited control over our personality but our character can be seen as the product of our own personal choices, at least to some degree.

Kevin Mitchell explains, on p239 of *Free Agents*: "the distinction between personality and character is a tricky one, especially because the two terms are used in overlapping fashion in common parlance...personality traits...refer to underlying psychological predispositions...these denote differences between individuals that are more or less neutral; that is, it is not necessarily *better* (author's emphasis) to be higher or lower in extraversion or openness to experience or even conscientiousness or neuroticism or agreeableness. There is no particular level of each of these traits or a single combination of levels that is optimal in all scenarios; it may, for example, be quite adaptive to be high in neuroticism in circumstances where threats abound...character traits, by contrast, are essentially defined as morally better or worse; in fact, they are typically categorised as virtues or vices. The virtues include things like honesty, fairness, courage, humility, generosity, steadfastness, loyalty, integrity, prudence, patience, forbearance, temperance, selflessness, and so on (and the vices their opposites)".

On pp239-40 Mitchell introduces the idea that positive character traits, or virtues, tend to be inherently prosocial, a notion we will return to when we discuss morality in Chapter 4: "virtues are essentially pro social traits: it's not that they are good or bad in an absolute sense or even that they are good or bad for the individual. It's that they're good or bad for everyone...in addition to pro- or antisocial aspects, the other main theme of character traits is one of self-control, as exemplified by patience, prudence, temperance, foresight, and perseverance. These traits represent the triumph of rationality over more basic drives (a capacity that may underpin more overtly prosocial behaviours)".

Mitchell asserts, on p241, that, unlike personality, our character is an aspect of our self over which we have some influence and for which we therefore bear some responsibility: "it is widely accepted that character traits are not just given but need to be actively developed and, moreover, that *individuals themselves* (author's emphasis) have both the power and the moral responsibility to engage in and direct that development". Later on p241 he invokes Cicero to explain that our character, the person we become, is the result of a number of factors specifically including our own existential choices: "for Cicero, character emerged from four sources...: human nature generally (including the capacity for rational thoughts and action); our own individual nature (my note: in other words, our specific genes and personality traits); events, experience, and the environment (my note: in other words, our own personal history and circumstances); and finally, the *accumulating effects of our own choices* (author's emphasis)".

This is why the way in which we choose to exercise personal agency in our daily life is so important – it is the decisions we make, and the actions we take, which ultimately come to define us.

PART C: How consciousness works

We may not be able to explain how consciousness works at the level of our brain's underlying biochemistry. But we know a great deal about various aspects of how it works in practice, or at least how we experience it working in practice, all of which can help us to enrich our understanding and, ultimately, self-knowledge.

Executive function and the rational brain

One of the most distinctive attributes of human consciousness is the group of faculties called "executive function", defined by the Merriam-Webster dictionary as: "the group of complex mental processes and cognitive abilities (such as working memory, impulse inhibition, and reasoning) that control the skills (such as organising tasks, remembering details, managing time, and solving problems) required for goal-directed behaviour".

The American social psychologist Jonathan Haidt describes this set of capabilities as "reasoning-why". It is distinctive to humans, contrasting with and indeed complementing "seeing-that" brain functionality, which humans share at least to some degree with other animals.

These distinctions echo those in our discussion of freewill, with "reasoning-why" corresponding loosely to Tomasello's "feedback control" cognitive mechanisms; and "seeing-that" corresponding to the kind of operant conditioning reflexes observed in Kandel's sea slugs

On pp50-51 of his 2012 book *The Righteous Mind* Haidt references the American social scientist Howard Margolis and his 1990 book *Patterns, Thinking, and Cognition*: "Margolis proposed that there are two very different kinds of cognitive processes at work when we make judgements and solve problems: 'seeing-that' and 'reasoning-why.' 'Seeing-that' is the pattern matching that brains have been doing for hundreds of millions of years. Even the simplest animals are wired to respond to certain patterns of input (such as light, or sugar) with specific behaviours (such as turning away from the light, or stopping and eating the sugary food). Animals easily learn new patterns and connect them up to their existing behaviours, which can be reconfigured into new patterns as well (as when an animal trainer teaches an elephant a new trick)...as brains get larger and more complex, animals begin to show more cognitive sophistication – making choices (such as where to forage today, or when to fly south) and judgements (such as whether a subordinate chimpanzee showed properly differential behaviour). In all cases, the basic psychology is pattern matching...Margolis also called this kind of thinking 'intuitive'...'reasoning-why,' in contrast, is the process 'by which we describe how we think we reach to judgement, or how we think another person could reach that judgement'. 'Reasoning-why' can occur only for creatures that have language and need to explain themselves to other creatures. 'Reasoning-why' is not automatic; it's conscious, it sometimes *feels* (Haidt's emphasis) like work, and it's easily disrupted by cognitive load".

Simply put, executive function is what enables us to take a strategic approach to a particular event or situation, rather than reacting purely in the moment. It gives us the ability to conceptualise and determine goals, which themselves can reflect both short and longer-term considerations. We can develop plans to achieve these goals, and then consider and evaluate options along the way. So far as we know, no other life-form can do these things, certainly not to the same extent, and this faculty obviously confers enormous benefit to our species overall and to each of us as individuals. Executive function is also critical in helping us to regulate our behaviour and exercise self-control, capabilities which are particularly relevant to the complex social interactions which dominate our experience as humans. Executive function, in short, is what enables us to heed Viktor Frankl's advice to "mind the gap" between a stimulus and the way we choose to respond.

The American neuroscientist John Cacioppo and his collaborator, science journalist William Patrick, suggest that executive function is at the heart of humanity's emergence as the dominant species. On p35 of their 2008 book *Loneliness*, they tell us that: "getting by as a happy and healthy human being requires the integrative intelligence exercised by the brain's frontal lobes, a function that neuroscientists and psychologists have labelled executive control. Remembering your name does not require this kind of intellectual coordination and integration, nor does simple arithmetic. Certain other tasks, such as reading your native language or playing a piece on the piano, you readily push out of executive control once you've mastered them. But more complex cognitive functions, including the complexities of social behaviour, demand lifelong self-regulation". On p37 they assert: "being able to self-regulate our emotions and our behaviours is a large part of what makes us human".

And on pp202-3 they describe the crucial role that the development of executive function played in our evolutionary past: "with the expansion of our brain and our field of vision came an even wider expansion – not just of a range of habitation, but of our range in terms of the global and temporal nature of our concerns. It is this expansion that lies at the heart of the Third Adaptation (my note: the Third Adaptation distinguishes humans from chimpanzees and bonobos, our closest evolutionary cousins). We became creatures not just of the moment, but of the future and the past. We could internalise lessons from experience, learn from our mistakes, and also plan ahead. We could defer gratification and we could keep mental accounts of treachery and of kindness extending back for generations, even centuries. With highly sophisticated and fully functional executive control, we could much more precisely sort out what served our own interests, while also taking into consideration our membership in various wider communities of interest, extending all over the world and into the future our great-grandchildren will inhabit. And thus, despite all the other human advantages, our most singularly beneficial adaptation remains the self-regulation and nuanced social cognition provided by our neocortex. The cornerstone of the Third Adaptation is executive function".

The importance of executive function to our ability to regulate our behaviour is illustrated by the celebrated, oft-quoted, case of Phineas Gage, a 19th century American railroad worker who had the misfortune to have a steel bolt accidentally fired through his skull.

Miraculously, he survived. Even more miraculously, his general health and cognitive faculties appeared to be unimpaired, even though the force of the steel bolt entering and then exiting his skull had taken with it part of his brain. There was a glaring exception to this normality, however. Before the accident, Phineas had been a popular and respected colleague and family man. After it, his behaviour changed, principally because he was no longer able to regulate it – the part of his brain which had been destroyed was the part of the frontal cortex most associated with executive function.

His predicament is summarised by Cacioppo and Patrick on pp37-8 of *Loneliness:* "an hour after the accident he was chatting about the experience. Within a couple of months he had recovered from his obvious injuries. But...he was no longer the responsible, personable young man, or the serious and conscientious young supervisor, he had been. He had become a foulmouthed hothead, incapable of holding a job or planning his future. His doctor described him as 'fitful, irreverent, indulging at times in the grossest profanity, which was not previously his custom, manifesting but little deference for his fellows, impatient of restraint or advice when it conflicts with his desires, at times pertinaciously obstinate, capricious and vacillating...a child in his intellectual capacity and manifestations, he has the animal passions of a strong man'. Despite the fact that his physical and general reasoning capabilities – attention, perception, memory, language, and intelligence – were intact, he could no longer make good choices. Because he could no longer incorporate social conventions and ethical concepts into his social interactions, his decisions no longer took into consideration the concerns of others, and, consequently, his decisions no longer served his own, or anyone else's, long-term interest".

Executive function, then, is the faculty, or set of faculties, which ultimately gives us the possibility to exercise existential choice over what we do and how we behave.

Learning and development

Our physical and cognitive development begin pretty much at the moment of our conception. Experience operates on our genes in quite a literal way, stimulating neural connections within our brain, connections which are in turn associated with growth across all of the physical, cognitive and psychosocial domains. The rate at which these neural connections proliferate is strongest during our early years, but new brain connections continue to be formed, and existing connections are strengthened or weakened, throughout our life. This means that the experiences we have in our formative years have a disproportionate effect on the person we become, but do not completely define us forever. Like the Universe itself, we are in an important sense in a state of flux throughout our life, with at least some continuing potential to change and, hopefully, progress as we pass through the various life stages from childhood to maturity and eventual old age.

Our physical body experiences considerable changes over time. To highlight a few, we are essentially helpless in our early years, which are also the time of our greatest physical and mental growth. We typically reach puberty around the age of 11 for girls and 12 for boys, although it can start as early as 8 for some individuals, in a process which can take as long as 4 years to complete. We reach our adult size and weight by our late teens, then starting at about the age of 30 and accelerating from about the age of 60 we start to lose muscle mass, and increase fat mass, at a rate of around 5% per year, albeit these effects can be at least partly mitigated through diet and exercise. Men in particular often start to experience thinning hair from quite early in their adult life. Both sexes typically start to lose height around the age of 40, at a rate of around 1 cm every 10 years, increasing after the age of about 70. Women experience the menopause, typically starting some time between the ages of 45 and 55, with symptoms lasting around 4 years on average.

What happens to our brain is more relevant to a discussion of consciousness, of course. And, as we might expect, the picture is nuanced. Essentially, our brain develops at a tremendous rate during our early years, absorbing many kinds of knowledge about the world, ranging from "basic" skills such as how to walk through to potentially sophisticated attitudes and cultural beliefs, many of which go on to form part of our subconscious mind in later life to the extent that they often become hard for our conscious brain to access. As we reach maturity, and then start to age, the rate of development slows but never fully stops, so that to some degree our brain continues to be open to, and shaped by, new experiences throughout our life. As we age, we accumulate experience and become less impressionable, for better and worse. But we do not altogether lose our ability to learn, nor our ability to challenge and change our entrenched beliefs should we choose to.

We saw earlier that a typical human brain contains about 86 billion neurons, and that it is the connections between these neurons, called synapses, which make us who we are. Particular experiences result in specific synaptic connections. Repetition then strengthens particular connections over time, and disuse weakens them.

The development of our brain begins in the womb, almost immediately after conception, so that by the time we are born we already have a certain amount of basic "wiring" in place. However, the brain we are born with is also highly plastic, and in effect wired to learn from the experiences we have.

American biologist John Medina explains, on pp60-61 of his book *Brain Rules*, published in 2008: "we are born into this world carrying a number of preset (neuronal) circuits. These control basic housekeeping functions like breathing, heartbeat, your ability to know where your foot is even if you can't see it, and so on. Researchers call this 'experience independent' wiring. The brain also leaves parts of its neural construction project unfinished at birth, waiting for external experience to direct it. This 'experience expectant' wiring is related to areas such as visual acuity and perhaps language acquisition. And, finally, we have 'experience dependent' wiring...where a great deal of the brain is hard-wired *not* (Medina's italics) to be hard-wired. Like a beautiful, rigorously-trained ballerina, we are hard-wired to be flexible".

Our "experience independent" wiring will in principle be similar to other people's, although of course there may nonetheless still be genetic differences between individuals. "Experience expectant" wiring will also be broadly similar for individuals undergoing similar experiences, such as literally learning how to see. This does not of course mean that everyone will have exactly the same experience. For example, on p146 of *The Human Brain* Susan Greenfield recounts the sad story of a young Italian boy who was permanently blind in one eye because he had a minor eye infection as a baby, the organ was bandaged for two weeks, and this turned out to overlap exactly with the critical period when his infant brain was making the neural connections to enable vision, such that: "sadly, the bandaging of the eye was misinterpreted by the brain as a clear indication that the boy would not be using that eye for the rest of his life", the neural connections for it to work were simply never made, and could not be retro-fitted.

It is the "experience dependent" neural connections which create the main opportunity for personalised development. As Medina explains, on pp61-2, it is impossible for any two people to have identical experiences, which means that their neural connections, and therefore their brains, will be physically different even if they share the same (virtually) identical genes: "even identical twins do not have identical brain wiring. Consider this thought experiment: suppose two adult male twins rent the Halle Berry movie *Catwoman*, and we...are viewing their brains while they watch. Even though they are in the same room, sitting on the same couch, the twins see the movie from slightly different angles. We find that their brains are encoding visual memories of the video differently, in part because it is impossible to observe the video from the same spot. Seconds into the movie, they are already wiring themselves differently...one of the twins earlier in the day read a magazine story about panned action movies, a picture of Berry figuring prominently on the cover. While watching the video, this twin's brain is simultaneously accessing memories of the magazine. We observe that his brain is busy comparing and contrasting comments from the text with the movie and is assessing whether he agrees with them. The other twin has not seen this magazine, so his brain isn't doing this. Even though the difference may seem subtle, the two brains are creating different memories of the same movie".

Medina summarises, on p62: "learning results in physical changes in the brain, and these changes are unique to each individual. Not even identical twins having identical experiences possess brains that wire themselves exactly the same way. And you can trace the whole thing to experience".

There is intriguing evidence that individual neurons may be critical to how we store particular experiences and ideas. Medina offers what he calls "the Jennifer Aniston neuron" as a concrete example, on pp60-2 of *Brain Rules*. He describes a man undergoing brain surgery, during which the surgeons are trying to map his brain to identify which specific neurons perform which functions, to help them guide the operation. The patient is conscious (remember, the brain has no pain receptors): "suddenly, one of the surgeons whips out a photo of Jennifer Aniston and shows it to the patient. The neuron in the man's head fires excitedly. The surgeon lets out a war whoop...Sound like a grade B movie? This experiment really happened. The neuron in question responded to 7 photographs of actress Jennifer Aniston, whilst it practically ignored the 80 other images of everything else, including famous and non-famous people...there is a neuron lurking in (this patient's) head that is stimulated only when Jennifer Aniston is in the room". The implications of the Jennifer Aniston neuron are not yet entirely clear, but it seems that what is being stored is a representation of the "idea" of Jennifer Aniston, in other words an abstract concept of her, rather than a specific image. The same neuron fired for all 7 pictures of Aniston, for example, but none of the 80 images of other people. In a related experiment with another person as the subject, a similar effect was observed when a single neuron fired in response to images of the actress Halle Berry, including one which did not show a picture of her but simply the letters spelling her name.

Whatever, it is our specific, personal, pattern of neural connections which make us who we are. And it is through the process of forming and selectively strengthening these connections that our experiences impact our genes.

How does this process unfold over time?

The highest level of activity in terms of growing new neurons happens in the womb. Specifically, on p122 of *The Human Brain* Greenfield tells us that during this time: "at maximum rates, cells will be dividing to give 250,000 new neurons per minute!"

Of course, a distinguishing feature of humans is that, unlike most other animals, much of our development, physical and mental, happens after we are born. Greenfield observes, on p130 of *The Human Brain*: "birth allows the brain to go on growing, since otherwise the head would soon become too big for the birth canal of the mother. At birth, the human head is roughly the same size as a chimpanzee...by six months, it will be half its eventual size, and by two years it will be three quarters the size of the adult head. At four years old the human brain is four times the size it was at birth".

Once we are born, the main emphasis within our brain shifts from growing new neurons to developing and reinforcing neural connections among those we already have, in response to experience. On p147 of *The Human Brain*: "as our development continues after birth, the jostling, restless neurons in the brain are very reactive as they form circuits to reflect whatever is happening in the individual outside world. Inside the brain, right up to 16 years of age, a bloody battle is being waged between neurons. It is a battle for establishing connections. If a new neuron does not make contact with a target neuron, or is insufficiently stimulated, then it dies...as we interact in this way with the environment, we become more adept at surviving in it, as more and more of the appropriate (that is, the most hardworking) neurons are connected to enable the most effective signalling".

And although the pace of development slows considerably as we get older, the mature brain nonetheless continues to make new neural connections, and strengthen existing ones, in response to continuing experiences throughout our life. Greenfield summarises, on p150-1 of *The Human Brain*: "although the brain is particularly impressionable while developing, such adaptability does not cease but merely lessens somewhat in maturity...... thus, as we live out our lives, we fashion the connections between neurons that endow us with an individual, unique brain. Nonetheless, by the time we arrive at middle-age we are fairly fixed as a personality, or we think we are… our brain continues to slow down in certain ways but to adapt and change in others".

The effect of all this development within our brain is that we experience both cognitive and psychosocial growth. The 20th century Swiss psychologist Jean Piaget offers probably the best-known theory of cognitive development, including the important insight that as children we actually think differently from adults. Piaget posited 4 stages of cognitive growth:

- *Birth to 2 years*: the sensorimotor stage, experiencing the world mainly through the physical senses, and learning mainly basic reflexes and motor responses
- *2 to 7 years*: the preoperational stage, when children begin to think symbolically, and language starts to emerge. However, children typically still think mainly in concrete terms, and are largely egocentric
- *7-11 years*: the concrete operational stage, when children start to embrace logic and also learn to recognise the perspectives of others (called Theory of Mind – more on this below)
- *12 and onwards*: the formal operational stage, in which the ability to think in abstract terms and to use deductive logic emerge, enabling consideration of moral, political and social issues as well as the ability to embrace hypotheses and nuance.

Psychosocial development deals specifically with our ability to relate to other people, in effect to function effectively as a member of a social group. Sophisticated social animals that we are, this capacity is critical to our ability to survive and thrive, as individuals and as a species, and is the focus of the next chapter. The main point for now is simply that developing social skills and a healthy sense of "self" is a critical element of our overall growth and development. Various frameworks exist to describe the main elements, although none is yet established as canonical. One of the most influential was proposed by the 20th century German-American psychologist Erik Erikson, who incidentally is also famous for coining the notion of a "personal identity crisis". Erikson suggested 8 stages of psychosocial development:

1. *Birth-18 months: Trust versus Mistrust* – the most fundamental stage. Developing a sense of trust at this early age has been shown to correlate with the ability to form healthy, enduring relationships later in life.
2. *2-3 years: Autonomy versus Shame and Doubt.* Success during this stage leads to a sense of autonomy and personal control, which as we saw earlier can have important associations with happiness later in life.
3. *3-5 years: Initiative versus Guilt.* Children who develop confidence in their ability to take the initiative again experience a sense of control, and develop an ability to lead, or at least influence, others.
4. *6-11 years: Industry versus Inferiority.* Children who feel validated in coping with social and academic challenges develop a sense of competence.
5. *12-18 years: Identity versus Confusion.* This is when we develop our specific sense of "self", wrapped up as it is with feelings of self-confidence and security.
6. *19-40 years: Intimacy versus Isolation.* The defining feature of this stage is our ability, or not, to create and sustain intimate relationships.
7. *40-65 years: Generativity versus Stagnation.* Success in this stage is based on accomplishments which produce a feeling of satisfaction and, possibly, legacy. Successfully raising children is one classic example.
8. *65-death: Integrity versus Despair.* People look back on their life and decide whether they are happy with how they have lived it.

The critical point is that our personal experiences shape us as a person, by stimulating particular neural patterns of connection in our brain. Arguably the clearest example of this is the process of operant conditioning, the focus of Kandel's experiments with sea slugs as we saw earlier. The concept of operant conditioning itself was developed and promoted by the Behaviourist school, which was dominant during the early and middle years of the twentieth century and remains influential to this day. Behaviourist ideas remain sufficiently influential that it is worth a brief digression to review them.

Behaviourism is summarised by Saul McLeod in a 2020 article titled *Behaviourist Approach*, published online on *Simply Psychology*: "Behaviourism...is a theory of learning which states all behaviours are learned through interaction with the environment through a process called conditioning. Thus, behaviour is simply a response to environmental stimuli...Behaviourism is primarily concerned with observable behaviour, as opposed to internal events like thinking and emotion".

Behaviourism is acknowledged to have begun as a movement in 1913, when the American psychologist John Watson published an article called *Psychology as the behaviourist views it*. Its leading proponent is generally considered to be another American psychologist, BF Skinner, who introduced "operant conditioning" as a concept, building on work by yet another American psychologist called Edward Thorndike, who was active at the end of the nineteenth century.

Operant conditioning essentially proposes that the consequences of a particular behaviour determine the probability that it will be repeated, specifically that a behaviour which is followed by pleasant consequences, in other words "rewarded", is likely to be repeated; and behaviour which is followed by unpleasant consequences, or "punished", is likely not to be.

Operant conditioning differs from classical conditioning, at least in concept, because it focuses on "voluntary" behaviours, for example, working hard at school; as distinct from "involuntary" ones, for example, salivating. As an aside, classical conditioning can nonetheless also be demonstrated, for example in the experiments of the Russian physiologist Ivan Pavlov and the eponymous "Pavlovian response", briefly referenced earlier. For example, Pavlov noticed that his experimental lab dogs would salivate in anticipation of food by associating it with the footsteps of the assistant who was bringing it, going on to train his dogs to salivate in response to a wide range of other behavioural triggers.

Behaviourism in its purest form was unabashed in its embrace of the *tabula rasa* concept that our mind is a blank slate at birth, and it is experience, and only experience, which then shapes it to produce the behaviours we demonstrate during the course of our life.

The process of operant conditioning has been shown to be effective in many conditions and species, certainly including humans. But Behaviourism also has its limitations, and these to some extent mirror our discussion of freewill. Perhaps most important, we have already seen that the mind is categorically not a *tabula rasa*: experience is important, certainly, but so are the underlying genes. And, on p171 of *How Emotions Are Made* Barrett is dismissive of the whole Behaviourist approach precisely because it takes insufficient account of the activity of our conscious mind: "thus began the most notorious historical period in psychology, called *behaviourism* (author's emphasis). Emotions were redefined as mere behaviours for survival: fighting, fleeing, feeding, and mating, collectively known as the "four Fs"... (behaviourism) declared that thoughts, feelings, and the rest of the mind were unimportant to behaviour or might not even exist...ultimately, most scientists rejected behaviourism because it ignores a basic fact: that each of us has a mind, and in every waking moment of life, we have thoughts and feelings and perceptions. These experiences, and their relation to behaviour, must be explained in scientific terms".

Returning to our main narrative, eventually our brain starts to decline, along with the rest of our body. We saw that we begin to lose muscle mass starting around the age of 30, and a somewhat similar process of degeneration happens to our brain. Thankfully this does not become apparent until considerably later in life, and even then the effects can be at least partly compensated by the remaining neurons forming new connections. Still, as life expectancy has increased many more people are living to experience cognitive decline. Greenfield summarises, on pp 151-2 of *The Human Brain*: "there is a 20 per cent loss in brain weight by age ninety, and even by age seventy there is a 5 per cent loss in brain weight. On the other hand...we know that the remaining neurons can take over certain roles".

The spectre looms of the brain disabilities which are unfortunately associated with ageing in our modern world, such as Alzheimer's and other forms of dementia. It is at least somewhat reassuring to know that, whilst sadly all too common, these conditions are not inevitable. Greenfield tells us, on p152 of *The Human Brain*: "it is important to realise that these diseases are actually illnesses; they are not a natural consequence of old age".

Finally, many attempts have been made to summarise what it is to be human as we progress through the various stages of our life. Different frameworks have been proposed with anything between 5 and 10 discrete but overlapping stages of development. No framework has yet emerged as definitive. We'll therefore give the floor to surely the most evocative, if not necessarily the most scientific, description, to wit Jacques' famous speech in

Shakespeare's *As You Like It*, written in 1599. The speech is taken from Act II, Scene vii, lines 139-166, and describes "the Seven Ages of Man", although if were being picky we might quibble that the number should be eight, as Jacques omits to mention the development of the embryo in the womb:

All the world's a stage,
And all the men and women merely players;
They have their exits and their entrances;
And one man in his time plays many parts,
His acts being seven ages. At first the infant,
Mewling and puking in the nurse's arms;
And then the whining school-boy, with his satchel
And shining morning face, creeping like snail
Unwillingly to school. And then the lover,
Sighing like furnace, with a woeful ballad
Made to his mistress' eyebrow. Then a soldier,
Full of strange oaths, and bearded like the pard,
Jealous in honour, sudden and quick in quarrel,
Seeking the bubble reputation
Even in the cannon's mouth. And then the justice,
In fair round belly with good capon lin'd,
With eyes severe and beard of formal cut,
Full of wise saws and modern instances;
And so he plays his part. The sixth age shifts
Into the lean and slipper'd pantaloon,
With spectacles on nose and pouch on side;
His youthful hose, well sav'd, a world too wide
For his shrunk shank; and his big manly voice,
Turning again toward childish treble, pipes
And whistles in his sound. Last scene of all,
That ends this strange eventful history,
Is second childishness and mere oblivion;
Sans teeth, sans eyes, sans taste, sans everything.

The point, from the perspective of this book, is that our consciousness is not a static thing, any more than our physical body is. Rather, we are in a constant state of change, and retain some capacity to develop and grow throughout the various stages of our existence, at least until the "last scene of all".

Joining up the dots – how our brain processes data

We have seen that our brain is essentially constructive, which is to say that it creates representations and predictions of external reality as the basis for instructing our body how to act.

This approach has of course proven over the course of evolutionary time to be extraordinarily effective. But it is not without its pitfalls. Simply put, our brain relies on data sampling to create its simulations, and then ascribes a particular meaning to a simulation as the basis for determining action. This creates the possibility of error if the data sample is somehow inaccurate, and also if the brain interprets a wrong or sub-optimal meaning.

To dig a level deeper, data sampling is the brain's response to a fundamental evolutionary design problem; namely, that the brain receives vastly more information than it is or could conceivably be capable of processing, particularly in the conscious mind. At any one moment, external reality assaults our senses with an almost infinite cacophony of sights, sounds, touches, tastes and smells. Specifically, the *Encyclopedia Britannica* tells us that in our waking moments our senses typically gather some 11 million bits of information every second from our environment. The eyes are responsible for the vast majority, capturing around 10 million bits per second. The skin is next with a million; the ears and nose capture 100,000 each; and the taste buds a comparatively meagre 1,000 bits per second.

Looking just at our eyes, these typically make about three movements each second, called saccades. Each interval between movements lasts around 200-300 milliseconds, and it is the information captured during these intervals which is transmitted to the brain. In effect the brain "sees" 3 snapshots of external reality every second, not a continuous reel. What is more, these snapshots focus on whatever objects the brain determines are most relevant at that particular moment. For example if we are looking for a taxi on a busy street, our brain will focus on capturing the visual data that is most relevant to this task, and will screen out much of the other data which might potentially be available. The point is that what our eyes capture is a fractional sample of the total visual information which is in theory available to them.

In any case, the processing capacity of our conscious mind has been assessed at only around 50 bits per second, equivalent to reading 300 words per minute: a tiny fraction of the volume of data our senses are taking in. Partly, the difference is explained by the fact that much of the sensory data never reaches our conscious mind but simply by-passes it and is used by the brain to drive activities which are largely unconscious, for example those of our autonomic nervous system which controls such things as our breathing, the activity of our heart and other vital organs, keeping us upright whilst we are walking, and so on.

Our brain also makes use of concepts to enable it to give meaning to the data it receives. For example, Barrett describes how the concept of a rainbow helps us to make sense of a stream of visual information, on p84: "when you look at a rainbow, you see discrete stripes of colour...but in nature, a rainbow has no stripes – it's a continuous spectrum of light, with wavelengths that range from approximately 400 to 750 nanometers. Why do you and I see stripes? Because we have mental *concepts* (author's emphasis) for colours like 'Red,' 'Orange,' and 'Yellow'. Your brain automatically uses these concepts to group together the wavelengths in certain ranges of the spectrum, *categorising* (again, author's emphasis) them as the same colour. Your brain downplays the variations within each colour category and magnifies the differences between categories, to perceive bands of colour".

On p85 she explains how concepts also help us to make sense of sound, specifically language and speech: "human speech also is continuous – (but) when you listen to your native language, you hear discrete words. How does that happen? Once again, you use concepts to categorise the continuous input. Beginning in infancy, you learn regularities in the stream of speech that reveal boundaries between phonemes, the smallest bits of sound that you can distinguish in a language (for example, the sound of 'D' or 'P' in English). These regularities become concepts that your brain later uses to categorise the stream of sound into syllables and words".

Concepts themselves are not necessarily rigidly or objectively defined, of course. Picking up on the rainbow example, on pp145-6 of *How Emotions Are Made* Barrett explains that different human cultures may have different ways of slicing and dicing the colour spectrum, so that a brain exposed to a different concept will actually "see" a different version of reality: "...if you visit the Russian Google...and search for the Russian word for rainbow...you'll see that Russian drawings contain seven colours, not six: the Western blue stripe has been subdivided into light blue and dark blue...concepts of colour are influenced by culture. In Russian culture, the colours 'blue' and 'sky blue' are different categories, as distinct as blue and green are to an American. This distinction is not due to inborn, structural differences in the visual systems of Russians versus Americans, but to culture-specific, learned concepts of colour. People raised in Russia are simply taught that light and dark blue are distinct colours with different names. These colour concepts become wired into their brains, and so they perceive seven stripes (in a rainbow)".

Obviously, the process of data sampling exposes the brain to error if the actual data sampled does not adequately reflect "true" reality – for example doesn't pick up on a tiger lurking in the bushes. There is also a possibility that the brain ascribes an inaccurate, or sub-optimal, meaning to the data it receives. Sometimes more than one meaning may be appropriate, as with the visual examples below:

Image 1: What do you see?

Image 2: What do you see?

Image 3: what do you see?

The first image can relatively easily be seen to be both a duck and a rabbit. The second features both the words "good" and "evil". The third, and for most people most complex, has representations of both an old and a young lady. The old lady is looking towards the viewer and towards the left of the page, with her dark hair partly covered by a white shawl. She has a large hooked nose and a prominent chin. The young lady is looking away from the viewer, also towards the left of the page. She also has dark hair partly covered by a shawl, but in her case with a delicate jawline, and a choker necklace where we might otherwise perceive the mouth of the older lady.

The point is that more than one meaning is possible for each of these. However, once our brain has joined up the dots in favour of a particular interpretation, it can be hard for it then to discern the second: our definition of reality tends to freeze onto whichever interpretation our brain first decides is "real". Admittedly, this can be influenced by the specific image: most people find it relatively easy to see both the duck and the rabbit, and harder to see both the young and old ladies.

A second potential source of fallibility relates to our brain's propensity to seek meaning through identifying "cause and effect" relationships. We saw earlier from Tomasello and especially from Baron-Cohen that this is a kind of human superpower. Success can obviously confer significant adaptive advantage, as evidenced by the possibly-overworked example of the prehistoric hunter on the savannah who sees some tall grass sway backwards and forwards with a motion which strikes him, or her, as unusual. Our hunter must decide whether what they are seeing is the effect of the breeze, in which case it can be ignored; evidence of a small herbivore, in which case it could make a tasty supper; or evidence of some large predator, in which case the hunter might risk themself becoming supper if they fail to beat a discreet retreat.

Powerful as this propensity is, it also carries risks. We might ascribe an incorrect meaning, for example concluding that the waving grass signifies a small herbivore when in fact it is hiding a lion.

Alternatively, we might project a meaning where none in fact exists, a propensity known as "pareidolia". An obvious example of the latter is "seeing" the face of the Man in the Moon, or seeing human or animal faces, or any object at all, in cloud formations. More colourfully, our propensity to look for patterns of causality underpins the conspiracy theories with which the internet is awash these days. For example: Shakespeare didn't write his own plays; JFK was killed by the CIA; the Moon landings were faked; Princess Diana was assassinated by the British Establishment; 9/11 was somehow staged; COVID-19 was a giant global hoax, and so on.

Miracles are another, perhaps more inflammatory, case of an illusory cause-and-effect, since as we discussed in Chapter 1 they are by definition impossible in a world which obeys entirely natural laws, with no exceptions.

Finally, in just the same way that the brain seeks to impose meaning on the external data received via our senses, so it also looks to interpret the information it gets from our body, through the process of interoception that we discussed earlier. On pp29-30 of *How Emotions Are Made* Barrett describes how "meaning" arises specifically from the way our brain conceptualises a physical sensation, so that the same sensation might be capable of producing very different meanings: "from your brain's perspective, your body is just another source of sensory input...(the) purely physical sensations inside your body have no objective psychological meaning. Once your concepts enter the picture, however, those sensations may take on additional meaning. If you feel an ache in your stomach while sitting at the dinner table, you might experience it as hunger. If flu season is just around the corner, you might experience that same ache as nausea. If you are a judge in a courtroom, you might experience the ache as a gut feeling that the defendant cannot be trusted. In a given moment, in a given context, your brain uses concepts to give meaning to internal sensations as well as to external sensations from the world, all simultaneously. From an aching stomach, your brain can construct an instance of hunger, nausea, or mistrust".

As an example of how this too can produce fallibility, later on p30 Barrett shares her own experience interpreting a physical symptom in a particular context: "back when I was in graduate school, a guy in my psychology program asked me out on a date. I didn't know him very well and I was reluctant to go because, honestly, I wasn't particularly attracted to him, but I had been cooped up too long in the lab that day, so I agreed. As we sat together in a coffee shop, to my surprise, I felt my face flush several times as we spoke. My stomach fluttered and I started having trouble concentrating. Okay, I realised, I was wrong. I am clearly attracted to him. We parted an hour later – after I agreed to go out with him again – and I headed home, intrigued. I walked into my apartment, dropped my keys on the floor, threw up, and spent the next seven days in bed with the flu".

In sum, our brain operates by "joining up the dots" from sampled data to create its own representation of external reality, combines this with the internal data it also receives about the state of our body, and then applies past experience and learned concepts to create "meaning" as the basis for determining how to instruct our body to act. This approach is undeniably successful in an evolutionary context but also exposes us to fallibility, for example if the data sampled is somehow unrepresentative or if the meaning we find turns out to be mistaken.

Instinct, emotion, and reason as triggers for behaviour

Instinct, emotion, and reason combine to prompt our behaviour. Each can have a different weight in different situations, and often they act in concert.

Instinct has the strongest claim to operate independently, regulating as it does our essential bodily functions such as breathing. There may nonetheless be particular situations in which it is appropriate for our conscious mind to intervene, for example choosing to take deep breaths to calm ourself in a crisis, or perhaps to regulate an instinctive "fight or flight" response to some emergency or other stress-inducing event.

More complex, it is clear that emotions play an important, often dominant, role in our decision-making, in ways that are often not obvious to our conscious mind. We are each programmed with a tendency to take cognitive short-cuts, prompted partly by a range of in-built, and again largely unconscious, biases. Often, what we experience as a rational decision may instead be our brain post-rationalising, that is to say creating a narrative to justify why we behaved the way we did, when the behaviour was in reality prompted by instinct or emotion.

This is by no means necessarily a bad thing. Instinctive, emotive responses meet strong adaptive needs, for example helping us move quickly to action with minimal cognitive effort and often serving to keep us safe in a crisis, or to act in ways which are socially appropriate.

Still, our instincts can also sometimes lead us astray, as when we act or speak on impulse then subsequently wish we had given more rational thought to our behaviour before it was too late. It is precisely in situations such as these that we do well to "mind the gap" between a stimulus and our response.

Cognitive bias

One way in which our instincts may frequently mislead us is through cognitive bias. This is defined by the *Cambridge English Dictionary* as: "the way a particular person understands events, facts, and other people, which is based on their own particular set of beliefs and experiences and may not be reasonable or accurate".

Arguably the most authoritative, and surely the most accessible, work on the topic is the book *Thinking Fast and Slow*, published in 2011 by American-Israeli psychologist Daniel Kahneman, drawing on his work over several decades with his colleague Amos Tversky who sadly died before the book was written. Famously, Kahneman is the only psychologist to have won a Nobel Prize for Economics, which he did in 2002, and *Thinking Fast and Slow* describes some of the many subconscious biases which tend to influence our personal economic decision-making. It is one of the canonical works in the emerging field of behavioural science and highly recommended reading, if you haven't already read it. And even if you have.

The central insight is to reinforce that many decisions which may seem to us to be coolly analytical and rational are in fact the product of cognitive short-cuts, which Kahneman calls "heuristics". These heuristics are in effect cognitive biases, and we are each prone to a bewildering variety of them, accepting that there will of course be considerable variation between individuals as to which specific biases most affect us, and in what way.

We can speculate that many of these biases may have conferred adaptive advantage to our remote ancestors, faced with the specific environments they inhabited. But in our modern world they can sometimes lead us astray.

To give a concrete example, Kahneman and Tversky's research identifies a bias they call "the framing effect", whereby the way a question or proposition is framed can have a big effect on how people typically respond. For instance, when asked to choose between alternative descriptions of a procedure to help tackle a hypothetical disease, an overwhelming majority of people say that they would choose an option framed as "80% of sufferers are saved" versus an alternative in which "20% of sufferers die", even though there is no mathematical difference between these two outcomes and the description of the procedure itself is identical in both framings.

The American economist Richard Thaler and law professor Cass Sunstein elaborate on the framing effect in their 2008 book *Nudge*. Their emphasis is on potential applications for public policy, specifically by proposing that more care be given to what they call "choice architecture", in other words paying more attention to how choices are framed. This has subsequently inspired governments around the world, including in the UK which in 2010 famously set up the "Nudge Unit" as part of the Cabinet Office, since spun out to become a separate "social purpose company".

An example of UK "nudge" in action is the decision to change the protocol for organ donation such that from May 2020 onwards people are required to opt out, rather than opt in as previously. Individuals still have the same exact choice, in that anyone who is happy to be a donor can be, and anyone who doesn't want to can easily not be. It is too early for concrete data on the impact of the change, but the expectation is that it will lead to a significant increase in the availability of organs for transplant, because the silent majority who are happy in principle to donate their organs but are not sufficiently motivated to make the effort previously needed to opt in will now automatically be part of the donor pool whereas previously they were not.

Thaler and Sunstein advocate that a change of this type – from "opt in" to "opt out" – could benefit people in a whole range of public policy applications, including for example participation in schemes for medical insurance and regular employee savings and pensions plans.

Applying the framing effect to our own lives as individuals, the insight is that how we choose to frame a particular decision which faces us may have a significant, if not necessarily obvious, effect on the conclusion we reach. The point is not that a particular framing is right or wrong, or even necessarily better or worse. The point is simply that how we frame a specific decision can influence the choice we end up making, and we do well to bear this in mind as we contemplate whatever decisions we are faced with, particularly if they are important.

Kahneman goes on to show how we tend to rely on heuristics in many other settings, often without being consciously aware that this is what we are doing. To take just one further example, we might sign up, or not, to a particular plan not because we have really analysed the numbers every which way (although we might also have done this), but because at a basic emotional level we trust, or not, the individual responsible. There is nothing intrinsically wrong with "backing the man, not the plan" (or woman of course; it just doesn't rhyme as well here). The point is that if this is what we are really doing, then it is surely best to be explicit, in our own mind above all. The potential pitfall is that we may delude ourselves that the basis for our choice is what we perceive to be a rigorous analysis of the pros and cons of the plan; when in reality it is our level of emotional trust in the individual who has conceived or must execute it.

Again, it is reasonable to assume that our propensity to use heuristics as the basis for much of our decision-making has adaptive advantages. Most obviously, they help us to reach an answer with a maximum of speed and a minimum of effort, both qualities we might expect evolution to value highly. The challenge comes from the fact that they are often not easily accessible to our conscious mind, and that these cognitive short cuts don't always give us the answer which we might consider to be most appropriate on mature reflection.

The list of potential biases is long. Kahneman's is by no means the only voice on the topic, and there is not yet and may never be a truly comprehensive catalogue. A Google search throws up lists which identify from as few as 50 to more than 180 different biases.

Fortunately, it is not necessary that we review all of them, or even any in detail. We will instead settle for highlighting some of the most prominent examples which have the potential to affect the way in which we exercise the kinds of personal existential choice we are discussing in this book. The implication is that we do well to watch out for the possible presence of these and other similar biases as we engage in our own personal decisions.

Examples include:

- *Availability bias*, in which we tend to over-weight things which come easily to mind, and under-weight things that do not. For example, on p130 of *Thinking, Fast and Slow*, Kahneman describes how dramatic events such as plane crashes temporarily alter our feelings about the safety of flight, even though the underlying probabilities have generally not changed. Similarly, personal experiences weight more highly than the reported experiences of others, or than mere statistics, in colouring our views positively or negatively

about a particular topic – the example Kahneman gives is our faith in the judicial system.
- *Confirmation bias*, whereby we tend to overweight data or opinions which confirm a pre-existing belief, and ignore or underweight data or opinions which contradict it. We are particularly prone to this if we have some deep emotional attachment to the belief, for example if it is somehow part of our sense of our own identity.
- *Recency bias*, whereby we tend to weight the impact of an experience which is more recent more highly than one that is not. This also partly underpins the "peak:end effect", a phenomenon we will discuss shortly when we look at memory.
- *Fundamental attribution error*, whereby we tend to put more weight on personality-based rather than situation-based factors in explaining the behaviour of other people. Specifically, we put more weight on "what kind of person" one is to explain their behaviour, rather than the social or environmental factors which may be influencing them. This can lead to undesirable, and unfair, attitudes such as racism, and class and gender prejudice.
- *Loss aversion*, whereby we tend to weight more highly the avoidance of loss than the possibility of gain. There is an evolutionary logic for this which harks back to our discussion of the hunter on the savannah who notices the movement of some grass and has to decide whether it denotes the presence of prey, a predator, or simply the wind. Clearly, there is asymmetric risk involved – if he concludes it is a predator and retreats then he has to find his supper elsewhere, but if he assumes it is prey or the wind and it turns out to be a predator the consequences may be terminal. So it is logical that he should weight the downside risk more highly than the upside opportunity. More generally, Kahneman cites a classic experiment in which people are asked to accept a bet or not based on the flip of a coin. If it comes up tails they lose $100, and the

question is what value of win is required if it comes up heads to persuade them to take the bet. Logically we might assume this to be as little as $101 (assuming that the loss of $100 would not cause them undue material hardship), since a 50% chance of winning $101 offset by a 50% chance of losing $100 equates to a probability that they will be 50 cents ahead. If 50 cents doesn't seem a big enough incentive, then we could substitute a higher value of say $110, equating to a probability of finishing $5 ahead. In reality, the value people say they would require turns out to be close to $200, on average.

- *Affinity bias*, whereby we tend to bias in favour of people we perceive are like ourselves in some way, and against people we perceive are different. This gives rise to the group behaviours which can be described as "tribal", or alternatively relating to "Ingroups" and "Outgroups", a phenomenon which we will explore in the next chapters.
- *Catastrophising*, in which we project our inner fears and insecurities onto a possible future event and give it a weight in our decision-making which is disproportional to the probability of it actually happening, and possibly to the impact it would have even if it does.
- *Overconfidence*, the reverse of catastrophising, in which we feel groundless optimism which may lead us to overweight the probability of a good outcome and underweight the possibility of a bad one. For example, Kahneman tells us that in surveys 95% of American drivers rate themselves "better than average".

It is not that we can somehow immunise ourself from these, or other, biases. They are hardwired into our consciousness. The point is rather that we are likely to make more informed choices if we cultivate some awareness of the particular biases to which we are personally most susceptible.

"Noise"

Our cognitive processes are subject not only to the systematic bias of various kinds discussed in the previous section, but also to random "noise". This "noise" results in additional errors in the form of inconsistent judgements and decisions in situations where we might reasonably expect consistency.

Daniel Kahneman has co-authored a book on this topic also, called *Noise, A Flaw in Human Judgement*, written with Olivier Sibony and Cass Sunstein and published in 2021. On p4, the authors explain the basic idea: "our topic is human error. Bias and noise – systematic deviation and random scatter – are different components of error...some judgements are biased; they are systematically off target. Other judgements are noisy, as people who are expected to agree end up at very different points around the target".

Elsewhere, the authors point out that we may also be "noisy" as individuals, that is, we may make different judgements about an issue at different times even though the issue itself remains the same. Amongst their examples are doctors making a medical diagnosis, and judges passing sentence: random variability is observed both between different doctors or judges presented with the same evidence in similar circumstances; and also in the judgements made by individual doctors or judges presented with similar cases over time.

The authors reinforce that noise is different from bias, on pp262-3: "we say that *bias* exists when most errors in a set of judgements are in the same direction. Bias is the *average error*, as, for example, when a team of shooters consistently hits below and to the left of the target; when executives are too optimistic about sales, year after year; or when a company keeps re-investing money in failing projects that it should write off...(however) eliminating bias from a set of judgements will not eliminate all error. The errors that remain when bias is removed are not shared. They are the unwanted divergence of judgements, the unreliability of the measuring instrument we apply to reality. They are *noise*. Noise is variability in judgements that should be identical" (authors' emphasis throughout).

Noise can be even more important than bias as a source of error, as the authors explain on p264: "of bias and noise, which is the larger problem? It depends on the situation. The answer might well turn out to be noise. Bias and noise make equal contributions to overall error...when the mean of errors (the bias) is equal to the standard deviations of errors (the noise). When the distribution of judgements is normal (the standard bell-shaped curve), the effects of bias and noise are equal when 84% of judgements are above (or below), the true value. This is a substantial bias, which would often be detectable in a professional context. When the bias is smaller than one standard deviation, noise is the biggest source of overall error".

Paradoxically, though, noise tends to receive less attention. This is because of what the authors describe on p305 as: "our excessive tendency...to seek and find coherence". They explain, on p369: "the human mind craves causal explanations. Whenever something goes wrong, we look for a cause – and often find it. In many cases, the cause will appear to be a bias...bias has a kind of explanatory charisma, which noise lacks. If we try to explain, in hindsight, why a particular decision was wrong, we will easily find bias and never find noise. Only a *statistical view* (authors' emphasis) of the world enables us to see noise, but that view does not come naturally – we prefer causal stories. The absence of statistical thinking from our intuitions is one reason that noise receives so much less attention than bias does".

Finally, the explanation for noise can often be found in our own underlying emotional mood – our "interoceptive feelings" as Barrett labelled them. Kahneman, Sibony and Sunstein comment, on p89 of *Noise*: "we need to emphasise an important truth: *you are not the same person at all times* (authors' emphasis). As your mood varies (something you are, of course, aware of), some features of your cognitive machinery vary with it (something you are *not* (again, authors' emphasis), fully aware of). If you are shown a complex judgement problem, your mood in the moment may influence your approach to the problem and conclusions you reach, even when you believe that your mood has no such influence and even when you can confidently justify the answer you found. In short, you are noisy". They give a number of examples, including research showing that physicians are significantly more likely to prescribe opioids at the end of a long day; that judicial sentences tend to be more severe when it is hot outside; and that college admissions officers pay more attention to the academic attributes of candidates on cloudier days and are more sensitive to nonacademic attributes on sunnier days.

Our mood can also influence our moral judgements. On pp88-9 the authors explain: "in one study, researchers exposed subjects to the footbridge problem, a classic problem in moral philosophy. In this thought experiment, five people are about to be killed by a runaway trolley. Subjects are to imagine themselves standing on a footbridge, underneath which the trolley will soon pass. They must decide whether to push the large man off the footbridge and onto the tracks so that his body will stop the trolley. If they do so, they are told, the large man will die, but the five people will be saved...the footbridge problem illustrates the conflict between approaches to moral reasoning. Utilitarian calculation, associated with English philosopher Jeremy Bentham, suggests that the loss of one life is preferable to the loss of five. Deontological ethics, associated with Immanuel Kant, prohibits killing someone, even in the service of saving several others. The footbridge problem clearly contains a salient element of personal emotion: physically pushing a man off a bridge into the path of an oncoming trolley is a particularly repugnant act. Making the utilitarian choice to push the man off the bridge requires people to overcome their aversion to a physically violent act against a stranger. Only a minority of people (in the study, fewer than one in ten) usually say they would do so...however, when the subjects were placed in a positive mood – induced by watching a five-minute video segment – they became three times more likely to say that they would push the man off the bridge. Whether we regard 'thou shalt not kill' as an absolute principle, or are willing to kill one stranger to save five should reflect our deepest values. Yet our choice seems to depend on what video clip we have just watched". We will discuss the "trolley problem" further in Chapter 4, when we explore morality more fully.

It is not that we can somehow avoid "noise". Like bias, it is an unavoidable part of being human, as the authors explain on p370: "the infinite variety of backgrounds, personalities, and experiences that make each of us unique is also what makes noise inevitable".

The point is rather that "noise" is an important additional potential source of error. We therefore do well to consider ways to mitigate its effects, both at a system level, for example in the operation of medical and judicial practice; and as individuals contemplating our personal existential choices. To take a simple, obvious, example, the awareness that we are likely to react in a different way if we are hungry or tired may allow us consciously to moderate our response to take account of this, or to eat or sleep before making an important decision.

The point is that we have some level of agency in the matter. Kahneman, Sibony and Sunstein conclude, on p375 of *Noise*: "judgement error may seem more tolerable when it is random than when we attribute it to a cause; but it is no less damaging. If we want better decisions about things that matter, we should take noise reduction seriously".

Categorisation

One of the most powerful features of our consciousness is the ability to categorise, that is to classify people or things into groups defined by whatever features we may consider to be similar, in turn allowing us to distinguish a particular group from others. This is one element of the capacity that we saw Baron-Cohen describes as "systemising", crucially enabling us to make sense of the mass of data about our world by compartmentalising it into relevant, manageable, segments.

To illustrate the broader point we'll consider the specific example of colour, building on Barrett's earlier discussion of rainbows. An article titled *How many colours are there in the world?* authored by Davey Gott and posted on 3 May 2019 on NCI News concludes that: "the answer is basically infinity...". What we perceive as different colours is in fact light of different wavelengths being reflected back off a particular surface, which is then processed by the optical machinery in our brain.

On p241 of his 2010 book *Through the Language Glass*, the Israeli linguist Guy Deutscher tells us that the spectrum of wavelengths visible to the typical human is "between around 380 and 750 nanometers (millionths of a millimetre)". Wavelengths outside this range, such as ultraviolet and infrared, are not visible to the typical human, accepting that in this as in most other cases there is some level of variation between the capacities of individual people. This might seem to imply that there is a specific number of unique colours we could each perceive, namely those wavelengths between whatever version of the 350 to 750 nanometer range we personally process. However, it turns out that our sensation of colour is produced not mainly by a "pure" light source of a particular wavelength (the technical term is "monochromatic") but rather by combinations of wavelengths, and there are an essentially infinite number of possible combinations. For those interested, Deutscher explains the technical details in the Appendix of *Through the Language Glass*, on pp241-9.

The point is that our ability to categorise is what enables us to make sense of this potentially infinite complexity. In fact our visual system could potentially distinguish about 10 million different colours, according to Davey Gott in the article referenced above. No wonder we can identify so many different shades of grey. However, most of us have no need for anything like this level of detail in our everyday life, and categorisation allows us to simplify to a level that is adequate for our practical needs. Specifically, Gott quotes 1969 research from Berlin & Kaye showing that in English there are 11 unambiguous colour terms: red, orange, yellow, green, blue, purple, pink, brown, grey, black and white. By definition, these 11 categories suffice for most of us, most of the time. Where they do not, they can be expanded. For example, Gott also tells us that Crayola makes 120 different colours of crayon, each with its own distinct colour name obviously, and he goes on to assert that in English a total of 1640 different colours have actually been named.

The example of colour serves to illustrate the power of categorisation to allow us to make practical sense of what might otherwise be potentially infinite complexity. And what is true for colour is true for almost every aspect of the world around us. Categorisation allows us to distinguish different types of human ("male/female", "tall/short", "fat/thin" etc); different kinds of emotion; different kinds of cloud formation, and so on and on.

Having said all this, as we might by now expect our propensity to categorise is also fallible. There is an obvious risk that we might mis-categorise, classifying people or things into groups inappropriately. Arguably a more pernicious risk is that we over-simplify, for example assuming that all the members we have classified into a group based on one particular feature, say the colour of their skin, must therefore be similar to one another, or different from non-group members, in other respects which are in reality not related to skin colour. We may also be misled into thinking that differences are categorical, or binary, when in fact they are simply points along a more nuanced spectrum: that they are black or white when in fact they may in reality be one of the many possible shades of grey.

To take one example, the British writer (and former national table-tennis champion) Matthew Syed writes in *The Sunday Times*, in an opinion piece called *Subtle stereotypes hit harder than a baton*, published on 7 June 2020, of an occasion when he was invited to take part in a panel discussion on the topic of "why are black people superior distance runners?" Some basic research on his part showed that people from many black communities do not tend to excel in distance running, for example people from the Caribbean or central Africa. When he shared this insight with the organiser the question was changed to "why are Kenyans superior runners?" But this turned out to be problematic too. Syed points out that there are almost no distance-running champions from eastern Kenya, or Nairobi, or the north or the west. Rather, almost all the distance-running success is concentrated in a tiny district called Nandi, in the Rift Valley. Syed summarises: "I mention this because it hints at a tendency in the human brain. We put people with dark skin in a box marked "black" and then assume that any trait shared by some (even a tiny minority) is shared by all – otherwise known as stereotyping".

Categorisation is crucial to our ability to make sense of disparate data, and therefore to derive meaning from it. We must beware the pitfalls, such as miscategorising or stereotyping. There is also an opportunity, as Barrett points out on p292 of *How Emotions Are Made*: "there is a kind of freedom in realising that we categorise to create meaning, and therefore it is possible to change meaning by recategorising".

PART D: Critical faculties which form part of consciousness

Reason

The capacity to reason is the faculty which, more than any other, has historically been viewed as setting humans apart from other species. Aristotle, for example, considered reason to be so important that he defined the highest human happiness as consisting of a life lived consistently and completely in accordance with its dictates. And much of the Western philosophical tradition came to accept reason as the preeminent human attribute, captured by Immanuel Kant's famous assertion in his 1781 masterwork *The Critique of Pure Reason* that: "all our knowledge begins with the senses, proceeds then to the understanding, and ends with reason. There is nothing higher than reason".

We have also seen that our decisions and actions are often driven, or at least heavily influenced, by predispositions and biases which are not easily accessible to our rational mind, famously leading the 18th century Scottish philosopher David Hume to the opposite conclusion that: "reason is, and ought only to be, the slave of the passions, and can never pretend to any other office than to serve and obey them" (*A Treatise of Human Nature*, Book III, Part III, Section IIII; published in 1739-40).

What to make of this apparent paradox?

It is clear that reason is indeed a kind of human superpower, enabling us to discern complex patterns of cause-and-effect relationships, and meaning more generally; to perform logical analysis; to plan for the future; and to develop technologies and other interventions which shape our environment and ultimately allow us to outcompete other species. Without reason there would be no scientific method, and no evidence-based theories of particle physics, evolutionary biology, neuroscience, or anything at all.

The answer, then, is clearly to seek to embrace and apply our capacity to reason whilst making appropriate allowance for the non-rational factors which also influence us. This does not, or at least should not, mean somehow separating reason entirely from emotion. In any event this would be next to impossible. Rather, it is by applying reason in the context of our emotions that we are most likely to find effective answers.

To dig a level deeper, the Cambridge English Dictionary defines reason as "the ability of a healthy mind to think and make judgements, especially based on practical facts". Other animals might be said to have "associative memory", a close cousin of operant conditioning, allowing them to regulate their behaviour based on a rudimentary sense of "cause-and-effect" phenomena – for example, a dog which has once been kicked may be wary of putting itself in a position in which the experience might be repeated. But as far as we know, only humans have the ability to use data as the basis for logical reasoning, to assemble facts, compare alternative explanations, model the future, develop options, and draw conclusions about which option will best suit the occasion and should therefore be actioned.

The *Stanford Encyclopedia of Philosophy* distinguishes between two kinds of reason, "practical" and "theoretical", in an entry titled *Practical Reason*, first published in 2003 and substantively revised in January 2020: "practical reason is the human capacity for resolving, through reflection, the question of what one is to do...theoretical reflection is concerned with matters of fact and their explanation". We might summarise this as "what?" and "why?" respectively.

The entry goes on: "the contrast between practical and theoretical reason is essentially a contrast between two different systems of norms: those for the regulation of action on the one hand, and those for the regulation of belief on the other". The same essential cognitive machinery is involved in both cases: "reasoning is an inferential process that takes as input some attitudes of a subject, and yields as output the formation or modification of other attitudes. Inferential processes of this kind are involved in the paradigmatic cases in which we exercise our capacities for (both) theoretical and practical reason...the difference is that theoretical reasoning leads to modifications of our beliefs, whereas practical reasoning leads to modifications of our intentions".

These two different kinds of reasoning can be linked, of course. For example, readers of this book may hopefully employ theoretical reasoning to scrutinise and if appropriate modify their personal beliefs about existence, then practical reasoning to determine what specific choices to make differently as a consequence.

The Canadian-American cognitive psychologist Steven Pinker mounts a spirited defence of the importance of reason in his 2021 book *Rationality*, asserting on ppxiiixiv of the Preface: "commentaries by the thousands have lamented our shortfall of reason, and it's become conventional wisdom that people are simply irrational. In social science and the media, the human being is portrayed as a caveman out of time, poised to react to a lion in the grass with a suite of biases, blind spots, fallacies, and illusions...yet as a cognitive scientist I cannot accept the cynical view that the human brain is a basket of delusions. Hunter-gatherers – our ancestors and contemporaries – are not nervous rabbits but cerebral problem solvers. A list of the ways in which we're stupid can't explain why we're so smart: smart enough to have discovered the laws of nature, transformed the planet, lengthened and enriched our lives, and, not least, articulated the rules of rationality that we so often flout".

Echoing Tomasello and Baron-Cohen, Pinker reminds us, on p2, that reason is a defining attribute of our evolutionary past and critical to defining humans as a species: "the cognitive wherewithal to understand the world and bend it to our advantage is not a trophy of Western civilisation; it's the patrimony of our species. The San of the Kalahari desert in South Africa are one of the world's oldest peoples, and their foraging lifestyle, maintained until recently, offers a glimpse of the ways in which humans spent most of their existence. Hunter-gatherers don't just chuck spears at passing animals or help themselves to fruit and nuts growing around them. The tracking scientist Louis Liebenberg, who has worked with the San for decades, has described how they owe their survival to a scientific mindset. They reason their way from fragmentary data to remote conclusions with an intuitive grasp of logic, critical thinking, statistical reasoning, causal inference, and game theory".

Reason has many facets, of course. At its heart lies a capacity for logical deduction, defined by Pinker (on p73) as: "inferring true statements (conclusions) from other true statements (premises)", and succinctly captured by Aristotle in his famous syllogism:

*"All men are mortal.
Socrates is a man.
Therefore, Socrates is mortal"*.

From here it is a relatively short step to Baron-Cohen's "systemising" and *"if-and-then"* causal analysis.

And, on p71 of *Rationality* Pinker reminds us that one of the most potent attributes of reason is the ability it confers to self-examine: "...the power of reason: (is that) it can reason about itself. When something appears mad, we can look for a method to the madness. When a future self might act irrationally, a present self can outsmart it. When a rational argument slips into fantasy or sophistry, an even more rational argument exposes it. And if you disagree – if you think there is a flaw in this argument – it's reason that allows you to do so".

Reason can operate prospectively or retrospectively. A prospective application might be to help us develop say a Theory of Relativity, or at a more mundane level to assess which holiday to choose, and how best to get there once we have chosen. It is also true that many thought processes of this kind can be heavily influenced by our emotions and underlying body state, often in a way that is close to invisible to our conscious mind. Still, the point is that reason has its role.

Retrospective applications help us to make sense of situations that have already happened, and of our own completed actions, through post-rationalisation. This can for example serve to mitigate the condition of cognitive dissonance, which we encountered earlier in our discussion of the potential consequences of denying personal agency.

Cognitive dissonance as a concept was first introduced in 1957 by the American social psychologist Leon Festinger and is defined by *Verywellmind* as "the mental discomfort that results from holding two conflicting beliefs, values, or attitudes". An article titled *Cognitive Dissonance* on the *Psychology Today* website tells us that, interestingly enough, among the examples Festinger used to illustrate his theory were doomsday cult members and their explanations for why the world had not ended as they had anticipated, the point being that rather than accept the world's continuing existence as evidence that their theory may be flawed they instead post-rationalised ways in which this could be explained without forcing them to give up their basic belief that the end of days was nonetheless imminent. We are all prone to experience cognitive dissonance in our everyday life at any time when our actions run contrary to some inner belief or value, such as telling a lie and then feeling uncomfortable because we see ourself as being fundamentally an honest person. Post-rationalisation helps us to square the psychological circle, for example by coming up with a rational explanation for why the lie was justified in the specific circumstances.

Of course, post-rationalisation is not the only way to resolve dissonance: another option might be to change our own behaviours or beliefs. The same *Psychology Today* entry offers two examples: "a man who learns that his eating habits raise his risk of illness feels the tension between his preferred behaviour and the idea that he could be in danger. He might ease this feeling by telling himself that the health warning is exaggerated or, more productively, by deciding to take action to change his behaviour. If a woman reads that her favourite politician has done something immoral, she could conclude that the charges have been invented by his enemies – or, instead, rethink her support".

The point is that post-rationalisation can help us to restore psychological harmony in cases where we are torn in different directions. The obvious potential pitfall is that we become too good at using, or too ready to use, our powers of reason to invent post hoc justifications for actions or beliefs which are inherently wrong or inappropriate when we would in fact be better served by changing these underlying actions or beliefs instead.

To conclude: we each have the precious gift of reason, to a greater or lesser extent, and it is up to us to make best use of it to help us make personal choices which bear the rational scrutiny both of our own "inner voice" and of other people we consider to be relevant. As Shakespeare's Hamlet says, in a quote from Act IV Scene IV lines 33-29 which forms the epigraph to Pinker's book:

"What is a man,
If his chief good and market of his time
Be but to sleep and feed? A beast, no more.
Sure he that made us with such large discourse,
Looking before and after, gave us not
That capability and godlike reason
To fust in us unus'd".

Emotion

Emotion might be defined as how we "feel", as opposed to what we "think", this being the product of reason. The *Cambridge English Dictionary* definition is: "a strong feeling such as love or anger, or strong feelings in general". *Oxford Languages*, which provides Google's English dictionary, offers: "a strong feeling deriving from one's circumstances, mood, or relationships with others...(an) instinctive or intuitive feeling as distinguished from reasoning or knowledge".

Emotions impact us in two important ways. First, stating the obvious, they colour our very experience of existence: what it feels like to be alive. Second, our emotions play a crucial role in determining how we behave, often without our conscious, rational mind being aware.

As so often, there is a balance to be struck. If we surrender entirely to our emotions then we are likely to have a vivid experience of life but also potentially be subject to extreme highs and lows and mood swings. We are also likely to make impulsive decisions, some of which we may later regret. On the other hand, to deny our emotions would be to deny our very humanity, and would surely dilute our capacity to enjoy our life. We may also sometimes find ourself over-thinking decisions, denying our instincts when in reality these might have an important role to play.

The solution, clearly, is to strive for some kind of "Goldilocks" ideal, in which we experience life in all its richness whilst also tempering our passions with the judicious application of reason, where appropriate.

In any case, it is easy to see how emotions might confer selective advantage in an evolutionary sense. They help us to make quick decisions, often using limited data, in a world where speed and efficiency were surely at least as important to our ancestors as they are to us today. Emotions are also vital to the way in which we engage with our fellow humans and even with ourself, and are therefore pivotal to all the main themes in the remainder of this book. For example, emotions serve to regulate, and reinforce, sociability, the focus of Chapter 3. One important role emotions play within the social sphere is to help anchor and give shape to a moral sense, the focus of Chapter 4. And what has come to be called "EQ" (or "Emotional Intelligence") is increasingly recognised as being as or more important than "IQ" ("Intelligence") in predicting success in life, admittedly begging the question of how "success" is most appropriately measured, a topics we will address in Chapter 5.

The classical view was that a discrete number of emotions exist, and are common to all humans. Notably, in the early 1960s the American psychologist Paul Ekman proposed six "universal" emotions: disgust, sadness, happiness, fear, anger and surprise. Ekman's approach has informed much of the discussion ever since, with many alternative suggestions for how best to define the canonical list. For example, in the 1990s Ekman himself suggested adding an additional 11 emotions: amusement, contempt, contentment, embarrassment, excitement, guilt, pride in achievement, relief, satisfaction, sensory pleasure, and shame.

Each emotion was thought to be accompanied by its own physiological "fingerprint", for example a particular facial expression. Lisa Feldman Barrett explains this idea, on p3 of *How Emotions are Made*: "each emotion is supposed to have a distinct pattern of physical changes, roughly like a fingerprint. Each time you grasp a doorknob, the fingerprints that you leave behind may vary depending on the firmness of your grip, how slippery the surface is, or how warm and pliable your skin is at that moment. Nevertheless, your fingerprints look similar enough each time to identify you uniquely. The 'fingerprint' of an emotion is likewise assumed to be similar enough from one instance to the next, and in one person to the next, regardless of age, sex, personality, or culture. In a laboratory, scientists should be able to tell whether someone is sad or happy or anxious just by looking at physical measurements of a person's face, body, and brain".

As we have already seen, however, Barrett rejects the classical view, arguing instead for what she calls the "theory of constructed emotion". Essentially, she proposes that our brain constructs our emotions in much the same way that it constructs our representations of external reality: by applying learned "concepts" to the data it receives about the state of our body, adjusted for whatever meaning it may perceive in the prevailing external environment.

This means that a given stimulus and physical state are capable of producing very different emotional interpretations, as Barrett describes on pp30-1: "an emotion is your brain's *creation* (author's emphasis) of what your bodily sensations mean, in relation to what is going on around you in the world...I call this explanation *the theory of constructed emotion* (again, author's emphasis): in every waking moment, your brain uses past experience, organised as concepts, to guide your actions and give your sensations meaning. When the concepts involved are emotion concepts, your brain constructs instances of emotion...if a swarm of buzzing bees is squeezing underneath your front door while your heart is pounding in your chest, your brain's prior knowledge of stinging insects gives meaning to the sensations from your body and to the sights, sounds, smells, and other sensations from the world, simulating the swarm, the door, and an instance of fear. The exact same bodily sensations in another context, like watching a fascinating film about the hidden lives of bees, might construct an instance of excitement. Or if you see a picture of a smiling cartoon bee in a children's book, reminding you of a beloved niece whom you took to a Disney movie, you could mentally construct the bee, the niece, and an instance of pleasant nostalgia".

Emotional concepts allow us to experience the range of emotions that we do, engaging the constructive machinery of the brain as Barrett explains on p31: "emotions are not reactions to the world. You are not a passive receiver of sensory input but an active constructor of your emotions. From sensory input and past experience, your brain constructs meaning and prescribes action. If you didn't have concepts that represent your past experience, all your sensory inputs would just be noise. You wouldn't know what the sensations are, what caused them, nor how to behave to deal with them. With concepts, your brain makes meaning of sensation, and sometimes that meaning is an emotion".

Barrett observes that two things are therefore critical to regulating our emotional life: our "body budget" and our repertoire of emotional concepts. On pp176-7: "the most basic thing you can do to master your emotions, in fact, is to keep your body budget in good shape. Remember, your interoceptive network labours day and night, issuing predictions to maintain a healthy budget, and this process is the origin of your affective feelings (pleasantness, unpleasantness, arousal, and calmness). If you want to feel good, then your brain's predictions about your heart rate, breathing, blood pressure, temperature, hormones, metabolism, and so on, must be calibrated to your body's actual needs. If they aren't, and your body budget gets out of whack, then you're going to feel crappy no matter what self-help tips you follow".

And on p180: "emotional intelligence is better characterised in terms of concepts. Suppose you knew only two emotion concepts, 'Feeling Awesome' and 'Feeling Crappy'. Whenever you experienced emotion or perceived someone else as emotional, you could categorise only with this broad brush. Such a person cannot be very emotionally intelligent. In contrast, if you could distinguish finer meanings within 'Awesome' (happy, content, thrilled, relaxed, joyful, hopeful, inspired, prideful, adoring, grateful, blissful...), and fifty shades of 'Crappy' (angry, aggravated, alarmed, spiteful, grumpy, remorseful, gloomy, mortified, uneasy, dread-ridden, resentful, afraid, envious, woeful, melancholy...), your brain would have many more options for predicting, categorising, and perceiving emotion, providing you with the tools for more flexible and functional responses. You could predict and categorise your sensations more efficiently, and better tailor your actions to your environment".

Barrett goes on to suggest, on p181, that the best way to expand our personal repertoire of emotional concepts is through language: "perhaps the easiest way to gain concepts is to learn new words. You probably never thought about learning words as a path to greater emotional health, but it follows directly from the neuroscience of construction. Words seed your concepts, concepts drive your predictions, predictions regulate your body budget, and your body budget determines how you feel. Therefore, the more finely grained your vocabulary, the more precisely your predicting brain can calibrate your budget to your body's needs".

We'll end our discussion of emotion with two observations. First, the theory of constructed emotion proposes that we literally create our own emotions, through the meaning that our brain ascribes to its representations of internal and external data. This leads to the important conclusion that "mindset matters", a topic we will explore further towards the end of this chapter. Suffice to say for now that how we interpret something can affect both how we feel about it, and even the physiological impact it has on us.

Of course, we don't always have conscious control over our interpretation, and there must always be some residual connection between our framing and the laws of physics: to paraphrase an earlier example, imagining a speeding train to be a marshmallow won't make it any less lethal when it hits us. Still, to the extent that we can, framing an event or experience constructively can make a meaningful difference to our emotional and potentially our physical reaction.

Second, notwithstanding the importance and power of reason, there are times when it is best just to surrender to the power of the emotional moment, especially when the emotions involved are positive or uplifting in some way.

The English Romantic poet John Keats was a strong advocate of this approach, recommending in an 1817 letter to his brothers the concept of "negative capability" in which reason is explicitly to be avoided in the pursuit of, in this case, poetic beauty. Keats defines "negative capability" as: "when a man is capable of being in uncertainties, mysteries, doubts, without any irritable reaching after fact and reason...with a great poet the sense of Beauty overcomes every other consideration, or rather obliterates all consideration".

To be clear, Keats does not suggest this is the appropriate response in every circumstance. We should simply recognise that there can sometimes be situations when words really do fail and we should just revel in the intensity of the emotion itself. Keats embodies this perfectly in the closing lines to his 1817 poem *Ode on a Grecian Urn*, concluding that, at least when contemplating the urn in question:

"Beauty is truth, truth beauty, - that is all
Ye know on earth, and all ye need to know".

Language

Language is critical to consciousness, to the extent that it is hard to imagine how sophisticated reasoning could happen without it. As the Austrian philosopher Ludwig Wittgenstein famously observed in his snappily-titled book *Tractatus Logico-Philosophicus*, published in 1921: "the limits of my language are the limits of my world".

This is not to imply that words alone are sufficient to capture the full richness of human communication. In the 1970s American psychologist Albert Mehrabian published his seminal findings that when an individual is speaking, the listener will typically focus only 7% of his or her attention on the words spoken, 38% on the manner of their delivery (the tone of voice, the emphasis or accentuation, and so on), and 55% on the speaker's facial expressions and "body language". How we say something clearly matters at least as much as what we actually say.

Still, words play a vital role. We saw earlier from Tomasello that the development of sophisticated, conventionalised language was an important factor in the evolution of human cognition; from Kahneman and others that how a choice is framed, even at the level of the specific words used, can have an important effect on what we eventually decide; and from Barrett how our personal repertoire of emotional concepts, defined in words, has a major bearing on how rich an emotional life we experience. And words obviously play the dominant role when it comes to any form of written communication, as well as to the introspective conversations we have with our own "little voice".

Words are on the one hand remarkable for their range and expressiveness, allowing us to capture and communicate complex thoughts and feelings on an almost infinite variety of topics; and at the same time imprecise, at best just a crude representation of the internal and external worlds that we seek to describe. Words are also ultimately arbitrary. "A rose by any other name would smell as sweet", as someone once wrote.

In *Through the Language Glass*, the Israeli linguist Guy Deutscher makes the case that language shapes our very perception of reality, so that two people experiencing the same phenomenon may have qualitatively different experiences of it if they are using different languages.

He gives many examples, but just one will serve to illustrate the point. On p210 Deutscher describes research showing that languages which assign genders to inanimate objects thereby subtly influence users' associations with those objects. For instance, bridges are feminine in German and masculine in Spanish, and the data show that: "German speakers tended to describe bridges as beautiful, elegant, fragile, peaceful, pretty and slender; Spanish speakers as big, dangerous, long, strong, sturdy, towering".

As an aside, Deutscher also challenges the literal truth of Wittgenstein's claim that "the limits of my language are the limits of my world", on the grounds that abstract concepts for which a language may lack a specific word can nonetheless be comprehensible to speakers of that language. He gives the concept of "schadenfreude" as one of several examples; it may of course also be argued that such a concept is accessible only because English possesses a set of words which allow it to be described, even if it does not have a single-word equivalent.

In any case, Deutscher's central conclusion is that the language we use to describe our world is fundamental to how we perceive it. His parting shot, on p232, is to suggest that differences in language may offer a more compelling explanation of differences between social groups than do underlying genes, which tend to show only superficial differecnes as we saw earlier: "the explanation for cognitive differences between ethnic groups has shifted over the last two centuries, from anatomy to culture...in the 19th century, it was generally assumed that there were significant inequalities between the hereditary, mental faculties of different races, and that these biological inequalities were the main reason for their varying accomplishments. One of the jewels in the crown of the 20th century was the recognition of the fundamental unity of mankind in all that concerns its cognitive endowment. So nowadays, we no longer look primarily to the genes to explain variations in mental characteristics among ethnic groups...but in the 21st-century, we are beginning to appreciate the differences in thinking that are imprinted by cultural conventions and, in particular, by speaking in different tongues".

Even within a particular language, specific words and phrases can be confusingly elastic, so that the same word in a given language may mean something very different to different people. The famous aphorism "divided by a common language" applies much more broadly than just to the lack of linguistic understanding between Americans and Brits. And one of the major challenges posed by the ambiguities inherent in any language is to communicate clearly, so that the meaning we intend when we "transmit" is the same meaning that is understood by those who are tuned to "receive".

Some words have evolved to be particularly elastic, and it is interesting to note that these include several with strong, but different, meanings in both a religious and secular context. To give a few examples:

- *"spiritual"*: either (a) relating to the divine, that is to say supernatural or (b) connecting with our inner consciousness in a purely secular sense, in ways which trigger deep emotions and can often transcend language e.g. contemplating a natural wonder or work of art.
- *"soul"*: either (a) our divine essence, separate from our mortal bodies and itself immortal or (b) our sense of secular "self" and, possibly, secular spirituality.
- *"divine"*: either (a) relating to God or another supernatural entity or (b) particularly lovely.
- *"religious"*: either (a) actively professing a specific religion or (b) a strong advocate of a particular, possibly secular, belief.

- *"destiny"*: either (a) a pre-determined outcome, possibly ordained by a Higher Authority or (b) the way things happened to turn out, which may seem to have been inevitable when viewed with the benefit of hindsight, but in reality was not.

Despite, or perhaps partly because of, its limitations, language can help us to connect with our deeper emotions, beyond the purely literal meaning of the words themselves. Said another way, language can open a window into our "soul", in a strictly secular sense. We might call this poetic insight, and the ability to convey it is surely one of the defining characteristics of "great" literature, not to mention "great" drama, film and even non-verbal art forms such as music and the visual arts.

There are many literary examples, but two will suffice. First, the celebrated opening lines of Tolstoy's *Anna Karenina* "Happy families are all alike; every unhappy family is unhappy in its own way". We may or may not agree with the literal meaning of these words. But the literal meaning is not the central point. Rather the lines set a powerfully sombre emotional tone, which subsequently permeates the entire novel. They also serve to cast an almost theatrical spotlight on the unique predicament and personality of Anna herself, in her own unhappy marriage, even though we have obviously not yet met her in the fictional flesh.

The second example is Ernest Hemingway's famous response to the challenge of telling a story in six words: "For Sale: baby shoes, never worn". The emotions he evokes travel far beyond the literal words on the page.

Finally, the challenge with language is not only to decide what specific words to use, but also how to put them together into combinations which convey the intended message clearly. As Chaucer's Host advises in *The*

Clerke's Tale, in an exhortation which resonates across more than 600 years:

*"Speketh so pleyn at this tyme, we yow preye;
That we may understonde what ye seye".*

The UK police force of the early 20th century set the bar even higher, as captured by this passage from *The Times* columnist Matthew Parris, in an article dated 31 March 2021: "Tom Windsor, HM Chief Inspector of Constabulary, sends me the most marvellous extract from an HMIC note...about writing well. The advice quotes from what it calls 'the golden rule of drafting', set down by the First Parliamentary Council in 1902: 'it is not enough to attain a degree of precision which a person reading in good faith can understand. It is necessary, as far as possible, to attain that degree of precision which a person reading in bad faith cannot misunderstand'".

The most practical advice on how to do this comes from George Orwell, the English novelist who might plausibly be said to have taken the quest for clarity and simplicity of expression more seriously than any other writer, at least one writing in English. In his 1946 essay *Politics and the English Language* Orwell offers the following sage counsel:

1. Never use a metaphor, simile, or other figure of speech which you are used to seeing in print (my note: his reasoning is that if you are used to seeing it in print, it will almost certainly be a tired cliché).

2. Never use a long word where a short one will do.

3. If it is possible to cut a word out, always cut it out.

4. Never use the passive where you can use the active.

5. Never use a foreign phrase, a scientific word, or a jargon word if you can think of an everyday English equivalent.

6. Break any of these rules sooner than say anything outright barbarous.

Readers will judge, I fear harshly, how far I have myself been able to follow this guidance.

Empathy and Theory of Mind

Amongst the most striking features of human consciousness are the capacity for empathy, that is the ability to experience the emotions of another being as though they were our own; and the ability to take on the cognitive perspective of another being, the technical term for which is "Theory of Mind". Both these capacities help us to make more effective choices, particularly as these relate to our interactions with other people.

The neurological basis for empathy is a set of "mirror neurons" in the brain, which as the name implies literally enable us to mirror another person's feelings and emotional state. And empathy is the faculty which ultimately enables us to connect and sustain close relationships with other individuals. *Psychology Today* summarises, in an article titled *6 Things You Need to Know About Empathy* posted on 23 January 2017: "Empathy. It's the bedrock of intimacy and close connection; in its absence, relationships remain shallow, defined largely by mutual interests or shared activities".

Our capacity for empathy is also vital to our lived human experience. For example, empathy enables us to appreciate fiction, by helping us to put ourself in the emotional shoes of, and therefore care about, the characters who populate a particular story, movie, TV drama, stage play, video game and so on.

A capacity for empathy is hard-wired into our brain through our genes, although as so often "nature" gives us a propensity which then needs to be reinforced by "nurture" if whatever latent capacity we possess is to be developed to its full potential. In an article for *Psychology Today* titled *The Four Moral Emotions* and posted online on 15 November 2009, Ilana Simons reinforces the importance of early childhood experiences in laying the foundation for a fully-developed capacity for empathy later in life: "infants learn to identify and regulate their emotions through successful dyadic interactions with their caretakers, primarily their mothers. An attuned mother who's receptive to her child's needs and cues is one who permits her baby to thrive and develop emotionally. By having his or her emotional states recognised and responded to, the groundwork is laid not just for the child's sense of self but sense of other. In time, that seed grows into empathy and the capacity for intimate connection".

However, it is typically not the case that we feel empathy consistently for all our fellow humans. Rather, we experience empathy most strongly for those to whom we already feel emotionally closest; and much less, potentially not at all, for strangers, especially those we perceive to be significantly different from ourself in some way. This is the psychological underpinning for our tendency to categorise people into "In groups" and "Out groups", with markedly different implications for our moral instincts towards the members of each group, a tendency we will explore further in chapters 3 and, particularly, 4.

As an example, a 2013 study led by James Coan, psychology professor at the University of Virginia (the full study appears in the August 2013 edition of *Social Cognitive and Affective Neuroscience*) found that fMRI brain scans showed similar brain response patterns when respondents were exposed to the threat of a (mild) electrical shock to themselves and separately to a friend. Coan comments: "the finding shows the brain's remarkable capacity to model self to others: that people close to us become a part of ourselves, and that is not just metaphor or poetry, it's very real." However, Coan's study did not find the same result when the threat was to a stranger. On the contrary, this provoked relatively little activity in the relevant areas of the subjects' brains.

A similar study conducted at the University of Zurich also concluded that we feel empathy more strongly for people whom we perceive to be members of the same group as us than we do for people we perceive to be strangers. In addition, it showed that relatively limited (positive) exposure to an individual stranger changes the picture considerably, leading the authors to conclude that empathy can be "learned", in the sense that if we first have the capacity for empathy then we can learn to extend it to individuals for whom we do not initially feel it, by the simple process of getting to know them better. The study was conducted by Grit Hein, Philippe Tobler, Jan Engelmann and Marius Vollberg) and reviewed online in *Science News* in a post called *Empathy with strangers can be learned,* dated 21 December 2015.

Finally, it is not the case that all humans have an equal capacity for empathy. For example, in Chapter 3 of *The Pattern Seekers* Simon Baron-Cohen describes the results of the UK Brain Study, in which 600,000 people were asked to complete questionnaires describing their personal profile with respect to empathy and, separately, systemising, which as you might recall is the capacity to apply *if-and-then* causal reasoning.

The researchers found a classic bell-curve distribution for both capacities, meaning that for empathy specifically some people exhibited a relatively high level, an equal number were low, and the statistical majority were clustered in the middle. Looking at empathy and systemising together, about 34% of the population exhibited relatively high empathy but relatively low systemising; 36% the reverse; and about 30% were balanced between the two.

We saw in the previous chapter that there are some cognitive differences on average between men and women and interestingly enough, 43% of women exhibited high empathy and low systemising but only 25% of men did; only 28% of women showed low empathy and high systemising whereas 44% of men did; and roughly 30% of both women and men were in the final, balanced, group. Within this, 3% of women were classified as showing "extreme empathy" compared to 1% of men; and 2% of women were classified as "extreme systemisers" compared with 4% of men.

Baron-Cohen explains these differences, concluding that there is, of course, a genetic component, and that experience also likely plays a role. He also quotes separate research identifying a correlation with the levels of prenatal testosterone to which a foetus is exposed in the womb, declaring on p57 that: "testosterone levels in the womb were associated with *both* (author's emphasis) systemising and empathising, but in opposite directions". He mentions on p54 that "male fetuses produce at least twice as much of this hormone as female fetuses do during prenatal life", and it seems that the higher the exposure, the more likely that the individual will develop a brain which is higher in systemising and also lower in empathy, and vice versa; the implication being that there is at least some level of biological trade-off between the two. This has implications beyond gender, of course: in general, to be strong on systemising is to have a higher probability of being low on empathising; and the converse is also true; notwithstanding that a (significant) minority of people exhibit a balanced profile.

American psychologist Jonathan Haidt highlights the specific if somewhat extreme case of psychopaths, on p72 of his 2012 book *The Righteous Mind*. Psychopaths are people whose capacity for empathy is severely restricted, or altogether missing, and whose behaviour tends to be characterised by high levels of egocentricity and impulsiveness: "roughly one in a hundred men (and many fewer women) are psychopaths. Most are not violent, but the ones who are commit nearly half of the most serious crimes, such as serial murder, serial rape, and the killing of police officers. Robert Hare, a leading researcher, defines psychopathy by two sets of features. There's the unusual stuff that psychopaths *do* – impulsive antisocial behaviour, beginning in childhood – and there are the moral emotions that psychopaths *lack*. They feel no compassion, guilt, shame, or even embarrassment, which makes it easy for them to lie, and to hurt family, friends, and animals". Haidt makes an explicit connection between empathy and feeling a sense of morality, a theme we will return to in Chapter 4.

Strikingly, psychopaths may not feel empathy, but they are typically otherwise cognitively normal and may often possess a superficial charm, which can mask their capacity for anti-social behaviour. Baron-Cohen describes this as having strong "cognitive" as distinct from "affective" empathy, on p68 of *The Pattern Seekers*. We might also say that they often retain a well-developed capacity for "Theory of Mind", which is to say that they can think their way into another person's metaphorical shoes even if they cannot share their emotions.

Theory of Mind is defined by American biologist John Medina on p67 of his 2008 book *Brain Rules* as: "the ability to understand the interior motivations of someone else and the ability to construct a predictable 'theory of how their mind works' based on that knowledge". American author Kendra Cherry offers an even more succinct definition: "thinking about thinking", in an article titled *How the Theory of Mind Helps Us Understand Others*, published online on *verywellmind* on 7 April 2020. Cherry offers the "Sally-Anne test" as an example of the kind of "false belief" test used by psychologists to assess an individual's (typically a child's) Theory of Mind capacity:

- Sally has a basket while Anne has a box
- Sally places a marble in her basket and then leaves the room
- While she is gone, Anne takes the marble from the basket and puts it in the box
- When Sally returns, children who have watched this scenario are asked where they think Sally will look for the marble

The correct answer is obviously that Sally will look in her basket. But to conclude this it is necessary to understand that Sally holds a "false belief" about the location of the marble, which the observer knows is in reality now in Anne's box. It is necessary to think about what Sally herself believes rather than the actual reality known to the observer. This may seem mundane, but in fact it is a remarkable cognitive skill which other species do not possess, as far as we know. It only seems mundane because as adult, or even adolescent, humans, it has already become second nature to most of us.

In the same article Cherry reinforces why Theory of Mind is such a big deal, especially for a highly-social species such as humans: "Theory of Mind allows people to infer the intentions of others, as well as to think about what's going on in someone else's head, including hopes, fears, beliefs and expectations. Social interactions can be complex, and misunderstandings can make them even more fraught. By being able to develop accurate ideas about what other people are thinking, we are better able to respond accordingly...in order to interact with others, it is important to be able to understand their mental states and to think about how those mental states might influence their actions".

Cherry explains how Theory of Mind is learned progressively, starting from about the age of 3. It is typically largely absent in children younger than this, who are characterised by ego-centricity. The learning curve is steep until about the age of 5, and continues at a gentler pace through adolescence and into early adulthood. Some of us who have passed beyond even that life stage may feel that the learning doesn't stop there.

Finally, Cherry lists the 5 main stages of Theory of Mind development, starting with the easiest, which is to say the component we learn first:

1. The understanding that the reasons why people might want something (i.e. desires) may differ from one person to the next.
2. The understanding that people can have different beliefs about the same thing or situation.
3. The understanding that people may not comprehend or have the knowledge that something is true.
4. The understanding that people can hold false beliefs about the world (obviously this is of particular relevance to this book).
5. The understanding that people can have hidden emotions, or that they may act one way while feeling another way.

The ability, and need, to think and feel our way into the metaphorical shoes of others also underpins our predilection for stories. Rosenberg describes how stories are central to the way in which make sense of the world, on p8 of *The Atheist's Guide to Reality*: "we are suckers for a good story – a description of events in the form of a plot with characters driven by motives. If information doesn't come in story form, we have trouble understanding it, remembering it, and believing it". For Rosenberg this is not necessarily a good thing, as he explains on p8 and then 14-5: "unfortunately for real science...(its) explanations never come in the form of stories...real science isn't a set of stories...and it can't be packaged into stories either. Real science is much more a matter of blueprints, recipes, formulas, wiring diagrams, systems of equations, and geometrical proofs. That's why we have a hard time following it, understanding it, accepting it, applying it, or even remembering it". We might of course counter that stories, or at least a clear narrative, might be exactly what is needed if science is to make its mysteries more accessible to the non-initiated.

In any case, on pp10-12 of *The Atheist's Guide* Rosenberg makes explicit the link between Theory of Mind and our focus on stories, in terms which echo Tomasello's thoughts about the evolution of group intentionality: "our brain was shaped by natural selection to take on board very early in life, or maybe even innately, a set of guesses about how other people operate...a theory of mind is part of nature's quick and dirty solution to a huge challenge for our species' survival – a 'design problem' that faced our hominin ancestors over the last few million years. Given our puny size, our conspicuous lack of speed or strength, we would have been easy pickings for African megafauna (lions and tigers and bears, oh my). The only way we were going to survive was through cooperation, coordination, and collaboration: warning each other and ganging up to protect ourselves or chase the predators away so we could scavenge their kills. That requires the sort of rudimentary ability to predict other people's behaviour that a theory of mind provides...when our ancestors lived in small family groups, predicting what family members were going to do made the difference between life and death and eventually between feast and famine. Later, when populations became large enough so that you were meeting strangers, there had to be further selection for the ability to predict behaviour. In the evolutionary past, if other people could pose a threat, then you needed to know what they wanted to do to you so that you could prevent them from doing it. If other people could do something nice for you, you needed to figure out how to motivate them to do it...long ago, these facts about the benefits and threats people pose to each other put further selective pressure on refining the theory of mind into a practice of plotting out other people's actions, to figure out their motives, their desires and goals, and their beliefs about how to realise them. There was, in effect, selective pressure on our ancestors that resulted in their telling themselves 'whodunnit' stories".

And on pp13-4: "humans tend to see everything in nature as organised by agents with motives, often malevolent ones. We are all natural-born conspiracy theorists...that's why we remember narratives and think of them as naturally easy to understand without any special knowledge or information. We all have a strong incentive to force anything we need to remember into a story with a plot".

Memory

Memory is so critical to our ability to function as a conscious being that the American psychologists Yana Weinstein and Megan Sumeracki, with collaborator Oliver Caviglioli, claim on p64 of their 2019 book *Understanding How We Learn*: "we would argue that *everything you do requires memory in some form or another*" (their emphasis).

Memory has tremendous practical value, of course, enabling us to operate day-to-day, for example by remembering whether we have or have not accomplished a certain task; to recall particular objects and people, including important details such as faces, names and personalities; and to learn from experience more broadly in a multitude of ways. Memory is core to our sense of identity and "self"; and also to our capacity to imagine the future, since it is mainly our recollection of experiences from the past which enable us to conceptualise possible alternative states which may be yet to come. In a similar way, memory is crucial to our ability to imagine more generally, since again our imagination functions by drawing on images and concepts which are familiar from our past, even if we then modify these impressions in interesting, possibly scary, ways.

It will come as no surprise, though, that our memory is as prone to fallibility as other aspects of our consciousness. And because memory plays such a critical role in enabling other cognitive functions, we will take some time to explore the topic.

The starting point is that memory is generally categorised into "explicit", or "declarative" on the one hand, that is memories which at least in principle we are able to summon to our conscious mind; and "implicit", or "procedural" on the other, which is to say memories of which we are not consciously aware, for example, how to move our fingers to grip something.

It is possible for "declarative" memories to become "procedural", usually as a result of repetition, examples being learning how to ride a bike, drive a car, swing a tennis racquet or golf club, and so on. And this distinction is important when we consider the impact of each type of memory on how we exercise personal choice. Calling on declarative memories by definition engages our conscious mind and is therefore compatible with and in a sense requires that we make a choice; whereas the main feature of procedural memories is that they are unconscious, promoting behaviour which is largely or entirely automatic.

As we have seen, embracing our capacity to exercise conscious choice is at the heart of living authentically. But this does not mean that engaging declarative memory is always preferable, because it requires considerably more mental effort and our mental resources are finite. It can therefore be in our best interests to "proceduralise" (or routinise) some decisions. This may sometimes also lead to more effective outcomes, as UK journalist Matthew Syed explains in an article titled *My battle with the biscuits shows willpower alone just isn't enough*, published in *The Sunday Times* on 22 January 2023: "I have discovered that willpower is a bit, well, overrated when it comes to resisting temptation. We do not need will; we need habits...it is remarkable that about 45% of human actions – and many of the most important ones – are not conscious but habitual. Think of brushing your teeth. Studies have shown that most people do not think about brushing their teeth at all, either in the build-up to the act, or even during the act itself. Rather, they are thinking about what they will talk about in tomorrow's meeting or have for breakfast...the reason is that the action has been repeated so often that it has become 'proceduralised'; it is encoded in a different part of the brain. It's a bit like driving to a familiar location. When you drive to your child's school, do you consciously work out which way to go? Or do you arrive at the car park without noticing that you have gone through a succession of complicated actions – using the mirror; giving right to oncoming traffic – to get there?...life can be difficult for those who haven't cultivated good habits: they have to summon the resolve each time, which is a daily battle that is treacherously easy to lose...the point is not that willpower is irrelevant, but that we have more of it available for the big battles that will always hit us in life if we can outsource the little, repeated stuff to habit".

Syed's "battle with the biscuits", by the way, ended with him concluding that it was more effective for him not to buy them in the first place rather than have them sitting in the cupboard inviting temptation. Which is not quite the same thing as invoking procedural memory. Still, the broader point stands: using declarative memory requires effort and is best focused on those occasions which merit expending it.

In any case even our explicit, declarative memories do not typically reside in our conscious mind for long. Rather, they can be segmented into 3 types:

• *sensory memory*, whereby we recall things in the immediate moment, but usually retain the information for less than a second.

• *short-term (also called "working") memory*. This allows us to recall information for a slightly longer period, of up to a few seconds. However, our capacity is quite limited. Most people can store only between 4 and 8 discrete items of information in this way. Interestingly how our mind defines an item of information is somewhat elastic. For example, most of us will find it easier to hold a telephone number in our working memory if we segment it into say 3 X 3-digit numbers rather than one long number, or a series of individual digits (e.g. 653-487-500, rather than 653487500, or 6-5-3-4-8-7-5-0-0).

• *long-term memory*. This stores truly enormous quantities of data, sometimes for our whole life once the experience has happened and the memory has formed. How and even where these memories are stored is not fully understood. It seems there is no specific area of the brain which acts as any kind of human "hard drive", although the hippocampus is important for the initial processing and encoding of the data to form a memory in the first place. Individual memories seem to be stored as connections between groups of neurons, which may themselves be distributed throughout the entire brain. Much of the activity associated with selecting and embedding memories seems to happen as we sleep, specifically during the non-REM portion of sleep (this is described in detail by Matthew Walker on pp109-120 of *Why We Sleep*: we will hear from him shortly about the importance of sleep to our consciousness overall). Frequently accessing a particular memory, say by thinking often of a specific telephone number, house address or life event, strengthens the neural pathways with which it is associated, and hence makes the item or event being remembered stronger and easier to recall. The reverse effect is also true: memories that we do not access frequently are likely to weaken and eventually disappear, in the sense that there comes a point when they defy conscious recall. Memories with a strong emotional weight tend to be more long-lasting and accessible than those with less.

On p251 of *Metazoa* the Australian philosopher Peter Godfrey-Smith proposes a somewhat modified categorisation of memory types, highlighting what he calls "episodic memory" as being particularly prone to fallibility: "psychology distinguishes between four or five main kinds of memory. Semantic memory is memory of facts – Paris is in France. Procedural memory retains the ability to do things – how to ride a bicycle. Episodic memory is memory of experienced events. Those forms of memory can persist for the long-term. There is also 'working' memory, the momentary retention of ideas and images as you manipulate them. Episodic memory is usually taken to have two main features: it is memory of particular events rather than generalities, and memory that is experienced or relived. A large and sometimes disturbing scientific literature describes how unreliable human memory is in many circumstances, and episodic memories can seem especially 'cooked up'".

This description leads us to perhaps the most important source of memory fallibility: like our consciousness more generally the process by which we store, and retrieve, long-term memories is reconstructive rather than being a photographic record of past reality. We do not take an objective "screenshot" of an experience or event and then retain it in a pure, unadulterated form. Rather what we store is our own subjective representation, which our brain subsequently reconstructs in order to bring it back into conscious awareness. Weinstein and Sumeracki explain, on p74 of *Understanding How We Learn*: "long-term memory is often talked about in terms of a four-stage model: encoding, consolidation, storage, and retrieval (Nader & Hardt, 2009). If a memory is never encoded, then it was never created in the first place, so there is nothing to retrieve...just because a memory is encoded, however, does not mean that it will be recallable later; it needs to be consolidated. And, consolidation of a memory is not a one-off event. When the memory is retrieved, it is reconstructed, re-activated, and reconsolidated (Sara, 2000)". On pp67-8 they explain what they mean by "reconstructive": "this is a key concept in long-term memory: the idea that every time you retrieve a memory, you are actually changing it...every time you tell the same story, it comes out a little more polished, with a few embellishing details added, or a few boring ones removed. The memory itself – not just the story – is changing, so that the next time you retrieve the memory of that event, it will be more like the story you last told, rather than the way it really was. Memory is reconstructive in nature, and every time a memory is activated, it is altered".

Daniel Gilbert provides an example of reconstructive memory in action, on pp79-80 of *Stumbling on Happiness*: "...the elaborate tapestry of our experience is not stored in memory – at least not in its entirety. Rather, it is compressed for storage by first being reduced to a few critical threads, such as a summary phrase ('dinner was disappointing') or a small set of key features (tough steak, corked wine, snotty waiter). Later, when we want to remember our experience, our brains quickly reweave the tapestry by fabricating – not by actually retrieving – the bulk of the information that we experience as a memory. This fabrication happens so quickly and effortlessly that we have the illusion...that the entire thing was in our heads the entire time...but it wasn't, and that fact can be easily demonstrated. For example, volunteers in one study were shown a series of slides depicting a red car as it cruises towards a give way sign, turns right, and then knocks over a pedestrian. After seeing the slides, some of the volunteers (the no-question group) were not asked any questions, and the remaining volunteers (the question group) were. The question these volunteers were asked was this: 'Did another car pass the red car while it was stopped at the stop sign?' Next, all the volunteers were shown two pictures – one in which the red car was approaching a give way sign and one in which the red car was approaching a stop sign - and were asked to point to the picture they had actually seen. Now, if the volunteers had stored their experience in memory, then they should have pointed to the picture of the car approaching the give way sign, and indeed, more than 90 percent of the volunteers in the no-question group did just that. But 80 percent of the volunteers in the question group pointed to the picture of the car approaching a stop sign. Clearly, the question changed the volunteers' memories of the earlier experience, which is precisely what one would expect if their brains were *reweaving* their experiences – and precisely what one would *not* expect if their brains were *retrieving* their experiences...this general finding – that information acquired *after* an event alters memory *of* the event – has been replicated so many times in so many different laboratory and field settings that it has left most scientists convinced of two things. First, the act of remembering involves 'filling in' details that were not actually stored; and second, we generally cannot tell when we are doing this, because filling in happens quickly and unconsciously" (author's emphases throughout).

Gilbert points out that the information our memory "chooses" to store is not necessarily that which is most representative of our everyday life. On the contrary: "the *least likely experience* is often the *most likely memory* (author's emphases)...most Americans know precisely where they were on the morning of 11 September 2001, but not on the morning of 10 September".

And there is strong evidence that we are inherently suggestible. For example, if we are repeatedly told, or repeatedly tell ourself, that a certain event happened in a certain way, or a certain person behaved in a particular manner, we may start to treat this narrative as a personal "memory", even though it may have no basis in historical reality and therefore cannot have been logged in our original memory of the event. Once internalised, however, this narrative, or "quasi-memory", becomes subjectively real to us, so that it may appear to be just as authentic as any of our other memories. We may be genuinely convinced that our version of whatever incident occurred is "right", and others who have a different recollection are "wrong". Of course, if other people were present they will also have memories which are subjective to them, and which may likewise be fallible in one way or another.

This is why conflicting witness testimony in a legal trial can happen even when all parties genuinely believe they are telling the truth – it can be possible that they are indeed each telling what they subjectively recall as "truth", but that their individual memories do not correspond to an historically accurate record. Some individuals seem to be more suggestible than others, and there is evidence that younger people and those who have suffered emotional trauma may be particularly prone.

Our memories also tend to be selective, filtered by our subjective self to construct a narrative which we find personally acceptable for whatever conscious or more likely unconscious reasons. We may not literally invent, at least not unless we are highly suggestible, but we are likely to emphasise some experiences and interpretations of experiences at the expense of others. This leads to the important, somewhat paradoxical, insight that "experience" and "memory" are not the same thing.

British journalist Tom McTague cites liberally from the work of Daniel Kahneman to help explain the difference, in an article called *The jabs success story may help Johnson bounce back,* published in *The Times on* Saturday 30 January 2021 (as the title suggests, the context for this article was a discussion of the political fortunes of then-UK Prime Minister Boris Johnson as the COVID-19 vaccination programme rolled out in the UK. But that is beside the point for our purpose – rather, what is of interest is McTague's summary of how memory works): "Daniel Kahneman, the Nobel prize-winning psychologist and economist, has talked about the 'cognitive trap' of confusing experience and memory. What we experience in life isn't what we remember. Instead, we form a story of what happened, to make sense of events. 'There is an experiencing self, who lives in the present and knows the present,' Kahneman says. 'Then there is a remembering self, and the remembering self is the one that keeps score'. Kahneman describes this remembering self as the story-teller, choosing the experiences we have been through and fitting them into a narrative that makes sense. What define these stories, he says, are big changes that happen, significant moments in our lives (my note: especially those which have significant emotional impact), and endings. 'Endings,' he notes 'are very, very important'...every country offers supporting evidence for Kahneman's thesis, picking bits of its national experiences to form its historical narrative. In the US, for example, the battle rages between two accounts: one of the land of the free born in 1776, of men created equal; the other of a country that emerged in 1619, a land of apartheid and slavery. A similar tension can be seen in France, which holds itself up as a nation of liberté and égalité but spends less time thinking of revolutionary terror, Algeria's colonisation or the many citizens who feel neither equal nor free today...in Britain, too, we are master storytellers: an island nation that ruled the waves, and the plucky underdog who defied the odds to prevail against mightier foes. We are the battle-hardened warriors of Agincourt, not the losers of the Hundred Years War; the civilised rulers of empire, in comparison with the ghastly Belgian or German butchers. But they are all stories, not accounts of actual experience. The events we choose to remember are the ones that tell the story we want to hear, those that reflect the values we hold today and the country we hope to be: Magna Carta and Henry VIII, two world wars and one World Cup. The terrible losses that dominated most of Britain's Second World War story are overwhelmed by the moments of glory that followed".

In *Thinking, Fast and Slow*, Kahneman expands on these themes, highlighting the importance of "associative memory" in constructing links in our minds which often happen below the level of conscious thought. He describes, on p380, a phenomenon he calls the "peak-end rule", briefly referenced earlier in the section on cognitive biases, and which Kahneman couples with "duration neglect" in this example. In a nutshell, our memories are disproportionately shaped by the intensity of an experience at its peak and then at its end, whilst we are remarkably insensitive to how long an experience lasted. To illustrate this, Kahneman gives the example of two patients both undergoing an intrusive medical procedure (a colonoscopy), who are asked to report on the level of pain they are feeling at 1-minute intervals throughout. We are invited to consider a case in which the first patient reports a consistently moderate level of pain throughout the procedure, which is moreover comparatively lengthy; and the second undergoes a shorter procedure in which they experience low pain at all times except for a short intense spike in the middle and right at the end. In an absolute sense, the first patient has suffered considerably more pain than the second. But it turns out that their subsequent memory of the pain is most accurately predicted by the average of (a) the peak level of pain they reported, regardless of when this occurred during the course of the procedure and (b) the level of pain they experienced right at the end. It is the second, shorter and on average objectively more benign, operation which is likely to be remembered as the more painful.

We are also prone to applying selective memory based on hindsight, using what the American psychologist Baruch Fischoff has called "creeping determinism". Essentially, this means that we recast our memory in light of how we know events actually turned out. As an example, Matthew Syed references an experiment conducted by Fischoff during the run-up to President Nixon's groundbreaking visit to China in 1972, in an opinion piece called *Sometimes scientists get it wrong. Believe it or not, that's a good thing*, published in the London *Times* on Saturday 30 January 2021. The context is that at the time he made it Nixon's visit was controversial, and seen to be a risky political move. Fischoff asked a number of experts to predict the consequences. Then once the trip was over he went back and checked their memories of what they had said. Sayed summarises: "in the event, the visit was a triumph, but what was astonishing was how experts remembered their original estimates. Those who were 60 per cent confident of success, for example, recalled being 'certain' that Nixon would pull it off. All their prior doubts had been obliterated by the dangerous illumination of hindsight. As Fischoff puts it 'subjects reconstructed having been less surprised by the events...than they really should have been'".

And when we have an experience that we find to be memorable for whatever reason, our brain may post-rationalise it in our mind, potentially influencing the way in which the "memory" is subsequently reconstructed in a manner similar to our earlier discussion of cognitive dissonance. Daniel Gilbert calls this the "Intensity Trigger", describing on pp180-1 of *Stumbling on Happiness* how we may rationalise really bad experiences to be somehow positive: "for example, volunteers in one study were students who were invited to join an extracurricular club whose initiation ritual required that they receive three electric shocks. Some of the volunteers had a truly dreadful experience, because the shocks they received were quite severe (severe-initiation group), and others had a slightly unpleasant experience, because the shocks they received were relatively mild (mild-initiation group). Although you might expect people to dislike anything associated with physical pain, the volunteers in the severe-initiation group actually liked the club more. Because these volunteers suffered greatly, the intensity of their suffering triggered their defensive systems, which immediately began working to help them achieve a credible and positive view of their experience. It isn't easy to find such a view, but it can be done. For example, physical suffering is bad ("Oh my God, that *really* hurt!"), but it isn't entirely bad if the thing one suffers for is extremely valuable ("But I'm joining a *very* elite group of *very* special people".

The more severe an irritation is, the more we are likely to recast it: "broken pencils may be annoying, but they do not pose a great threat to our psychological well-being, and hence do not trigger our psychological defences. The paradoxical consequence of this fact is that it is sometimes more difficult to achieve a positive view of a *bad* experience than of a *very bad* experience" (Gilbert's emphases throughout).

The Intensity Trigger leads in turn to what Gilbert calls: "the Inescapability Trigger", whereby we change things we can change, and rationalise things we can't: "when the experience we are having is not the experience we *want* to be having, our first reaction is to go out and have a different one, which is why we return unsatisfactory rental cars, check out of bad hotels and stop hanging around with people who pick their noses in public. It is only when we *cannot change the experience* that we look for ways to *change our view of the experience*, which is why we love the clunker in the driveway, the shabby cabin that's been in the family for years and Uncle Sheldon despite his predilection for nasal spelunking" (author's emphases throughout; p183 of *Stumbling on Happiness*).

Last but not least, the way in which memory works may degrade as we age, with potentially profound consequences. For example, it is not uncommon for older people suffering some form of dementia to retain clear memories of their childhood whilst being unable to recognise their own loved ones, or to remember a conversation from even a few minutes previously. Ultimately, memory degradation impacts our sense of "self", and therefore amongst other things our ability to exercise personal choice, precisely because, as Kahneman puts it on p390 of *Thinking, fast and slow*: "odd as it may seem, I am my remembering self, and the experiencing self, who does my living, is like a stranger to me".

In sum, our memory is crucial to both our experience of existence and to the effective operation of many of our other cognitive functions. Powerful as it is, though, like many of our other faculties memory is essentially reconstructive and therefore potentially fallible.

Imagination

Our consciousness enables us not merely to process sensory data and look for rational patterns and causal connections in the "real" world, but also to imagine what might be, largely independent of underlying reality. This opens up an essentially infinite range of possibilities, with implications for almost every aspect of our existence. For example, we might imagine our own or others' future; we might create some kind of fantasy world in which the laws of Nature do not fully apply, or alternatively a world in which they do but the characters and events are entirely fictional; or we might engage in abstract thinking, for example musing on "what to believe if we don't".

This is not to say that our capacity to imagine is itself infinite. On the contrary, what we are able to imagine usually conforms at some level to what we might call the "meta conventions" of our everyday commonsense world. For example, if we imagine a ghost, it typically takes human form, or at least accords with our notions of how humans might think and feel. Reports of sightings of extra-terrestrial beings are usually consistent with the conventions of the genre, such as elliptical "flying saucer"-shaped spaceships, quasi-human body parts and mannerisms, and so on.

The ability to imagine is closely connected with our capacity for abstract thought, that is to conceive of concepts which have no material or objective reality. For example, the concepts of "justice", or "good and evil". Imagination also allows us to create entire fictional and fantasy worlds, including of course the notion of a supernatural realm.

And our imagination relies heavily on our memory, for the obvious reason that without remembered experiences it would be virtually impossible to project potential future ones because we would have no frame of reference. Godfrey-Smith highlights episodic memory specifically (that is, our memory of experienced events), later on p251 of *Metazoa*: "the Canadian psychologist Endel Tulving, who named episodic memory...observed that a patient with severe amnesia affecting his episodic memory, Kent Cochrane, also had another problem; he could not imagine events in the future. Cochrane was the first of several patients studied who had these paired problems. Clive Wearing, an English expert on early music, acquired amnesia in 1985 due to an infection, and ended up with largely intact semantic and procedural memories but highly impaired episodic memory, along with a distressing near-permanent sense that he had just woken up. Imagined futures...are as inaccessible to Wearing as remembered pasts".

We have seen that our cognitive functions can be fallible in important ways, and in *Stumbling on Happiness*, Daniel Gilbert points out that similar potential pitfalls exist for our imagination. For example, on p24: "just as our eyes sometimes lead us to see things as they are not, our imaginations sometimes lead us to foresee things as they will not be". On p114 Gilbert introduces the separate notion of "presentism", namely the idea that the interoceptive feelings we experience at a particular moment in time exert a powerful influence on how we imagine the future. Specifically: "most of us have a tough time imagining a tomorrow that is terribly different from today, and we find it particularly difficult to imagine that we will ever think, want or feel differently than we do now". A classic everyday example is visiting the supermarket whilst feeling hungry: we are likely to buy more, and potentially different, items than if we shop whilst replete precisely because it is hard to separate our imagined future ("what shall we eat for dinner tomorrow?") from our current state.

The ability to imagine is surely one of consciousness' richest gifts. It offers tremendous functional benefits, enabling us to achieve a degree of control over our environment by re-imagining the status quo rather than meekly accepting or reacting to it. On top of this, our imagination gives us the possibility of a stimulating and endlessly varied mental life.

At the same time, we must guard against the risk that because we imagine something and give it a kind of subjective reality inside our own mind, this somehow implies that it exists in an objective, real-world sense. In other words, we must not allow "imagined reality" to become "delusion".

Motivation and drive

The exercise of personal existential choice is all well and good, but it doesn't amount to much unless we take meaningful action as a consequence.

There may of course be situations in which the best course of action is inaction, for example by choosing not to escalate a potential confrontation. But even then the point stands that the ability to make a conscious decision and follow it through is paramount. And this in turn requires a certain level of determination actively to embrace an available choice rather than to lapse into passivity or fatalism; coupled with the energy to follow through on an action once a choice has been made.

Motivation and drive are of course celebrated as being important qualities in life. The English-Canadian journalist Malcolm Gladwell, billed as "the world's most influential thinker" by no less an authority than GQ magazine, famously introduced us to the 10,000 hours rule ("the magic number of greatness"), in his 2008 book

Outliers. This essentially states that excellence in any discipline requires a great deal of commitment, well beyond mere natural talent, calibrated as 10,000 hours of meaningful relevant experience, and requiring a level of dedication beyond that demonstrated by less motivated and therefore ultimately less successful practitioners.

In a similar vein American psychologist Angela Duckworth claims in her 2016 book *Grit: The Power of Passion and Perseverance*, that "grit" (a mix of passion and perseverance, as the title of the book suggests) is a better predictor of performance than underlying IQ in situations as diverse as academic achievement in US schools; the performance of cadets at the US West Point military academy; and the rankings achieved by American children in spelling bee competitions.

Subsequent research suggests a more nuanced picture, for example showing that hours of practice do not provide a complete explanation for differences in violin virtuosity. But the central points of both authors are hard to refute, namely that an individual's level of motivation and drive has an important impact on the outcomes he or she is likely to achieve, independent of whatever innate level of competence they may have.

What then is the source of motivation and drive?

Naturally, there is an important genetic component, described by Duckworth on pp96-7 of *Grit*: "very recently, researchers in London let me know they administered the Grit Scale to more than two thousand pairs of teenage twins living in the United Kingdom. This study estimated the heritability of the perseverance subscale to be 37 percent...in the simplest terms, this means that some of the variation in grit in the population can be attributed to genetic factors, and the rest can be attributed to experience".

Duckworth goes on to show, starting on p100, that on average "grittiness" increases with age. She suggests this is because as we mature and gain life experience we become better at focusing on the things we really care about; and also more resilient, able to rise above and be less distracted by life's challenges. She proposes a number of factors with the potential to improve an individual's capacity for perseverance, for example: "follow your passion", within whatever constraints you may face and accepting that it may take time and some experimentation to discover passions which are both personally inspiring and pragmatically viable; focus as far as possible on activities which carry some sense of purpose (in Chapter 5 we will see how activities and achievements which have personal meaning are also amongst the most important determinants of our likely happiness); engage in what Duckworth calls (on p145) "deliberate" practice, meaning practice which specifically aims at improvement not just repetition; and have "hope", defined (on p203) as: "the expectation that our own efforts can improve our future".

Our motivation may also be affected by a combination of extrinsic and intrinsic factors, which are themselves likely to impact us differently in different situations.

In his 2009 book *Drive: The Surprising Truth About What Motivates Us*, the American author Daniel Pink proposes that we each have three "operating systems", which together provide our psychological motive force.

The first comprises our basic biological urges: to find food and shelter, and to reproduce. In the industrial world the first two of these no longer present the same degree of existential challenge as our ancestors faced, at least for the majority of the population.

The second focuses on seeking reward ("pleasure") and avoiding punishment ("pain"). Pink notes that what he calls "carrot and stick" approaches based on rewarding desired outcomes and penalising undesired ones permeate much of our modern world, from the way we bring up children, to how the judicial system operates in most countries, to the way employees are managed at work. And there is considerable science which supports the view that such triggers can be effective, going back to the seminal work on "operant conditioning" by BF Skinner and his fellow-Behaviourists.

Pink highlights that both these first two operating systems are essentially "extrinsic", meaning that they rely mainly on external stimuli for their impact.

He then proposes a third operating system, which he calls "intrinsic motivation", because its source is within the individual him or herself.

Pink makes the important point that these different sources of motivation are likely to have different, potentially even opposing, effects in different situations. He gives a number of examples of situations in which an extrinsic "carrot and stick" approach not only fails to increase the effectiveness of a particular outcome but actually reduces it because it runs counter to the underlying intrinsic motivation, and this turns out to be more fundamental at least in the cases he highlights.

To take just one example, on p37 of *Drive* Pink describes a 1970s study by the American psychologists Mark Lepper and David Greene, assisted by Robert Nisbett, who reviewed a group of pre-school children all of whom chose to spend their free time drawing. The researchers divided these children into 3 groups, one of which was told they would receive a "Good Play" certificate to reward their efforts at the end of each free time session; a second which was not told this but was awarded one anyway; and a third group which was neither told to expect a certificate nor received one. After two weeks the first group was seen to be spending materially less time drawing, whereas groups two and three continued unabated. The explanation was that the offer to Group 1 of a "carrot" in the form of a certificate had somehow turned "play" into "work" and thereby reduced the appeal of the activity itself. As Pink comments, on p38, this effect only applied when the reward was contingent, that is, there was an explicit promise that "if you do this, you'll get that". The children in the second group who received a reward but didn't expect one did not demonstrate any decline in their intrinsic motivation.

Pink points out, on p46, that a carrot-and-stick approach is typically most appropriate in cases where there is a high degree of predictability and an overriding need to focus on a repetitive, narrowly-defined task at hand. Conversely, intrinsic motivation is likely to be more effective in situations for which a degree of creativity is needed. Indeed, at such times carrot-and-stick may be not just ineffective but counterproductive, as it was for the first group of children in the experiment just described: "...extrinsic rewards can be effective for algorithmic tasks - those that depend on following an existing formula to its logical conclusion. But for more right-brain undertakings - those that demand flexible problem-solving, inventiveness, or conceptual understanding - contingent rewards can be dangerous. Rewarded subjects often have a harder time seeing the periphery and crafting original solutions".

Finally, Pink defines intrinsic motivation as having three components:

- *autonomy*, defined as individuals having some meaningful level of control over what they do, when they do it, how they do it, and who they do it with.
- *mastery*, defined as the desire to get better and better at things which are "autotelic" in nature, meaning that

the activity is its own reward, as experienced by the individual.

- *purpose*, defined as doing things that matter, again from the perspective of the individual, and likely to involve engaging in activities which the individual perceives are in some sense "larger" than them.

In sum, motivation and drive help us to engage actively with our world and to ensure that whatever existential choices we make are appropriately followed through. In this as in other things we each have a certain latent propensity resulting from the combination of our genes and personal experiences. Beyond this, we are likely to find inspiration from a combination of extrinsic and intrinsic sources, with the specific answer as to which is most effective depending largely on the particular situation we are in at the time.

PART E: Enablers and inhibitors of consciousness

We have seen that human consciousness gives us the freedom to exercise an important degree of existential choice over our life; discussed some of the ways in which consciousness is prone to fallibility; and reviewed some of the faculties with which consciousness endows us and which are most important in helping us to make effective use of our fundamental freedom to choose.

We'll now turn to two factors which can enormously impact how our consciousness functions in practice: sleep and stress.

Sleep

Sleep could be said to be the opposite of consciousness, because by definition we are obviously unconscious for the period that we are actually asleep. But in fact the two states are closely connected. If we don't get enough sleep, or more accurately enough sleep of sufficient quality, then both our cognitive and physiological functioning will quickly be seriously impaired during our waking hours. Conversely, a healthy sleep pattern can boost our cognitive and physical performance. The implication is that at the most basic level life choices which give us the best chance of having sufficient quantity and quality of sleep are amongst the most important we can make.

Given that we spend roughly one-third of our lives asleep it is surprising that it has only relatively recently become a major topic for research and public health debate. A notable contribution, certainly in terms of its accessibility to the general population, is the 2017 book *Why We Sleep*, by Matthew Walker, a British neuroscientist and the Director of the Sleep and Neuroimaging Laboratory at the University of California in Berkeley. We will draw on his insights throughout this section.

Walker is unequivocal that research proves sleep to be the single most important foundation for health. For example, on p8 of *Why We Sleep* he tells us: "based on a rich, new scientific understanding of sleep, we no longer have to ask what sleep is good for. Instead, we are now forced to wonder whether there are any biological functions that do *not* (author's emphasis) benefit by a good night's sleep. So far, the results of thousands of studies insist that no, there aren't…sleep is the single most effective thing we can do to reset our brain and body health each day".

In the same vein, on p107 Walker imagines sleep as a remarkable new scientific "discovery":

"AMAZING BREAKTHROUGH: Scientists have discovered a revolutionary new treatment that makes you live longer. It enhances your memory and makes you more creative. It makes you look more attractive. It keeps you slim and lowers food cravings. It protects you from cancer and dementia. It wards off colds, and

the flu. It lowers your risks of heart attacks and stroke, not to mention diabetes. You'll even feel happier, less depressed, and less anxious. Are you interested?"

The point is that effective sleep is vital to enable our brain, and our body, to recharge. It is so fundamental to life that all animals are observed to sleep in one way or another, although as we would expect the specifics take many forms across species: some species of sharks, for example, must famously keep swimming forwards even while they sleep, because forward motion is essential to allow them to continue to oxygenate.

Examples of benefits that sleep is proven to bring to humans include strengthening the immune system, enabling us to resist disease; enhancing the consolidation of the memories and learning acquired during our waking hours; and producing improved cognitive and physical functioning more generally.

Conversely, sleep deprivation is detrimental to our mental and physical health in a variety of ways. On p133, Walker lists some examples, and it's a long and weighty list: "Alzheimer's disease, anxiety, depression, bipolar disorder, suicide, stroke and chronic pain...cancer, diabetes, heart attacks, infertility, weight gain, obesity, and immune deficiency".

Beyond these serious disorders, inadequate sleep can have a significant practical impact on our everyday life. For example, on p139 Walker quotes 2016 research from the AAA Foundation in Washington DC showing that drivers with less than 4 hours sleep are on average more than 11 times more likely to crash than drivers with 8 hours or more. Even a driver with between 6 and 7 hours sleep is 30% more likely to crash than a driver with 8 hours or more. On p140, Walker summarises: "1.2 million (vehicle) accidents are caused by sleepiness each year in the United States. Said another way, for every 30 seconds you've been reading this book, there has been a car accident somewhere in the US caused by sleepiness".

Walker is clear that for him 8 hours of sleep a night is the right benchmark for almost all of us, and that those who think that they can somehow thrive on significantly less are simply wrong. The further below 8 hours, the less likely that it is possible to thrive. On p145 Walker quotes his research colleague Dr Thomas Roth, of the Henry Ford Hospital in Detroit: "the number of people who can survive on five hours of sleep or less without impairment, and rounded to a whole number, is zero".

The challenge is that comparatively few people in today's world regularly enjoy 8 hours sleep a night, at least in the industrialised countries which is where most of the research has so far been done. On p296 Walker summarises the scale of the problem: "a hundred years ago, less than 2 percent of the population of the United States slept six hours or less a night. Now, almost 30% of American adults do...circumnavigate the globe, and things look no better. In the UK and Japan, for example, 39 and 66 percent respectively of all adults report sleeping fewer than seven hours...taken as a whole, one out of every two adults across all developed countries (approximately 800 million people) will not get the necessary sleep they need this coming week".

The potential consequences are severe. On p340, as part of his concluding statements, Walker asserts: "this silent sleep loss epidemic is the greatest public health challenge we face in the twenty-first century in developed nations". He wrote this before anyone knew of the Covid-19 pandemic which brought the world to a virtual standstill in 2020. But it seems reasonable to suppose this would not change his view – he would simply point out the underlying importance of sleep to a healthy immune system, and hence to an individual's ability to resist the Covid virus along with other health threats.

The sleep statistics that currently exist tend to focus on length of sleep, partly because this is relatively easy to measure. But sleep quality matters too, defined as getting enough of the right kinds of sleep. Walker explains, starting on p43, how during the course of a night we alternate between two very different kinds of sleep, "NREM" (Non-Rapid Eye Movement, which itself has four stages) and "REM" (Rapid Eye Movement). As the names imply, these different sleep states are characterised by different levels of eye activity. During REM sleep our eyes dart rapidly from side to side under their lids, whereas during NREM sleep our eyes do not move around. Brain scans show that during REM sleep our brain is remarkably active, to a level almost the same as when we are wide awake. And, as we might therefore predict, REM sleep is intimately connected with "the experience we call dreaming", as Walker puts it, on p42.

Interestingly, as REM sleep begins the brain emits a neurotransmitter (called glycine) which has the effect of putting the body into a temporary state of paralysis, presumably so that we cannot harm ourself by reacting physically to whatever dreams we may experience. The body can still move "involuntary" muscles, for example those used for breathing and the beating of our heart. But our arms, legs and other "voluntary" muscles are in effect frozen, until such time as the REM sleep finishes, or we wake up, at which point we regain full bodily function.

During sleep we oscillate between NREM and REM sleep in recurring 90-minute cycles. Within each cycle, the early stages comprise the four successive stages of NREM, culminating in "deep NREM", and the final stage of each cycle is REM. However, the proportions change over successive cycles, such that we experience relatively more NREM sleep in the early cycles, and relatively more REM in the later ones.

Our brain derives different benefits from these different kinds of sleep, so that a full quota of both kinds is necessary if we are to reap the full rewards. There is not yet consensus on what the specific benefits of each kind are, although Walker suggests, on p44, that there may be an important linkage to memory: "one theory I have offered is that the uneven back-and-forth interplay between NREM and REM sleep is necessary to elegantly remodel and update our neural circuits at night, and in doing so manage the finite storage space within the brain. Forced by the known storage capacity imposed by a set number of neurons and connections within their memory structures, our brain must find the 'sweet spot' between retention of old information and leaving sufficient room for the new. Balancing this storage equation requires identifying which memories are fresh and salient, and which memories that currently exist are overlapping, redundant, or simply no longer relevant...a key function of deep NREM sleep, which predominates early in the night, is to do the work of weeding out and removing unnecessary neural connections. In contrast, the dreaming stage of REM sleep, which prevails later in the night, plays a role in strengthening those connections".

One of the implications of this asymmetric balance between NREM and REM sleep during the course of the night is that cutting short our sleep may have a disproportionate impact one or other kind. The maths can be surprisingly stark, as Walker explains on p46: "let's say that you go to bed this evening at midnight. But instead of waking up at 8 am, getting a full eight hours of sleep, you must wake up at 6 am... What percent of sleep will you lose? The logical answer is 25%, since waking up at 6 am will drop off two hours of sleep from what would otherwise be a normal eight hours. But that's not entirely true. Since your brain desires most of its REM sleep in the last part of the night... you will lose 60 to 90% of all your REM sleep, even though you are losing 25% of your total sleep time. It works both ways. If you wake up at 8 am, but don't go to bed until 2 am, then you lose a significant amount of deep NREM sleep".

Why do people not get enough sleep, of the right kind? We asserted earlier that sleep has not been an area of general focus until comparatively recently, and it may simply be that as a consequence we are guilty of taking sleep for granted and not paying enough attention to the consequences of disrupting it.

To the extent we do think about sleep, we may be prone to various misconceptions. For example, an individual might consider themselves to be an exception to the general rule, such that whilst the population overall may need 8 hours a night they personally can make do with significantly less. Walker flatly contradicts this possibility, mentioning anecdotally that famous exemplars such as Margaret Thatcher and Ronald Reagan sadly ended their lives in the twilight world of advanced dementia.

A second example is the macho appeal of "pulling an all-nighter" to meet deadlines. To Walker, this merely demonstrates a fundamental misunderstanding of the restorative powers of sleep on performance, and the reduction in cognitive and physical ability which is the inevitable consequence of sleep deprivation.

A third misconception is the belief that sheer willpower, or alternatively drugs of different kinds, can allow us to conquer the effects of sleep deprivation. Walker shows that this is ultimately not possible, and also that attempting it can have tragic consequences.

Finally, there is the notion that we can make up for at weekends whatever sleep we may have "lost" during the week. Walker shows that we can't, although this is not to say that getting good sleep at the weekend is a bad idea, simply that it is a mistake to think that it will compensate fully for sleep that has been lost during the working week.

Walker is a self-professed sleep evangelist. For example, on p8 he tells us: "I should note that I am in love with sleep...(and) with communicating the astonishing brilliance of it to the public". Not all his fellow-scientists agree with every detail of his claims. In particular, American paleoanthropologist Daniel Lieberman challenges what he calls the "myth" that we each require an average of 8 hours sleep per night, on p82 of his 2020 book *Exercised – The Science of Physical Activity, Rest and Health*: "numerous studies...have confirmed that people who sleep about seven hours tend to live longer than those who sleep more or less. In no study is eight hours optimal, and in most of the studies people who got more than seven hours had shorter life spans than those who got less than seven hours (an unresolved issue, however, is whether it would be beneficial for long sleepers to reduce their sleep time)". Lieberman quotes from several studies which show that around 7 hours is the average in a variety of modern non-industrial populations, the closest we can get to assessing what is likely to have been typical for our evolutionary ancestors.

Lieberman is also clear that there is some variation in how much sleep different individuals need, hence his caveat at the end of the quote above that just because studies show that on average 7 hours per night may be preferable, this does not mean that individuals who find they are regularly sleeping for longer should necessarily cut down. He doesn't comment on how much variation is to be expected, and therefore does not contradict Walker's assertions that 5 hours a night or less is likely to be too little. As an aside, Lieberman also reminds us that sleep patterns can and do vary across individuals, most notably distinguishing the "larks", whose body-clocks make it natural for them to rise, and therefore go to bed, early from the "owls" for whom the reverse is true.

In any case, Lieberman is at pains to reinforce that he does not dispute the central message that getting the right quantity and quality of sleep is essential for our health. On p74 of *Exercised* he says: "adequate sleep is profoundly important for health, and in no way do I wish to trivialise the real and serious problems of those who cannot or do not get enough sleep". He proposes a rough-and-ready way to assess whether we are ourselves getting enough sleep, on p94: "if you are unsure about your own sleep health, sleep researchers suggest you ask yourself five simple questions:

Are you satisfied with your sleep?
Do you stay awake all day without dozing?
Are you asleep between 2:00 and 4:00 am?
Do you spend less than 30 minutes awake at night?
Do you get between six and eight hours of sleep?

If your answers to these questions are 'usually or always', then you should sleep contentedly knowing that you generally get enough sleep".

All things considered, we surely do well to heed Walker's closing call to arms, on p340 of *Why We Sleep*, by making it our personal priority to get a consistent amount of "proper" sleep each night, which in deference to Lieberman we might define as 7-8 hours. Walker makes a compelling case that there are few, if any, decisions we can make which will have a bigger impact on the quality and even duration of our existence: "the decimation of sleep throughout industrialised nations is having a catastrophic impact on our health, our life expectancy, our safety, our productivity, and the education of our children...I believe it is time for us to reclaim our right to a full night of sleep, without embarrassment or the damaging stigma of laziness. In doing so we can be reunited with that most powerful elixir of wellness and vitality, dispensed through every conceivable biological pathway. Then we may remember what it feels like to be truly awake during the day, infused with the very deepest plenitude of being".

What practical steps can we take to achieve this nirvana? In his Appendix, Walker offers "Twelve Tips for Healthy Sleep", which I paraphrase to save space:

1. *Stick to a sleep schedule.* Go to bed and wake up at the same time each day.
2. *Exercise is great*, but not too late in the day...not later than two to three hours before your bedtime.
3. *Avoid caffeine and nicotine*, especially in the afternoon. The effects of caffeine specifically can take as long as eight hours to wear off fully.
4. *Avoid alcoholic drinks before bed.* On pp82-3 Walker explains that alcohol suppresses REM sleep specifically, and therefore inhibits the retention of new learning and memories. Heavy alcohol consumption is bad for sleep whatever time of day it is consumed.
5. *Avoid large meals and beverages late at night.*
6. *If possible, avoid medicines that delay or disrupt your sleep.* At intervals throughout the book, and in particular in a diatribe starting on p285 and called "Sleeping pills - the bad, the bad, and the ugly", Walker warns vigorously against the use of sleeping pills on the grounds that they provide "sedation", which is by no means the same as, or an adequate substitute for, "natural" sleep. In fact he devotes the whole of Chapter 14 to this topic, including the warning, on p282: "sleeping pills do not provide natural sleep, can damage health, and increase the risk of life-threatening diseases".
7. *Don't take naps after 3pm.*
8. *Relax before bed.*
9. *Take a hot bath before bed.*

10. *Dark bedroom, cool bedroom, gadget-free bedroom.* On p275 Walker makes the specific observation: "to successfully initiate sleep, your core temperature needs to decrease by 2 to 3 degrees Fahrenheit, or about 1 degree Celsius".

11. *Have the right sunlight exposure*...try to get outside in natural sunlight for at least thirty minutes each day. In chapter 2 Walker explains that we need this so that our personal "circadian clock" can reset daily to the 24-hour cycle that we actually live by. Without it, we will each default to a personal cycle of sleeping and waking which will reflect our own specific biology, and will on average be a bit longer than 24 hours, and therefore progressively become out of synch with the cycle of the Earth.

12. *Don't lie in bed awake*...the anxiety of not being able to sleep can make it harder to fall asleep.

The point is simple and, hopefully, obvious. Getting enough quantity and quality of sleep should be a priority for all of us, because it will enhance our waking experience of existence and improve our cognitive and physical performance, including of course helping us to make more effective existential choices.

Stress

Stress is part of the zeitgeist of 21st century life, particularly in the industrial, urbanised world. For example, a Google search of the word produces the following response: "about 1,010,000,000 results (0.88 seconds)". This tells us something about the power of Google too. But Google does not create all this content, it merely aggregates what others have written.

Stress is often represented as being malign, a problem to be solved. And there is no question that excessive or unrelenting stress can be associated with unpleasant consequences; for example, substantially degrading the quality of our day-to-day life; reducing life expectancy;

and laying us open to, or accelerating, the onset of a host of stress-related psychological and physical disorders.

At the same time, it is wrong to portray stress as being unequivocally or always bad. For one thing, it is built into our biology, and is therefore an inescapable fact of our existence. We have no option but to learn to live with it. Just as important, our physiological stress responses are associated with a number of important adaptive benefits, for example helping to keep us safe in an emergency, and to perform under pressure. And often, so long as we survive them, experiences which are stressful in the moment are also those that we learn the most from, and look back on as having been particularly intense and satisfying, especially if we came through them with some degree of eventual success. In short, experiencing an appropriate amount of stress both helps us to perform effectively and builds our resilience.

The implication is twofold. Of course we should each do what we can to avoid excessive or unnecessary stress, and to develop coping mechanisms for those situations in which we unavoidably experience it. At the same time, we should welcome what we might call a healthy level of stress as a necessary, even desirable, feature of existence.

One of the leading authorities on the topic is the American neurologist Robert Sapolsky, whom we met in the previous chapter when discussing agency and freewill. For much of what follows we will draw on Sapolsky's influential book *Why Zebras Don't Get Ulcers*, first published in 1994 and updated and revised in a third edition published in 2004. All quotes in this section are from this book, unless specifically otherwise attributed.

Sapolsky describes three different categories of stress, on pp4-5. These are: "acute physical", such as a zebra, and presumably most other animals, might experience when being chased by a lion; "chronic physical", such as experiencing an extended period of drought or famine; and "psychological and social", which mainly, although not exclusively, applies to humans because: "we humans live long enough, and are smart enough, to generate all sorts of stressful events purely in our heads".

It is this third type of stress, psychological and social, which can often be the most problematic. This is because our bodies have evolved mainly to deal with the challenges of acute physical stress, manifesting in the classic "fight or flight" physical response and typically quickly resolved; and chronic physical stressors, which eventually produce compensatory changes in our underlying metabolism.

The problem with psychological and social stress is that it is often chronic, which is to say that it continues for a long period of time, and whilst it can and does produce physical changes in our human body, such as the ulcers which zebras do not get, these changes do little or nothing to alleviate, much less solve, the psychological root cause.

We understand a great deal about the body chemistry associated with "fight-or-flight". When we are confronted by an acute physical threat, say the sudden appearance of a tiger, our brain arranges for the release of hormones which rebalance the distribution of resources between the two parts of our autonomic nervous system, which regulates involuntary bodily functions such as heartbeat, blood flow, breathing and digestion. These hormones simultaneously stimulate the "sympathetic" nervous system, and deactivate or at least dial down the "parasympathetic" nervous system, until such time as the stress-inducing event has been resolved, at which point our stress-response should in theory switch off so that the process reverses and what Sapolsky calls "allostatic balance" is restored (the Merriam-Webster dictionary defines "allostasis" as "the process by which a state of internal, physiological equilibrium is maintained by an organism in response to actual or perceived environmental and psychological stressors").

Simply put, the effect of the "fight-or-flight" stress response is to direct energy to those parts of our body which are likely to need it most during a crisis, and away from those parts more focused on what might be described as investments in the longer term. Sapolsky summarises, on pp22-3 of *Why Zebras Don't Get Ulcers*: "the sympathetic nervous system kicks into action during emergencies, or what you think are emergencies. It helps mediate vigilance, arousal, activity, mobilisation...the other half of the autonomic nervous system plays an opposing role...(it) mediates calm, vegetative activities...it promotes growth, energy storage, and other optimistic processes".

The American psychologist Kelly McGonigal offers a complementary description, on p50 of her 2015 book *The Upside of Stress*: "a fight-or-flight stress response starts when your sympathetic nervous system kicks in. To make you more alert and ready to act, the sympathetic nervous system directs your whole body to mobilise energy. Your liver dumps fat and sugar into your bloodstream for fuel. Your breathing deepens so that more oxygen is delivered to your heart. And your heart rate speeds up to deliver the oxygen, fat, and sugar to your muscles and brain. Stress hormones like adrenaline and cortisol help your muscles and brain take in and use that energy more efficiently".

This kind of stress response is ideal for the kind of situation in which it presumably evolved – for example, to send maximum energy to the leg muscles and vital organs of the putative zebra, pursued by a lion, to help it have the best chance of escape. For that matter, a similar stress response also helps the lion, by ensuring its physiology literally responds to the thrill of the chase. The important point is that this kind of stress response is usually short-term. Once the crisis has passed, the zebra can go back to grazing more or less happily on the plains, assuming of course that it survived the encounter in the first place. Its heartbeat returns to normal, its digestive system resumes business as usual, growth hormones are restored to normal levels, and so on.

The problem for a human suffering from chronic psychological stress is that these parasympathetic systems continue to be suppressed, in favour of the adrenaline-fuelled processes which are needed in an emergency but unhelpful, or worse, once this is over. Sapolsky summarises, on p6 of *Zebras*: "this is the critical point of this book: if you are that zebra running for your life, or that lion sprinting for your meal, your body's physiological response mechanisms are superbly adapted for dealing with such short-term physical emergencies. For the vast majority of beasts on this planet, stress is about a short-term crisis, after which it's either over with or you're over with. When we sit around and worry about stressful things, we turn on the same physiological responses – but they are potentially a disaster when provoked chronically. A large body of evidence suggests that stress-related disease emerges, predominantly, out of the fact that we so often activate a physiological system that has evolved for responding to acute physical emergencies, but we turn it on for months on end, worrying about mortgages, relationships and promotions".

As we might expect from our earlier discussion of the way in which our brain constructs external reality by creating representations of it, it is not the potentially-stressful stimulus itself which determines our response but rather the way our mind interprets and reacts to it: in other words, our psychology. Sapolsky reinforces the point, on p263: "...it's not just the external reality; it's the meaning you attach to it...".

And in our modern world psychological stressors are by far the most important source of likely stress, at least for most of us, as Sapolsky describes on p373: "...a central concept of this book is that stress is heavily rooted in psychology once you are dealing with organisms who aren't being chased by predators, and who have adequate shelter and sufficient calories to sustain good health".

Of course, this is not to suggest that the causes of stress are entirely the product of our own mind. A diagnosis of advanced cancer is a diagnosis of advanced cancer, for example, and the death of someone we love is a categorical reality. The point is that even in situations like these where there is a high inherent potential for stress, it is nonetheless our own reaction to the situation which ultimately determines the level and kind of stress we experience. Two people undergoing a similar event might have very different physiological reactions precisely because they have different psychological reactions. As Sapolsky puts it, on p254 for both quotes: "...the physiological stress-response can be modulated by psychological factors. Two identical stressors with the same extent of allostatic disruption can be *perceived*, can be *appraised* differently"; and: "in the absence of any change in physiological reality – any actual disruption of allostasis – psychological variables alone could *trigger* the stress-response" (author's emphasis throughout).

Sapolsky asserts that a particular cause of psychological stress, in humans and other primates, is relative social rank, as perceived or experienced by the individual. We will return to this topic when we discuss hierarchy, in the next chapter. He further asserts, on p364, that for humans there is also a vital link to poverty, so that: "if you want to see an example of chronic stress, study poverty". On p373 he makes the point that in this case also what matters most is not an individual's absolute level of poverty but rather their perception of their own situation relative to others, within whatever social group or society they are part of: "it's not about being poor. It's about *feeling* poor, which is to say, it's about feeling *poorer* than others around you". And on p375 he extrapolates this to inequality more generally, and what he calls "being *made* to feel poor" (again, author's emphasis throughout).

Sapolsky identifies five critical psychological factors which research shows influence the level of stress we are likely to experience from a given stimulus:

- *Predictability*. If we have advance knowledge that something will happen, even something bad, we are likely to experience it as less stressful than if it comes out of the blue. As one of several examples, on p260 Sapolsky describes the experience of London residents during the "Blitz" bombing raids in 1940: "...during the onset of the Nazi blitzkrieg bombings of England, London was hit every night like clockwork. Lots of stress. In the suburbs the bombings were far more sporadic, occurring perhaps once a week. Fewer stressors, but much less predictability. There was a significant increase in the incidence of ulcers during that time. Who developed more ulcers? The suburban population. (As another measure of the importance of unpredictability, by the third month of the bombing, ulcer rates in all the hospitals had dropped back to normal)".

- *Control*. If we perceive that we have some measure of control over a situation, then we are likely to experience a stimulus as less stressful, even though the control we have may not extend to preventing it from happening in the first place. What is more, linking to our earlier discussion of freewill, the perception that we have control seems to matter more than necessarily exercising it, and possibly whether the control is even genuine, so long as we don't discover that it isn't: "...place two people in adjoining rooms, and expose both to intermittent noxious, loud noises; the person who has a button and believes that pressing it decreases the likelihood of more noise is less hypertensive. In one variant on this experiment, subjects with the button who did not bother to press it did just as well as those who actually pressed the button. Thus, the *exercise* of control is not critical; rather it is the *belief* that you have it" (p261; author's emphases).

- *A perception of things worsening, for the individual.* If we think that our situation is or might be in danger of deteriorating, then we are likely to feel stress. This tends to apply at a parochial level, rather as we saw a moment ago that perceptions of relative poverty seem to matter more than the absolute level. Specifically, what typically triggers stress is our perception of how a particular event will impact our own personal situation. For example, on p263: "a version of this can be observed among the baboons I study in Kenya. In general, when dominance hierarchies are unstable, resting glucocorticoid levels rise (my note: elsewhere Sapolsky shows that elevated levels of glucocortinoids provide a clear biological indication of increased stress). This makes sense, because such instabilities make for stressful times. Looking at individual baboons, however, shows a more subtle pattern: given the same degree of instability, males whose ranks are *dropping* have elevated glucocortinoid levels, while males whose ranks are *rising* amid the tumult don't show this endocrine trait".

- *Finding outlets for frustration.* When once we experience stress, how we respond can affect the psychological and physiological consequences. Sapolsky quotes various animal and human studies showing that finding an effective outlet to vent our frustration can alleviate many of the negative symptoms. For example, on p255: "...we humans...deal better with stressors when we have outlets for frustration – punch a wall, take a run, find solace in a hobby...a central feature of an outlet being effective is if it distracts from the stressor. But, obviously, more important is that it also be something positive for you – a reminder that there is more to life than whatever is making you crazed and stressed at the time". Sapolsky advocates exercise as one particularly effective stress antidote. He recalls his image of a zebra running from the hungry lion, later on p255: "...the stress-response is about preparing your body for an explosive burst of energy consumption *right now* (author's emphasis); psychological stress is about doing all the same things to your body for no physical reason whatsoever. Exercise finally provides your body (with) the outlet that it was preparing for". As a less appealing but nonetheless common alternative, Sapolsky also highlights the tactic of "stress-induced displacement of aggression", in other words relieving one's own stress by taking it out on something or someone else. Sapolsky explains, on p256: "...stress-induced displacement of aggression...the practice works wonders at minimising the stressfulness of a stressor...a male baboon loses a fight. Frustrated, he spins around and attacks a subordinate male who was minding his own business. An extremely high percentage of primate aggression represents frustration displaced onto innocent bystanders. Humans are pretty good at it, too, and we have a way of describing the phenomenon in the context of stress-related disease: 'he's one of those guys who doesn't get ulcers, he gives them'. Taking it out on someone else – how well it works at minimising the impact of a stressor".

- *Social support.* Social species that we are, it turns out that our network of close personal relationships can play a significant role in helping us to deal with the effects of stress, a phenomenon which is also seen in other primates. For example, on p254 Sapolsky describes research showing that a baby monkey which is able to cry in its mother's arms exhibits a lower stress response to a stimulus than one which is not. And of course it is not only babies for whom this is true (on p256): "an additional way we can interact with another organism to minimise the impact of a stressor on us is considerably more encouraging for the future of our planet than is displacement aggression. Rats only occasionally use it, but primates are great at it. Put a primate through something unpleasant: it gets a stress response. Put it through the same stressor while in a room full of other primates and... it depends. If those primates are strangers, the stress response gets worse. But if they are friends, the stress response is decreased. Social support networks – it helps to have a shoulder to cry on, a hand to hold, an ear to listen to you, someone to cradle you and to tell you it will be okay". Indeed, on p257: "people with spouses or close friends have longer life expectancies". A cautionary note is appropriate, however. By no means all relationships achieve the kind of shared intimacy and trust needed to provide helpful support. A dysfunctional relationship can be a source of stress in its own right, with measurable impact in terms of poorer health outcomes. Sapolsky notes, on p407: "for women, being in a *bad* (his emphasis) marriage is associated with immune suppression". He leaves intriguingly open the question of what happens to men in a similar situation. Nonetheless, his conclusion is clear, also on p407: "a close, intimate relationship with the wrong person can be anything but stress-reducing".

Finally, Sapolsky describes, on p302, how unremitting stress can lead to a psychological condition called "learned helplessness", in humans and many other species: "it takes surprisingly little in terms of uncontrollable unpleasantness to make humans give up and become helpless in a generalised way". This is a highly undesirable state, obviously, characterised by symptoms similar to those associated with clinical depression, and causing the sufferer to become passive and withdrawn, potentially with impaired cognitive functioning. For example, on p301: "animals (with learned helplessness) have a motivational problem – one of the reasons that they are helpless is that they often do not even attempt a coping response when they are in a new situation...animals with learned helplessness also have a cognitive problem, something awry with how they perceive the world and think about it. When they do make the rare coping response, they can't tell whether it works or not".

McGonigal describes something similar on p155 of *The Upside of Stress*, summarising the effects of what she calls the "defeat response" to a stressful situation: "you lose motivation, hope and the desire to connect with others. It becomes impossible to see meaning in your life, or to imagine any action you could take that would improve the situation".

The key to avoiding "learned helplessness", or the "defeat response", lies in cultivating an appropriate sense of personal agency, what Sapolsky calls an "internalised locus of control". On p303 he cites a study by the American psychologist Donald Hiroto which sought to stimulate learned helplessness in its subjects: "Hiroto had given the students a personality inventory beforehand. Based on that, he was able to identify the students who came into the experiment with a strongly 'internalised locus of control' – a belief that they were the masters of their own destiny and had a great deal of control in their lives – and, in contrast, the markedly 'externalised' volunteers, who tended to attribute outcomes to chance and luck. In the aftermath of the uncontrollable stressor, the externalised students were far more vulnerable to learned helplessness. Transferring that to the real world, with the same external stressors, the more that someone has an internal locus of control, the less the likelihood of a depression".

Leaving aside the apparent irony of Sapolsky advocating for a healthy sense of personal agency given his resistance to the idea of genuine freewill, discussed earlier, an appropriate feeling of personal "locus of control" is associated not just with avoiding depression but also positively linked to feeling happier and more fulfilled, a topic we will return to in Chapter 5.

And, switching tack, it's important to recognise that in many situations stress, or more accurately our response to it, is not only not harmful but potentially beneficial. "Whatever does not kill you makes you stronger", as Kelly McGonigal puts on p182 of *The Upside of Stress*. Indeed, this could be taken as a central theme of her book, the subtitle of which is: *Why Stress is Good for You (and How to Get Good at It)*. As an example, on p183 she references the American psychologist Mark Seery who: "challenged the widespread belief that traumatic events always increase the risk of depression, anxiety and illness. Instead, he showed that a history of negative life events can actually protect against these outcomes. Adversity, he claimed, can create resilience".

The key is, again, not so much the adverse experience itself but rather how we react to it. On p49 McGonigal gives two contrasting examples of possible responses to a potentially-stressful stimulus, which she labels "challenge", tending to be confrontational at some level; and "tend-and-befriend", which inclines towards conciliation and possibly nurturing. As McGonigal puts it: "alongside the familiar fight-or-flight response, these make up your stress response repertoire".

However, whilst both the "challenge" and "tend-and-befriend" responses have the potential for positive impact on our body and mental state, the effects are markedly different: "the specific cardiovascular changes, ratio of hormones released, and other aspects of a stress response can vary widely. Differences in your physical stress response can create very different psychological and social responses...for example, a *challenge response* increases self-confidence, motivates action, and helps you learn from experience; while a *tend-and-befriend response* increases courage, motivates caregiving, and strengthens your social relationships".

McGonigal reinforces how a "challenge" response can enhance performance under pressure, on p51 of *The Upside of Stress*: "people who report being in a flow state – a highly enjoyable state of being completely absorbed in what you are doing – display clear signs of a challenge response. Artists, athletes, surgeons, video gamers, and musicians all show this kind of stress response when they're engaged in their craft or skill. Contrary to what many people expect, top performers in these fields aren't physiologically calm under pressure; rather, they have strong challenge responses. The stress response gives them access to their mental and physical resources, and the result is increased confidence, enhanced concentration, and peak performance".

She concludes, on p58 of *The Upside of Stress*: "different types of stressful situations typically provoke different responses. For example, social stress usually increases oxytocin more than other kinds of stress. That's good, because it motivates social connection. In contrast, performance stress is more likely to increase adrenaline and other hormones that give you energy and focus. That's also good, because it's what you need to do your best. Ideally, your responses will be flexible and fine-tuned, and your body will respond to each stressful situation in a way that best uses your resources. A trial lawyer about to give summary statements should have a challenge response. When she gets home, if her kids are fighting over her attention, a tend-and-befriend response will soothe them and herself. And if the fire alarm goes off in the middle of the night, a fight-or-flight response will get her and the rest of the family out of the house safely".

Given all this it is no surprise to find evidence suggesting that it is possible to have too little stress in our life. On pp183-4 of *The Upside of Stress*, McGonigal elaborates on Seery's research showing that people who experience modest levels of adversity, as measured by how many of a list of 37 "traumatic events" they had experienced, how many times, tend to be happier and healthier not just than those who experience high levels of trauma but also than people who report few or none: "Seery looked at whether the number of traumatic events people had lived through predicted their well-being over the four-year study. One possibility was a direct and negative relationship: the more adverse events, the lower a person's well-being. Instead, Seery found a U-shaped curve, with those people in the middle the best off. People who had experienced a moderate level of adversity had the lowest risk of depression, the fewest physical health problems, and the greatest satisfaction with life. People at the extremes – either the lowest or highest levels of adversity – were more depressed, had more health problems, and were less satisfied with their lives. Although many people idealise a life without adversity, those who actually have one are less happy and healthy than those who have faced some hardship".

And on pxxi of the Introduction to *The Upside of Stress* McGonigal underscores that it is often the things which matter most to us in life which also constitute the biggest potential sources of stress: "*stress is what arises when something you care about is at stake* (author's emphasis)...stress and meaning are inextricably linked. You don't stress out about things you don't care about, and you can't create a meaningful life without experiencing some stress". "A meaningful life is a stressful life", as she titles her Chapter 3, an observation which will take on particular significance when we consider the critical importance of meaning to happiness, in Chapter 5.

McGonigal cites a number of large-scale, cross-cultural studies showing that high levels of self-reported stress are often associated with high levels of self-reported happiness and fulfilment, and conversely that low levels of reported stress tend to correlate with low reported happiness. She summarises, on p64: "I call this the *stress paradox* (her emphasis). High levels of stress are associated with both distress and well-being. Importantly, happy lives are not stress-free, nor does a stress-free life guarantee happiness. Even though most people view stress as harmful, higher levels of stress seem to go along with things we want: love, health, and satisfaction with our lives".

Finally, McGonigal reinforces that our attitude to stress can impact its effects. On pxii of the Introduction she quotes a 1998 US study of 30,000 adults which compared reported levels of stress with a range of health outcomes, including death: "high levels of stress increased the risk of dying by 43 percent. But...that increased risk applied only to people who also believed that stress was harming their health. People who reported high levels of stress but who did not view their stress as harmful were not more likely to die. In fact, they had the lowest risk of death of anyone in the study, even lower than those who reported experiencing very little stress".

What are we to make of all this?

Just like sleep, stress can have a major impact on how our consciousness functions, for better and worse, and therefore on our ability to embrace and make the various existential choices which confront us. Stress is an inherently personal experience, and of course there is no silver bullet which can help all personalities to deal with it, in all situations. Still, some helpful themes emerge:

1. *Cultivate a positive, albeit realistic, attitude to stress.* As McGonigal reminds us, stress is something to be embraced, within reason. "A meaningful life is a stressful life", and experiences which may be stressful at the time are often also those we look back on later as being especially important, intense, and, at least sometimes, fulfilling. We saw that the more we are able to cultivate an "internalised locus of control", the less we are likely to experience the negative consequences of stress. And when the chips really are down we do well to follow Sapolsky's advice (on p415 of *Why Zebras Don't Get Ulcers*), to temper hope with realism: "hope for the best and let that dominate your emotions, but at the same time let one small piece of you prepare for the worst".

2. *Control what you can control – take action where you think it can help.* Fatalism and anything resembling "learned helplessness" or a "defeat response" are to be avoided as far as possible. "Just do it", as Sapolsky advises, on p414. He adds "...beyond it not being abusive to those around you"; for example, avoiding displaced aggression as a coping mechanism.

3. *Cultivate outlets for frustration.* By definition, these will be personal. As we saw, Sapolsky advocates exercise as one particularly effective avenue, albeit he caveats, on p401, that: "exercise is (only) stress reducing so long as it something you actually want to do", and, on p402: "exercise needs to occur on a regular basis and for a sustained period...a minimum of twenty to thirty minutes at a time, a few times a week, to really get the health benefits". He suggests that meditation can also be an effective outlet, for those for whom it is.

4. *Ask for help; and give help to others.* Sapolsky emphasises, on p407, that the act of giving support to someone who is suffering from stress can have positive consequences for the donor, not just the recipient: "often, one of the strongest stress-reducing qualities of social support is the act of *giving* (his emphasis) social support, to be needed...in a world of stressful lack of control, an amazing source of control we all have is the ability to make the world a better place, one act at a time".

PART F: Implications of consciousness for existence

In this, the final part of this chapter, we'll review five implications of consciousness for our existence:

- The fact that we have the freedom to exercise personal existential choice in our life means that we should actively embrace it, and then take responsibility for the choices we make;
- The fact that our consciousness is fallible means that in making choices we should consider the possibility of bias and error;
- "Luck" is a fact of life, whereas "destiny" isn't;
- Mindset matters: how we think about our existence has a material impact on, although of course does not completely determine, both the likely outcomes and how we feel about them.
- Expectations matter: how we think about ourself and others can change what we and they feel and do.

To take each in turn:

The fact that we have the freedom to exercise personal existential choice in our life means that we should actively embrace it, and then take responsibility for the choices we make.

This belief reached perhaps its purest form of expression in the Existentialist philosophy movement, which flourished in the middle part of the 20th century and is an inspiration for many of the ideas in this book.

Existentialism takes as its starting premise that the Universe and everything in it is essentially "absurd", that is lacks any kind of objective meaning or purpose. Our consciousness is the key to constructing our own, subjective, meaning; and the series of existential choices we make in our life are ultimately what define us.

The Existentialist approach is summarised on p284 of *The Philosophy Book*, published in 2011, in an entry focused on the French novelist and playwright Albert Camus, one of the leading proponents of the school: "on the one hand, we are conscious beings who cannot help living our lives as if they are meaningful. On the other hand, these meanings do not reside out there in the universe, they reside only in our minds. The universe as a whole has no meaning and no purpose. It just is. But because, unlike other living things, we have consciousness, we are the kinds of beings who find meaning and purpose everywhere…it is only once we accept the fact that life is meaningless and absurd that we are in a position to live fully".

Faced with this uncompromising reality of a universe without objective meaning, we may experience "existential angst", a phrase attributed to the 19th century Danish philosopher Soren Kierkegaard, who is generally considered to be the first existentialist philosopher even though he did not himself use this label. "Angst" is defined by the Lexico online dictionary as: "a feeling of deep anxiety or dread, typically an unfocused one about the human condition or the state of the world in general".

If we do experience some form of angst, the Existentialists do not advocate that we surrender to it.

Arguably the most extreme form of surrender would be suicide, as Camus acknowledges in the opening lines of his 1942 book *The Myth of Sisyphus*: "there is but one serious philosophical problem and that is suicide". However, he unequivocally rejects this as a solution, in the Preface to the same work: "it is legitimate and necessary to wonder whether life has a meaning; therefore it is legitimate to meet the problem of suicide face to face. The answer, underlying and appearing through the paradoxes which cover it, is this: even if one does not believe in God, suicide is not legitimate". True to this, neither Camus himself nor any of his main fictional characters pursue suicide as any kind of answer to their existential challenges.

More broadly, Existentialists advocate that far from surrendering one should "rebel" against the absurdity of the Universe, by creating our own personal meaning in full knowledge and acceptance that this is personal and subjective. Camus captures this sentiment in a quote taken from *Three Interviews*, in *Lyrical and Critical Essays*, dated 1970: "accepting the absurdity of everything around us is one step, a necessary experience; it should not become a dead end. It arouses a revolt that can become fruitful".

To illustrate the point, Camus offers the Myth of Sisyphus, a figure in Ancient Greek mythology who is condemned by the gods to roll a heavy stone up a steep hill only to find that each time he reaches the top the stone rolls back down to the bottom and he must start all over again, for all eternity with no hope of remission. Incidentally, the reason the gods had sentenced Sisyphus to this terrible fate was that he had attempted, sadly unsuccessfully, to put Death in chains so that no human need ever die. For Camus, the point is that Sisyphus still has existential choice, even though he can hardly be described as "free" in any other respect. And this choice gives him the ability to embrace the reality of his situation and rise above it, on p111 of *The Myth of Sisyphus*: "the struggle itself towards the heights is enough to fill a man's heart. One must imagine Sisyphus happy".

In similar fashion the French philosopher Jean-Paul Sartre, another celebrated voice of the Existentialist school, asserts that humans can and must shape their own meaning in a famous passage centring on the phrase "existence precedes essence". The quote is taken from a lecture called *Existentialism is a Humanism*, published in 1946: "existence precedes essence...man is nothing else but what he makes of himself...man is responsible for what he is. Thus, the first effect of existentialism is that it puts every man in possession of himself as he is, and places the entire responsibility for his existence squarely upon his own shoulders".

In the same lecture Sartre also rejects a passive or fatalistic response to our existential predicament, arguing that action is ultimately what defines us: "quietism is the attitude of people who say 'let others do what I cannot do'. The doctrine I am presenting before you is precisely the opposite of this, since it declares there is no reality except in action. It goes further, indeed, and adds, 'Man is nothing else but what he purposes, he exists only in so far as he realises himself, he is therefore nothing else but the sum of his actions...Existentialism cannot be regarded as a philosophy of quietism since it defines man by his action...nor is it an attempt to discourage man from action since it tells him that there is no hope except in his action, and that the one thing which permits him to have life is the deed".

Finally, our actions are of course determined by the choices we make in our life, day by day and even minute by minute. Elsewhere in the lecture Sartre makes the important observation that we have no option but to take responsibility for these choices, because: "...what is not possible is not to choose...I must know that if I do not choose, that is also a choice".

In sum, the Existentialist view, shared by this book, is that we are fundamentally alone in an amoral Universe which lacks objective meaning, and that consciousness gives us the freedom to respond by creating ("choosing") subjective meaning to define our own existence, a meaning which is ultimately manifested through and defined by our actions and behaviours. This freedom to choose is in effect an obligation, since: "if I do not choose, that is also a choice".

The fact that our consciousness is fallible means that when making choices we should give appropriate consideration to the possibility of bias and error.

Whatever choices we make in our life must be made with an appropriate degree of humility, grounded in the awareness that the potential for bias and error exists. To recap, the two main potential sources of fallibility are:

- we may have a mistaken view of external reality. For example, our brain might "join up the dots" to see a cause-and-effect relationship where in fact none exists, or where the data our brain perceives to be causal is in fact due to mere coincidence. We may over-interpret patterns, as when we see a "face" in a cloud formation. Or we may see a particular interpretation of an object or event as definitive when in fact more than one interpretation is possible, as with the visual images on pages 312-314.
- we are prone to a wide range of internal cognitive biases which influence the decisions we make and the actions we take. Generally, this is because our decisions are being driven at an instinctive or emotional level, below that of our conscious mind. It is not that such decisions are always bad, simply that in many situations

it can be helpful to "mind the gap" between an external stimulus and our behaviourial response, so that we can exercise choice consciously, in a considered rather than purely instinctual way.

"Luck" is a fact of life, whereas "destiny" isn't.

Random chance plays an important role in our lives, even in situations where we may feel that we have a measure of control. But it is important to distinguish between "luck", that is the impact of random chance; and "destiny", a sense that a certain outcome was predetermined and therefore inevitable. "Luck" is an inescapable aspect of existence, whereas "destiny" is not.

"Luck" essentially reflects the uncertain, probabilistic nature of the world, plus that the fact that we seldom have complete information about a situation such that we could predict an outcome with certainty even if it were indeed truly mechanistic.

This is not to suggest that we can or should rely on luck, merely that we are forced to accept that there will almost always be some element of it in whatever outcomes we achieve. In particular, as we have seen the genes we inherit and particular experiences we have, especially in our early, formative, years, predispose us to act in certain ways, for better or worse. Obviously, we can take no personal credit for our genes, and little or none for our formative experiences: our inheritance of this can only be ascribed to luck, in the sense we are using the term here. There may of course also be things we can do "to make our own luck" and influence the odds of a particular situation in our favour, or at least to reduce our reliance on random chance. For example, the champion golfer Arnold Palmer is often credited with the witticism: "people say I'm a lucky golfer, and I find that the more I practice the luckier I get". There is uncertainty whether

Palmer was the true source of this line, but whoever said it first doesn't dilute the essential truth.

Luck can also manifest as a specific outcome amongst a sequence of events which are individually random but collectively tend towards predictability. This phenomenon is reflected in the Law of Large Numbers, which states that whilst the outcome of an individual event may be subject to random chance, a large number of instances will predictably give an average result close to the expected mathematical value of the outcome, and the larger the number of instances, the closer the match will be. For example, over an extended period a casino can predict with considerable accuracy what its take from say a roulette wheel will be. The casino knows that on average it will win, because the mathematical odds are stacked (transparently) in its favour, given that a winning number pays out at 36:1 but there are 37 possible numbers including zero, and 38 for tables with a double zero. However the casino cannot have the same level of confidence that it will win on any given spin. The individual punter is subject to "luck", and the casino ultimately isn't, unless it accepts individual bets so large that they are capable of bankrupting it before the Law of Large Numbers can apply. Of course, if an individual punter plays often enough then they will ultimately be subject to the Law of Large Numbers as well, although the same maths will effectively guarantee that they lose modestly, at a predictable percentage of their cumulative stake which will in turn be a function of how many zeroes the tables at their preferred casino has.

It is tempting to assume that our luck evens out over the course of our life. However, on p81 of *Determined* Robert Sapolsky makes the sobering argument that for many people the reverse is true and bad luck compounds over time: "bad luck doesn't get evened out...it amplifies instead. Have some particular unlucky gene variant, and you will be unluckily sensitive to the effects of adversity during childhood. Suffering from early-life adversity is a predictor that you'll be spending the rest of your life in environments that present you with fewer opportunities than most, and that enhanced developmental sensitivity will unluckily make you less able to benefit from those rare opportunities – you may not understand them, may not recognise them as opportunities, may not have the tools to make use of them, or to keep you from impulsively blowing the opportunity. Fewer of those benefits make for a more stressful adult life, which will change your brain into one that is unluckily bad at resilience, emotional control, reflection, cognition...bad luck doesn't get evened out by good. It is usually amplified until you're not even on the playing field that needs to be levelled".

The same argument applies in reverse. If we are born with a "lucky" gene variant and our early life experiences are stimulating and nurturing then we will be well positioned to take advantage of whatever opportunities might come our way, and so embark on a cycle of self-reinforcing success and fulfilment with a similar, but in this case positive, compound effect.

Having said all this, whatever probabilities we end up assessing remain just probabilities, so that sometimes an outcome can surprise us against the odds. For example, if we choose to jump out of an aeroplane without a parachute at 18,000 feet, there is an overwhelming probability that we will meet a sticky end. Remarkably, there is also some tiny probability of survival, evidenced by the British tail-gunner Nicholas Alkemade who survived exactly this experience with nothing more than a sprained leg to show for it when he jumped without a parachute to escape the flames of his burning plane over Germany in March 1944. The point is obviously not that Alkemade's experience should encourage others to try the same thing with any reasonable hope of repeating his success. It is simply that even in situations where the odds of a particular outcome look hopeless, luck can still sometimes surprise, albeit by definition the more hopeless the odds the more rarely this will happen. By the same token we can sometimes experience bad luck, so that what seemed like a sure thing fails.

"Destiny" is a different matter, at least in the sense we are using it here: which is to imply that the outcome of a particular event was pre-determined, with no element of chance or possibility of an alternative outcome. We discussed earlier, and ultimately rejected, the notion of physical predeterminism, the idea that everything that happens in the Universe is the inevitable result of a prior cause. One implication of rejecting this is that there is room for probability and chance to intervene, as they do for example at the most fundamental level of reality in the form of quantum randomness.

There is nonetheless room for linguistic ambiguity, as usual. When an event involves a fundamental Law of Nature we can predict with confidence that it will happen, within the bounds of whatever quantum probabilities might apply. In this sense, we might say that it is the "destiny" of the Moon to orbit the Earth, or that it is the "destiny" of all living things, including humans, to die.

Linguistically, we may also describe something as "destiny" which is already a matter of historical fact. Here, the fact that something has actually happened may create an impression that the outcome was inevitable, for example "he was destined to die young" or "she was destined for greatness". In reality, however, in such situations we are commenting about probabilities not certainties. "He was likely to die young", or "the odds of achieving greatness were stacked in her favour" would be more accurate summaries.

In sum, luck is an inescapable part of life albeit we may also be able to make choices which increase our odds of success. Conversely, "destiny" is an illusion, unless expressed in the broadest terms in relation to the fundamental Laws of Nature.

Mindset matters: how we think about our life obviously affects how we feel about it, and can also influence outcomes.

Our attitude to something by definition determines the specific meaning we attach to it, and this can become self-fulfilling in that it can affect the impact it has, psychological and even physical. Hence, our mindset can influence not only how we feel about our life, but also the actual outcomes we experience, at least to some degree.

For example, we saw in our earlier discussion of stress that our psychology can play an important role. If we perceive or interpret something to be threatening, our body will activate stress and defence responses, whereas if we perceive the self-same event to be non-threatening, it won't. Clearly, we are likely to be at risk if we fail to perceive something as threatening when in fact it is. But the reverse is true — we can equally expose ourself to risk if we systematically perceive things as threatening when they are not, or don't need to be.

One example of the way in which our attitude can affect our health is the famous placebo effect. For example, patients given a non-active substance as part of a control panel in a clinical trial frequently report improved medical outcomes from the drug they imagine they have taken, even though in fact they have not. A variation on the same theme is that patients may also report feeling side-effects, even though they have received an inert substance not an active drug. The American evolutionary biologist Joseph Henrich testifies to the surprising power of placebo effects, on p273 of his 2016 book *The Secret of*

Our Success, how culture is driving human evolution, domesticating our species, and making us smarter: "decades of research now make it clear that...depending on a person's beliefs, desires, and prior experiences, taking a placebo or experiencing any 'sham' medical procedure, including fake surgery, can activate biological pathways in the body. Often these pathways are the very same pathways triggered by the active chemicals in popular drugs. Placebos can reduce pain, activate the immune system, mitigate irritable bowel symptoms, improve motor coordination in Parkinson's patients, and ameliorate asthma. However, the action and effectiveness of a placebo often depends entirely on how much faith the patient puts in a particular placebo or medical treatment. The more you believe it will work, the more it may actually work. Not only that, there appears to be a synergistic interaction between the size of the placebo effects, and the size of the chemical effects; that is, the more one believes a drug like morphine will reduce pain (measured by using placebo-morphine), the more effective real morphine actually is. Some drugs don't work at all if administered *without* (author's emphasis) the patient's conscious knowledge – that is, the drug requires some placebo effect to catalyse the chemical effects". Henrich takes the argument further, observing on p277 that: "witchcraft...can actually cause material responses in our bodies if we believe it can".

It is but a short step from here to the topic of positive thinking. The Mayo Clinic lists a wide range of potential positive thinking benefits, catalogued on its Stress Management home page: "increased lifespan; lower rates of depression; lower levels of distress; greater resistance to the common cold; better psychological and physical well-being; better cardiovascular health and reduced risk of death from cardiovascular disease; better coping skills during hardships and times of stress".

In the same vein, researchers from Boston University School of Medicine summarise the results of a study showing that an optimistic mindset is associated with significantly greater longevity, in an article titled *New evidence that optimists live longer* published online by *Science News* on 26 August 2019: "the study was based on 69,744 women and 1,429 men. Both groups completed survey measures to assess their levels of optimism, as well as their overall health and health habits such as diet, smoking and alcohol use. Women were followed for 10 years, while the men were followed for 30 years. When individuals were compared based on their initial levels of optimism, the researchers found that the most optimistic men and women demonstrated, on average, an 11 to 15% longer lifespan, and had 50-70% greater odds of reaching 85 years old compared to the least optimistic groups. The results were maintained after accounting for age, demographic factors such as educational attainment, chronic diseases, depression and also health behaviours, such as alcohol use, exercise, diet and primary care visits".

Finally, on pp4-5 of *The Upside of Stress*, Kelly McGonigal shares the remarkable results of research by American psychologist Alia Crum into weight loss among hotel housekeepers. In a section called *The Effect You Expect Is the Effect That You Get*, McGonigal explains how Crum recruited housekeepers from seven hotels across the US for a study of how their beliefs about the nature of their work could affect their actual health and weight: "housekeeping is strenuous work, burning over 300 calories an hour...in comparison, office work...burns roughly 100 calories an hour...and yet, two-thirds of the housekeepers Crum recruited believed they weren't exercising regularly...(and) one-third said they got no exercise at all. Their bodies reflected this perception. The average housekeeper's blood pressure, waist-to-hip ratio, and bodyweight were exactly what you'd expect to find if she were truly sedentary". Crum divided the housekeepers into two groups, and engaged the first group in a "mindset intervention" which explained the health benefits of their activities and explicitly encouraged them to start to think of their work as a form of physical exercise. The second, control, group received similar communication on the generalised benefits of exercise but, crucially, no suggestion was made that their own work qualified as exercise. McGonigall summarises: "four weeks later, Crum checked in with the housekeepers. Those who had been informed that their work was exercise had lost weight and body fat. Their blood pressure was lower. They even liked their jobs more. They had not made any changes in their behaviour outside work. The only thing that had changed was their perception of themselves as exercisers. In contrast, housekeepers in the control group showed none of these improvements".

To be clear, there is plenty of evidence that a positive attitude can affect our own physiology, but none whatever that it can impact the external physical world more broadly. The laws of nature are immutable, after all, and not susceptible to the influence of "mind over matter". On p6 of *The Upside of Stress* McGonigal is explicit that the key to the outcomes seen in the housekeeper experiment is that it aligns the psychology of the participants with their actual physical reality: "does this mean that if you tell yourself that watching television burns calories, you can lose weight? Sorry, no. What Crum told the housekeepers was true. The women really were exercising. Yet when she met them, they didn't see their work that way. Instead, they were more likely to view housekeeping as hard on their bodies".

Powerful as it can be, then, positive thinking has practical limits. For example, on p404 of *Why Zebras Don't Get Ulcers*, Robert Sapolsky warns us against "John

Henryism", quoting Sherman James of Duke University: "(John Henry) refers to the American folk hero who, hammering a six-foot-long steel drill, tried to outrace a steam drill tunnelling through a mountain. John Henry beat the machine, only to fall dead from the superhuman effort. As James defines it, John Henryism involves the belief that any and all demands can be vanquished, so long as you work hard enough". And later on p404 Sapolsky reinforces the John Henry insight that positive thinking can be positively harmful if taken too far: "it is clearly a travesty to lead cancer patients or their families to believe, misinterpreting the power of the few positive studies in this field, that there is more possibility for control over the causes and courses of cancer than actually exists. Doing so is simply teaching the victims of cancer and their families that the disease is their own fault, which is neither true nor conducive to reducing stress in an already stressful situation".

In much the same vein prayer has been shown to be not only ineffective but potentially harmful, conclusions which both arise from a remarkable study dubbed the "Great Prayer Experiment". This was led by the American cardiologist and pioneer of "mind-body medicine" Dr Herbert Benson, beginning in 1998 with results reported in 2006, and is described in some detail by Richard Dawkins in his combative 2006 book *The God Delusion*. Incidentally, Dr Benson was and apparently somehow remains an advocate of the positive power of prayer, hence, as Dawkins puts it: "the study was in good hands, unlikely to be spoiled by sceptical vibrations". The research was designed according to rigorous "double-blind" scientific principles. Around 1,800 patients undergoing heart bypass surgery in six American hospitals were each assigned to one of three groups and prayed for, or not, by the congregations of three churches selected with sufficient geographic separation that direct contact was unlikely between patients and congregation members. The first patient group were prayed for but were not told so; those in group 2 were not prayed for and were also not told; and those in group 3 were both prayed for and told that this was happening.

Dawkins summarises the outcome, on pp86-8 of *The God Delusion*: "the results, reported in the *American Heart Journal* of April 2006, were clear cut. There was no difference between those patients who were prayed for and those who were not". Which is to say there was no difference in the health outcomes recorded for Groups 1 and 2: prayer had no effect, either positive or negative. There was however a twist: "there was a difference between those who knew they had been prayed for (that is, Group 3) and those who did not know one way or the other (Groups 1 and 2); but it went in the wrong direction. Those who knew they had been the beneficiaries of prayer suffered significantly more complications than those who did not... it seems more probable that those patients who knew they were being prayed for suffered additional stress in consequence: 'performance anxiety', as the experimenters put it. Dr Charles Bethea, one of the researchers, said, 'It may have made them uncertain, wondering am I so sick they had to call in their prayer team?'"

The experiment demonstrates clearly enough the unsurprising result that prayer has no impact on outcomes. Perhaps more unexpectedly it also serves to reinforce that mindset does, or at least can, as the patients in Group 3 attest.

Returning to the secular, material world, the key is to cultivate a positive mindset whilst keeping within the bounds of practical reality. As the American psychology journalist Kendra Cherry reminds us, in an article called *Understanding the Psychology of Positive Thinking* and published on *verywellmind* on 26 November 2019, there can be a vital distinction between positive thinking and what she calls "positive psychology", and it is surely preferable to cultivate the latter: "positive psychology certainly tends to focus on optimism, but it also notes that while there are many benefits to thinking positively, there are actually times when realistic thinking is more advantageous". And even: "in some situations, negative thinking can actually lead to more accurate decisions and outcomes". In other words, it can be helpful to adopt a positive mindset, but not always, and certainly not at the cost of facing whatever is the underlying reality.

Cherry offers four specific suggestions on how we can turn all this into practical action, in an article titled *How to Think Like an Optimist and Stay Positive*, published on *verywellmind* on 9 December 2019:

1. Avoid negative self-talk. We have seen that how things are framed can make a significant difference to how we then react to them, and this applies to the little voice inside our head just as much to the broader outside world. American journalist Dana Sparks highlights some common self-talk pitfalls, in an article titled *Mayo Mindfulness: Overcoming negative self-talk*, published on the Mayo Clinic website on 29 May 2019. These are: *filtering*, which is to say screening out positive facts and focusing instead only on negative ones; *personalising*, that is being too ready to blame ourself when something bad happens (for example, you learn that friends have cancelled an evening out with you and assume that it's because they don't want to be around you); *catastrophising*, which as we saw earlier involves fixating on the worst possible outcome even though the probability of it happening may be very low; and *polarising*, seeing things as either definitively good or bad, with no nuance or middle ground - for example, as the Mayo Clinic puts it "you feel that you have to be perfect or you're a total failure". On the other side of the ledger American psychologist Elaine Mead offers ten examples of positive self-talk statements and phrases "just to get you started", in an article titled *What is Positive Self-Talk?* published on positivepsychology.com on 18 February 2021:

i. I have the power to change my mind.
ii. Attempting to do this took courage and I am proud of myself for trying.
iii. Even though it wasn't the outcome I hoped for, I learnt a lot about myself.
iv. I might still have a way to go, but I am proud of how far I have already come.
v. I am capable and strong, I can get through this.
vi. Tomorrow is a chance to try again, with the lessons learned from today.
vii. I will give it my all to make this work.
viii. I can't control what other people think, say or do. I can only control me.
ix. This is an opportunity for me to try something new.
x. I can learn from the situation and grow as a person.

2 Try humour. Laughter can sometimes be the best medicine, as the saying goes. Cherry observes: "even when you are facing challenges, it is important to remain open to laughter and fun...sometimes, simply recognising the potential humour in a situation can lessen your stress and brighten your outlook".

3. Cultivate optimism. The key to this is the "explanatory style" we typically use to explain the events in which we are involved, which has some echoes of the "locus of control" factors described by Sapolsky in our discussion of stress. As Cherry puts it: "optimists tend to have a positive explanatory style. If you attribute good things that happen to your skill and effort, then you are probably an optimist. Pessimists, on the other hand, usually have a negative attributional style. If you credit these good events to outside forces, then you likely have a more pessimistic way of thinking". The reverse is also true. When something bad happens, optimists tend to give more weight to external factors rather than themselves as being causally responsible, whereas pessimists are quicker to shoulder the blame personally, as we saw in the discussion of "self-talk". Obviously, there is a balance to be struck. A mindset which attributed good outcomes entirely to our own merit and bad ones entirely to uncontrollable external forces would clearly take things too far, especially since as we saw earlier that whatever successes or failures we may experience are largely attributable to the luck inherent in our genes and personal history, as well as in the particular circumstances of the situation itself.

4. Keep practicing. Cherry again: "there is no on:off switch for positive thinking. Even if you are a natural-born optimist, thinking positively when faced with challenging situations can be difficult. Like any goal, the key is to stick with it for the long-term...".

Expectations matter: how we think about ourself and others can materially change what we and they feel and do.

There is an important caveat to the assertion that our mindset cannot impact the external physical world. When other humans are involved then the expectations we project, for others and also for ourself, can indeed have an impact on how things turn out, in ways which may not always be obvious or consciously intended.

As one example, in his 2020 book *Humankind, a hopeful history*, Dutch historian Rutger Bregman describes a classic 1960s experiment in which the American psychologist Bob Rosenthal showed that in tests laboratory rats labelled as brighter started to outperform those labelled as less bright, even though, unbeknownst to the lab assistants, the initial classifications had in fact been entirely arbitrary. The explanation was people-centric, not rat-centric: the lab assistants had unconsciously begun to treat the "brighter" rats differently, giving them more care and attention, and thereby inducing genuinely superior performance.

Buoyed by this success, Rosenthal decided to extend his experimental range to human children, and Rutger takes up the story, on pp259-61 of *Humankind*: "when the new school year started, teachers at Spruce Elementary (my note: a school in California) learned that an acclaimed scientist by the name of Dr Rosenthal would be administering a test to the pupils. This 'Test of Inflected Acquisition' indicated who would make the greatest strides at school that year. In truth it was a common or garden IQ test, and, once the scores had been tallied, Rosenthal and his team cast them all aside. They tossed a coin to decide which kids they would tell teachers were 'high-potentials'. Kids, meanwhile, were told nothing at all. Sure enough, the power of expectation swiftly began to work its magic. Teachers gave the group of 'smart' pupils more attention, more encouragement and more praise, thus changing how the children saw themselves, too. The effect was clearest among the youngest kids, whose IQ scores increased by an average of twenty-seven points in a single year. The largest gains were among boys who looked Latino, a group typically subject to the lowest expectations in California. Rosenthal dubbed his discovery the Pygmalion Effect, after the mythological sculptor who fell so hard for one of his own creations that the gods decided to bring his statue to life. Beliefs we're devoted to – whether they're true or imagined – can likewise come to life, effecting very real change in the world…just as positive expectations have very real effects, nightmares can come true, too. The flipside of the Pygmalion Effect is what is known as the Golem Effect, named after the Jewish legend in which a creature meant to protect the citizens of Prague instead turns into a monster. Like the Pygmalion Effect, the Golem Effect is ubiquitous. When we have negative expectations about someone, we don't look at them as often. We distance ourselves from them. We don't smile at them as much. Basically, we do exactly what Rosenthal's students (my note: in other words, the lab assistants) did when they released the 'stupid' rats into the maze. Research on the Golem Effect is scant, which is not surprising, given the ethical objections to subjecting people to negative expectations. But what we do know is shocking. Take the study done by psychologist Wendell Johnson in Davenport, Iowa, in 1939. He split twenty orphans up into two groups, telling one that they were good, articulate speakers and the other that they were destined to become stutterers. Now infamously known as 'The Monster Study', this experiment left multiple individuals with lifelong speech impediments".

Bregman concludes: "the Pygmalion and Golem Effects are woven into the fabric of our world. Every day, we make each other smarter or stupider, stronger or weaker, faster or slower. We can't help leaking expectations, through our gazes, our body language and our voices. My expectations about you define my attitude towards you, and the way I behave towards you in turn influences your expectations and therefore your behaviour towards me".

One framework which can be helpful in framing our own and others' mindset in particular situations is the "Drama Triangle", proposed in the late 1960s by American psychologist Stephen Karpman, building on a concept called Transaction Analysis developed in the 1950s by Canadian psychiatrist Eric Berne. The Drama Triangle suggests that in many situations we are each prone to assign ourself one of three basic roles: "Victim", in which we act as the helpless and hapless sufferer; "Persecutor", in which we act in some sense as a hierarchical superior to the "Victim", for example proactively pointing out their faults; and "Rescuer", in which we seek to help the "Victim" by solving whatever problem for them. The underlying assumption is that all parties have positive intentions in all cases; so that for example a Persecutor may be motivated by a spirit of "tough love", believing that they have the best interests of the Victim at heart.

Two features of the model are noteworthy. The first is that the roles are exactly that – roles. The model posits that each person adopts the mindset associated with the role, usually subconsciously. However, there is nothing inherent in the situation which forces them to do this.

The second, important, point is that all three roles can be counter-productive, making a successful resolution less likely. By choosing a "Victim" mindset, a person deprives themself of agency, similar in some ways to the "Defeat" and "Learned Helplessness" responses in our earlier discussion of stress. A "Victim" may even actively seek out a "Persecutor", to validate their sense of victimhood. And the impact of a "Persecutor" is indeed likely to reinforce the "Victim's" sense of helplessness and reduce their sense of agency. Less obviously, a "Rescuer" also potentially contributes to the problem because the effect of solving, or even simply trying to solve, the "Victim's" problem for them is likely to be to increase the Victim's dependency and further erode their sense of agency.

To escape this doom loop, Karpman advocates a conscious shift of attitude for each party. The "Victim" instead becomes a "Creator", which is to say adopts a more active focus on what actions he or she might take to mitigate or improve the situation. The "Persecutor" becomes a "Challenger", focused on helping the "Creator" to clarify their own needs in order to move forwards. And the "Rescuer" becomes a "Coach", helping the Victim to frame and exercise their own personal choices, rather than seeking to solve whatever problem, or make whatever choices, for them. The main point for our purposes is that the mindset we adopt in a particular situation can contribute materially to the way we and others respond to it.

Finally, British journalist Emma Duncan reinforces the power our mindset can wield over our own behaviour, suggesting that if we are too quick to attribute undesirable outcomes to external or uncontrollable forces, in effect adopting the mindset of a victim, then we risk diluting our sense of personal agency and therefore our ability to take positive action. The example she uses is the challenge of obesity, and the associated societal pressure to avoid "body shaming" people who are overweight. In an article titled *We shouldn't be pretending it's fine to be fat*, published in *The Times* on 20 May 2022, Duncan acknowledges that whilst pushback to body shaming may be well-intentioned, there is a risk that it is also ultimately counter-productive precisely because it may undermine our sense of personal responsibility and choice. At the same time, Duncan acknowledges that there is a balance to be struck: "it's a good thing the fashion industry no longer encourages everybody to look like a rake, and in most ways it's a good thing that society has become kinder. When I was growing up, disabled people were spastic, dyslexic people were stupid and dyspraxic people were clumsy. I don't want to go back to that world. There is a downside to this progress, though. As we have become more understanding, so we have become less willing to hold people responsible for their choices. We view people increasingly as the victims of social forces rather than as agents with the power to shape their own fates. You can see that in our language. Health services describe people as 'living with' obesity, as though it were a creature that had crept in through the back door when nobody was watching, not the consequence of years of caramel frappuccinos with whipped cream and marshmallows. This tendency to regard obesity as society's fault, not the result of individual choice, seems to be exacerbating the problem. Studies show that the fatter people are, the more inclined they are to blame their weight on outside forces and the less control over it and responsibility for it they feel they have".

Duncan concludes that, yet again, the issue comes back to our ability to embrace and exercise a realistic level of agency: "if people believe they are powerless to lose weight, they are less likely to change their behaviour".

Chapter summary

Human consciousness defines our experience of existence, enabling us to survive and thrive as individuals and as a species whilst also enjoying a rich and textured inner life.

Consciousness is the material product of our material brain. It gives us the possibility, and in a sense the obligation, to exercise personal agency: to make conscious decisions about the person we want to be and how we choose to behave. At the same time, consciousness is subjective and fallible. We do well to cultivate an awareness of our own inevitable predispositions and biases so that we may make some appropriate level of allowance for these in the decisions we make and the choices we take in our day-to-day life.

Specific "beliefs" about consciousness include:

- Consciousness is entirely material. There is no such thing as an immortal soul: our mortal life as a conscious being on Earth is our entire existence.

- Consciousness gives us the existential freedom to choose what we do and how we behave. In particular, executive function enables us to "mind the gap" between a stimulus and how we choose to respond.
- Exercising this freedom to choose can only be done by engaging our sense of "self", filtered through our own unique personality.
- Learning happens when our lived experiences act on our genes to form networks of neural connections, which are then strengthened or weakened over time. Our specific network of neural connections is unique to us. The most intense period for forming these is when we are young, but we continue to form new pathways, and strengthen or weaken others, throughout our life. This means that the experiences we have in our early years have a disproportionate impact on, but do not completely determine, the person we eventually become; and that some level of continuing growth and development remains possible even as we age.
- Consciousness is ultimately subjective. Our senses transmit data from the outside world, which our brain then uses to create a representation of "reality" inside our mind, as the basis for determining how best to respond to a given situation. Whilst this process is highly effective and efficient overall, it also lays us open to fallibility in important ways:

– our brain works on the basis of "data sampling", which is to say that it takes a subset of the total amount of data which is in theory available, and uses this to create a representation of reality inside. The picture our brain creates may not always be an accurate interpretation of the data. More than one valid interpretation may be possible from a particular set of data.

– our brain looks for patterns to make sense of the world around us. These often take the form of "cause-and-effect" relationships. We can be fooled into "seeing" a wrong pattern, or seeing a pattern where none exists.

- our brain tends to categorise, even though what it is dealing with is often (but not always) a continuum. This can lead us to think of things as binary, or rigidly defined, when in fact they are nuanced.
- Our behaviours are driven by a combination of instinct, emotion and reason. Whilst these are mainly processed in different parts of our physical brain, they also interact in important ways. Emotions are a powerful stimulus, although their effects often take place below the level of our conscious mind. We are prone to a (large) number of cognitive biases, which can mislead us into thinking we are acting rationally when in fact we are not.
- Consciousness gives us a number of important faculties, including:
- reason: the ability to think critically and analytically;
- emotions: which have a powerful effect on our behaviour, and largely define our experience of existence;
- language, without which it is hard to see how reason could work, but which also inevitably has limitations and can be prone to ambiguity or unclear meaning;
- a capacity for empathy, enabling us to experience the emotions of other people as if they were our own; and the ability to think ourself into others' shoes, called Theory of Mind. These faculties are particularly important to our ability to live as members of complex social groups, as well as to enjoying a textured mental life.
- memory, which is crucial to learning and our sense of self. However, memories are essentially reconstructions made by our brain, and can also be selective and fallible.
- imagination, specifically the ability to imagine concepts and things which are not currently and may never be real. This has enormous benefits, but also creates a challenge in for example clearly differentiating between fiction and fact.
- motivation and drive, which help us to take decisive action and get things done.

- Two factors stand out as having a big impact on how our individual consciousness functions:
  - sleep is fundamental to both our brain and body. But many of us do not put sufficiently high priority on getting enough sleep, of sufficient quality.
  - high levels of sustained stress can be associated with impaired brain function and undesirable health outcomes. At the same time, a "healthy" level of stress can be beneficial. Our own mindset can play an important role in how we experience stress.
- Consciousness has important implications for our personal existence:
  - the fact that we have the freedom to exercise personal existential choice means that we should actively embrace it, and then take responsibility for the choices we make.
  - the fact that our consciousness is fallible means that in making choices we should give appropriate consideration to the possibility of bias and error.
  - "luck" is a fact of life, whereas "destiny" isn't.
  - mindset matters: how we think about our life obviously affects how we feel about it, and can also influence outcomes.
  - expectations matter: how we think about ourself and others can change what we and they feel and do.

Of course, our consciousness does not operate in a vacuum but rather in whatever environment we are fortunate, or unfortunate, to live. And, because we are human, the defining characteristic of this environment is likely to be social above all. In the next chapter we will explore our capacity, and need, for sociability, and the implications this has for how we might exercise our existential choices about how to behave.

Chapter 3:

Sociability

"Only connect..."
E.M Forster, 1910

"No man is an island," the 17th century English metaphysical poet John Donne famously observed, as it happens not in one of his poems but rather in Meditation XVII, part of his prose *Meditations upon Emergent Occasions*, published in 1624.

Indeed, we are social animals first and foremost. Our propensity to cooperate, especially with strangers with whom we have no underlying genetic connection, has profoundly shaped our cognition, as we saw in the last chapter. It is also the behaviour which most distinguishes humans from other species.

Cooperation enables us to learn from and participate in the vast suite of cultural adaptations which have ultimately come to define our species, for example technologies, such as cooking; ways of doing things, such as (in the historical context) hunting and gathering; and novel organisational forms, such as living in extended bands, tribes, and eventually complex industrial societies. And our ability to survive and thrive as individuals is largely defined by our capacity to live and engage productively as a member of a social group.

It is no coincidence that evolution has equipped us with a powerful emotional need for social affiliation. Love, friendship, and simple fellowship, accompanied by a sense of truly belonging, are perhaps the most powerful and fulfilling emotions it is possible to experience; and conversely their mirror image of social alienation, estrangement, and loneliness can be amongst the most harrowing. These pro-social emotions encourage us to behave in pro-social ways, suggesting in turn that those of our remote ancestors' generations who developed the emotional range to reinforce collaboration out-survived and out-reproduced those who did not.

Of course, having a propensity to cooperate does not mean that this is our default behaviour, on all occasions and under all circumstances. Manifestly it is not. A capacity for selfishness remains an important part of our make-up, with an accompanying predilection for anti-social behaviours such as hierarchy, status and dominance, not to mention bullying, intimidation and even violence.

And what is true at the level of our species is also true for each of us as individuals. We each have some capacity for *both* cooperative and selfish behaviours, even though our specific individual profile, social needs and aptitudes, and behavioural "triggers" of course vary based on our own unique genes and experiences.

The net of all this is that the existential choices we make between when to cooperate and when to behave selfishly, or "compete", are among the most important that we face, precisely because they bear on the social relationships which themselves largely condition our existence.

Nor is it the case that selfish behaviours are automatically or always wrong. There are many situations in which if we do not look out for our own interests, at least at some level, we cannot be confident that anyone else will. The harsh reality is that to behave consistently selflessly regardless of circumstance is to invite exploitation, and might legitimately be called naïve. And the same evolutionary logic applies. The fact that both cooperative and selfish behaviours survive in our modern world, and that at least the impulse for both remains hard-wired into each of us as individuals, strongly suggests that those of our remote ancestors' generations who adopted a mixed strategy of cooperation-with-selfishness out-competed those of their compatriots who were either consistently selfish, or consistently selfless.

The point is that we each have within us elements of both Dr Jekyll and Mr Hyde, the competing personalities of the single fictional protagonist of the 19th century British novelist Robert Louis Stevenson. In the previous chapter we discussed how freewill, in particular our brain's executive function, enables us to exercise some level of existential choice over our own behaviour. In this chapter we will explore how our sociable nature means that many of the most important choices we face are specifically between "cooperative" behaviours, which is to say those in which we privilege the needs, wants and feelings of other people; and "selfish" ones, in which our behaviour is more attuned to our own personal interests.

These decisions are "existential" in that they directly affect how our life unfolds, and often also how we feel about ourself as a consequence of whatever choice we make. However, they are certainly not rare. On the contrary, we each face choices of this kind many times every day, often in quite mundane settings.

Finally, in contemplating these decisions there is a balance to be struck. For sure, if we place too great an emphasis on our own interests we run the risk that we will eventually meet a bigger bully, or that we will fail to build the deep personal connections which can enrich and provide meaning for our life. On the other hand, a strategy of "always cooperate" will simply lay us open to exploitation. A bias towards cooperation is likely to serve us well, but a single default response towards it in all circumstances is unlikely to. When it comes to making a specific choice in a particular situation, context is all.

Part A. Pro-social behaviours

Why sociability matters

Humans may be among the most "groupish" of animals, but a tendency to sociability does not by itself make us unique. In fact, there is a solid evolutionary logic for why we might expect groupishness to develop more generally in nature, stretching back right to the earliest life forms.

The American psychologist Joshua Greene summarises, on p20 of his 2013 book *Moral Tribes*: "why should any creature be social? Why not just go it alone? The reason is that individuals can sometimes accomplish things together that they can't accomplish by themselves. This principle has guided the evolution of life on earth from the start. Approximately four billion years ago, molecules joined together to form cells. About two billion years later, cells joined together to form more complex cells. And then a billion years later, these more complex cells joined together to form multicellular organisms. These collectives evolved because the participating individuals could, by working together, spread their genetic material in new and more effective ways. Fast-forward another billion years to our world, which is full of social animals, from ants to wolves to humans. The same principle applies. Ant colonies and wolf packs can do things that no single ant or wolf can do, and we humans, by cooperating with one another, have become the earth's dominant species".

In a modern human context social groups create the potential for major gains in economic productivity, through the division and specialisation of labour. This was famously explained by the 18th century Scottish economist Adam Smith, in his book *The Wealth of Nations*, published in 1776. Smith gives the example of a factory making pins, in which, if every worker works alone they will each produce 20 pins per day, whereas 10 workers who each specialise in different aspects of the process will have a daily output of 48,000. Whilst the maths behind this impressive leap in productivity may not be entirely clear the broader point certainly is: individuals working together can often achieve a great deal more than if they work alone.

And evolution has wired us as humans to be "obligatorily gregarious", harnessing all of our neurology, our physiology, and our emotions in service of the sociable cause. American neuroscientist John Cacioppo and writer William Patrick summarise, on p127 of their 2008 book *Loneliness*: "our brains and bodies are designed to function in aggregates, not in isolation. That is the essence of an obligatorily gregarious species. The attempt to function in denial of our need for others, whether that need is great or small in any given individual, violates our design specifications...social connection is not just a lubricant that, like motor oil, prevents overheating and wear. Social connection is a fundamental part of the human operating (and organising) system itself".

There are complications, naturally. In particular, pro-social behaviours which are in the interests of the group may not always be in the interests of each individual member. To take an obvious if stark example, sharing food is all well and good when there is enough to go around, but what about times when there isn't and one or more individuals must starve? Also, groupishness creates the possibility and therefore incentive for what the literature calls "freeloading", in which an individual benefits from shared resources without contributing his or her share of the effort needed to acquire them, leaving the individual themself with surplus energy to spend on other things. We may regard this as invidious behaviour, but as we will explore in the next chapter, evolution does not concern itself with morality, just with survival and the reproduction of offspring who themselves survive. And it is not hard to find examples of freeloading behaviour in everyday life, even in quite mundane instances such as the person who pushes to the front of a queue whilst others wait patiently in line.

Culture as the defining human attribute

In the previous chapter we heard from Michael Tomasello about the importance of culture in enabling our species' success, benefiting from the "ratchet effect" whereby cultural innovations are shared within groups and across generations and, mostly, progressively enhanced over time.

Humans are unique in being the only species to have crossed what the American evolutionary biologist Joseph Henrich describes as a "Rubicon", after which cultural evolution rivals, or arguably surpasses, genetic evolution in importance; to the extent that culture can even drive genetic adaptation.

We briefly met Henrich in Chapter 2 when discussing positive thinking and the power of placebos. On p3 of his book *The Secret of Our Success* Henrich explains how culture came to define our species, and therefore the social environment in which individuals live out their existence: "the key to understanding how humans evolved and why we are so different from other animals is to recognise that we are a *cultural species* (author's emphasis). Probably over 1 million years ago, members of our evolutionary lineage began learning from each other in such a way that culture became cumulative. That is, hunting practices, tool-making skills, tracking know-how, and edible-plant knowledge began to improve and aggregate – by learning from others – so that one generation could build on and hone the skills and know-how gleaned from the previous generation. After several generations, this process produced a sufficiently large and complex toolkit of practices and techniques that individuals, relying only on their own ingenuity and personal experience, could not get anywhere close to figuring out over their lifetime...once these useful skills and practices began to accumulate and improve over generations, natural selection had to favour individuals who were better cultural learners, who could more effectively tap into and use the ever-expanding body of adaptive information available. The newly produced products of this cultural evolution, such as fire, cooking, cutting tools, clothing, simple gestural languages, throwing spears, and water containers, became the sources of the main selective pressures that genetically shaped our minds and bodies. This interaction between culture and genes, or what I'll call *culture-gene coevolution* (again, author's emphasis), drove our species down a novel, evolutionary pathway, not observed elsewhere in nature, making us very different from other species – a new kind of animal".

The most acute pressure in a culture-led environment is to be able to learn from others, putting a premium on having a brain adapted to this purpose, as Henrich explains on p35: "culture, and cultural evolution, are...a consequence of genetically evolved psychological adaptations for learning from other people. That is, natural selection favoured genes for building brains with abilities to learn from others".

What is "culture" exactly? On p34 of *The Secret of Our Success* Henrich offers a definition: "the suites or packages of skills, beliefs, practices, motivations, and organisational forms that permit people to survive, and often thrive, in diverse and challenging environments".

And on p36 he gives some concrete examples of what he calls "domains of cultural learning":

- Food preferences and quantity eaten
- Mate choices (individuals and their traits)
- Economic strategies (investments)
- Artefact (tool) functions and use
- Suicide (decision and method)
- Technological adoptions
- Word meanings and dialect
- Categories ("dangerous animals")
- Beliefs (e.g. about gods, germs, etc.)
- Social norms (taboos, rituals, tipping)
- Standards of reward and punishment
- Social motivations (altruism and fairness)
- Self-regulation
- Judgement heuristics

Once started, cultural developments in these and other areas created what Henrich describes as an "autocatalytic" process, whereby as our brainpower grew so further cultural developments were produced, in turn stimulating our brains to develop further still, and so on. On p57 he says: "the central argument in this book is that relatively early in our species' evolutionary history, perhaps around the origins of our genus (*homo*) about 2 million years ago, we first crossed this evolutionary Rubicon, at which point cultural evolution became the *primary driver of our species' genetic evolution* (author's emphasis). This interaction between cultural and genetic evolution generated a process that can be described as *autocatalytic* (again, author's emphasis), meaning that it produces the fuel that propels it. Once cultural information began to accumulate and produce cultural adaptations, the main selection pressure on genes revolved around improving our psychological abilities to acquire, store, process, and organise the array of fitness-enhancing skills and practices that became increasingly available in the minds of the others in one's group. As genetic evolution improved our brains and abilities for learning from others, cultural evolution spontaneously generated more and better cultural adaptations, which kept the pressure on for brains that were better at acquiring and storing this cultural information. This process will continue until halted by an external constraint".

For most, perhaps all, other species it is genetic adaptation which allows them to survive in diverse environments, ultimately leading to the emergence of entirely new species when the environments are sufficiently different. By contrast, humans exhibit remarkably little genetic diversity even though we have expanded to live in almost every land-based environment available. Rather, it is culture, and our ability to adapt culture to the needs of a particular environment, which has been the driving force. Crucially, culture requires not only that our brains are adapted to learning it, but also that we live in social groups of some size so that we have people to learn from; and that group members behave in sufficiently pro-social ways that the learning can occur.

And rates of cultural development are highly sensitive to both group size and the degree of inter-connectedness within it. Larger, better-connected groups create what Henrich terms a "collective brain", in which the whole is greater than any individual member could achieve, regardless of how personally brilliant a single individual might be. He explains, on p212: "once individuals evolve to learn from one another with sufficient accuracy (fidelity), social groups of individuals develop what might be called *collective brains* (author's emphasis). The power of these collective brains to develop increasingly effective tools and technologies, as well as other forms of nonmaterial culture (e.g. know-how), depends in part on the size of the group of individuals engaged and on their social interconnectedness. It's our collective brains operating over generations, and not the innate inventive power or creative abilities of individual brains, that explain our species' fancy technologies and massive ecological success".

Henrich goes on to illustrate these effects. On p213 he addresses group size: "the most obvious way that the size of a group can matter is that more minds can generate more lucky errors, novel recombinations, chance insights, and intentional improvements. To see this in starkest terms, consider how group size influences the chance of coming up with an invention, say using feathers to fletch an arrow. Suppose any one individual operating alone will only figure out – by luck or effort – 'arrow fletching' once in one thousand lifetimes. The chance that at least one person in a group of 10 people will figure out fletching in their lifetimes is then 1%. So, on average, a group of 10 persons will take 100 generations to come up with this invention (2,500 years). In a group of 100 people, at least one person will devise it 10% of the time in one lifetime. Consequently, on average, it will take 11 generations for the group to figure this out (275 years). For 1000 people, there's a 63% chance they will get it in one generation, and on average, they will figure it out in 1.6 generations (40 years). If you can unite 10,000 minds, you will have fletching in one generation (well, technically, a 99.995% chance). So, bigger groups have the potential for more rapid cumulative cultural evolution, especially since these effects further compound when you consider that many inventions require combining several elements, so their rate of emergence depends on the slowest element".

Heinrich then describes the surprising power of interconnectedness and how this can often mean that "it is better to be social than smart", on pp213-4: "(all) this, of course, assumes that the members of (a) group are sufficiently socially connected to other members of the group, so that their improvements can rapidly spread through the group. The bigger the group, the more implausible this assumption is. To see the importance of this sociality, imagine that every person is a social island, who keeps any insights he has secret from all others. What happens? Well, not much. Some individuals will make slightly better tools, but then they will die and their improvements will go with them. No fancy tools will emerge. And the size of the group doesn't matter. This is the case for most animals...thus, along with group size, the degree of social interconnectedness is very powerful in generating cumulative, cultural evolution, even more powerful than individual smarts. Consider two very large pre-human populations, the *Geniuses* and the *Butterflies*. Suppose the Geniuses will devise an invention once in 10 lifetimes. The Butterflies are much dumber, only devising the same invention once in 1000 lifetimes. So, this means that the Geniuses are 100 times smarter than the Butterflies. However, the Geniuses are not very social and have only one friend they can learn from. The Butterflies have 10 friends, making them 10 times more social. Now, everyone in both populations tries to obtain an invention, both by figuring it out for themselves and by learning from friends. Suppose learning from friends is difficult: if a friend has it, a learner only learns it half the time. After everyone has done their own individual learning and tried to learn from their friends, do you think the innovation will be more common among the Geniuses or the Butterflies? Well, among the Geniuses a bit fewer than 1 out of 5 individuals (18%) will end up with the invention. Half of those Geniuses will have figured it out all by themselves. Meanwhile, 99.9% of Butterflies will have the innovation, but only 0.1% will have figured it out by themselves. Keep in mind that the Geniuses were 100 times smarter than the Butterflies, whereas the Butterflies were only 10 times more social. Bottom line: if you want to have cool technology, it's better to be social than smart. Now, suppose the invention mentioned above is the bow and arrow, and the Butterflies and the Geniuses come into conflict over territory. Who would win, the smarter group, or the more social one? It's unclear, but the Butterflies would have a good chance, since they would all be armed with bows and arrows, but only 18% of the Geniuses would".

As an aside, the importance of passing cultural knowledge down the generations potentially also helps to explain the unusual prevalence of grandparenting among humans. For most species grandparenting is simply not a practical option because evolution has decreed that once an individual passes beyond their own reproductive years they soon die, presumably based on the unsentimental logic that if they were to continue living the benefits that would accrue to the gene pool would be more than outweighed by the extra resources they would consume. Conversely, Henrich explains on pp133-4 of *The Secret of Our Success* that for humans: "the longer we live, the more information we accumulate, and the potentially more valuable we are as transmitters of this wisdom, provided the world is relatively stable during one lifetime (which it probably was for most of our species' evolutionary history). Under these conditions, natural selection should favour extending our lives in order to give us time to transmit our accumulated know-how to our children and grandchildren, and to make sure that they have the time and opportunity to learn what they will need. As individuals, our cultural stock is going up over the decades while our physical skills are going down, as are our abilities to produce high-quality babies. At a certain point, those lines cross, and it's time to stop reproduction and focus all of our efforts on the current children and grandchildren. However, given our declining physical abilities, one of the major ways we can help our younger relatives, especially in traditional societies, is by dispensing our accumulated wisdom. This is why humans, but not other primates, live for decades beyond when we stop reproducing, and even live past when we stop being economically productive. This longevity not only emerges in modern societies, but has also now been shown among hunter-gatherers and other small-scale societies, and likely dates back tens or even hundreds of thousands of years into the Paleolithic. By contrast, chimpanzees and other primates do not possess a long post-reproductive life. Death usually follows in relatively short order after reproduction ends".

For completeness, grandparenting makes humans unusual but not unique. For example, it has also been observed among elephants, presumably for similar adaptive reasons relating to the sharing of experience. In a 2016 study of South Asian elephants published in the journal *Scientific Reports*, Finnish biologist Mirkka Lahdenpera found that the calves of young (and therefore inexperienced) elephant mothers were eight times more likely to survive if their grandmothers lived near them than if they didn't, although the same effect was not observed with the calves of older, more experienced mothers (taken from an online article by Mara Grunbaum called *Do Any Animals Know Their Grandparents*, published on *Live Science* dated 9 March 2019).

The broader point is that as culture became progressively more important to human success, so it started to exert selective pressure on our genes. To take one example from many, on p69 of *The Secret of Our Success* Henrich describes how the advent of culinary innovations such as fire and cooking led to dramatic changes in our digestive system. This in turn had the dual effect of freeing up resources that our body could redeploy to other, more adaptive, areas, particularly bigger brains; as well as eventually making it challenging for us to survive without access to cooked food: "our repertoire of food-processing methods altered the genetic selection pressures on our digestive system by gradually supplanting some of its functions with cultural substitutes. Techniques such as cooking actually increase the energy available from foods and make them easier to digest and detoxify. This effect allowed natural selection to save substantial amounts of energy by reducing our gut tissue, the second most expensive tissue in our bodies (next to brain tissue), and our susceptibility to various diseases associated with gut tissue. The energy savings from the externalisation of digestive functions by cultural evolution became one component in a suite of adjustments that permitted our species to build and run bigger and bigger brains".

Culture also changes our body in ways which although not genetic, which is to say that do not automatically pass from one generation to the next, are clearly biological, in other words have a material and lasting impact on the way our body works. Again, one example will suffice from many. Henrich describes how literacy changes our brain, on pp260-1: "highly literate people have different brains than those who are illiterate because they've trained their brains to read. Learning to read specialises your brain for visually processing whatever writing system you are working on. The better you can read, the more specialised the wiring of your brain is for reading...(for example) it thickens the corpus callosum, the information highway that connects the left and right sides of the brain". There is an, inevitable, trade-off, however: "these enhancements don't come without costs. Skilled readers are probably worse at identifying faces...I was personally glad to hear this, as I now have an excuse for why I forget faces so often – I've recycled some of my facial recognition neuronal firmware to support my reading addiction".

The critical point from the perspective of this book is that culture enables, and in turn requires, social groups in which individuals behave prosocially, at least much of the time. Without this, there would simply be no-one to learn from. The fact that larger and more connected groups are conducive to better, faster, cultural development creates adaptive pressure for larger social structures and more collaborative individual behaviours, stretching well beyond our own immediate genetically-based kin group. This again sets humans apart from other species, including other primates, as Henrich describes on pp162-4 of *The Secret of Our Success*: "perhaps the most important feature of social life in human hunter-gatherers, in contrast with other primates, is that individuals are socially connected into an immense network of other people scattered across numerous other groups. In many foraging societies, band membership itself is quite fluid. If an individual or family wants to leave their band, due to some acute social tensions, drought, or just to visit friends, they can tap a network of contacts who can open the doors to extended visits in other bands. By contrast, chimpanzees live in troops that patrol and defend a territory...intruders are attacked and killed on sight, unless they are young females, who are permitted to move among troops...the vast tribal social networks that mobile hunter-gatherers rely on, for example, in times of drought and war, are largely constituted and nourished by social (my note: we might also say 'cultural') norms of various types, including those related to rituals, marriage, and exchange".

In sum, early in our species' development culture came to define us to an extent not seen in any other species. The consequences were profound, including: larger brains capable of engaging in social learning across a complex range of aspects of culture; social groups of sufficient size and inter-connectedness to enable such learning to occur; and pro-social behavioural norms which reinforced group cohesion and individual learning.

Sociability as the defining human behaviour

As we saw in our discussion of the evolution of human cognition, what makes humans unique in terms of sociability is not the fact of our groupishness but rather the nature of it.

Specifically, we have the capacity to cooperate in an intentional way, with a broad range of fellow-humans including people to whom we have no particular genetic connection. This distinguishes us on the one hand from eusocial species such as ants and bees, which create enormous colonies with individual specialisation of roles but are united by a strong shared genetic inheritance since all members of the colony are descended from the same queen; and on the other from social species such as lions, wolves and other primates, which typically cooperate within limited groups, generally reflecting some element of kin connection, and still with a primary focus on within-group competition.

The American anthropologist Herman Pontzer explains how the specific capacity to share food sets humans apart from even our closest evolutionary cousins the other apes, conferring distinct, and ultimately decisive, evolutionary advantages. The passage is taken from pp131-2 of *Burn*: "what makes hunting and gathering so successful isn't the *hunting* or the *gathering*, it's the *and*. More than just *man the hunter* or *woman the gatherer*, we are *human the sharer*. In stark contrast, the living apes hardly ever share. Sure, mothers of all ape species will occasionally share some food with their infants or young children. Orangutan mothers in the wild share food with their young kids about one out of every 10 meals, usually foods that are difficult to obtain...sharing among adult apes is even less common. Gorillas have *never* been observed sharing food among adults in the wild. Adult chimpanzees in the Sonso community in the Budongo forest of Uganda share food about once every two months, and much of what passes for 'sharing' is more like tolerated theft. Bonobos share the most, but even they fall well short of the human norm. At the site of Wamba in Congo, Japanese researcher Shinya Yamamoto found that adult bonobos (mostly females) share a particular fruit, the large and fleshy junglesop, about 14% of the time...apes, despite their intricate, lifelong social relationships, live lives of dietary solitude. When it comes to food, they are on their own. Consequently, they are compelled to go for the sure thing, to make certain that they get enough food each day to keep from starving. And there's little upside to pursuing big game or gathering more than they need; anything they can't shove in their mouths *right now* will go to waste or be pilfered by beggars, who are unlikely to ever return the favour...(on the other hand) humans are social foragers. We routinely bring home more than we need, with the intention of giving it away to our community. That means we have one another as a safety net; if someone comes home empty-handed, they won't go hungry. This allows us to diversify and take risks, to develop complementary foraging strategies – hunting and gathering – that maximise the potential for big gains while limiting the consequences of failure...and the foundation of it all is the inviolable, ironclad, unspoken understanding that we will share...sharing is the glue that binds hunter-gatherer communities together and provides the fuel that makes them run" (author's emphasis throughout).

Once a tendency to cooperate became established, it is easy to see how evolutionary pressures might reinforce and accelerate it, in much the same way that the increasing importance of culture created pressure for the larger brains and collaborative behaviours needed to learn. On pp56-7 of *Loneliness*, Cacioppo and Patrick quote the evolutionary biologist George Williams: "in his book *Adaptation and Natural Selection* (1966)...George Williams summed up the idea with a direct contradiction of Hobbes's notion of early human existence as a constant state of battle: 'simply stated, an individual who maximises his friendships and minimises his antagonisms will have an evolutionary advantage, and selection should favour those characters that promote the optimisation of personal relationships'".

Cacioppo and Patrick explain, on pp14-15 of *Loneliness*, that there is still some variation between individual humans in our propensity, and need, for sociability: "each of us inherits from our parents a certain level of need for social inclusion (also expressed as a sensitivity to the pain of social exclusion), just as we inherit a certain basic body type and basic level of intelligence. (In each case, the influence of the environment on where that genetic inheritance takes us is also vitally important.)...some people love hot sauce – they crave it on everything. For others, a hint of jalapeño sends them gasping for ice water. Human variation in the desire for connection is similarly broad".

These differences arise, of course, from the differences in our individual genetic profiles and the unique set of experiences to which we are each exposed. And on pp23-5 the authors conclude that, as with many other traits, our specific sociability profile is attributable roughly 50% to our genes, and 50% to our experiences: "the standard way to sort out the heritable (genetic) component from the environmental component of any human characteristic – including the relative intensity of our appetite for social connection – is to do long-term studies of (identical) twins...when we found loneliness in one member of a pair of these identical twins, our prediction of loneliness in the second member of the pair was right approximately forty-eight percent of the time...heritability in human behaviour means that the genes set the course, but that the environment still strongly influences the final destination. The influence of genes on a purely physical characteristic such as eye colour is generally 100 percent, as is the influence of genes on certain conditions such as Huntington's disease. In those cases, genes are in fact destiny; the environment is never going to change the outcome. With the genetic bias towards a greater need for feelings of connection, however, a genetic contribution of forty-eight percent allows for a fifty-two percent contribution from the world we encounter".

As an aside, Cacioppo and Patrick also assert, on p24, that a roughly 50:50 balance between genetic and environmental effects is an appropriate rule of thumb for other aspects of our personality: "it so happens that a heritability coefficient around .48 also holds true for most of the other genetically influenced major personality characteristics such as neuroticism, agreeableness, and anxiety".

The point is that we are each programmed to be sociable, to a greater or lesser extent. But this is not at all to say that we are programmed *only* to cooperate. On the contrary, cooperation must occur in the context of a Darwinian world characterised above all by an unending competition for resources, across and within species. Individual success depends on reaping the benefits of cooperation without ignoring entirely the potential rewards from selfishness, or at least taking into account not just our own behaviours but also those of other people. Cacioppo and Patrick summarise, on p62 of *Loneliness*: "all of life represents a working out of the cost-benefit ratio of cooperation versus aggression. As the evolutionary biologist Martin Nowak suggests, 'perhaps the most remarkable aspect of evolution is its ability to generate cooperation in a competitive world'.

We humans are at the top of the food chain because we are the species most adept at behaving generously whilst also accruing the benefits of competition".

And what is true for "all of life" is true for each of us as individuals. We are repeatedly called on to choose between cooperating or behaving selfishly in particular situations, to the extent that these are perhaps the most important choices that we make.

The evolution of human sociability, and society

We discussed in the previous chapter how human cognition developed hand-in-glove with increased levels of collaboration and sociability, specifically a move from the "competitive foraging" which characterises our modern ape cousins and, we hypothesise, our last common ancestor; to intentional "joint foraging" and, eventually, cooperative "group foraging" as the rainforests retreated and proto-humans adapted to life on the savanna.

As we saw in Chapter 1, humans are a branch of the primate family, which has its origins around 65 million years ago, diverging from other mammals around the time of or perhaps slightly after the extinction of the dinosaurs. Early primates were small, tree-dwelling animals, existing exclusively on fruit and vegetables. Apes diverged from other primates around 21 million years ago, and were successful for a long time, spawning dozens of species. Then around 7 million years ago most ape species died out, and around the same time hominids, which is to say proto-humans, diverged from other apes. This was a period of considerable climate change, in which the African rainforests gradually started to retreat, being replaced by more open grassland known as savanna, and it seems reasonable to assume that the various significant changes in the ape lineage were related to the changes taking place in the physical environment more broadly.

Our closest surviving cousins the chimpanzees and bonobos retreated with the rainforests, along with the other great apes, the gorillas and orangutans. This strategy was successful in that these species survive, outcompeting other ape species which became extinct.

Hominids, however, took a different approach, adapting to the new savanna environment and spending progressively less time in trees and more on the ground. At some point our ancestors also made the transition from hierarchy-dominated competition for mates and promiscuity to (relatively) faithful pair-bonding. It was far from obvious that such a fundamental shift would occur, as the Russian-born American physicist turned biologist Sergey Gavrilets explains in his article *Human origins and the transition from promiscuity to pair-bonding*, published on the *NIH (National Library of Medicine)* website dated 29 May 2012: "a crucial step in recent theories of human origins is the emergence of strong pair-bonding between males and females accompanied by a dramatic reduction in the male-to-male conflict over mating and an increased investment in offspring. How such a transition from promiscuity to pair-bonding could be achieved is puzzling. Many species would, indeed, be much better off evolutionarily if the effort spent on male competition over mating was redirected to increasing female fertility or survivorship of offspring. Males, however, are locked in a 'social dilemma', where shifting one's effort from 'appropriation' to 'production' would give an advantage to free-riding competitors and therefore, should not happen".

Improbable as it may have been, the shift to pair-bonding occurred within the early human population. Gavrilets suggests that it might have been fuelled by sexual selection: specifically females, the "choosier" sex because of their relatively greater investment in reproduction, adopting a preference for males willing to make a larger investment in parenting. Gavrilets explains that, somewhat paradoxically, these would most likely have been lower-ranked males within whatever dominance hierarchy existed, and that, furthermore, the evolutionarily stable equilibrium would be for strong but not total fidelity to the pair-bond: "(the) benefits (of pair-bonding) are most pronounced for low-ranked males who have a low chance of winning a mate in competition with top-ranked males. One, therefore, should expect that it is low-ranked males who will attempt to buy mating by provisioning...top-ranked males can easily beat out or chase away the low-ranked males and steal the paternity, making the investment of low-ranked males in production wasteful. However, after females start developing preferences for being provisioned, the low-ranked males' investments start to pay off...male provisioning and female faithfulness coevolve in a self-reinforcing manner. At the end, except for a very small proportion of the top-ranked individuals, males invest exclusively in provisioning females who have evolved very high fidelity to their mates. Overall, females are not predicted to become completely faithful, but rather, the level of their faithfulness is expected to be controlled by a balance between selection for better genes (potentially supplied by top-ranked males) and better access for food and care (provided largely by low-ranked males)".

Gavrilets suggests that the change to pair-bonding likely happened soon after the divergence of the hominid lineage, around 6-7 million years ago: "new palaeontological data on 4.4 million-year-old fossils of *Ardipithecus ramidis* show that this species already had a reduced sexual size dimorphism and strong reduction in upper canine teeth. This finding and a loss of morphological adaptations to sperm competition in humans suggest that strong decline in the intensity of male-to-male conflict, which is one of the consequences of the transition to pair-bonding, happened soon after the hominins/chimpanzees divergence".

Whatever the timing, the ramifications were significant, as Gavrilets, again, explains: "the transition to strong pair-bonding opened a path to intensified male parental investment, which was a breakthrough adaptation with multiple anatomical, behavioural, and physiological consequences for early hominins and all of their descendants. The establishment of pair-bonding shifted competition between males for mates, which was potentially destructive for the group, to a new dimension which is beneficial for the group – competition to be a better provider to get better mates. Pair-bonding provided a foundation for the later emergence of the institution of modern family as an outcome of additional processes, such as wealth accumulation and inheritance. Pair-bonding also made possible the recognition of male kin, dramatically expanding the efficiency of kin selection and helping by grandparents, leading to stronger within-group coalitions and alliances, and allowing for subsequent evolution of widespread cooperation in general".

A second important change which accompanied our ancestors move from trees to savanna was the crucial evolutionary adaptation to become bipedal, which is to say to walk upright on two legs. This may have happened as long ago as around 4 million years. As we briefly reviewed in Chapter 1, bipedalism is more economical for covering long distances, and allowed for better sight across a savannah terrain. Complementary adaptive developments at around this time included: sweat glands covering the entire skin, providing an advantage for movement in hot sun; loss of body hair, aiding the evaporation of sweat; and greater pigmentation of skin and eyes, protecting nuclear DNA from the higher UV levels in the new more open environment.

Around 2.5 million years ago we see the earliest clear evidence of hominid cooperation and sharing: the shift to collaborative foraging and the "joint intentionality" described by Tomasello. Herman Pontzer takes up the story, on pp124-34 of *Burn*: "...from the fossil record we know that the earliest hominins walked on two legs and had stubby, less lethal canine teeth. Otherwise, they were very apelike: chimpanzee-sized bodies and brains; long arms, long fingers, and grasping feet for scrambling high up in the trees...but around 2.5 million years ago, hominins started behaving in strange, un-apelike ways. Rather than hunting the occasional monkey or small antelope, they began targeting much larger game – zebras and other big animals. Stone tools begin to show up all across East Africa in large numbers, and animal fossils from sites in Kenya and Ethiopia show signs of butchery. Meat was no longer a rare delicacy, it was a regular part of the menu. This was the dawn of hunting and gathering...it marks the early emergence of our genus, *Homo*. But the crucial cognitive leap was not the hunting or the tools – after all, chimpanzees and bonobos hunt and make tools, and it hasn't led to any radical departure from their ape-ish ways. The big dietary innovation that would change our metabolism and our evolutionary destinies wasn't the food these hominins ate, it was the food they gave away...despite the long odds against it, in a population of ape-brained hominins some two and a half million years ago, somewhere in eastern Africa, the right combination of conditions, diet, and behaviour aligned. Sharing became the norm".

Once established, sharing became part of a positive feedback loop, enabling the hunter-gatherer lifestyle; which itself enabled a more secure and more varied diet, with greater quantities of meat. These extra high-energy calorie sources fuelled a gradual increase in brain size, helped by the fact that the changes in diet made digestion easier, so that the body's resources could be rebalanced: as our brain grew larger so our digestive system shrank.

Larger, more complex brains led to the cognitive developments we reviewed in Chapter 2, in turn producing innovation such as more sophisticated tools and hunting weapons; for example hand axes around 1.5 million years ago, and the earliest spears around 700,000 years ago. At some point, tentatively dated to around 4-500,000 years ago, fire was harnessed, changing the chemical composition of food in ways which again made it easier to digest, enabling more calories to be absorbed for relatively less effort.

And all the while, as we heard from Tomasello, the motive force driving the increase in brain size and cognitive ability was the need to engage in increasingly complex levels of cooperation with other hominins. Cacioppo and Patrick take up the theme, on pp64–5 of *Loneliness*: "as they worked their way out of the forest and onto the plains, early humans lived in an environment of evolutionary adaptation in which the most perplexing challenge no longer came from the flora and fauna surrounding them. Reading one another, sometimes deceiving one another, maintaining peace with one another despite the quirks of human sentiments and ever-increasing human intelligence – this was the next major arena in which natural selection would separate the most advantageous genes from ones that biased us towards less adaptive characteristics. In determining whether or not your genes would make it into the next generation, being slow to catch on to the social vibe became a more common threat than being mauled by a lion or bitten by a snake".

The most important, and distinctive, aspect of human sociability is the capacity to cooperate with "strangers", which is to say with individuals with whom we do not share a close genetic bond. We saw earlier that Tomasello dates the start of this crucial behavioural development to as recently as 100,000 years ago. Whatever the date, the French neuroscientist Stephanie Cacioppo (she shares a surname with John because they were married) explains, on pp18-9 of her 2022 book *Wired for Love*: "at some point in evolutionary history...our human ancestors took a giant leap, socially speaking. They adapted the skills used to build their own relationship (perspective-taking, planning, cooperation) and generalised them, forming bonds with other primates who were neither their reproductive partners nor their offspring. In other words, they made friends...these early humans needed friends because they occupied a vulnerable position in the food chain. They couldn't fly. They had no camouflage or armour. They lacked the strength, speed, and stealth of other species in the animal kingdom. They spent most of their time scavenging for food and avoiding predators. All they had, really, was an unusual talent for connection, a special knack for navigating the most complex environment in nature: the social world. This was quite the superpower – and in the intervening eons, as anthropoid primates evolved, it would prove more decisive than their opposable thumbs, their skills at making tools, or the fact that they walked upright. As war and climate change made life on earth harsher, some species had trouble surviving; but these difficulties actually played to the strengths that early humans were developing. Their social skills helped them build complex groups and eventually whole societies undergirded by mutual aid. People learnt how to sort out friends from foes; to avoid predators; to anticipate the actions of neighbours; to privilege long-term interests over short-term desires; to use language to communicate; to manage mating relationships that were shaped not only by the female's ovulatory cycle but by different factors like affection and empathy. Finally, they learned how to trust and say 'I love you'".

None of this is to say that the evolution of human sociability was straightforward or somehow inevitable. Indeed, the very fact that the trait is so distinctive to humans suggests quite the opposite: sociability the way humans practice it is vanishingly rare in the animal kingdom and hence statistically unlikely. Pontzer, again, explains, on pp133-5 of *Burn*: "it would have taken a very particular set of circumstances for sharing to prevail in the human lineage: the costs of acquiring more food than you could eat had to be lower than the benefits of giving it away. Foraging for extra food means less energy for yourself, more for someone else – not the sort of thing that natural selection, Darwin's amoral accountant, usually favours. To the extent that the recipient is related to you and shares the same genes, their reproductive success is partly yours. But the discounting is steep: even your child shares only half your genes. The costs of acquiring extra food would need to be low, and the payoff to the receiver really high, for sharing to be worth it. It's easy to understand why no other apes – in fact, hardly any other species at all – have hit upon sharing as a successful strategy...sadly, the details of its origins may be too fine-grained to be caught in the rough sieve of the fossil record...the earliest hard evidence for sharing comes from cut-marked bones on large animals like zebra. No hominin could eat a zebra by himself, no matter how hungry. And targeting a zebra, dead or alive, would require teamwork, either to hunt it or to push other hungry carnivores off the corpse. Teamwork pays only if there is an agreement to share the spoils. Perhaps hominin sharing grew from apelike hunting, with some individuals giving more than the limited, grudging scraps we see with chimpanzees...or perhaps hominin sharing grew from the sort of fruit-sharing behaviour we see among female bonobos...a strong case can be made that wild tubers, the distant cousins of the potatoes and yams in our supermarkets today, were an important shared food early on. Tubers are a dietary staple for the Hadza (my note: an indigenous hunter-gatherer tribe living in northern Tanzania, much-studied by modern anthropologists including Pontzer) and other hunter-gatherer populations around the world. And they are calorific starch bombs, hard for small kids to dig from the ground but easy enough to harvest in surplus for adults. Just as orangutan mothers tend to share foods that are hard for young offspring to get, hominin mothers (or fathers) could have made a habit of feeding tubers to their kids. Perhaps older females, past their childbearing years, began to channel their maternal efforts into sharing food with their daughters and grandchildren...whether it was meat, plant foods, or some combination, this strange act of foraging for others had profound consequences for human evolution. Sharing meant more energy for life's essential tasks. Survival and reproduction, the currencies of natural selection, improved. The sharing hominids and their kin outcompeted their less generous neighbours...we are the descendants of these early, sharing hominins".

As sharing became established, so it exerted increasing selection pressure on individuals to develop the relevant cognitive and social skills. Cacioppo and Patrick summarise, on p11 of *Loneliness*: "...most neuroscientists now agree that, over a period of tens of thousands of years, it was the need to send and receive, interpret and relay increasingly complex social cues that drove the expansion of, and greater interconnectedness within, the cortical mantle of the human brain. In other words, it was the need to deal with other people that, in large part, made us who and what we are today".

They add, on p160: "...our big brains did not evolve in order to evaluate art or to solve quadratic equations.

They evolved because it was to our adaptive advantage to be able to process and manage complex and dynamic *social* (authors' emphasis) information".

And, on pp67–8 of *Loneliness*: "historically, individuals with behavioural dispositions less well adapted to the environment did not survive – or they survived only marginally, or they did not survive long enough to produce as many offspring as those who were better adapted. Individuals with better-adapted behavioural repertoires lived to produce more children, or at least more children who themselves lived long enough to reproduce, allowing the genes responsible for those better-adapted traits to be passed along more widely...among ancestral humans, bonding with the larger group became the norm, but for different reasons depending on gender. Bonding gave hunter-gathering females a survival advantage: the group meant safety, but it also meant being able to share maternal duties while taking care of other necessary business...among early human males, puny scavengers who relied on sharp sticks as weapons, bonding together to form alliances became the norm for its political advantages (and political dominance led to better mating opportunities), and also because it provided strength in numbers for safety. But the greatest advantage of social connection and coordination may have been in the acquisition of large amounts of concentrated protein. Lions are anatomically much more formidable than humans when it comes to aggression, and even they rely on highly coordinated teamwork to bring down prey larger than themselves".

Henrich elaborates on the increase in brain size specifically, on p62 of *The Secret of our Success*: "our brains evolved from the size of a chimpanzee's, at roughly 350 cm^3, to 1350 cm^3 in about 5 million years. Most of that expansion, from about 500 cm^3 upward, took place only in about the last 2 million years. That's fast in genetic evolutionary terms. This expansion was finally halted about 200,000 years ago, probably by the challenges of giving birth to babies with increasingly bulbous heads. In most species, the birth canal is larger than the newborn's head, but not in humans. Infant skulls have to remain unfused in order to squeeze through the birth canal in a manner that isn't seen in other species. It seems our brains only ceased expanding because we hit the stops set by our primate body plan; if babies' heads got any bigger, they wouldn't be able to squeeze out of mom at birth. Along the way, natural selection came up with numerous tricks to circumvent this *big-headed baby problem* (author's emphasis), including intense cortical folding, high-density interconnections (which permit our brains to hold more information without getting bigger) and a rapid postbirth expansion. Specifically, newborn human brains continue expanding at the faster pre-birth gestational rate for the first year, eventually tripling in size. By contrast, newborn primate brains grow more slowly after birth, eventually only doubling in size".

The effect of all these changes was to increase the odds that an individual would be biologically more successful if they behaved prosocially at least some of the time. This had particular implications for males, being naturally more physical and aggressive. Cacioppo and Patrick, again, summarise, on pp70-2 of *Loneliness*: "along the route to *Homo sapiens*, other epoch-making innovations emerged – the ability to walk upright, an opposable thumb for grasping, a shoulder good for throwing – that allowed our ancestors to increase the range of their immediate concerns. These anatomical features provided for both perception and action at a distance, which put a further premium on being able to think, plan, and communicate. Greater intelligence meant physically larger brains, which meant larger heads on infants, which demanded a wider pelvis on the mothers giving birth. But upright posture favoured a relatively narrow pelvis to facilitate walking...to resolve these competing anatomical demands, natural selection favoured human infants that came into the world before their brains were fully formed. Cranial capacity could be kept to a reasonable level before birth, but the trade-off would be that cognitive, emotional, and social development would have to continue during the first months – even years – of life. This meant that all human infants would be born, to some extent, 'half baked' and therefore utterly helpless for an extended period of time. Chimp babies can at least cling to their mothers from day one, but not so human babies. This prolonged period of complete dependency created intense pressure on the mothers, who still had to avoid predators and continue to forage for food – in pre-agricultural societies it is the women's gathering of roots and berries that provides the tribe's most reliable source of calories – all while feeding and otherwise caring for the helpless child...this placed an even greater premium on bonding and on parental investment. For males as well as females, those who felt compelled to bond with their offspring and take care of them, even if they themselves had to subsist on less and endure more hardships, left behind more surviving relatives who carried their 'socially connected' genes. Assuming normal variation in the genetically biased need for social connection, an ancestral male from, say, a hundred thousand years ago, might have had a social thermostat set so low that he could hoard food for himself without feeling much in the way of shame, guilt, or pain. He could have gone off on a three-day hunt, found a place where the antelope play, and simply never come back. He might have been oblivious to the absence of his family, or to the knowledge that they might be starving. Inured to loneliness as a signal of distress, hunting only to feed himself, he might have been better nourished than those who carried food back to camp and contributed to the good of all. But if his children did not survive long enough to mature and reproduce and nurture their own young, neither did his genes. (If his tribe did not survive, his children also would be less likely to survive.) The older, more purely selfish genes persisted, but their influence in the population at large shrank by reproductive attrition. Individual success was now driven by the ability to transcend selfishness and act on behalf of others. The selfish gene had given rise to a social brain and a different kind of social animal".

As we saw in Chapter 1, modern humans that is to say *homo sapiens*, arrived on the scene around 200,000 years ago, co-existing and even inter-breeding for a long time with other proto humans, most notably the Neanderthals. Groups of *homo sapiens* expanded out of Africa from about 60,000 years ago, reaching the Americas, the last continent to be populated, maybe 25,000 years ago. *Homo sapiens* and Neanderthals co-existed in parts of what is now Europe for thousands of years before the Neanderthals finally became extinct around 40,000 years ago.

It is possible, although necessarily speculative, that what ultimately enabled *homo sapiens* to outcompete Neanderthals and other hominids was specifically their (perhaps we should say, our) more developed sociability, as Stephanie Cacioppo suggests on pp19-20 of *Wired for Love*: "about seventy thousand years ago...our own species, *Homo sapiens*, moved from East Africa to the Arabian peninsula and Eurasia. There they met other hominids, most famously the Neanderthals. The Neanderthals were fearsome competition: bigger, stronger, with better vision and brains that may have been slightly larger than those of humans. But the neural architecture of the Neanderthals and *Homo sapiens* differed in important ways. Neanderthals had more space dedicated to vision and motor skills – they were ideal physical warriors. But the *Homo sapiens* were ideal social warriors: they could understand the intentions of others, they could consider a choice from two sides, they learned quickly from their mistakes...all this allowed them to compensate for their shortcomings in strength. And, as a result, the epic evolutionary matchup between the Neanderthals and *Homo sapiens* wasn't even close".

In the interests of balance, as we saw in Chapter 1 there is an alternative hypothesis that climate changes wiped out both the Neanderthal and *homo sapiens* populations in Europe, resulting in the extinction of Neanderthals since this was the main region they inhabited, and the eventual re-population of Europe by descendants of *homo sapiens* who had already ventured further afield and thus survived whatever localised climate apocalypse. Of course these two hypotheses are not mutually exclusive.

For the millions of years for which hunter-gathering was the dominant human lifestyle, people lived in quite small groups, often called "bands". In *The Secret of Our Success* Henrich suggests that at some point the bonds holding band members together became cultural rather than biological, which is to say that they promoted genetic diversity by emphasising "marriage" type relationships rather than close biological family linkages. On p155 he references research into members of two contemporary hunter-gatherer bands, the Ache from Paraguay, comprising 21 members; and the Ju/'hoansi from Africa, with 15 members. The conclusion is that: "about threequarters of band relationships are based on something besides genetic relatedness...(of the) other unrelated band members...two-thirds are spouses and affines (my note: elsewhere Henrich defines an "affine" as an "in-law"). That is, marriage norms create over half the ties in adult relationships within a band. Arguably, primates who pair-bond may create bonds that are spouse-like, but...no evidence suggests that primate affines hold any special relationships. Perhaps surprising to some, the evolution of in-laws may be one of the key features that make humans special".

Henrich's conclusions are consistent with the findings of a research paper titled *Ancient genomes show social and reproductive behaviour of early Upper Paleolithic foragers*, published on the *Science* website dated 5 October 2017 and reported on the Cambridge University website in an entry called *Prehistoric humans are likely to have formed mating networks to avoid inbreeding*. The Cambridge authors comment: "the study...examined genetic information from the remains of anatomically modern humans who lived during the Upper Palaeolithic, a period when modern humans from Africa first colonised Western Eurasia (my note: the specific remains are of four humans apparently buried at the same time and estimated to have lived around 34,000 years ago; the site where they were found is called Sunghir, in modern Russia). The results suggest that people deliberately sought partners beyond their immediate family, and that they were probably connected to a wider network of groups from within which mates were chosen, in order to avoid becoming inbred...the people at Sunghir may have been part of a network similar to that of modern day hunter-gatherers, such as Aboriginal Australians and some historical native American societies. Like their Upper Palaeolithic ancestors, these people live in fairly small groups of around 25 people, but they are also less directly connected to a larger community of perhaps 200 people, within which there are rules governing with whom individuals can form partnerships".

The authors speculate that this cultural development may have been an alternative reason which helped our early human ancestors to outcompete Neanderthals, among whom such evidence as exists suggests that inbreeding remained prevalent. Be that as it may, the authors conclude: "the results...show that Upper Palaeolithic human groups could use sophisticated cultural systems to sustain very small group sizes by embedding them in a wide social network of other groups".

Life within many of these bands was likely relatively egalitarian, as anthropologists observe that it is in many of the surviving "primitive" civilisations which began to be studied at the margins of Empire from the 19th century onwards ("primitive" is in inverted commas because by definition all these civilisations have in fact been evolving over exactly the same timespan that ours has). This is not at all to imply, however, that similar cultural norms were common across groups. Indeed, the American anthropologist Jared Diamond asserts on p8 of his 2012 book *The World Until Yesterday* that the opposite is true: "traditional societies are far more diverse in many of their cultural practices than are modern industrial societies".

And as an aside, recent evidence challenges the conventional view that the hunter-gatherer lifestyle necessarily or always entailed a strict division of gender roles. In an article titled *Hunter-gathering wasn't a man's world*, published in *The Times* on Friday 30 June 2023, UK science journalist Rhys Blakely writes: "an ancient stereotype – that prehistoric hunting was work reserved for men – appears to have been debunked. For decades, researchers have known of isolated Amazonian tribes where females equipped with bows and blades bring home the meat. A new study suggests that far from being exceptional, this kind of arrangement is the norm in modern hunter-gatherer societies, with women hunting in nearly 80 per cent of them. These females were typically highly skilled, with grandmothers frequently among the best hunters of the village, said Professor Cara Wall-Scheffler of Seattle Pacific University, who led the research. The findings may provide a glimpse of how our own ancestors lived before the invention of farming about 12,000 years ago, Wall-

Scheffler said: 'the myth of 'man the hunter' ostensibly describes the division of labour in subsistence human groups, with men doing the hunting and women doing the gathering. Any time people describe men as being...strong, dominant, they are typically using a 'man the hunter' narrative that suggests men have evolved to behave in aggressive ways, because it made them better hunters. This still comes up regularly in our society'.

She and her colleagues trawled through multiple reports, dating back to the 1800s, and almost 400 hunter-gatherer communities. Reports on 63 communities were found to contain details on how tasks were split between the sexes. There were records of women hunting in 50 of those communities, making it clear that they were setting out to hunt intentionally. Women hunted in every society where hunting was considered the main source of livelihood, and for 18 communities there were descriptions of them multitasking – by hunting and looking after children at the same time. Men hunted, but also helped to gather. 'The collected data...directly opposes the traditional paradigm that women exclusively gather, and men exclusively hunt', Wall-Scheffler and her co-authors conclude in a paper published in the journal *PLOS One*. This work follows on from research by Professor Randy Haas of the University of California, Davis. In 2020 he investigated a 9000-year-old burial site in the Peruvian Andes, and found a 'big-game hunting kit', including what appear to be stone spear heads and a blade. The individual laid to rest there was a teenage girl. Haas then looked at another 27 burials (sic) sites in the Americas, dating from about 13,000 years ago, containing similar weapons – 11 were female and 15 were male. He said the findings had forced him to 'rethink the most basic organisational structure of ancient hunter-gatherer groups'".

Whatever the gender roles may have been among hunter-gatherers, there is no doubt that human society changed dramatically with the advent of agriculture, sometime around 10,000 BCE.

It is not that agriculture necessarily improved the lot of the individuals who practiced it. On the contrary, there is considerable evidence that it often did not. For example, on p168 of *The Third Chimpanzee*, Jared Diamond tells us: "palaeopathologists studying ancient skeletons from Greece and Turkey found...(that)...the average height of hunter-gatherers in that region towards the end of the Ice Age (my note: around 13,000 years ago or so) was a generous 5 foot 10 inches for men, 5 foot 6 inches for women. With the adoption of agriculture, height crashed, reaching by 4,000 BC a low value of only 5 foot 3 inches for men, 5 foot 1 inches for women. By classical times, heights were very slowly on the rise again, but modern Greeks and Turks have still not regained the heights of their healthy hunter-gatherer ancestors".

Agriculture appears to have prospered as a technology because it had the crucial advantage that it was more economically efficient. It could therefore support a much larger population, which could then easily outcompete local hunter-gatherers for the resources available in any particular geographic location. Diamond again, on p171 of *The Third Chimpanzee*: "farming could support far more people than hunting, whether or not it also brought on the average more food per mouth. (Population densities of hunter-gatherers are typically one person or less per square mile, while densities of farmers average at least ten times higher.) Partly, this is because an acre of field planted entirely in edible crops produces far more tons of food, and allows one to feed far more mouths, than an acre of forest with scattered edible wild plants. Partly, too, it is because nomadic hunter-gatherers have to keep their children spaced at four-year intervals by infanticide and other means, since a mother must carry her toddler until it is old enough to keep up with the adults. Because sedentary farmers do not have that problem, they can and do have a child every two years".

Farming obviously required a more settled lifestyle, and also enabled the production of economic surpluses. This fuelled the development of larger, fixed or semi-fixed communities, which we might call villages. Still, there were limits to how large these settlements could be, and how long they could last. The *Britannica* website summarises, in an entry titled *City*: "in the Neolithic period (New Stone Age; roughly 9,000 to 3,000 BCE), humans achieved relatively fixed settlement, but for perhaps 5,000 years such living was confined to the semipermanent peasant village – semipermanent because, when the soil had been exhausted by the relatively primitive methods of cultivation, the entire village was usually compelled to pick up and move to another location. Even when a village prospered in one place, it would commonly split in two after the population had grown relatively large so that all cultivators would have ready access to the soil".

Eventually, technological developments enabled larger, more permanent communities, as the same *Britannica* entry describes: "the evolution of the Neolithic village into a city took at least 1,500 years – in the Old World from 5,000 to 3,500 BCE. The technological developments making it possible for humankind to live in urban places were at first mainly advances in agriculture. Neolithic-era domestication of plants and animals eventually led to improved methods of cultivation and stock breeding, which eventually produced a surplus and made it possible to sustain a higher population density while also freeing up some members of the community for craftsmanship and the production of non-essential goods and services".

These surpluses also created the conditions for social hierarchies to appear. Indeed, the argument could be made that some form of hierarchy was required as group size increased, to direct the efforts of group members so that the productivity of the whole would exceed the sum of the individual parts. As Diamond, again, puts it, on p13 of *The World Until Yesterday*: "with increasing population size and population density, the acquisition of food and other necessities tends to become intensified. That is, more food is obtained per acre by subsistence farmers living in villages than by small nomadic groups of hunter-gatherers, and still more is obtained per acre on the intensive irrigated plots cultivated by higher-density peoples and on the mechanised farms of modern states. Political decision-making becomes increasingly centralised, from the face-to-face group discussions of small hunter-gatherer groups to the political hierarchies and decisions by leaders in modern states. Social stratification increases, from the relative egalitarianism of small hunter gatherer groups to the inequality between people in large centralised societies".

It is not universally accepted that hierarchy was, or is, inevitable as social complexity increased. For example, in their 2021 book *The Dawn of Everything*, the British-American anthropologist David Graber and British archaeologist David Wengrow make the case that many examples exist of pre-agrarian societies which achieved high levels of complexity without explicit hierarchy, in particular a number of Native American populations.

Nonetheless, once established, hierarchy became pervasive. Societies grew larger, although generally not more equal. Family groups became clans, with chieftains at their head. Tribes formed, with tribal chiefs as leaders, although strictly speaking the concept of a "tribe" has a range of meanings and has proved notoriously difficult to define with any precision. Still larger units followed, which we might call kingdoms, similarly with anointed, or likely often self-appointed, leaders called "kings" and, occasionally, "queens". Elites were created, aggregating to themselves a disproportionate share of the available wealth, and otherwise dominating societies which became increasingly segmented into distinct social ranks.

As we saw in Chapter 1 the earliest settlements that we might recognise as cities date from around 3,500 BCE in Sumeria, in what is now the Middle East. Eventually from around 2,350 BCE the first empires emerged – the Akkadian empire, which included the Sumerians; the Assyrians; the Babylonians; the Hittites and of course ancient Egypt. Writing appeared around 3,000 BCE, meaning that by definition it is around this time when recorded history begins. The most ancient texts that have survived largely consist of records of business transactions: we may hypothesise that language was originally invented by, or at least for, accountants.

Through into modern times kingdoms and empires waxed and waned, often through a kind of dialectical process involving attritional or pre-emptive violence of one kind or another. Eventually the Industrial Revolution signalled the beginning of a process of mass urbanisation, which is still ongoing. The concept of the nation state emerged. There is lively dialogue about when this idea took hold and even how a nation state should properly be defined. But most pundits agree that it took root in 19th century Europe, and the concept has since become the dominant form of political structure globally. With a handful of exceptions, authoritarian government of one sort or another was the norm throughout history, until democracy of various kinds gradually became established in many, but by no means all, places during the course of the 20th century.

The Industrial Revolution also saw major shifts in how most people spent their time, moving from agriculture to factories, and eventually in many "advanced" economies, to the provision of services. Urbanisation continued, to the point where today the majority of the world's population live and work in a city or at least a town. The pace of this transition has been remarkable. According to UN statistics quoted by UK sociologist Ken Plummer on p62 of his 2010 book *Sociology the Basics*, in 1950 746 million people lived in a town, representing around 30% of the global population. By 2014 this had grown to 3.9 billion, around 50% of all the people on the planet.

Slavery, in the sense of humans legally owning other humans, was a fact of life in many societies throughout recorded history until it began to decline from the 18th century onwards, at least in the industrial world. The long process of female emancipation began, and more recently of minority rights more generally.

Viewed at the level of the species, the results of all this change are little short of dramatic. To start at the lowest possible point, in Chapter 1 we saw that humanity has experienced more than one population bottleneck, and whilst there is not agreement on the specifics the most extreme estimates suggest there may have been as few as 2,000 individuals at some point around 100,000 or so years ago. Whatever the details, humanity obviously survived, just. From this low point, the population is projected to have increased to something in the range 1 to 15 million globally by the time agriculture began, around 12,000 years ago. Numbers grew steadily, reaching maybe 2-300 million at the dawn of the Common Era. There were occasional severe setbacks, for example the Black Death pandemic in the 14th century CE, which reduced the global population from an estimated 450 million in 1340 to as low as 350 million in 1400, a loss of almost 25%. We have of course only recently emerged from the Covid pandemic which caused such disruption in the early 2020s and it is sobering to reflect that a Covid mortality rate similar to the Black Death would have killed something in the order of 2 billion people, that is, 25% of a total global population of around 8 billion. This compares with a World Health Organisation estimate of around 15 million global excess deaths directly and indirectly associated with Covid between January 2020 and December 2021, published in May 2022. The point of this comparison is not to suggest that Covid was or is somehow trivial, but rather to underscore that it in no way represents a worst-case example of the potential impact of a global pandemic.

Although the overall trend was for species growth, medieval cities faced a continuing challenge to maintain their population levels, mainly because of the high mortality rate from infectious diseases. Still, it is estimated that there were around 1 billion people in the world by about 1800 CE. Since then there has been exponential growth, especially during the 20th century, and today the United Nations estimates that the population totals around 8 billion people globally.

This is a lot of people, obviously. Still, humans account for only around 0.01 percent of all the biomass on Earth, according to an article called *Humans make up just 0.01% of Earth's life – what's the rest?*, authored by Hannah Ritchie and published by *Our World in Data* on 24 April 2019. Trees represent by far the largest source of biomass, accounting for around 82%; and the next largest category is bacteria, at 13%. At the same time, humans constitute about 9 times the biomass of all wild mammals put together; and the livestock reared to feed human populations have a biomass over 14 times that of all wild mammals, and therefore 1.5 times that of the humans they sustain.

Of course the experience of what it is to be human has also undergone profound change over this timeframe. Materially, there is no question that there has never been a time when so many people globally have had it so good, notwithstanding the many challenges we continue to face as a species. Most notably, the last 200 years have seen a major increase in average global life expectancy, from around 30 in 1800 to around 73 today, according to Leigh Shaw-Taylor, in an article called *Covid 19 – the long view*, published in the Cambridge University alumni newsletter in June 2020. Indeed, Shaw-Taylor tells us that as recently as 1800 no country on Earth had an average life expectancy much above 40. Of course, this does not imply that 30 (or 40 in the best-performing countries) was somehow an upper age limit - it is an average, and in this case risks masking the underlying picture of high rates of child mortality offset by a natural lifespan of somewhere between 50 and 70 for those fortunate enough to survive childhood. The Swedish public health expert Hans Rosling reinforces this point, on p54 of his book *Factfulness*, published posthumously in 2018, and co-written with his son and daughter-in-law, Ola Rosling and Anna Rosling Ronnlund: "back in 1800, when Swedes starved to death and British children worked in coal mines, life expectancy was roughly 30 years everywhere in the world. That was what it had been throughout history. Among all babies who were ever born, roughly half died during their childhood. Most of the other half died between the ages of 50 and 70. So the average was around 30. It doesn't mean most people lived to be 30. It's just an average, and with averages we must always remember that there is a spread".

Still, this increase in average life expectancy represents a remarkable improvement for a large number of people, most obviously those individuals who might otherwise have died young, and the family and friends who would have mourned them. Many people are also living longer, beyond the 70 years which Rosenberg sets as an upper age limit historically, and especially in the industrialised world. As the UK *Centre for Ageing Better* puts it, in an online article titled *The State of Ageing 2023-24* and admittedly focusing just on England: "for many people today, living longer is not just a hope but an expectation. Gains in life expectancy in past decades mean that millions more of us are living into our 70s, 80s, 90s and beyond, with record numbers of centenarians...".

These increases have been achieved by a combination of factors, including the economic benefits of industrialisation becoming available to more people so that, for example, food and shelter are more widely accessible; a reduction in levels of violence, at least when measured as a proportion of the population; and dramatic improvements in sanitation and our ability to combat infectious disease, mainly through vaccines.

An important consequence is that most contemporary societies now have a much higher proportion of older people than did any previous generation, a trend which is continuing and even accelerating. For example, in *Sociology the Basics*, Plummer quotes UN statistics showing that the world population of people aged 60 or more grew from 9.2% in 1990 to 11.7% in 2013. In absolute numbers, the over-60 cohort is projected to grow from 841 million in 2013 to over 2 billion by 2050.

Prosperity has also increased for a huge number of people, even though poverty remains a challenge. In an article for *Our World in Data* called *Global Extreme Poverty*, published in 2013 and revised in 2019, economists Max Roster and Esteban Ortiz-Ospina write: "the available long-run evidence shows that in the past, only a small elite enjoyed the living conditions that would not be described as 'extreme poverty' today. But with the onset of industrialisation and rising productivity, the share of people living in extreme poverty started to decrease. Accordingly, the share of people in extreme poverty has decreased continuously over the course of the last two centuries. This is surely one of the most remarkable achievements of humankind".

The benchmark for extreme poverty is set at 1.90 international $ (that is, $ adjusted for purchase power parity) per day, and the statistics quoted by the authors show that currently about 10% of the global population live below this level. What this means is that, measured this way, the number of people in extreme poverty fell from nearly 1.9 billion in 1990 to about 650 million in 2018, even as the global population increased from around 5.3 billion to 7.7 billion over the same period.

In *Factfulness* Hans Rosling and his co-authors amplify this theme, demonstrating with a wealth of statistics and considerable nuance just how far human society has come in improving the quality of everyday life for the majority of its members. The authors describe four levels of income, with the lowest, Level 1, equating to extreme poverty – effectively basic subsistence. Level 1 is set at an income of $0-2 per day; Level 2 is $2-8; Level 3 is $8-32; and Level 4 is over $32. These may not seem like big numbers but the authors explain that moving up the levels tends to confer concrete benefits which are highly meaningful at each stage, for example improved access to clean water, better means of transport and cooking facilities, and improved diet and healthcare. Like Roster and Ortiz-Ospina, they point out that for most of human existence until relatively recently almost everyone effectively scraped a subsistence living, on the equivalent of Level 1. Nowadays, however most, albeit not yet all, of the world has reached levels 2 and 3, usually with a mix between these levels in any given population.

This is a truly remarkable achievement when measured in terms of the alleviation of human suffering, and the potential this in turn creates for individual happiness and fulfilment. A surprising feature is that the authors remind us how comparatively recent many of these improvements are even in the advanced industrial nations, and conversely how well-established in many countries which might historically have been thought of as "undeveloped". Specifically, they point out that the majority of people in the West existed in a range between income levels 2 and 3 as recently as the 1950s. They conclude, on p38 of *Factfulness*: "human history started with everyone on Level 1. For more than 100,000 years nobody made it up the levels and most children didn't survive to become parents. Just 200 years ago, 85% of the world population was still on Level 1, in extreme poverty…today the vast majority of people are spread out in the middle, across Levels 2 and 3, with the same range of standards of living as people had in Western Europe and North America in the 1950s. And this has been the case for many years".

In similar vein, the British social scientist Bobby Duffy explains that major improvements in living conditions have occurred in the relatively recent past even in an "advanced" society such as the UK. The quote is taken from an article called *Here is the real news: things are getting better all the time*, published in *The Sunday Times* on Sunday, 31 July 2022: "…my daughter is keen to never see the news again – and she's far from alone in that. A recent Reuters Institute study shows the selective avoidance of news has doubled in the past five years, to 46 per cent in the UK. I didn't have the energy to try to convince my daughter that there are at least as many good news stories in the world, and that it is a much better place than it has been in the recent past. But I would have had a lot of evidence to draw on. In 1950, when her grandparents were her age, 30 in 1,000 infants died before their first birthday; now the figure is three in 1,000. Life expectancy at birth back then was about 65 years; for babies born in 2020 it's about 89. Cancer survival rates have doubled in the past 40 years, and heart disease deaths have decreased by almost half since

2005. Despite the talk of a 'dementia tsunami', there has been a 20 per cent fall in the past two decades. Greenhouse gas emissions in the UK have halved between 1990 and 2020, and Britain's woodlands now cover as much of the country as they did during the Middle Ages, thanks to 20th-century forestry and rewilding practices. Unemployment rates are the lowest since 1974 and, while my daughter's grandparents left school at 15 for work in factories, mines and steelworks, about half of young people today go to university, 10 times the level seen in the 1960s. Society today is also much safer, despite what we think and what we're told. The murder rate in the UK has declined substantially over the past 20 years, but in studies by the polling firm Ipsos for my 2018 book *The Perils of Deception*, only 19 per cent of people correctly identified that's the case, while twice as many think it's increased. And we forget the progress we've made on all sorts of social and cultural norms. It seems incredible that only 11 per cent of the UK public thought homosexuality was 'not wrong at all' when I was growing up in the 1980s, partly because it's changed so much: now seven in 10 are of that view".

These increases in health and material wealth have been accompanied by significant increases in leisure time, at least in the developed world. British psychologist Bruce Hood tells us, on p141 of his 2024 book *The Science of Happiness*: "in the West, the average working week declined from 60-to-70 hours per week in 1870, to the current 30-to-40 hours per week. We also have more holidays than we did 150 years ago".

Duffy goes on to explain in the article referenced above that much of this good news is poorly understood, partly because of a cognitive bias most of us have to emphasise bad news rather than good: "one of our most powerful biases is our inbuilt focus on what we view as negative information. There is an evolutionary element to this.

Negative information tends to be more urgent, even life-threatening: in our cave people past, we needed to take note when we were warned about a lurking sabre-toothed tiger – and those who didn't were edited out of the gene pool. We are therefore at the end of a long chain of people who've succeeded by taking these negative cues seriously, as shown in neuroscience experiments that track electrical activity in subjects' brains. We react more strongly to images such as mutilated faces or dead cats, and process them with different intensity in different parts of the brain. We are then, on average, very attuned to bad news. As one recent opinion piece in the Washington Post put it, 'negativity is clicky'. In contrast, we have much less interest in slow, positive trends".

And none of this is to deny that significant challenges remain. For example, as we saw around 10% of the world remains trapped in extreme poverty, equating to about 800 million individual people. Two-thirds of the global population live on less than 10 international $ per day - riches when compared with countless generations throughout history, but not when the comparison is with contemporary living standards in the most advanced economies. And wealth inequality is perhaps most starkly illustrated by a statistic taken from the 2021 *World Inequality Report*, quoted in a *Fortune* magazine article called *World's richest people now own 11% of global wealth* by journalist Nicole Goodkind, published on 7 December 2021. Goodkind tells us that: "the top 0.01% richest individuals – the 520,000 people who have at least $19 million – now hold 11% of the world's wealth". The gap is also growing: "the top 1% have grabbed 38% of all additional wealth accumulated since the mid-1990s, while the bottom 50% captured just 2% of it".

In any case, material living standards are only part of the story because the changes in social structure and environment associated with industrialisation and urbanisation also impose novel psychological challenges. For example, for most of history, most individuals would grow up and live in a fairly stable community, accepting that individuals might move between communities so that as discussed earlier the composition of specific social groups would by no means be entirely kin-based. Everyday travel would typically be restricted to a radius of a few miles, albeit with some exceptions such as soldiers journeying to war, and a small number of itinerant merchants.

British anthropologist Robin Dunbar has suggested, in 1992, that the social conditions which prevailed through most of human evolution have given each of us the cognitive ability to maintain an average of around 150 stable social relationships, coinciding with the estimated average size of a Neolithic farming village. This "Dunbar number" is hypothesised to have remained relatively constant even as our social environment has changed beyond recognition.

But these days for most people in the industrial world it makes more sense to think of an individual as belonging to multiple overlapping social groups, rather than being defined mainly by their membership of a single geographically-based family or village community. People still have families of course, but family sizes are smaller and adult family members tend to be physically more dispersed than they were in the past. People obviously live in a particular location with specific neighbours, but relationships are more fragmentary and transient, especially in large cities. Individual social life is therefore spent relatively less in long-established relationships with family and long-term neighbours, and relatively more with colleagues and friends from work, and from shared interest groups such as sports, hobbies, churches and so on. In the last decade or so, the internet and especially the proliferation of social media have dramatically expanded the possibility set for social connections, albeit with important qualitative differences in the type of social relationships they foster.

In short, as individuals living in the modern world most of us are exposed to more people, across a more diverse range of environments, with a higher level of transience, than was usual for our ancestors. Most of us spend relatively less of our time with people we have known for a long time, and relatively more with people we have met more recently. And, just because it is important to us to feel a sense of belonging to one or more social groups does not mean that this is easy to achieve. Our evolutionary history has provided us with some vital, foundational, capabilities. But almost all the world's societies have changed enormously since the dawn of agriculture, and at breakneck pace since the start of the Industrial Revolution not much more than 200 years ago. Genetic adaptation rarely moves at that kind of speed. And as we have seen, whilst some aspects of social living might be thought of as universal, many more are specific to a particular society or social group, defined by the elusive term "culture". They are also by definition man-made, that is to say subjective and changeable. All of which is to say that, whilst the changes in society have brought about unprecedented material improvements for a huge number of people, it is no surprise that, at least in some populations and for some individuals, they are accompanied by a significant increase in feelings of alienation and existential "angst".

The net of all this is that, whilst evolution has wired each of us to be sociable in a variety of ways, the changing nature of our social environment also presents us with novel opportunities and challenges. Simply put, we are confronted with more complexity, but with the benefit that we also have greater economic and social freedom to exercise agency over our own life than most of our ancestors enjoyed. Daniel Gilbert summarises, on p235 of *Stumbling on Happiness:* "most of us make at least three important decisions in our lives: where to live, what to do, and with whom to do it. We choose our towns and our neighbourhoods, we choose our jobs and our hobbies, we choose our spouses and our friends. Making these decisions is such a natural part of adulthood that it is easy to forget that we are among the first human beings to make them. For most of recorded history, people lived where they were born, did what their parents had done and associated with those who were doing the same. Millers milled, Smiths smithed, and little Smiths and little Millers married whom and when they were told. Social structures (such as religions and castes) and physical structures (such as mountains and oceans) were the great dictators that determined how, where, and with whom people would spend their lives, which left most people with little to decide for themselves. But the agricultural, industrial, and technological revolutions changed all that, and the resulting explosion of personal liberty has created a bewildering array of options, alternatives, choices, and decisions that our ancestors never faced. For the very first time, our happiness is in our (own) hands".

This is clearly a great opportunity, if once we are willing to take it.

Part B. Anti-social behaviours

Sociability may be the behaviour which most distinguishes humans as a species, but of course this does not mean that it is somehow the only, or even the default, behaviour of which humans are capable.

On the contrary, we are also prone to all manner of anti-social behaviours. As Cacioppo and Patrick point out, on p55 of *Loneliness*: "no one can deny that competitiveness, envy, hatred, cruelty, and betrayal are aspects of human nature, and that these negatives are all well represented in human history..." They are quick to add that: "...the driving force of our advance as a species has not been our tendency to be brutally self-interested, but our ability to be socially cooperative". But the point is nonetheless that we are manifestly capable of behaving in both pro and anti-social ways.

It is easy to see why this should be so. The Darwinian world in which we live is one in which at the most basic level every organism is pitted against every other, across and within species, in an unending struggle to survive and thrive. On p189 of *Leviathan* Thomas Hobbes memorably summarises the natural state of humankind as: "...a condition of war of everyone against everyone".

We may feel this overstates the case, but it does not necessarily fundamentally misrepresent it. Individuals are in essence nothing more than Dawkins' "survival machines", competing for finite resources. Those best able to succeed in a given environment (the "fittest") survive and pass on copies of their genes to the next generation. Nature itself has no moral laws to constrain how an organism achieves success: the end always justifies the means, and all that matters in an evolutionary sense is the empirical fact of an organism's survival and successful reproduction. And if a particular organism succeeds in outcompeting others through anti-social, "selfish" methods, it follows that the genes which code for that kind of behaviour will themselves spread into the next generation. The more successful the selfish, or partly selfish, individual is relative to his or her competitors, the relatively more copies of these genes there will be. Ultimately, it is reasonable to infer that anti-social behaviours have survived because they confer some adaptive advantages to the individuals who display them, at least in some circumstances, and no matter how much we might wish this were not the case.

Cacioppo and Patrick comment, on p182 of *Loneliness*: "in the external world, love and kinship mingle with resentment and competition at every juncture...parents love all their children, in theory, and, at least in theory, they love each child equally. Adults in the family try to encourage brothers and sisters to show affection for each other, and to share resources equitably among themselves. But parents and children have only a fifty percent overlap in their genetic interest. Each child has his own evolutionary agenda, which begins with extracting all the parental love and resources he can. Mothers and infants squabble about the amount of time spent breastfeeding. Littermates fight over access to the nursing mother, and the runts get shoved to the end of the line. Young chicks sharing a nest will often fight and may push their weaker siblings out. In some species nestlings peck one another to death while the parent placidly observes".

And there is evidence that bullying can be a winning strategy, at least if we accept the parallel example of our chimpanzee cousins amongst whom, admittedly, dominance strategies tend to be the only viable way to get ahead. British journalist Rhys Blakely comments, in an article titled *It's the law of the jungle...bullies are successful*, published in *The Times* on 25 April 2023: "wild male chimpanzees scale the social ladder more successfully if they have more bullying, greedy, and irritable personalities, according to a study...these boorish types are also better at siring offspring than their more deferential counterparts. The research drew on data collected over several decades in Gombe National Park, Tanzania, including observations made in the 1970s by Jane Goodall, the primatologist...the latest study shows that male chimps with high dominance and low conscientiousness tendencies tend to do better in life".

We may consider ourselves fortunate not to live among chimpanzees, but still the point is that some level of tension between sharing and selfishness is latent within each of us as individuals. On p183 of *Loneliness*, Cacioppo and Patrick remind us that: "for the same sorts of reasons that natural selection maintains a certain amount of variation in the behavioural attributes of any given population, natural selection favours a certain behavioural flexibility in each of us. Thus we find that, even in those who generally reach first for kindness and generosity in the toolkit of social skills, there reside vestiges of dishonesty and duplicity held in reserve".

Our dual nature is well captured in a modern parable recounted by Rutger Bregman on pp9-10 of *Humankind*: "floating around the Internet is a parable of unknown origin. It contains what I believe is a simple but profound truth: an old man says to his grandson: 'there's a fight going on inside me. It's a terrible fight between two wolves. One is evil – angry, greedy, jealous, arrogant, and cowardly. The other is good – peaceful, loving, modest, generous, honest, and trustworthy. These two wolves are also fighting within you, and inside every other person too'. After a moment, the boy asks, "which wolf will win?" The old man smiles. 'The one you feed'".

And the decision which wolf to feed happens not once but many times, every day, often in quite mundane settings. This is why the personal existential choices that we make between prosocial ("cooperative") and anti-social ("selfish") behaviours turn out to be amongst the most important we are faced with.

Our starting point as we contemplate these choices will be to ground the discussion by reviewing some of the most common forms of anti-social behaviour, namely:

- hierarchy and status
- violence, bullying and intimidation

- the capacity to manipulate and deceive

Hierarchy and status

The word "hierarchy" has come to be regarded as pejorative in many contexts, presumably because it is so easily associated with characteristics that many of us would see as undesirable; such as inequality, the interests of a privileged "few" being pursued at the expense of those of the "many", barriers to social mobility, and even outright repression.

Nonetheless, hierarchy of various kinds is pervasive throughout Nature, and a salient feature of most human societies. Why should this be?

One potential explanation is that, as we saw earlier, increased scale can generate substantial increases in economic productivity, and it turns out that at least some forms of hierarchy can be an effective way to harness scale, an attribute which as we saw became more salient for humans once the invention of agriculture created the possibility for economic surpluses.

More generally, in a paper called *The evolutionary origins of hierarchy*, submitted on 23 May 2015, data scientists Henok Mengistu, Joost Huizinga, Jean-Baptiste Mouret and Jeff Clune assert that hierarchy is an effective organizational solution to the problem of what they call "connection costs". The authors comment: "in computational simulations, we find that networks without a connection cost do not evolve to be hierarchical...however, with a connection cost, networks evolve to be both modular and hierarchical".

Simply put, hierarchy evolved because it made a group with a lot of "network connections" (that is to say, a larger group, with more complex interactions) more productive, enabling it to out-compete other, less-hierarchical groups. And this in turn meant that individuals within a group who were attuned to hierarchy tended to prosper at the expense of those who were not, with the result that our genetic inheritance essentially hardwires us to be sensitive to hierarchy. Authors Jessica Koski, Hongling Xie and Ingrid R. Olson assert in an article titled *Understanding Social Hierarchies: The Neural and Psychological Foundations of Status Perception*, published on 20 February 2015 on the PMC website of the *US National Library of Medicine*: "the ease with which we perceive status cues and assign rank to others reflects a general preference for a hierarchical social organisation...the purpose of social hierarchies is to organise social groups in order to allocate limited resources, such as mates and food, facilitate social learning, and maximise individual motivation...importantly, the organisation of social groups into a hierarchy serves an adaptive function that benefits the group as a whole".

In Nature more broadly, dominance hierarchies may reinforce inequity but may also bring a measure of stability, as Robert Sapolsky explains on p355 of *Why Zebras Don't Get Ulcers*: "resources, no matter how plentiful, are rarely divvied up evenly. Instead of every contested item being fought for with bloodied tooth and claw, dominance hierarchies emerge. As formalised systems of inequities, these are great substitutes for continual aggression between animals smart enough to know their place".

In such societies status is often largely a function of individual physical prowess and therefore body size, and a psychological propensity for aggression; in other words, to the capacity to inflict and withstand violence. Even then, hierarchy may come in many flavours, as Sapolsky point outs on pp355-6 of *Why Zebras Don't Get Ulcers*: "hierarchical competition has been taken to heights of animal complexity by primates. Consider baboons, the kind running around savannas in big social groups of a hundred or so beasts. In some cases, the hierarchy can be fluid, with ranks changing all the time; in other cases, rank is hereditary and lifelong. In some cases, rank can depend on the situation – A outranks B when it comes to a contested food item, but the order is reversed if it is competition for someone of the opposite sex. There can be circularities in hierarchies – A defeats B defeats C defeats A. Ranking can involve coalitional support – B gets trounced by A, unless receiving some well-timed support from C, in which case A is sent packing. The actual confrontation between two animals can include anything from a near fatal brawl to a highly dominant individual doing nothing more than shifting menacingly and giving subordinates the willies".

In any case, humans have evolved to be somewhat more subtle and significantly more complex in how we determine hierarchical status, particularly as adults. Joseph Henrich posits at least two distinct forms: "dominance", of course, and "prestige". Prestige arises from our need to learn aspects of culture from those with most to offer on a particular topic, as Henrich describes on pp118-9 of *The Secret of Our Success*: "once humans became good cultural learners, they needed to locate and learn from the best models. The best models are those who seem to possess the information most likely to be valuable to learners, now or later in their lives. To be effective, learners must hang around their chosen models for long periods and at crucial times. Learners also benefit if their models are willing to share nonobvious aspects of their practices, or at least not actively conceal the secrets of their success. As a consequence, humans reliably develop emotions and motivations to seek out particularly skilled, successful, and knowledgeable models and then are willing to pay deference to those models in order to gain their cooperation (pedagogy), or at least acquiescence, in cultural transmission. This deference can come in many forms, including giving assistance (e.g. helping with chores), gifts and favours (e.g. watching the children), as well as speaking well of them in public (thus broadcasting their prestige). Without some form of deference, prestigious individuals have little incentive to allow unrelated learners to be around them, and would not be inclined to provide any preferential access to their skills, strategies, or know-how".

"Dominance", by contrast, requires very different protocols, on pp120-1: "we humans also possess a *dominance psychology* (Henrich's emphasis), which was inherited from our primate ancestors, and is thus much older than prestige. In both primates and humans, individuals attain dominance status when others fear them and believe they will use physical violence or other means of coercion if they do not receive deference in the form of appeasement displays and preferred access to mates and resources (e.g. foods). In these hierarchies, subordinates signal their acceptance of a lower rank with displays involving diminutive body positions, including narrowed shoulders and a downward gaze. Dominant individuals remind subordinates of who the boss is with expansive body positions, upright torsos, widely spread limbs, and broadened chests. In some primates, high rank is achieved purely through fighting ability, which is based mostly on size and strength, though coalition partners and kinship also play a role. In chimpanzees, alliances are also often crucial, as pairs or trios establish coalitions in order to secure the top spots in the dominance hierarchy. These rankings are not the unstable products of continuous fighting, but often provide a relatively stable social order that is established after periods of fierce conflict. High dominance rank in both males and females generally leads to greater reproductive success, as measured by numbers of surviving offspring".

In *Understanding Social Hierarchies* Koski, Xi and Olson make the important point that: "particularly in humans, rank is not limited to the actual observation of a dominant or valued trait, but is often the product of group consensus, or reputation. As a result, the structure of human hierarchies is multidimensional, largely context or group dependent, and self-reinforcing". They describe a number of what they call the "perceptual" and "knowledge-based" cues typically used by humans to assess status, asserting that many of the perceptual cues in particular are common not just to human cultures but also to many other social species. Among non-humans, the main perceptual cues tend to be physical characteristics, such as body size; and "dominant actions", such as biting, hitting, chasing and open-mouth threats (among primates). These may in turn link to personality attributes which themselves are associated with different levels of particular neurotransmitters such as dopamine and testosterone, impacting an individual's willingness to engage in violence, or to affiliate and ally with fellow-creatures, or some combination of the two. Among humans, the authors list factors such as male height (for example, referencing research suggesting that taller US Presidential candidates are more likely to receive popular votes and be re-elected); perceptions of physical attractiveness; the propensity to maintain eye-contact whilst speaking, or alternatively whilst listening; the use of dominant gestures, and body-language more generally; the use of language and speaking style (for example: "speaking quickly and confidently, avoiding nonstandard speech and too much politeness, and utilising sophisticated vocabulary and proper enunciation can communicate high status"); and facial characteristics and expressions (for example, it seems that across cultures "facial masculinity" is associated with high status, in both sexes). Examples of "knowledge-based" cues include factors such as income, occupation, intelligence, popularity and prestige, all of which can be "learned" directly or from other people – in other words, by dint of social reputation: "reputations and labels tend to carry status information and sometimes the only information used to make status judgements is what we learn about someone from others". In short, human hierarchy is a complicated business and status cues, which may be subtle, can often matter as much or more than physical characteristics or overt dominance cues, at least in many cultures.

Human males and females both exhibit a propensity for hierarchy, although there are some gender-specific differences in how this typically plays out. Koski, Xi and Olson, again: "same-sex female hierarchies are somewhat less stable, showing more frequent fluctuations in rank among mid-ranking and top-ranking members compared to male groups, yet the salience and function of the hierarchy is comparable across genders...there might be early gender differences in the type of aggression used to establish dominance but both genders engage in behaviours used to establish a hierarchy".

Finally, it seems that, like many things, our capacity for hierarchy is a product of both nature, that is our genes; and nurture, our experiences and environment. There is emerging evidence, referenced in the same article by Koski, Xi and Olson, that we are born with the cognitive machinery enabling us to develop the neural circuits to recognise status cues from an early age, rather as we are born with the innate capacity to acquire language. But, our definition of what actually constitutes status changes as we mature, in ways which echo Henrich's distinction between "dominance" and "prestige". Koski, Xi and Olson comment: "even very young children are sensitive to perceptual cues signifying dominance...by the end of the first year of life, infants possess the belief that size is associated with strength or dominance, and they use this information to anticipate the outcome of a conflict interaction...in real-life social settings, 1-2-year-old children display dyadic dominance relations themselves, from which members of a group can be ranked along a linear hierarchy...this highlights the inherent nature of social hierarchies, and an early respect for socially dominant behaviour...by early adolescence, peer groups become more differentiated in terms of status rating by peers and the salience and importance of social status beyond other achievements peaks".

Neuroscientists Jasmin Cloutier and Tainyi Li amplify, in an article published online on *sciencedirect.com* titled *Neuroimaging Investigations of Social Status and Social Hierarchies*: "whereas research suggests that young children tend to ascribe higher status to individuals perceived to be more dominant, adults base their judgements of others' social status on a wide range of socially valued dimensions that may or may not be perceptually available. For example, individuals believed to be immoral or bad tend to be assigned lower status. Although what conveys social status may not always generalise across individuals and social groups, perceived differences in standing typically appear to be based on social dimensions valued by members of a given group".

The general effect of all this social pressure is to create a high level of cognitive complexity, reinforcing the hypothesis that the main reason humans developed a larger, more powerful brain relative to our body size is that it was necessary for and in turn enabled by progressively more sophisticated social interactions and social learning. Eventually, social aptitude rather than raw physical power became the primary means of succeeding in life and therefore passing on one's genes to the next generation; and our brain activity came to be dominated by social considerations above all.

The British science writer Matt Ridley comments, on p321 of his 1994 book *The Red Queen: Sex and the*

Evolution of Human Nature: "as Horace Barlow of Cambridge University has pointed out, the things of which we are conscious are mostly the mental events that concern social actions; we remain unconscious of how we see, walk, hit a tennis ball or write a word". And on p322 Ridley quotes a passage from George Eliot's 1866 novel *Felix Holt, the Radical* which captures the complexity involved in social dealings with other humans, and reinforces why a sophisticated brain might be needed to deal with it: "fancy what a game of chess would be if all the chessmen had passions and intellects, more or less small and cunning; if you were not only uncertain about your adversaries men, but a little uncertain also about your own...you would be especially likely to be beaten, if you depended arrogantly on your mathematical imagination, and regarded your passionate pieces with contempt. Yet this imaginary chess is easy compared with a game a man has to play against his fellow-men with other fellow men for instruments".

As an aside, Ridley also de-bunks the hypothesis that large brains developed in humans as a function of and in parallel with advanced tool-making. He highlights that humans are not the only animals found to use primitive tools – most notably, chimpanzees do, and also a number of bird species. If tool-use were the key, we might expect that these species too would have developed larger brains. Equally important, the fossil record shows that human brains began to increase in size around 3 million years ago. But complex tool use began only around 200,000 years ago, around the time that *homo sapiens* arrived on the scene.

Prior to this, Ridley points out, on p314 of *The Red Queen*, that although there is evidence of primitive tool use over long periods of time, there is little sign of the kind of technological innovation which might be expected to be linked to advanced cognition: "the first stone tools, the Oldowan technology of *homo habilis*, which appeared about two and a half million years ago in Ethiopia, were very simple indeed: roughly chipped rocks. They barely improved at all over the next million years, and far from experimenting, they gradually became more standardised. They were then replaced by the Acheulian technology of *homo erectus*, which consisted of hand axes and tear-drop shaped stone devices. Again, nothing happened for a million years and more...".

As a second aside, in another of his books, *The Origins of Virtue*, published in 1996, Ridley tells us that, hierarchical as we may be, humans are nonetheless relatively egalitarian when compared with most other species. He suggests, on p165, that the development of weapons may be at least partly responsible: "it has been obvious for years to anthropologists that weapons make dominance a chancy business, and thus require a leader to lead more by persuasion than by coercion".

Returning to the main narrative, just because hierarchy may be endemic, and serve an important evolutionary purpose by enabling large, complex social groups to function effectively, this does not mean that we should expect a particular hierarchy to be equally beneficial for all the individuals within it. On the contrary, a defining feature of any hierarchy is that resources are not distributed evenly, and that rank confers some level of privileged access to them. As Koski, Xie and Olson put it in *Understanding Social Hierarchies*: "hierarchy refers to the ranking of members in social groups based on the power, influence, or dominance they exhibit, whereby some members are superior or subordinate to others...by definition, some individuals within the hierarchy – those at the top – will be afforded more resources and benefits than others". We may regard this as being inherently undesirable, but the authors point out that this has not stopped hierarchies from becoming more or less ubiquitous in society: "despite that fact that there are always losers in this scenario, social hierarchies are highly pervasive across human cultures and they appear to emerge naturally in social groups".

Still, it may be stating the obvious to assert that occupying low status within a particular hierarchy can be bad news, associated for example with poorer health outcomes and lower life expectancy when compared with those of higher status. A landmark study which illustrates the point is the so-called "Whitehall Study", which looked at a range of outcome metrics over time for a sample of British Civil Service employees, drawn from the full range of clearly-demarcated hierarchical "grades" for which this organisation is noted. Indeed, historically the British Civil Service grade system offers about as pure a form of explicit, measurable, hierarchy as one could wish to find, almost as though it were designed with the specific experiment in mind. In fact there were two Whitehall studies. The first started in 1967 and lasted 10 years. The results showed that overall mortality rates were relatively higher for people with relatively lower employment grades, yielding a statistical correlation between morbidity and grade such that the higher the grade one was, the longer one might expect to live, and vice versa. This correlation held even after controlling for risk factors such as drinking alcohol, smoking, and so on. A second, updated, study was conducted between 1985-8, and drew exactly the same conclusions, as reported in the leading British medical *The Lancet* in an abstract published on 8 June 1991 and now available online: "between 1985 and 1988 we investigated the degree and causes of the social gradient in morbidity in a new cohort of 10,314 civil servants (6,900 men, 3,414 women) aged 35-55 (the Whitehall II study)...in the 20 years separating the two studies there has been no diminution in social class difference in morbidity...we found an inverse correlation between employment grade and (various diseases are listed)...self-perceived health status and symptoms were worse in subjects in lower-status jobs".

This does not mean that all is necessarily lost for individuals who may be low down in a particular hierarchy. We heard extensively in the last chapter from the American biologist Robert Sapolsky, and he has a lot to say on this topic also. The main conclusions relevant to our discussion are:

• Many humans living in "modern" societies are members of a number of different social groups, and our personal experience of hierarchy may be different in each, largely because our actual position in the pecking order may well be. For example, on p363 of *Why Zebras Don't Get Ulcers* Sapolsky suggests that: "the lowly subordinate in the mailroom of the big corporation may, after hours, be deriving tremendous prestige and self-esteem from being the deacon of his church, or the captain of her weekend softball team, or may be at the top of the class at the adult-extension school".

• When a hierarchy is unstable or under great pressure, those of higher rank may in fact experience more stress than their subordinates. Admittedly, when a hierarchy is stable those closer to the top indeed have a more enjoyable experience than those nearer the bottom: "people at the top give ulcers, rather than get them", as Sapolsky puts it on p362 of *Why Zebras Don't Get Ulcers*. For this reason, he asserts that "executive stress syndrome" is often a myth – it is the individuals at the bottom who typically experience the most stress and therefore the worst outcomes, which is of course consistent with the findings of the Whitehall Study among many others. But if once a hierarchy becomes unstable a very different picture emerges. Sapolsky gives the twin examples of wild dogs and dwarf mongooses, on p359: "being dominant in those species doesn't mean a life of luxury, effortlessly getting the best of the pickings and occasionally endowing an art museum...instead, being dominant requires the constant reassertion of high rank through overt aggression - one is tested again and again". An inherently stable hierarchy may also become temporarily unstable, with a corresponding increase in stress levels for those aspiring to high status. On p361 Sapolsky gives an example taken from his favoured species of baboons, but which he surely intends to have echoes for humans: "some key individual has died, someone influential has transferred into the group, some pivotal coalition partnership has formed or come apart – and a revolution results, with animals changing ranks right and left. Under those conditions, it is typically the dominant individuals who are in the very centre of the hurricane of instability". A third possible scenario is when some shock to the external environment disrupts the status quo and again disproportionately increases stress for those of high status, described on p360: "another example concerns male baboons where, as noted, subordinates normally have the elevated glucocortinoid levels (my note: a clear indication of acute stress) – except during a severe drought, when the dominant males were so busy looking for food that they didn't have time or energy to hassle everyone else (implying, ironically, that for a subordinate animal, an environmental stressor can be a blessing, insofar as it saves you from a more severe social stressor)".

- How we feel about our position in a hierarchy depends critically upon our specific personal experiences within it. Sapolsky again, on p360-1 of *Why Zebras Don't Get Ulcers*: "another critical variable is an animal's personal experience of both its rank and society. For example, consider a period when an immensely aggressive male has joined a troop of baboons and is raising hell, attacking animals unprovoked left and right. One might predict stress-responses throughout the troop thanks to this destabilising brute. But, instead, the pattern reflects the individual experience of animals – for those lucky enough never to be attacked by this character, there were no changes in immune function". What is more, the prevailing, group-specific, culture which regulates behaviours within a particular hierarchy can make a big difference to the experiences of individual members, across all status levels: "one example is found among female rhesus monkeys, where subordinates normally take a lot of grief and have elevated basal glucocortinoid levels – except in one group that was studied, which, for some reason, had high rates of reconciliatory behaviours among animals after fights. The same is found in a baboon troop which just happened to be a relatively benign place to be a low-ranking individual".

- How we feel about a hierarchy can be affected by the personal meaning we attach to it. Sapolsky again, on pp361 and 363 of *Why Zebras Don't Get Ulcers*: "...while rank is an important predictor of individual differences in the stress-response (to hierarchy), the meaning of that rank, the psychological baggage that accompanies it in a particular society, is at least as important...consider a marathon being observed by a Martian scientist studying physiology and rank in humans. The obvious thing to do is keep track of the order in which people finish the race. Runner 1 dominates 5, who clearly dominates 5,000. But what if runner 5,000 is a couch potato who took up running just a few months ago...but finished, exhausted and glowing? And what if runner 5 had spent the previous week reading in the sports section that someone of their world-class quality should certainly finish in the top three, maybe even blow away the field. No Martian on earth could predict correctly who is going to feel exultantly dominant afterward".

Finally, Sapolsky makes an important and unambiguous exception to all of the above for the case of people who live in poverty, on p364: "if you want to see an example of chronic stress, study poverty". He describes how being at, or close to, the bottom of the socioeconomic scale exposes people to many of the triggers for chronic stress, and reduces or eliminates their ability to access the appropriate stress-relief mechanisms, with correspondingly negative implications for their health. Even here though, he goes on to assert that the challenges are again at least partly psychological, at least for individuals whose basic subsistence needs are met, that is who are not living in what we defined earlier as "extreme poverty". Sapolsky makes a distinction between "being poor" and "feeling poor", and suggests that a high level of inequality in a society in which overall there is plenty is tantamount to "being made to feel poor" for those at the bottom of the scale.

The conclusion from all this is that hierarchy of one kind or another is an inevitable part of our existence. Human hierarchies share important characteristics with those of other species but we also differ in at least three important respects. First, human status tends to be determined with a greater emphasis on social rather than purely physical attributes: "prestige" rather than just "dominance". Second, as humans we tend to be members not of a single hierarchy, or social group, but rather of several, and our personal status may be different in each. Third, an important component of our experience of hierarchy is ultimately subjective: the meaning we attach to it within our own mind.

There is no denying the suffering we may personally experience if we find ourself caught in a hierarchy which we feel to be toxic in some way, especially if we also feel that we occupy a subordinate role with little or no power to change things. At the same time, we may have at least the possibility of exercising some degree of personal agency over, for example, which social groups we choose to be part of; which individuals we choose to associate with within them; and the meaning that we ascribe to our own, and others', positions.

Violence, bullying and intimidation

It's a sad fact of life that violence, bullying and intimidation have been prevalent throughout human history, and continue to be all too visible today.

The natural world itself offers no shortage of examples of violent behaviour. As Steven Pinker puts it, on pp38-9 of *The Better Angels of Our Nature*: "anyone who has ever seen a hawk tear apart a starling, a swarm of biting insects torment a horse, or the AIDS virus slowly kill a man has firsthand acquaintance with the ways that survival machines callously exploit other survival machines. In much of the living world, violence is simply the default, something that needs no further explanation. When the victims are members of other species, we call the aggressors predators or parasites. But the victims can also be members of the same species. Infanticide, siblicide, cannibalism, rape, and lethal combat have been documented in many kinds of animals".

Where violence is the norm, we might say that the law of the jungle prevails, with potentially devastating consequences for those caught up in it. We heard earlier from the 17th century English philosopher Thomas Hobbes, and here he is again, describing his vision of human life in a state of nature in perhaps the most celebrated, bleakest, passage from his 1651 book *Leviathan*, on p186: "...and that which is worst of all, continual fear, and danger of violent death; and the life of man, solitary, poor, nasty, brutish, and short".

We may ask what are the primal impulses which give rise to violent behaviours. On p208 of *Loneliness*, Cacioppo and Patrick explain how in the case of our close evolutionary cousins, chimpanzees, competition for sex, which is to say for mating opportunities, leads to an evolutionary need for physical dominance, at least among males: "for chimpanzees, the males' need to compete heavily for sex (combined with the preferences females exercise in their choice of sexual partners) has led to the evolution of males that are big, strong, and frequently brutal. The indirect result of these two social factors – male competition and female choice – is male dominance, which then feeds back into the interplay of sexual selection and natural selection. Dominant males have more and better reproductive options, and therefore it is in a female's genetic interest to mate with the biggest and strongest, if only to increase the odds that her male offspring also will be big and strong, with the wider reproductive options that accrue to big strong males, and on and on from one generation to the next".

And in humans too, the data shows that males are typically more prone to violence than females. For example, men accounted for just over 80% of all US arrests for violent crime in 2014, and a study of US homicide statistics between 1980 and 2008 showed that men perpetrated around 90%.

Still, we saw that humans have evolved to value social status, or prestige, above pure physical dominance, and on p209 of *Loneliness* Cacioppo and Patrick point out that social attributes are relevant even in the fundamentally violent world of the chimpanzee: "an often overlooked fact about dominance is the extent to which the alpha at the top of the social pyramid relies on his or her ability to self-regulate and to co-regulate. A dominant chimpanzee usually gains his top-dog position with more than a little help from his friends, cousins, and brothers. They, in turn, gain greater access to sexual privileges as a form of political patronage. So while attaining and maintaining alpha status definitely requires genetic brawn, it also depends on a genetic endowment for the kinds of executive-control functions that, as we have seen, are challenged by feelings of social exclusion: attention focus, self-restraint, impulse control, social awareness, even social sensitivity...alpha status depends on male-male corporation, so even among apes, senior management requires insight, trust building, ability to detect treachery, and reciprocation. This is the only way that the leadership can establish and maintain 'minimally winning coalitions' that preserve important roles, and attractive benefits, for all members of the team. As every ape learns sooner or later, a social system built on 'winner take all' is never viable for long".

As an aside, the authors point out that a social system built on violence is also not without its costs to the individuals involved, in terms of both life experience and expectancy: "for chimps, regulating social interactions through constant battle comes at a price. The single male that winds up atop the hierarchy does not suddenly become immune to the competition that drives the selection process...life for male chimpanzees is incredibly stressful. Researchers often see young males trembling in fear, screaming, and suffering diarrhea because of their anxiety. Not surprisingly, in chimp society, even though male and female infants are born in equal numbers, there are usually twice as many adult females as males".

Cacioppo and Patrick explain, on p211, that female chimpanzees also maintain a dominance hierarchy, albeit one less based on physical violence: "among female chimps...rank most often is based on personality and age, so there is little to fight over, and the hierarchy is largely undisputed. And yet the pressures of self-regulation and co-regulation remain strong. Even in captivity, when female chimps are brought into research labs for a learning experiment, one will always defer to the other as her superior. She will hold back, and will not touch the puzzle box, or the computer, or whatever else is offered, until the dominant female leads the way".

Human females may also be less prone to physical violence, but this does not mean that they are free from aggression more generally. In an article titled *Aggression in Women: Behaviour, Brain and Hormones*, dated 2 May 2018 and published online by *Frontiers in Behavioural Neuroscience*, authors Denson, O'Dean, Blake and Beames assert: "women tend to engage in more indirect forms of aggression (e.g. spreading rumours)...in laboratory studies, women are less aggressive than men, but provocation attenuates this difference. In the real world, women are just as likely to aggress against their romantic partner as men are, but men cause more serious physical and psychological harm".

The authors point out that female aggression has been far less studied than has male aggression, and conclude: "research consistently reports that women use *indirect aggression* (authors' emphasis) to an equivalent or greater extent than men. Indirect aggression occurs when someone harms another while masking the aggressive intent. Specific examples of indirect aggression include spreading false rumours, gossiping, excluding others from a social group, making insinuations without direct accusation, and criticising others' appearance or personality. Girls' use of indirect aggression exceeds boys' from age 11 onward. This difference persists into adulthood...thus, in the real world aggression is common in women and girls, but the form it takes is largely indirect compared to men's aggression".

Stepping back, US psychologists David Buss and Todd Shackleford propose 7 "adaptive problems" for which human aggression might have evolved as a solution, in their 1997 paper *Human aggression in evolutionary psychological perspective*. These are: co-opting the resources of others; defending against attack; inflicting costs on same-sex rivals; negotiating status and power hierarchies; deterring rivals from future aggression; deterring mates from sexual infidelity; and reducing the resources expended on genetically-unrelated children.

It is not that violence is necessarily the automatic answer in these situations. Rather, the optimal solution to a particular circumstance depends on a kind of evolutionary calculus, explained by Steven Pinker on p39 of *The Better Angels of Our Nature*. He addresses the question: "why nature does not consist of one long, bloody melee", with the response: "animals are less inclined to harm their close relatives, because any gene that would nudge an animal to harm a relative would have a good chance of harming a copy of *itself* (Pinker's emphasis) sitting inside that relative...more important,...any organism that has evolved to be violent is a member of a species whose other members, on average, have evolved to be just as violent. If you attack one of your own kind, your adversary may be as strong and pugnacious as you are, and armed with the same weapons and defences. The likelihood that, in attacking a member of your own species, you will get hurt is a powerful selection pressure that disfavours indiscriminate pouncing or lashing out...organisms are selected to deploy violence only in circumstances where the expected benefits outweigh the expected costs".

Of course, a tendency towards violence in modern humans is also likely to be moderated by prestige considerations, namely that, as already discussed, our personal social capital tends to be critical to our chances of success within a particular group, and in many, although sadly not all, social groups it would be seriously damaging to our reputation if we were to develop a reputation for brutality.

Our social systems have also developed to moderate the incidence of physical violence. Hobbes' *Leviathan* makes the case that one of the principal benefits of the modern state is that it essentially exercises a monopoly on violence, increasing the costs to would-be perpetrators and so changing their calculus. Pinker summarises, on p42 of *The Better Angels of Our Nature*: "the title of (Hobbes') master work identified a way to escape (violence): the Leviathan, a monarchy or other government authority that embodies the will of the people and has a monopoly on the use of force. By inflicting penalties on aggressors, the Leviathan can eliminate their incentive for aggression, in turn defusing general anxieties about pre-emptive attack and obviating everyone's need to maintain a hair trigger for retaliation to prove their resolve. And because the Leviathan is a disinterested third party, it is not biased by the chauvinism that makes each side thinks its opponent has a heart of darkness while it is as pure as the driven snow".

In any case, there are grounds for optimism. The full title of Pinker's book is *The Better Angels of Our Nature: Why Violence Has Declined*, and during the course of it he presents a wealth of statistical data leading to the conclusion that rates of violence among humans are in long-term decline, and that the last 50 years or so may well have been the least violent of our entire history as a species, at least when considered in relative terms, that is to say looking at rates of violence proportional to the size of the population. Admittedly there has subsequently been some challenge to Pinker's methodology and data sources. For example, on pp90-91 of *Humankind*, Rutger Bregman raises specific concerns which lead him to the general conclusion that Pinker is wrong to assert that levels of violence have declined over time because

Pinker's estimates of how much violence existed in ancient times are too high.

Whatever the long-term trend, few would argue that it would not be desirable for the violence which exists in contemporary society to reduce. And Pinker suggests some useful checklists which can help us to think about the topic, both in the round and when it comes to our own personal proclivities and triggers.

Specifically, in Chapter 8 of *Better Angels*, Pinker posits five "inner demons", each of which might lead us to commit violent acts:

- Predation: violence deployed as a means to an end, usually involving the seizure of resources of one kind or another.
- Dominance: "the urge for authority, prestige, glory and power".
- Revenge: "the moralistic urge towards retribution, punishment, and justice".
- Sadism: "the deliberate infliction of pain for no purpose but to enjoy a person's suffering".
- Ideology: "a shared belief system, usually involving a vision of utopia, that justifies unlimited violence in pursuit of unlimited good".

In Chapter 9, he proposes four "Better Angels", which, properly applied, can help us to control whatever violent demons we may personally harbour, and which link to topics we have or shortly will discuss:

- empathy: "feel the pain of others and...align their interests with our own".
- self-control: "anticipate the consequences of acting on our impulses and...inhibit them accordingly".
- the "Moral Sense": which "sanctifies a set of norms and taboos that govern the interactions among people in a culture". (Pinker points out that in some contexts these

can also sanctify violence: we will explore morality more fully in the next chapter.)
- reason: which "allows us to extract ourselves from our parochial vantage points".

Finally, in Chapter 10 Pinker outlines five "historical forces", each of which he asserts serves to rebalance the calculus that a violent approach will ultimately serve their own best interests for both institutions and individuals:

- the Leviathan: the Hobbesian idea, reviewed above, that modern nation states which exercise a monopoly on violence can inhibit violence among their citizens.
- the growth of commerce, with an important implication being that "other people become more valuable alive than dead".
- feminisation: increasing respect for "the interests and values of women", who as we saw are less prone to physical violence, if not necessarily to aggression overall.
- cosmopolitanism, helping "prompt people to take the perspectives of people unlike themselves and to expand their circle of sympathy to embrace them". We will explore this idea further in the next chapter, as part of our discussion of "In-Groups" and "Out-Groups".
- "the Escalator of Reason": specifically: "intensifying application of knowledge and rationality to human affairs" which "can force people to recognise the futility of cycles of violence, to ramp down the privileging of their own interests over others', and to reframe violence as a problem to be solved rather than a contest to be won".

The capacity to influence, manipulate and deceive

Hierarchy and dominance are not the only options available to us in seeking to persuade other people to behave as we wish them to. An alternative to is to deploy what we might call our social skills to influence, or alternatively manipulate, other people. Indeed, we saw earlier that it is likely that our big human brains developed largely for this purpose.

We quickly run into a potential problem of language. The very word "manipulate" has a pejorative association, implying that the purpose is to enable the individual to achieve their own, implied-to-be-nefarious, ends. To "influence", however, makes no such presumption, even though the behaviours and social skills involved may be more or less identical. In any case, the distinction is not necessarily as clear-cut as the different words may make it sound - one person's "persuasion" can easily be interpreted as another's "manipulation".

The broader point is that as individual humans we possess extraordinarily sophisticated capacities to engage with other humans, to sense what they might want or need, and to use this understanding to find non-violent ways to encourage them to behave in ways we would like them to. And our focus in what follows will be on our generalised capacity to influence other people, regardless of our ultimate motives for doing so. As far as possible, words like "manipulation" will therefore be used in a strictly neutral, technical sense.

Of course, humans are by no means the only species to practice manipulative behaviour. As Richard Dawkins and John Krebs point out in their contribution to the 1978 Blackwell Scientific Publications book *Behavioural Ecology, An Evolutionary Approach*, in a chapter titled *Animal Signals: Mind-Reading and Manipulation*: "many of the externally visible features of animals, many of their behaviour patterns, many chemical substances and most of the sounds given off by them, are best interpreted as being adapted –'designed by natural selection'- to influence the behaviour of other animals".

We can broaden the point and assert that communication of all kinds often has the goal of manipulation, which is to say of encouraging others to behave in a certain way, rather than simply of transferring information. For example, a bird may sing long and eloquently to persuade a female to mate with him, or to encourage a rival to keep clear of his territory. If he were merely passing on information, he need not make the performance so elaborate. Indeed, animal communication, say Dawkins and Krebs: "is more like human advertising than like airline timetables. Even the most mutually beneficial communication, like that between a mother and a baby, is pure manipulation, as every mother who has been woken in the night by a desperate sounding infant that merely wants company knows".

And Matt Ridley quotes Geoffrey Miller, a Stanford University psychologist, on p323 of *The Red Queen*: "all apes and monkeys show complex behaviour replete with communication, manipulation, deception and long-term relationships", and also gives surely the most succinct summary of the main point: "...as Lord Macaulay put it 'the object of oratory alone is not truth, but persuasion'".

Still, for the reasons already discussed we humans have developed particularly sophisticated ways to manipulate and potentially deceive, so much so that these things are an integral part of our everyday experience. For example, in an article titled *Effects of deception in social networks*, dated 7 September 2014 and published online by the Royal Society, authors Iniguez, Govezensky, Dunbar, Kaski and Barrio quote a US study in which a randomised representative sample of 1000 Americans recorded an average 1.65 lies per person per day, equating to 550 per person per year. They quote another study in which 92% of people say they have lied at some time to a partner. It's hard not to wonder whether the other 8% are themselves telling the truth.

Of course, developing a reputation as a serial liar is likely to be as, or possibly even more, damaging to our social capital as making a name for systematic violence. But this may again be at least partly to do with the semantics of the word "liar". In fact, it is hard to imagine society functioning without the ability for individuals to exercise discretion and a regard for their interlocutor in what they choose to say and how they choose to say it. And if we define a lie as any statement which is not a literal truth, then it is easy to think of everyday examples in which a "lie" can grease the social wheels in ways which are arguably beneficial to all parties. For example, when asked by a work colleague "how are you today?" most of us would probably reply "fine thanks, how are you?", almost regardless of how we actually feel. We interpret that our inquisitor is merely observing social convention, and unlikely to relish being regaled with details of our ailments, family troubles or financial worries; and the same convention requires that we say we feel fine even if we don't. There is of course a multitude of situations in which we might consider a technical lie to be the most appropriate response: for example, inventing an imaginary excuse to end a phone call without hurting the other party's feelings ("I must go now because I need to put some more money in the parking meter..." as distinct from the more truthful "I am bored of this conversation"); tactfully complimenting someone on a new outfit into which they have obviously put a lot of emotional capital even though this may not accurately reflect our true opinion; or, to take a more high-stakes situation, telling a hostile visitor who knocks on the door with violent intent that the person they are seeking is not at home, even though in fact they are. And so on.

What this points to is that not all deception is the same. A capacity to deceive can be used for a range of purposes, many of which we might consider to be benign or indeed beneficial. In the same Royal Society article, Iniguez and colleagues summarise: "social psychologists commonly characterise the degree of human deception by distinguishing four types of lying: (i) *prosocial* – lying to protect someone, or to benefit or help others; (*ii*) *self-enhancement* – lying to save face, to avoid embarrassment, disapproval or punishment, or to gain an advantage (these lies are not intended to hurt anyone, rather they benefit the self); (*iii*) *selfish* – lying to protect oneself at the expense of another and/or to conceal a misdeed; and (*iv*) *antisocial* – lying to hurt someone else intentionally".

The point is simply to acknowledge that a capacity to influence, or alternatively manipulate, is fundamental to our ability to operate effectively in a social context, especially one in which social relationships are more nuanced than mere physical hierarchy and dominance. Of course it matters what kind of deception we practice. Used appropriately, prosocial deception, the celebrated "white lie", clearly has the potential to strengthen social fabric; whilst selfish or antisocial deception must surely undermine it, at least in the event that it is detected.

Part C: "Me" versus "Us"

We have seen that a capacity for sociability is the behaviourial characteristic which most defines humans relative to other species, defined as the ability to cooperate and share in an intentional way with individuals with whom we bear no special genetic bond. We have also seen that this is balanced at least to some extent by a capacity for anti-social, selfish behaviours; and that as individuals we possess the capacity to behave both pro and anti-socially.

It is now time to combine this with the central insight from Chapter 2, that human consciousness gives us an opportunity, in effect an obligation, to exercise existential choice in our life – over what we do, and how we behave.

The specific link is that our freedom to exercise existential choice largely boils down to a series of decisions about when to cooperate, in other words to behave in a pro-social way which at some level privileges the interests of others rather than, or in addition to, our own; and when to compete, in other words to behave "selfishly", and to pursue our own interests even to the extent that these are in conflict with those of other people. In his 2013 book *Moral Tribes* the American psychologist Joshua Greene memorably frames this as a choice between privileging "Me" versus "Us".

The question is relevant to each of us, every single day. Virtually every social interaction that we have, no matter how trivial, presents us with some form of this choice.

In many situations what is right for us as an individual can also be beneficial to other people, indeed to society overall: the classic "win:win". As Adam Smith famously observed in *The Wealth of Nations* Book 1, Chapter 2: "it is not from the benevolence of the butcher, the brewer, or the baker, that we expect our dinner, but from their regard to their own interest". In cases like these there is no real choice to be made. All that matters is that an individual is motivated to be productive, regardless of whether the source of this motivation is personal gain or a desire to help others.

However, in many other cases there is an element of "win:lose", in other words the interests of the individual do not align elegantly with those of the group. And here there is a genuine choice to be made. For example, when resources are finite and a decision must be made on how to allocate or divide them; or, to elaborate on Smith's metaphor, if an individual baker goes rogue and decides to cheat his or her customers by serving them adulterated bread. In such a case, the more productive they are, the worse it is likely to be for those around them.

How to decide when to privilege "Me", and when "Us", in other words "others"? The answer turns out to be highly situational, as we will now explore.

Cooperate or compete - the critical existential choice

The canonical work on the topic of cooperation versus competition is generally acknowledged to be *The Evolution of Cooperation*, a book written by the American political scientist Robert Axelrod, originally published in 1984 and revised in 2006. Axelrod will therefore be our main guide.

Axelrod's work has spawned a healthy level of critical admiration. Richard Dawkins, the passionate advocate of evolutionary theory whom we met in chapter 1 is an admirer, and provides an excellent and detailed summary of Axelrod's main ideas in Chapter 12 of *The Selfish Gene*. Dawkins' chapter title, *Nice guys finish first*, gives a strong clue to the counter-intuitive nature of Axelrod's main conclusions, specifically that a strategy of cooperation will often enable the individuals who pursue it to out-compete others who adopt a more adversarial, nakedly selfish, approach.

Dawkins also wrote the Foreword to the revised 2006 edition of *The Evolution of Cooperation*, and on pvii he summarises Axelrod's central message: "in a Darwinian world, that which survives survives, and the world becomes full of whatever qualities it takes to survive. As Darwinians, we start pessimistically by assuming deep selfishness at the level of natural selection, pitiless indifference to suffering, ruthless attention to individual success at the expense of others...and yet from such warped beginnings, something can come that is in effect, if not necessarily in intention, close to amicable brotherhood and sisterhood. This is the uplifting message of Robert Axelrod's remarkable book".

Axelrod's research centres on a version of a modern parable called the Tragedy of the Commons, a term coined in an 1833 essay by the British economist William Forster Lloyd and popularised more than a century later in a 1968 article by the American ecologist Garrett Hardin. An unspecified number of herders are assumed to be grazing their cattle on an area of common land (a "commons"). Each individual herder tries to do the best for him or herself and so grazes their animals for maximum productivity, increasing their herd size as far as they can. The eventual, inevitable, result is that the land is overgrazed, at which point everyone loses out. The "tragedy" is that whilst each individual herder is acting in a way which is rational to them the cumulative effect is disaster for the group, and therefore ultimately for each individual member.

There are parallels to many real-world situations, obviously including the highly topical question of the sustainability of Planet Earth itself. Harvard Business School online lists five everyday examples, at least some of which likely involve each of us personally, in an article titled *Tragedy of the Commons: What It Is & 5 Examples*, dated 6 February 2019. The list includes: coffee consumption, leading to "significant" environmental impacts such as habitat loss; overfishing ("posing significant risks to marine ecosystems"); fast fashion, leading to "extreme" product surplus; traffic congestion ("as more people decide that roads and highways are the fastest way to travel to work, more cars end up on the roads, ultimately slowing down traffic and polluting the air"); and groundwater use ("the (US) groundwater supply is decreasing faster than it can be replenished").

Axelrod focuses on a computerised simulation of a gamified version of the Tragedy of the Commons, called the Prisoner's Dilemma. The "game" element turns out to be important because it allows for quantification and therefore a rich analysis of alternative strategies. Indeed, Axelrod's work has become a central pillar in the discipline now known as Game Theory.

The term Prisoner's Dilemma itself was coined by Canadian mathematician Albert Tucker in the 1950s, building on earlier work by the American mathematicians Merrill Flood and Melvin Dresher. The setup is that two prisoners are accused of a serious crime. The authorities lack sufficient evidence to convict either unless they can persuade one prisoner to inform against the other. They do however have evidence to convict both of a lesser crime. The authorities therefore give each prisoner a one-time opportunity to inform on the other with respect to the more serious crime. The deal each is offered is that if they inform and the other stays silent, then the informant will go free and the person who is informed against will be convicted of the serious crime and receive a lengthy jail sentence. If both inform, both will receive a lengthy jail sentence but with some modest reduction to reflect the fact that they were each helpful in securing the conviction of the other. If both stay silent, both will be convicted of the lesser offence, and therefore both receive a relatively light jail sentence. No communication is allowed between the prisoners.

The "dilemma" arises from the fact that the only logical choice for each of the prisoners is to inform on their accomplice - in other words, to behave selfishly, and "compete" rather than "cooperate" with each other, despite the fact that cooperation would result in a better overall outcome. This is because if Prisoner A assumes that Prisoner B will denounce them, then informing on B will result in A receiving a lengthy prison sentence but less than if they stayed silent. Conversely, if A assumes B will stay silent, then by themself informing A will walk away scot-free as opposed to the short jail sentence they would receive if they also stayed silent. The same logic obviously applies in reverse to Prisoner B. Hence, if both parties act purely logically in their own self-interest then both must inevitably choose "Me", even though this outcome dooms them to a worse combined fate than if they had both chosen "Us".

Axelrod's version of the Prisoner's Dilemma assigns numerical scores to the different outcomes, and then repeats over multiple rounds - what he calls an "iterated" version of the game. Specifically, two protagonists face off and must each choose whether to "cooperate" (the equivalent of staying silent in the original game: the cooperation is with the other prisoner, not with the authorities) or to "defect" (the technical word for acting selfishly, and the equivalent of informing in the context of the original game). Obviously, no conferring is allowed - each must make this choice without knowing what the other will do. Importantly, as with the original Prisoner's Dilemma, the incentives are arranged in such a way that no matter what the other party does, on any single turn defection (acting selfishly) always receives the highest reward, and a player who cooperates when the other party defects receives the lowest. Solo defection also scores higher than the reward available for each party if both cooperate, and if both parties defect, then both do worse than if they had both cooperated. An important ground rule is that each player is playing to "win" in a Darwinian sense, in other words their only consideration is to seek to maximise their own score.

The specific values which Axelrod assigns are that if both players cooperate on a given turn, they each receive 3 points. He calls this "R", the reward for mutual cooperation. If both defect, they each get 1 point, "P", the punishment for mutual defection. If one defects whilst the other cooperates, the defector receives 5 points ("T", the temptation to defect) and the cooperator gets zero ("S", the sucker's payoff). It would of course be possible to assign different values to each of T, R, P and S, but this doesn't affect the general conclusions as long as the relative order is maintained that T is worth more than R, which is worth more than P, which is worth more than S.

If Axelrod's version of the game is restricted to a single turn then the only logical course of action for each player is to defect, as in the original Prisoner's Dilemma. To run through the maths, if a player assumes that the other party will cooperate, then by themselves defecting they secure the maximum reward "T" – 5 points, higher than the 3 points available for "R", mutual cooperation. Alternatively, if they assume the other party will defect, then by defecting themself they secure reward "P", the punishment for mutual defection, which at 1 point is still relatively more than the alternative of zero for reward "S", for cooperating when an opponent defects.

However, in an "iterated" game, played over multiple rounds, many different strategies are possible and there is not the same overwhelming logic for mutual defection. Examples of possible, simple, strategies are: "always cooperate", or alternatively "always defect". A more sophisticated approach might be "always cooperate, except defect on every Nth move to benefit from the element of surprise", or "cooperate if the opponent cooperated on the previous move, but if they ever once defect then always subsequently defect yourself since they clearly can't be trusted".

There is of course an inherent tension. Defection in any given round creates the possibility of securing the maximum 5 points available from "suckering" an opponent in that round, whilst also avoiding any risk of being "suckered" oneself. At the same time, a decision to defect eliminates the possibility of securing the 3 points available from mutual cooperation for that round, and risks antagonising the opponent such that, having once been "suckered", they may be less likely to cooperate in subsequent rounds.

In 1980, Axelrod had the idea to invite fellow scientists to participate in a competitive Iterated Prisoner's Dilemma, to be played over 200 iterations, or rounds. Each entrant was asked to submit a computer programme coding the relevant instructions for their chosen strategy, and 14 entries were received. Axelrod then ran a computer simulation in which each strategy was matched against each of the others received, and also against a clone of itself, plus an additional, control, strategy called "Random", in which as the name implies each move was determined by random chance.

Over multiple rounds the highest value strategy in theory would be "always defect", if, and only if, the other party chose to cooperate on every turn (in other words, they used a strategy of "always cooperate"). In such a scenario "always defect" would secure the maximum 5-point haul for reward "T" every round, yielding 1000 points over 200 rounds. Of course, in such a case the strategy of "always cooperate" would achieve precisely zero points, receiving the sucker's payoff on every one of the 200 turns. It is obvious even from this simplistic example that a strategy of "always cooperate, regardless of circumstance" is naïve and would inevitably lay its user open to exploitation, at least in the context of Axelrod's game. No rational competitor would cooperate indefinitely with an opponent implacably committed to consistent defection.

A more realistic benchmark score is therefore one in which both parties find a way to cooperate. The way the game was structured, if they both do this on every one of the 200 turns then they would each receive reward "R" of 3 points per turn, yielding 600 points each across 200 rounds, and a total of 1200 points for both players combined. This is of course higher than the combined total of 1000 points achieved in the first scenario.

The winning strategy from the entries received for Axelrod's first tournament was famously called Tit for Tat, submitted by Anatol Rapoport, an American mathematical psychologist. This also happened to be the simplest strategy submitted (for obvious reasons no-one entered "always cooperate", or even "always defect"). Tit for Tat always cooperated on the first turn and thereafter, as its name implies, simply did whatever the opponent had done on the previous turn.

Axelrod analysed the results of this initial tournament, and drew a number of important conclusions which turn out to be relevant to the broader themes of this chapter. In particular, he noted that the 8 strategies which scored best out of the 15 submitted (comprising 14 competitors plus "Random") were all what he called "nice", and the 7 which scored lowest were all "nasty". The definition of a "nice" strategy was technical not moralistic, specifically that it was never the first to defect, but only ever defected in response to an opponent doing so. A "nasty" strategy was the exact opposite - it was willing to be the first to defect, without any "provocation" from its adversary.

Quantifying the results across the 200 rounds showed a marked difference in outcomes. Tit for Tat scored 504 points in total, not far short of the benchmark 600 points for a game in which both parties collaborated on every turn. The lowest-performing "nice" strategy scored 472, and the best-performing "nasty" strategy scored 401.

Axelrod also determined that a characteristic of higher-performing strategies was that they were what he called "forgiving". This means that when they came up against an opponent who was prone to defect, they found ways to avoid getting trapped in a prolonged cycle of retaliation. Importantly, "forgiving" did not mean "turn the other cheek". As we saw a moment ago, a strategy of "always cooperate regardless of what the counterparty does" would simply invite exploitation. Nonetheless, Axelrod observed that strategies tended to do better across the course of the game if they engaged in what we might call proportional retaliation, giving the counterparty a chance to resume cooperation, rather than punitive retaliation, which was more likely to result in both parties ending up locked in a prolonged cycle of mutual attrition.

Tit for Tat obviously meets the criterion for "forgiving", because its policy of copying the previous move of the opponent means that if an opponent who has chosen to defect subsequently switches to "cooperate", then Tit for Tat automatically does the same on the very next turn. In fact, Axelrod took this notion of "forgivingness" further, calculating that in this initial tournament Tit for Tat itself would have been outscored by a strategy of Tit for Two Tats, had one been submitted. Tit for Two Tats cooperated for two turns after an opponent had defected. Only if the counterparty then defected for a second consecutive time would Tit for Two Tats itself defect.

Axelrod then invited entries for a second tournament, sharing with all comers the results of the first including his conclusions about the saliency of "niceness" and "forgivingness". The second tournament attracted 62 entries, making 63 in all with the addition of Random. Interestingly, the field split between entries which took the lessons from tournament 1 at face value and sought to embrace "niceness" and "forgivingness" in various ways, and others which instead pursued some form of "nasty" approach, presumably reasoning that they might be able to prosper by second guessing (that is to say, exploiting) those who would faithfully but perhaps naively adopt the "nice" playbook that had proved successful in tournament 1. Tit for Two Tats was an entry into this second tournament, submitted by no less a person than the British evolutionary biologist John Maynard Smith.

One important modification to Tournament 2 was that it was announced to be over an unspecified number of rounds, unlike the first tournament which was fixed in advance to 200 rounds exactly. This is because logicians had quickly deduced that a finite number of rounds should rationally lead both parties to conclude that they would have to defect on move 200, for the reasons we reviewed earlier relating to a single-round game, which is effectively what move 200 would become. However, if each party knew that the other would certainly defect on move 200, then logically they should also both defect on move 199, and so on in a remorseless chain of logic back to move 1. The number of rounds in tournament 2 was therefore determined probabilistically, with a 0.00346 chance of the game ending after any given move.

The winner of the Tournament 2 was...Tit for Tat, again. This time Tit for Tat scored a remarkable 576 points, 96% of the "benchmark" level of 600.

Overall, "nice" strategies again did definitively better than "nasty" ones. All but one of the fifteen highest-scoring strategies were "nice", and all but one of the fifteen lowest-scoring were "nasty". Interestingly, Tit for Two Tats didn't do as well this time, ranking twenty-fourth overall and falling victim to some new entries which had been explicitly designed to prey on the finding from tournament 1 that "niceness" and "forgivingness" are innately desirable. An example was a strategy called TESTER, which consistently alternated between Cooperate and Defect on successive turns, thereby never triggering Tit for Two Tats to retaliate, whilst "suckering" it 50% of the time.

An important lesson is that, faced with an opponent who is willing to behave selfishly and defect, it turns out that it is possible to be too "nice" and too "forgiving", certainly in the context of Axelrod's tournament. Said another way, it is not enough to be "nice", without also having some way of engaging productively with other parties who are themselves "nasty". Axelrod himself summarises, on p44 of *The Evolution of Cooperation*: "there were a number of rules (my note: or 'strategies') in the second...tournament that deliberately used controlled numbers of defections to see what they could get away with. To a large extent, what determined the actual rankings of the "nice" rules was how well they were able to cope with these challengers". We saw earlier that Dawkins titled the chapter of his own book in which he discusses Axelrod's ideas *Nice guys finish first*, but a more accurate summary might be *Nice guys finish first, but not if they are so nice as to be naïve*.

The reason Tit for Tat performed better than other strategies was not because it ever outscored them head-to-head. It never once did this, nor was it likely to since like all "nice" strategies it was programmed never to be the first to defect. It scored consistently well when paired with other "nice" strategies of course – both would always score an average reward of "R", or 3 points, on every turn. But this was not differentiating when compared with these other "nice" strategies, because by definition they all cooperated in every round when paired together.

What enabled Tit for Tat to stand out was precisely that it was relatively better at avoiding being exploited by "nasty" strategies. Tit for Tat was less susceptible to being "suckered", that is to say to cooperating when its opponent defected; and relatively more effective at influencing "nasty" opponents to cooperate, so that fewer of Tit for Tat's games descended into a vendetta-style cycle of recurring mutual defection. Said a different way, Tit for Tat proved most adept at increasing the size of the overall pie, so that even though its share for any given turn was generally the same as or smaller than that of its immediate opponent, this nonetheless translated to more pie for Tit for Tat in the game overall when measured over multiple rounds and multiple opponents.

Axelrod points out that part of the way Tit for Tat achieved these superior outcomes was by being not only "forgiving", but also what he calls "retaliatory". Tit for Tat immediately and always "punished" a defection from another player by defecting itself, ignoring whatever track record of cooperation or defection the other player may previously have established. We might say that Tit for Tat was not sentimental, and even, at the risk of stretching the point, that it reacted purely on observed behaviour and not any attempt to analyse motive. Equally important, as we also saw, if the opponent then mended their ways and started to cooperate then Tit for Tat was equally quick to "forgive". We might say that it did not bear grudges.

A separate insight is that the effectiveness of a particular strategy for the iterated game could only be assessed in the context of the strategy population within which it was required to compete. For example, we know that Tit for Two Tats would have won the first tournament, had it been entered, but came unstuck in the second tournament, precisely because a different mix of alternative strategies was present in the game population.

Tit for Tat was itself successful in the context in which it was assessed, that is with the particular population of alternative strategies submitted, and under the operating condition that each strategy met each of the other strategies just once. But this does not mean that Tit for Tat is somehow the perfect strategy, or would flourish under all conceivable conditions. Indeed, it is easy to demonstrate that this is not the case. For example, if Tit for Tat were to meet "Always Defect", which didn't happen to be submitted to either of Axelrod's tournaments but one could imagine to be a plausible, Hobbesian, strategy, then in the first round Tit for Tat would cooperate, and Always Defect would, of course, defect. Hence Tit for Tat would score zero points, and Always Defect would score 5. In the second and every subsequent round, both strategies would defect, each achieving 1 point. Whenever the end of the game arrived, Tit for Tat would inevitably have 5 fewer points than Always Defect. As an isolated case in a population featuring many alternative strategies and in which each strategy meets each of the others just once - the case for both Axelrod's tournaments - this might not matter much to the overall result. Tit for Tat would likely encounter plenty of other opponents whom it could "persuade" to cooperate, or who would simply choose to cooperate with it, and thereby boost its average score. Always Defect would be doomed to a series of attritional encounters in which it rarely scored highly, unless it were lucky enough to meet naïve opponents playing something close to a version of "Always Cooperate". But if we hypothesise a game population comprising *only* copies of Always Defect, except for the single copy of Tit for Tat, then Tit for Tat would obviously flounder, and would inevitably finish last. The overall scores for all players combined would be much lower than for those in a game where cooperation was more prevalent, but that wouldn't make the outcome any better for Tit for Tat in the particular game environment.

It follows that the optimal strategy in an iterated game of Prisoner's Dilemma can only be defined by reference to the other strategies present in the game population. And if the relative proportion of strategies changes over time, then so might the relative effectiveness of any given strategy. In an iterated game, as in life more broadly, there is no such thing as a single "winning" strategy, which would be sure to prosper against all comers and under all scenarios.

To explore this aspect further, Axelrod took the same 63 strategies which were entered in his second tournament and ran a series of "competitions" designed to simulate the effects of Darwinian evolution on the game population over time. The idea was that successful strategies would propagate at the expense of less successful ones, which might eventually go extinct, so simulating natural selection. Specifically, at the end of each round each strategy was rewarded with relatively more or less "offspring" (i.e. copies of itself), based on how the strategy had performed in that round. So, instead of facing each alternative strategy just once, as happened in the first two versions of the tournament, high-performing strategies would face progressively more encounters with other high-performing strategies over time, including clones of themselves, and relatively fewer with strategies which had already proved to be less successful, to the extent that these might disappear entirely. And since, as we saw, all strategies fare better against some types of opponent than others, the fortunes of individual strategies might wax and wane during the course of a competition, as the mix of strategies itself evolved over successive rounds.

The specific goal was to see not just which strategy would score highest, but also to assess whether some form of stability might be reached, after which the mix of strategies in a game population would reach some level of equilibrium: the equivalent of John Maynard Smith's Evolutionarily Stable State or "ESS", in which a population mix is stable in a given environment, at which point it will predictably be reinforced rather than undermined by the impact of continuing selection pressures so long as the environment itself remains stable. In the context of Axelrod's Iterated Prisoner's Dilemma, this might mean that a particular strategy ultimately prevailed and all others went extinct, or it might be that a mix of strategies in some proportion became the established and stable norm.

Axelrod ran 6 versions of his putative "Tournament 3", each with different starting population mixes designed to create environments which would test individual strategies in different ways. It will come as no surprise that Tit for Tat scored highest in 5 out of the 6 simulations, and second highest in the sixth.

In general, the aggressive strategies designed to exploit overly cooperative, "naïve" opponents (such as the hapless Tit for Two Tats) did well in the early rounds, but then started to decline as the strategies that were their "prey" began to diminish in number and themselves go extinct. After about 1,000 rounds the population mix indeed typically became stable, so that an ESS was achieved. "Nasty" strategies fared consistently badly, generally succumbing to extinction by about round 200, although one (called "Harrington") lasted until nearly round 1,000 before finally disappearing. Axelrod comments, on p117: "the lesson is that not being nice may look promising at first, but in the long run it can destroy the very environment it needs for its own success".

Of course, this is all very encouraging for those of us who would like to believe in a world where nice (even if not naïve) guys really can finish first, or at least be sustainably successful. But Axelrod went on to explore one further critical question: is it possible that "nice" strategies could evolve and prosper in a world which was predominantly "nasty"?

He concluded, more soberingly, that if a strategy as "nasty" as Always Defect once becomes dominant in a population, there is no way for a single player using a "nice" strategy to defeat it. In such a world, a "nice" guy would inevitably be doomed to finish last, as we saw earlier with the specific if extreme example of a single Tit for Tat adrift in a population of Always Defects.

However, Axelrod also showed how relatively small clusters of "nice" individuals representing as little as 5% of the total population could survive and even thrive, so long as they interacted disproportionately, although not exclusively, with one another. Axelrod highlights that in the real world, trust is typically the vital ingredient needed to underpin mutual cooperation. He suggests that, in the real world, the best way to build and sustain trust is to structure frequent, repetitive contact over an extended timeframe, as distinct from occasional, intermittent contact; and it is moreover helpful if the value at stake in any specific interaction is modest and therefore the temptation for either party to defect is low on any specific transaction or "turn".

Finally, Axelrod underscores the importance of what he calls "the shadow of the future". Simply put, most players will, and logically should, value the outcome of a current round more highly than the possible future outcomes of possible future rounds; and the further into the future one looks, the higher the discount one should apply. For one thing, as we saw the number of rounds over which the game would be played was uncertain. This means there is some probability, however small, that any given round, or transaction, will be the last. In addition, basic economics and "the time value of money" tell us that value today is (almost) always worth more by some amount than an equivalent face value in the future. Axelrod tells us that, depending how large a "discount rate" we apply to the future, and the specific ratios between the assigned values of T, R, P and S, there are scenarios in which it is rational to defect immediately even in an iterated game.

The overall conclusions from all this work are ultimately optimistic, certainly in Axelrod's own view, and also that of Dawkins, as we saw earlier. They show that cooperation can be predicted to exist and indeed flourish even in a world driven entirely by rational self-interest, at least in situations where the conditions are similar to those of the game, which is to say that the rewards available are "non-zero-sum", and it is therefore rational for all parties to pursue some form of "win:win" rather than a purely "win:lose" approach.

To bring the discussion further to the realm of the practical, Axelrod offers four suggestions to help guide decision-making in situations in which we find ourself facing some version of a Prisoner's Dilemma in real life. Which is to say, all of us, often. The suggestions are:

1. *Don't be envious.* Humans are wired to compete, at least in part. One implication is that we can be prone to assume that for us to "win", someone else must "lose", and conversely that if we see another person flourishing this must somehow be coming at our own expense. Of course, some situations really are zero-sum. But as we saw earlier there are many others which are not, or need not be. In these, the possibility exists that the those involved will do better over time by cooperating than by adopting an adversarial approach. Rather than seeking to "beat" a counterparty, our own interests may be best served by helping them to succeed, much as Tit for Tat almost never scores more highly than the other player in any individual game but rather avoids being exploited and is better at influencing other players to cooperate.

2. *Don't be the first to defect.* One of the most counterintuitive findings from Axelrod's work is that "nasty" strategies consistently perform poorly, in virtually every scenario. The reason is that they provoke early retaliation, in turn making it hard to establish a subsequent pattern of "trust" and collaboration. In general, then, a bias to initial cooperation is likely to serve

us well. There are some important caveats, however, which mean that it would be going too far to assert that we should never even consider pre-emptive defection. As we saw, if we know that the "game" will only last one round then defection is the only logical move, at least if we do not assign much weight to intangibles such as our longer-term relationship with the counterparty, or our social reputation more broadly. More subtly, even in an iterated game, "the shadow of the future" is a critical factor, and can make early defection logical under specific circumstances. Still, these are caveats which should not detract from the central point that in most circumstances it is best to start by cooperating: to presume trust, as it were, at least until such time as the counterparty shows that this is misplaced.

3. *Reciprocate both cooperation and defection.* As we saw, Dawkins calls the chapter in which he summarises Axelrod's work *Nice guys finish first.* Crucially, the definition of "nice" here is Axelrod's, and refers specifically to strategies (or "guys") who avoid being the first to defect. He is explicitly *not* talking about people who are "nice" in a more general sense, for example who systematically turn the other cheek when provoked. On the contrary, an important insight is that if another player "provokes" by defecting, then it is important to retaliate promptly, and to "punish" them by defecting oneself. Having said this, Axelrod proposes that such retaliation should be proportionate, and as far as possible at a level of intensity slightly below the original provocation, to signal good intent. The idea is to find ways to avoid what might otherwise have been an isolated case of defection from turning into a longer-term vendetta, assuming that the other player also wants or can be brought to want to avoid this themself. Hence, as we saw, successful strategies demonstrate a capacity for what Axelrod calls "forgiveness". Actions speak louder than words, especially when dealing with emotionless computers, and

the best way to signal forgiveness is to reciprocate cooperation even if the counterparty has demonstrated a willingness to defect.

4. *Don't be too clever.* It is telling that Tit for Tat was one of the simplest strategies submitted to either of Axelrod's tournaments. Simplicity helps, in Axelrod's view, because it makes behaviour relatively transparent and predictable, to a computer algorithm and perhaps more importantly to a human counterparty in real life.

Applying Axelrod to our social reality

Axelrod's work has important implications as we consider our own fundamental existential choices between cooperation and selfishness. The basic message is that often, but not always, behaving cooperatively turns out to be in our own best interests as well as those of the people with whom we interact. We might draw a number of conclusions besides:

- *Beware assuming that a situation is "zero sum" when it may not be, or at least may not need to be.* We might equally well argue the reverse, of course – seeking a "win:win" solution to a situation in which this is structurally impossible is unlikely to produce a good outcome. Still, it is surely the case that cooperation delivers the best outcome for all parties in many situations in life, especially when involving a series of interactions over time. Conversely, if we start with a mindset that success requires us to get one over on the other guy, we risk initiating a self-fulfilling doom loop in which our dealings with others become "win:lose" not because this was inevitable, but rather because we ourself made it so.

- *Presume trust, but only sustain it to the extent that this is merited by the actual behaviour of the person being trusted.* We saw that one of Axelrod's main lessons was "don't be the first to defect", because by doing so we make it more likely that a doom loop will develop whereby the person or people we are dealing with will themselves defect in response, in turn risking an attritional cycle of mutual reprisal. We also saw that if our initial cooperative, prosocial, behaviour is met with "defection", which is to say antisocial, behaviour from the person we are dealing with, it is important that we modify our approach, not simply keep on blindly trusting or cooperating. To continue to cooperate in the face of a counterparty who does not reciprocate is to risk being naïve, and lays us open to exploitation. Cacioppo and Patrick elaborate on this point, on p197 of *Loneliness*: "for many reasons...the most adaptive strategy is to maintain both the ability to detect cheating or betrayal and the ability to carefully modulate one's response...the distinctive human adaptation is to be socially cooperative in a way that allows us to optimise the advantages of the group while retaining our own individuality".

- *Focus energy disproportionately on people who can themselves be trusted to cooperate.* Recall that Axelrod shows that a cooperative approach can succeed even in a world where as few as 5% of the total population are themselves consistently cooperating, so long as those of a cooperative bent interact mainly, but not necessarily exclusively, with one another.

- *Don't bear grudges.* One of Axelrod's most important insights is that the strategies which flourish in his game world are those which most effectively encourage cooperative behaviour in others. In the real world this may involve all kinds of difficult judgements. But the central message holds that if someone who has previously behaved selfishly shows a genuine willingness to modify their behaviour and cooperate instead, it is in our interests as well as theirs to encourage this, not rebuff it.

PART D: "Only connect" – love and affection

"All you need is love," The Beatles famously sang. As an existential insight, it's quite profound. Love is arguably the strongest, most intense emotion we are capable of feeling, with friendship and fellowship not far behind.

These things are so critical that if we regularly experience them then we are likely to feel that our life is worthwhile, and that we are in some important sense fulfilled. Conversely, if we don't get enough of them to meet our own personal threshold needs then we are likely to be miserable, or at least to feel that something important is missing from our life. In short, a capacity, and need, for love and affection is a large part of what it means to be human; to the extent that in the rare cases in which an individual's capacity for these things is distorted or severely reduced we are likely to diagnose them as suffering from some serious mental, or emotional, disorder, and may even regard them as being "inhuman".

It is easy to see how emotions such as love and affection might have evolved. These feelings predispose us to behave in cooperative ways, at least towards those for whom we feel them, and for at least part of the time (as we saw earlier it is certainly not the case that a propensity for adversarial behaviour has been eliminated from the human genome, or from our own personal makeup as individuals). This predisposition to cooperate in turn helps us to develop a virtuous circle of mutual cooperation, at a minimum with a core group of family and friends. We saw from Axelrod in the previous section that it is possible for cooperation to sustain within a relatively small group even if the broader environment is dominated by individuals more inclined to behave selfishly, so long as whatever transactions undertaken are disproportionately focused among other members of the cooperative group.

We also saw that, where cooperation sustains over time, it is likely to prove more successful than a purely adversarial approach – "nice guys finish first", as long as they are not naive. Hence, we may infer that those of our ancestors' generations who experienced the gradual stirrings of love and affection were more disposed to cooperate with one another than those who did not, and that this in turn helped the "loving" cooperators to out-compete their peers, ultimately ensuring that the genes which code for these emotions passed down into the modern gene pool at the expense of genes which do not.

The same logic holds for negative emotions such as loneliness and feelings of social alienation. These can be seen as prompts for us to change our behaviour to become more actively pro-social, in much the same way as feelings of physical pain prompt us to moderate a behaviour which is causing them. Those ancestors who experienced incipient feelings of loneliness were also paradoxically prompted to behave in more pro-social ways in order to mitigate them, and by doing this were able to out-compete their contemporaries who did not experience such feelings, passing down to subsequent generations the genes which code for them.

This brings us to arguably the most important advice in this book, courtesy of the English novelist E.M. Forster and the epigraph to his 1910 novel *Howards End* in which he exhorts us to: "only connect...".

Personal connection is vital not only because it is likely to help us engage effectively with other members of whichever social group or groups we happen to be part, but also because it is likely to be crucial to achieving personal happiness, as we will explore in Chapter 5.

Perhaps the closest Forster himself came to defining what he meant exactly was in his essay *What I Believe*, written in 1938 as the storm clouds gathered over Europe, and reproduced in a collection of essays called *Two Cheers for Democracy*, published in 1951. On p87 Forster describes what he calls an "aristocracy": "not an aristocracy of power, based upon rank and influence, but an aristocracy of the sensitive, the considerate and the plucky. Its members are to be found in all nations and classes, and all through the ages, and there is a secret understanding between them when they meet. They represent the true human tradition, the one permanent victory of our queer race over cruelty and chaos...they are sensitive for others as well as for themselves, they are considerate without being fussy, their pluck is not swankiness but the power to endure, and they can take a joke".

Of course, many different kinds of "connection" are possible. No canonical categorisation exists, but for our purposes it may be helpful to distinguish four kinds. First and most obvious is romantic love, closely linked with our evolutionary need to pair-bond. Second is parental and sibling love, typically linked to shared genes. Third is friendship, what Stephanie Cacioppo calls "companionate love", on p64 of *Wired for Love*. Finally, there is what we might call "fellowship" – a sense of belonging to a particular social group, even though one might not have a personal relationship with many, or in an extreme case even any, of its individual members. This in turn links to the concept of "In-groups", a topic we will explore more fully in the next chapter.

The definition of what constitutes fellowship may be deep, but can also be quite arbitrary and shallow. For example, on p164 of her 2020 book *Friendship*, American science journalist Lydia Denworth references: "...a raft of laboratory experiments showing how quickly and easily people formed in-group bonds, even where the group they were 'in' had been made up by researchers on trivial grounds (think red shirts versus green shirts)". The point is that in all these situations, the feeling of affection that we experience is likely not only to make us feel good in the moment, but more importantly (at least in an evolutionary context) to prompt us to behave more cooperatively towards those individuals, or categories of individual, for whom we feel it.

In any case, the specific type and level of social connection we need remains highly personal. It is a universal truth that meeting our companionship needs is likely to make us happy; and failing to meet them to make us unhappy. But what these needs are exactly is particular to us, reflecting our unique combination of genes and experiences as we might expect. As Cacioppo and Patrick put it, on p23 of *Loneliness*: "those who are highly vulnerable to sensing disconnection can be socially satisfied, and those lower in the need for connection can be lonely. The problems arise simply when there is a mismatch between the level of social connection desired and the level the environment provides".

Finally, "only connect..." is highly relevant to our exercise of personal existential choice in our life – where, and on whom, to focus our time and emotional energy, and how to show up behaviourally when we do.

It is important that we sense some element of reciprocal connection. As we saw, a relationship in which we bias towards Axelrodian cooperation and our counterparty consistently does not is unlikely to be either fulfilling or sustainable and may lead to us being exploited.

It is surely helpful to embrace the possibility of connection when we meet new people, projecting openness and reciprocating whatever overtures that they might make to us, assuming some spark on both sides.

Last but not least, we do well to invest discretionary energy in nurturing and reinforcing existing relationships in which we sense some element of connection, so that these remain active and flourish; rather than taking such relationships for granted by sitting passively by or assuming that the other party will make all the running.

Sociability feels good and is good

On pp18-9 of *Loneliness* Cacioppo and Patrick highlight the benefits of what they term "social satisfaction": "one of our most intriguing findings about feeling socially satisfied is that this disposition, free of social pain and the distorted social cognitions such a pain can cause, also places the individual on a very even – and very healthful – keel. When we feel connected we are generally less agitated and less stressed than when we feel lonely. In general, feeling connected also lowers feelings of hostility and depression. All of which can have profoundly positive influences on our health".

The authors summarise, on p201: "a great deal of what it means to be human, perhaps a great deal more than philosophy, religion, or even science realised until very recently, is to be social".

This is reinforced by the results of a remarkable Harvard University study called The Study of Adult Development, referenced by Lydia Denworth in *Friendship*. The project was started in 1937 by a physician called Arlie Bock, had run for no less than 75 years by the time of Denworth's book, which as a reminder was published in 2020, and continues to this day. It looks in detail at the lives of 724 men across virtually their entire lifetimes, with a view to identifying the characteristics of what made these people happy, from a wide range of variables.

The original scope did not anticipate looking at health outcomes specifically, but these were added during the course of the work. Denworth summarises, starting on p327: "Bock's original grand intention was to focus not on ill health but on what it took to live well. And decades later, the answer was quite clear. In 2008 longtime study director George Vaillant was asked, "What have you learned?" His response was emphatic: *'that the only thing that really matters in life are your relationships to other people'*" (the emphasis is mine).

Denworth also quotes the current (at the time of her book) study director, Robert Waldinger, on the lessons from 75 years of research: "first, that social connections are really good for us, and that loneliness kills...the second lesson is that quality (of relationship) matters as much or more than quantity...conflict is bad for your health, good warm relationships are protective...the third lesson is that good relationships don't just protect our bodies; they also protect our brains".

To complete the full circle of evolutionary logic, there is evidence to suggest that a capacity for friendship may also be related to reproductive success, even in a rigidly hierarchical, dominance-based society such as that of baboons. Denworth references statistical analysis carried out by the behavioural ecologist Joan Silk, using data from the Amboseli Baboon Research Project, which has also been running continuously since it was set up in 1971 by the primatologist couple Jeanne and Stuart Altmann. Denworth observes that "although it's professionally frowned upon to liken animals to humans, the dirty secret of primatology is that nearly everyone does".

And so to the summary of Silk's findings, in an extract beginning on p177 of *Friendship*: "by then the Amboseli Project had complete life histories for more than one hundred females... choosing the outcome for the analysis was easy. Since reproductive success is the critical evolutionary measure, they would count each female's surviving infants and measure that against what they called a sociability index. It was an assessment Alberts had designed that combined and weighted all social behaviours. 'That gave us a number, which reflects the strength of social bonds', says Silk. 'It's basically how often females interacted nicely'. After months of organising the data, Silk came to the moment of truth, when she had to calculate the final result...she had been quite prepared to see nothing much. Where evolutionary processes are concerned, picking up an effect – a measurable signal in the data – is exceedingly rare. But the signal was loud and clear. Having more and better 'friends' was significantly related to reproductive success. Furthermore, *strong social bonds mattered more than rank* (again, my emphasis), which everyone had assumed was the most influential variable in the hierarchical world of monkeys". The study was later repeated at another monkey study site called Moremi, with the same results.

Stephanie Cacioppo reinforces that strong social connections are good for our brain, in humans and in many other species, on p21 of *Wired for Love*: "neuroimaging studies...show that the size of core regions of the brain like the amygdala and the frontal and temporal lobes correlates with the size of our individual social networks. Similar findings reinforcing the value of social connections appear in studies of social species across the animal kingdom. If you raise a fish alone in an aquarium, its brain cells will be less complex than those of the same species of fish raised in a group. A desert locust's brain, when it's part of a swarm, grows by an impressive 30%, presumably to accommodate the additional information-processing demands of a more complicated social environment. Chimpanzees learn how to use new tools much faster when they are in groups than in isolation".

The point is that, as the header of this section asserts, meeting our personal social needs not only feels good but is good for us, in a multitude of ways.

Romantic love

A central theme of poets since time immemorial is that romantic love is the most intense form of emotional attachment it is possible for a human to feel, making it the strongest form of "connection". Of course there is a corresponding potential for heartbreak if we once discover that our feelings are not reciprocated, or not to the extent that we might wish. Whatever, it is easy to see how romantic love reinforces pair-bonding, a behaviour that we saw earlier probably emerged in our ancestors around 6 or 7 million years ago and represents an important milestone in the evolution of our species.

Neuroscience confirms that whilst romantic love is similar in many ways to other forms of emotional attachment, it is indeed more intense. For example, Stephanie Cacioppo describes the results of a "meta-analysis" of fMRI studies conducted on love, with the goal being "to make a kind of map of love in the brain", also on p21 of *Wired for Love*: "my co authors and I spent weeks in front of the computer, digging into the weeds of the methodology of earlier studies. When we finished crunching the numbers, we found that love seemed to activate twelve specific brain regions...we then compared the brain map of romantic love to that of companionate love (the kind we feel for friends) and the only other type of love that had been studied extensively by neuroscientists, maternal love. All twelve regions in the 'love network' were activated by the three different types of love, but the intensity and pattern of activation were different...romantic love triggered both the brain's pleasure centres and the cortical regions that manage our sense of self, like the angular gyrus, much more intensely than friendship".

On p114 Cacioppo explains how romantic love can alter and extend our very conception of our "self": "you'll notice that couples in love often refer to the other person as their soulmate or 'better half'. They talk about themselves using the pronoun 'we' instead of 'I'. They stand very close together, often linking their arms and hands automatically, as if becoming a single unit were the most natural thing in the world. For couples deeply and passionately in love, the usual, transactional give-and-take that characterises other social relationships doesn't apply. They experience their partner's victories as their own; they *feel* their partner's pain in defeat or loss. They think nothing of giving up something valuable, or enduring some discomfort, if there is a net benefit to the relationship, even if it accrues only to their partner...this is more than empathy. This is the result of what psychologists term *self-expansion*. A theory developed by the husband-and-wife social psychologist team Arthur and Elaine Aron, self-expansion assumes two interlocking truths about human nature: (1) people have an innate drive to broaden themselves – by following their curiosity, honing their abilities, or exploiting new opportunities, and (2) the primary way they do this is through close relationships, particularly romantic relationships, in which the idea of the self ('me') expands to *include* the other person ('we'). Self-expansion gives you the ability to experience someone else's identity as your own" (Cacioppo's emphasis throughout).

Cacioppo goes on to describe how romantic love is linked with important health benefits, on p127: "a growing body of research from social neuroscience and other fields shows that love literally makes us stronger – not just emotionally and cognitively, as we've already discovered, but also physically. Let me count the ways. Compared to single people, those in satisfying, healthy long-term romantic relationships sleep better. They have a better immune function. They exhibit fewer addictive behaviours. They suffer fewer recurrent strokes. They even have a better survival rate for some diseases (including some cancers)".

Desire is important, of course. Stephanie Cacioppo comments, on p90 of *Wired for Love*: "in scientific paper after scientific paper, we were discovering that love and desire were activating complementary parts of the same brain regions, reinforcing the idea that they are not necessarily opposing forces but have the potential to grow out of the other".

However, neuroscience also suggests that the brain chemistry which underpins romantic love changes over time, in ways which largely correspond to the time periods needed to conceive and then nurture a child. The specifics are explained in an article by Melissa Hogenboom on the BBC website titled *The sinister reason why people fall in love*, dated 15 February 2016.

Hogenboom describes how romantic love typically starts with sexual desire, triggering the release of feel-good chemicals in the brain. As initial "lust" gives way to something closer to what we might define as "love", the brain's limbic system pumps out the chemical dopamine and the hormone oxytocin, which has the specific effect of binding people together emotionally. At the same time, parts of the prefrontal cortex involved in rational decision-making are deactivated, and levels of serotonin, which makes us feel calm, are suppressed. As Hogenboom puts it, at this stage people are literally "crazy in love". After a few months – enough time to conceive a child, at least from a purely biological standpoint – serotonin and dopamine levels normalise and the emotions move towards something closer to "companionship", not unlike the bond between a parent and their child, or indeed the "companionate love" referenced earlier by Stephanie Cacioppo. Oxytocin levels remain elevated, however, reinforcing the closeness of this emotional bond, and reinforcing the conclusion that romantic love is similar to but often more intense than other forms of emotional attachment such as family bonds and friendships.

As an aside, Hogenboom also cites evidence that if oxytocin levels are artificially suppressed in other pair-bonding species (she mentions the prairie vole) then the animals stop being monogamous, a topic we will explore further shortly. In any case, it seems that in many pair-bonding species there is a distinction between "sexual monogamy", where as the name implies pair-bonded couples only have sex with each other; and "social monogamy", in which couples stay together to rear their offspring but remain open to sexual encounters with third parties. Defined in this way, the majority of pair-bonded species are observed to be socially rather than sexually monogamous. Many non-human species also pair-bond specifically for the time it takes to bring up offspring to be independent, not necessarily for life.

The British "relationship expert" Tracey Cox comments on how our brain chemistry changes as a romantic relationship matures, in an article titled *How NOT to rescue your sex life!* published by the *Mail Online* on 3 August 2022, which as the title implies focuses on the implications for a couple's sex life: "'spontaneous desire' - the sort we all think of as desire – happens at the start of relationships and is biologically based. It's driven by hormones that release for a purpose (to get us to procreate) then fade away. If you're a couple who've been together 10 years, spontaneous desire – feeling a random and uncontrollable desire to rip each other's clothes off and have sex – happens about once a year. If you're lucky. Most couples realise sex changes with time and is fuelled by more than 'sparks' but few truly embrace the 'responsive desire' model which functions in most long-term relationships. Responsive desire means rather than feel like sex and then seek it out, you feel like sex after sexual stimulation has already started. Desire shows up after arousal".

In summary, romantic love is the most intense form of personal connection we are capable of feeling. Physical desire is likely to be an important part of the equation, especially in the early stages of a relationship; but the role this plays changes and typically reduces as the relationship matures, reflected in changes to our brain chemistry and in ways which need not at all imply any weakening of the underlying emotional bond.

Sex and the capacity to entertain

Whatever its evolution over the course of a relationship, it is hardly an insight to observe that sex is fundamental to the human experience. Famously, for Sigmund Freud sex explains almost everything there is to know about human behaviour, and whilst few modern psychologists would take such an extreme view, few would also disagree that sex plays an important role in our psyche.

Beyond its obvious importance for procreation, what does sex have to tell us about our evolution as fundamentally social animals? Earlier we met Matt Ridley and his book *The Red Queen: Sex and the Evolution of Human Nature*. Ridley's provocative, and entertaining, thesis is that sexual attraction plays a fundamental role in explaining how and why our brains developed as they did.

The Red Queen starts by reviewing the evolutionary logic for sex to exist at all. After all, many species are asexual, consisting only of "females" who essentially reproduce clones of themselves. Other species are hermaphrodite, meaning the individual organism can assume either a female or male role depending on the situation, but is again self-sufficient in matters of reproduction. There are some evolutionary advantages to these modes of reproduction. Most obviously, an asexual species will reproduce at twice the rate of a sexual one, assuming equal rates of fertility.

However, it turns out that there are offsetting evolutionary advantages for species which reproduce sexually, as we discussed in Chapter 1. In particular, they are better equipped to participate in the biological arms race with parasites, a fact which turns out to be highly significant in a world where all successful species act as a magnet for some form of parasite or other. The advantage derives from the fact that sexual reproduction promotes genetic diversity from one generation to the next, allowing a species to stay one step ahead of adaptation by whatever parasites it may face. Conversely, whilst asexual reproduction may be more efficient in the short run it promotes genetic similarity across generations, such that if a more effective parasite evolves, the impact on the host species can be catastrophic.

For most sexually-reproducing species there are imbalances of role, as we also saw in Chapter 1. Females typically make a bigger investment in carrying and rearing offspring and hence are the "choosier" species. This in turn gives rise to the phenomenon of "sexual selection", in which, if it once becomes established, subjective female preference for a particular characteristic, such as a magnificent tail on a male peacock, creates adaptive pressure for males to compete on that basis, irrespective of whatever purely functional benefit may or may not also accrue.

As an aside, a few species have been observed in which males take on a disproportionate role in child-rearing, and are therefore the "choosier" sex. For these species the same dynamic operates in reverse – it is the females who compete for male favour: females tend to be larger than males, and sexual selection tends to be driven by male preference, for example the magnificence of female plumage in the case of a species of migratory wading bird called red phalaropes, found in the Arctic regions of North America and Eurasia.

Whatever, Ridley's central metaphor in *The Red Queen* is the eponymous character from *Alice in Wonderland* who famously runs all day but never gets anywhere because the landscape moves with her. This symbolises the arms race at the heart of human mating, whereby males compete for female favour by developing and displaying whatever characteristics females find most attractive; female preferences themselves adapt further over time as more males become more proficient; this stimulates males to develop yet further; and so on until some form of equilibrium is reached.

Ridley makes the intriguing suggestion that at some point in human evolution females developed a preference for males to impress not with the splendour of their plumage but rather with their capacity to entertain – in effect, their wit. As this became established, it created increasing pressure for males to develop relevant cognitive skills, and for females to develop a corresponding cognitive ability to recognise and appreciate their efforts when they did. Ridley proposes that this hypothesis explains some features of human cognition which are hard to account for on a purely functional basis, for example, music, humour, and general repartee. He summarises with another quote from Geoffrey Miller, on p327 of *The Red Queen*: "I suggest that the neocortex is not primarily or exclusively a device for tool-making, bipedal walking, fire-using, warfare, hunting, gathering, or avoiding savanna predators. None of these postulated functions alone can explain its explosive development in our lineage and not in other closely related species...the neocortex is largely a courtship device to attract and retain sexual mates: its specific evolutionary function is to stimulate and entertain other people, and to assess the stimulation attempts of others".

We saw earlier that Tomasello suggests the evolution of human cognition was fuelled primarily by lifestyle changes to joint and then collective foraging. These hypotheses need not necessarily be mutually exclusive. It is plausible that as the human brain developed it enabled, and was in turn stimulated by, more than one adaptive function; and "entertainment as courtship" certainly adds an engaging twist.

Extramarital sex

We just saw that many non-human species who pair-bond engage in "social" rather than "sexual" monogamy, meaning that both males and females are open to some level of extra-marital sex, at least in some circumstances. (For the purposes of this discussion we'll assume that marriage and pair-bonding are synonymous). We also saw that, whilst pair-bonding became the norm in humans as long ago as 6 to 7 million years, the research nonetheless predicts that the evolutionarily stable strategy retains an incentive for some residual level of "cheating" on the part of both males and females: males in order to father more offspring than is likely in a pair-bond alone, and females to have the possibility of accessing "better" genes.

This prompts the question: to what extent does observed human behaviour align with this prediction?

It is not an easy question to answer, for the obvious reason that people tend to be coy about their sex lives in general, and we might expect this to be particularly the case when admitting to a behaviour which would typically be frowned on publicly, at least in the majority of modern societies. Yet much of the data which is available is necessarily based on survey techniques of one kind or another, with the accompanying risk that respondents may be misrepresenting the reality.

Jared Diamond asserts that whilst "marriage", that is pair-bonding, is common to all known human societies and can therefore be taken as a human behaviourial norm, so is at least some level of extramarital sex. On pp53-4 of *The Third Chimpanzee*, he tells us: "pursuit of extramarital sex is obviously greatly influenced by each individual's particular upbringing and by the norms of the society in which the individual lives. Despite all that cultural influence, we are left with having to explain the fact that *both* the institution of marriage *and* (Diamond's emphasis in both cases) the occurrence of extramarital sex have been reported from all human societies; but that extramarital sex is unknown in gibbons, although they do practice 'marriage' (that is, lasting male/female pairing to rear offspring); and that the question of extramarital sex is meaningless for chimpanzees because they do not practice 'marriage'".

On p71 of *The Third Chimpanzee* Diamond observes that: "any social system with rules of conduct is open to the risk of individuals cheating when they find the advantages of cheating to outweigh the burden of sanctions". There are of course echoes here of freeloading and our Axelrodian choices between "cooperation" and "defection", or in this case "fidelity" and "cheating".

And on pp72-3 Diamond provides an empirical answer, largely based on the results of a remarkable US medical study which did not rely on survey techniques but rather produced hard facts, albeit as what Diamond describes as "a totally unexpected by-product". The study was conducted in the late 1940s by a doctor whom Diamond calls "Dr X" because the individual preferred to remain anonymous even half a century later, presumably because of what he regarded as the controversial nature of the subject-matter.

Diamond takes up the story: "Doctor X was studying the genetics of human blood groups, which are molecules that we acquire only by inheritance...the study's research plan was straightforward: go to the obstetrics ward of a highly respectable US hospital; collect blood samples from 1000 newborn babies and their mothers and fathers; identify the blood groups in all the samples; and then use standard genetic reasoning to deduce the inheritance patterns. To Dr X's shock, the blood groups revealed nearly ten per cent of those babies to be the fruits of adultery! Proof of the babies' illegitimate origin was that they had one or more blood groups lacking in both alleged parents. There could be no question of mistaken maternity – the blood samples were drawn from an infant and its mother soon after the infant emerged from the mother. A blood group present in a baby but absent in its undoubted mother could only have come from its father. Absence of the blood group from the mother's husband as well showed conclusively that the baby had been sired by some other man, extramaritally. The true incidence of extramarital sex must have been considerably higher than ten per cent, since many other blood-group substances now used in paternity tests were not yet known in the 1940s, and since most bouts of intercourse do not result in conception".

Diamond continues: "(Dr X's) results have more recently been confirmed by several similar genetic studies whose results did get published. Those studies variously showed between about five and thirty per cent of American and British babies to have been adulterously conceived. Again, the proportion of the tested couples of whom at least one practised adultery must have been higher, for the same two reasons as in Dr X's study".

Diamond concludes, on p73 of *The Third Chimpanzee*: "we can now answer the question...whether extramarital sex is for humans a rare aberration, a frequent exception to a 'normal' pattern of marital sex, or so frequent as to make a sham of marriage. The middle alternative proves to be the correct one. Most fathers really are raising their own children, and human marriage is not a sham. We are not just promiscuous chimpanzees pretending to be otherwise. Yet it is also clear that extramarital sex is an integral, albeit unofficial, part of the human mating system".

Finally, on p83 Diamond touches briefly on the underlying morality. The topic of morality more broadly will be the focus of the next chapter. For now, Diamond makes the important observations that ethics are essentially a human construct, not something inherent in nature; but that our ability to recognise and apply them is nonetheless one of the things which most distinguishes humans from other species: "...we evolved, like other animals, to win the reproduction game. That contest has a single aim, to leave as many descendants as possible. Much of the legacy of that game strategy still with us. But we have also chosen to pursue ethical goals, which can conflict with the goals and methods of the sexual contest. Having that choice among goals represents one of our most radical departures from other animals"

In other words, it is essentially up to us, as individuals and as a society, to decide how we feel both about these statistics and the topic of extramarital sex itself.

Altruism

If "cheating" is one aspect of human sociability which bears investigation, then altruism is surely another. We have repeatedly seen that evolutionary biology predicates a remorselessly competitive state of nature, in which individual organisms within and across species strive to secure the resources they need to survive and reproduce, in competition with all other organisms and species. We have also seen that in many circumstances a strategy of what we might call "enlightened", as distinct from "naïve", cooperation can enable an individual to prosper through participating in "win:win" solutions.

But none of this explains altruistic behaviour in its purest sense: an individual who acts in a way which is not just in others' interests but is directly contrary to their own. An obvious, if dramatic, example would be a passer-by who snatches a toddler from the path of a speeding car at the cost of their own life.

Altruistic behaviour can be seen in many species beyond humans. In many groupish species, for example, an individual who spots a predator will utter a warning; alerting its fellows to the risk, and the predator to it.

And it turns out that there is an adaptive, evolutionary explanation for this kind of behaviour, relating to the genes and gene-combinations which we saw in Chapter 1 are the basic unit of selection. Specifically, altruistic behaviour is clearly highly prosocial, and the benefits to a group of a genetic predisposition towards hyper-sociality can outweigh the costs, even if the result is that some individuals sometimes pay the ultimate price.

Cacioppo and Patrick, again, explain, on pp56-7 of *Loneliness*: "like Darwin, Hamilton (my note: the 20th century British biologist William D Hamilton) could observe that a bird or a prairie dog that gives a warning call to save the group makes itself the one most likely to be carried off by the approaching hawk. One way that such 'other-directed' behaviour makes evolutionary sense is this: the prosocial gene or constellation of genes that drives an animal to sound the alarm, even at the cost of its own life, is shared by many of its closest relatives, including the selfless lookout's nieces or nephews. So even if the lookout dies young in the process, having lots of surviving nieces and nephews improves the rate of propagation of the genes that biased the lookout to do what it did. Over time, a characteristic that even modestly increases the survival and reproductive rate of individuals carrying the particular genes for a particular characteristic can spread until that characteristic becomes 'species typical'. Hamilton's theory for how a gene for helping others, even at the cost of one's own life, could be passed along was first called 'kin selection' and is now called 'inclusive fitness'. It led to a broader concept called 'reciprocal altruism'. Humans extend altruistic acts to people who are not their blood relatives. Such behaviour is species typical because altruism reinforces social connection, and social connection, along with the genetic dread of loneliness that is its flipside, helped our ancestors survive".

Still, however beneficial it may be for the species, altruism clearly has its limits from the perspective of an individual. In his 2013 book *Give and Take*, American psychologist Adam Grant expands on this point, classifying people into what he calls "Givers", "Takers" and "Matchers". As the names imply, "Givers" are people who put a high emphasis on the needs of others rather than their own, in other words have a higher propensity to behave altruistically; "Takers" are the exact opposite; and "Matchers" pursue a strategy of strict reciprocity, a sort of "you scratch my back and I'll scratch yours" approach which has echoes of the Tit for Tat strategy in Axelrod's Prisoner's Dilemma.

Grant spends the bulk of the book demonstrating that, all other things being equal, individual "Givers" are likely to be both happier and more successful than people in either of the other two categories. Still, it is possible to take things too far and Grant counsels against what he calls "selfless giving", equating this with "pathological altruism", which is in turn reminiscent of the "naïve cooperation" strategies which Axelrod found are typically so ineffective. Specifically, on pp324-5 of the Kindle edition of *Give and Take* Grant explains: "there are two types of givers, and they have dramatically different success rates. Selfless givers are people with high other-interest and low self-interest. They give their time and energy without regard for their own needs, and they pay a price for it. Selfless giving is a form of pathological altruism, which is defined by researcher Barbara Oakley as 'an unhealthy focus on others to the detriment of one's own needs', such that in the process of trying to help others, givers end up harming themselves...most people assume that self-interest and other-interest are opposite ends of one continuum. Yet in my studies of what drives people at work, I've consistently found that self-interest and other-interest are completely independent motivations: you can have both of them at the same time...if takers are selfish and failed givers are selfless, successful givers are *otherish* (Grant's emphasis): they care about benefiting others, but they also have ambitious goals for advancing their own interests. Selfless giving, in the absence of self-preservation instincts, easily becomes overwhelming. Being otherish means being willing to give more than you receive, but still keeping your own interests in sight, using them as a guide for choosing when, where, how, and to whom you give".

The point is that altruism and selflessness are qualities which are likely to benefit the group and also have the potential to benefit the individuals who practice them; so long as they are not exaggerated to the point where they become "pathological", or in Axelrod's language "naïve".

Loneliness and solitude

If love and affection are central to a fulfilling existence, loneliness is the spectre at the feast. To experience loneliness is to experience at least some level of misery, and possibly despair.

The starting point is that the normal human state is a condition of being "not lonely". Loneliness is of course the central theme of John Cacioppo and William Patrick's book of that name, and on pp7-8, the authors assert that feeling "not lonely" is indeed so typical that we have no word to describe it: "in English, we have a word for pain and a word for thirst, but no single, specific terms that mean the opposite. We merely reference the absence of these aversive conditions, which makes sense, because their absence is considered part of the normal state. Our research suggests that 'not lonely' – there is no better, more specific term for it – is also, like 'not thirsty' or 'not in pain,' very much part of the normal state. Health and well-being for a member of our species requires, among other things, being satisfied and secure in our bonds with other people, a condition of 'not being lonely' that, for want of a better word, we call social connection".

Experiencing loneliness is neurologically similar to experiencing physical pain, as the authors explain on p8: "...this idea of loneliness as social pain is more than a metaphor. Functional magnetic resonance imaging (fMRI) shows us that the emotional region of the brain that is activated when we experience rejection is, in fact, the same region – the dorsal anterior cingulate – that registers emotional responses to physical pain".

It is important not to confuse loneliness with solitude, that is simply being alone. The authors point out, on p13: "being alone does not necessarily mean being lonely. In his book *Solitude*, the psychiatrist Anthony Storr explains – in fact recommends – the pleasures of sometimes being by yourself. Think of a naturalist doing research in the rainforest, or a pianist in a marathon practice session, or a bicyclist training in the mountains".

James Marriott makes a similar point, in an article titled *Sociability is vital but true solitude is precious*, published in *The Times* on 21 January 2025. Empathising with what he calls: "sensible scepticism of the inanities of small talk", Marriott opines that: "many compulsively sociable characters must go out every evening because they cannot stand their own company; they hope to lose, not find, themselves in other people. The ersatz sociability of social media serves a similar function". He acknowledges that: "loneliness is a scourge", but goes on to assert that: "solitude – voluntary, genuine, well-used solitude – is one of life's high pleasures", partly because: "it is only when we are really alone, that we see ourselves".

Loneliness emerges, then, as a psychological state: a product of the meaning we attach to a particular set of social circumstances. This is why it is possible to feel lonely even when surrounded by a crowd.

And there is no question that experiencing loneliness can have devastating consequences for those unfortunate enough to suffer it. They are likely to feel miserable, of course, but also potentially to suffer from worse health and even lower life expectancy. Stephanie Cacioppo explains, on p131 of *Wired for Love*: "in social species ranging from fruit flies to human beings, social isolation decreases life expectancy. Scientists used to believe that it was the risky and harmful health behaviours that loners engaged in that accounted for their poorer health outcomes. But evidence is building that loneliness *itself* (Cacioppo's emphasis) – and not the things lonely people do – has damaging effects on our health through the way it changes our brain chemistry and sets off a cascade of biological booby-traps...a meta-analysis of seventy studies involving more than three million participants who were followed for an average of seven years showed that being lonely increased the odds of an early death by 25 to 30 percent - roughly the same level as obesity".

The psychology of loneliness is such that, once established, in can trap the person experiencing it in a kind of doom loop, distorting their perceptions of the world in ways which reinforce a fundamentally negative outlook and hence risk becoming self-fulfilling. Cacioppo and Patrick comment, on pp15-6 of *Loneliness*: "whatever our own individual sensitivity, our well-being suffers when our particular need for connection has not been met. Because early humans were more likely to survive when they stuck together, evolution reinforced the preference for strong human bonds by selecting genes that support pleasure in company and produce feelings of unease when involuntarily alone. Moreover...evolution fashioned us not only to feel good when connected, but to feel secure. The vitally important corollary is that evolution shaped us not only to feel bad in isolation, but to feel insecure, as in physically threatened...once these feelings arise, social cognition can take the sense of danger and run with it. The person who starts out with a painful, even frightening sensation of being alone may begin to see dangers everywhere on the social landscape. Filtered through the lens of lonely social cognition, other people may appear more critical, competitive, denigrating, or otherwise unwelcoming. These kinds of interpretations quickly become expectations, as loneliness turns the perfectly normal fear of negative evaluation into a readiness to fend off blows. And then the plot thickens. The fear that can force us into a defensive crouch can also cost us some of our ability to self-regulate. When loneliness is protracted, impaired regulation, combined with distorted social cognition, makes us less likely to acknowledge someone else's perspective. We may become less able to evaluate other people's intentions, which can make us socially awkward, but can also make us vulnerable to manipulation by anyone trying to conceal ulterior motives. At the same time, fear of attack fosters a greater tendency to pre-emptively blame others. Sometimes this fear makes us lash out. Sometimes it makes us desperate to please, and sometimes it causes us to play the victim...the sad irony is that these poorly regulated behaviours, prompted by fearful sensations, often elicit the very rejection that we all dread the most. Even more confounding, over time, the feeling of vulnerability that comes with loneliness can make us more likely to be dissatisfied with, and distrustful of, whatever social connections we have".

Around a third of adults in the world say they feel lonely at least some of the time, as reported in an article by researcher Simona Varella titled *Feeling of loneliness among adults 2021, by country,* dated 4 November 2021 and published on *statista.com*: "according to a global survey, about 33 percent of adults experienced feelings of loneliness worldwide. Brazil had the highest percentage of people experiencing this, with 50 percent of respondents declaring that they felt lonely either often, always, or sometimes. Turkey, India, and Saudi Arabia followed, with 43 percent to 46 percent of respondents having experienced loneliness at least sometimes. On the contrary, the Netherlands, Japan, Germany, and Russia registered the largest share of interviewees which did not feel lonely".

And there is evidence to suggest that, perhaps surprisingly, younger adults are more likely than older people to experience loneliness. In an article titled *Is there a loneliness epidemic?*, published online by *Our World in Data* on 11 December 2019, researcher Esteban Ortiz-Ospina cites data from a UK study showing that: "those aged 16 to 24 are the group most likely to report feeling lonely, with 10% feeling lonely 'often or always'. In contrast, those aged 65 years and older are the group least likely to report feeling lonely, with 3% feeling lonely 'often or always'".

In fact, the incidence of loneliness seems to decrease steadily as people get older, until about the age of 75 after which it starts to increase again, albeit for reasons which tend to be specific to individuals, such as the loss of a partner, rather than being an otherwise inevitable consequence of ageing. Later in the same *Our World in Data* article Ortiz-Ospina reviews the results of a study by the American research scientist Louise Hawkley published in the journal *Psychology and Aging*: "they found that after age 50 – which is the earliest age of participants in the study – loneliness tended to decrease, until about 75, after which it began to increase again. The authors explain in the paper that the increase in loneliness after 75 was explained by a decline in health and the loss of a spouse or partner. When adjusting for these factors, they found that loneliness continued declining into 'oldest old age'".

Ortiz-Ospina explains the forces behind this: "...there are two forces at play. On the one hand, there seems to be a direct relationship between age and loneliness, whereby loneliness *decreases* (author's emphasis) with age as our social expectations adapt, and we become more selective about relating with contacts who bring positive emotions. On the other hand, there seems to be an indirect association pushing in the opposite direction, whereby loneliness *increases* (again, author's emphasis) with age, because our health deteriorates and we lose relatives and friends. In our middle age the direct effect dominates, but once we enter advanced old age, the negative indirect effect starts dominating".

Finally, levels of loneliness appear to be broadly stable over time, contrary to some narratives and at least in the US from which the research is drawn. Ortiz-Ospina comments, in the same *World in Data* article: "in the 'loneliness epidemic' narrative, it is often implied that if we compare two individuals of the same age – one today and another one a generation ago – we would find that the one today is more likely to feel lonely. This is based on the idea that there have been societal changes – such as the rise of living alone – that make newer generations more likely to feel lonely. In their study, Louise Hawkley and co-authors searched for evidence of these 'cohort trends' in the US, but didn't find any. There was very little difference in self-reported loneliness of people born in different generations. Those that were born in 1920-1947 experienced the same changes of loneliness throughout their lives as those born in 1948-1965. It's not the case that loneliness is increasing across generations". Admittedly, the results of this study pre-date the full impact of the exponential rise of social media, with consequences which are yet to be fully understood but may paradoxically include a greater sense of isolation, at least for some users.

The potential to experience loneliness is the price we pay for our inherently social human nature. Although only a minority of people report experiencing it and the probability of feeling lonely reduces as we get older, it is a large minority and the effects can be severe.

Ultimately, the implication for each of us as individuals is the same as the conclusion from our discussion of love, friendship and fellowship: to prioritise personal and social relationships; make active, sustained efforts to "connect"; and invest discretionary energy accordingly.

Relationships and subjective interpretation

Relationships are of course subject to the same foibles that we have seen characterise our consciousness overall.

In particular, a large part of the action happens inside our own mind and is ultimately subjective; defined largely by whatever meaning we ascribe to the signals we pick up from other people, as well as the way in which they interpret the signals we send out ourself. As Cacioppo and Patrick state at the beginning of *Loneliness*, on Pix of the Acknowledgments: "we quickly surmised that it was an individual's *perceptions* (my emphasis) of the social situation that mattered most".

Cacioppo and Patrick elaborate, on p77: "the role of subjective meaning in our sense of social connection is not all that different from the role of individualised, personal meaning in other aspects of our lives...you can have all the 'right' friends in terms of social prestige, in-group cachet, or business connections, or a spouse who is rich, brilliant, and fabulous looking, but if there is no deep, emotional resonance – specifically for you – then none of these relationships will satisfy the hunger for connection or ease the pain of feeling isolated".

The reverse is also true. It is self-evidently possible to connect meaningfully with someone who may not have high social prestige or be rich or famous. What ultimately matters is the way we subjectively experience them.

And this is in turn a product of the way our brain interprets a particular individual or situation, and therefore subject to the same kind of pitfalls that we saw in the previous chapter complicate our perception of reality in general, as Cacioppo and Patrick explain on pp176-7. "human beings are inherently meaning-making creatures, and the lonely are hardly unique in interpreting social cues through a highly subjective lens. The human brain must take disparate, atomistic snips of sensory input and weave them all into a 'theory of the case,' an interpretation of time and space, cause and effect, that allows us to survive today, plan for tomorrow, and make sense of the past. Ideally, the narrative we construct aligns with objective reality well enough for us to appropriately address the problems confronting us in the real world. However, there is no guarantee. Reflexively, the hypersocial human brain registers three dots in a triangular pattern as representing a human face, but sometimes a pattern of three dots is merely three dots".

Expectations matter, of course. The key is not necessarily to lower these but rather to seek to ensure that they are realistic, as Stephanie Cacioppo suggests on pp98-9 of *Wired for Love*: "so much of our social experience, especially when it comes to romance, has to do with expectations...applying this expectation formula to love relationships, the more we love without expecting any rewards in return, the more we will increase our chance of happiness. This is in line with a large body of research showing that setting realistic expectations leads to greater relationship satisfaction...adjusting your expectations does not necessarily mean lowering them. It's more about letting go of the social pressure that often drives us to pursue unrealistic expectations without understanding what it is we really want or need, and what we can do without".

The expectations we have for a relationship may also play an important role in shaping it, rather as we saw in Chapter 2 that the expectations of teachers who were told that a group of randomly-chosen children had high potential caused them unconsciously to adjust their own behaviour such that the prophesy became self-fulfilling.

For example, on p9 of *Humankind* Rutger Bregman explains that: "if we *believe* (Bregman's emphasis) most people can't be trusted, that's how we'll treat each other, to everyone's detriment". He continues, at a more general level: "few ideas have as much power to shape the world as our view of other people. Because ultimately, you get what you expect to get". And Andrew Grant highlights, on p60 of the Kindle edition of *Give and Take*, that consistent with the evolutionary bias towards loss aversion which we discussed earlier, we may be programmed systematically to assume the worst of others and so inadvertently risk this becoming similarly self-fulfilling: "the fear of exploitation by takers is so pervasive, writes the Cornell economist Robert Frank, that 'by encouraging us to expect the worst in others it brings out the worst in us: dreading the role of the chump, we are often loath to heed our nobler instincts'".

What to do in the face of all this potential for mental distraction and misinterpretation?

Cacioppo and Patrick advise, on p18 of *Loneliness*, that the solution is to keep our attention focused externally rather than on our own "psychological business", and to curb our tendency to feel threatened, assuming of course that the situation allows : "the secret to gaining access to social connection and social contentment is being less distracted by one's own psychological business – especially the distortions based on feelings of threat. When any of us feels connected, the absence of social pain and the sense of threat allows us to be truly *there* (authors' emphasis): in sync with others. This lack of negative arousal leaves us free to be more genuinely available for and engaged by whatever real connection might develop. If a feeling of connection biases cognition, it is in a positive and generous direction that lifts us up whilst also giving a boost to others. Being socially contented will not necessarily make us the life of the party, but such a generous and optimistic influence often means that others will find us more pleasant and even more interesting".

In short, the chances that we "only connect..." are substantially increased if we are open to the possibility of connection in the first place.

Experiencing love

We've spent this chapter exploring how sociability is the behaviour which most distinguishes humans from other species, and how evolution has equipped us with the emotions of love and affection on the one hand, and loneliness on the other, all of which ultimately serve to reinforce pro-social behaviours. Powerful as they are, like everything else we experience these emotions are filtered through the medium of our consciousness, and are therefore ultimately subjective and fallible.

It seems appropriate to close with a comment on what it is subjectively to experience love. If there is a common theme it is that for those fortunate enough to know and embrace love, it has the power to transcend in a way that few, if any, other experiences do. Conversely, being rejected or otherwise losing love can be the most devastating of life's ordeals.

Love has inspired countless generations of poets and other artists: this is surely a topic for which poetic insight can credibly claim the most powerful voice. But, having thus opened Pandora's box, we will be brief and give the floor to just two of many possible candidate poets.

First, we have the Bard himself, specifically Sonnet 116, published in 1609 as part of a sequence of 154 sonnets which would surely have established Shakespeare as a literary great even if he had never written a single play:

"Let me not to the marriage of true minds
Admit impediments; love is not love
Which alters when it alteration finds,
Or bends with the remover to remove.
O no; it is an ever-fixed mark
That looks on tempests and is never shaken;
It is the star to every wandering bark,
Whose worth's unknown, although his height be taken.
Love's not Time's fool, though rosy lips and cheeks
Within his bending sickle's compass come;
Love alters not with his brief hours and weeks,
But bears it out even to the edge of doom.
If this be error and upon me proved,
I never writ, nor no man ever loved."

And we'll close with the celebrated couplet from *In Memoriam AHH*, by the 19th century British poet Alfred, Lord Tennyson, in memory of his close friend Arthur Henry Hallam who died in 1833, aged 22. The entire work contains 2,916 lines, organised into 133 cantos, and this couplet closes Canto 27 with a resonant summary of what we might call the human condition:

"'Tis better to have loved and lost
Than never to have loved at all".

Chapter summary

We are social beings first and foremost. Our capacity to cooperate in an intentional way, including with people with whom we share no special genetic relationship, is the behaviour which most distinguishes us from other species. Evolution has equipped us with powerful emotions which tend to prompt and reinforce pro-social behaviours - in particular, love and affection, which reward social connection in ways few other things can match; and loneliness, which alerts us to its absence.

The implication is that many of the most important existential choices we make are social in nature – which individuals to associate with, or alternatively to avoid; and when to cooperate or alternatively to compete with specific individuals, in particular situations.

Beyond these headline conclusions are a series of more-or-less concrete "beliefs":

• Humans are fundamentally social animals. The extent and manner of our capacity to cooperate sets us apart from other species, even though at a generic level cooperation is widespread in nature.
• Sociability is important for transmitting culture, enabling humans to share acquired knowledge between different groups and to accumulate it over generations.

Sociability also promotes the sharing of resources, enabling and requiring that humans cooperate to an extent and in ways not seen in other species.

- Our success, as individuals and a species, is closely linked to our ability to develop and sustain strong social connections. Nonetheless, our specific propensity, and need, for connection is unique to us as an individual, a product of our genes and personal experiences.
- For most of our evolutionary existence as a species, humans lived in small bands practicing a hunter-gather lifestyle. The development of agriculture around 10,000 BCE led to economic surpluses and the growth of larger, more complex social units, generally organised according to some form of hierarchy. This in turn fuelled explosive growth in population leading to rapid change in our social environment, particularly in recent centuries.
- We retain considerable capacity for anti-social behaviours, as individuals and as a species. Notably:

- a tendency towards hierarchy and status. Low status can be associated with high levels of stress, albeit this is significantly influenced by the psychology and mindset of the individual experiencing it.

- a capacity for violence, bullying and intimidation, although there are also potentially indications that over the long run levels of physical violence are declining.

- a capacity to influence and persuade, which can also mean to manipulate and deceive.

- As members of a social group, or groups, we are frequently confronted by the need to make existential choices between behaviours which are "cooperative" (in the interests of the group overall, or of specific other group members) versus "selfish" (in our own interest). The individual decisions are often small and may seem inconsequential. But collectively the decisions we make come to define us.
- It is often in our own self-interest to cooperate, as well as in the interests of the group more broadly. However,

this is only true so long as we are confident that our counterparty will reciprocate cooperation. If we consistently cooperate and they do not, there is an obvious risk, over time a probability, that we will be exploited as "naïve".

- Cooperation is likely to be most productive if we act on four core principles:
  - don't be envious: accept that cooperation will benefit others, sometimes as much as or possibly even more than it benefits us.
  - don't be the first to "defect", which is to say to behave selfishly.
  - reciprocate both cooperation and defection. Don't simply "turn the other cheek" if someone else behaves selfishly; at the same time, be proportionate in responding, and be "forgiving" if they demonstrate willingness to change their own behaviour.
  - don't be too clever: don't make it too hard for another party to see what we are doing, and why.
- Even if we find ourself in an environment dominated by selfish behaviour it may be possible to reap the rewards from a cooperative approach if we can find a core group willing to cooperate reliably with us, and then ensure that the majority, although not necessarily all, of our transactions are with members of this group.
- Evolution has shaped some of our most powerful emotions to reinforce sociability, in particular love and affection, encouraging us to behave pro-socially towards individuals for whom we feel these things; and loneliness and social alienation, which encourage us to build social connections, but make us feel miserable if we fail.
- "Only connect": a satisfying level of social connection is critical for our mental health, and also good for our physical health. The clear implication is that we should place a high priority on cultivating and sustaining personal relationships with those with whom we feel a connection.

- Romantic love is the most intense form of connection, reinforcing the core evolutionary pair-bond. Neuroscience shows that broadly similar areas of the brain are activated in a similar way, albeit at a lower level of intensity, by other kinds of emotional connection such as parental love and friendship.
- Sexual attraction is an important part of romantic love, particularly during the early stages. An intriguing hypothesis suggests that our brains may have evolved in the way they have at least partly in response to a female preference to be entertained as part of courtship ritual.
- Evolutionary theory predicts that in some circumstances both males and females have a biological incentive to seek sex outside "marriage", which is to say outside a particular pair-bond. There is clear evidence that a material number of people in modern societies indeed do this, albeit not to the extent that it is the norm.
- Altruism also has an evolutionary explanation: in the right environment the genes for extreme pro-social behaviour can spread even if the particular individual who carries them does not themself survive.
- Loneliness is bad for both our mental and physical health. The good news is that the natural state is one of social fulfilment, and being alone does not necessarily imply feeling lonely. Still, around one-third of adults globally report feeling lonely at least some of the time.
- Our emotions are ultimately triggered by subjective perceptions, and are therefore susceptible to the mind traps which are an integral part of human consciousness. Expectations can also influence outcomes. We do well to strive for expectations which are realistic, and to guard against an innate tendency to assume the worst about others. If and when we feel lonely, we should beware entering a negative spiral of thoughts in which personal feelings of isolation cause us to adopt a systematically negative interpretation of events, and potentially to

behave in ways which deepen our isolation rather than mitigate it.
- Love, including but not limited to romantic love, has the potential to transcend; albeit it can also cause great misery when it is lost or rejected. Still, it is actively to be sought, and in the final analysis: "'tis better to have loved and lost; than never to have loved at all".

In this and the preceding chapters we have focused mainly on an empirical discussion of how our Universe and we ourselves "work": the behaviours we typically exhibit, and the underlying biological and psychological foundations. We now turn to the more subjective topic of morality: whether and under what circumstances our behaviours might be considered appropriate.

Chapter 4:

Morality

"There is nothing either good or bad, but thinking makes it so"

Hamlet, William Shakespeare, 1603

Social creatures that we are, our thoughts and especially our behaviours are heavily influenced by moral instinct, in other words a feeling that some things are fundamentally "right" and others "wrong", in ways that transcend the merely expedient question of the impact something might have on our own immediate personal circumstances. Often, our moral instinct drives our behaviour in ways which are not readily accessible to our conscious mind, as we might by now expect.

Our capacity for moral feeling is innate, hardwired into us by evolution and observable across all human cultures, and even in babies. It is also critical to our identity. As Thomas Jefferson put it, in a letter to his nephew Peter Carr dated August 1787: "the moral sense, or conscience, is as much a part of man as his leg or arm".

Moral instinct is therefore another defining characteristic of what it means to be human, so much so that if we are unfortunate enough to encounter one of the rare individuals who are seriously deficient in this regard we are likely to think of them as lacking in humanity and possibly even as "inhuman". Certainly, we would not consider them to be "neurologically normal", a phrase borrowed from the American psychologist Paul Bloom, from whom we'll hear more later.

The general effect of our moral feelings is to encourage us to behave pro-socially, resolving our Axelrodian choices in favour of "cooperation", especially with respect to other people whom we consider to be members of our own social group. For example, as we saw in Chapter 2 humans everywhere demonstrate a capacity for "empathy", which is to say to put themselves in the emotional shoes of others. We are similarly each programmed with an innate sense of "fairness". Of course, we do not all possess these capacities in the same way or to the same degree. The point is that as humans almost all of us possess them to a greater or lesser extent.

However, there are also a number of important complications which, taken together, mean that sadly we cannot be confident that our moral instincts will always prompt us to behave in ways which our rational self might consider appropriate. These are:

1. *Morality is ultimately relative, not an absolute law of nature.* We all share generalised moral capacities such as empathy, but culture has a big impact on how these are translated into specific moral norms. We may experience these as "absolute" because of the powerful emotions they engender, or because a particular religion claims divine revelation as its infallible source. But in fact they are not.

2. *Moral instinct is instinctive – we feel first, and reason later.* Often, the role our rational brain plays is simply to invent a post-hoc justification for an action which was in reality based on unconscious instinct.

3. *Our instincts do not always prompt us to behave "morally".* Our moral feelings exert a strong influence on our behaviour, but we are also prone to behave in ways which violate whatever norms we may in principle espouse. Specific moral norms may also conflict, for example if we are unfortunate enough to be in a situation

in which violence, or even killing another person, is the only way to protect ourself, or our loved ones, from harm.

4. *Morality is often nuanced and contextual.* Moral choices which may seem intuitively clear are often not when inspected in the cold light of reason.

5. *Morality inherently prompts us to privilege other members of our own social group at the expense of members of other groups.* The American social psychologist Joshua Greene calls this "the tragedy of commonsense morality", the point being that whatever moral norms we may subscribe to we tend to apply mainly, or at least differently, to people whom we perceive to be members of our own "ingroup", as distinct from "outsiders".

6. *Moral norms are not stable, but rather change over time.* The implication being that we need to remain open to the possibility of evolving our own moral thinking as our circumstances, and we ourself, evolve.

The point is that our moral instincts are ultimately subjective, relative and fallible, even as they also exert a powerful influence on our behaviour. It is not that we should somehow seek to avoid their promptings, nor would this even be possible. Rather, we do well yet again to heed Viktor Frankl's advice to "mind the gap" between a moral instinct and our behaviourial response, particularly since in the final analysis only we can decide what we believe to be truly moral in a given situation.

We'll start the chapter with a discussion of what morality is and why it matters. We'll then explore the complications, and close with some thoughts on the practical implications.

PART A: What is moral instinct?

Definition of morality

The *Cambridge English Dictionary* defines morality as: "a set of personal or social standards for good or bad behaviour and character: the quality of being right, honest, or acceptable". The crucial points being, first that the defining characteristic of moral standards is that they are designed to influence behaviour; and second, that the context is inherently social, which is to say that morality specifically defines behaviour which is, and is not, "acceptable" within a particular society or social group.

The Stanford Encyclopedia of Philosophy distinguishes between what it calls "descriptive" and "normative" morality, in the entry on *The Definition of Morality*, first published 17 April 2002 and substantively revised 8 September 2020. The distinction is between morality as it applies to a particular social group, and which might therefore potentially be different from the moral norms observed by other, different, groups; and what we might call a "universal" morality, applicable to the whole of humanity:

"...the term 'morality' can be used either

1. descriptively to refer to certain codes of conduct put forward by a society or a group (such as a religion), or accepted by an individual for her own behaviour, or
2. normatively to refer to a code of conduct that, given specified conditions, would be put forward by all rational people".

The article goes on to highlight that morality is just one of several mechanisms which help regulate behaviour within a social group: "even in small homogenous societies that have no written language, distinctions can sometimes be made between morality, etiquette, law, and religion. And in larger and more complex societies these distinctions are often sharply marked".

We might think of etiquette as a kind of "morality lite", without the emotional intensity – behavioural guidelines with much lower stakes for transgressors.

We might also hope for a reasonable degree of overlap between morality and the law, for example proscribing murder in both cases. But there are obviously practical limits to how much can realistically be legislated, particularly in modern multi-cultural societies comprising many sub-groups each with their own specific moral norms and customs.

As for religion, the world's most popular faiths have undeniably had enormous impact in shaping the moral frameworks to which we are heir. And to reject a religious explanation for the world we live in, as this book does, is not necessarily to reject the whole of religiously-inspired moral thinking, with the important caveat that we might classify many of the norms associated with a particular religion as "descriptive" rather than "normative" in the *Stanford Encyclopedia of Philosophy* parlance, and certainly reject the claim many religions make that they somehow have privileged access to a form of singular, objective, moral "truth".

Morality as sociability

The common thread in all of this is the critical role that morality plays in helping complex social groups to function. Specifically, moral codes tend to help resolve the Axelrodian dilemma of "cooperate" versus "compete" that we explored in the previous chapter in favour of consistently prosocial, "cooperative" behaviours.

The American social psychologist Jonathan Haidt summarises, on p314 of his 2012 book *The Righteous Mind*: "...my approach starts with Durkheim (my note: a

French sociologist active in the 19th and early 20th centuries), who said: 'what is moral is everything that is a source of solidarity, everything that forces man to...regulate his actions by something other than...his own egoism'".

Haidt goes on to offer his own definition of morality, providing as he does a helpful catalogue of the diverse range of elements which help define and reinforce particular moral codes: "moral systems are interlocking sets of values, virtues, norms, practices, identities, institutions, technologies, and evolved psychological mechanisms that work together to suppress or regulate self-interest and make cooperative societies possible".

Joshua Greene reinforces the importance of context when assessing the choice of whether to cooperate or to compete, in his 2013 book *Moral Tribes* (all quotes in this paragraph are from p20).

Greene's starting point is that: "the problem of cooperation is the central problem of social existence". Sometimes it is obvious that cooperation is the only sensible option: "suppose that two people, Art and Bud, are at sea in a rowboat, trying to stay ahead of a violent storm. Neither will survive, unless both row as hard as possible. Here, self-interest and collective interest (in this case, a collective of two) are in perfect harmony".

In other situations cooperation may be out of the question, so that it is equally clear that it is literally every person for him or herself: "in other cases, cooperation is impossible. Suppose, for example, that Art and Bud's boat is now sinking, and that they've only one life vest, which can't be shared".

Of course, things get more complicated when we find ourself somewhere in the middle: "cooperation becomes a challenging but solvable problem when...individual interest and collective interest, are neither perfectly aligned, nor perfectly opposed...the problem of cooperation, then, is the problem of getting collective interest to triumph over individual interest".

Greene goes on to suggest, on p21, that it is this third, complicated, category, which tends to dominate our actual experience of sociality: "most cooperation among humans is of the interesting kind, the kind in which self-interest and collective interest are partially aligned...more generally, it's rare to find a cooperative enterprise in which individuals have no opportunity to favour themselves at the expense of the group. In other words, nearly all cooperative enterprises involve at least some tension between self-interest and collective interest, between Me and Us. And thus, nearly all cooperative enterprises are in danger of eroding".

Greene emphasises that moral instinct tends above all to regulate in favour of cooperation, on pp23-6: "morality is a set of psychological adaptations that allow otherwise selfish individuals to reap the benefits of cooperation...the essence of morality is altruism, unselfishness, a willingness to pay a personal cost to benefit others...morality is nature's solution to the problem of cooperation within groups, enabling individuals with competing interests to live together and prosper". Matt Ridley makes a similar point, on p38 of *The Origins of Virtue*: "all human beings share a fascinating taboo...against selfishness. Selfishness is almost the definition of vice. Murder, theft, rape and fraud are considered crimes of great importance because they are selfish or spiteful acts that are committed for the benefit of the actor and the detriment of the victim. In contrast, virtue is, almost by definition, the greater good of the group. Those virtues (such as thrift and abstinence) that are not directly altruistic in their motivation are few and obscure. The conspicuously virtuous things we all praise – cooperation, altruism, generosity, sympathy, kindness, selflessness – are all unambiguously concerned with the welfare of others. This is not some parochial Western tradition. It is a bias shared by the whole species".

These universal moral instincts are themselves the product of evolution, as Rosenberg describes on p107 of *The Atheist's Guide to Reality*: "the idea that the moral core has huge consequences for survival and reproduction should not be controversial. Any long-standing norm (and the behaviour it mandates) must have been heavily influenced by natural selection. This will be true whether the behaviour or its guiding norm is genetically inherited, like caring for your offspring, or culturally inherited, like marriage rules. That means that the moral codes people endorse today almost certainly must have been selected for in a long course of blind variation and environmental filtration. Because they had an impact on survival and reproduction, our moral norms must have been passed through a selective process that filtered out many competing variations over the course of a history that goes back beyond *Homo erectus* to our mammalian ancestors".

Specifically, we may infer that a kind of virtuous cycle developed whereby as humanity became progressively more "groupish", individuals who demonstrated cooperative behaviour were selected for at the expense of those who did not. These individuals had more surviving offspring, which further populated the gene pool with "groupish" genes, and so on. Moral instinct developed as an adjunct to genes which coded for "groupish" behaviour; and its specific role was and remains to reinforce "groupishness", although not naivete.

As Greene puts it, on p24 of *Moral Tribes*: "we today are morally minded beings only because our morally minded ancestors outcompeted their less morally minded neighbours". Similarly, Joseph Henrich asserts, on p154 of *The Secret of Our Success*: "to the degree that we are more cooperative than other mammalian species (and we are), it's because culturally evolved norms constructed social environments that, over eons, penalised and gradually weeded out aggressive, antisocial types (norm violators), while rewarding the more sociable and docile among us".

Finally, the impact that morality has on behaviour within a social group can be so profound as to have important consequences for the success, or failure, of the group itself. British journalist Matthew Syed gives a contemporary example, in an article titled *The Renaissance informs us Boris did not create economics without ethics*, published in *The Sunday Times* on 13 February 2022: "in the 1950s an American called Edward Banfield had travelled to southern Italy to solve a conundrum that had long vexed economists: why did the area have such low growth compared with the prosperous north? After detailed study he realised that it had nothing to do with investment or capital but something quite different: moral education...in (southern) Italy young people were taught to be suspicious of others and to expect them to act in bad faith. Banfield alluded to stories such as the one in the novel that tells of a father putting his six-year-old son on a high ledge. 'Jump and don't worry: Daddy will catch you,' the father says. When the boy jumps, the father allows him to fall to the ground. 'Remember one thing,' he tells his injured son. 'In this life, never trust anyone.'...in this context mutually beneficial activity is obliterated. People don't want to cooperate with others, fearing they will be swindled. They don't trust judges to act impartially when enforcing contracts. Worst of all, the expectation of being cheated means that people get their retaliation in first, corroding trust still further. The net result is that social networks shrink, the rule of law is weakened and growth collapses

- a pattern seen in southern Italy for centuries...in the north firms and individuals acted according to self-interest but within a different ethical context. A more trusting context. A context where selfishness was constrained by honesty, reliability and doing the right thing even when it might pay to do the wrong. And this expresses a curious phenomenon absent from classical economics: when a critical mass of people act in a trustworthy way, it enlarges the potential of everyone. This is why the Renaissance happened in the north, not the south...don't take my word for it. A seminal study in 1998...showed that a 15% increase in the nation's belief that 'most people can be trusted' adds a full percentage point to growth every year – a staggeringly large effect. 'If trust is low,' the authors write, 'economic growth is unachievable'".

Morality, then, is "designed" by Nature to reinforce cooperation within a group; and the more effectively it does this, the more successful the group is likely to be.

Universal moral triggers

A capacity for moral instinct is innate, hardwired into the brains of all normally-functioning humans, rather as we are born with a generalised capacity for language. American psychologist Steven Pinker explains, in an article titled *The Moral Instinct,* published in *The New York Times* magazine on 13 January 2008, and referencing work by Marc Hauser and John Mikhail who themselves drew on an idea first developed by the philosopher John Rawls: "according to Noam Chomsky, we are born with a 'universal grammar' that forces us to analyse speech in terms of its grammatical structure, with no conscious awareness of the rules in play. By analogy, we are born with a universal moral grammar that forces us to analyse human action in terms of its moral structure, with just as little awareness".

Pinker elaborates: "the idea that the moral sense is an innate part of human nature is not far-fetched. A list of human universals collected by the anthropologist Donald E. Browne includes many moral concepts and emotions, including a distinction between right and wrong; empathy; fairness; admiration of generosity; rights and obligations; proscription of murder, rape, and other forms of violence; redress of wrongs; sanctions for wrongs against the community; shame; and taboos....though no one has identified genes for morality, there is circumstantial evidence they exist. The character traits called 'conscientiousness' and 'agreeableness' are far more correlated in identical twins separated at birth (who share their genes but not their environment) than in adoptive siblings raised together (who share their environment but not their genes). People given diagnoses of 'antisocial personality disorder' or 'psychopathy' show signs of morality blindness from the time they are children. They bully younger children, torture animals, habitually lie, and seem incapable of empathy or remorse, often despite normal family backgrounds".

And this notion that even very young children possess a basic moral sense is supported by the American psychologist, Paul Bloom, in an interview conducted by journalist Gareth Crook published in *Scientific American* on 12 November 2013 and titled *The Moral Life of Babies*: "morality is not just something that people learn, argues Yale psychologist Paul Bloom: it is something we are all born with. At birth, babies are endowed with compassion, with empathy, with the beginnings of a sense of fairness...the earliest signs are the glimmerings of empathy and compassion – pain at the pain of others, which you can see pretty soon after birth. Once they're capable of coordinated movement, babies will often try to soothe others who are suffering, by patting and stroking...the sort of research that I've been involved with personally, looking at the origins of moral judgement, is difficult to do with very young babies. But we have found that even three-month-olds respond differently to a character who helps another than to a character who hinders another person. This finding hints that moral judgement might have very early developmental origins...I think the strongest evidence that morality has a genetic component has...everything to do with human universals. Every normal person has a sense of right and wrong, some appreciation of justice and fairness, some gut feelings that are triggered by kindness and cruelty".

What form does our moral instinct typically take? There is not a canonical list of features. But at the broadest level, significant similarities are seen across cultures, as Pinker highlights in his *Moral Instinct* article: "when anthropologists like Richard Shweder and Alan Fiske survey moral concerns across the globe, they find that a few themes keep popping up from amid the diversity. People everywhere, at least in some circumstances and with certain other folks in mind, think it's bad to harm others, and good to help them. They have a sense of fairness: that one should reciprocate favours, reward benefactors, and punish cheaters. They value loyalty to a group, sharing and solidarity among its members and conformity to its norms. They believe that it is right to defer to legitimate authorities, and to respect people with high status. And they exalt purity, cleanliness and sanctity while loathing defilement, contamination, and carnality". He concludes: ""the exact number of themes depends...but (Jonathan) Haidt counts five – harm, fairness, community (or group loyalty), authority and purity – and suggests that they are the primary colours of our moral sense. Not only do they keep reappearing in cross-cultural surveys, but each one tugs on the moral intuitions of people in our own culture".

Rosenberg expresses a similar view that a "core morality" is innate to all humans, on p104 of *The Atheist's Guide to Reality*. He suggests that the main elements are so obvious that we mostly take them for granted: "a more accurate way to think about core morality begins by recognising those norms that no one has ever bothered to formulate because they never come into dispute...if we set out to express them, we might start out with candidates like these:

- Don't cause gratuitous pain to a newborn baby, especially your own.
- Protect your children.
- If someone does something nice to you, then, other things being equal, you should return the favour if you can.
- Other things being equal, people should be treated the same way.
- On the whole, people being better off is morally preferable to their being worse off.
- Beyond a certain point, self-interest becomes selfishness.
- If you earn something, you have a right to it.
- It's permissible to restrict complete strangers' access to your personal possessions.
- It's okay to punish people who intentionally do wrong.
- It's wrong to punish the innocent".

Finally, Pinker describes what he calls the two "hallmarks" of moralisation: "the first hallmark of moralisation is that the rules it invokes are felt to be universal. Provisions of rape and murder, for example, are felt not to be matters of local custom but to be universally and objectively warranted. One can easily say, 'I don't like brussels sprouts, but I don't care if you eat them,' but no one would say, 'I don't like killing, but I don't care if you murder someone'...the other hallmark is that people feel that those who commit immoral acts deserve to be punished. Not only is it allowable to inflict pain on a person who has broken a moral rule; it is wrong *not* (Pinker's emphasis) to, to 'let them get away with it'. People are thus untroubled in inviting divine retribution or the power of the state to harm other people they deem immoral. Bertrand Russell wrote, 'the infliction of cruelty with a good conscience is a delight to moralists – that is why they invented hell'".

This instinct to "punish" perceived transgressors of course carries echoes of Axelrod's finding that the most effective cooperation strategies involve not simply tuning the other cheek but rather standing up to defectors in some appropriate, proportionate way. Moral norms must be enforced, it seems, if they are to be effective.

In sum, our capacity for moral sense ultimately derives from our genes, at such a fundamental level that the basic elements are universal for all "neurologically normal" humans. But this is not at all to say that as individuals we each possess a moral instinct in exactly the same way or to the same degree. As we have seen multiple times our particular genes and experiences are unique to each of us as individuals, and we would therefore predict there will be differences in the extent to which different individuals are predisposed to act morally. Jefferson reinforces exactly this point, in the same letter to his nephew quoted at the beginning of this chapter, pointing out that moral instinct is: "given to all human beings in a stronger or lesser degree".

Nor is it the case that whatever moral instincts we may possess dominate to the extent that we always act in accordance with them. Indeed, we would not expect this in the Darwinian, Axelrodian world that we inhabit. For example, as Axelrod shows, morality may typically encourage cooperation but sometimes it may be more appropriate to act "selfishly", especially if we are faced with a counterparty who is clearly committed to behaving this way themself. And in any case there can often be a situational temptation to "defect", in Axelrod-speak, to achieve some short-term personal gain or simply avoid the risk that we will be taken advantage of.

Last but by no means least, we may share universal moral instincts at the generalised level described by Pinker and Rosenberg but when it comes to specific norms is entirely possible that two equally-morally-minded individuals might disagree on what is or is not "moral" in a particular situation. To take just one, mundane, example: is it or is it not ok to keep a £20 note that you find on the street? This gives rise to what Greene calls "the tragedy of commonsense morality", a topic we will explore in more detail shortly.

For now, the main point is that we are each born with an innate moral sense, in effect a "conscience". This manifests in a set of behaviourial triggers which generally serve to reinforce cooperation and conformity within our particular social group; as well as to motivate us to sanction perceived transgressors.

Two triggers with particular relevance to this book are our capacity for "empathy", leading to a moral sentiment that we should avoid harming those people for whom we feel it; and our sense of "fairness", underpinning norms about the nature, and limits, of cooperation.

Empathy and "do no harm"

We encountered empathy in chapter 2, when we discussed how this, along with the ability to conceptualise a "Theory of Mind", are critical aspects of human consciousness.

The connection to morality is obvious. Empathy underpins close, cooperative relationships by allowing us to share another person's emotions at a visceral level, lifting us above the purely transactional. Empathy enables and in a sense forces us to consider the impact of our actions on others. From here it is a relatively short step to a basic morality in which doing things which harm other people is "bad", and doing things which benefit them is "good". This in turn gives rise to the moral precept of "do no harm", and the so-called "Golden Rule", exemplified in the gospel of Matthew, Chapter 7 Verse 12: "do unto others as you would have them do unto you". In fact the Golden Rule has been formulated in different ways by many influential thinkers before and after Matthew, at least as far back as early Confucian times around 500 BCE. It is arguably the most important moral principle to emerge in human society, in the past, present and likely future.

There is however an important caveat. As we saw in Chapter 2, we tend to feel empathy mainly for people with whom we have some kind of existing emotional connection, and much less, or not at all, for people whom we regard as strangers, particular if they are members of what we identify as an "Outgroup". Far from feeling empathy we have an innate bias to dehumanise members of outgroups, as we also saw in Chapter 3; an unfortunate adaptation which poses particular challenges in today's globally connected inter-dependent world.

As usual, it is important to be precise in our use of language. Canadian author Tamara Lechner makes a distinction between "empathy", "sympathy" and "compassion", in an article entitled *The Danger of Confusing Empathy or Sympathy with Compassion*, published online by *Positive Psychology* and dated 13 July 2018: "empathy refers to feeling what another person is feeling. Sympathy means you understand what the other person is feeling even without feeling it yourself. Compassion means your feelings have prompted you to take action to relieve the suffering of another person".

With these definitions in mind, Paul Bloom encourages us to strive for "compassion" in preference to "empathy" in our everyday life; and moreover to engage reason to combat our tendency to bias in favour of those people whom we perceive to be members of our own social group. Bloom comments, in an interview published by *Vox* on 16 Jan 2019 and referencing his 2016 book *Against Empathy: The Case for Rational Compassion*: "empathy and compassion activate different parts of the brain...in the moral domain, empathy leads us astray...empathy is biased...I feel a lot less empathy for people who aren't in my culture, who don't share my skin colour, who don't share my language...(as an example) I could not imagine a better recipe for bias and unfair sentencing decisions than (empathy applied to witness statements)...if the victim is an articulate, attractive white woman, it's going to be so much more powerful than if the victim is a sullen, African-American man who doesn't like to talk about his feelings....I think that when it comes to moral reasoning, empathy is just a bad idea...I want to make the case for the value of conscious, deliberative reasoning in everyday life, arguing that we should strive to use our heads rather than our hearts".

And Lechner points out that empathy alone can actually be harmful to the person experiencing it, because of its essential passivity. She cites as an example a study showing that 60% of the US medical profession has suffered from "empathy burnout", associated with symptoms such as anxiety, stress and depression.

The point is that whilst empathy may enable individuals to share the emotional pain of another person, this may be counter-productive if we do not also feel some level of agency, in other words some ability to take meaningful action to help alleviate it. Compassion, by contrast, is often associated with an emotional lift for the person experiencing it precisely because it leads to them taking some action which is helpful to the suffering party and therefore to their own sense of self-worth.

Fairness

"Fairness" is a concept so ingrained into our evolutionary past that we appear to share it with other primates. For example, captive Capuchin monkeys will happily accept a reward of cucumber for performing a simple task, and if they see that the monkey in the next cage is enjoying the same reward then all is well. But if they see that the next-door monkey is receiving what they perceive to be a superior reward, say banana, for the same task for which they themselves are receiving cucumber, they become agitated and may refuse to co-operate at all.

Our sense of fairness can act as a kind of higher goal, causing us to behave in ways which unequivocally pro-social. A classic example is the celebrated psychological experiment, sometimes called the Ultimatum Game, in which a respondent is told they must divide a potential gift of say $100 between themselves and a randomly-selected stranger, whom they do not know and are unlikely ever to meet again. The rules are simple: the respondent is allowed to make just one offer, which the stranger must then either accept or reject. If the stranger accepts, then the $100 is divided between them in whatever proportion was agreed. If the stranger rejects the offer, then neither party gets anything.

An economically rational respondent would clearly offer a split in which they get the lion's share of value, say they get $90 and the stranger gets $10, or even $99:$1; on the grounds that an economically-rational stranger should in theory accept any offer above zero since they are obviously better off with something rather than nothing.

In fact, experiments repeatedly show that in a majority of cultures a high proportion of offers are quite generous, with a significant proportion being 50:50 or even weighted in favour of the stranger. Conversely when more miserly offers are made they tend to be rejected by a significant proportion of strangers, who prefer to punish the respondent for what they perceive as morally "unfair" behaviour even at the cost of losing an opportunity to make a modest economic gain themselves. For completeness, there are some exceptions. For example, Joseph Henrich tells us on p192 of *The Secret of Our Success*: "the smallest-scale human societies tend not to offer very much nor reject low offers because they lack social norms for monetary exchanges with strangers or anonymous others".

And in the real world an outcome is likely to be influenced by perceptions of the relationship between the different parties involved. Specifically, other experiments show that we experience "fairness" primarily in local rather than universal terms, which is to say that we experience it mainly in comparison with others whom we perceive to be in some way similar to ourself. For example, if we happen to be an hourly-paid manual worker it will likely matter more to us whether we are paid relatively more, or less, than a co-worker on the same shift than how much less, or more, we earn than the factory manager, or the local judge. Intriguingly, our capuchin monkeys seem to have a similar sense. What they perceive as being "fair" relates entirely to the treatment accorded to other neighbouring monkeys. It does not seem to matter to them that the human experimenter who is providing the rewards has access to as much banana as they want, without even needing to complete a task to earn it.

PART B: Complications

Unfortunately we cannot always rely on our moral instinct prompting us to behave in ways that our rational self might consider appropriate, a problem compounded by the fact that our moral sense also tends to elicit strong, even visceral, emotions.

At the start of the chapter we reviewed a number of specific challenges, which we will now discuss, with the intention that understanding them will put us in a better position to make informed existential choices which take appropriate account of our moral sentiments without however surrendering blindly to them.

1. *Morality is ultimately relative, not an absolute law of nature.*

"Man is the measure of all things" the Greek philosopher Protagoras said, sometime in the 400s BCE. And this is certainly true when it comes to morality.

As members of the human species we each share innate universal moral instincts, as we already saw. But we are the sole species to exhibit this to any level of sophistication, accepting that elements of what we might call a rudimentary moral instinct can also be observed amongst a handful of others, in particular our closest cousins the other apes.

How these universal moral instincts translate into specific norms varies widely by culture. For example, in *The Righteous Mind* Jonathan Haidt explores differing attitudes to violence: the degree to which violence is acceptable as a way to resolve disputes; whether and under what circumstances it is acceptable that such violence is lethal or non-lethal; and whether some sub-groups might be treated differently from others within the overall group – for instance, whether corporal punishment is acceptable for both sexes, only for one sex, or not at all. Haidt summarises, on p31 of *The Righteous Mind*: "we're born to be righteous, but we have to learn what, exactly, people like us should be righteous about".

It follows that what we experience as moral instinct is a product of both "nature" – our universal instincts, which are innate; and "nurture" – the particular environment and culture in which we are raised and live, these obviously being what drive our personal experiences.

It is perhaps intuitive to assume that cultural differences in moral norms might most readily be defined along geographic lines: people who live in the same location might have similar norms, and these might be different at least in some ways from those living in some faraway place. This may of course often be true. However, on pp22-6 of *The Righteous Mind* Haidt demonstrates that it is not necessarily always the case, and that, at least in today's industrialised world, relative socio-economic status may provide a better indicator. He describes an experiment with the specific aim of identifying similarities and differences in moral views, conducted among respondents living in Philadelphia, in the US; and in Recife and Porto Alegre, two contrasting cities in Brazil. The hypothesis was that people living in each of these places would have views similar to one another, and different along at least some dimensions from those living in the other two. However, a different, surprising, picture emerged. Haidt summarises, on p25: "unexpectedly, the effect of social class was much larger than the effect of city. In other words, well-educated people in all three cities were much more similar to each other than they were to their lower-class neighbours. I had flown five thousand miles south to search for moral variation when in fact there was more to be found a few blocks west of campus, in the poor neighbourhood surrounding my university".

In any case, the broader point is that morality as a concept applies almost exclusively to humans. In an important sense it is a human "invention", although of course I do not suggest that a particular prehistoric individual sat down and simply thought of it – moral instinct would surely have developed in gradual, incremental steps like everything else in evolution.

We can explicitly reject any idea that morality is some kind of objective or universal truth, existing outside of or independent from human experience. Rather, morality is entirely subjective and relative. In principle, we have complete freedom to decide what we personally define as "moral", although in practice of course we have no choice but to work within the cognitive and physiological parameters that evolution has bequeathed us; and, as individuals living in social groups, we have at least to be aware of the specific moral norms of whichever group or groups we happen, or choose, to be part.

We can reject any notion of natural, much less divine, "justice". Nature itself is inherently amoral: there is no sense in which it is objectively "just" whether or not the lioness catches the baby gazelle on a given day, or whether the skies rain or not on a particular parade. The evolutionary algorithm (replicate, vary, select) rewards only outcomes, and we might therefore assert that in Nature the end always justifies the means, although it might be more accurate to say rather that the end is simply blind to the means.

Of course, none of this is to deny the importance of morality in the context of human society. The notion of "justice", to continue with that example, is obviously pivotal to our ability to regulate affairs in our complex social groups. Nor does the fact that we are in principle free to decide for ourself what is "moral" mean that we can simply ignore whatever social and community norms may be part of the particular world we happen to live in. To do so may pass some abstract test of philosophical purity but would clearly be naïve. It is simply that we cannot assume that "justice", or any other aspect of morality, is somehow an independent Law of Nature or imbued with objective meaning. Whatever meaning it has is the meaning that we ourselves, as humans, give it.

It follows that morality is also robustly relative, meaning that there is no truly objective basis for determining that the norms of one culture are inherently superior to those of another. This is reflected in the doctrine of moral relativism, a school which may have its origins in the Ancient Greece of Protagoras but gained traction in the modern world early in the 20th century, largely as a reaction to and rejection of the colonial view that "European", or alternatively "Christian", values were somehow inherently superior to all others.

As an aside, moral relativism is not quite the same thing as cultural relativism, a notion rejected by Richard Dawkins with characteristic forcefulness on p36 of his 1995 book *River Out of Eden*: "show me a cultural relativist at 30,000 feet and I will show you a hypocrite". His point is, of course, that when it comes to culture, what we might call the scientific approach can be objectively demonstrated to be more effective at least in material terms than alternative approaches based for example on faith in the supernatural. Specifically, a culture which is using science to make, test and then refine objectively-verifiable conclusions can produce a working aeroplane; and a culture which is relying mainly on "magic" or some other kind of faith-based belief system cannot.

Be that as it may, *The Stanford Encyclopedia of Philosophy* defines moral relativism as the belief that: "the truth or falsity of moral judgements, or their justification, is not absolute or universal, but is relative to the traditions, convictions, or practices of a group of persons...(for example) a moral judgement such as 'polygamy is morally wrong' may be true relative to one society, but false relative to another. It is not true, or false, simply speaking". In other words, whilst many of us brought up in a Western tradition might feel intuitively that polygamy is wrong, in fact it, like any other moral norm, is only "moral" or "immoral" within the context of a culture which decides that it is.

Many attempts have been made to develop from first principles a kind of universal moral code which can be shown to be logically valid at the level of the entire human species, but none have succeeded. Indeed, many whom we might think qualified for the attempt have given up even trying. *The Stanford Encyclopedia of Philosophy* offers the definitional possibility of a "normative", or universal, morality. But is also tells us that: "explicit attempts, by philosophers, to define (a universal) morality are hard to find, at least since the beginning of the twentieth century". It is beyond the scope of this book, not to mention the capacities of the author, to fill this void, and in any case the point is that such an attempt would be doomed to fail.

We'll discuss moral relativism further when we come to discuss the implications of our moral sense for our everyday life later in this chapter. We'll see that as a practical matter in today's inter-connected, multi-cultural world we have little alternative other than to find constructive ways to arbitrate between conflicting norms, at least in those cases where the differences are incompatible and threaten the cohesion of the broader social group. The main point for now, though, is that even as we do this we must accept that there is no truly objective basis for determining that one moral norm is inherently superior to another.

2. *Moral instinct is instinctive – we feel first, and reason later.*

Our moral judgements tend to be the product of our intuition, prompted by our unconscious mind. We often experience them viscerally, as being somehow obvious with little room for discussion or doubt. To the extent that we engage it at all our rational brain is often the "slave to our passions", as David Hume memorably put it.

In *The Righteous Mind* Haidt distinguishes between two cognitive processes relevant to moral judgements which he calls "seeing-that", corresponding to instinct; and "reasoning-why", corresponding to reason. He describes a number of imaginary situations and invites us to decide whether the characters involved have behaved morally or not. As an example, on p4 he tells us: "a man goes to the supermarket once a week and buys a chicken. But before cooking the chicken, he has sexual intercourse with it. Then he cooks it and eats it".

Haidt explains that many people presented with this narrative react with a strong instinctive feeling of disgust, prompting a judgement that the man has indeed behaved immorally. But they then struggle to explain this reaction rationally: no-one, and no animal, has been hurt; there is no social or reputational dimension because no-one else knows what has happened; and even "as some of my (Haidt's) research students pointed out", the story involves "a kind of recycling that is...an efficient use of natural resources".

The conclusions to be drawn from this and the many other examples in Haidt's book are that our moral judgements are often based wholly or at least largely on an instinctive feeling; that we may then find it difficult to explain this feeling in a rational way; and that this difficulty seldom dilutes the clarity or intensity of the moral feeling itself. To the extent that we engage our rational brain at all, its role is to construct a post-hoc justification for why we felt and acted the way we did. Haidt concludes, on p47 of *The Righteous Mind*: "people made moral judgements quickly and emotionally. Moral reasoning was mostly just a post hoc search for reasons to justify the judgements people had already made".

We saw earlier from Lisa Barrett how the interoceptive "affect" we are experiencing at a particular moment can influence our view of a situation, sometimes profoundly; and Haidt makes the case that our moral judgements are similarly susceptible. For example, on pp70-71 of *The Righteous Mind*: "Alex Jordan, a grad student at Stanford, came up with the idea of asking people to make moral judgements while he secretly tripped their disgust alarms. He stood at a pedestrian intersection on the Stanford campus and asked passers-by to fill out a short survey. It asked people to make judgements about four controversial issues, such as marriage between first cousins...Alex stood right next to a trash can he had emptied. Before he recruited each subject, he put a new plastic liner into the metal can. Before half the people walked up (and before they could see him), he sprayed...fart spray twice into the bag, which 'perfumed' the whole intersection for a few minutes. Before other recruitments, he left the empty bag unsprayed. Sure enough, people made harsher judgements when they were breathing in foul air".

Haidt summarises by quoting UVA colleague Jerry Clore, on p71: "when we're trying to decide what we think about something, we look inward, at how we're feeling. If I'm feeling good, I must like it, and if I'm feeling anything unpleasant, that must mean I don't like it".

And moral instinct is inherently emotive. We heard in Chapter 2 from Ilana Simons and her article titled *The Four Moral Emotions*, these being guilt, shame, embarrassment and pride. Simons proposes that these four emotions serve to help regulate our behaviour with respect to other people, and are largely unique to humans as a species. Indeed she asserts that these "moral" emotions are what "make (human) societies work". Simons contrasts them with what she calls the six "basic" emotions, namely: anger, disgust, fear, joy, sadness and surprise, suggesting that these mainly help us to survive as individuals in the quotidian Darwinian struggle for survival, and are not unique to humans but rather can also be observed in at least some other species. This framing is not entirely consistent with Lisa Barrett's notion of "constructed emotion", which we reviewed in Chapter 2, and we might also quibble that "disgust" specifically can be associated with moral sentiment, as it is in Haidt's example of the supermarket chicken. But the broader point stands that we often experience our moral sentiments in visceral emotional terms, and that at least some of our emotions are rooted in our sense of morality.

Emotional intensity is not always helpful. British columnist James Marriot warns that elevated levels of moral sentiment may paradoxically sometimes undermine sociability, in an article titled *Feeling virtuous doesn't mean you're good*, published in *The Times* on 24 February 2022: "'moral righteousness' and even 'moral fury' are still terms of praise or admiration but our moral convictions are an unreliable guide to treating other people well. An analysis published in the *Journal of Personality and Social Psychology* by behavioural scientists at the University of Illinois found that strong moral feelings predict increased 'intolerance'; 'lower levels of goodwill and cooperativeness' towards those with different beliefs; and a 'greater inability' to 'resolve disagreements'".

And through it all there is an important role for reason to play, challenging as this can be given the strength of emotions which are often involved. On pp53-4 Haidt introduces the metaphor of an elephant and its rider, to represent his two types of moral cognition: "I called these two kinds of cognition the rider (controlled processes, including 'reasoning-why') and the elephant (automatic processes, including emotion, intuition, and all forms of 'seeing-that'). I chose an elephant rather than a horse, because elephants are so much, bigger – and smarter – than horses. Automatic processes run the human mind, just as they have been running animal minds for 500 million years, so they're very good at what they do, like software that has been improved through thousands of product cycles. When human beings evolved the capacity for language and reasoning at some point in the last million years, the brain did not rewire itself to hand over the reins to a new and inexperienced charioteer. Rather, the rider (language-based reasoning) evolved because it did something useful for the elephant...the rider can do several useful things. It can see further into the future (because we can examine alternative scenarios in our heads), and therefore it can help the elephant make better decisions in the present. It can learn new skills and master new technologies, which can be deployed to help the elephant reach its goals and sidestep disasters. And, most important, the rider acts as the spokesman for the elephant, even though it doesn't necessarily know what the elephant is really thinking. The rider is skilled at fabricating post hoc explanations for whatever the elephant has just done, and it is good at finding reasons to justify whatever the elephant wants to do next".

3. *Our instincts do not always prompt us to behave "morally".*

It is an article of faith for some people that humans are innately "good", and therefore that any moral failing must be a product of the environment and not the individual. Is this the case?

At a philosophical level it turns out to be something of a trick question, because as discussed earlier "good" is one of those slippery words which sounds like it ought to be absolute but is in fact robustly relative, at least when used in a moral sense. On a strictly technical, if pedantic, level therefore we cannot assert that all humans are good because we cannot provide a consistent, objective, definition of what "good" actually looks like. This problem is challenging if we just consider the norms which characterise a particular social group. It is greatly increased if expand the definition to include different norms, from different groups.

Still, this feels a bit like sophistry, and is certainly not satisfying from an everyday practical perspective. So let us attempt a more pragmatic answer.

It is clearly not the case that all our behaviour is "moral", all of the time. We know that moral codes tend to reinforce and reward cooperative behaviours and penalise selfish ones. Yet, as we discussed earlier, anti-social behaviours such as violence, bullying, intimidation and various forms of manipulation persist.

We saw in chapter 2 that our consciousness has evolved to give us a "conscience" – the little voice inside our heads which amongst other things helps us to assess our own behaviour, and connect with corresponding emotions such as satisfaction, pride, guilt or shame. The fact that we each experience at least some examples of the latter two, at least some of the time, reinforces that we do not subjectively perceive ourself as behaving in a uniformly moral or "good" way.

The question really turns, then, on the degree to which we can and should be held responsible for the "immoral" (or "non-moral") actions we commit. And here the matter becomes intensely practical, because plainly if we do not hold ourselves and others personally responsible for our individual actions, at least in large measure, then we have no basis for ordering and regulating behaviour in our social groups at all, as we saw in Chapter 2.

Fortunately, as we also discussed in chapter 2, it is reasonable to believe that consciousness gives us each some element of "freewill". Our individual genetic inheritance and the specific environment in which we grow and live certainly predispose us to behave in certain ways in response to particular situations. But ultimately we retain agency, the ability to decide for ourself how to behave. As we discussed, this is specifically what makes it possible, and legitimate, to hold ourself and others responsible for the choices we and they make, and the actions which result; even as we might also make some appropriate allowance for the potentially significant effects of genes, experiences, and environment.

If we allow that we have an important measure of freewill, and we accept that our individual behaviours are not consistently "good" (or "moral"), then it is a relatively short step to admit at least some measure of individual responsibility for our "bad" (or "immoral") behaviours. To deny this would be to assert that only "good" behaviours are the product of freewill, and all "bad" behaviours are driven by mitigating factors such as genes and environment. This is logically possible. But it is also something of a tautology, and at odds with our subjective experience in which our conscience often tells us that we made a deliberate choice. In any case, we have said that our chief concern in this line of argument is one of practicality, and as we already saw it is simply not practical to deny the concept of personal responsibility for "bad" actions, because it would remove any basis for regulating our social interactions.

So we have our answer. If we accept that humans are capable of and indeed frequently perform morally "bad" actions, and also that we can legitimately be held accountable for them to at least some degree, then we are forced to conclude that we cannot consider ourselves innately "good".

Of course this is not to say that we are innately "bad" either. Our conscience may experience guilt and shame, but it also experiences the warm glow of satisfaction that comes from feeling we have behaved with integrity or in some other way that we, and likely others around us, consider to be virtuous.

We are capable of, and responsible for, both "good" and "bad" behaviours, as it is logical to suppose we should be in a world in which our very existence requires that we continually make Axelrodian choices between cooperative ("good") behaviours and selfish ("bad") ones.

None of this is to deny the potential importance of mitigating factors such as genes and environment in predisposing us to act in certain ways. As we have seen, these effects are real and often significant, and must be given appropriate weight in our judgments of when and to what extent to hold an individual, including ourself, morally accountable for a particular action. There is a balance to be struck, and some measure of empathy, or sympathy, or even compassion, for a transgressor is often likely to be appropriate.

We'll give the last word to George Orwell, in his essay *The Art of Donald McGill,* published in *Horizon* in 1941. As so often, Orwell cuts through the complexity to offer a pithy summary: "on the whole human beings want to be good, but not too good, and not quite all the time".

4. *Morality is often nuanced and contextual.*

The strength of our moral emotions may prompt us to act as though an issue is categorically "right" or "wrong". But if once we subject a choice to rational scrutiny it can often turn out to be nuanced and highly contextual.

An example is the classic psychological thought experiment known as the Trolley Experiment, which we briefly met in chapter 2, in our discussion of "Noise". Many versions of this exist, but the simplest is that you are standing by the side of a railway track and see that a runaway truck (or trolley) is hurtling down the line towards a group of two railway workers, who are blissfully unaware of this. If you do nothing the truck will certainly kill them both, and there is no time to shout a warning. However, you happen to be standing next to a lever which, if you pull it, will divert the truck down a siding where there is just one worker. If you pull the lever, this single worker will certainly be killed instead. To summarise, if you do nothing two strangers will die, and if you pull the lever one stranger will.

What do you do?

Many people hesitate to pull the lever. The rational brain shows a clear and obvious utilitarian trade-off in favour of doing so because it will result in just one stranger's life being lost instead of two. But this is often more than offset by a strong emotional aversion to having the kind of personal agency in causing human death which pulling the lever involves, and standing passively by somehow does not. Logically, not pulling the lever can also be said to be making a choice, consistent with Sartre's reminder in Chapter 2 that: "I must know that if I do not choose, that is still a choice", but somehow it doesn't feel that way emotionally, at least for a lot of people.

Circumstances alter cases, as the proverb says, and the context in which the Trolley Game is framed can have a significant effect on the outcome. For example, what if rather than 2 workers being saved by pulling the lever to divert the runaway truck the number saved is 3, or 5, or 10, or whatever number you care to think of, still at the cost of the solitary life of the individual stranger in the siding? What if the truck is heading towards just a single person, and there are 2 (or 3, 5 or 10) people working in the siding, but the single person is your lover, your parent, or your child? A good but not particularly close friend? An attractive-looking stranger of whichever sex you find most appealing? The permutations are endless.

The point is that there are no objectively "right" or "wrong" answers to these moral dilemmas. We are likely to feel that the answer is intuitively clear in some cases, and less clear obvious in others. Our rational brain may also be in conflict with our emotional self. Ultimately you, the respondent, are forced to make a choice in each case, bearing in mind that to do nothing is itself to choose. The choice is ultimately binary – you either pull the lever or you don't. But the basis on which you have to make it is in many cases shrouded in nuance, and both rational and emotional complexity.

It is unlikely that any of us will find ourself in the specific situation imagined by the Trolley Experiment. But it is not hard to think of similarly amorphous moral choices in our everyday lives. To offer some admittedly trivial examples, is it OK to cut into a queue of slow-moving traffic if it is safe to do so, we have been waiting a while, and no-one has proactively offered us a space? What if we have a passenger in urgent need of medical treatment and we are in a rush to get to a hospital? What if the traffic is moving a bit faster and there is a probability that we will force another vehicle to brake, albeit conditions are such that we would reasonably expect the driver to have plenty of time to do this without undue risk? Or maybe there is some element of risk, but we judge it to be modest...there are simply not black-and-white answers even to these mundane questions.

To take another, more emotive, example, many people would agree that "thou shalt not kill" is an important moral principle. As an aside, this is not quite the same thing as the idea that "all human life is sacred", a notion which evolved during the course of the 20th century but was not commonplace in earlier eras. But they amount to much the same thing for the purposes of our discussion.

And the complication quickly arises that most people, in most cultures, would also agree that there are particular circumstances in which killing another person can be morally OK, although what these circumstances are exactly might be a matter for debate. For example, many people would feel that it is morally acceptable to kill another person in self-defence and assuming there is no viable alternative, accepting that this then begs inevitable questions about how to establish the severity of the threat and the viability of alternative responses. What if it is not ourself who is threatened but rather a child (of ours), a lover, or a close family member? A stranger, or a group of several strangers? Should it make any difference if the would-be murderer, whom we are about to kill because there is no other way to stop them killing, is themselves a child, a lover, or a close family member? And so on. We rapidly find ourselves on a kind of moral spectrum. It is obvious that a line must be drawn somewhere, but it is far from clear where exactly it can or should be.

The complexity only increases when we broaden our scope to include questions of state-sanctioned killing. It is easier to pose questions on this topic than to provide definitive answers. For example, is it ever morally acceptable that the state should take someone's life through execution, perhaps to satisfy a public thirst for vengeance in response to some horrible crime, or alternatively "pour encourager les autres" as the 18th century French writer Voltaire so memorably phrased it (obviously, in this context the purpose of an execution would be to provide an example with the intention to *dis*courage others from committing a similar crime, begging the question of what evidence exists if any that capital punishment indeed has such an effect). What about the hotly-debated questions of abortion, and assisted dying? Can either of these ever be justified, under any circumstances? If so, where exactly should we draw the line?

Last but not least, even if we think we are clear on a particular moral principle, further complexity may be involved as we seek to apply it consistently in the everyday world. For example, it turns out that what psychologists call "immediacy" and "accessibility" have a big impact on our likely instinctive reaction.

To illustrate this, we'll briefly review another thought experiment, also described in Joshua Greene's *Moral Tribes*, paraphrased from p258. You happen to walk by a swimming pool in which a lone child, whom you do not know, is clearly struggling and about to drown. There is no-one else around, and no time to seek help. Even if you can't swim you can easily save the child's life at no risk to your own because the swimming pool is shallow enough for you, an adult, to be safely within your depth even though the child is out of theirs. However, you happen to be wearing an expensive suit which you only recently bought. It will be ruined if you jump into the water to save the child.

What do you do?

Most people have little hesitation in answering that of course they would jump into the water, and too bad for the suit. The moral calculus at stake is that the life of an unknown child is worth more than the price of the suit.

The complication comes when we consider the parallel case of a child in some faraway land, who we do not know and cannot see, but whose life we can be confident we will save if we donate the price of our suit to a specified charity. These cases are morally equivalent in a literal sense: the life of a child we do not know is saved, at the cost of the price of the suit. We can vary the terms of the experiment by suggesting that maybe the price of the suit, and therefore the value of the donation to the charity, will save 2 faraway children's lives, or 3 or 4, compared with the one life we save by jumping into the pool.

Yet most of us have a harder time deciding to donate the price of the suit, in thought experiments and in everyday life. There seem to be at least three effects which help explain why:

- the drowning child is concrete – we can see and (if we jump into the water) touch them, whereas the child in the faraway land is abstract.

- only we can save the drowning child, whereas we can hope that someone else will make the donation to the charity (psychologists call this the "bystander effect" – there is some evidence that we are on average more likely to help someone if we are the only person present rather than one of a crowd; admittedly this evidence has recently been disputed).

- the drowning child is a one-off need, that is to say that once we have saved them there is no reason to suppose there will be any additional need to save additional drowning children. By contrast, if we once donate the price of our suit to the charity, why stop there? There will be other children's lives which can be saved by bigger or subsequent donations, and it is not clear where we should draw the line short of donating all our material wealth down to subsistence level. This is of course what some philosophies and religions have advocated in the past, but few people in history have been observed actually to do.

5. Morality inherently prompts us to privilege other members of our own social group at the expense of members of other groups ("the tragedy of commonsense morality").

In chapter 3 we reviewed how our tendency to categorise people into "ingroups" and "outgroups" biases our unconscious mind in important ways. We deferred until this chapter the role played by, and impact on, morality.

It turns out that distinctive moral norms can be some of the most important features in helping a group to define its own unique identity, and also that particular norms may be set specifically in order to be different from those of other groups, meaning that will certainly be different and may even be in direct opposition. We know that moral instincts are often highly emotive. When we combine all this with our instinctive bias to privilege "ingroup" members and disfavour or even demonise people we perceive to be part of an "outgroup", the result is a major challenge to cross-group cooperation with, sadly, no obvious or easy solution.

This dichotomy is the focus of Joshua Greene's 2013 book, *Moral Tribes*. In brief, Greene asserts that morality, and the emotions in which it is rooted, has evolved to do an effective job of moderating behaviour within a given social group – what he calls "Me versus Us". It therefore plays a vital role in solving or at least mitigating the Tragedy of the Commons, so long as there is only one, relatively homogenous, social group grazing a particular commons.

Where things get much trickier, though, is when the definition of what is "moral" is different across two different social groups, and it becomes necessary to arbitrate between them. Greene calls this "the tragedy of commonsense morality", the tragedy being that both groups can behave morally according to their own definition of the term, and still clash.

There is no requirement for overt "cheating" or "betrayal" for there to be tension and potentially confrontation. Rather, tension is structurally inevitable because the groups have different views on what they define as moral in the first place. Both are likely to experience a level of emotional outrage when they perceive they are behaving "morally" and the other group "immorally" according to their own definition; especially when there is no truly objective basis for determining that one set of norms is "better" than the other.

It is one thing for these kinds of tensions to exist between groups who have limited contact or interaction with one another. The scale of the challenges, as well as the importance of finding acceptable resolutions, is greatly amplified when the groups are in frequent contact, as they tend to be in today's inter-connected global and multi-cultural world.

Greene's point is not simply that this cross-group tension exists, but that it is an explicit product of human evolution, helping bind individuals more closely to their particular "tribe" whilst simultaneously magnifying the differences with other groups. He summarises, on pp24-5 of *Moral Tribes*: "insofar as morality is a biological adaptation, it evolved not only as a device for putting Us ahead of Me, but as a device for putting Us ahead of Them...as a device for intergroup competition".

To bring all this to life, in his introduction Greene describes The Parable of the New Pastures, which then serves as the central metaphor for his book. He imagines a forest is cleared to become arable land, and four previously-isolated tribes of herders descend from North, East, South and West to graze their cattle on the new pasture. Each tribe has evolved distinctive moral norms to help it cope with the Tragedy of the Commons ("Me versus Us") in its original homeland, and each set of norms has worked more or less effectively for that tribe in the isolated environment in which they hitherto lived.

There are however crucial differences between these norms. In the East, the rule is that each family gets the same number of sheep to graze, regulated by a Council of Elders which has for example been called on to sanction a family which started to breed exceptionally large sheep. In the West, the size of a family's flock is determined by the size of the family, also regulated by a Council of Elders which for example had to rule on cases where one family had 12 healthy children whereas another only had 6, 5 of whom died young. In the North, each family has its own plot of land, surrounded by a fence. Some plots are more fertile than others, of course, and over time successful families have increased the size of their plots at the expense of less successful families, so that by now significant disparities exist, and in a harsh winter some poorer tribe members sometimes die from hunger and cold. There is a Council of Elders here too, but they don't do much beyond enforcing property rights. Finally, in the South, all the sheep are shared among the whole tribe, and each tribe member receives an equal share of the fruits of their collective labour. The Council of Elders in the South is very busy, assigning people to work, monitoring outcomes, and mediating disputes, for example responding to frequent complaints from some tribe members that others are not pulling their weight.

As each tribe expands onto the new, shared, pasture, they come into contact with the others. There is inevitably competition for grazing, and each tribe naturally looks to resolve disputes using the moral norms to which they are accustomed. The problem (the "tragedy"), is of course that each is using different norms, and the different moral systems are incompatible. For example, none of the other tribes likes it when herders from the North build fences around areas of the new land. To the other tribes this is "wrong" and "unfair", whereas to tribesmen from the North it is simply how things are.

The seemingly-inevitable result is violent conflict, because the differences are experienced as moral violations, giving rise to strong, primal, emotions. Greene comments: "the tribes of the new pastures are engaged in bitter, often bloody conflict, even though they are all, in their different ways, moral peoples...(they) are, in many ways, very similar. For the most part they want the same things: healthy families, tasty and nutritious food, comfortable shelter, labour-saving tools, leisure time to spend with friends and family...even as they fight one another, their minds work in similar ways. What they perceive as unjust makes them angry and disgusted". The point is, summarised on p4 of *Moral Tribes*: "they fight not because they are fundamentally selfish but because they have incompatible visions of what a moral society should be".

Of course Greene's scenario is fictional, a modern parable as he says. But it illustrates a fundamental truth about the everyday world in which we live. And, as we saw earlier, this "tragedy of commonsense morality" can and does apply to different social groups within a single society, not just or even mainly to people living in different geographic areas.

Indeed, Greene points out that differences in moral worldview is a powerful lens through which to observe what many commentators have identified as the increasing polarisation of US society (and of other contemporary societies, it is just that Greene's own example focuses on the US).

As an example, on pp6-8 he describes an exchange from the 2012 US Republican Presidential primaries. A journalist called Wolf Blitzer asked Texas congressman Ron Paul how the state should respond to a (hypothetical) case in which an apparently-healthy 30 year old with a good, well-paid, job decides not to take out personal medical insurance, and subsequently becomes seriously ill. Should society (that is, the state) give them medical treatment, or should it let them die?

This is clearly an emotive framing, and Greene describes how, as an experienced politician, Paul avoided giving a straightforward answer. His response was along the lines that the man should exercise his individual choice on whether or not to take out an insurance policy, then suffer the consequences if he chose not to, whilst also expressing the hope that in the specific circumstances described he might be helped by the intercession of his family, or his church, or some other social group of which he was a member. However, it seems that some Paul-supporting members of the audience shouted a more definitive response: "yeah, let him die!", predictably outraging members of the liberal opposition.

The point here is not to resolve the debate, but rather to reinforce how two moral principles which most of us would consider to be reasonable - "individual freedom of choice is sacred, and with it comes responsibility for the consequences of your choices" and "human life is sacred" – can be incompatible, certainly in the specific context of Greene's example.

There are, of course, many examples of moral norms which differ across social groups and are fundamentally incompatible. *The Stanford Encyclopedia of Philosophy* lists some salient examples of practices which are "moral" in some societies, but which it describes as "sharply at odds with moral outlooks common in the United States", in an entry on *Moral Relativism* first published on 19 February 2004 and substantively updated on 20 April 2015. The list includes: "polygamy, arranged marriages, suicide as a requirement of honour or widowhood, severe punishments for blasphemy or adultery, female circumcision...and so on". An obvious addition might be the treatment of minorities in many societies.

Greene's point is that morality has evolved specifically to reinforce not just cooperation within social groups, but also competition between them. On p186 of *Moral Tribes* he explains: "...morality evolved to promote cooperation, but that's not the whole story...morality evolved (biologically) to promote cooperation *within groups* for the sake of *competition between groups* (Greene's emphasis in both cases). The only reason that natural selection would favour genes that promote cooperation is that cooperative individuals are better able to outcompete others. This highlights a more general point about the function of morality, which is that its ultimate function, like that of all biological adaptations, is to spread genetic material. Evolution is not aimed at promoting cooperation per se. It promotes cooperation only insofar as cooperation helps propagate the genes of the cooperators".

And one important effect of this is that we may instinctively feel that the moral norms which govern interactions within our own "ingroup" do not apply, or not in the same way, to people whom we perceive to be members of "outgroups". This in turn helps to explain the phenomenon we saw in Chapter 2 that we tend to feel empathy only for people we recognise as somehow being linked to us, and not towards strangers, much less those we perceive to be members of an "outgroup".

To return to the example of "thou shalt not kill", most cultures have evolved the notion that killing within the group is to be discouraged, unless in certain specific contexts. Killing members of an "outgroup", however, may not simply be less problematic but may even be something to be actively welcomed and encouraged. Matt Ridley comments, on pp192-3 of *The Origins of Virtue*: "no less an authority than Margaret Mead asserted that the injunction against murdering human beings is universally interpreted to define human beings as members of one's own tribe. Members of other tribes are subhuman. As Richard Alexander has put it, 'the rules of morality and law alike seem not to be designed explicitly to allow people to live in harmony within societies but to enable societies to be sufficiently united to deter their enemies'...when Joshua killed twelve thousand heathen in a day and gave thanks to the Lord afterwards by carving the ten commandments in stone, including the phrase 'Thou shalt not kill', he was not being hypocritical. Like all good group-selectionists, the Jewish God was as severe towards the out-group as he was moral to the in-group".

The tragedy of commonsense morality was tragic enough in the historical world, in which social groups were often separated by geography and relatively self-contained, meaning that, much as one social group might disagree with the moral norms of another, a policy of "live and let live" was at least practicable. It is of existential importance in our modern world, inter-connected as we increasingly are in both a physical and virtual sense. It is not overstating the case to assert that effective cooperation across societies, at the level of the human species, is increasingly a requirement; not simply to capture the benefits of scale that we have seen that cooperation typically brings but also, perhaps more important, to avert the catastrophic downside risks of a "tragedy of the global commons" arising from the impact of 8 billion and counting increasingly-industrialised and technologically-capable humans on the planet.

Greene summarises, on pp25-6 of *Moral Tribes*: "two moral tragedies threaten human well-being. The original tragedy is the Tragedy of the Commons. This is a tragedy of selfishness, a failure of individuals to put Us ahead of Me. Morality is nature's solution to this problem. The new tragedy, the modern tragedy, is the Tragedy of Commonsense Morality, the problem of life on the new pastures. Here morality is undoubtedly part of the solution, but it's also part of the problem. In the modern tragedy, the very same moral thinking that enables cooperation within groups undermines cooperation between groups...Us versus Them".

The challenge, then, is twofold.

As individuals, we need to beware our instinctive tendency to categorise other people into "ingroups" and "outgroups", and the largely unconscious bias which flows from this to assume that ingroup members are somehow inherently "good" and outgroup members "bad" or even "subhuman".

As societies, we must face the fact that we cannot rely on our inherited moral instincts to promote global mutual understanding, world peace or a universal brotherhood of humankind. Rather, we need to accept that moral differences between groups are an inevitability, practice tolerance where we believe differences can reasonably co-exist, and find constructive ways to resolve differences where this is not the case.

Both challenges are made all the greater, of course, by the emotive nature of the topic - the important role that moral norms play in helping define the identity of each group, and of each of us as individual group members; and the correspondingly strong emotional defence mechanisms which are likely to be triggered when changes are required.

6 *Moral norms are not stable, but rather change over time.*

The challenge of change is made all the more acute by the fact that moral codes must and do themselves evolve over time, to take account of changing contexts, societal circumstances and preferences. An obvious example is slavery, regarded by most of antiquity as simply part of the natural order, and now universally abhorrent in the modern industrial world.

In chapter 2 we saw that we continue to learn and, potentially, to grow as individuals throughout the course of our lives. The same is true for our personal moral compass: as we ourself change, and the world we live in changes, we need to remain open to revisiting and where appropriate changing our moral attitudes.

This is not likely to be easy, of course, because as we have seen many of these instincts are buried in our subconscious mind, and changes will potentially trigger strong emotions since the underlying beliefs may be integral to our sense of personal identity. This is presumably why the contemporary "culture wars" engender such strength of feeling on all sides. Still, movements like #metoo and #blacklivesmatter, alongside more amorphous voices challenging for example those of us who live in former imperial powers to question this legacy, invite us to reexamine some pillars of our personal moral framework. We surely do well to embrace this opportunity with an open mind, paying particular attention to the ingroup/outgroup biases which may lurk below the surface of our conscious mind, and anticipating the emotional barriers we are likely to experience in contemplating personal change.

Beyond this, as a modern society at the point we have reached in human history we find ourselves confronted by a large number of important questions that no previous society has faced, certainly not in anything like their contemporary form, and which none of our historical moral codes is designed for or adequate to address. These issues are not necessarily entirely, or even mainly, moral in nature; but there is nonetheless a moral discussion to be had in each. Our challenge as a society, therefore, is not simply to navigate "the tragedy of commonsense morality" with respect to differences in existing moral norms, but also to develop satisfactory new norms which respond to these pressing new questions. For example:

- how to deploy and regulate artificial intelligence in a host of applications including military.

- how to address the potential global existential crisis relating to biodiversity and climate change, and the natural environment more broadly.
- how to address social inequality, especially in a world where we face a realistic prospect that machines will increasingly take over many jobs previously done by humans, without necessarily creating offsetting opportunities for those who are displaced.
- whether and how to embrace technological advances in the field of genetics, for example in areas such as genetically-modified crops, animals and, especially, humans.
- whether and in what circumstances to engage in "assisted dying", especially considering that ageing populations coupled with medical advances increasingly make it possible that longevity can far outrun quality of life, and that a life otherwise well-lived can end in considerable but avoidable pain and distress in the final months or even years.
- birth regulation and control, including the fraught questions surrounding abortion particularly in a world where medical advances mean that foetuses which would historically have been unviable no longer are but the individuals who are born as a result may have unavoidably low quality of life.
- personal privacy in the digital information age.
- and so on, and on...

The overall point is that morality is not and cannot be static or somehow immutable. The times they are a changin', and our challenge is to change with them, as individuals and societies. What is more, many of the specific moral challenges we face are new. They apply broadly across many social groups, and in at least some cases are likely to require effective global cooperation to solve. We may look to past traditions, and to our own moral instincts, for guidance. But we cannot expect the past to provide clear, robust answers, even if we could be confident that our inherited traditions and instincts were broadly consistent across social groups, which as we have seen they are not.

PART C: Practical implications

Human consciousness gives us the ability to exercise some level of existential choice over our life and, in particular, our own behaviour; and many of our most important choices relate to whether to behave prosocially or "selfishly". We each possess a powerful moral instinct, the general effect of which is to encourage us to behave prosocially but which is also susceptible to a number of complications exist which, taken together, mean that we cannot always trust our moral instincts when it comes to deciding how to behave.

How to proceed in light of this? We'll close the chapter by discussing four potential implications for each of us as individuals:

- *Embrace a moral principle*: to help us simplify, without of course falling into the trap of being simplistic.

- *Live and let live*, as far as realistically possible: accept the reality that different groups are likely to have different norms, whilst remaining open to confronting, in a constructive way, situations where competing norms are fundamentally incompatible or socially divisive.

- *Let reason, not emotion, determine the answer to complex moral issues*: Joshua Greene proposes a process he calls "Deep Pragmatism", or alternatively "Enlightened Utilitarianism".

- *"Mind the gap"*: exercise our freedom to use the "space" between a stimulus and our response – in this case, by engaging our rational brain to help determine our behaviour in a particular situation, rather than reacting purely on the basis of an unfiltered moral instinct or emotion.

Embrace a moral principle

We are free to choose our own moral principle or principles, at least in theory. Indeed, we might think of this as one of the most important personal existential choices we can make. In practice, of course our choices are likely to be limited to principles which are compatible with the social groups in which we live.

What are some options?

The leading candidate is surely The Golden Rule, which we briefly discussed earlier in the chapter. The biblical formulation of this is: "do unto others as you would have them do unto you". As we also discussed, however, the underlying idea is by no means exclusive to Christianity but rather has many formulations across many cultures, certainly pre-dating the New Testament. It therefore has a legitimate claim, if not quite to universality, then at least to saliency across a wide range of human populations and eras.

A second, or perhaps supplementary, candidate principle is the sentiment memorably enshrined in the American Declaration of Independence: "we regard this truth as self-evident, that all men (nowadays we might prefer to say all people) are created equal". It is a seductive claim. It is manifestly untrue, of course. Some people are born with the genes to be taller and stronger than others; some with the potential to be more intelligent, or cunning; and some are born into wealth and privilege and others into poverty and challenge. Still, if we interpret the phrase as meaning something like "all people matter equally in terms of their individual existence", then this is hard to beat as a moral principle on which to construct the rules for a civilised society.

Beyond these two standout candidate principles, there have been various attempts to catalogue "universal" moral norms observed across multiple cultures, somewhat echoing the musings of Pinker and Rosenberg earlier in this chapter. Such norms might legitimately be said to be universal not because they can be objectively "proven" but simply because they are empirically observed in a majority of human societies. For example, the University of Oxford highlights *Seven moral rules found all around the world*, in an article of that name published on the university website dated 11 February 2019. These are: "help your family, help your group, return favours, be brave, defer to superiors, divide resources fairly, and respect other's property". The entry comments that: "the rules...were found in a survey of 60 cultures from all around the world...the research found, first, that these seven cooperative behaviours were always considered morally good. Second, examples of most of these morals were found in most societies. Crucially, there were no counter-examples – no societies in which any of these behaviours were considered morally bad. And third, these morals were observed with equal frequency across continents; they were not the exclusive preserve of 'the west' or any other region".

Alternatively, the website *verywellmind* website lists the following suggestions, in an entry titled *Types of Moral Principles and Examples of Each*, dated 14 March 2023:

- Don't kill
- Speak the truth
- Be careful what you say and do to others
- Respect the property of others
- Treat people in need or distress as we would want to be treated if our situation were reversed

Of course, to be memorable a moral principle must be short, but this inevitably risks it becoming simplistic. And as we have seen the devil is often in the detail when it comes to interpreting the implication of a particular moral norm for the nuanced demands of a specific situation. As we discussed earlier, for example, "don't kill" will almost certainly serve us well in the overwhelming majority of situations we are (hopefully) likely to encounter, but it is also easy to think of extreme circumstances in which it might not prove inviolable.

In sum, we may find it helpful to embrace our own moral principle, or short list of principles, to help guide our existential choices; the caveat being that whatever we land on we will then need to apply judiciously in the hurly-burly of everyday reality.

Live and let live

A basic policy of tolerance is the logical response to the doctrine of moral relativism: the belief that morality is fundamentally a human construct; that different social groups develop different norms as part of their culture and group identity; and that there is no truly objective way to determine that one moral norm is inherently "better" than another.

And tolerance is surely the appropriate default response for a wide range of moral differences. For example, eating certain meats, or even meat of any kind, is proscribed in some cultures and not in others; some cultures embrace alcohol and soft drugs whilst others do not; the same can be said of gambling; and there are wide variations in what is considered acceptable in terms of dress code and body adornment. We may of course be able to think of particular instances of some of these things which we might personally consider to be beyond the pale: eating dogs springs to mind as one example in the canine-loving "West". But in general it is hard to make a case that other people should do as we do just because we happen to have grown up that way, any more than we feel inclined to abandon our own distinctive practices just because others do it differently.

Tolerance is of course easier to practice when people live in relatively closed societies, so that out of sight can largely also be out of mind. This was the situation throughout most of human history, when individual communities and cultures tended to be separated geographically with limited opportunity even to communicate, much less intermingle. Admittedly, many pre-modern empires held sway over vast territories and peoples, but even then it was generally possible for particular cultures to live largely in isolation from one another in their day-to-day lives.

In today's more inter-connected, multi-cultural world, a policy of tolerance alone is more challenging to sustain, however; the problem being that the Tragedy of Commonsense Morality may drive sub-groups apart, potentially inflaming passions and threatening social cohesion. To take an extreme, hypothetical, example, it would clearly not be acceptable that a particular group in one part of town practiced human sacrifice whilst all other citizens were expected to go calmly about their everyday business. We might feel the same way about so-called "honour" killing.

Less dramatically, as discussed earlier we may accept that there is no philosophical basis for asserting that polygamy is objectively "wrong", but this does not imply that it would be desirable, or acceptable, behaviour if practiced by adherents of a particular culture living in a broader society which in general opposes it. Similar arguments might apply to any number of other topics, such as the persecution of adulterers, people engaging in premarital sex, homosexuality, and so on. For completeness, it is possible to make the same argument in reverse – if we happen to live in a society which endorses some or all these things, we might consider it a problem that some sub-groups do not.

The critical point for now is the potential that incompatible moral norms have to be socially divisive. What to do when this is the case?

We must obviously guard against an instinctive assumption that "our" morality is somehow inherently or automatically better than "theirs", simply because it is "ours". We must also recognise that whatever differences exist are likely to engender strong emotions on both sides, possibly linking to notions of personal and group identity. Still, whilst a bias towards tolerance as our default response may be appropriate, a policy of "always tolerate" has its limitations, rather as Axelrod shows that a strategy of "always cooperate" is unsustainable and naive in most environments.

If social cohesion is really threatened then we need a sensible way to resolve whatever differences may exist, and for this we will turn to an approach suggested by Joshua Greene, which he calls "Deep Pragmatism".

Let reason, not emotion, determine the answer to complex moral issues.

Deep Pragmatism advocates that the most practical way to resolve substantive moral difference is to strive to put emotion to one side and instead use reason as the mediating force. Of course, this is only likely to work if all the relevant parties themselves engage rationally, and as we have already seen this may itself present a substantial challenge given the strength of emotion which moral issues often engender.

Be that as it may, Deep Pragmatism proposes a process in which the net impact of alternative solutions to a particular moral issue are weighed in the balance. Greene proposes that the fundamental measure - what he calls the "common currency" - should be the impact each solution has on the overall quality of human experience, calculated by multiplying the scale of impact by the number of people impacted, of course subtracting out any negative impacts, and crucially counting each individual as having equal significance.

Deep Pragmatism is based on the philosophical tradition of Utilitarianism, as Greene acknowledges. This is best remembered for the phrase used by its founder, the 18th century English philosopher and social reformer Jeremy Bentham, on p393 of his 1776 book *A Comment on the Commentaries and a Fragment on Government*: "it is the greatest happiness of the greatest number that is the measure of right and wrong". *The Stanford Encyclopedia of Philosophy* describes Utilitarianism as: "one of the most powerful and persuasive approaches to normative ethics in the history of philosophy...though there are many varieties of the view discussed, utilitarianism is generally held to be the view that the morally right action is the action that produces the most good...on the utilitarian view one ought to maximise the overall good – that is, consider the good of others as well as one's own good" (this appears in an entry called *The History of Utilitarianism*, first published 27 March 2009 and substantively revised 22 September 2014).

An important feature of Utilitarianism is that it is consequentialist, that is, it focuses ultimately on the *impact* of a particular action. It does not seek to assert that something is inherently "right" or "wrong", but rather that its "rightness" or "wrongness" is a consequence of the impact it has. Greene points out that this means that it lends itself to logical analysis: the conclusions it reaches are susceptible to, and indeed depend on, careful examination of whatever evidence may be available about actual or projected outcomes.

A second important feature is that the Utilitarian calculus treats all individuals as having equal weight, in line with the "self-evident" belief expressed in the American Declaration of Independence. In the entry referenced above, *The Stanford Encyclopedia of Philosophy* describes Utilitarianism as being: "distinguished by impartiality and agent-neutrality. Everyone's happiness counts the same...my good counts for no more than anyone else's good. Further, the reason I have to promote the overall good is the same reason anyone else has to so promote the good. It is not peculiar to me".

In this important respect Utilitarianism echoes the view of another influential 18th century philosopher, Immanuel Kant, described by *The Stanford Encyclopedia of Philosophy* as "the central figure in modern philosophy", in its entry titled *Immanuel Kant*, first published 20 May 201 and substantively revised 28 July 2020. Kant is celebrated for his assertion of the Categorical Imperative, introduced in his 1785 book *Groundwork of the Metaphysics of Morals*, and formulated as "act only according to that maxim by which you can at the same time will that it should become a universal law", and also as: "so act as to treat humanity, whether in your own person or in another, always as an end and never only as a means".

It is worth highlighting in passing that in other important ways Kant's thinking was quite different. His ambition was to create a deontological moral framework, which is to say one in which the consideration of whether a particular action is right or wrong can be made in strictly abstract terms by refence to objectively-derived rules, and not by subjective reference to its consequences as is the case for Utilitarianism. As we have already seen, and notwithstanding Kant's brilliance, a deontological approach is ultimately doomed to fail because morality is a human construct, with no truly objective basis in nature more broadly. The point here is therefore simply that both Kant and Utilitarianism align on the specific, important, principle that all individuals should be regarded as being equal when weighing the impact of moral choices.

In Bentham's original formulation of Utilitarianism, the currency which morality should seek to optimise is human happiness, the focus of our next, and final, chapter. For now, Bentham himself framed happiness in terms of maximising "pleasure" and minimising "pain", imagining these in fairly concrete, even hedonistic terms. For example, in his 1780 book *An Introduction to the Principles of Morals and Legislation*, Bentham asserts, on p1 of the section called *Of the Principle of Utility*: "nature has placed mankind under the governance of two sovereign masters, pain and pleasure. It is for them alone to point out what we ought to do, as well as to determine what we shall do. On the one hand the standard of right and wrong, on the other the chain of causes and effects, are fastened to their throne. They govern us in all we do, in all we say, in all we think...".

The 19th century British philosopher John Stuart Mill refined Bentham's approach in important ways, in particular introducing the idea that not all pleasures should be regarded as equal, but that we might rather conceive of a hierarchy of "higher" and "baser" pleasures, with higher ones obviously carrying more weight in the calculation of ultimate utility. Mill did not, however, dilute the principle that all individuals should be given equal weight.

And modern thinking, admittedly inspired by ideas first formulated in Ancient Greece, broadens Bentham's definition of happiness beyond just pleasure and pain, to include what in Chapter 5 we will call "wellbeing" and which Greene terms "experience".

Building on these foundations and returning to Deep Pragmatism as a methodology, on p149 of *Moral Tribes* Greene consolidates the historical thinking down to a succinct principle with which to resolve moral questions: "...simply do *whatever works best*" (Greene's emphasis). Lest this sound too simplistic, he adds some important qualifiers, on p153: "Utilitarianism is more than an injunction to be pragmatic. First, 'pragmatism' may imply a preference for short-term expediency over long-term interests. This is not what we have in mind. Utilitarianism says that we should do whatever *really* (again, Greene's emphasis) works best, in the long run, and not just for the moment. Second, 'pragmatism' may suggest nothing more than a flexible management style, one that can be deployed in the service of any values. A staunch individualist and a staunch collectivist could both be 'pragmatists' in the colloquial sense. Utilitarianism, by contrast, is about core values. It's about taking 'pragmatism' all the way down to the level of first principles. It begins with a core commitment to doing whatever works best, whatever that turns out to be, and even if it goes against one's tribal instincts".

Greene highlights the importance of taking a consequentialist approach: "consequentialism says that consequences – 'results,' as a pragmatist might say - are the only things that ultimately matter. Here the word "ultimately" is very important. It's not that things other than consequences - things like being honest, for example - don't matter, but rather that other things matter, when they do, because of *their* (Greene's emphasis) consequences".

Finally, Greene addresses the topic of happiness as the ultimate metric of success, anticipating some of the discussion we will have in the next chapter by redefining it as experience more broadly, and celebrating it as a "common currency" which can then be used to assess alternative solutions to a particular moral problem: "if we combine the idea that happiness is what matters with the idea that we should try to maximise good consequences, we get utilitarianism" (*Moral Tribes* p155). On pp156, 160 and 161 he asserts that: "what utilitarian philosophers mean by 'happiness' is far broader than what we think of when we think about 'happiness'...happiness is not (just) ice cream and warm summer evenings at the lake house. One's happiness is the overall quality of one's experience, and to value happiness is to value everything that improves the quality of experience, for oneself and for others – and especially for others whose lives leave much room for improvement...the utilitarian conception of happiness is very broad, encompassing all positive aspects of experience as well as the removal of negative aspects...Bentham and Mill's real insight, in my opinion – is that happiness is the *common currency* (Greene's emphasis) of human values".

Greene explains the full details of the Deep Pragmatism methodology in Chapter 11 of *Moral Tribes*, the penultimate chapter, and readers who may want a complete explanation are referred there.

The headline is that when faced with a challenging moral question Greene advocates that we should engage in a strictly rational assessment of which of the various solutions will deliver the greatest net good (or "happiness", broadly defined along the lines of "experience") for the greatest number of people, putting aside our intuitions and emotions as far as we are able.

He provides a worked example using the vexed, and emotive, question of abortion. This case study occupies 18 pages of his book, from p309 to p327, and it is impossible to do full justice to it in a short discussion here. Nonetheless, for readers who may not have time for or access to the original, I'll attempt a summary.

Greene first considers, and rejects, the main arguments typically used to support the main competing positions: "pro-choice", specifically, a woman's right to choose what happens to her body, including to have an abortion if that is what she wants; and "pro-life", a foetus's right to life, and therefore anti-abortion. His point is that neither camp succeeds in advancing a truly compelling argument, because both are typically ultimately appealing to deontological, rights-based arguments which can neither be proved nor in any meaningful way analysed or compared. For example, he highlights the logical inconsistency of a "pro-choice" stance that abortions during the first trimester are acceptable whereas abortions during the third trimester are not; and demonstrates that the biological evidence does not support a "pro-life" belief that something magical, such as what Greene calls "ensoulment", happens at the moment of conception, and that there is therefore no logical basis for concluding that a fertilised egg is somehow sacred in a way that an unfertilised one, or indeed an individual sperm, is not.

Greene explores the psychology of abortion, noting in particular our inherent aversion to doing harm to a creature with recognisably human movement and features, especially eyes. He suggests that this is why a "pro-choice" advocate might be accepting of an early-stage abortion, when the foetus resembles "just a cluster of cells", but uncomfortable with a late-term abortion, by which time the foetus looks and to some extent even behaves like a "real baby". This poses a practical problem of course, because "looking babylike is a matter of degree": the change is gradual and there is no specific moment when the foetus changes from being a "cluster of cells" to a "real baby".

He describes, on p222, how Deep Pragmatism focuses not on appeals to "rights" but rather on the potential consequences of alternative options: "...we start with a different set of questions: What happens if we restrict legal access to abortion? What happens if we don't? And what impact would these policies have on our lives?".

Then Greene works systematically through the answers to these questions. To give a flavour, also from p222: "these are complex empirical questions, difficult to answer, but we can begin with some educated guesses...If abortion were outlawed, people would adjust their behaviour in one of three general ways. First, some people would change their sexual behaviour. Some would abstain from sex completely, at least for a time. Others would have sex less frequently, and others would take further measures to reduce the likelihood of pregnancy. Second, some people would seek abortions by other means, illegally or abroad. Third, some people would give birth to babies who would otherwise not be born. Of these people, some would give their babies up for adoption and some would choose to raise these children themselves".

Greene keeps digging, exploring the likely second and third-order consequences of these behaviourial changes. One passage, from p323, will suffice to give a flavour: "how does all of this add up? Let's start with people who change their sexual behaviour. For most adults, nonprocreative sex is a highly enjoyable and fulfilling part of life. Nonprocreative sex is a major source of happiness, not only for the young and the restless, but for couples in stable monogamous relationships. For fertile couples, non-procreative sex is made possible by contraception, but as we all know, contraception provides no guarantee, even when used responsibly. Thus, for millions of sexually active adults, the option to have an abortion provides an important safeguard against unwanted pregnancy...on the other side of the pragmatic ledger, some sex is harmful, and there might be less harmful sex if abortion were outlawed. Examples of harmful sex include emotionally damaging sex between consenting adults, sex between teenagers who are not emotionally ready to have sex, incest, and rape. Avoiding sex for fear of pregnancy might also have the beneficial side-effect of reducing the spread of sexually transmitted disease. What's less clear is whether outlawing abortion would substantially reduce the amount of harmful sex. It seems unlikely that rapists will be deterred by the knowledge that their victims couldn't get abortions. Certainly, outlawing abortion would prevent some teenagers from having sex, though it's not clear whether this would be, on balance, good or bad. The teenagers who are most mindful of the consequences of their choices are, presumably, the ones who are most ready to be sexually, active...in sum, when it comes to changing people's sexual behaviour, making abortion illegal would take a big toll on millions of sexually active adults without any clear, compensating benefit, as measured in terms of happiness".

He takes a similar approach to explore the potential consequences of a range of related questions, including for example policy alternatives to abortion and the impact of higher birth rates were abortion to be outlawed.

Eventually, Greene reaches a conclusion. On p326, 17 pages into his case study, he comes down in favour of a pro-choice approach not too different from the legal policy which prevails in most, although certainly not all, industrial countries today: "disrupting people's sex lives, disrupting people's life plans, and forcing people to seek international or illegal abortions are all very bad things that would make many people's lives much worse, and in some cases much shorter. And that's why, in the end, I believe that deep pragmatists should be pro-choice. I make no appeal to 'rights,' just to a realistic consideration of the consequences".

We may or may not agree with Greene's specific answer, our reaction likely reflecting at least partly our starting position on the issue and the degree to which we are successful or not in suspending the emotions with which we are almost certainly invested. The point, though, is not to strive for consensus on abortion specifically, but rather to illustrate Deep Pragmatism as a process, and hopefully show how a rigorous, dispassionate analysis of alternatives and consequences can provide a practical way for people who may have very different starting points to engage constructively and have the best chance of resolving otherwise irreconcilable differences.

Greene acknowledges that engaging in Deep Pragmatism is likely to feel uncomfortable precisely because it is a rational process and our moral feelings tend to be highly instinctual and emotive. He therefore suggests that we reserve Deep Pragmatism just for the most complex and socially divisive moral questions, which he labels questions of "Us versus Them". It may of course also be helpful as we contemplate the kinds of emerging moral questions which we referenced earlier, and which are not yet divisive but certainly have the potential to be, for example the ethics of Artificial Intelligence, genetic engineering and so on.

Greene advocates that for more straightforward moral choices, which is to say those that more naturally fall within the norms of our own particular social group and involve only other members of this group, we should continue to rely on our gut instincts as a reliable behavioural prompt: "when the problem is Me versus Us (or Me versus You), we should trust our moral gut reactions, also known as *conscience* (Greene's emphasis): don't lie or steal, even when your manual mode thinks it can justify it. Cheat on neither your taxes nor your spouse. Don't 'borrow' money from the office cash drawer...when it's Me versus Us, trust your automatic settings (the moral ones, not the greedy ones!)".

Finally, Greene considers appeals to human rights as an alternative way to resolve moral differences. He is ultimately dismissive of "rights", and their companion concept, "duties", because he points out that they tend to enshrine an instinctive feeling about something and then render it inaccessible for rational debate,. As one example, on p302 of *Moral Tribes* he points out that: "appeals to 'rights' function as an intellectual free pass, a trump card that renders evidence irrelevant". Deep Pragmatism, by contrast, is not only open to but critically dependent on finding and appropriately scrutinising whatever relevant evidence is available. Green summarises, on p304 of *Moral Tribes*: "the difference...is that claims about what will or won't promote the greater good, unlike claims about rights, are ultimately accountable to *evidence* (Greene's emphasis)".

For completeness, Greene goes on to acknowledge the role that some rights causes play in advancing what most people would agree to be a moral agenda. He concludes that, whilst the concept of rights is not helpful in resolving moral questions where there are genuine grounds for disagreement, it can nonetheless sometimes be helpful as a metaphorical "weapon" with which to bludgeon those who continue to resist a position which is otherwise broadly accepted. For example, on p305: "what about selling little girls into prostitution? What about torturing people for expressing their beliefs?...arguing about rights may be pointless, but sometimes arguing is pointless. Sometimes what you need is not arguments, but weapons. And that's when it's time to stand up for rights".

So there we have it. When tolerance is not a viable option, Greene's Deep Pragmatism offers a rational, evidence-based way to resolve moral differences. The critical requirement is that we set aside our instincts and emotions and engage reason instead, something which is admittedly easy to say but demonstrably hard to do.

"Mind the gap" between moral instinct and behavioural response.

Thus far in this section we have focused mainly on what we might call Big Moral Questions. But we should not close without recognising that there are also many moments in our everyday life when we experience a flash of moral emotion and must decide in the moment how to react. Perhaps someone pushes ahead of us in a queue, or drops out of a commitment at short notice, or with what we consider insufficient apology, or an apology which we feel to be inadequate or insincere. Or someone takes the only chocolate biscuit from the plate as it passes among the group when we have been silently eyeing it and hoping it would reach us, and surely everyone knows we are partial to a chocolate biscuit...the list of potential triggers is virtually infinite, and often infinitely trivial.

It is entirely natural, indeed inevitable, that we should experience such feelings. The question is therefore not how to avoid them, but rather what to do when they occur, the risk obviously being that our subconscious moral instinct prompts us to behave in the heat of the moment in a way that we subsequently regret.

And it is precisely at such times that we do well, yet again, to heed the advice of Viktor Frankl to "mind the gap" between a stimulus, in this case our moral instinct, and how we choose to respond. As a reminder from Chapter 2: ""between stimulus and response lies a space. In that space lie our freedom and power to choose a response. In our response lies our growth and our happiness".

Chapter summary

As we contemplate our existential choices between "cooperation" and "competition" we cannot help but be influenced by our moral instincts. These are innate, exert a powerful influence on our emotions and our behaviour, and often operate at a level below that of our conscious mind. At the same time, morality is a product of human evolution, not a fundamental Law of Nature. It is ultimately for us each to decide as individuals when and how to respond to our moral instincts and "to our own self be true".

Specific "beliefs" about morality include:

- Morality is a fundamental aspect of what it is to be human, to the extent that to seek to deny it would literally be to be "inhuman" in some important sense.
- Morality serves to regulate behaviour with human social groups, generally reinforcing cooperation in preference to competition, at least between members of the same group albeit not necessarily between different groups.
- All "neurologically normal" humans share some high-level moral instincts to a greater or lesser degree, including for example a capacity for empathy for people with whom we feel some level of connection; and a sense of fairness, experienced mainly locally, which is to say with respect to others whom we perceive are similar to us.
- However, specific moral norms vary widely across cultures.
- Several factors complicate our ability to apply moral instinct in our everyday life, including:

– morality is ultimately a human construct, not an absolute law of nature. One important implication is that morality is relative: there is no truly objective basis on which to demonstrate that one set of moral norms is superior to another.

– moral instinct is instinctive – we feel first, and reason later. Often, the role our rational brain plays is simply to provide a post-hoc narrative to justify actions which have in reality been prompted by our subconscious mind.

– our instincts do not always prompt us to behave "morally".

– morality is often nuanced and contextual: moral choices which seem intuitively clear may often turn out not to be on closer, rational, examination.

– morality typically prompts us to privilege other members of our own group at the expense of members of other groups, even prompting us to dehumanise people we regard as "other". This is "the tragedy of commonsense morality".

– moral norms are not stable, but rather change over time. Technological and social changes are creating important emergent moral questions for which there is no obvious historical precedent, and for which tradition is therefore unlikely to provide the answers.

- There are four potential implications for each of us as individuals:

– embrace a moral principle, for example The Golden Rule.

– live and let live, as far as realistically possible. Maintain humility and respect when confronting differences, and remain open to changing our own position on moral topics.

– let reason, not emotion, determine the answer to complex moral issues, specifically the Deep Pragmatism approach advocated by Joshua Greene.

– "mind the gap" between the emotional stimulus of a moral instinct and our behavioural response.

Chapter 5:

Happiness

"Live, love, laugh and be happy"
Harry Woods, 1926

"Happiness is the meaning and purpose of life, the whole aim and end of human existence". This stirring call to arms is attributed to Aristotle, expressed in his master work *Nicomachean Ethics*, written around 340 BCE. In this, final, chapter we'll embrace Aristotle's insight and explore the consequences for our own life.

The context is what we have seen in previous chapters to be the boundary conditions of our existence. As humans we are the product of an unequivocally material Universe; consciousness gives us the ability, and in an important sense the obligation, to exercise personal agency in choosing what we do and how we behave; we are primarily social animals, so that our relationships with other people and how we choose to behave towards them have particular significance; and our decisions are shaped by a powerful although often unconscious moral sense, which is ultimately relative and subjective and serves to bind us to others within our own group but also to set us apart from people we consider to be "other".

We will see that happiness is likely to lie mainly in embracing the business of everyday living, through a combination of maximising pleasure, broadly defined, and minimising pain; meeting our fundamental needs;

and ultimately creating our own personal "meaning" for our existence.

The good news is that happiness is eminently achievable. We are each unique and there is no single recipe for success, but we are nonetheless likely to find four things in particular helpful:

- achieving some threshold level of wealth, health and security;
- enhancing the quality and quantity of our personal relationships and sense of belonging;
- achievements which we find personally meaningful, and
- behaving in ways which are congruent with what we consider to be our authentic "Self".

Happiness is possible even in the most unpromising circumstances, although there is also no doubt that our environment influences the odds of success.

Last but not least, we must ultimately take responsibility for our own happiness. This is best exercised by adopting a positive but realistic attitude; embracing whatever opportunities our existence affords us; and cultivating a resilient, but not resigned, approach to confronting the setbacks and suffering which are an inescapable part of the human condition.

Of course, we will not prescribe categorical answers for what we should each ultimately do to achieve personal happiness. If you have made it through the book this far, it is hopefully abundantly clear already that our life choices are inherently personal and subjective. You are the only person who can choose how you should live your life, how you should behave in a given situation, and what will ultimately make you happy, remembering always that "if I do not choose, that is also a choice".

This may seem daunting, but is also a remarkable opportunity if once we are ready to take it.

PART A: Happiness as the goal of human existence

In part vii of Book 1 of the *Nicomachean Ethics* Aristotle explains that happiness can justifiably be regarded as the goal of human existence because it is the only thing that can truly be seen as an end in itself, rather than a means to some further end: "we always choose (happiness) for itself, and never for any other reason. It is different with honour, pleasure, intelligence and good qualities generally. We do choose them partly for themselves...but we choose them also for the sake of our happiness, in the belief that they will be instrumental in promoting it". He concludes, a few lines later: "happiness, then, is found to be something perfect and self-sufficient, being the (ultimate) end to which our actions are directed". (These quotes are taken from the JAK Thomson translation, first published in 1953.)

We saw earlier that Utilitarianism also celebrates happiness, appropriately defined, as the legitimate goal of existence and the basis for resolving questions of morality. Greene describes happiness as the "common currency of human values", on p161 of *Moral Tribes*.

And happiness is famously enshrined as an "unalienable right" in the US Declaration of Independence, drafted by Thomas Jefferson in 1776. Specifically: "we hold these truths to be self-evident, that all men are created equal, that they are endowed by their Creator with certain unalienable Rights, that among these are Life, Liberty and the pursuit of Happiness".

As an aside, Jefferson also asserted that the main aim of government should be to maximise the happiness of its citizens: "the care of human life and happiness...is the sole legitimate object of good government". And whilst the focus of this book is on the beliefs we might hold as individuals, and the consequences for our personal behaviours and actions, there is no question that governments, and other institutions, indeed have a vital role in creating an environment within which individual happiness can flourish.

In any case, it is hard to think of a reasonable alternative to happiness as an ultimate life goal. Religious tradition might offer options such as "the glorification of God" or "use this life to prepare for the next". But these obviously do not apply in a world where our starting point is that the Universe is entirely material and that neither God nor an afterlife exist.

There are surprisingly few alternative secular candidates. We might consider "the propagation of our species", which is logical from an evolutionary standpoint but clearly prosaic. Other possible options, such as seeking wisdom, or to "do good" in the world, tend to be susceptible to Aristotle's caveat that they can ultimately be argued to be at least partly means to the end of bringing us personal fulfilment and therefore happiness, even if they may also be desirable in their own right.

We will therefore not dedicate space to an extended discussion of whether a superior alternative to happiness exists as the goal of human existence. Rather, we will take Aristotle's assertion at face value and devote this chapter to exploring the implications for each of us as individuals, addressing questions such as: what do we mean by "happiness"?; what makes us believe it is achievable?; and, most important, what practical things can we do as individuals to build and sustain it?

PART B: Defining Happiness

Pain and pleasure

The most basic definition of happiness is to maximise pleasure and minimise pain.

This has a noble philosophical heritage stretching back at least to Ancient Greece. Early advocates included Aristippus, active around 400 BCE and founder of the Cyrenaic school; and Epicurus, active a little before 300 BCE, which is to say a few decades after Aristotle, who gave rise to the influential school which came to be known as Epicureanism, of particular interest to this book because surprisingly enough it was based squarely on a materialist view of the Universe. Epicureanism took as its starting point the atomic materialism of Democritus, who together with his mentor Leucippus first suggested, sometime around the low 400s BCE, that all matter in the Universe is composed of indivisible atoms with no need for any kind of supernatural explanation. And in the modern era Jeremy Bentham, the father of Utilitarianism, memorably described pain and pleasure as the "two sovereign masters", as we saw in the previous chapter.

To assert that happiness is intimately connected with pleasure is of course to beg the question how "pleasure" itself should be defined. This has been the subject of much debate through the ages, with general agreement that an appropriate definition entails something more than mere gratification of the senses.

Epicurus, for example, suggested that pleasure is the product of a simple, moderate lifestyle which focuses on minimising exposure to pain and fear whilst specifically avoiding sensory excess. Admittedly, this is not how he has come to be remembered, because in the ancient world Epicureanism faced a kind of Darwinian struggle against other philosophical schools, most notably Stoicism which ultimately prevailed; and Epicurus came to be characterised by his opponents as advocating unbridled hedonism. Somehow this reputation stuck, proof if any were needed that life can be unfair and history is often written by the eventual winners.

Aristotle also pointed out, somewhat sneeringly, the limitations of a life in which pleasure is defined merely as personal gratification: "the many, the most vulgar, seemingly conceive the good and happiness as pleasure, and hence they also like the life of gratification. Here they appear completely slavish, since the life they decide on is a life for grazing animals" (p7 of the 1985 translation of the *Nicomachean Ethics* by T Erwin).

To be clear, it is not that sensory pleasure is somehow inimical to happiness. Life is for living, after all, and there is much to be said for the enjoyment of a warm bath, a good meal, and the pleasures of the flesh more generally. And the feelings of "positive affect" that they engender are indeed associated with a broader experience of happiness, as we will shortly see. The point is not that these things are not pleasurable, then, nor that it is somehow wrong to enjoy them for what they are, but rather that experience shows that they are unlikely to be enough by themselves to satisfy us entirely.

An obvious enhancement is to expand our definition to include aesthetic pleasures: appreciating "beauty", for example in music or art, or in Nature more generally.

And studying the underlying neurochemistry enables us to make two further observations. First, *anticipation* of an expected reward stimulates the highest release of dopamine, the neurotransmitter most involved with our sensation of pleasure, more even than actually achieving the reward. This effect is not limited to our experience of pleasure: something similar happens with the anticipation of pain, in particular an effect known as "stress-induced hyperalgesia", described by Robert Sapolsky on p198 of *Why Zebras Don't Get Ulcers*: "just seeing the nurse take the cap off the hypodermic needle for the blood draw makes your arm throb".

Second, novelty also plays a role, so that we experience higher levels of pleasure from an experience which is relatively new than from the same experience once it has become familiar. This is not to say that it can't still be pleasurable, simply that the intensity is likely to reduce as familiarity increases. In the same way, experiences which we may find terrifying when we first encounter them become less so with repetition, for example making a parachute jump.

Our starting point, then, is that experiencing a combination of sensory and aesthetic pleasure whilst minimising our exposure to pain provides a foundation for happiness; and that both anticipation and novelty will tend to heighten the intensity of whatever positive or negative experiences we have.

Fundamental needs

Beyond our in-the-moment experience of pleasure or pain we also have a set of fundamental needs, and the extent to which we are able to satisfy these is likely to have a material effect on our happiness.

The seminal work on this topic is by the American psychologist Abraham Maslow, in particular his famous idea that we each have a personal "hierarchy of needs", and that happiness consists in progressively meeting these and hence ascending the hierarchy.

Maslow first introduced this concept in a paper called *A Theory of Human Motivation*, published in the *Psychological Review* in 1943. He continued to refine it until his untimely death in 1970. The specifics of

Maslow's work are not without controversy from a scientific perspective. Nonetheless, his influence continues to be considerable, and his core ideas to be widely embraced. We will therefore take some time to review them, including in due course reviewing the main scientific concerns.

We will draw heavily on the work of the British psychologist Saul McLeod and his article *Maslow's Hierarchy of Needs*, published by *Simply Psychology* and most recently updated 29 December 2020. All quotes in this section are from that article, unless specified otherwise.

Maslow's hierarchy of needs

Maslow's basic original ideas are that a hierarchy of fundamental human needs exists; that achieving happiness requires progressively meeting these needs; and that more "basic" needs, such as food and shelter, must be met before "higher" needs, such as say love and belonging, become truly relevant or realistically attainable. Conversely, as "basic" needs are met, so "higher" needs take on greater importance, with the highest level being what Maslow called "self-actualisation", loosely translated as achieving one's own personal full potential.

Maslow's proposed hierarchy defines a generic set of needs relevant to all humans. At the same time though, he suggests that in practice no individual has the same exact needs as any other. Rather, we each have our own unique profile, which is moreover likely to change over time as our life circumstances and we ourself change.

McLeod explains the "needs pyramid" thus: "Maslow's hierarchy of needs is a motivational theory in psychology comprising a five-tier model of human needs, often depicted as hierarchical levels within a pyramid. Needs lower down in the hierarchy must be satisfied before individuals can attend to needs higher up...Maslow posited that...'it is quite true that man lives by bread alone - when there is no bread. But what happens to man's desires when there is plenty of bread and when his belly is chronically filled? At once other (and 'higher') needs emerge and these, rather than physiological hungers, dominate the organism. And when these in turn are satisfied, again new (and still 'higher') needs emerge and so on. This is what we mean by saying that the basic human needs are organised into a hierarchy of relative prepotency' (Maslow, 1943, P375)".

McLeod summarises the needs, as articulated in Maslow's original, five-tiered pyramid. Maslow subsequently proposed some modifications, as we will shortly review. But the original is nonetheless often still used as the canonical version:

1. "*Physiological needs* - these are biological requirements for human survival, e.g. air, food, drink, shelter, clothing, warmth, sex, sleep. If these needs are not satisfied the human body cannot function optimally. Maslow considered physiological needs the most important as all the other needs become secondary until these needs are met.

2. *Safety needs* - once an individual's physiological needs are satisfied, the needs for security and safety become salient. People want to experience order, predictability and control in their lives. These needs can be fulfilled by the family and society (e.g. police, schools, business and medical care). For example, emotional security, financial security (e.g. employment, social welfare), law and order, freedom from fear, social stability, property, health and well-being (e.g. safety against accidents and injury).

3. *Love and belongingness needs* - after physiological and safety needs have been fulfilled, the third level of

human needs is social and involves feelings of belongingness. The need for interpersonal relationships motivates behaviour. Examples include friendship, intimacy, trust, and acceptance, receiving and giving affection and love, affiliating, being part of a group (family, friends, work).

4. *Esteem needs* are the fourth level in Maslow's hierarchy - which Maslow classified into two categories: (i) esteem for oneself (dignity, achievement, mastery, independence) and (ii) the desire for reputation or respect from others (e.g., status, prestige). Maslow indicated that the need for respect or reputation is most important for children and adolescents and precedes real self-esteem or dignity.

5. *Self-actualisation needs* are the highest level in Maslow's hierarchy, and refer to the realisation of a person's potential, self-fulfilment, seeking personal growth and peak experiences. Maslow (1943) describes this level as the desire to accomplish everything that one can, to become the most that one can be. Individuals may perceive or focus on this need very specifically. For example, one individual may have a strong desire to become an ideal parent. In another, the desire may be expressed economically, academically or athletically. For others, it may be expressed creatively, in paintings, pictures, or inventions".

We might note that the first and second level needs, physiological and safety, overlap at least partly with our discussion of pleasure and pain in the previous section; and the third level, "love and belongingness" with our innate predilection for sociability, which was the focus of Chapter 3. Be that as it may, Maslow characterised the first 4 levels of his pyramid as "deficit" needs, meaning that they arise due to deprivation, and that our motivation further to satisfy the need reduces the closer it comes to being met at some threshold level. For example, if we are hungry then we need to eat, but as we do so our need to continue eating reduces until finally we are completely satisfied, at least for a while. Conversely, Maslow characterised the fifth and highest need, "self-actualisation", as a "growth" need, meaning that the more of it we obtain the more we are likely to want.

It is important to reinforce that although the pyramid is represented as a hierarchy, and Maslow's initial suggestion was that an individual could not progress to meeting higher level needs until those on a lower level were fully met, he also suggested that progress is far from assured and it is entirely possible to move back down the levels. McLeod explains: "every person is capable and has a desire to move up the hierarchy toward a level of self-actualisation. Unfortunately, progress is often disrupted by a failure to meet lower level needs. Life experiences, including divorce and loss of a job, may cause an individual to fluctuate between levels of the hierarchy. Therefore, not everyone will move through the hierarchy in a uni-directional manner but may move back and forth between the different types of needs".

In any case, Maslow later modified his initial belief that the needs hierarchy is rigidly progressive, adopting a more dynamic view in which the relative importance of particular needs may vary with circumstance; and also that needs may act in combination rather than being entirely separate.

McLeod summarises: "Maslow (1943) initially stated that individuals must satisfy lower level deficit needs before progressing on to meet higher level growth needs. However, he later clarified that satisfaction of a need is not an 'all-or-none' phenomenon, admitting that his earlier statements may have given 'the false impression that a need must be satisfied 100 percent before the next need emerges' (1987, p69)... Maslow continued to refine his theory based on the concept of a hierarchy of needs over several decades (Maslow, 1943, 1962, 1987)...regarding the structure of his hierarchy, Maslow (1987) proposed that the order in the hierarchy 'is not nearly as rigid' (p. 68) as he may have implied in his earlier description...Maslow noted that the order of needs might be flexible based on external circumstances or individual differences. For example, he notes that for some individuals, the need for self-esteem is more important than the need for love. For others, the need for creative fulfilment may supersede even the most basic needs...Maslow (1987) also pointed out that most behaviour is multi-motivated and noted that 'any behaviour tends to be determined by several or all of the basic needs simultaneously rather than by only one of them' (p. 71)".

For completeness, Maslow eventually proposed new, more sophisticated versions of his pyramid, expanding from the original 5 levels to 7 and then 8. This can be confusing, since the original 5 level framework remains in wide circulation, as already noted. Still, McLeod points out that: "it is important to note that Maslow's (1943, 1954) five-stage model has been expanded to include cognitive and aesthetic needs (Maslow, 1970 a) and later transcendence needs (Maslow, 1970 b). Changes to the original five-stage model...include a seven-stage model and an eight-stage model; both developed during the 1960s and 1970s.

1. *Biological and physiological needs* - air, food, drink, shelter, warmth, sex, sleep, etc.

2. *Safety needs* - protection from elements, Security, order, law, stability, freedom from fear.

3. *Love and belongingness needs* - friendship, intimacy, trust, and acceptance, receiving and giving affection and love. Affiliating, being part of a group (family, friends, work).

4. *Esteem needs* - which Maslow classified into two categories: (i) esteem for oneself (dignity, achievement, mastery, independence) and (ii) the desire for reputational respect from others (e.g., status, prestige).

5. *Cognitive needs* - knowledge and understanding, curiosity, exploration, need for meaning and predictability.

6. *Aesthetic needs* - appreciation and search for beauty, balance, form, etc.

7. *Self-actualisation needs* - realising personal potential, self-fulfilment, seeking personal growth and peak experiences. A desire "to become everything one is capable of becoming" (Maslow, 1987, p. 64).

8. *Transcendence needs* - a person is motivated by values which transcend beyond the personal self (e.g., mystical experiences and certain experiences with nature, aesthetic experiences, sexual experiences, service to others, the pursuit of science, religious faith, etc)".

In this expanded model, "cognitive", "aesthetic" and "transcendence" are all characterised as "growth" needs in the same way as "self-actualisation", meaning that our appetite to meet the need continues to increase rather than ever being sated.

The critical point from our perspective is not so much the detail of how many levels or even which specific needs exist, but rather the general principles which underpin Maslow's thinking. McLeod proposes four of these, reflecting Maslow's more nuanced approach and incidentally also going a long way towards addressing the scientific criticism of his earlier work:

a) "human beings are motivated by a hierarchy of needs.

b) needs are organised in a hierarchy of prepotency in which more basic needs must be more or less met (rather than all or none) prior to higher needs.
c) the order of needs is not rigid but instead may be flexible based on external circumstances or individual differences.
d) most behaviour is multi-motivated, that is, simultaneously determined by more than one basic need".

Self-actualisation

"Self-actualisation" is the highest order need in Maslow's original 5 level pyramid and remained central to his thinking in subsequent versions. The idea builds on work by the German psychiatrist Kurt Goldstein earlier in the 20th century. Ultimately it harks back all the way to Aristotle, again, who asserted not simply that the goal of human existence is to achieve happiness but also that this can best be achieved through realising one's individual latent potential to the fullest possible extent – to become the best Self that one is capable of being.

The form that self-actualisation takes is specific to the individual, of course, because by definition our specific potential is unique to us. What is more, we have an important degree of personal agency in deciding which aspects of whatever potential we feel we possess should take priority. McLeod quotes Maslow's definition: "'it refers to the person's desire for self-fulfilment, namely, to the tendency for him to become actualised in what he is potentially. The specific form that these needs will take will of course vary greatly from person to person. In one individual it may take the form of the desire to be an ideal mother, in another it may be expressed athletically, and in still another it may be expressed in painting pictures or in inventions' (Maslow, 1943, p. 382-383)".

Maslow believed that only a small minority of people succeed in self-actualising, somehow quantifying this as roughly two per cent of the population. Happily, subsequent thinkers have taken a more optimistic view, as we will shortly discuss. Sticking with Maslow for now, though, he went on to identify the characteristics and behaviours which in his view defined successful self-actualisers. His list comes with a major health warning in that this aspect of his work is subject to particular criticism as lacking in scientific rigour. Still, anecdotal as we might consider it to be, the list is worth scanning as we look for creative inspiration relevant to our own life choices. Our source is again Saul McLeod's article:

Characteristics of self-actualisers:
1. They perceive reality efficiently and can tolerate uncertainty;
2. Accept themselves and others for what they are;
3. Spontaneous in thought and action;
4. Problem-centred (not self-centred);
5. Unusual sense of humour;
6. Able to look at life objectively;
7. Highly creative;
8. Resistant to enculturation, but not purposely unconventional;
9. Concerned for the welfare of humanity;
10. Capable of deep appreciation of basic life-experience;
11. Establish deep satisfying interpersonal relationships with a few people;
12. Peak experiences;
13. Need for privacy;
14. Democratic attitudes;
15. Strong moral/ethical standards

Behaviour leading to self-actualisation:
a) Experiencing life like a child, with full absorption and concentration;

b) Trying new things instead of sticking to safe paths;
c) Listening to your own feelings in evaluating experiences instead of the voice of tradition, authority or the majority;
d) Avoiding pretence ('gameplaying') and being honest;
e) Being prepared to be unpopular if your views do not coincide with those of the majority;
f) Taking responsibility and working hard;
g) Trying to identify your defences and having the courage to give them up.

Finally, although Maslow believed full self-actualisation to be an extremely rare occurrence, he did not suggest that it is a binary state of being; nor did he propose that an individual who successfully self-actualised was necessarily likely to be morally superior to others as a result. Rather, self-actualisation simply involves achieving, or "actualising", whatever it is that we personally identify as our full human potential. McLeod summarises: "...self-actualisation is a matter of degree, 'there are no perfect human beings' (Maslow, 1970a, p. 176)...it is not necessary to display all 15 characteristics to become self-actualised, and not only self-actualised people will display them. Maslow did not equate self-actualisation with perfection. Self-actualisation merely involves achieving one's potential. Thus, someone can be silly, wasteful, vain and impolite, and still self-actualise".

Critical assessment of Maslow's ideas

The main criticism of Maslow's work centres on the unscientific nature of some of his methodology, in particular his definition of the characteristics and behaviours associated with self-actualised people.

McLeod again provides the summary: "the most significant limitation of Maslow's theory concerns his methodology. Maslow formulated the characteristics of self-actualised individuals from undertaking a qualitative method called biographical analysis. He looked at the biographies and writings of 18 people he identified as being self-actualised. From these sources, he developed a list of qualities that seemed characteristic of this specific group of people, as opposed to humanity in general. From a scientific perspective, there are numerous problems with this particular approach. First, it could be argued that biographical analysis as a method is extremely subjective as it is based entirely on the opinion of the researcher. Personal opinion is always prone to bias, which reduces the validity of any data obtained. Therefore Maslow's operational definition of self-actualisation must not be blindly accepted as scientific fact...furthermore, Maslow's biographical analysis focused on a biased sample of self-actualised individuals, prominently limited to highly educated white males (such as Thomas Jefferson, Abraham Lincoln, Albert Einstein, William James, Aldous Huxley, Beethoven)...another criticism concerns Maslow's assumption that the lower needs must be satisfied before a person can achieve their potential and self-actualise. This is not always the case, and therefore Maslow's hierarchy of needs in some aspects has been falsified...through examining cultures in which large numbers of people live in poverty (such as India), it is clear that people are still capable of higher-order needs such as love and belongingness...also, many creative people, such as authors and artists (e.g., Rembrandt and Van Gogh) lived in poverty throughout their lifetime, yet it could be argued that they achieved self-actualisation".

These important criticisms notwithstanding, McLeod highlights that subsequent research validates Maslow's central thesis that universal needs exist across different human groups, whilst also reinforcing that these needs can operate on multiple levels rather than in a rigid hierarchy, a modification that Maslow himself came to embrace as we have seen: "...contemporary research by

Tay and Diener (2011) has tested Maslow's theory by analysing the data of 60,865 participants from 123 countries, representing every major region of the world. The survey was conducted from 2005 to 2010...respondents answered questions about six needs that closely resemble those in Maslow's model: basic needs (food, shelter); safety; social needs (love, support); respect; mastery; and autonomy. They also rated their well-being across three discrete measures: life evaluation (a person's view of his or her life as a whole), positive feelings (day-to-day instances of joy or pleasure), and negative feelings (everyday experiences of sorrow, anger, or stress)...the results of the study support the view that universal human needs appear to exist regardless of cultural differences. However, the ordering of the needs within the hierarchy was not correct. 'Although the most basic needs might get the most attention when you don't have them,' Diener explains, 'you don't need to fulfil them in order to get benefits (from the others)'. Even when we are hungry, for instance, we can be happy with our friends. 'They're like vitamins,' Diener says about how the needs work independently. 'We need them all'".

Self-actualisation for all

Carl Rogers, whom we met in Chapter 2 in connection with our concept of Self, democratised the idea of self-actualisation, suggesting that it is something to which we can *all* realistically aspire, in contrast to Maslow's view that it is accessible only to a tiny minority. What is more, Rogers proposed that self-actualisation is not simply the highest-order need, but dominates all the others.

Saul McLeod summarises again, this time from the entry on *Carl Rogers* in *Simply Psychology*, updated in 2014: "Carl Rogers...believed that humans have one basic motive, that is the tendency to self-actualise - i.e., to fulfil one's potential and achieve the highest level of 'human beingness' we can...Rogers believed that every person could achieve their goal".

McLeod also points out that for Rogers this striving to fulfil our personal potential is not just some lofty ambition but rather a critical part of our experience of everyday life: "'the good life is a process, not a state of being. It is a direction not a destination'. (Rogers, 1967, p. 187)".

Taking Maslow's and Rogers' ideas together, we may conclude that we each have a personal hierarchy of needs, which is likely to conform to a greater or lesser extent to the general hierarchy Maslow proposes; that our happiness will be enhanced by our ability to meet these needs over time; that if we are successful in meeting more basic needs our aspirations are likely to increase to encompass new ones; and that we can and should aspire to "self-actualise" as our ultimate goal, which is to say to realise our own personal full potential as a human being, accepting that it is for we ourself to define this potential.

Armed with these more sophisticated ideas about happiness, we are now ready to attempt an overall synthesis, specifically by redefining "happiness" more broadly as "wellbeing".

Happiness as wellbeing

Wellbeing as a concept essentially combines two philosophical approaches to happiness which yet again have their roots in Ancient Greece: "hedonia" and "eudaemonia", loosely translated as "pleasure" and "flourishing" respectively. As an aside, "hedonic" should not be confused with "hedonistic", which implies a focus on self-gratification, usually of the physical senses, and typically involving serial and unsustainable excess. But there is no reason why hedonic pleasures have to take this extreme form. Separately, "eudaemonia" is sometimes rendered as "eudaimonia" and also "eudemonia" – when quoting from other authors we will use whichever spelling they do.

The concept of hedonia is closely linked to our earlier discussion of pleasure and pain. American psychologist Cynthia Vinney explains, in an article titled *What's the Difference Between Eudaimonic and Hedonic Happiness?*, published on the *ThoughtCo* website and updated on 14 February 2020: "the idea of hedonia dates back to the fourth century B.C., when a Greek philosopher, Aristippus, taught that the ultimate goal in life should be to maximise pleasure...psychologists who study happiness from a hedonic perspective cast a wide net by conceptualising hedonia in terms of pleasures of both the mind and body. In this view, then, happiness involves maximising pleasure and minimising pain".

The concept of eudaemonia traces back to Aristotle, again, and finds echoes in Maslow's notion of self-actualisation. Vinney comments, in the same article referenced above: "like hedonia, the concept of eudaemonia dates back to the fourth century B.C., when Aristotle first proposed it in his work, *Nicomachean Ethics*. According to Aristotle, to achieve happiness, one should live their life in accordance with their virtues. He claims people are constantly striving to meet their potential and be their best selves, which leads to greater purpose and meaning".

British psychologist Catherine Moore provides more details in her article *What is Eudaemonia? Aristotle and Eudaemonic Well-Being*, published on *Positive Psychology.com* on 5 March 2021: "the distinction between eudaemonia and hedonia is examined in great depth by Huta and Waterman in their 2013 review of the happiness literature. For those after a quick, broad distinction between the two, here are the authors' given examples of eudaemonia, based on literature review:

- authenticity;
- excellence;
- meaning; and
- growth.

Contrast and compare these with their examples of hedonia, and you'll see that very, very roughly, the second is much less value-laden and is somewhat more experiential:

- an absence of distress;
- comfort;
- enjoyment; and
- pleasure.

...with regard to hedonia, while 'absence of distress' wasn't always an important element, '... there is a clear consensus that pleasure/enjoyment/life satisfaction is core to the definition' (Huta & Waterman, 2013, p.1448)".

Modern research shows that these two components of happiness are not in opposition to each other. People who strive for a combination of hedonic and eudaemonic wellbeing are more likely to "flourish" than people who focus just on one or the other, or indeed neither. Moore comments, in the same article referenced above: "according to Schotanus-Dijkstra and colleagues (2016), flourishing describes people who have both high levels of EWB (note: this acronym stands for "Eudaemonic WellBeing"), *and* (my emphasis) hedonic well-being. While activities related to both are shown to be important for 'flourishers', it's interesting to note that even having the intention to pursue both may impact on our well-being (Huta & Ryan, 2010). That is, out of four groups (hedonic motives only, eudaimonic motives only, both, or no motives at all)...individuals with both high hedonic and high eudaimonic motives – as compared to individuals in the other three groups – had the most favourable outcomes".

Finally, the question of timespan is relevant. It is good to be happy for an hour, or a day; but obviously much preferable to be happy for a lifetime, or at least for a majority of it. Aristotle, again, was early to appreciate this. In section vii of Book 1 of the *Nicomachean Ethics* he observes that: "one swallow does not make a summer; neither does one day. Similarly neither can one day, or a brief space of time, make a man blessed and happy".

Lifespan is also important in a more technical sense when comparing happiness across populations, for example across countries, perhaps with a view to formulating policy recommendations to help governments increase the happiness of their people as Jefferson advises. The British-based economists Richard Layard and Ekaterina Oparina amplify this point, in Chapter 8 of the *World Happiness Report 2021*, titled *Living Long and Living Well: the WELLBY approach*: "most accounts of well-being focus on the experience of the living. But, if we are to judge the overall welfare of a country, we must also consider how long people live...the well-being approach to these issues is simple. People want to live well, and they want to live long. Therefore, we should judge a society by the extent to which it enables people to experience lives that are long and full of well-being. For any individual, the measure of this is simply the well-being she experiences each year summed up over all the years that she lives". A refinement is to take into account not just total lifespan but also "healthy lifespan", since unsurprisingly good health is a contributory factor to overall happiness, as we will in due course see.

So finally we have our definition of happiness-as-wellbeing. There are three main elements:

- how we feel in a particular moment, including the extent to which we are experiencing sensory or psychological pleasure or pain. We have encountered this before as positive or negative "affect".
- the degree to which we feel our life has meaning and purpose and that we are achieving our personal potential as a human being, whatever we define this to be.
- the healthy lifespan over which we experience, or might reasonably expect to experience, these two elements of happiness.

We can apply this definition at the level of a single individual, or an entire society.

PART C: Happiness in the world

Recent decades have seen a good deal of attention being paid to assessing the extent to which people in the world can be said to be happy, together with building an understanding of the underlying root causes and therefore what actions, by governments and individuals, might have the greatest impact on improving happiness in a population.

The topic is not straightforward to measure, subjective as it obviously is. We'll therefore start this section with a brief review of the methodologies which researchers have developed to tackle the challenge, with the intention that this will build confidence for when we come on to discuss the actual data.

Measuring happiness

The subjective nature of happiness means that the only realistic way to find out how happy someone is, and why, is to ask them, through some kind of survey. Of course this raises important challenges, in particular relating to the potential ambiguity of language, particularly when research spans multiple geographies so that survey questions must be translated into different languages. Even seemingly-simple questions like "are you happy?" or "does your life have meaning?" have obvious potential for interpretative difference.

Researchers have put a great deal of thought into resolving, or at least mitigating, this challenge. They tend to tackle the potential for ambiguity in two ways. First, rather than asking a single question they ask a range, addressing both how a person is feeling in the moment ("positive or negative affect") as well as how they assess their life from a more analytical standpoint, for example whether they consider their life to have meaning.

As an example, on pp409-427 of their article *Measuring Subjective Wellbeing: Recommendations on Measures for use by National Governments*, published by the *Journal of Social Policy*, Vol 41, Issue 02, April 2012, British behavioural scientists Paul Dolan and Robert Metcalfe propose four standard questions which cover all the elements of Subjective Wellbeing discussed in the previous section:

(i) "Overall, how satisfied are you with your life nowadays?
(ii) Overall, how happy did you feel yesterday?
(iii) Overall, how anxious did you feel yesterday?
(iv) Overall, how worthwhile are the things that you do in your life?"

Second, a graduated scale is often used for responses, rather than simply asking for a binary "yes:no" reply. The most prominent example is the Cantril Self-Anchoring Scale, otherwise known as the Cantril Ladder, developed by the American psychologist Hadley Cantril in 1965. A respondent might be told: "please imagine a ladder with steps numbered from zero at the bottom to 10 at the top. The top of the ladder represents the best possible life for you, and the bottom of the ladder represents the worst possible life for you. On which step of the ladder would you say you personally feel you stand at this time?"

Finally, some research probes for insights into the psychological characteristics which have been shown to correlate with happiness, rather than, or in addition to, asking direct questions about happiness itself. One of the most widely used such approaches is the Ryff Scale of Psychological Wellbeing, first introduced in 1989 by the American psychologist Carol Ryff. American academic Tricia Seifert explains, in an entry titled *The Ryff Scales of Psychological Well-Being*, posted on the website of the Center of Enquiry at Wabash College, University of Iowa, and dated Spring 2005: "well-being is a dynamic concept and includes subjective, social, and psychological dimensions as well as health-related behaviours. The Ryff scales of psychological well-being is a theoretically-grounded instrument that specifically focuses on measuring multiple facets of psychological well-being. These facets include the following:

- Self-acceptance,
- The establishment of quality ties to other (people),
- A sense of autonomy in thought and action,
- The ability to manage complex environments to suit personal needs and values,
- The pursuit of meaningful goals and a sense of purpose in life,
- Continued growth and development as a person."

Overall, we can be confident that happiness research based on these techniques provides us with meaningful data. Economists Esteban Ortiz-Ospina and Max Roser confirm, in an article titled *Happiness and Life Satisfaction* which appears in *Our World in Data*, first published in 2013, and substantively revised in May 2017: "self-reports about happiness and life satisfaction are known to correlate with things that people typically associate with contentment, such as cheerfulness and smiling...experimental psychologists have also shown that self-reports of well-being from surveys turn out to correlate with activity in the parts of the brain associated with pleasure and satisfaction. And various surveys have confirmed that people who say they are happy also tend to sleep better and express positive emotions verbally more frequently...the main conclusion from the evidence is that survey-based measures of happiness and life satisfaction do provide a reasonably consistent and reliable picture of subjective well-being".

Are people happy?

So what does the research tell us about the state of happiness in the world today?

Our main sources are two of the leading ongoing global happiness studies. The first is the *World Happiness Report*, produced annually by the United Nations every year since 2012 with the stated aim to "give more importance to happiness and well-being in determining how to achieve and measure social and economic development". The *World Happiness Report* itself draws on data from the *Gallup World Poll*, which produces an annual "league table" of happiness by country based on what Gallup tells us is "the most comprehensive and farthest-reaching survey of the world. The survey connects with more than 99% of the world's adult population through annual, nationally representative surveys with comparable metrics across countries".

The second main source is the *World Values Survey*, founded in 1981 by American political scientist Robert Inglehart and his team, and "devoted to the scientific and academic study of social, political, economic, religious and cultural values of people in the world".

The good news is that on average a majority of people report that they are happy, albeit this obviously also means that a minority do not. For example, the 2025 *World Happiness Report*, the most recent available at the time of writing, shows that respondents report an average life evaluation score of 5.0 or higher, that is above the mid-point on the Cantril scale, in 100 out of 147 countries covered, or 68% of countries (on a point of detail, all individual country scores are based on 3-year average data). Of course, it follows that 47 countries, or 32%, score below the mid-point on average. At the headline level, these results mirror those of a *Global Happiness Study* published in August 2019 by *Ipsos Global Advisor* covering 28 countries and showing that 64% of adults reported themselves to be "very" (14%) or "rather" (50%) happy; meaning of course that 36% did not.

The differences between countries are significant. To take the extremes, in the 2025 report Finland ranks highest (for the eighth year in a row) averaging 7.7 on the Cantril scale; and Afghanistan ranks lowest, at 1.4. For what it is worth the ten countries which rank highest are:

1. Finland: 7.7
2. Denmark: 7.5
3. Iceland: 7.5
4. Sweden: 7.3
5. Netherlands: 7.3
6. Costa Rica: 7.3
7. Norway: 7.3
8. Israel: 7.2
9. Luxembourg: 7.1
10. Mexico: 7.0

And the ten which rank lowest, in ascending order from the bottom:

147. Afghanistan: 1.4
146. Sierra Leone: 3.0

145. Lebanon: 3.2
144. Malawi: 3.3
143. Zimbabwe: 3.4
142. Botswana: 3.4
141. DR Congo: 3.5
140. Yemen: 3.6
139. Comoros: 3.8
138. Lesotho: 3.8

For the record, selected others include:

11. Australia: 7.0 New Zealand: 7.0
12. Switzerland: 6.9
18. Canada: 6.8
21. Germany: 6.8
22. United Kingdom: 6.7
23. United States: 6.7
32. Saudi Arabia: 6.6
33. France: 6.6
40. Italy: 6.4
55. Japan: 6.1
66. Russia: 5.9
68. China: 5.9
118. India: 4.4

To back this up, the *Gallup World Poll* routinely asks two additional questions aimed at assessing the degree to which respondents experience positive and negative affect in the moment, in contrast to the more reflective nature of the life evaluation question. The general form for these affect questions is: "did you experience the following feelings during a lot of the day yesterday?" Positive affect is measured by the average of individual yes or no answers about three emotions: laughter, enjoyment, and interest; and negative affect by the average of individual yes or no answers about whether people experienced worry, sadness, and anger. The 2023 *World Happiness Report* authors conclude that:

"positive emotions are more than twice as frequent (global average of 0.66) as negative emotions (global average of 0.29), even during the three Covid years 2020–2022".

There is evidence that levels of happiness have been generally increasing, albeit not everywhere and with some recent evidence which points in the other direction, at least in some countries.

Esteban Ortiz-Ospina and Max Roser conclude, in an article titled *Happiness and Life Satisfaction* published by *Our World in Data*, first appearing in 2013 and revised in May 2017: "the *World Values Survey* collects data from a series of representative national surveys covering almost 100 countries...in the majority of countries the trend is positive: in 49 of the 69 countries with data from two or more surveys, the most recent observation is higher than the earliest". Obviously, this also means that happiness had at best not increased for 20 countries. The authors of the 2024 *World Happiness Report* also comment that: "looking...at the global average across countries, life evaluations have improved very slightly across all age groups".

In the 2025 *World Happiness Report*, however, the most recent picture, the authors tell us that: "in general, the western industrialised countries are now less happy than they were between 2005 and 2010. Fifteen of them have had significant drops, compared to four with significant increases. Three western countries had drops exceeding 0.5 on the 0-10 scale (the United States, Switzerland, and Canada) putting them among the fifteen largest losers".

Of course, there is no reason to expect that average happiness levels should increase over time as if this were somehow inevitable. And the 2021 *World Happiness Report* highlights the specific example of the US, in which levels of average happiness have been in decline for some considerable time, even as the country has continued to prosper economically, at least in a relative sense. Indeed, the entire fifth chapter is devoted to this issue, authored by American psychologist Jean Twenge and somewhat soberly titled *The Sad State of Happiness in the United States and the Role of Digital Media*.

Twenge comments: "the years since 2010 have not been good ones for happiness and well-being among Americans. Even as the United States economy improved after the end of the Great Recession in 2009, happiness among adults did not rebound to the higher levels of the 1990s, continuing a slow decline ongoing since at least 2000 in the General Social Survey (Twenge et al, 2016)...this decline in happiness and mental health seems paradoxical. By most accounts, Americans should be happier now than ever. The violent crime rate is low, as is the unemployment rate. Income per capita has steadily grown over the last few decades. This is the Easterlin paradox: as the standard of living improves, so should happiness - but it has not".

As an aside, the Easterlin paradox was formulated in 1974 by the American economist Richard Easterlin, who noted that whilst at any given point in time reported happiness tends to correlate with levels of material wealth, increases in wealth over time do not systematically correlate with increases in happiness. There is some confusion and even controversy around these observations, which we will explore shortly.

Meantime, it is not clear why the US picture is as it is. Various theories have been proposed, including: growing inequality; declining physical health with the rise of obesity and the opioid crisis; and declining mental health, itself the product of factors which remain speculative but may include the fragmentation of communities and the alienating effects of the precipitous rise of social media, the hypothesis proposed by Twenge in her 2021 *World*

Happiness Report entry mentioned above. Perhaps the answer lies in a combination of all these things.

Whatever the explanation, the US serves to remind us that whilst the headline data suggests that happiness may be eminently achievable for a majority of people, it certainly cannot be taken for granted, even in the wealthiest, and arguably most developed, of nations.

PART D: What makes people happy?

What helps individuals to be happy?

It will come as no surprise that there is no "silver bullet" solution to happiness, but rather a range of potential factors which contribute to a greater or lesser extent, depending on an individual's profile and circumstances. Still, as usual there are averages and statistical patterns which can help to guide us. The story starts at the beginning, of course, with the genes we inherit.

1. Genes

We saw in Chapter 1 that our genes exercise a significant, although not entirely deterministic, influence on our life, and it turns out that this applies to our happiness also. We are each born with a certain genetic propensity to feel happy, and at least some differences in the specific triggers that are likely to make us happy or sad. Each individual has a unique genetic profile and therefore set of propensities, and so it goes.

The American social scientist Arthur Brooks suggests that we each have our own happiness "set point", in an article titled *The Three Equations for a Happy Life, Even During a Pandemic*, published in *The Atlantic* on 9 April 2020. The idea is that particular experiences may make us feel temporarily happier or more miserable, but in the long run we each tend to return to our own default level of happiness, this being heavily influenced by our genes.

Brooks explains: "personally, I dislike the idea that happiness is genetic; I dislike the idea that *anything* (author's italics) about my character or personality is genetic, because I want to be fully in charge of building my life. But the research is clear that there is a huge genetic component in determining your 'set point' for subjective well-being, the baseline you always seem to return to after events sway your mood. In an article in the journal *Psychological Science* reporting on an analysis of twins - including identical twins reared apart and then tested for subjective well-being as adults - the psychologists David Lykken and Auke Tellegen estimate that the genetic component of a person's well-being is between 44% and 52%, that is, about half".

The notion of a "happiness set point" links to the idea of a "hedonic treadmill", originally introduced in 1971 by the psychologists Philip Brickman and Donald Campbell, Canadian and American respectively, with the "treadmill" metaphor itself added by the British psychologist Michael Eysenck 20 years later. Seph Pennock, who introduces himself as "the business mind behind *Positive Psychology.com*", explains, in an entry on that website titled *The Hedonic Treadmill – Are We Forever Chasing Rainbows?*, dated 7 April 2021: "along with Brickman and Campbell's original research (1971), a notable piece of research on the hedonic treadmill studied two sets of people: one was a group of people who won large lottery prizes, and the other was a group of accident victims who were now paralysed (including quadriplegic and paraplegic people)....the research revealed that, in the long term, neither group appeared to be happier than the other. (Brickman, Coates, and Janoff-Bulman, 1978). Of course, the lottery winners and paralysis victims experienced initial reactions of happiness and sadness, respectively....the effects didn't turn out to be long-lasting, and people in both groups shortly reverted to their previous levels of happiness. In the original theory of the hedonic treadmill, Brickman and Campbell propose that people immediately react to good and bad events but in a short time return to neutrality (1971)".

Subsequent research suggests a more nuanced picture. Individuals do indeed have different basic happiness "set points", but under some conditions a set point can change, more or less permanently. Even here there is individual variation, in that different people have different propensities to return to their personal set point, or not, in reaction to particular experiences.

Still, the key point is that some life events may have lasting impact on our underlying propensity for happiness. The examples of things which change our "set point" are often negative, that is to say experiences which make us permanently less happy, for example unemployment. But some experiences can also have lasting positive impact, a perhaps-surprising example being divorce. Conversely, some experiences which we might predict to have a lasting impact on happiness and therefore to change our happiness "set point" turn out to be neutral over the long run, which is to say that on average people tend to return to their original level of happiness. An example of this is marriage.

Ortiz-Ospina and Roser explain, in their article *Happiness and Life Satisfaction*, referenced above: "do people tend to adapt to common life events by converging back to a baseline level of happiness?...single life events do tend to affect happiness in the short run, but people often adapt to changes. Of course, there are clear differences in the extent to which people adapt. In the case of divorce, life satisfaction first drops, then goes up and stays high. For unemployment, there is a negative shock both in the short and long run, notably among men. And for marriage, life satisfaction builds up before, and fades out after the wedding".

The authors address the specific case of paraplegia, again drawing a nuanced conclusion: "in general, the evidence suggests that adaptation is an important feature of well-being. Many common but important life events have a modest long-term impact on self-reported happiness...a number of papers have noted that long-term paraplegics do not report themselves as particularly unhappy, when compared to non-paraplegics....however, comparing differences in self-reported life satisfaction among people with different disability statuses is not an ideal source of evidence regarding the effect of tragedy on happiness. Non-paraplegics are potentially different to paraplegics in ways that are hard to measure. A better source of evidence are longitudinal surveys where people are tracked over time...Oswald and Pawdthavee (2008) use data from a longitudinal study in the UK to explore whether accidents leading to disability imply long-term shocks to life satisfaction...those entering disability suffer a sudden drop in life satisfaction, and recover *only partially* (my emphasis). This supports the idea that while adaptation plays a role for common life events, the notion of life satisfaction is indeed sensitive to tragic events".

Finally, our mindset, which is to say the way we interpret events and experiences, can have an important effect on our happiness, similar to the way we saw that "mindset matters" in the case of stress. Seph Pennock explains, in the *Hedonic Treadmill* article referenced above: "an individual's definition of an event (threat or challenge), his or her interpretations, and the ways in which he or she continues to think about the event (e.g., with a sense of tragedy, a sense of humour, ruminating about the past) can have a big impact on his or her outlook...in Sonja Lyubomirsky's research on this subject, she found that happy individuals perceive, interpret, and subsequently think about life events and life circumstances in more positive ways than negative ones (1998). These differences in cognitive processes may, in turn, reinforce and promote people's affective dispositions...happy individuals can evaluate events (especially negative ones) in positive and productive ways. Unhappy individuals tend to dwell on the negative aspects of events, finding things that are 'wrong' about positive events, or ruminate on how things were better before".

2. Sense of personal agency ("locus of control")

As we briefly noted during our discussion of freewill in Chapter 2, our happiness can be affected by the degree to which we do or do not feel we have some appropriate level of personal agency, and therefore some ability to control or at least influence our environment. Psychologists call this our "locus of control".

The Goldilocks Principle applies: the happiest people tend to be those who feel they have a level of agency which is appropriate to their actual circumstances and therefore real in a practical sense. Extreme "externals", that is people with a very low sense of agency, are likely to be less happy than their peers; and so are people who have an inflated sense of agency, beyond what their actual situation can reasonably justify.

Authors Kurt April, Babar Dharani and Kai Peters comment, in an article titled *Impact of Locus of Control Expectancy on Level of Well-Being*, published in the *Review of European Studies* dated June 2012: "the lack of well-being for extreme externals is...linked to depression, powerlessness...helplessness and also learned helplessness...and hopelessness". The article also describes how "the maximum level of happiness is achieved by individuals with a bi-local expectancy", bi-local being defined as a sense of agency which is appropriate to one's actual circumstances. Individuals with an exaggerated sense of agency, beyond what their personal situation reasonably supports, also report lower feelings of subjective well-being than do people whose sense of agency corresponds more closely to their underlying reality.

Our sense of agency, then, is important not only in enabling us to take responsibility for our own life by embracing our opportunity to exercise existential choice, but also to our ability to achieve happiness in the process.

3. Life stage

Whatever "set point" level of underlying happiness we may individually possess, it is typically not stable during the course of our life.

Rather, a U-curve exists, whereby on average we tend to be at our happiest as a young adult, aged around 18-20; our happiness levels dip through middle age, with a low point typically around 45-50; then increase again as we continue to age, all the way through to our 70s or 80s and even beyond. To be clear, the implication is not that we become *unhappy* in middle age, merely that we report lower happiness at that time relative to the levels reported by those younger and older than us; or than the levels reported by our younger and older self, in the case of the few longitudinal studies available.

There is a good deal of evidence to support the existence of this U-curve, but it is not entirely clear why it should occur, nor is it seen everywhere in the world. There are many theories for why it should happen, of course, including that our middle adult years are typically when we are subject to the greatest amount of stress, from a combination of career and family pressures. Alternatively, that at a psychological level during our early adulthood we have the optimism, or possibly naivete, of youth; during our middle years we are gradually finding out about our "real Self"; and eventually, if we are lucky, we grow into progressively greater self-knowledge and self-acceptance.

This U-curve effect is well established, but there is also evidence that in very recent times it may be eroding, at least in some places. This is because younger people in these places are less happy on average than people in their age cohort used to be. For example, the 2024 *World Happiness Report* comments: "for the United States, Canada, Australia and New Zealand, happiness has decreased in all age groups, but especially for the young (my note: defined here as those under 30), so much so that the young are now, in 2021-2023, the least happy age group. This is a big change from 2006-2010, when the young were happier than those in the midlife groups, and about as happy as those aged 60 and over".

The cause of this change is not yet clear, but many commentators point to the rise of social media as the culprit. For example, the UK journalist Caroline Scott writes, in an article titled *Jonathan Haidt: How we can save our children from smart phones*, published in *The Sunday Times* on 5 January 2025: "economists have known for decades that the happiest people are the young and the old...a vast amount of literature...supports this U-shaped curve in human well-being across the world. But not any more...economist and UN advisor Danny Blanchflower...reported last year that it had changed. The wellbeing of adults under 26, especially young women, went into precipitous decline beginning around 2017, with some evidence suggesting it was as early as 2014. Now young adults, on average, are the least happy people, Blanchflower says. Evidence for this transformation first became apparent in the US and the UK, but it is now true in 82 countries".

Scott goes on to propose a connection with the rise of social media and the widespread adoption of smartphones among the young, in turn referencing the

2024 book *The Anxious Generation*, authored by the same Jonathan Haidt from whom we heard in previous chapters. In this latest book Haidt suggests that smartphone usage specifically has resulted in a major shift in adolescent behaviour, replacing live social interaction with "five hours of 15-second videos", and creating entirely novel cognitive pressures on adolescent brains at a time when they are still relatively plastic and only partly formed, as we saw in Chapter 2.

This reduction in happiness among young people in many developed societies is obviously cause for concern, albeit its recency makes it hard to assert with confidence what is really behind it.

In the meantime, the main point from the perspective of this book is that we should expect our underlying level of happiness to change as we age; and, encouragingly, that whatever our personal baseline we can reasonably hope for our golden years to be amongst our happiest.

4. Relationships

Social animals that we are, it is no surprise that the quantity, and especially the quality, of our personal relationships should link strongly to our happiness; and conversely that loneliness makes us miserable. It bears repeating that EM Forster's advice to "only connect..." is arguably the most important advice in this book.

Having said this, the centrality of our relationships to our existence is such an important topic that we have covered most of the relevant ground earlier in the book. We will therefore limit the discussion here to a brief recap of some of the major themes.

For example, in Chapter 3 we encountered the Harvard Study of Adult Development, which has been running for 75 years with the stated goal "to enable people to live healthier lives filled with meaning, connection and purpose". When asked to summarise what he had learned from all this research, Director George Vaillant answered simply: "that the only thing that really matters in life are your relationships to other people".

In similar vein, a later Director, Robert Waldinger, shared his "three main lessons": "first, that social connections are really good for us, and that loneliness kills...second...that quality (of relationship) matters as much or more than quantity...conflict is bad for your health, good warm relationships are protective...third...that good relationships don't just protect our bodies; they also protect our brains".

Relationships come in many shapes and flavours, of course. There is no single ideal form: what matters is simply that they work subjectively for us, and presumably also for the other party if they are to last. American academic Arthur Brooks reinforces this important point, in the *Three Equations for a Happy Life* article referenced above: "...there is no magic formula for what shape your family and friendships should take. The key is to cultivate and maintain loving, faithful relationships with other people...people who have loving relationships with family and friends thrive; those who don't, don't".

Finally, some level of reciprocity is advisable. This is likely to make for a richer and more sustainable relationship in the first place, of course, and certainly one with healthier power dynamics. Also, a two-way street enables us to benefit from support when we need it, and also to offer our own support when that is appropriate, which can itself paradoxically enhance our own sense of wellbeing. To reprise Robert Sapolsky, on p256 and then p407 of *Why Zebras Don't Get Ulcers*: "it helps to have a shoulder to cry on, a hand to hold, an ear to listen to you, someone to cradle you and to tell you it will be okay" and also: "often, one of the strongest stress-reducing qualities of social support is the act of *giving* (author's emphasis) social support, to be needed".

5. Health

Healthier people tend to be happier, and vice versa.

This seems obvious at an intuitive level, and the statistical data fully supports the intuition for a change. Authors Nathan Hudson, Richard Lucas and Brent Donnellan conclude, in an article titled *Healthier and Happier? A 3-Year Longitudinal Investigation of the Prospective Associations and Concurrent Changes in Health and Experiential Well-Being* published by the *Personality and Social Psychology Bulletin Vol 45* in 2019: "a substantial body of research has examined the associations between health and global well-being...many studies have converged on the finding that global well-being and health are positively associated with correlations ranging from $r = .10$ to $.50$...moreover, recent research suggests that these associations are evident in more than 30 countries".

What is less clear from the data is which is the metaphorical chicken and which the egg – does being healthy make us more likely to be happy, or is it rather that if we are happy we are more likely to be healthy?

The general view is that benefits flow both ways. *BetterHelp*, self-described as "the world's largest therapy platform" summarise, in an entry on their website titled *Health and Happiness: Uncovering the Connection*: "over time, studies have shown that health and happiness are intrinsically linked. When you feel physically healthy, your mood may also improve, and vice versa...according to researchers at the University of Texas Health Science Centre at Houston, 'feeling sad can alter levels of stress-related opioids in the brain and increase levels of inflammatory proteins in the blood that are linked to increased risk of comorbid diseases, including heart disease, high blood pressure, stroke, and metabolic syndrome'... happiness also seems to be a factor in boosting the efficacy of the immune system, with research showing that mood affected cytokine response to flu viruses. One form of happiness (a sense of life meaning) was linked to lower reported pain levels, and less distress in those who live with chronic pain. We do know that less stress plays a positive role in promoting better health (for example, those who report less stress have a lower risk for health problems like heart attack), but researchers also report that those who are happier are also more likely to engage in behaviours that contribute to make them healthier overall, such as regular exercise, and healthy eating habits".

The implication is that we do well to nurture our own health, obvious as this is. There is no shortage of advice to be had on the topic, and it is beyond the scope of this book to engage in any detail on how best we might do this. We will limit our discussion mainly to a recap of some ideas we have already encountered:

- First, sleep is critical. Quantity and quality both matter, as we saw in Chapter 2.

- Second, diet is important. As with sleep, both quality and quantity are relevant.

- Third, exercise, or at least movement, matter. There is a growing body of evidence to suggest that even a modest amount of movement is beneficial to our health, such as taking the stairs rather than the elevator for a couple of flights; that simple exercise such as walking is helpful even if we cannot bring ourselves to work out more energetically; and that a balanced programme which includes regular vigorous exercise will achieve the best results. On the specific topic of controlling weight, diet matters more than exercise, although both potentially have a role.

- Fourth, stress and how we react to it can affect our physical health, as we discussed in Chapter 2. Our psychological reaction to a potential stressor importantly influences its impact, and in any case the goal is not to eliminate stress from our life altogether but rather to embrace healthy stress which can enhance performance and enjoyment, and also build resilience so that "what doesn't kill us makes us stronger".

Finally, one further topic is the effect that our breathing can have on our health. The case for this is made forcefully by the American science journalist James Nestor in his 2020 book *Breath, the new science of a lost art*. Space does not permit that we explore his ideas in detail, so we will settle for a single quote: "while some of us may be genetically predisposed toward one disease or another, that doesn't mean we're predestined to get these conditions. Genes can be turned off just as they can be turned on. What switches them are inputs in the environment. Improving diet and exercise and removing toxins and stressors from the home and workplace have a profound and lasting effect on the prevention and treatment of the majority of modern, chronic diseases...breathing is a key input. From what I've learned in the past decade, the 30 pounds of air that passes through our lungs every day and the 1.7 pounds of oxygen our cells consume is as important as what we eat or how much we exercise. Breathing is a missing pillar of health". Nestor rounds off the argument by himself quoting "the famed doctor" Andrew Weil, who apparently said: "if I had to limit my advice on healthier living to just one tip, it would be simply to learn how to breathe better". Interested readers will need to consult Nestor's book for the specifics.

6. Money

It may be true that money can't buy happiness, but the data suggests that it certainly helps. In fact, contrary to some perceptions, it seems that the richer you are the likelier you are to be happy, with no obvious ceiling. There is even evidence that the Easterlin Paradox, which we encountered earlier in this chapter, may not be such a paradox after all.

The core, uncontroversial, point (uncontroversial from an analytical if not necessarily a social perspective) is that on average people living in rich countries tend to be happier than people living in poor ones. Ortiz-Ospina and Roser observe, in their article *Happiness and Life Satisfaction*, referenced above: "if we compare life satisfaction reports from around the world at any given point in time, we immediately see that countries with higher average national incomes tend to have higher average life satisfaction scores. In other words: people in richer countries tend to report higher life satisfaction than people in poorer countries...this correlation holds even if we control for other factors: richer countries tend to have higher average self reported life satisfaction than poorer countries that are comparable in terms of demographics and other measurable characteristics...the same tends to be true within countries: richer people within a country tend to be happier than poorer people in the same country...while less strong, there is also a correlation between income and happiness across time. Or, put differently, as countries get richer, the population tends to report higher average life satisfaction".

This last point, that happiness increases as wealth does, has been the subject of considerable debate. Seminal 2010 research by Daniel Kahneman, of *Thinking, Fast and Slow* fame, and the British-American economist Angus Deaton famously proposed the existence of a plateau effect, whereby happiness increases up to a certain threshold level of wealth but not thereafter. At the time of their research, the authors estimated this plateau to start at around $75,000 annual income, equating to around $90,000 in today's money. And this finding has since become anchored in the public consciousness, perhaps because it serves to reinforce a commonsense intuition, with echoes of Maslow, that there is a point after which you have enough money to satisfy your basic needs and having more won't make you happier. As an aside, the British comedian Spike Milligan once ventured that: "money can't buy you happiness, but it does bring you a more pleasant form of misery". But that is a different point. And this bon mot has been attributed to many fathers besides Milligan, including Groucho Marx.

Returning to our main narrative, things become more nuanced when we dig into the detail, not that we have to dig very far. The paper in which Kahneman and Deaton published their findings was titled: *High income improves evaluation of life but not emotional well-being*, published by *PNAS* (*Proceedings of the National Academy of Sciences of the United States of America*), dated 21 September 2010. And what the authors found was exactly what their title says, specifically that the happiness measure we previously called "positive or negative affect" and which they label "emotional well-being" seems to plateau at a certain level of wealth; but that what they call the "evaluation of life", specifically the measure which uses the Cantril scale, does not.

Kahneman and Deaton are quite explicit: "we find that emotional well-being (measured by questions about emotional experiences yesterday) and life evaluation (measured by Cantril's Self-Anchoring Scale) have different correlates...when plotted against log income, life evaluation rises steadily. Emotional well-being also rises with log income, but there is no further progress beyond an annual income of ~$75,000".

In the original research, then, one measure of happiness is shown to plateau as wealth increases, and the other does not. It is not clear why these two different measures of happiness should yield such different outcomes, but we'll resist the temptation to speculate and be content with the observation that they do.

Both measures are generally accepted to be legitimate assessments of happiness, as we saw earlier. It is not necessary to choose one or the other as preeminent, although to the extent we might like to there is no reason to suppose that life evaluation (which we might paraphrase as "how happy I feel about my life overall") is somehow inferior to "emotional well-being" (which we might paraphrase as "how happy or sad I felt yesterday"). Indeed, the *World Happiness Report* chooses life evaluation as *the* critical measure on which to base its annual country comparisons.

On a point of detail, what Kahneman and Deaton found is that life evaluation continues to increase indefinitely with income in a logarithmic relationship, which is to say that a similar level of increase in reported happiness is observed with every *doubling* in income. In other words, whatever starting income two individuals might have, they would each need to double this if they are both to experience the same quantum of increase in happiness. Conversely, if income were to increase by a specific amount the happiness impact would be greater for someone starting at a relatively lower level of income in the first place. To illustrate, an increase of say $10,000 per year would double the income of an individual who was only earning $10,000 to start with, but would represent an increase of just 1% to an individual who was earning $1,000,000. In this more technical sense, then, we might predict that the wealthier someone is to start with, the harder it is for further wealth to make them happier, at least presuming that it is more difficult for someone earning say $1,000,000 to double their income than it is for someone earning much less to double theirs.

In any case, more recent research challenges the idea that a plateau effect exists even for emotional wellbeing ("how happy or sad I felt yesterday"). The American psychologist Matt Killingsworth reports on a study of 33,391 employed US adults aged 18-65, in which respondents were asked to use their smartphones to provide multiple real-time data on how happy they were feeling, responding to randomly-timed requests during their waking hours, and answering questions about both their emotional wellbeing and life evaluation. The quote is from an article titled *Experienced well-being rises with income, even above $75,000 per year*, also published by PNAS, dated 26 January 2021: "past research has found that experienced well-being does not increase above incomes of $75,000 per year. This finding has been the focus of substantial attention from researchers and the general public, yet is based on a dataset with a measure of experienced well-being that may or may not be indicative of actual emotional experience (retrospective, dichotomous reports; my note: 'dichotomous' means using binary, 'yes:no' questions). Here, over 1 million real-time reports of experienced well-being from a large US sample show evidence that experienced well-being rises linearly with log income, with an equally steep slope above $80,000 as below it. This suggests that higher incomes may still have potential to improve people's day-to-day well-being, rather than having already reached a plateau for many people in wealthy countries".

It is also not clear that there is any kind of plateau effect even at very high levels of wealth. American author Peter Cohan cites 2018 research conducted exclusively among (American) millionaires, in an undated article titled *This*

Harvard Study of 4,000 Millionaires Revealed Something Surprising About Money and Happiness, published online by *Inc.*: "does money buy happiness?...Harvard Business School researchers Grant Donnelly and Michael Norton penned their answer in the *Wall Street Journal*...what made their research unique was their survey of 4,000 millionaires...what they found is that people with a net worth of $10 million are significantly happier than those in the $1 million to $2 million range".

There is nonetheless a twist, which serves to reinforce further the importance to happiness of feeling a sense of personal agency: "...not all decamillionaires are equally happy. The one factor that makes some of them happier than their equally wealthy peers comes as no surprise - making the money themselves instead of inheriting or marrying into it". Elsewhere in the article, Donnelly and Norton point out that the differences in reported happiness at these high levels of wealth are "modest". Still, the point is that they exist at all.

Finally, all this would appear to contradict the Easterlin paradox, which as we saw earlier states that whilst at any given point in time reported happiness tends to correlate with levels of material wealth, increases in wealth over time do not systematically correlate with increases in happiness.

And Ortiz-Ospina and Roser do indeed explicitly reject the paradox, in the same article called *Happiness and Life Satisfaction* referenced above. As part of their argument, they also propose an explanation for why increases in average wealth have not produced increased levels of happiness in the US over time – because on rising inequality, specifically that we are dealing yet again with averages and the increases in wealth have not been equally distributed around the average.

Specifically, Ortiz-Ospina and Roser explain that: "the observation that economic growth does not always go together with increasing life satisfaction was first made by Richard Easterlin in the 1970s. Since then, there has been much discussion over what came to be known as the 'Easterlin paradox'...at the heart of the paradox was the fact that richer countries tend to have higher self-reported happiness, yet in some countries for which repeated surveys were available over the course of the 1970s, happiness was not increasing with rising national incomes...notably, Easterlin and other researchers relied on data from the US and Japan to support this seemingly perplexing observation. If we look closely at the data underpinning the trends in these two countries, however, these cases are not in fact paradoxical...(in) the case of Japan...the life satisfaction questions in the "life and nation surveys" changed over time, making it difficult - if not impossible - to track changes in happiness over the full period...the correlation between GDP and happiness growth in Japan is positive within comparable survey periods. The reason for the alleged paradox is in fact mismeasurement of how happiness changed over time. In the US, the explanation is different, but can once again be traced to the underlying data. Specifically, if we look more closely at economic growth in the US over the recent decades, one fact looms large: growth has not benefited the majority of people. Income inequality in the US is exceptionally high and has been on the rise in the last four decades, with incomes for the median household growing much more slowly than incomes for the top 10%. As a result, trends in aggregate life satisfaction should not be seen as paradoxical: the income and standard of living of the typical US citizen has not grown much in the last couple of decades".

It should be acknowledged that Easterlin himself does not accept this, or other, rebuttals of his paradox, pointing mainly to methodological differences, or sometimes plain misunderstandings, to explain the disagreement. For example, in a paper titled *Paradox Lost?*, published as IZA discussion Paper No 9676 in January 2016, Easterlin states unequivocally: "Paradox Lost?...or Paradox Regained? The answer is Paradox Regained. New data confirm that for countries worldwide long-term trends in happiness and real GDP per capita are not significantly positively related. The principal reason the Paradox critics reach a different conclusion, aside from problems of data comparability, is that they do not focus on identifying long-term trends in happiness. For some countries their estimated growth rates of happiness and GDP are not trend rates, but those observed in cyclical expansion or contraction".

Paradox or not, the main point is clear. Money may not be able to buy happiness, but it surely makes it statistically more likely, with no obvious ceiling.

7. Work

"Since most of us spend a great deal of our lives working, it is inevitable that work plays a key role in shaping our levels of happiness", is the opening line of an article titled *Does Work Make You Happy? Evidence from the World Happiness Report*, which appeared in the *Harvard Business Review* dated 20 March 2017, authored by economists Jan-Emmanuel De Neve and George Ward. De Neve and Ward also authored a chapter on this topic in the 2017 *World Happiness Report* itself.

They elaborate: "the importance of having a job extends far beyond the salary attached to it. A large stream of research has shown that the non-monetary aspects of employment are also key drivers of people's well-being. Social status, social relations, daily structure, and goals all exert a strong influence on people's happiness".

The authors go on to make a number of observations which are pertinent to our present discussion.

First, they find a statistical correlation between reported job satisfaction and overall reported happiness: "we see a moderate correlation (0.28, where a perfect correlation would be 1.0) between job satisfaction responses and life evaluation for individuals in the Gallup world poll". This may be a "moderate" correlation from a technical, statistical standpoint. However, as already observed in the cases of genes and material wellbeing, it would be surprising were any single factor to have a dominant, much less total, effect on happiness. De Neve and Ward's "moderate" correlation provides firm evidence of the important role work plays in influencing happiness.

Second: "people working blue-collar jobs report lower levels of overall happiness in every region around the world." This reinforces the observation in Chapter 2 that individuals who are relatively lower in a social, or economic, hierarchy, tend to experience higher levels of chronic stress and report lower happiness than those higher up; the very opposite of the pervasive image of the stressed-out leader with the cares of the world on his or her shoulders. This is not to belittle the stress that many leaders undoubtedly feel. It is merely to note that on average people towards the top of a hierarchy tend to report higher happiness than those further down.

Third, self-employment is associated with lower happiness in the developing world, and conversely with higher overall happiness but also increased negative affect (anxiety, worry and so on) in the developed world. We might speculate that in the developing world self-employment is often precarious and oriented to subsistence; conversely in the developed world happiness may be higher because of relatively greater feelings of autonomy and control, albeit somewhat offset by higher anxiety because of the relatively higher level of personal responsibility and risk.

Fourth, as we already saw in a different context, unemployment has pernicious and often lasting consequences for happiness: "one of the most robust findings in the economics of happiness is that unemployment is destructive to people's well-being. We find this is true around the world. The employed evaluate the quality of their lives much more highly on average as compared to the unemployed. Individuals who are unemployed also report around 30% more negative emotional experiences in their day-to-day lives...not only are the unemployed generally unhappier than those in work, we find in our analyses that people generally do not adapt over time to becoming unemployed. More than this, spells of unemployment also seem to have a scarring effect on people's well-being, even after they have regained employment".

These conclusions are supported by a great deal of other research pointing to the inescapable conclusion that long-term unemployment in particular has sustained negative impact on both the happiness and health of those unfortunate enough to experience it.

Finally, the authors comment that even though the data show that employment correlates with happiness, and that those in employment demonstrate relatively high levels of job satisfaction on average, especially in the industrialised world, this does not mean that employees are necessarily engaged emotionally with their employer: "in contrast to the relatively high job satisfaction numbers...the number of people noting that they are actively engaged is typically less than 20%...job satisfaction can perhaps be reduced to feeling content with one's job, but the notion of (active) employee engagement requires individuals to be positively absorbed by their work and fully committed to advancing the organisation's interests".

In sum, for most people work is an important factor in their happiness, for reasons which overlap both social and financial wellbeing as well as potentially conferring a sense of self-worth. Conversely, unemployment can be highly damaging, especially if it is prolonged.

8. Religion

There is some evidence to suggest that on average religious people report higher levels of happiness than non-religious. The data are not entirely consistent, however; and to the extent a correlation between religion and happiness exists the underlying causes seem to be mainly the opportunities that religion affords to build community and social relationships rather than the underlying beliefs involved.

At a headline level British journalist Kaya Burgess writes, in an article published in the *Times* and dated 9 October 2023: "a report by Gallup, the American research and polling firm, has found that around the world people who see religion as being 'important in their daily life' tend to score more highly than non-religious people on key measures of well-being, holding true even in nations classed as 'less religious countries'...the researchers created a score after polling people with questions including 'did you smile or laugh a lot yesterday?', 'did you learn or do something interesting yesterday?' and scoring how much 'enjoyment' they experienced the previous day. In the most religious countries, devout people reported an average score for 'positive experiences' of 67.1 compared to 58.7 for non-religious people. Even in less religious countries, those for whom religion is important scored 70.8 compared to 70.2 for the non-religious. An analysis by broad region found the same held true globally, with a score of 67.4 for religious people in Europe and Central Asia, compared to 67.3 for non-religious people".

The same research showed the UK to be an outlier, for reasons which are unclear. The title of Burgess' article is *Non-believers happier than the faithful – but only in the UK* and she goes on to say: "UK data revealed that religious people scored 72.7 (out of 100), lower than the score of 75.4 for non-religious people....a second measure, dubbed the "social life index", asked if "you have relatives or friends you can count on" and if people were "satisfied with the opportunities to meet people and make friends"...in this category, the UK was again an exception, with religious people scoring 86.1 compared to 87.5 for non-religious people".

In any case, this British exceptionalism appears to be of recent origin. Journalist Catherine Snowden, writing in the *Huffington Post UK* on 2 February 2016 in an article titled *Official "Well-Being" Statistics Show Religious People Are Happier Than Atheists* reports on a study by the British Office for National Statistics which looked at personal wellbeing data for more than 300,000 UK adults over 3 years, from 2012-2015 and concluded not only that religious people were on average happier than non-religious at that time but even rank-ordered the impact of different religions: "the average response for happiness (using the Cantril scale) was 7.38 out of 10. Hindus scored 7.57, Christians 7.47, Sikhs 7.45 and Buddhists 7.41. Then came Jews at 7.37, Muslims at 7.33, those who follow "any other religion" at 7.26, and people with "no religion" at 7.22". Admittedly, it is not clear which differences are statistically significant, if any.

Other studies show a more nuanced global picture. For example, American social scientist Joey Marshall comments, in an article titled *Are religious people happier, healthier? Our new global study explores this question*, published by the *Pew Research Center* on 31

January 2019: "actively religious people are more likely than their less religious peers to describe themselves as 'very happy' in about half of the countries surveyed. Sometimes the gaps are striking: in the US, for instance, 36% of the actively religious describe themselves as 'very happy,' compared with 25% of the inactively religious and 25% of the unaffiliated. Notable happiness gaps among these groups also exist in Japan, Australia and Germany".

The definitions in this study are noteworthy. "Actively religious" are defined as people who identify with a religion and attend religious services at least once per month; "inactives" are those who identify with a religion and attend less often; and "unaffiliated" are those who do not identify with a religious group. The source data is *World Values Surveys*, 2010-2014. 26 countries are included, although it's not clear why they were chosen specifically. All the countries included are what we might think of as "major", but the scope excludes, for example, France, Italy and the UK.

The picture is mixed, then. But there is at least some evidence to suggest that in some places and times religious people report higher levels of happiness than their non-religious fellow-citizens, prompting the question: why might this be?

Various theories have been proposed, and we will touch briefly on the two most prominent.

The first is that it is not religious belief per se which correlates to increased happiness but rather active participation in religious gathering, with the crucial benefit that this reinforces social bonds and a sense of community and "belonging" – factors which themselves correlate strongly with happiness, as we have seen. In those cases where religious people may be happier, then, it is potentially for social, essentially secular, reasons.

Science journalist Stephanie Pappas, explains, in an article titled *Why Religion Makes People Happier (Hint: Not God)*, published in *Live Science* on 7 December 2010: "religious people are more satisfied with their lives than non-believers, but a new study finds it's not a relationship with God that makes the devout happy. Instead, the satisfaction boost may come from closer ties to earthly neighbours...according to a study published...in the journal *American Sociological Review*, religious people gain life satisfaction thanks to social networks they build by attending religious services....study researcher Chaeyoon Lim, a sociologist at the University of Wisconsin-Madison, (said): 'we show that (life satisfaction) is almost entirely about the social aspect of religion, rather than the theological or spiritual aspect of religion... we found that people are more satisfied with their lives when they go to church, because they build a social network within their congregation'". (My note: this study was conducted in 2006 among a nationally representative sample of 3,108 American adults. In 2007 the same individuals were called again, and 1,915 of them answered a second time).

The second theory is that religious faith can help people to cope with earthly stress, and the benefits of this are proportionally greater for individuals living in societies with high underlying levels of stress, which in turn tend to be those societies which are less materially developed and less socially and politically cohesive. This explanation helps to address what might otherwise be a paradox, that countries with the highest average levels of reported happiness consistently tend also to be those with the lowest levels of religiosity.

The Irish-American biopsychologist Nigel Barber explains, in a blog called *Are Religious People Happier?*, published by *Psychology Today* on 20 November 2012: "why are the happiest countries also the least religious ones? Both happiness and religiosity are affected by the highly developed character of these countries. All score close to the top of the UN's human development index that measures the overall quality of life in terms of health, wealth and education...residents of highly developed countries are happy because their quality of life is better. The key factor may be an expectation of living to old age without fear of extreme poverty. Because they are confident in their own welfare, they have less need of religion as a salve for the difficulties of their lives...such confidence increases in societies where there is a well-developed welfare state that redistributes income from the wealthy to the less fortunate. This could help explain why the US - with significant gaps in its government safety nets - is more religious than Europe despite having a similar level of economic development".

He goes on to assert that: "the basic function of religion is coping with anxiety. More specifically, it helps people to deal with the stress of uncertainty from third-world living conditions. In countries with a better standard of living, basic anxieties about food supply and illness recede and religion fades along with them...in very religious places, there is a great deal of misery because the quality of life is abysmal. Think of Afghanistan, or Somalia. Within that environment, the security blanket of religion may be the only effective anti-anxiety agent around. As a result, people who are deeply religious can achieve a level of calm that eludes their less religious neighbours...in developed countries, there are two key differences. First, the quality of life is so much better that large numbers of people (even the majority) can turn their backs on religion. Second, there are many other avenues for anxiety reduction that range from anti-anxiety drugs to endless entertainment".

Barber's conclusion is unequivocal: "in the grand scheme of global differences, religious people are actually quite miserable. Yet, thanks to religious beliefs and practices they are less miserable than they would otherwise be. If you want to be happier, the last thing you should do would be to move to a religious country. You might consider living in a country like Sweden instead where most people are happy atheists".

What helps societies to be happy?

Chapter 2 of the 2024 *World Happiness Report* describes six factors which show a strong statistical correlation with the data on reported happiness by country. The *World Happiness Report* has as its stated objective to help governments as they seek to set policy, and the factors it chooses to highlight naturally reflect this. The chosen factors are highly consistent with those we have just reviewed as being most relevant at the level of the individual, even if the specific metrics might be different: with, for example, "GDP per capita" being a proxy for "money". The authors tell us that: "taken together, these six variables explain more than three-quarters of the variation in national annual average ladder scores among countries and years, using data from 2005 through 2023", which is statistically a strong correlation indeed. The six factors are:

1. *Gross Domestic Product (GDP) per capita*, measured in terms of Purchasing Power Parity (PPP) adjusted to constant international dollars.

2. *Healthy life expectancy*, using data provided by the World Health Organisation (WHO).

3. *Social support*, measured as "the national average of the binary responses (0 = no, 1 = yes) to the Gallup World Poll (GWP) question 'if you were in trouble, do you have relatives or friends you can count on to help you whenever you need them, or not?'" The *World Happiness Report* authors note that there may be specific

aspects of the social culture in some societies which reinforce, or in other cases serve to restrict, happiness. For example: "on average, the countries of Latin America...have mean life evaluations that are significantly higher (by about 0.5 on the 0-10 scale) than predicted by the model. This difference has been attributed to a variety of factors, including some unique features of family and social life in Latin American countries".

4. *Freedom to make life choices*, measured as "the national average of binary responses to the GWP question 'are you satisfied or dissatisfied with your freedom to choose what you do with your life?'"

5. *Generosity*, measured as "the residual of regressing the national average of GWP (my note: "*Gallup World Poll*") responses to the donation question 'have you donated money to a charity in the past month?' on log GDP per capita". This ties to the idea that the act of giving can serve to increase our own personal happiness, as well as benefiting the recipient.

6. *Perceptions of corruption*, measured as "the average of binary answers to two GWP questions: 'is corruption widespread throughout the government or not?' and 'is corruption widespread within businesses or not?' Where data for government corruption are missing, the perception of business corruption is used as the overall corruption-perception measure".

It is hardly surprising that citizens are on average likely to be happier living in a society which is wealthier, healthier, more cohesive, freer, in which people are more prone to help their fellows who may be in need, and in which government and businesses are felt to have lower levels of corruption. Still, there is surely value in identifying that these specific factors are indeed critical, with the caveat that the report also notes that some additional factors may be relevant but cannot currently reliably be measured on a global basis, for example unemployment, inequality, and the extent to which people feel they have a sense of purpose in their life.

Finally, on inequality specifically, the jury remains out on the extent to which this does or does not correlate statistically with average levels of happiness. A case that it does is made forcefully in the 2009 book *The Spirit Level*, authored by the British social scientists Richard Wilkinson and Kate Pickett. However, their arguments were swiftly rebutted by another book, *The Spirit Level Delusion*, published in 2010 by the British journalist Christopher Snowdon. Snowdon points out (on p54) that nowhere in their original book do Wilkinson and Pickett actually show a statistical correlation between happiness and inequality, then goes on to make exactly this comparison for a sample of 28 countries for which reliable data is available, incidentally using the *World Values Survey* as the source for happiness. Snowdon's analysis shows no correlation.

PART E: Personal meaning

The factors we have reviewed in the previous two sections all demonstrate a statistical correlation with happiness. Correlation does not always imply causation, of course, but it is reasonable to conclude nonetheless that the more of these things we have the happier we are likely to be, and vice versa.

Still, they do not explain everything about what it is to be truly fulfilled. As humans we are "inherently meaning-making creatures", as Cacioppo and Patrick put it on pp176-7 of *Loneliness*. We search for patterns of meaning in our external environment, to help us survive and thrive; and also in our own self, seeking self-knowledge as the Delphic Oracle exhorts and driven by a fundamental need to feel that who we are, and what we do, matters: in other words, has "meaning".

Psychologists Steger, Kashdan, Sullivan, & Lorentz provide a pithy summary: "the search for meaning... expresses the deep-seated human desire to understand, integrate, and synthesise experience", in an article with the admittedly non-pithy title of *Understanding the Search for Meaning in Life: Personality, Cognitive Style, and the Dynamic Between Seeking and Experiencing Meaning*, published in the *Journal of Personality 76:2* in April 2008.

Whatever meaning we find will necessarily be personal and subjective, living as we do in a Universe which itself lacks objective purpose as we discussed in Chapter 1. It follows that in seeking meaning we must look not externally but rather inside ourself. As we will see, on this as on other topics research can help us to identify things that people on average find meaningful. But only we can decide what is truly relevant to us.

The good news is that the data suggests that, like happiness more broadly, personal meaning is eminently achievable. What is more, for most of us success is unlikely to require grand gestures or heroic acts, but rather will be found in the everyday business of living – the simple pleasures that life has to offer; achievements that we feel enable us to fulfil our personal potential; and most of all through the personal relationships and sense of "belonging" that we are able to create and sustain.

The Meaning of Life

Our starting point is that to search for "The Meaning of Life" in the conventional sense is to embark on a futile quest. As we have explored in some detail, the Universe is inherently random and amoral, and although the natural Laws of Physics are a source of legitimate enquiry and wonder there is no sense in which they are the product of any kind of intentional Grand Plan.

It is therefore no surprise that some of the most memorable answers to the question "what is the meaning of life?" are provided by satirists. Famously, British author Douglas Adams gives the answer to "The Ultimate Question of Life, the Universe and Everything" at the end of his 1979 novel *The Hitchhiker's Guide to the Galaxy*. The answer is (spoiler alert): 42; spawning an extensive subsequent literature on why Adams chose this number specifically.

Whatever the origin of the specific number, in the world Adams creates the fact that 42 is shown to be the answer serves only to spark the realisation that the Ultimate Question which has produced it is itself unknown. This is discovered at the end of the next novel in the series, *The Restaurant at the End of the Universe* (second spoiler alert): "what do you get when you multiply six by nine?"

In similar vein, in 1983 the British comedy team Monty Python released an entire movie rejoicing in the title *The Meaning of Life*. And sure enough, towards the end this "meaning" is duly revealed (final spoiler alert): "well, it's nothing very special. Try and be nice to people, avoid eating fat, read a good book every now and then, get some walking in, and try and live together in peace and harmony with people of all creeds and nations".

There's really nothing to add, except perhaps to observe that modern dietary advice suggests that eating an appropriate amount of the right kind of fat might actually be ok.

Meaning in life

American psychologists Laura King and Joshua Hicks propose a way to "escape the quandaries" associated with searching for the Meaning of Life, in their article *The Science of Meaning in Life*, published by *The Annual Review of Psychology*, dated 8 September 2020. The authors suggest reframing the quest such that rather than seeking "the meaning of life" the focus is instead on finding "meaning in life".

This may feel semantic, although precision in language can be important, as we discussed in Chapter 2. The authors indeed go on to explain, on p562, that the semantics are the point, because the new framing captures the inherently subjective nature of the topic: "one way to escape these quandaries is to focus on prepositions, separating the meaning of life from the meaning in life. The meaning of life implies one principle that somehow provides a final answer, the profound secret through which human life, at last, makes sense or matters. In contrast, when we talk about meaning in life, we are talking about an experience, a mental state. Klinger (1977, P. 10) captured this idea: 'the meaningfulness of someone's life cannot be inferred just from knowing his or her objective circumstances. Meaningfulness is something very subjective, a pervasive quality of a person's inner life. It is experienced both as ideas and as emotions. It is clear, then, that when we ask about the meaningfulness of someone's life we are asking about the qualities of his or her inner experience'".

King and Hicks continue, on p563: "understanding meaning in life requires that we surrender the vague, mysterious domain of the meaning of life to philosophers and theologians (my note: they might have added, and satirists) and instead satisfy ourselves with a more circumscribed terrain. The science of meaning in life, as a subjective experience, begins with the assumption that people experience to varying degrees something they recognise as meaning in their lives and they can report on that experience".

They go on to discuss how subjective meaning can best be measured. Suffice to say that, as with our earlier discussion of happiness and wellbeing more broadly, on p564 they conclude that a survey-based approach can work: "a multitude of studies conclude that whatever people mean when they say their lives are meaningful has important implications".

On p565 the authors define "meaning": "King and colleagues (2006, P. 180) summarised scholarly definitions of meaning as follows: 'lives may be experienced as meaningful when they are felt to have significance beyond the trivial or momentary, to have purpose, or to have a coherence that transcends chaos'. Similarly Steger (2012, p. 165) defined meaning as 'the web of connections, understandings, and interpretations that help us comprehend our experience and formulate plans directing our energies to the achievement of our desired future. Meaning provides us with the sense that our lives matter, that they make sense, and that they are more than the sum of our seconds, days, and years'".

Finally, on pp565-8 King and Hicks describe what they call "three primary components of meaning in life", specifically:

- *Comprehension/coherence* – "humans are motivated to understand and make sense of their lives and the world more broadly (e.g., Fiske 2018, Yalom 1980)...at its most basic level, coherence arises when one understands experience".

- *Purpose* – "purpose reflects the feeling that one's behaviour is guided by personally valued goals (Klinger 1977, McKnight & Kashdan 2009). Purposeful goal pursuits are often consistent with core aspects of identity and may contribute to the development of self-knowledge itself (Bronk 2011)".

- *Existential mattering/significance* – "the notion of existential mattering or significance refers to the extent to which a person believes their life counts - i.e. that their existence has and will have a lasting impact on the world. Mattering is tied to the belief that one's existence will continue to influence others across time and space".

Will to meaning

We have repeatedly heard from Viktor Frankl, the 20th century Jewish-Austrian psychiatrist who encouraged us to embrace the existential freedom which lies in the "gap" between a stimulus and how we choose to respond. Frankl also proposed that what he called a "will to meaning" is the fundamental and preeminent human need, and that fulfilling this need is what ultimately enables us to find true happiness. Of course, to find personal meaning we must look internally, taking us to the very centre of the metaphorical onion described in the Introduction to this book.

Our discussion of meaning will be guided extensively by Frankl's ideas, in particular his book *Man's Search for Meaning*, published in 1992 and comprising a collection of texts written in the preceding decades. These include *Experiences in a Concentration Camp*, first published in 1946, in German, which draws on the more than three years Frankl spent as an inmate of Auschwitz and other Nazi concentration camps during the Second World War; *Logotherapy in a nutshell*, first published in 1962; and *The Case for a Tragic Optimism*, the text of a speech given in 1983. All quotes and page references relate to the 1992 edition of *Man's Search for Meaning*.

Frankl called his overall approach "logotherapy" after the Greek word "logos" which he translates as "meaning". On p117 of *Man's Search for Meaning*, he summarises his central idea: "it is one of the basic tenets of logotherapy that man's main concern is not to gain pleasure or to avoid pain but rather to see a meaning in his life".

His approach was sometimes dubbed "the Third Viennese school of psychology" and on p104 he explicitly compares his own thinking with that of the other two notable Viennese schools: "according to logotherapy, this striving to find a meaning in one's life is the primary motivational force in man. That is why I speak of a *will to meaning* in contrast to the pleasure principle (or, as we could also term it, the *will to pleasure*) on which Freudian psychoanalysis is centred, as well as in contrast to the *will to power* on which Adlerian psychology, using the term 'striving for superiority,' is focused" (author's emphases throughout).

Frankl does not propose that there is such a thing as a single universal Meaning. On the contrary, he asserts that whatever meaning we may find will inevitably be specific to us as an individual. What is more, our personal meaning will not necessarily remain constant over time. Rather, we must work to shape and "actualise" it, through the choices we make and the actions we take, day by day. On p113 he says: "the meaning of life differs from man to man, from day to day and from hour to hour. What matters, therefore, is not the meaning of life in general but rather the specific meaning of a person's life at a given moment. To put the question in general terms would be comparable to the question posed to a chess champion: 'tell me, Master, what is the best move in the world?' There simply is no such thing as the best or even a good move apart from a particular situation in a game and the particular personality of one's opponent. The same holds for human existence. One should not search for an abstract meaning of life. Everyone has his own specific vocation or mission in life to carry out a concrete assignment which demands fulfilment. Therein he cannot be replaced, nor can his life be repeated. Thus, everyone's task is as unique as is his specific opportunity to implement it".

We are each free to choose our own meaning, and then to actualise it through our everyday behaviours. Frankl's experience of life in the death camps provides a stark illustration, described on p135: "a human being is not one thing among others; *things* determine each other, but *man* (Frankl's emphasis in both cases) is ultimately self-determining. What he becomes - within the limits of endowment and environment - he has made out of himself. In the concentration camps, for example, in this living laboratory and on this testing ground, we watched and witnessed some of our comrades behave like swine while others behaved like saints. Man has both potentialities within himself; which one is actualised depends on decisions but not on conditions".

Finally, on pp140-1, happiness may be the legitimate end goal but meaning is the means by which it can be achieved: "happiness cannot be pursued; it must ensue. One must have a reason to 'be happy'. Once the reason is found, however, one becomes happy automatically...a human being is not one in pursuit of happiness but rather in search of a reason to become happy".

Experiencing meaning

A majority of people indeed report that they experience meaning in their life.

King and Hicks explain, on pp564-5 of *The Science of Meaning in Life*, referenced above: "to find out how meaningful life is, on average, Heintzelman & King (2014a) gathered descriptive statistics from various data sets including measures of meaning in life. Drawing on large-scale representative surveys, they found the levels of meaning in life espoused were typically rather high, above the midpoint of the rating scales used. For example, the Centers for Disease Control and Prevention administered three items from the MLQ presence subscale to a representative sample of North Americans (N > 5,000; Kobau et al. 2010). Average endorsement was significantly higher than the midpoint rating scale. For instance, the item 'my life has a clear sense of purpose' (which had the lowest average endorsement) was rated a 4 or 5 on a 1-5 scale by nearly 60% of the sample. Beyond the United States, a Gallup World Poll conducted on representative samples of 132 nations included the item 'does your life have a special purpose or meaning?' and averaging across nations, 91% of the pollees responded in the affirmative (Oishi & Diener 2014)". (My note: MLQ stands for "Meaning in Life Questionnaire"; this was developed by Steger et al. in 2006 and according to the authors has since "emerged as the most widely used measure of meaning in life").

Finding personal meaning is associated with a host of physical and psychological benefits, described by psychologists Lambert, Stillman, Hicks, Kamble, Baumeister, and Fincham in their 2013 article *To Belong is to Matter: Sense of Belonging Enhances Meaning in Life*, published in *Personality and Social Psychology Bulletin 39* by the Society for Personality and Social Psychology, Inc: "some people's search to find meaning is more fruitful than it is for others...the belief that one's life lacks meaning is associated with a number of negative mental and physical outcomes, whereas the belief that one's life is full of meaning is associated with a number of positive variables (see Steger, 2012, for a comprehensive review). The negative consequences of low meaning include psychopathology (Crumbaugh & Maholick, 1964), stress (Mascaro & Rosen, 2006), need for therapy (Battista & Almond, 1973), suicidal ideation (Harlow, Newcomb, & Bentler, 1986), and depression (Debats, van der Lubbe, & Wezeman, 1993; Mascaro & Rosen, 2005). In contrast, high levels of meaning are associated with good physical health and general well-being (Reker, Peacock, & Wong, 1987; Wong & Fry, 1998; Zika & Chamberlain, 1987, 1992)".

In sum, experiencing meaning in one's life might be described as the Holy Grail of existence. Unlike the Grail, however, a quest for meaning is eminently achievable, albeit certainly not guaranteed. Whatever meaning we find will inevitably be personal and subjective, and we should expect it to change both over time and from one circumstance to another.

We'll close this chapter, and the book, by reviewing first Viktor Frankl's suggestions and then more recent research on the topic.

Sources of meaning

Sources of meaning - Frankl

Frankl proposes three ways in which personal meaning may be discovered, on p115 of *Man's Search for Meaning*: "(1) by creating a work or doing a deed; (2) by experiencing something or encountering someone; and (3) by the attitude we take toward unavoidable suffering". He also highlights the importance of "actualising" our own latent potential, reinforcing that it is our actions which ultimately come to define us.

1. Creating a work or doing a deed.

Frankl asserts, later on p115, that it is "quite obvious" what is meant by his first source of meaning: "the way of achievement or accomplishment". And indeed it needs little elaboration. There is of course a virtually infinite list of potential candidate deeds and works, some of which may be lifetime goals but most of which are likely to be relevant to a particular context and period of time. Entrepreneurs may be inspired, or feel compelled, to create businesses or other institutions; artists to create; and those with a vocation to pursue it, such as doctors, nurses, teachers or indeed priests. At a more mundane but not necessarily less important level are everyday accomplishments such as striving to be a good spouse, parent or friend; pursuing a career; or engaging in a hobby, for example tending an allotment. Speaking personally, researching and writing this book has been an important source of meaning for me for the five years or so I have been engaged on it.

Frankl offers a poignant example of his own, crediting his survival in the death camps against all the odds to his passion to see his work on logotherapy come to some kind of fruition. He had developed his ideas in the years immediately before the Second World War and he tells how on entering his first camp he was carrying a manuscript intended to be his first book, which soon after his arrival was taken from him. Recreating it became a burning, and sustaining, passion. On pp109-110 he relates: "as for myself, when I was taken to the concentration camp of Auschwitz, a manuscript of mine ready for publication was confiscated. Certainly, my deep desire to write this manuscript anew helped me to survive the rigours of the camp I was in. For instance, when in a camp in Bavaria I fell ill with typhus fever, I jotted down on little scraps of paper many notes intended to enable me to re-write the manuscript, should I live to the day of liberation. I am sure that this reconstruction of my lost manuscript in the dark barracks of a Bavarian concentration camp assisted me in overcoming the danger of cardiovascular collapse". The book was eventually published in 1955, titled *The Doctor and the Soul: an Introduction to Logotherapy*.

2. Experiencing something or encountering someone.

Frankl explains his second potential source of meaning later on p115: "the second way of finding a meaning in life is by experiencing something – such as goodness, truth and beauty – by experiencing nature and culture or, last but not least, by experiencing another human being in his very uniqueness – by loving him".

We have already discussed both these topics. It will suffice here to recall Keats' insight that, at least in some circumstances "beauty is truth and truth beauty"; and Forster's exhortation to "only connect...". Echoing Tennyson, Frankl also suggests that love for another person can continue to be a source of meaning in our own life even if our loved one dies. On p117 of *Man's Search for Meaning* he says: "once, an elderly general practitioner consulted me because of his severe depression. He could not overcome the loss of his wife who had died two years before and whom he had loved above all else. Now, how could I help him? What should I tell him? Well, I refrained from telling him anything but instead confronted him with the question, 'what would have happened, Doctor, if you had died first, and your wife would have had to survive you?' 'Oh,' he said, 'for her this would have been terrible; how she would have suffered!' Whereupon I replied, 'you see, Doctor, such a suffering has been spared her, and it was you who have spared her this suffering - to be sure, at the price that now you have to survive and mourn her'. He said no word but shook my hand and calmly left my office".

3. The attitude we take to unavoidable suffering.

It is hardly surprising that reaction to suffering featured prominently in Frankl's thinking, given. Having experienced more than three years of unrelenting horror in the Nazi death camps he was eventually freed to discover that his wife, both his parents, his brother and much of his extended family had died in them, not to mention countless friends and acquaintances. Survival and liberation also brought their own challenges in re-integrating to a "normal" life, as he describes movingly on pp94-100 of *Man's Search for Meaning*.

He explains how our reaction to suffering can be a source of meaning, on p116: "we must never forget that we may also find meaning in life even when confronted with a hopeless situation, when facing a fate that cannot be changed. For what then matters is to bear witness to the uniquely human potential at its best, which is to transform a personal tragedy into a triumph, to turn one's predicament into a human achievement. When we are no longer able to change the situation – just think of an incurable disease such as inoperable cancer – we are challenged to change ourselves".

And, suffering more generally is something we all experience, even though of course we may hope never to undergo the particular horrors that Frankl and other Holocaust victims did. To an extent, in a Universe without objective meaning "to live is to suffer", as the American psychologist Gordon Allport puts it on p9 of his preface to the 2004 edition of *Man's Search for Meaning*: "it is here that we encounter the central theme of existentialism: to live is to suffer, to survive is to find meaning in the suffering. If there is a purpose in life at all, there must be a purpose in suffering and in dying".

To be clear, Frankl does not suggest that suffering is somehow desirable. On the contrary, on p177 he asserts that it should be avoided wherever possible: "let me make it perfectly clear that in no way is suffering *necessary* to find meaning. I only insist that meaning is possible even in spite of suffering - provided, certainly, that the suffering is unavoidable. If it *were* avoidable, however, the meaningful thing to do would be to remove its cause, be it psychological, biological or political. To suffer unnecessarily is masochistic rather than heroic (Frankl's emphasis in both cases)".

The point is that even in situations as extreme as the death camps we still have freedom to choose our response, and meaning can be found in how we exercise this choice. Frankl explains, on pp74-6: "the experiences of camp life show that man does have a choice of action. There were enough examples, often of a heroic nature, which proved that apathy could be overcome, irritability suppressed. Man can preserve a vestige of spiritual freedom, of independence of mind, even in such terrible conditions of psychic and physical stress...we who lived in concentration camps can remember the men who walked through the huts comforting others, giving away their last piece of bread. They may have been few in number, but they offer sufficient proof that everything can be taken from a man but one thing: the last of the human freedoms - to choose one's attitude in any given set of circumstances, to choose one's own way...it is this spiritual freedom - which cannot be taken away - that makes life meaningful and purposeful".

The meaning to be found in suffering, then, resides largely in how we choose to react to it when we must accept it as inevitable. Once again, personal relationships and meaningful deeds can be relevant, as Frankl explains on p88, incidentally quoting Nietzsche in the process: "a man who becomes conscious of the responsibility he bears toward a human being who affectionately waits for him, or to an unfinished work, will never be able to throw away his life. He knows the 'why' for his existence, and will be able to bear almost any 'how'".

4. *"Actualising" our personal potential.*

Later in *Man's Search For Meaning* Frankl describes a fourth potential source of meaning: striving to "actualise" our latent potential, in ways which carry a clear reminder of Maslow's "self-actualisation". We might paraphrase this as "to be the best we can be".

Frankl explains, on p110, that this inherent tension between what we are and what we might become can be a major source of motivation and energy: "it can be seen that mental health is based on a certain degree of tension, the tension between one what one has already achieved and what one still ought to accomplish, or the gap between what one is and what one should become. Such a tension is inherent in the human being and therefore is indispensable to mental well-being. We should not, then, be hesitant about challenging man with a potential meaning for him to fulfil. It is only thus that we evoke his will to meaning from its state of latency. I consider it a dangerous misconception of mental hygiene to assume that what man needs in the first place is equilibrium or, as it is called in biology, "homeostasis," i.e., a tensionless state. What man actually needs is not a tensionless state but rather the striving and struggling for a worthwhile goal, a freely chosen task. What he needs is not the discharge of tension at any cost but the call of a potential meaning waiting to be fulfilled by him".

And an emphasis on "actualisation", in other words action, can produce a level of fulfilment which has the potential to transcend ageing and even our eventual death, as Frankl outlines on p124-5: "those things which seem to take meaning away from human life include not only suffering but dying as well. I never tire of saying that the only really transitory aspects of life are the potentialities; that as soon as they are actualised, they are rendered realities at that very moment; they are saved and delivered into the past, wherein they are rescued and preserved from transitoriness. For, in the past, nothing is irretrievably lost but everything irrevocably stored...logotherapy, keeping in mind the essential transitoriness of human existence, is not pessimistic but rather activistic. To express this point figuratively we might say: The pessimist resembles a man who observes with fear and sadness that his wall calendar, from which he daily tears a sheet, grows thinner with each passing day. On the other hand, the person who attacks the problems of life actively is like a man who removes each successive leaf from his calendar and files it neatly and carefully away with its predecessors, after first having jotted down a few diary notes on the back. He can reflect with pride and joy on all the richness set down in these notes, on all the life he has already lived to the fullest. What will it matter to him if he notices that he is growing old? Has he any reason to envy the young people who he sees, or wax nostalgic over his own lost youth? What reasons has he to envy a young person? For the possibilities that a young person has, the future which is in store for him? 'No, thank you,' he will think. 'Instead of possibilities, I have realities in my past, not only the reality of work done and of love loved, but of sufferings bravely suffered. The sufferings are even the things of which I am most proud, though these are things which cannot inspire envy'".

Sources of meaning – post Frankl

In their article *The Science of Meaning in Life*, referenced above, King and Hicks offer a contemporary take on what they describe as: "the most empirically supported antecedents of meaning in life", adding the caveat that their list is "not exhaustive". There is some overlap with Frankl's suggestions and indeed with our earlier review of happiness in the round, but for the main part their list is complementary. Specifically, King and Hicks list six factors which research shows correlate statistically with people experiencing meaning in their lives:

- Positive affect
- Social connections
- Religion and worldviews
- The Self
- Mental time travel
- Mortality awareness

5. Positive affect.

Simple enjoyment of life's pleasures can make us feel good in the moment, of course, but can also enhance our sense of meaning and fulfilment more broadly. King and Hicks explain, on pp569 and 571: "positive affect (i.e., feelings of happiness, cheerfulness, enjoyment, fun) is a robust, if controversial, antecedent of meaning in life...the strong link between positive affect and meaning in life suggests that the hedonic versus eudaemonic distinction may not carve the good life at its joints".

Correlation does not necessarily imply causation, as we have seen before; and it is in any case a moot point which direction whatever causality might exist is travelling: is it that experiencing life's pleasures leads to a deeper sense of fulfilment, or that feeling fulfilled makes it more likely that day-to-day life will be pleasurable? It could of course be a combination of the two. Either way, the point is that enjoying life day-to-day is statistically associated with feelings of deeper fulfilment.

6. Belonging.

The notion of "belonging" clearly reinforces our need for sociability, a topic we discussed extensively in Chapter 3 and also earlier in this chapter.

Still, "belonging" adds an additional dimension, and therefore merits brief elaboration. The essential point is that whilst forming close personal relationships and being a member of one or more social groups are both good for our happiness, neither is sufficient. It is also important that we feel we are truly accepted by and fit into whatever group.

American psychologists Lambert, Stillman, Hicks, Kamble, Baumeister, and Fincham explain, on p1418 of an article titled: *To Belong is to Matter: Sense of Belonging Enhances Meaning in Life*, published in *Personality and Social Psychology Bulletin 39* by the Society for Personality and Social Psychology, Inc, dated 2013: "many theorists have suggested that the human drive for social relationships such that forming and maintaining social bonds reflects an innate tendency that is adaptive and crucial for survival (Ainsworth, 1989; Axelrod & Hamilton, 1981; Barash, 1977; Baumeister & Leary, 1995; Bowlby, 1969; Buss, 1990s; Moreland, 1987). In fact, there are physical and mental health repercussions of failing to form interpersonal attachments (for a review, see Baumeister & Leary, 1995). They chose the phrase *need to belong* (author's emphasis) to describe the pervasive human drive to form positive, close attachments. This article has been widely cited, and the term *need to belong* (again, author's emphasis) has therefore been used as a general term for the desire to form relationships. Of course, it is possible to have positive relationships, thereby satisfying the need to belong in a general sense, yet still not feel that one is fully accepted. In other words, satisfying a general need for positive social relationships - for instance, by participating in a fraternity or sorority - does not guarantee the subjective experience of belonging. In the present investigation, our interest in belonging went beyond whether one has positive relationships and extends to the subjective experience of having relationships that bring about a secure sense of fitting in. We refer to this as having a sense of belonging". This definition is reinforced on p1425: "having a sense of belonging is to have a relationship with people, or a group of people, that brings about a secure feeling of fitting in. As such, sense of belonging is not the same as simply having social relationships. Nor is it synonymous with having positive, close relationships. Our use of the term *belonging* is similar to that suggested by Brewer (2008), who proposed that *belonging* is appropriate for describing group membership, whereas *bonding* is preferable when discussing close attachments. The current work suggests that belonging, in the sense of fitting in with others, is closely related to finding meaning in life (authors' emphasis throughout)".

The most important source of a sense of belonging turns out to be family, at least for the young college-educated American adults among whom the relevant research was conducted. The findings are reported by almost the same team of American psychologists (Lambert, Stillman, Baumeister, Fincham, Hicks & Graham) in a paper titled *Family as a salient source of meaning in young adulthood*, published by *The Journal of Positive Psychology*, and dated 20 October 2010. The authors summarise, on p373: "across five studies, we found evidence that family relationships are a potent source of meaning in life and contribute to a sense of meaning. Study 1 demonstrates the salience of family relationships for creating meaning. We found that 68% of participants reported family to be the one thing that brought the most meaning to their lives, while the next most commonly cited source of meaning (friendships) was endorsed by 14% of respondents. When allowed to mention three sources of meaning in life, 90% of participants mentioned family as contributing to meaning in their lives, compared to 66% who mentioned friends. Thus, family was the most prevalent and salient contributor to meaning for these participants...in Study 2, we hoped to increase the breadth of our findings by comparing the contribution of family relationships with 11 likely alternative sources of meaning. We found that participants rate family as being more important to meaning than any other alternative source presented". (My note: on p369 the authors tell us that the full list of potential sources of meaning from which respondents were invited to select was: family; friends; happiness; religious faith; achievements; self-acceptance; personal growth; self-worth; justice/fairness; personal goals; intimacy; and helping others.)

7. *Religious and other worldviews.*

Having a coherent "worldview", literally a view of how the world works, is also statistically associated with finding meaning in our life.

Organised religions tend to specialise in offering a ready-made worldview, and on pp571-2 of *The Science of Meaning in Life*, referenced above, King and Hicks comment that religiosity indeed correlates with experiencing meaning in life: "worldviews are overarching belief structures that provide a sense of how the world works...they help us make sense of experiences, they tell us what goals have value, and they provide us with a place in the grand scheme...religiosity is positively related to meaning in life".

Of course, earlier in this chapter we also saw that the evidence for a correlation between religiosity and happiness more broadly is mixed, and in those cases where a link is observed it may be best explained by the social connections that religious observance enables rather than by the underlying religious belief itself.

In any case, it is not necessary to embrace religion to develop a coherent worldview, as King and Hicks attest:

"although they have received scant empirical attention, nonreligious worldviews might also serve as sources of meaning in life". Indeed, it is the immodest hope of the author that this book might contribute to a coherent, robustly secular, worldview.

8. The Self.

Experiencing meaning in our life is associated with feeling that we are authentic: that there is some level of congruence between our self-image and ideal-self, as Carl Rogers puts it. In effect, this is statistical evidence to support the wisdom of Polonius' advice "to thine own self be true", with the important addition that this applies most appropriately to our ideal, or "best" self.

King and Hicks observe, on pp572-3 of *The Science of Meaning in Life*: "feeling a strong connection to one's self may...help us make sense of our lives. Often understanding one's self goes hand-in-hand with an overarching sense of purpose, as it helps identifying what one is meant to do (e.g., McAdams & Olson 2010)...a rich literature speaks to the role of autobiographical memories in helping us find purpose and coherence in our lives (e.g., James 1893, Pasupathi 2001)... many scholars posit that authenticity is crucial to a meaningful existence (e.g., McGregor & Little 1998, Ryan & Deci 2001). Early research supported these ideas, showing that narratives describing meaningful experiences often contain themes of being connected to oneself (compared to themes of self-disconnection in narratives of meaninglessness)".

The authors caveat, however, on p573, that this may not always be as easy as it might sound, particularly for those facing some form of social stigma: "...for people who exist in unjust social systems, who face the challenges of prejudice and negative stereotypes, authenticity may be a complicated path to meaning in life".

9. *Mental time travel.*

The sense of continuity we get from comparing our current Self to past or possible, imaginary, future Selves is also associated with experiencing our life as meaningful, accepting that both memory and imagination are prone to fallibility as we saw earlier. King and Hicks comment, on p573 of *The Science of Meaning in Life*: "a diverse line of literature suggests that the ability to mentally project oneself in the past, in the future and even into alternative realities can enhance the feeling that life is meaningful...placing one's self in a different reality can facilitate strong connections between one's current and distal selves, creating a sense of self-continuity and coherence".

10. *Mortality awareness.*

In our material world death is the final frontier, and as Gordon Allport reminded us in his Introduction to *Man's Search for Meaning* if we are find meaning in our life we must necessarily somehow come to terms with our own mortality, and with that of those we love.

King and Hicks elaborate, on p574 of *The Science of Meaning in Life*: "no treatment of the experience of meaning in life would be complete without considering death...the relationship between mortality awareness and meaning is at the heart of many perspectives in existential philosophy (e.g., Heidegger 1982 (1927)). These perspectives often overlap to suggest that acknowledging one's inevitable demise, paradoxically, has the potential to lead people to live a more authentic and meaningful existence (De Carvalho 2000). Perspectives in the psychological sciences draw similar conclusions".

On pp574-5 they explain how awareness of our own mortality may underpin our urge to transcend: "Terror

Management Theory (TMT) is the most prominent theory in psychology to explicitly address a link between mortality awareness and meaning (see Routledge & Vess 2018 for a review). According to TMT, awareness of mortality has the potential to evoke paralysing anxiety. From this perspective, we fend off this terror by investing in cultural worldviews (and self-esteem), attaching our existence to structures whose existence transcends our time on earth".

Finally, on p575 they reassure us that knowledge of the inevitability and finality of death does not inhibit, and may even enhance, our ability to find meaning in our life: "in sum, the awareness that life is finite - that even very good lives will end - does not inevitably destroy meaning in life. Rather, the fact that life ends appears to enhance its value or preciousness, potentially enhancing its ultimate subjective meaning".

Meaning as everyday experience

Whatever meaning we find in our life, the likelihood is that we will experience it not as some blinding revelation but rather through the minutiae of everyday existence. On p578 of *The Science of Meaning in Life* King and Hicks comment: "research has provided a sense of what meaning in life is and where it comes from. Meaning in life is a subjective sense that one's life makes sense, has purpose, and matters to others. Each of these aspects of meaning can emerge from everyday experiences such as the enactment of routines, the pursuit of goals, and engagement in social relationships. Meaning in life appears to be somewhat commonplace: on average, people rate their lives as pretty meaningful. The things that make life meaningful are resources that are widely available to most people - including being in a good mood, engaging in social relationships, and having religious faith" (my note: recall that they also highlight that what they call "nonreligious worldviews" may serve a similar end, obviously an important caveat given the thrust of this book).

King and Hicks' bottom line is perversely encouraging: "everyday people appear to be living lives of meaning despite the best efforts of academic psychologists and philosophers to persuade them that meaning in life is rare or that there is, in fact, no meaning in life".

In sum, personal meaning is subjective and may even be somewhat arbitrary. But it is certainly there to be found, if once we choose to look.

Chapter summary

Happiness is the legitimate goal of our existence, appropriately defined as physical and especially psychological "wellbeing".

It is incumbent on each of us as individuals to find our own happiness, looking inside ourself for answers rather than to some external agency. Our odds improve if we are able to meet our basic needs such as food, shelter and security; and if we are able to sustain some level of health and material wealth. Ultimately, our happiness depends on us finding personal, subjective, meaning, which may change over time and will most likely be found mainly in the business of everyday living. There is no universal formula, but important elements may include: building and sustaining personal relationships of love, friendship and fellowship, which also enable a sense that we truly belong; achievements which we consider to be meaningful; and behaving in ways which satisfy our "inner voice" and help us feel that we have been true to our authentic Self.

Encouragingly, the research suggests that achieving personal happiness and meaning are eminently achievable for the majority of people, although they are certainly not inevitable. Ultimately, it is the choices we make and the actions we take which define us.

Specific beliefs include:

- "Happiness is the meaning and purpose of life, the whole aim and end of human existence".
- We each have a set of fundamental needs, with a profile which is unique to us. Happiness requires meeting these needs, to a greater or lesser extent. They are likely to form a loose hierarchy whereby higher-order needs become more relevant as more basic needs are met. Self-actualisation is at the top of the pile, defined as achieving one's personal full potential: being the best Self one feels one is capable of being, the closest possible to one's "ideal Self".
- Happiness is more appropriately defined as "wellbeing", comprising "hedonia", which tends to be more sensory in nature; and "eudemonia", which tends to be more psychological.
- Happiness is achievable: a majority of people report experiencing it.
- It is not realistic to pursue happiness directly. What is realistic is to pursue reasons to be happy, such that happiness then "ensues".
- A number of factors correlate statistically with individual happiness:
  - genes
  - life stage
  - relationships
  - health
  - money
  - work
  - religiosity, although the data here are not consistent, and to the extent a correlation with happiness is seen it may be based at least partly on the opportunities for social connection that religious practice affords

- Six factors have been identified which can be measured robustly and correlate to increased happiness at the level of a society:
  - material wealth, measured as GDP per capita
  - healthy life expectancy
  - social support
  - freedom to make life choices
  - generosity in the community
  - perceptions of corruption
- Beyond these, the key to happiness is to find personal meaning for our existence. To do this we need to look inside ourself. The evidence is that a large majority of people succeed.
- Finding meaning is ultimately subjective and personal. Nonetheless, research identifies a number of likely potential sources:
  - creating a work or doing a deed which has particular significance to us
  - experiencing something or encountering someone, in particular the quality and quantity of our social relationships
  - the attitude we take to unavoidable suffering
  - "actualising" personal potential: being the best Self we can be
  - experiencing positive affect: maximising pleasure and minimising pain
  - belonging: feeling truly accepted as a member of a social group
  - establishing a coherent "worldview", which may be religious but can also be secular
  - building authenticity, that is, cohesion between our self-image and our "ideal-Self"
  - mental time travel: building cohesion between our current and past or future Self
  - using awareness of our own and others' mortality to reinforce rather than undermine our sense of meaning

- Meaning and happiness are likely to be found through, and rooted in, the everyday business of living.
- We are each responsible for our own happiness: the choices we make and the behaviours we demonstrate are ultimately what define us.

Summary of beliefs discussed

The core belief of this book is that we each have a precious opportunity, amounting to an obligation, to take responsibility for our own existence by embracing our ability to exercise existential choice in our life, in particular over what we do and how we behave.

We must do this in the knowledge, or more accurately belief, that we are fundamentally alone in an entirely material and therefore uncaring Universe, and so must ultimately look inside *ourself* for answers.

Happiness is our eventual goal, and the good news is that this is eminently achievable, although by no means certain. Ultimately it is the choices we make, and the actions we take, which define us.

A number of specific beliefs are explored in each chapter:

Nature

The core belief about Nature is that "we are living in a material world", with no need of or room for any element of supernatural explanation. Underpinning beliefs are:

– the Universe is governed by a set of inviolable natural laws, notably including quantum theory, which is inherently probabilistic not deterministic; and relativity, which reveals that even a concept as fundamental as time which may seem to us to be absolute is in fact relative.

– all life, including human life, is a product of the natural process of biological evolution, mediated through our genes and gene-combinations. Experience acts on our genes to make us who we are, predisposing us to think and act in particular ways; and since our specific genetic profile and personal experiences are obviously unique to each of us as individuals it follows that we are ourself ultimately unique.

Specific beliefs are:

- The Universe, including human life, is entirely natural, which is to say that it is entirely material, governed by a set of natural laws which are themselves inviolable. The supernatural is "real" only within the subjective world of the human mind, not in any objective external sense.
- All matter throughout the Universe, including human beings, is composed of fundamental particles, more accurately "wave-particles", which are themselves an expression of, and interchangeable with, underlying force fields which permeate the Universe. The total amount of energy these particles represent does not change, even as their distribution does.
- At a microscopic scale reality is probabilistic, meaning that random chance plays an important role.
- Things we may subjectively experience as absolute are in fact relative, specifically including Time and Space.
- Nature is inherently amoral, subject to the evolutionary algorithm: "replicate; vary; select".
- Humans are just of one of many species which all ultimately developed from a common ancestor in the 3.5 billion years or so since life on Earth began. Humans are not a "chosen" species, simply one which has been successful at out-competing other species, albeit for a relatively short period in terms of evolutionary time.
- As individuals, we each have a specific genetic profile which is unique to us, inherited from our biological parents. Our genes significantly affect, but do not completely determine, who we are. Our experiences and environment are important influences too.
- The natural world is in a constant state of flux, and there is much that we cannot predict or control, implying

amongst other things that we ourself should remain open to change.
- We are each part of a remarkable story which starts with Big Bang 13.6 billion years ago and continues right through until...us.

Consciousness

The core belief about consciousness is that "I am the captain of my soul", meaning that we each have some level of personal agency and are ultimately free to choose our own actions. However, our freedom is constrained in important ways, and our judgement can be fallible. Underpinning beliefs are:

- human consciousness creates agency: the possibility, and in a sense the obligation, to exercise conscious choice over what we do and how we behave; although this freedom is constrained by the fact that our genes and experiences predispose us to respond in certain ways to particular triggers.

- consciousness is fallible. In exercising personal choice, we face the possibility of cognitive error, psychological bias and random "noise", often operating below our conscious mind. We do well to cultivate self-knowledge about our own personal predilections.

Specific beliefs are:

- Consciousness is entirely material. There is no such thing as an immortal soul: our mortal life as a conscious being on Earth is our entire existence.
- Consciousness gives us the existential freedom to choose what we do and how we behave. In particular, executive function enables us to "mind the gap" between a stimulus and how we choose to respond.

- Exercising this freedom to choose can only be done by engaging our sense of "self", filtered through our own unique personality.
- Learning happens when our lived experiences act on our genes to form networks of neural connections, which are then strengthened or weakened over time. Our specific network of neural connections is unique to us. The most intense period for forming these is when we are young, but we continue to form new pathways, and strengthen or weaken others, throughout our life. This means that the experiences we have in our early years have a disproportionate impact on, but do not completely determine, the person we eventually become; and that some level of continuing growth and development remains possible even as we age.
- Consciousness is ultimately subjective. Our senses transmit data from the outside world, which our brain then uses to create a representation of "reality" inside our mind, as the basis for determining how best to respond to a given situation. Whilst this process is highly effective and efficient overall, it also lays us open to fallibility in important ways:

– our brain works on the basis of "data sampling", which is to say that it takes a subset of the total amount of data which is in theory available, and uses this to create a representation of reality inside. The picture our brain creates may not always be an accurate interpretation of the data. More than one valid interpretation may be possible from a particular set of data.

– our brain looks for patterns to make sense of the world around us. These often take the form of "cause-and-effect" relationships. We can be fooled into "seeing" a wrong pattern, or seeing a pattern where none exists.

– our brain tends to categorise, even though what it is dealing with is often (but not always) a continuum. This can lead us to think of things as binary, or rigidly defined, when in fact they are nuanced.

- Our behaviours are driven by a combination of instinct, emotion and reason. Whilst these are mainly processed in different parts of our physical brain, they also interact in important ways. Emotions are a powerful stimulus, although their effects often take place below the level of our conscious mind. We are prone to a (large) number of cognitive biases, which can mislead us into thinking we are acting rationally when in fact we are not.
- Consciousness gives us a number of important faculties, including:
- reason: the ability to think critically and analytically;
- emotions: which have a powerful effect on our behaviour, and largely define our experience of existence;
- language, without which it is hard to see how reason could work, but which also inevitably has limitations and can be prone to ambiguity or unclear meaning;
- a capacity for empathy, enabling us to experience the emotions of other people as if they were our own; and the ability to think ourself into others' shoes, called Theory of Mind. These faculties are particularly important to our ability to live as members of complex social groups, as well as to enjoying a textured mental life.
- memory, which is crucial to learning and our sense of self. However, memories are essentially reconstructions made by our brain, and can also be selective and fallible.
- imagination, specifically the ability to imagine concepts and things which are not currently and may never be real. This has enormous benefits, but also creates a challenge in for example clearly differentiating between fiction and fact.
- motivation and drive, which help us to take decisive action and get things done.
- Two factors stand out as having a big impact on how our individual consciousness functions:
- sleep is fundamental to both our brain and body. But many of us do not put sufficiently high priority on getting enough sleep, of sufficient quality.

– high levels of sustained stress can be associated with impaired brain function and undesirable health outcomes. At the same time, a "healthy" level of stress can be beneficial. Our own mindset can play an important role in how we experience stress.

• Consciousness has important implications for our personal existence:

– the fact that we have the freedom to exercise personal existential choice means that we should actively embrace it, and then take responsibility for the choices we make.

– the fact that our consciousness is fallible means that in making choices we should give appropriate consideration to the possibility of bias and error.

– "luck" is a fact of life, whereas "destiny" isn't.

– mindset matters: how we think about our life obviously affects how we feel about it, and can also influence outcomes.

– expectations matter: how we think about ourself and others can change what we and they feel and do.

Sociability

The core belief about sociability is "only connect...", meaning that we should focus our discretionary energy on building and sustaining meaningful personal relationships above all else. Underpinning beliefs are:

- we are social animals first and foremost. We are hardwired to behave in "groupish", which is to say cooperative, ways, anchored by powerful emotions such as love, friendship and fellowship. We are also each capable of anti-social, "selfish", behaviour.

– some of the most important existential choices we make are when to cooperate, privileging the interests of other people; and when to behave "selfishly", privileging our own. We do well to bias towards cooperation, but also to recognise that the appropriate choice in any particular situation is circumstantial.

Specific beliefs are:

- Humans are fundamentally social animals. The extent and manner of our capacity to cooperate sets us apart from other species, even though at a generic level cooperation is widespread in nature.
- Sociability is important for transmitting culture, enabling humans to share acquired knowledge between different groups and to accumulate it over generations. Sociability also promotes the sharing of resources, enabling and requiring that humans cooperate to an extent and in ways not seen in other species.
- Our success, as individuals and a species, is closely linked to our ability to develop and sustain strong social connections. Nonetheless, our specific propensity, and need, for connection is unique to us as an individual, a product of our genes and personal experiences.
- For most of our evolutionary existence as a species, humans lived in small bands practicing a hunter-gather lifestyle. The development of agriculture around 10,000 BCE led to economic surpluses and the growth of larger, more complex social units, generally organised according to some form of hierarchy. This in turn fuelled explosive growth in population leading to rapid change in our social environment, particularly in recent centuries.
- We retain considerable capacity for anti-social behaviours, as individuals and as a species. Notably:
− a tendency towards hierarchy and status. Low status can be associated with high levels of stress, albeit this is significantly influenced by the psychology and mindset of the individual experiencing it.
− a capacity for violence, bullying and intimidation, although there are also potentially indications that over the long run levels of physical violence are declining.

- a capacity to influence and persuade, which can also mean to manipulate and deceive.
• As members of a social group, or groups, we are frequently confronted by the need to make existential choices between behaviours which are "cooperative" (in the interests of the group overall, or of specific other group members) versus "selfish" (in our own interest). The individual decisions are often small and may seem inconsequential. But collectively the decisions we make come to define us.
• It is often in our own self-interest to cooperate, as well as in the interests of the group more broadly. However, this is only true so long as we are confident that our counterparty will reciprocate cooperation. If we consistently cooperate and they do not, there is an obvious risk, over time a probability, that we will be exploited as "naïve".
• Cooperation is likely to be most productive if we act on four core principles:
- don't be envious: accept that cooperation will benefit others, sometimes as much as or possibly even more than it benefits us.
- don't be the first to "defect", which is to say to behave selfishly.
- reciprocate both cooperation and defection. Don't simply "turn the other cheek" if someone else behaves selfishly; at the same time, be proportionate in responding, and be "forgiving" if they demonstrate willingness to change their own behaviour.
- don't be too clever: don't make it too hard for another party to see what we are doing, and why.
• Even if we find ourself in an environment dominated by selfish behaviour it may be possible to reap the rewards from a cooperative approach if we can find a core group willing to cooperate reliably with us, and then ensure that the majority, although not necessarily all, of our transactions are with members of this group.

- Evolution has shaped some of our most powerful emotions to reinforce sociability, in particular love and affection, encouraging us to behave pro-socially towards individuals for whom we feel these things; and loneliness and social alienation, which encourage us to build social connections, but make us feel miserable if we fail.
- "Only connect": a satisfying level of social connection is critical for our mental health, and also good for our physical health. The clear implication is that we should place a high priority on cultivating and sustaining personal relationships with those with whom we feel a connection.
- Romantic love is the most intense form of connection, reinforcing the core evolutionary pair-bond. Neuroscience shows that broadly similar areas of the brain are activated in a similar way, albeit at a lower level of intensity, by other kinds of emotional connection such as parental love and friendship.
- Sexual attraction is an important part of romantic love, particularly during the early stages. An intriguing hypothesis suggests that our brains may have evolved in the way they have at least partly in response to a female preference to be entertained as part of courtship ritual.
- Evolutionary theory predicts that in some circumstances both males and females have a biological incentive to seek sex outside "marriage", which is to say outside a particular pair-bond. There is clear evidence that a material number of people in modern societies indeed do this, albeit not to the extent that it is the norm.
- Altruism also has an evolutionary explanation: in the right environment the genes for extreme pro-social behaviour can spread even if the particular individual who carries them does not themself survive.
- Loneliness is bad for both our mental and physical health. The good news is that the natural state is one of social fulfillment, and being alone does not necessarily

imply feeling lonely. Still, around one-third of adults globally report feeling lonely at least some of the time.
- Our emotions are ultimately triggered by subjective perceptions, and are therefore susceptible to the mind traps which are an integral part of human consciousness. Expectations can also influence outcomes. We do well to strive for expectations which are realistic, and to guard against an innate tendency to assume the worst about others. If and when we feel lonely, we should beware entering a negative spiral of thoughts in which personal feelings of isolation cause us to adopt a systematically negative interpretation of events, and potentially to behave in ways which deepen our isolation rather than mitigate it.
- Love, including but not limited to romantic love, has the potential to transcend; albeit it can also cause great misery when it is lost or rejected. Still, it is actively to be sought, and in the final analysis: "'tis better to have loved and lost; than never to have loved at all".

Morality

The core belief about morality is that: "there is nothing either good or bad, but thinking makes it so": morality itself is essentially a human invention and therefore subjective and relative. Underpinning beliefs are:

- we each have an innate moral sense, which drives our feelings and behaviour in significant, often unconscious, ways, generally serving to reinforce pro-social, which is to say cooperative, behaviours especially towards people we perceive to be members of our own social group.

- however, moral judgements that we may experience as being binary may often turn out to be nuanced and circumstantial when subjected to closer scrutiny. Our moral instincts can be particularly problematic when it comes to people we perceive as "other", often serving to alienate rather than bind us.

Specific beliefs are:

- Morality is a fundamental aspect of what it is to be human, to the extent that to seek to deny it would literally be to be "inhuman" in some important sense.
- Morality serves to regulate behaviour with human social groups, generally reinforcing cooperation in preference to competition, at least between members of the same group albeit not necessarily between different groups.
- All "neurologically normal" humans share some high-level moral instincts to a greater or lesser degree, including for example a capacity for empathy for people with whom we feel some level of connection; and a sense of fairness, experienced mainly locally, which is to say with respect to others whom we perceive are similar to us.
- However, specific moral norms vary widely across cultures.
- Several factors complicate our ability to apply moral instinct in our everyday life, including:
  - morality is ultimately a human construct, not an absolute law of nature. One important implication is that morality is relative: there is no truly objective basis on which to demonstrate that one set of moral norms is superior to another.
  - moral instinct is instinctive – we feel first, and reason later. Often, the role our rational brain plays is simply to provide a post-hoc narrative to justify actions which have in reality been prompted by our subconscious mind.
  - our instincts do not always prompt us to behave "morally".

- morality is often nuanced and contextual: moral choices which seem intuitively clear may often turn out not to be on closer, rational, examination.
- morality typically prompts us to privilege other members of our own group at the expense of members of other groups, even prompting us to dehumanise people we regard as "other". This is "the tragedy of commonsense morality".
- moral norms are not stable, but rather change over time. Technological and social changes are creating important emergent moral questions for which there is no obvious historical precedent, and for which tradition is therefore unlikely to provide the answers.

• There are four potential implications for each of us as individuals:
- embrace a moral principle, for example The Golden Rule.
- live and let live, as far as realistically possible. Maintain humility and respect when confronting differences, and remain open to changing our own position on moral topics.
- let reason, not emotion, determine the answer to complex moral issues, specifically the Deep Pragmatism approach advocated by Joshua Greene.
- "mind the gap" between the emotional stimulus of a moral instinct and our behavioural response.

Happiness

The core belief about happiness is "live, love, laugh and be happy", in other words that we should take responsibility for our own happiness by embracing the opportunities that life affords. Underpinning beliefs are:

– personal happiness is the legitimate goal of our existence, broadly defined as achieving a sense of well-being, which includes both sensory and aesthetic pleasure as well as deeper psychological fulfilment.

Happiness is eminently achievable, although certainly not guaranteed.

– it is for us each to take responsibility for our own happiness. The specific answer will be unique to each of us as indiviudals. For most people it will be found mainly through embracing the business of everyday living; and, social creatures that we are, relationships will be at the core. Important elements are likely to include:

- doing what we can to secure our health, material wealth, and security.
- building personal relationships and a sense of belonging.
- striving for achievements which we consider to be personally meaningful.
- and behaving in ways which are congruent with our sense of Self.

Specific beliefs are:

- "Happiness is the meaning and purpose of life, the whole aim and end of human existence".
- We each have a set of fundamental needs, with a profile which is unique to us. Happiness requires meeting these needs, to a greater or lesser extent. They are likely to form a loose hierarchy whereby higher-order needs become more relevant as more basic needs are met. Self-actualisation is at the top of the pile, defined as achieving one's personal full potential: being the best Self one feels one is capable of being, the closest possible to one's "ideal Self".
- Happiness is more appropriately defined as "wellbeing", comprising "hedonia", which tends to be more sensory in nature; and "eudemonia", which tends to be more psychological.
- Happiness is achievable: a majority of people report experiencing it.

- It is not realistic to pursue happiness directly. What is realistic is to pursue reasons to be happy, such that happiness then "ensues".
- A number of factors correlate statistically with individual happiness:
  - genes
  - life stage
  - relationships
  - health
  - money
  - work
  - religiosity, although the data here are not consistent, and to the extent a correlation with happiness is seen it is based at least partly on the opportunities for social connection that religious practice affords
- Six factors have been identified which can be measured robustly which correlate statistically to increased happiness at the level of a society:
  - material wealth, measured as GDP per capita
  - healthy life expectancy
  - social support
  - freedom to make life choices
  - generosity in the community
  - perceptions of corruption
- Beyond these, the key to happiness is to find personal meaning for our existence. To do this we need to look inside ourself. The evidence is that a large majority of people succeed.
- Finding meaning is ultimately subjective and personal. Nonetheless, research identifies a number of likely potential sources:
  - creating a work or doing a deed which has particular significance to us
  - experiencing something or encountering someone, in particular the quality and quantity of our social relationships

- the attitude we take to unavoidable suffering
- "actualising" personal potential: being the best Self we can be
- experiencing positive affect: maximising pleasure and minimising pain
- belonging: feeling truly accepted as a member of a social group
- establishing a coherent "worldview", which may be religious but can also be secular
- building authenticity, that is, cohesion between our self-image and our "ideal-Self"
- mental time travel: building cohesion between our current and past or future Self
- using awareness of our own and others' mortality to reinforce rather than undermine our sense of meaning

- Meaning and happiness are likely to be found through, and rooted in, the everyday business of living.
- We are each responsible for our own happiness: the choices we make and the behaviours we demonstrate are ultimately what define us.

Acknowledgments

What to Believe When You Don't is in many senses the product of my personal life story so far, hence a complete list of acknowledgements would exceed that of the most gushing Academy Awards acceptance speech. And the book is already long enough. So I'll keep this part brief and apologise upfront to the many people I might have named and haven't.

The starting point is the myriad of individuals who have helped me to become me, for better and worse: my parents, of course, Sam and Mary Rogers, who provided a secure, loving environment and encouraged me to develop an enquiring mind even when this led me to conclusions with which they didn't always agree; my sister Jill and brother Stephen; my teachers at primary and secondary school, most notably John "Bill" Hunt and Iain "Spike" MacLeod; my university tutors; my work colleagues in my various itinerant jobs and then at Procter & Gamble and Bain & Company, where I also had the privilege of working with many inspiring clients; those I have met over the years through my various sporting and other social activities; my first wife Gill, and our wonderful sons Jamie and Douglas; and most of all Gilly, with whom I have been lucky to feel the greatest connection of all, and her children, my stepchildren, Jamie and Chess Johnston. All of this adds up to the Chaucerian cast of characters with whom I have had the pleasure of experiencing personal connection over time and many of whom I am fortunate still to count as friends to this day (you know who you are because by definition there is some degree of reciprocal feeling, or at least that is my hope and impression...). All of you have enriched my life immeasurably, and all of you have contributed to my learning in the Great School of Life. Thank you.

Then there are the people who have contributed directly to the book manuscript. Obviously, I owe a tremendous debt to the many eminent authors from whom I quote in the text, those listed in the bibliography, and many others besides. Several people have given specific feedback and encouragement as the various iterations of the manuscript progressed, notably Peter Ullmann, Paul "Louis" Cornelius, Duncan Duff, and my mum Mary; as well as Chess who helped provide source material for Chapter 5, where I found academic papers to be important but hard to access, and Rupert Sanders, who saved me from a number of false steps regarding the science of Chapter 1 in particular. Thanks to all of you for finding the time and headspace to engage amongst all your other commitments, and for your insightful comments and support.

A number of people have helped bring the manuscript to market, a daunting process at least for me. In particular, James Essinger of The Conrad Press, who has acted as publisher, editor and general partner in crime; Zoe Verner, the Conrad Press publicist; Alison Wressell, doyenne of online; Emma Lockley, for help compiling the Indices; Gregory Motton for design and typesetting; Clays for the printing; Gardners for distribution, and last but not least Jamie Johnston and Sarah Cole for their help shooting content. Without all of you, the book would have remained a solitary document buried in the electronic files on my laptop. Thank you for your professional expertise, energy and support.

Finally, it would be remiss not to acknowledge the reader. If you have made it this far, you have most likely read the full text of the book. This was of course ultimately your personal choice, and I appreciate you making it. Thank you for engaging, and I hope you found it worthwhile.

Bibliography and Index

Bibliography

In this section I list the books which I have personally found interesting, to a greater or lesser degree. Readers may find it an eclectic list, and it is what it is. For reasons of practicality I have included only published books, and not referenced other sources, such as academic papers, articles from journals, newspapers or online blogs, or the various online lecture series which it has been my pleasure to engage with. However, where appropriate I have referenced all these other sources in the main body of the book itself. This may risk this bibliography looking unbalanced, as my main sources for Chapter 5 in particular were these alternative channels rather than traditional books.

As far as possible I have allocated specific books to the chapter to which they are most relevant, apart from a handful which don't neatly fit my chapter structure and I have therefore classified under "miscellaneous". Even then, some of the books classified under a particular chapter may be relevant to other chapters.

Finally, I've included a section on Religion since, although this book is not about religion, I nonetheless find it fascinating to explore what religious people typically believe ("what to believe if you do", as it were), and how it is that religion remains so pervasive in so much of the world despite the position of this book being that "there is no need for that hypothesis".

The books are arranged in alphabetical order of author within each section of the bibliography. The exception is that I have highlighted at the start of each section that book (or those books, in the case of Chapters 1 and 3) which I personally found particularly insightful and compelling. A reader wishing to explore the chapter subject matter in more detail might choose to start with these, although I hasten to add that many of the other listed titles well repay the effort to read them.

Chapter 1 – Nature

The Selfish Gene, Richard Dawkins
The Universe in Your Hand, Christophe Galfard

The Man from the Future, the visionary life of John von Neumann, Ananyo Bhattacharya
Eve: How The Female Body Drove 200 Million Years Of Human Evolution, Cat Bohannon
A Short History of Nearly Everything, Bill Bryson
The Epigenetics Revolution, Nessa Carey
Why Does E=MC2?, Brian Cox and Jeff Forshaw
The Quantum Universe; Everything that can happen does happen, Brian Cox and Jeff Forshaw
On the Origin of Species, Charles Darwin
The Extended Phenotype, Richard Dawkins
The Blind Watchmaker, Richard Dawkins
River Out of Eden, Richard Dawkins
Climbing Mount Improbable, Richard Dawkins
A Devil's Chaplain, Richard Dawkins
The Ancestor's Tale, Richard Dawkins
The Magic of Reality, Richard Dawkins
The rise and fall of the third chimpanzee, Jared Diamond
Gut, Giulia Enders
The Age of Entanglement, Louisa Gilder
In Search of Schrodinger's Cat, John Gribbin
A Brief History of Time, Stephen W. Hawking

The Grand Design, Stephen W. Hawking
The Case Against Reality – how evolution hid the truth from our eyes, Donald D. Hoffman
The Rules of Contagion, Adam Kucharski
More Sex is Safer Sex, Steven E. Landsburg
The Revenge of Gaia, James Lovelock
Limits to Growth, Donella Meadows, Jorgen Randers, Dennis Meadows
Stuff Matters, Mark Miodownik
How to Teach Quantum Physics to your Dog, Chad Orzel
How to Teach Relativity to your Dog, Chad Orzel
Copernicus' Secret, Jack Repcheck
Nature via Nurture, Matt Ridley
The Atheist's Guide to Reality, Alex Rosenberg
Seven Brief Lessons on Physics, Carlo Rovelli
Reality is Not What it Seems, Carlo Rovelli
Helgoland, Carlo Rovelli
A Brief History of Everyone Who Ever Lived, Adam Rutherford
Particle Physics Brick by Brick – Atomic and Subatomic Physics explained in Lego, Dr Ben Still
The Beak of the Finch, Jonathan Weiner

Chapter 2 - Consciousness

The Human Brain – a guided tour, Susan Greenfield
Thinking, Fast and Slow, Daniel Kahneman

The Brain, Ammar Al-Chalabi, Martin R. Turner, R. Shane Delamont
The Pattern Seekers, Simon Baron-Cohen
How Emotions are Made, Lisa Feldman Barrett
Consciousness Explained, Daniel C. Dennett
The Tiger That Isn't, Michael Blastland, Andrew Dilnot
The Body, Bill Bryson
Psychology – A Very Short Introduction, Gillian Butler and Freda McManus
Quiet, Susan Cain

The Mind is Flat, Nick Chater
Darwin's Dangerous Idea, Daniel C. Dennett
Through the Language Glass, why the world looks different in other languages, Guy Deutscher
Grit, Angela Duckworth
Evolutionary Psychology, Robin Dunbar, Louise Barret, John Lycett
The Brain, David Eagleman
An Introduction to Jung's Psychology, Frieda Fordham
Stumbling on Happiness, Daniel Gilbert
Blink, Malcolm Gladwell
Outliers, Malcolm Gladwell
Metazoa – Animal Minds and the Birth of Consciousness, Peter Godfrey-Smith
Emotional Intelligence, Daniel Goleman
The Private Life of the Brain, Susan Greenfield
Switch – how to change things when change is hard, Chip & Dan Heath
The Rough Guide to Psychology, Dr Christian Jarrett
Who Moved My Cheese, Dr Spencer Johnson
Noise, A Flaw in Human Judgement, Daniel Kahneman, Olivier Sibony & Cass Sunstein
How We Decide, Jonah Lehrer
Exercised, Daniel Lieberman
The Organized Mind, Daniel Levitin
The Upside of Stress, Kelly McGonigal
Brain Rules, John Medina
Not Born Yesterday – the science of who we trust and what we believe, Hugo Mercier
Free Agents – how evolution gave us freewill – Kevin Mitchell
Breath – The New Science of a Lost Art, James Nestor
The Mind, Dr. Raj Persaud
Rationality, Steven Pinker
The Smartest Kids in the World, Amanda Ripley
Why Zebras Don't Get Ulcers, Robert M. Sapolsky
Why People Believe Weird Things, Michael Shermer
Nudge, Thaler & Sunstein

A Natural History of Human Thinking, Michael Tomasello
Why We Sleep, Matthew Walker
Understanding How We Learn, Yana Weinstein and Megan Sumeracki with Oliver Caviglioli

Chapter 3 - Sociability

The Evolution of Cooperation, Robert Axelrod
Loneliness – Human Nature and the Need for Social Connection, John T Cacioppo & William Patrick

The Origin of Wealth, Eric D. Beinhocker
Humankind, A Hopeful History, Rutger Bregman
The Social Animal, David Brookes
Wired for Love, Stephanie Cacioppo
Friendship, Lydia Denworth
Guns, Germs & Steel, Jared Diamond
Why is Sex Fun?, Jared Diamond
The World Until Yesterday, Jared Diamond
The Dawn of Everything, A New History of Humanity, David Graeber and David Wengrow
Give and Take - A Revolutionary Approach to Success, Adam Grant
The Secret of Our Success; How Culture is Driving Human Evolution, Domesticating Our Species, and Making Us Smarter, Joseph Henrich
Anthropology – the basics, Peter Metcalf
Drive, Daniel H. Pink
The Better Angels of our Nature, Steven Pinker
Sociology – the basics, Ken Plummer
Burn – the misunderstood science of metabolism, Herman Pontzer
The Red Queen – Sex and the Evolution of Human Nature, Matt Ridley
Factfulness, Hans Rosling, with Ola Rosling and Anna Rosling Ronnlund

The Spirit Level, Richard Wilkinson & Kate Pickett
The Spirit Level Delusion, Christopher Snowdon

Chapter 4 - Morality

Moral Tribes, Joshua Greene
The Origins of Virtue, Matt Ridley

Causing Death and Saving Lives, Jonathan Glover
The Righteous Mind, Jonathan Haidt

Chapter 5 – Happiness

Man's Search for Meaning, Viktor E. Frankl

Nicomachean Ethics, Aristotle
The Science of Happiness – Seven Lessons for Living Well, Bruce Hood
TA Today – A New Introduction to Transactional Analysis, Ian Stewart and Vann Jones

Miscellaneous

The Philosophy Book, Camilla Hallinan (Managing Editor), published by Dorling Kindersley
Lingo, Gaston Dorren
Sapiens, Yuval Noah Harari
Homo Deus, Yuval Noah Harari
Made to Stick, Chip Heath & Dan Heath
Exercised – The Science of Physical Activity, Rest and Health, Daniel Lieberman
Freakonomics, Steven D. Levitt & Stephen J. Dubner
Weapons of Math Destruction, Cathy O'Neil
Anaximander, Carlo Rovelli
Fermat's Last Theorem, Simon Singh
The Diet Myth, Tim Spector
Bounce, Matthew Syed

The Wisdom of Crowds, James Surowiecki
Affluence without Abundance, James Suzman
The Black Swan, Nassim Nicholas Taleb
Narconomics, Tom Wainwright

Religion

A History of God, Karen Armstrong
Islam – A Short History, Karen Armstrong
A Short History of Myth, Karen Armstrong
Muhammad, Prophet for our Time, Karen Armstrong
The Great Transformation – the world in the time of Buddha, Socrates, Confucius and Jeremiah, Karen Armstrong
The Bible – the biography, Karen Armstrong
Religion Explained – the evolutionary origins of religious thought, Pascal Boyer
Atheism – A Very Short Introduction, Julian Baggini
Religion for Atheists, Alain de Botton
The Early Church, Henry Chadwick
The God Delusion, Richard Dawkins
Why Gods Persist, Robert A. Hinde
God is not Great, Christopher Hitchens
Making Sense of God – an invitation to the sceptical, Timothy Keller
Judaism, Nicholas de Lange
Conceiving God – the cognitive origin and evolution of religion, David Lewis-Williams
The Gnostics, Sean Martin
The Gnostic Gospels, Elaine Pagels
The Templar Revelation, Lynn Picknett & Clive Prince
Rescuing the Bible from Fundamentalism, John Shelby Spong
The Jesus Dynasty, James D. Tabor

Index of topics

10,000 hours rule 309–310

A
abortion 559–562
actively religious 620
actualisation 639
    self 574, 576–577, 584–585, 639, 649, 664
actualising 634, 639, 650
acute physical stress 325
aesthetic needs 579
aesthetic pleasure 19, 573, 663
affection 466–497
affinity bias 260
agency 215, 217–220, 325, 362, 601–602, 654
    personal 157, 199–220, 229, 272, 334–335, 361–362, 434, 567, 580, 601–602, 613, 654
aggression 437, 439
    female 437
    indirect 437
    male 437
agreeableness 112, 227–228
agriculture 143, 150, 197, 402–403, 406, 415, 498
alleles 88, 119
allowed states 47
altruism 483–486, 500, 508–509, 660
altruistic behaviour 484
Alzheimer's 244
androgen insensitivity syndrome 107
animals 137, 148, 159, 161, 164, 167, 185, 215, 230, 238, 269, 316, 369, 372, 438, 442, 471
anti-electron 65
antimatter 65–68
anti-neutrinos 66
anti-photons 66
anti-quarks 66
anti-selves 65–66
anti-social behaviour 290, 416–466, 498, 530, 657–658
apes 93–94, 139, 147, 180–184, 186, 189, 193, 382, 385–386,

392, 436, 443, 521
aristocracy 468
artificial selection 76, 121
asexual reproduction 104, 478
associative memory 269, 303
asteroids 69, 138
atheism 11, 83
atomic structure of matter 33–40
atoms 33, 35–41, 53, 58, 62, 69, 84, 134–135
autonomy 616
autonomy versus shame and doubt 241
availability bias 258–259
Axelrodian cooperation 469

B
baboons 421, 431–432, 471
bacteria 138
bad behaviours 531–532
basic needs 574, 580, 610
behavioural triggers 367, 516
behaviourism 242–244
belief 13–16, 497
    religious 12, 620
belonging 620, 626, 641–644, 664, 666
belongingness 575–576, 578
bias 260–262, 264, 365
    affinity 260
    availability 258–259
    cognitive 255–260, 303, 364
    confirmation 15, 259
    unconscious cognitive 15
Big Bang 66, 133–135, 146–147, 201–202, 654
Big 5 personality profile 112, 226
biochemistry 153, 215, 229
    neural 153
biological computer 173
biological female 109–110
biological male 109, 117
biological reproduction 72–73
biological sex 103–117, 124
biology 33, 83, 103

bipedalism 139, 148, 388
Black Death 406–407
Black Holes 60–61, 69, 135
blacks 96, 98
bonobos 382, 386, 389, 392
Bose Einstein condensate 53
Bosons 34, 41–42, 69, 134
bottom quark 34
brain 153, 156, 161, 164–179, 202, 204, 211, 216, 219, 235–237, 239–240, 242, 244, 246–253, 277–278, 289, 298, 300, 305, 318–319, 328, 363–365, 368, 374, 379, 390, 396, 413, 427, 473, 480, 660
    collective 374–375
    female 111
    human 127, 208, 210, 235
    male 111
    mammalian 168
    rational 168, 229–233
    reptilian 168
brain processes 163
breathing 608
bullying 434–441, 498, 658
Butterflies 376–377
butterfly effect 132

C

Cambrian Explosion 138
camel's hump bi-modal pattern 109, 116
Cantril Ladder 590, 593, 610
Capuchin monkey 519–520
carbon 37, 40, 84, 136
carrot and stick approach 312–313
catastrophising 260
Categorical Imperative 555
categorisation 265–268
causal relationships 197–198
causality 197–198, 209, 252
cause and effect relationships 251, 363, 655
cerebral cortex 166–169, 223
CERN 34, 41, 64, 66
challenge response 336

Chaos Theory 132
character 225–229
Charles II (King of Spain) 118
charm quark 34
chimpanzees 91–93, 100, 139, 181, 194, 230, 239, 378, 380, 382, 386, 388–389, 392, 394, 418–419, 423, 427, 435–436, 472, 481
choice architecture 256
chromosomes 85–89
    sex 86
    X 86–87
    Y 87
chronic physical stress 325
clans 405
classical conditioning 243
classical physics 44, 47, 51, 62
climate change 139, 385, 391, 398, 547
cognition 154, 164, 181, 209, 213, 215, 217, 366, 495
    human 156, 160, 180–199, 281, 381, 385, 427, 479–480
    moral 528
    reflective 212
    social 182–183, 192, 470, 489
cognitive bias 255–260, 303, 364, 656
    unconscious 15
cognitive capacity 180–181, 215
cognitive differences 289
cognitive dissonance 218, 273, 305
cognitive functions 295, 306, 308
cognitive hierarchy 212
cognitive needs 579
cognitive neuroscience 174
cognitive trap 302
coherence 51
    quantum 52
collaborative hunting 186
collective brain 374–375
comets 69
common ancestor 94–95
communication 191–192
companionate love 468, 475
companionship 469, 475

compassion 517–518
competition 185, 192, 447, 506, 565, 662
competitive foraging 385
concepts 248–249
concrete operational stage 240
conditioned stimulus 206
confirmation bias 15, 259
conscientiousness 112, 226, 228
conscious experience 151
conscious mind 215, 220, 243, 247, 254, 258, 295, 344, 364,
    546, 565, 656
conscious thoughts 214
consciousness 14, 151–365, 492, 496, 567, 655–657
    human 16–17, 146, 286, 314, 362, 445, 500, 516, 548,
        654, 661
    inner 283
consequentialism 557
constructed emotions 528
controlled inbreeding 121
cooperation 366, 369, 384, 447, 463–465, 467, 481, 499, 503,
    506–507, 509, 516, 565, 659, 662
    Axelrodian 469
    mutual 450
cooperative behaviours 368, 465, 506, 509, 530
core morality 514
corruption 624, 650, 665
cosmopolitanism 441
Covid-19 317, 406–407
Creator 13, 29, 70
creeping determinism 304
cultural evolution 372–376, 379
cultural group 185, 187
culture 187, 205, 282, 371–381, 415, 432, 513, 519, 521–522,
    524, 550–552, 636, 658
    human 194, 248, 424, 429
    Western 195
cumulative cultural revolution 194

D
dark energy 65, 67–68
dark matter 65, 67–68

Darwin Finches 74–76, 90
Darwinian evolution 137, 459
Darwinism 96
data 246–253, 268–269, 282, 297
    external 279
    internal 253, 279
    sensory 247, 307
death camps 635, 637–638
deceive 441–445
declarative memories 295–297
Deep Pragmatism 548, 553–554, 557–559, 562–563, 566, 663
defeat response 334
defection 451–452, 456, 463, 465, 481, 499, 659
    mutual 450–451
deleterious gene 120
dementia 244, 306
depression 130–131, 335, 337, 470, 634, 636
    inbreeding 117–118
destiny 284, 345, 348–349, 365
diet 607–608
differences in sexual development (DSD) 106–107, 116
dinosaurs 94, 138–139, 147
diversity 142, 513
divine 283
DNA (deoxyribonucleic acid) 40, 82–90, 92, 100, 126, 128, 142, 389
do no harm 516–519
dog 159–160
dominance 422–423, 425, 433, 440–441, 445
    male 435
dominance hierarchies 421
dominant genes 119
down quark 34–35
Drama Triangle 359
drive 309–314, 364
dualism 162

E

Earth 29–30, 35–40, 50, 55–57, 59, 70–72, 81, 93–94, 135–138, 142, 145–147, 162, 348, 362, 369, 407–408, 653–654
East Asians 98

Easterlin paradox 596, 609, 613–614
ego-centricity 292
electromagnetic field 42, 49, 65
electromagnetism 41, 61, 134
electron neutrino 34
electrons 34–43, 45, 48–49, 53, 65, 69
    anti 65
elites 405
emotional concepts 277–279, 281
emotional self 534
emotional wellbeing 610–612
emotions 15, 159, 161, 163, 243, 254, 267, 269, 274–280, 283, 286, 290, 364, 367, 370, 496, 499–500, 503, 512, 521, 540, 553–564, 656–657, 661
    constructed 528
    moral 290, 527, 532, 549
    negative 467
    pro-social 367
    universal 276
empathy 286–294, 364, 440, 503, 512, 516–519, 532, 543, 565, 656
empathy burnout 518
empathy circuit 198
empires 405
employment 617
    self 616
    un 617–618, 625
Enlightened Utilitarianism 548
environment 126–129, 131, 133, 146, 158, 164, 170, 180, 205, 213, 239, 242, 309, 383–384, 394, 413, 417, 499, 522, 531–532, 568, 632, 653
    social 414–415
environmental influences 131
environmental stimuli 205
Epicureanism 571
epigenetics 126
episodic memory 298, 308
EQ (emotional intelligence) 275, 278
Escalator of Reason 441
essential self 220–225
esteem 576

    self 578
esteem needs 579
ethnic groups 103, 282–283
ethnicity 103
eudemonia 585–586, 649, 664
eugenics 71, 125
eukaryotic cell 103–104, 136–137, 147
Europe 96, 99
European colonialists 96
Europeans 96, 99
evolution 27, 70–81, 83, 154, 168, 205, 216–217, 367, 369–371, 377, 381, 384, 392, 415, 473, 477, 489, 495, 497, 499, 502, 509, 543, 660
    cultural 372–376, 379
    Darwinian 137, 459
    genetic 373–374
evolutionary algorithm 84–85, 90, 105, 119, 137, 146
evolutionary change 77–78, 80
evolutionary process 74–75, 95
evolutionary psychology 114–115
evolutionary selection 75
evolutionary stable state 79, 459–460
evolutionary stable strategy (ESS) 79
evolutionary theory 77–79, 447, 500, 660
executive control 160, 231
executive function 229–233
executive stress syndrome 430
exercise 607–608
existential choice 156–157, 233, 314, 342, 367–368, 446–464, 498, 565, 659
    personal 156–157, 199–229, 258, 264, 309, 340, 365, 419, 469, 549, 657
existentialism 341, 343, 637
experience dependent neural connections 236
experience expectant wiring 236
experience independent wiring 236
experiences 126–129, 131, 146, 151, 163, 205, 233–234, 259, 275, 300, 302–303, 305–306, 308, 310, 335, 367, 531, 556, 597, 600, 629, 653
    conscious 151
    openness to 112

experiencing love 495–497
experiencing meaning 632–634
external data 279
external reality 14, 16, 28–33, 43, 53, 132, 156, 178–179, 246–247, 253, 277, 284, 328, 344
external stimuli 312
extinction 142
extramarital sex 480–483
extraversion 112, 227
extreme poverty 409–411, 413, 433, 622
extroversion 226

F

fairness 503, 519–520
false belief 291
farming 402–403
feedback control cognition 208
fellowship 468, 492
female aggression 437
female brains 111
females 103–104, 112–113
        biological 109–110
feminisation 441
Fermions 34, 41, 69, 134
fertilisation 87
fight or flight response 254, 326–327, 337
First Law of Thermodynamics 49
Fisher Principle 79
fitness 73, 90, 97, 119
forced sterilisation 125
formal operational stage 240
framing effect 256
fraternal (dizygotic) twins 87, 129
freeloading 370–371, 481
freewill 17, 157, 199–220, 230, 243, 325, 330, 335, 368, 530–531, 601
friendship 471, 473, 492
fundamental attribution error 259
fundamental forces 41–43, 134
fundamental needs 573–574, 649
fundamental particles 33–34, 37, 47, 69, 145

fungi 94, 105, 137–138

G

Gage, Phineas 232–233
galaxies 39, 69, 134–135, 203
Gallup World Poll 592, 594, 616, 623–624, 633
Game Theory 449
gametes 105–106
gender 116, 282, 394
gender differences 112
gender identity 103–117
gender roles 400, 402
gene pool 90
General Relativity 53, 60–61, 64
General Theory 54
General Theory of Relativity 56, 65
generativity versus stagnation 241
generosity 624
genes 81–83, 88–93, 96, 98–100, 102, 108–109, 119, 124–129, 151, 155, 234, 283, 287, 345, 357, 367, 372, 374, 378, 384, 387, 392, 394, 397, 417, 425, 467, 480, 498, 512, 515, 531, 543, 549, 597, 608, 616, 649, 652–654, 658, 665
    deleterious 120
    dominant 119
    recessive 119, 123–124
    selfish 397
genetic determinism 124
genetic differences 90–95, 97–100, 103–104, 113
genetic diversity 118, 121, 144, 374, 398
genetic drift 122
genetic evolution 373–374
genetic overlap 91–92
genetic similarities 90–95
genetic variation 92–93, 96–99, 115
genetics 81–83, 95–103, 117, 123–125, 216
Geniuses 376–377
genome 84–85, 87–91, 99, 105, 122–123
genotype 82
Givers 485–486
gluons 42–43, 49, 69
God 200, 283, 342, 621

The Goldilocks Principle 24, 275, 601
Golem Effect 359
good behaviours 531–532
gorillas 93, 381, 386
GPS navigation systems 55–56
gravity 41–42, 54–56, 61, 64, 68, 134
greenhouse gas emissions 412
grit 310–311
group behaviour in I-mode 193
group foraging 385
group intentionality 181, 293
groupishness 369–370, 381, 509

H
Happiness 19, 22, 567–666
Hawthorne effect 45
health 606–608, 634, 648–649, 664–665
healthy life expectancy 623
hedonia 585–587, 649, 664
hedonic treadmill 598–599
hedonism 572
Heisenberg Uncertainty Principle 44
helium 35–38, 134
heredity 81–83, 90, 126
hermaphrodites 106, 477
heuristics 255, 257–258
hierarchy 404, 419–434, 436, 441, 445, 498, 573–575, 577–580, 584–585, 616, 658, 664
    cognitive 212
    dominance 421
    human 425, 433
    social 421, 429
hierarchy of needs 573–580, 583, 585
higher needs 574, 580
historical race theory 95
hominids 139–142, 147–148, 181, 186, 293, 385–390, 392–393, 397
homo erectus 141, 147–148, 428, 509
homo habilis 428
homo heidelbergensis 186
homo sapiens 140–142, 149, 196, 395, 397–398, 427

hormones 108, 127
human behaviour 45, 477
human brain 127, 208, 210, 235
human cognition 156, 160, 180–199, 281, 381, 385, 427, 479–480
human consciousness 16–17, 146, 286, 314, 362, 445, 500, 516, 548, 654, 661
human cultures 194, 248, 424, 429
human hierarchy 425, 433
human sexuality 88
human sociability 385–416, 483
humanistic self-concept 222
humanity 502, 509, 555, 583
humans 11–13, 17, 27–29, 32, 70, 80–82, 85, 88, 90–95, 99–100, 105, 123, 128, 132, 137, 141–143, 146, 150, 158–161, 164, 167, 180, 182, 184, 186, 196, 198, 200, 208, 212–213, 215, 238, 243, 264, 266, 268–269, 271, 275–278, 291, 294, 307, 316, 326, 329, 331–333, 343, 357, 369, 371, 377–378, 380–383, 385, 387, 390–392, 395, 397, 399, 407, 416, 420, 422–424, 426–427, 430–433, 438–439, 442–443, 445, 462, 466, 471–473, 480, 482–485, 489, 495, 497–499, 508, 514–515, 529, 567, 574, 625, 632, 638–639, 653, 658
hunter-gatherer lifestyle 140, 143, 148, 389, 400, 498, 658
hunter-gatherers 271, 378, 380, 382, 393–394, 398–399, 402, 404
    nomadic 402, 404
hydrogen 35–40, 58–59, 84, 134

I
ideal-self 222–223, 645, 649–650, 664, 666
idealism 177
identical (monozygotic) twins 87, 95, 128–130, 237
identity versus confusion 241
ideology 440
imagination 307–309, 364, 646, 656
immoral 515
inbreeding 117–124, 399
    controlled 121
inbreeding depression 117–118
incest 124

income 611
income inequality 614
indeterminacy principle 44
indirect aggression 437
individual intentionality 180, 192
industrial nations 411
Industrial Revolution 96, 405, 415
industrial societies 400
industrialisation 409, 413
industry versus inferiority 241
inequality 420, 433, 596, 613, 625
    income 614
influence 441–445
ingroups 287, 441, 468, 504, 537–538, 543–546
inhuman 466, 502, 565
initiative versus guilt 241
inner consciousness 283
inner demons 440
integrity versus despair 241
intensity trigger 305
interdependence 186
internal data 253, 279
interoception 175, 252
interoceptive 175
interoceptive feelings 263
intersex 104, 106
intimacy versus confusion 241
intimidation 434–441, 498, 658
intrinsic activity 174–175
intrinsic motivation 312–313
intrinsic networks 175
introspection 154, 174, 199, 212
IQ 101, 275, 310, 358

J

Jennifer Aniston neuron 237–238
John Henryism 352–353
joint foraging 385
joint intentionality 180

K

Khelif, Imane 107
kingdoms 405
kings 405

L

language 158, 248, 279–286, 364, 424–425, 442, 511, 518, 529, 589–590, 628, 656
    standardisation of 190
Laplace's demon 62
last Ice Age 143, 150
law of large numbers 346
laws of nature 307, 348–349, 352, 523, 565, 662
laws of physics 28, 30, 201, 211, 626
learned helplessness 333–334
learning 234–246
Leviathan 439, 441
life expectancy 408–409, 422, 429, 436, 488, 665
    healthy 623
life stage 602–604
little voice 151, 158, 161, 191, 199, 225, 281, 355
locus of control 334–335, 339
logotherapy 631, 640
loneliness 383, 396, 467, 471, 485–492, 495, 500, 604–605, 660
long-term memory 297
loss aversion 259–260
love 466–497, 575–576, 578, 661
    companionate 468, 475
    experiencing 495–497
    romantic 473–477, 500–501, 660–661
luck 345–349, 365

M

macroscopic quantum behaviour 50
macroscopic quantum effect 51–52
male 104, 112–113
    biological 109, 117
male aggression 437
male brains 111
male dominance 435

mammalian brain 168
mammals 82, 94, 100, 138–139, 147, 166, 208
manipulate 441–445
Mars 136
mass urbanisation 405
Matchers 485
maturity 235
meaning as everyday experience 647–648
meaning in life 628–630, 632–633, 640, 644
meaning of life 626–628
meiosis 87, 105
memory 294–308, 315, 319, 323, 364
    associative 269, 303
    declarative 295–297
    episodic 298, 308
    long-term 297
    personal 301
    procedural 298
    quasi 301
    reconstructive 299
    selective 304
    semantic 298
    sensory 297
    short-term (working) 297–298
    subsequent 304
memory degradation 306
men 103
meta conventions 307
microbes 69
microorganisms 136
Middle Ages 412
migration 141
    Out of Africa 141, 149
Milky Way 135
Mind the Gap 219, 254, 345, 363, 504, 548, 564, 566, 654, 663
mirror neurons 286
mitochondrial Eve 100, 149
molecules 38–40, 69
money 609–615, 623, 649, 665
monkey 94, 185, 193, 443, 472
    Capuchin 519–520

The Monster Study 359
mood 263–264
Moon 50, 136, 348
moral cognition 528
moral education 510
moral emotions 290, 527, 532, 549
moral feelings 503, 526
moral instinct 502–523, 525, 527, 545, 548–549, 564–566, 662
moral judgment 513, 525–527, 661
moral norms 503–504, 506, 509, 515, 522, 538, 542, 545–546, 550–551, 553, 565–566, 662–663
moral principle 549–551
moral reasoning 526
moral relativism 524–525, 551
moral sense 440, 515, 521, 525
moral thinking 504
moral triggers 511–516
moralisation 514
morality 14, 18, 290, 371, 441, 483, 501, 502–566, 569, 661–663
    core 514
mortality 646–647, 650, 666
mortality rate 407, 429
motivation 309–314, 364
motor neurons 177–178
muon 34
muon neutrino 34
mutations 73–74, 76, 79, 85, 90, 100, 105
mutual cooperation 450
mutual defection 450–451

N

nasty strategy 453–456, 460, 462
nation state 405
natural laws 12, 27, 70, 252
natural selection 70–73, 76, 83, 90, 114–115, 120, 209, 293, 377, 379, 390, 392–393, 395–396, 419, 435, 442, 447, 509, 543
natural world 31–32, 44
Nature 16, 27–150, 287, 294, 417, 420–421, 425, 434, 483,

497, 503, 511, 522–523, 556, 565, 572, 636, 652–654
    laws of 307, 348–349, 352, 523, 565, 662
Neanderthals 140–142, 149, 194, 397–399
nebulae 39
negative capability 280
negative emotions 467
neocortex 167–168, 171, 479
Neolithic period 403
neon 38
neural biochemistry 153
neurologically normal 502, 515, 565, 662
neurons 127, 169–175, 177, 179–180, 207, 223, 235, 237–239, 244, 297, 319
    Jennifer Aniston 237–238
    mirror 286
    motor 177–178
    sensory 177–178
neuroscience 154, 214
    cognitive 174
neuroticism 112, 227–228
neurotransmitters 169, 171
neutrons 35, 41, 49, 69, 206
Newton's Laws of Gravity 60
nice strategy 453–456
nitrogen 40, 84
noise 261, 265, 592, 654
nomadic hunter-gatherers 402, 404
nonprocreative sex 560
NREM sleep 318–319
nuclear fission 58–59
nuclear fusion 58–59, 134
nuclei 36, 39
nucleus 37, 48, 136
nurture 98, 101–102, 109, 114, 124–125, 128, 131–132, 287, 425, 522, 607

O

obesity epidemic 110
objective reality 493
observer effect 44
OCEAN framework 226

Oganesson 35
openness 226–227
openness to experience 112
operant conditioning 208, 242–243, 312
orangutans 93, 181, 381, 386, 393
organism 73, 75, 84–87, 90, 94–95, 104–105, 137, 144, 165, 167, 170, 209–211, 214, 327, 329, 333, 369, 417, 438, 477, 483, 575
Other 18, 566, 567, 662–663
outgroups 287, 441, 517, 537–538, 543–546
Out of Africa migration 141, 149
overconfidence 260
overlapping camel's hump 112
oxygen 37–40, 84, 137, 174

P

pain 159, 166, 304–305, 311, 350, 440, 470, 487, 512, 514–515, 518, 556, 571–573, 576, 589, 650, 666
painful stimuli 207
pair-bonding 386–388, 473, 476, 480–481, 500, 660
pareidolia 252
Paris Olympics (2024) 107
particles 37, 42, 45–46, 49–51, 67, 133–135
    fundamental 33–34, 37, 47, 69, 145
    quantum 44, 48, 203
    sub-atomic 28, 33, 46–47, 63, 133
    wave 28, 37, 47, 50, 145, 653
peak-end rule 303
Persecutor 360
persona 224
personal agency 157, 199–220, 229, 272, 334–335, 361–362, 434, 567, 580, 601–602, 613, 654
personal existential choice 156–157, 199–229, 258, 264, 309, 340, 365, 419, 469, 549, 657
personal identity 115–116
personal identity crisis 241
personal meaning 625–648
personal memory 301
personal relationships 383, 468, 499, 568, 604, 626, 638, 642, 660, 664
personality 129, 131, 157, 221, 223, 225–229, 240

phenotype 82
phosphorus 40, 84
photons 42, 46, 49, 69
    anti 66
photosynthesis 137–138
physical characteristics 97
physical predeterminists 200
physics 32–33
physiological needs 575, 578
physiological stress 325–326
placebo effect 349
planets 69, 203
plants 94, 105, 137–138
pleasure 70, 159, 276, 311, 473, 487–489, 556, 571–573, 576, 585, 592, 650
    aesthetic 19, 573, 663
    sensory 19, 572–573, 589, 663
plutonium 58
population bottlenecks 142–144, 149
positive affect 641
positive thinking 354, 357
positive psychology 355
positron emission tomography (PET) scanners 67
positrons 67
post-rationalisation 273–274
poverty 329, 331, 409, 433, 549, 583
    extreme 409–411, 413, 433, 622
pragmatism 557
    Deep 548, 553–554, 557–559, 562–563, 566, 663
prayer 353–354
predictions 178–179
prefrontal cortex 171, 212, 475
preoperational stage 240
presentism 308
prestige 422, 425, 433, 435
primates 94, 182, 184, 212, 332–333, 378, 380–381, 385, 391, 395, 398, 421, 423, 519
Prime Mover hypothesis 12
Prisoner's Dilemma 448–452, 458–459, 462, 485
procedural memory 298
pro-choice 559, 561

prokaryotic cell 137
pro-life 559
propensities 131
pro-social behaviours 369–416, 419, 496–497
pro-social emotions 367
proteins 82, 88–89, 91
protons 35, 41, 49
psyche 162
psychological stress 328–329, 332
psychopaths 290
psychotherapy 219
puberty 107–108
punctuated equilibrium 80
Pygmalion Effect 358–359

Q
quantum 63–64, 153
quantum coherence 52
quantum effects 43–53
quantum field theory 42, 69
quantum fields 41–43, 46–49, 65
quantum leaps (quantum jumps) 47–48, 63
quantum levitation (Meissner effect) 53
quantum mechanics 28, 37, 53, 61–65, 68–70, 202
quantum particles 44, 48, 203
quantum physics 50–51
quantum theory 16, 51, 63, 65, 652
quantum-to-classical transition 203
quantum uncertainty 46, 203–204
quantum wavefunctions 50
quantum world 45–47, 132, 204
quarks 34, 41–42, 49, 69
    anti 66
    bottom 34
    charm 34
    down 34–35
    strange 34
    top 34
    up 34–35
quasi-memory 301

R

race 95–103, 114, 141
    white 96, 98
racial engineering 71
racial groups 96
ratchet effect 187–188, 371
rational brain 168, 229–233
realism 177, 339
reality 176–178, 248, 251, 262, 281, 299, 307, 341, 363, 655
    external 14, 16, 28–33, 43, 53, 132, 156, 178–179, 246–247, 253, 277, 284, 328, 344
    objective 493
    social 464–466
    subjective 309
    true 249
reason 268–274, 441
reasoning-why 229–230
recessive genes 119, 123–124
reconstructive memory 299
reflective cognition 212
relationships 492–495, 604–606
    causal 197–198
    cause and effect 251, 363, 655
    personal 383, 468, 499, 568, 604, 626, 638, 642, 660, 664
    social 492, 618, 642–643, 647, 650, 665
relativity 16, 49, 53–65, 70, 153
    General 53, 60–61, 64
    General Theory of 56, 65
    Special 53–55, 58
    Special Theory of 54, 57
Relativity Theory 28
religion 12, 618–623
religiosity 621–622, 644, 649, 665
religious 283, 644–645
    actively 620
religious belief 12, 620, 623, 644
REM sleep 318–319, 323
reproduction 477–478
    asexual 104, 478
    biological 72–73

      sexual 104–105, 478
reptilian brain 168
Rescuer 360–361
responsive desire model 476
revenge 440
right 502, 513, 534
RNA (ribonucleic acid) 83
romantic love 473–477, 500–501, 660–661
Royal House of Hapsburg 117–118, 124
Rubicon 371
Ryff Scale of Psychological Wellbeing 591

S

sadism 440
safety needs 575, 578
Sally-Anne test 291
scientific racism 125
seeing-that 229–230
selective breeding 125
selective memory 304
self 116, 155, 157, 163, 220–225, 240–241, 283, 295, 306, 363, 474, 568, 580, 584, 645–646, 648–650, 655, 664, 666
    emotional 534
    essential 220–225
    ideal 222–223, 645, 649–650, 664, 666
self-actualisation 574, 576–577, 584–585, 639, 649, 664
self-control 440
self-employment 616
self-esteem 578
self-estimated intelligence (SEI) 113
self-expansion 474
self-image 223, 645
self-knowledge 22, 226, 229
self-talk 355–357
self-worth 222, 618
selfish behaviours 368, 445, 499, 657
selfish genes 397
selfishness 511, 659
selflessness 486, 508–509
semantic memory 298
sensorimotor stage 240

sensory data 247, 307
sensory inputs 277–278
sensory memory 297
sensory neurons 177–178
sensory organs 165
sensory pleasure 19, 572–573, 589, 663
sensory stimuli 204
sex 477–480
    biological 103–117, 124
    extramarital 480–483
    nonprocreative 560
sex chromosomes 86
sex ratio 79
sexual behaviour 560–561
sexual monogamy 476, 480
sexual reproduction 104–105, 478
sexual selection 77–78, 386, 435, 478
sexual size dimorphism 77
shadow of the future 461, 463
short-term (working) memory 297–298
simulations 246
skin colour 97–100
slavery 406
sleep 314–324, 338, 365, 607, 656
    NREM (Non-Rapid Eye Movement) 318–320
    REM (Rapid Eye Movement) 318–319, 323
sleep deprivation 316, 320
smartphones 603–604, 612
sociability 17, 275, 365, 366–501, 506–511, 528, 657–661
    human 385–416, 483
social affiliation 367
social behaviours 472
social cognition 182–183, 192, 470, 489
social connection 370, 383, 394, 396, 469, 471–472, 485, 487, 490, 493, 495, 497–498, 644, 658, 660
social environment 414–415
social expectations 491, 494
social groups 143, 147, 159, 182–183, 187, 190, 193, 240, 282, 330, 366, 369, 380, 414–415, 421–422, 426, 428–430, 433–434, 437–438, 467–468, 498, 504–505, 516, 518, 523, 525, 537–538, 541–542, 544, 547–548, 551, 562, 565,

642, 650, 656, 659, 662, 666
social hierarchies 421, 429
social media 488, 596, 603
social monogamy 476, 480
social networks 472
social norms 520
social reality 464–466
social relationships 492, 618, 642–643, 647, 650, 665
social satisfaction 470
social selection 186
social stress 326
social support 623
sociality 508
Solar System 135, 162
solitude 486–492
soul 152, 162, 164, 219, 283
soundwaves 30
sources of meaning 640–647
Space 28, 37–39, 48, 56, 61, 136, 146, 653
space dilation 57
Spacetime 54–55, 60–62, 134
Spacetime dilation 58
Special Relativity 53–55, 58
Special Theory of Relativity 54, 57
spiritual 283
Standard Model of Physics 61, 64–65
standardisation of language 190
status 420–434
stereotyping 268
stimulation 178–179
stimuli 177–178, 242
    environmental 205
    external 312
    painful 207
    sensory 204
stimulus 154, 180, 206–207, 219, 254, 277, 328, 330, 333, 335, 654
    conditioned 206
    unconditioned 206
stimulus-response linkages 208
stoicism 572

Stonehenge 196
strange quark 34
strangers 288, 294, 333, 366, 390, 517, 519–520, 533, 535, 543
stress 314, 324–340, 349–350, 356, 365, 607–608, 621, 657
    acute physical 325
    chronic physical 325
    physiological 325–326
    psychological 328–329, 332
    social 326
stress response 336
strong nuclear force 41, 134
struggle for existence 72
sub-atomic particles 28, 33, 46–47, 63, 133
sub-atomic realm 33–40
subjective interpretation 492–495
subjective reality 309
subsequent memory 304
suffering 637, 666
sulphur 40
Sun 37, 58, 67, 134–135
superconductivity 53
superfluidity 53
supernova 36
survival machines 83
synapses 169, 235
systemising 195–197, 272, 289

T

Takers 485
tau 34
tau neutrino 34
Terror Management Theory (TMT) 646–647
testosterone 110
theory of constructed emotion 276
Theory of Mind 157, 188, 286–294, 364, 516, 656
Third Adaptation 232
Time 28, 146, 653
Tit for Tat 453–458, 460–461, 464, 485
top quark 34
tragedy of commonsense morality 538, 541, 544, 546, 552,

Tragedy of the Commons 448, 538–539, 544
Transaction Analysis 359
transcendence needs 579
transgender 116
Tree of Life 80, 83, 93
tribal organisation 187
tribes 404, 539–540
triggers 151, 155–156, 219, 243, 254, 312, 331, 433, 440, 516, 654
    behavioural 367, 516
    intensity 305
    moral 511–516
Triune model 168
Trolley Experiment 532–534
true reality 249
trust versus mistrust 241

U

Ultimatum Game 519
unconditioned stimulus 206
unconscious cognitive bias 15
unconscious mind 14
unemployment 617–618, 625
universal emotions 276
Universe 11–13, 16, 27–29, 32–36, 39–41, 43, 49–50, 53–54, 58, 60–62, 65–70, 133–135, 144–145, 152, 163, 169, 179, 200–202, 234, 341–342, 344, 348, 501, 567, 570, 626, 652–653
up quark 34–35
Upper Palaeolithic 399
urbanisation 406, 414
    mass 405
uranium 35, 58
US 98
Utilitarian calculation 263
Utilitarianism 554–558, 569, 571
    Enlightened 548

V

velocity 54–55

Victim 360–361
violence 434–441, 498, 504, 521, 658

W

wave-particle duality 46
wave particles 28, 37, 47, 50, 145, 653
wave theory 47
weak nuclear force 41, 134
wealth 609–613, 648, 664–665
wellbeing 585–592, 596, 598, 601–603, 605–606, 610, 617–619, 629, 634, 639, 648–649, 663
    emotional 610–612
Western culture 195
white race 96, 98
Whitehall Study 429
will to meaning 630–632
work 615–618, 634, 649–650, 665
wrong 502, 513, 534

X

X chromosome 86–87

Y

Y-chromosomal Adam 100, 149
Y chromosome 87
Yu-ting, Lin 107

Index of authors quoted.

A
Adams, Douglas 627
Al-Chalabi, Ammar 169
Alexander, Richard 543
Alkemade, Nicholas 347
Allport, Gordon 637, 646
Altman, Jeanne 471
Altman, Stuart 471
Andersen, Tim 204
Anderson, Mike 98
Andrews, Glenda 113
April, Kurt 601
Aristippus 571, 586
Aristotle 125, 268, 272, 567, 569–572, 580, 586, 588
Aron, Arthur 474
Aron, Elaine 474
Aspect, Alan 45
Axelrod, Robert 447–454, 456–457, 459–466, 485–486, 515–516, 553

B
Baird, Christopher 50
Banfield, Edward 510
Barber, Nigel 621–622
Barlow, Horace 427
Baron-Cohen, Simon 180–181, 195–198, 251, 265, 271–272, 288–290
Barrett, Lisa Feldman 153, 168, 174–175, 177–179, 224, 243, 247, 252–253, 263, 265, 268, 276–279, 281, 527–528
Barrio, Rafael A 443–444
Baumeister, Roy F 633, 642
Beames, Joanne R 437
Belk, Russell 221
Bell, John Stewart 45
Benson, Herbert 353
Bentham, Jeremy 263, 554, 556, 558, 571
Berkeley, George (Bishop) 29–30, 32
Berne, Eric 359
Bethea, Charles 354
Bettiza, Sofie 108
Blake, Khandis R 437
Blakely, Rhys 400, 418
Blanchflower, Danny 603
Blitzer, Wolf 541
Bloom, Paul 502, 512, 518
Bock, Arlie 470–471
Bohannon, Cat 86, 111
Bonaparte, Napoleon (Emperor) 13
Boole, George 195
Bouchard, William 129
Bregman, Rutger 357–359, 419, 439, 494
Brewer, Marilynn 643
Brickman, Philip 598–599
Brooks, Arthur 597–598, 605
Browne, Donald E 512

Burgess, Kaya 618–619
Buss, David 437

C

Cacioppo, John 231, 233, 370, 383–384, 390, 393, 395, 416, 418–419, 435–436, 465, 469–470, 484, 487, 489, 492–493, 495, 625
Cacioppo, Stephanie 391, 397, 468, 472–475, 488, 494
Cambridge English Dictionary 13–14, 81–82, 158, 221, 225, 255, 269, 274, 505
Campbell, Donald 598–599
Camus, Albert 341–342
Cantril, Hadley 590
Carr, Peter 502
Carroll, Sean 61, 64
Caviglioli, Oliver 294
Chater, Nick 154, 172–174
Chaucer, Geoffrey 284
Cherry, Kendra 158–159, 290–292, 354–357
Chomsky, Noam 511
Christal, RM 226
Christiansen, Jen 126
Cicero 228–229
Clore, Jerry 527
Cloutier, Jasmin 426
Clune, Jeff 420
Coan, James 287–288
Cochrane, Kent 308
Cockcroft, George 217
Cohan, Peter 612
Covey, Stephen 219
Cox, Tracey 476
Coyne, Jerry 99, 103, 105
Crick, Francis 82
Crook, Gareth 512
Crum, Alia 351–352

D

Darwin, Charles 70–72, 74, 76–77, 80–83, 90, 94, 124, 132, 392, 484
Dawkins, Richard 74, 83, 94, 218, 353–354, 417, 442–443, 447, 456, 462–463, 524
Deaton, Angus 609–611
Delamont, R Shane 169
Democritus 571
De Neve, Jan-Emmanuel 615
Dennett, Daniel 164
Denson, Thomas F 437
Denworth, Lydia 468, 470–471
Descartes, Rene 162
Deutscher, Guy 265–266, 281–282
Devlin, Hannah 142
DeYoung, Colin 109, 112, 114–115
Dharani, Babar 601
Diamond, Jared 400, 402, 481–482
Diener, Ed 584

Dispentiere, Joseph 63
Dolan, Paul 590
Donne, John 366
Donnellan, Brent 606
Donnelly, Grant 613
Dresher, Melvin 449
Duckworth, Angela 310–311
Duffy, Bobby 411–412
Dunbar, Robin 443–444
Duncan, Emma 361–362
Durant, Will 177

E
Easterlin, Richard 596, 614–615
Einstein, Albert 47, 49, 53–55, 57–60, 63, 68
Ekman, Paul 276
Eliot, George 427
Encyclopedia Britannica 246
Engelmann, Jan 288
Epicurus 571–572
Erikson, Erik 241
Evans, Gavin 99–101
Eysenck, Michael 598

F
Festinger, Leon 273
Fincham, Frank D 633, 642
Finlay, Barbara 169
Fischetti, Mark 126
Fischoff, Baruch 304–305
Fisher, Ronald 79
Fiske, Alan 513
Flinders, Matthew 122
Flood, Merrill 449
Flynn, Jim 101
Forster, EM 366, 467–468, 604, 636
Frank, Robert 494
Frankl, Viktor 219, 231, 504, 564, 630–632, 634–647
Freud, Sigmund 477

G
Gabaldon, Toni 104
Galfard, Christophe 32–33, 36–40, 42–46, 48–49, 55–57, 59, 66, 68–69
Galton, Francis 124–125, 129
Gavrilets, Sergey 386–388
Gilbert, Daniel 176–177, 299, 301, 305–306, 308, 416
Gladwell, Malcolm 309
Godfrey-Smith, Peter 160, 162, 298, 308
Goldstein, Kurt 580
Goodall, Jane 418
Goodkind, Nicole 413
Gott, Davey 265–266
Govezensky, Tzipe 443–444
Grant, Adam 485–486, 494

Grant, Peter 74–75
Grant, Rosemary 74–75
Greene, David 312, 369
Greene, Joshua 446, 504, 507–509, 516, 536, 538–542, 544, 548, 553–554, 556–563, 566, 569, 663
Greenfield, Susan 161, 164–165, 167, 169, 171, 236, 238–239, 244
Grunbaum, Mara 378

H
Haas, Randy 401
Haidt, Jonathan 229–230, 290, 506–507, 513, 521–522, 526–528, 604
Hallam, Arthur Henry 497
Hamilton, William D 79, 484–485
Hardin, Garrett 448
Hare, Robert 290
Hauser, Marc 511
Hawking, Stephen 32
Hawkley, Louise 491–492
Hein, Grit 288
Heisenberg, Werner 44
Hemingway, Ernest 284
Henrich, Joseph 349–350, 372–380, 394, 399, 422, 425, 510, 520
Hicks, Joshua 628–629, 632–633, 640–642, 644–648
Hiroto, Donald 334

Hirsh, Jacob 109, 112, 114–115
Hobbes, Thomas 383, 417, 434, 439
Hoffman, Donald 31, 176
Hogenboom, Melissa 475–476
Holmes, Oliver Wendell 23
Hood, Bruce 412
Hudson, Nathan 606
Huizinga, Joost 420
Hume, David 268, 526

I
Inglehart, Robert 592
Iniguez, Gerardo 443–444

J
James, Sherman 353
James, William 213–214, 221–222
Jefferson, Thomas 502, 515, 569, 588
Johansen, Wilhelm 81–82
Johnson, Wendell 359
Juarrero, Alicia 210

K
Kahneman, Daniel 255–261, 263, 265, 281, 302–303, 306, 609–611
Kamble, Shanmukh 633, 642
Kandel, Eric 206, 230, 242
Kandler, Otto 104
Kant, Immanuel 177, 264,

268, 555–556
Karpman, Stephen 359–360
Kashdan, Todd B 626
Kaski, Kimmo 443–444
Keats, John 280, 636
Kierkegaard, Soren 341
Killingsworth, Matt 612
King, Laura 628–629, 632, 640–641, 644–648
Klinger, E 628
Koski, Jessica 421, 424–425, 428
Krebs, John 442–443

L
Lahdenpera, Mirkka 378
Lambert, Nathaniel M 633, 642
Langevin, Paul 55
Langford, Cooper Harold 195
Laplace, Pierre-Simon 12–13, 62, 201
Layard, Richard 588
Lechner, Tamara 517–518
Lepper, Mark 312
Leucippus 571
Lewis, Clarence Irving 195
Li, Tainyi 426
Liebenberg, Louis 271
Lieberman, Daniel 321–322
Lim, Chaeyoon 621
Linnaeus, Carl 97
Lloyd, WF 448
Lorentz, Danielle 626
Lorenz, Edward 132
Lucas, Richard 606
Lykken, David 598
Lyubomirsky, Sonja 600

M
MacLean, Paul 168
Madonna 27
Margolis, Howard 230
Marin, Frederic 123
Maroja, Luana 99, 103, 105
Marriott, James 487–488, 528
Marshall, Joey 619
Maslow, Abraham 573–586, 610, 639
McGonigal, Kelly 327, 334–339, 351–352
McLeod, Saul 221–223, 242, 574–575, 577–585
McTague, Tom 302
Mead, Elaine 355
Mead, Margaret 543
Medina, John 235–237, 290
Mehrabian, Albert 281
Mendel, Gregor 81
Mendeleev, Dmitri 35
Mengistu, Henok 420
Merriam-Webster Dictionary 221, 229
Metcalf, Peter 97
Metcalfe, Robert 590
Michelson, Albert 54

Mikhail, John 511
Mill, John Stuart 556, 558
Miller, Geoffrey 443, 479
Milligan, Spike 610
Mitchell, Kevin 167, 170–171, 202–203, 209–216, 227–228
Moore, Catherine 586–587
Mouret, Jean-Baptiste 420

N

National Genome Research Institute 88
Nestor, James 608
Neumann, David 113
Newton, Isaac 20, 46, 60, 62, 68
Nietzsche, Friedrich 638
Nisbett, Robert 312
Norton, Michael 613
Nowak, Martin 384

O

Oakley, Barbara 486
O'Dean, Siobhan M 437
Olson, Ingrid R 421, 424–425, 428
Oort, Jan 67
Oparina, Ekaterina 588
Opfer, Chris 223
Ortiz-Ospina, Esteban 409–410, 490–491, 591, 595, 599, 609, 613–614
Orwell, George 285, 532
Orzel, Chad 48

P

Palmer, Arnold 345–346
Pappas, Stephanie 621
Parris, Matthew 285
Patrick, William 231, 233, 370, 383–384, 390, 393, 395, 416, 418–419, 435–436, 465, 469–470, 484, 487, 489, 492–493, 495, 625
Pausanias 220
Pavlov, Ivan 243
Peirce, Charles Sanders 195
Pennock, Seph 598, 600
Perlmutter, Saul 68
Peters, Kai 601
Piaget, Jean 240
Pickett, Kate 625
Pink, Daniel 311–313
Pinker, Steven 270–272, 434, 438–440, 511–516, 550
Plummer, Ken 406, 409
Pogge, Richard 56
Pontzer, Herman 128, 166, 381, 389, 392–393
Powell, Corey 61, 64
Protagoras 521, 524

R

Rapoport, Anatol 453
Rawls, John 511
Reilly, David 113
Rettner, Rachael 126
Ridley, Matt 90–92, 125–126, 129, 131, 426–428,

443, 477, 479, 508, 543
Riess, Adam 68
Rogers, Carl 222, 584–585, 645
Rosenberg, Alex 34, 153, 174, 201, 205–206, 208, 212, 214, 292–293, 408, 509, 514, 516, 550
Rosenthal, Bob 358–359
Roser, Max 591, 595, 599, 609, 613–614
Rosling, Hans 408, 410
Rosling, Osla 408
Rosling Ronnlund, Anna 408
Roster, Max 409–410
Roth, Thomas 317
Russell, Bertrand 515
Ryff, Carol 591

S

Sapolsky, Robert 116, 126–127, 130–131, 201–202, 204–205, 208, 214–216, 218, 325, 327–334, 339, 346, 352–353, 356, 421, 430–433, 573, 605
Sartre, Jean-Paul 533
Schmitt, Brian 68
Schopenhauer, Arthur 207
Scott, Caroline 603
Seery, Mark 335, 337
Shackleford, Todd 437
Shakespeare, William 220, 245, 274, 496, 502
Shaw, Alfie 119, 123
Shaw-Taylor, Leigh 408
Shweder, Richard 513
Sibony, Olivier 261, 263, 265
Silk, Joan 471–472
Simons, Ilana 287, 527
Skinner, BF 125, 242, 312
Smith, Adam 370, 446
Smith, Cameron 123
Smith, John Maynard 79, 455, 459
Smolin, Lee 203
Snowden, Catherine 619
Snowdon, Christopher 625
Soule, Michael 122
Sparks, Dana 355
Spinoza, Baruch 207
Stanford Encyclopedia of Philosophy 270, 505–506, 524–525, 542, 554–555
Steger, Michael F 626, 629
Stevenson, Robert Louis 368
Stillman, Tyler F 633, 642
Storr, Anthony 487
Sullivan, Brandon A 626
Sumeracki, Megan 294, 299
Sunstein, Cass 256–257, 261, 263, 265
Syed, Matthew 267, 296, 304, 510

T

Tay, Louis 584

Tellegen, Auke 598
Tennyson, Alfred 497, 636
Thaler, Richard 256–257
Thomas, Drew 98
Thorndike, Edward 242
Tobler, Philippe 288
Tolstoy, Leo 284
Tomasello, Michael 180–193, 198, 208–209, 212–215, 230, 251, 271, 281, 293, 389–391, 480
Tucker, Albert 449
Tulving, Endel 308
Tupes, Douglas 226
Turner, Martin R 169
Tversky, Amos 255–256
Twenge, Jean 596

U
UK Centre for Ageing Better 408–409

V
Vaillant, George 471, 605
Varella, Simona 490
Venter, Craig 99
Verde, Clelia 203
Vinney, Cynthia 586
Vollberg, Marius 288
Voltaire 535

W
Waldinger, Robert 471, 605
Walker, Matthew 298, 315–324

Wall-Scheffler, Cara 400–401
Ward, George 615
Watson, James 82
Watson, John 242
Wearing, Clive 308
Weil, Andrew 608
Weiner, Jonathan 74
Weinstein, Yana 294, 299
Weisberg, Yanna 109, 112, 114–115
Wellcome Trust Sanger Institute 85
Wheelis, Mark 104
Wilkinson, Richard 625
Williams, George 383
Wittgenstein, Ludwig 280, 282
Woese, Carl 104
Wong, Yan 94
Woods, Harry 567

X
Xie, Hongling 421, 424–425, 428

Y
Yamamoto, Shinya 382